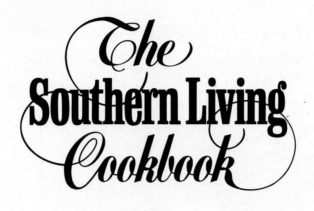

The
Southern Living
Cookbook

The Southern Living Cookbook

From the Foods Staff of Southern Living *magazine*

Compiled and Edited by
SUSAN CARLISLE PAYNE

Foreword by JEAN WICKSTROM LILES

Oxmoor House

Library of Congress Catalog Number: 87-060990
ISBN: 8487-0709-5

Manufactured in the United States of America
Second Printing 1987

Southern Living®
   Foods Editor: Jean Wickstrom Liles
   Associate Foods Editors: Susan Payne, Deborah Lowery
   Assistant Foods Editors: Phyllis Young Cordell,
      Susan Dosier, B. Ellen Templeton
   Editorial Assistants: Catherine Garrison, Karen Brechin,
      Jodi Jackson
   Test Kitchens Director: Kaye Adams
   Test Kitchens Staff: Jane Cairns, Diane Hogan, Judy Feagin,
      Peggy Smith, Patty Vann
   Photo Stylists: Beverly Morrow, Cindy Manning
   Senior Foods Photographer: Charles E. Walton IV
      Additional photography by Sylvia Martin, pages 4, 7, 14, 269;
      John O'Hagan, page 315.
   Production: Clay Nordan, Wanda Butler

Oxmoor House, Inc.
   Executive Editor: Ann H. Harvey
   Production Manager: Jerry Higdon
   Associate Production Manager: Rick Litton
   Art Director: Bob Nance
   Production Assistant: Theresa Beste

The Southern Living *Cookbook*

   Senior Editor: Joan Erskine Denman
   Editorial Assistants: Donna A. Rumbarger, Pam Beasley Bullock
   Designer: Faith Nance
   Illustrator: Carol Middleton
   Indexer: Melinda West

*Back cover: These recipe classics will
delight your family now and for years to
come. From front, Shrimp Scampi (page
235), No-Knead French Bread (page 96),
and Strawberry Shortcake (page 118).*

*Page ii: Select foods from each of the food
groups every day to help you eat a healthy
and well-rounded diet.*

CONTENTS

Foreword

For over 20 years, *Southern Living* magazine has presented the South with delicious recipes and wonderful entertaining ideas. In a region where people enjoy cooking and entertaining in their homes, Southern hospitality has always been a strong tradition. And *Southern Living* has played an important role in strengthening this tradition as Southerners have turned to our recipes to please family and friends.

THE SOUTHERN LIVING COOKBOOK is the culmination of a much-cherished wish. Indeed it's a dream come true! THE SOUTHERN LIVING COOKBOOK is our proud collection of over 1,300 favorite classic recipes depicting the South's good food and gracious lifestyle.

Many of the selected recipes have been family treasures passed down from generation to generation, and they have been updated for this book to reflect current trends and cooking techniques. Additional recipes were newly-developed specifically with you and your busy lifestyle in mind.

For our entire foods staff, producing this cookbook was much like taking a lengthy trip throughout the Southern states. First, it was a momumental task and a great challenge to vividly recall the thousands and thousands of wonderful recipes we've tested from the South's best cooks. Next, as the foods staff retested, tasted, and evaluated each recipe for this book, we once again shared the food celebrations, legends, and traditions so loved all over the South.

When many people think of Southern food, images of country ham, cornbread, and fried okra come to mind. These are still favorites, but Southern food is much, much more. From crab cakes and clam fritters to Texas chili and Kentucky burgoo, the food of the South is as varied as its people and its regions.

Besides offering you traditional Southern favorites, and many of these with a new twist, this book brings you the best in microwave adaptations, quick-and-easy recipes, plus party ideas, menu plans, and preparation tips.

THE SOUTHERN LIVING COOKBOOK maintains our standard of excellence and represents the best of *Southern Living.* We are proud that this cookbook continues the tradition started by *Southern Living* in 1966 to share the South's treasured recipes and gracious entertaining ideas.

JEAN WICKSTROM LILES

Preface

THE SOUTHERN LIVING COOKBOOK has been the working title of a book affectionately dreamed of for years by the foods staff of *Southern Living* magazine. Now that dream is a reality.

As the most comprehensive foods book *Southern Living* has ever published, it includes more than 1,300 recipes, organized into 17 chapters. Within each chapter, recipes were organized to begin with the most basic and end with the most detailed.

The book is much more than a recipe book, however; it's a complete guide to cooking. Within each food category chapter, such as Vegetables or Meats, you'll find straightforward information pertinent to the food and techniques within that chapter, such as equipment you'll need, procedure and ingredient information, freezing and storing particulars, and microwave adaptabilities. You'll also find solutions to common cooking problems, as well as creative hints for garnishing and serving. Each chapter is packed with photographs, too—over 450 of them.

There's also a chapter with useful information about food, equipment, and appliances. In addition you'll find advice to help you plan balanced menus that look good and are good for you. And no matter how big a party you plan to have, the entertaining guide will direct you step by step through initial planning, food preparation, decorating, and serving.

Obviously, a book of this nature isn't put together overnight. In fact, the book has been several years in the making, with contributions from the entire foods staff of *Southern Living* magazine. Recipe selection was nurtured by Foods Editor Jean Liles, who seems to have a memory bank to rival that of a computer. She noted for the book favorite recipes she remembered from her 15 years on the foods staff.

Kaye Adams, test kitchens director, did the bulk of the recipe testing herself. Patty Vann, assistant test kitchens director, pitched in to help meet the deadline. The entire foods staff closely scrutinized each recipe before giving it a stamp of approval.

Kaye prepared over 2,500 total recipes for the book. According to Kaye, the criteria used to evaluate the recipes was the strictest ever imposed. "Not only did we want to include a recipe for pecan pie in the book—it had to be the *best* pecan pie possible."

Charles Walton, Senior Foods Photographer, and Beverly Morrow, Photo Stylist, helped set the look of the book—an updated classic *Southern Living* look. You'll see the results in vivid color throughout THE SOUTHERN LIVING COOKBOOK.

Thanks are due these and all the other people who helped make the dream for this book a reality. We hope it becomes an indispensable source of information and pleasure for you in your kitchen.

SUSAN CARLISLE PAYNE

COOKING BASICS

Whether you're a beginning cook or a seasoned professional, you'll agree that the secret to being a good cook starts with the basics—using the right ingredients, equipment, and techniques. This chapter will help you gain the knowledge and confidence you need when cooking any meal—from a simple family supper to a fancy dinner party for 12.

ORGANIZE YOUR KITCHEN

You can reduce the time and energy you spend in the kitchen just by organizing it to fit your needs. First read this chapter in its entirety to help you inventory what you need to make your kitchen a comfortable and efficient workspace. Then make use of the following suggestions to help you clean up, throw out, and reorganize.

● Clean out your pantry. Check all the canned items. Canned foods older than a year tend to lose their nutritional value and flavor.

● Organize your recipe files. Try those recipes you've been saving. Discard the ones you know you'll never use.

● Store utensils and small appliances near the place in your kitchen where you'll be using them. For example, store your mixer, measuring spoons and cups, and mixing bowls near the area where you would mix a cake. Keep pot holders, cooking spoons, and pans near the cooktop.

● Arrange wooden spoons and spat-

Whether you're working on a simple task like measuring spices or a more complicated technique like piping whipped cream, having the right equipment and knowing about the food you're working with is essential to its success.

ulas in a decorative container. Place the container close to, if possible, the cooktop, and you'll always have

cooking utensils at your fingertips.

● Organize the utensil drawers. Invest in plastic drawer trays to store pancake or egg turners, wire whisks, and specialty items, such as a garlic press or zester.

● Store knives in a knife block where they will be safe, easily accessible, and less likely to be dulled. Keeping them in a drawer not only dulls the blades, it's dangerous. If knives must be kept in a drawer, a protective covering over the blades provides a safety feature.

● Clean out the freezer. Bring older items to the front and use them before recently purchased ones. Also, label frozen foods with the date you bought them or the date you prepared them.

● Check spices by smelling each one. If the aroma has faded, it's time to buy more. We store our spices and seasonings in the freezer. This keeps them fresh and away from the heat and humidity of the kitchen. You can measure them straight from the freezer, since they don't freeze solid.

Equipment

How well a kitchen is equipped is often related to how much the cook enjoys cooking. If the cook invests in the necessary tools, many tasks can be performed easily and efficiently.

When purchasing kitchen equipment, buy the best you can afford; in general, a higher price indicates a sturdier, longer-lasting product. Here's a brief guide to help you stock your kitchen with most of the basic items you'll need.

Preparation Equipment

Basting brush: Basting brushes come in all sizes and are useful for brushing on marinades and glazes.

Bowls: You can never have enough mixing bowls. Choose bowls in graduated sizes so they're easier to stack and store. Plastic bowls work well for most jobs, but you'll have to have a stainless steel, glass, or copper bowl for beating egg whites.

Bulb baster: This gadget will efficiently suck up pan juices and splash them back over food to keep it juicy while cooking.

Chopping board: Wood is considered the best medium for chopping, but requires meticulous cleaning to prevent cross-contamination. There are some good plastic chopping surfaces on the market, too; they're considered easier to clean.

Colander: A metal or sturdy plastic colander is essential for draining foods like pasta.

Funnel: You'll want a large and small funnel to simplify the process of transferring easy-to-spill foods.

Grater: Invest in a sturdy upright grater with several sizes of grating holes.

Juicer: A hand-juicer simplifies the process of squeezing citrus fruits. If you use fresh juice often, you might like to invest in an electric model.

Kitchen shears: Kitchen scissors cut many foods more easily than a knife.

Ladle: Large cup-shaped ladles transfer liquids without spills.

Mallet: Choose a stainless steel mallet for pounding meat and other foods.

Measuring cups: Select a set of metal or plastic dry measuring cups in graduated sizes of 1 cup, ½ cup, ⅓ cup, and ¼ cup. You'll need liquid measuring cups in glass or clear plastic that have a rim above the last cup level to prevent spilling. They come in 1-cup, 2-cup, and 4-cup sizes.

Measuring spoons: Measuring

spoons come in sets with spoon sizes that graduate from ⅛ teaspoon to 1 tablespoon.

Mixing spoons: You'll need several large metal or sturdy plastic spoons for stirring. Also purchase some wooden spoons; they won't conduct heat when you're stirring a hot mixture on the cooktop.

Openers: An electric can opener is standard stock in most kitchens, but you'll also want a hand model to rely on when the power goes out. You'll also need a bottle opener and corkscrew.

Pastry bag and tips: This equipment is not essential, but you might like to have a set if you enjoy creative baking and garnishing.

Pastry blender: This makes a quick job of incorporating fat into flour mixtures.

Potato masher: A sturdy potato masher will do a fast job of mashing cooked potatoes and other soft foods.

Rolling pin: A large, heavy rolling pin is essential for rolling dough properly.

Rotary egg beater: A rotary egg beater can be useful for small mixing tasks.

Ruler: A ruler is an essential tool for rolling dough to the proper thickness and dimensions.

Shaped cutters: You'll need a round cutter of about 2 inches for cutting biscuits and other breads and pastries. You might enjoy a set of cutters in varied shapes if you make a lot of specialty cookies, breads, and pastries.

Sifter: You'll need a sifter for sifting cake flour and powdered sugar. The kind with a trigger that you squeeze is simpler to use than the kind with the crank. Don't wash the sifter every time you use it; just shake out the excess residue, and store sifter in a plastic bag.

Spatulas: You'll want a thin metal spatula for spreading soft foods, and rubber spatulas for scraping bowls clean.

Strainer: Buy a large and small strainer for such ingredients as tea.

Thermometer: You'll want a thermometer for meat and a combination candy/frying thermometer. In general, the more they cost, the more accurate and durable they are.

Timer: If your oven doesn't have a built-in timer, invest in a freestanding one. Good cooks don't cook without one.

Tongs: Tongs are useful for removing pieces of food from liquids and for turning foods you don't want to pierce with a fork.

Vegetable parer: Sharp metal parers quickly remove fruit and vegetable peels.

Whisk: Invest in several balloon-shaped wire whisks for fast and efficient hand-beating.

ALL ABOUT KNIVES

A good set of knives is essential for efficient slicing and chopping. While food processors are good for many chopping and slicing needs, there are times when only a knife will do. For instance, when garnishing a dish with nuts, you can chop more uniform pieces with a knife. Also, carrots and green peppers can be more uniformly sliced or chopped by hand.

In the best quality knives, the tang (part of the blade that extends into the handle) is the same thickness as the blade, the same length as the knife handle, and is attached to the handle with at least three rivets.

The sharpness of the cutting edge is determined by the steel in the blade. Blades made from high-carbon steel sharpen well but tend to rust without proper care. Stainless steel blades won't rust but are hard to keep sharp. A good compromise is knives made from a high-carbon steel alloy like vanadium steel.

Our home economists recommend washing knives by hand rather than in the dishwasher. The high heat of the dishwasher can dull blades and ruin handles. To keep knives sharp, use a ceramic hone regularly. Proper storage is important, too. Keep them in a knife block or in a special case designed for knives.

You'll find knives available in a variety of shapes, lengths, and edges designed for an array of specific tasks. The knives pictured and described on this page are considered to comprise a basic set.

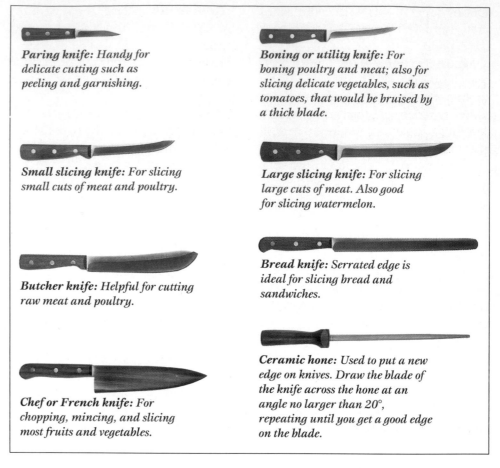

Paring knife: *Handy for delicate cutting such as peeling and garnishing.*

Small slicing knife: *For slicing small cuts of meat and poultry.*

Butcher knife: *Helpful for cutting raw meat and poultry.*

Chef or French knife: *For chopping, mincing, and slicing most fruits and vegetables.*

Boning or utility knife: *For boning poultry and meat; also for slicing delicate vegetables, such as tomatoes, that would be bruised by a thick blade.*

Large slicing knife: *For slicing large cuts of meat. Also good for slicing watermelon.*

Bread knife: *Serrated edge is ideal for slicing bread and sandwiches.*

Ceramic hone: *Used to put a new edge on knives. Draw the blade of the knife across the hone at an angle no larger than 20°, repeating until you get a good edge on the blade.*

Cookware

Some of the most important utensils in the kitchen are the pots and pans. With the variety of materials and looks now available, investing in cookware can be a difficult decision. We encourage you to get the best cookware you can afford; it's wise to buy quality that will last.

Choose pots and pans of heavy gauge or thickness and sturdy construction—those that will not warp, develop hot spots, or dent easily. The gauge usually determines the quality, and the heavier the better.

To be energy efficient, look for cookware with straight sides, tight-fitting lids, and flat bottoms for best contact with the heat source. Handles and knobs should be sturdy and attached securely to the pot or pan, and the handle should be strong enough to support the weight of the utensil when it's filled. Look for cookware with handles and knobs that are heat resistant.

Select at least 1-, 2-, and 3-quart saucepans, as well as a large Dutch oven, all with lids. You'll also want a 6- to 8-inch and 10-inch covered skillet. A double boiler is nice to have, but not essential. Also you might like to invest in a nonstick skillet for making omelets and crêpes.

Bakeware

Shiny aluminum or stainless steel bakeware usually turns out the best baked goods. They conduct heat evenly and give baked goods a brown crust. Dark pans sometimes cause overbrowning. For piepans, use glass, ceramic, or dull metal.

Always use the pan size specified in a recipe. If the size isn't indicated on your pan, measure it from the inside top edges.

To make sure you have all the bakeware you'll need for most tasks, invest in the following pieces:

Baking pans and dishes: Most common are 13- x 9- x 2-inch, 12- x 8- x 2-inch, and 11- x 7- x 2-inch sizes. You'll also often have use for both 8- and 9-inch square pans. The most frequently used cakepan is 9 inches in diameter; you'll need two of these for most cakes, three for some. Eight-inch round cakepans are periodically specified. Ten-inch tube and Bundt pans are needed for pound cakes and other one-piece cakes. The capacity of these pans varies, and they are not always interchangeable; use only what the recipe calls for.

Baking sheets: Purchase at least two large baking sheets, sometimes called cookie sheets. You'll also frequently need a 15- x 10- x 1-inch jellyroll pan. Choose heavy grade baking sheets for long-term use.

Loafpans: Pans of 9 x 5 x 3 inches are most typically used. Pans of 8 x 4 x 3 inches are not uncommon.

Muffin pans: Pans 2 inches in diameter are most common, although it's handy to have a set of miniature muffin pans.

Pieplates: If your recipe calls for a pieplate, use a glass one. If it calls for a piepan, that means a metal pan. Pies of 9 inches in diameter are most common; 10- and 8-inch sizes are sometimes needed.

Specialty pans: For specialty baking, purchase a springform pan with removable sides, a tart pan with removable bottom, and a pizza pan.

Wire rack: This is an essential baking accessory to keep baked goods from becoming soggy while cooling.

Small Appliances

Certain appliances can be real time-savers for the busy cook. The following information about common appliances may help you decide whether or not to invest in them.

Deep-fat fryer: If you do a lot of frying, you might like to have an electric fryer. Available in small to large sizes to fit the frying needs of your family, electric fryers hold oil at an even, accurate temperature for frying.

Electric blender: The blender is your best appliance for making milkshakes and other beverages, and for whirling salad dressings and sauces. A blender will also make breadcrumbs and finely chop nuts and other dry ingredients. If you own a food processor and you don't make a lot of beverages and sauces, you may find you can do without a blender.

Electric mixer: While you can cream butter and make a cake without an electric mixer, you probably wouldn't want to do it often. A heavy-duty model is your best bet for fast and thorough mixing. Some models have special attachments for making pastry, kneading dough, and juicing citrus. You might also like to have an electric or battery-operated handheld mixer to help with small jobs and to mix things as they cook on the cook surface.

Electric skillet: This appliance is helpful when your cook surface has fewer burners than you need, or when you want to cook in areas other than your kitchen.

Food processor: This appliance has revolutionized cooking. It chops, slices, grates, grinds, and mixes. It is especially time-saving when processing large quantities of food.

Some models have attachments that juice citrus fruit and make fine purees and homemade pasta. Check each model to see what specific tasks it will perform.

Toaster/toaster oven: A toaster is still the best way to toast bread, but it doesn't do much else. A toaster oven will toast bread, and some models even cut off automatically when the toast is done. A toaster oven can double as a small secondary oven as well. It's handy for reheating a single serving of food, and for when you want to cook in rooms other than the kitchen.

Waffle iron and griddle: This is an appliance for the waffle and pancake lover. The griddle also makes great toasted sandwiches and fried patties.

The Microwave Oven

A microwave oven can perform a multitude of cooking chores or it can just sit on the counter and be used occasionally to reheat a cup of cold coffee.

To help you get the most from your microwave oven, we offer this in-depth information about their selection and use.

FEATURES TO CONSIDER

Microwave ovens are available with some basic features, such as variable power and defrost cycles, as well as some special options. When you're looking for a microwave, consider what you'll be using the oven for—whether it's for reheating or preparing whole meals. If the microwave is going to be your main cooking appliance, the following features will be helpful:

An oven with **variable power** has several different power levels; this lets you cook foods that need to cook more slowly than does the HIGH setting. These levels can be selected by dial or touch controls. Touch controls may be more expensive, but they are usually more accurate and allow more cooking options.

A **defrost cycle** lets you defrost food without cooking it. Defrost cycles vary in operation; some ovens decrease power as the food defrosts, while others cycle on and off to defrost and prevent cooking.

A **turntable** is a tray or shelf in the microwave that automatically rotates during cooking to allow for even cooking or browning. This features speeds up cooking time and makes it easier, but it often limits space in the oven cavity.

A **browning unit** is available at the top of the oven cavity on some

models. You can also buy a browning dish.

A **temperature probe** is placed in a food or beverage, and the plug is inserted into a socket on the oven wall. Set the final temperature you want, and when it is reached, the oven automatically turns off. Some ovens will maintain a specific internal temperature for an hour if food is kept in the oven with the probe inserted.

Humidity and weight sensors select the power level and cooking time. By setting controls for the type and amount or weight of food, the cooking is done automatically. Or, after pressing a control, a burst of steam from the food being cooked calculates the right power level and cooking time needed.

The **memory control** feature keys in several steps that will work in sequence without continually reprogramming your oven.

Delay start lets you preset your oven to start cooking at a certain time without you being there.

Oven shelves are racks in the oven cavity that allow you more food space. They will help if reheating several foods, but will lengthen cooking time because of the increased amount of food.

A **combination convection/microwave** combines the speed of microwave cooking with the browning capability of convection cooking. Combination cooking works well for some foods, but converting conventional recipes to a convection oven may involve some experimenting.

A **conventional/microwave** is a combination oven that lets you use the oven conventionally or as a microwave. With this combination, a

continuous or self-cleaning feature is usually not an option. And often, the microwave feature has lower wattage and doesn't allow a faster cooking time.

HOW MICROWAVES WORK

The first step to mastering microwave cookery is to understand how it differs from conventional cooking. To put it simply, microwaves agitate molecules in the food, creating heat, which is then conducted throughout the food. So the food cooks by internal heat rather than by contact with hot air or a hot pan as in conventional cooking.

The finished product will depend largely on the techniques you use while cooking. The following tips will help you achieve top results with your microwave oven.

CONTAINERS FOR THE MICROWAVE

Although metal pans commonly used in conventional cooking are unsafe in the microwave, there are a variety of containers safe for use.

● Paper products, such as paper plates and cups, can be used for defrosting; for heating snacks, sandwiches, or beverages; and for cooking bacon or other foods requiring short cooking times. When left in the oven for long cooking periods, especially with foods with a high fat content, they may catch fire. Avoid using items that are made from recycled paper.

● Most ceramic, porcelain, and oven glass products are safe for defrosting, heating, and cooking processes.

● Some plastic products and dinnerware are usable, but not all are of the same quality. Look for labels that indicate "Safe for Microwave."

• A number of products are designed especially for use in the microwave. These are generally made of glass or heavy-duty plastic and are available in department stores.

• Oven cooking bags, freezer bags, and packages should be pierced for use in the microwave. Remove metal twist ties before placing bags in the microwave.

• To check a dish for safety in the microwave, pour 1 cup water into a glass measure. Place the measure in the microwave next to the dish being tested. Microwave at HIGH for 1 minute. If the dish being tested is warm and the water cool, the dish is unsafe. Do not test dishes containing metal decor as they are not safe for use.

COVERING FOOD

Covering food is a key for achieving good microwave results.

• Paper towels and napkins absorb moisture and grease, prevent spattering, and promote even heating.

They are useful when cooking bacon and heating sandwiches or bread. As with other paper products, they should be avoided for long cooking periods.

• Wax paper holds in heat when cooking meat, chicken, fruit, and some vegetable casseroles.

• Heavy-duty plastic wrap holds in steam and heat when cooking vegetables and fish. It is also useful for bowls that have no cover. Place the wrap loosely over the dish, and fold back one corner to prevent excessive steam buildup.

• The container's lid is useful when cooking types of food that require long, slow cooking.

TECHNIQUES FOR GOOD RESULTS

A few special techniques make microwaving simple and assure good results.

• Food arrangement is crucial. Since microwave energy first enters the food at the edge of the dish, arrange foods such as chicken pieces

so meatier portions are positioned around the outside of the dish.

• Unless your microwave has an automatic turntable, rotate dishes periodically during the cooking period to cook more evenly. When rotating, give the dish a quarter to half turn.

• Be sure to prick foods with thick skins (potatoes and zucchini) or membrane coverings (chicken livers and egg yolks) to allow steam to escape; otherwise, they may burst when heat builds up inside the food.

• Stir foods to mix the heated portions of food with unheated portions. Foods that require constant stirring when cooked conventionally, such as sauces, will require stirring only once or twice during microwaving.

• Food continues to cook after removal from the microwave, so standing time is required on many microwaved foods. Microwave recipes usually give a range for standing time, 5 to 7 minutes for example.

• Shielding with thin strips of lightweight aluminum foil to prevent overbrowning is useful when cooking unevenly shaped foods like poultry or portions of thin foods like fish. Check your manual to make sure it's safe to use foil in your model.

DEFROSTING IN THE MICROWAVE

• Test meat often as it defrosts. If warm to the touch, the meat has started to cook and should be prepared immediately. If defrosting for later use, we suggest partially defrosting in the microwave, then placing the meat in the refrigerator.

• When defrosting meat, place the meat in its original plastic or paper-wrapped package on a microwave rack in a shallow baking dish. Microwave at MEDIUM LOW (30%

Arrange food to be cooked in the microwave with thicker or tougher portions to the outside of the dish, leaving food parts that cook more quickly toward the inside.

Prick potatoes and other food with thick skins several times with a fork to allow steam to escape. If not pricked, these foods can burst when steam builds up inside the food.

Shielding with thin strips of lightweight aluminum foil prevents overcooked edges in dishes with corners or when cooking unevenly shaped foods like ham halves. Smooth the foil down so it doesn't wrinkle.

power), removing the package and wrappings as soon as possible. Cover loosely with wax paper after half the time, turning the meat over on the rack. Shield the edges of the meat with aluminum foil to help prevent overcooking. If thawing a roast, continue microwaving until a skewer can be inserted into the center.

● Always put poultry and fish on a microwave rack for defrosting so the bottom of the food doesn't start to cook in the liquid that drains off. When partially thawed, plunge poultry or fish into cool water.

● Place frozen blocks of soup in a casserole or soup bowl. Cover and microwave until the frozen block is partially thawed, gradually breaking apart with a fork.

TECHNIQUES FOR REHEATING
● Individual plates of food reheat best at lower power settings. Arrange thick or dense foods to the outside of the plate. Softer, more delicate foods should be placed toward the center. Cover with wax paper or plastic wrap to hold in heat and moisture.

● Never reheat meat at HIGH power; this will cause it to toughen. Most refrigerated main dishes should be reheated at MEDIUM (50% power).

● Bread can be reheated in just seconds; it will become tough if heated too long. Always wrap bread in a paper towel to absorb moisture.

● Wedges of quiche or egg casserole can be reheated satisfactorily, but scrambled eggs cook too quickly to be reheated; it is best to start over with scrambled eggs.

● To reheat rice, just add several tablespoons of water, and microwave at MEDIUM HIGH (70% power) for a few minutes. Fluff the hot rice lightly with a fork just before serving.

USING OUR MICROWAVE RECIPES
When our test kitchen home economists tested each recipe conventionally for this book, they also tested it in a microwave oven. This gave them a comparison of the two end products and the time saved, and let them evaluate whether to recommend microwave directions for the recipe. When we don't give a microwave conversion, it either took longer in the microwave or the end product wasn't as good.

When the initial microwave results had potential, we retested the recipe until the directions were perfected, and then tested it in a different wattage microwave oven. (One oven cooks with 700 watts, and the other with 600 watts.) This allowed us to get a cooking time range to suggest. To prevent overcooking, always check for doneness at the lower end of the range.

Ingredients

About Staples

Selecting just the right ingredient is a key factor in being a good cook. The following guide lists many of the basic foods called for in our recipes and describes their many available forms.

BREADCRUMBS
You can purchase breadcrumbs commercially prepared or you can make your own at home. Pay attention to the specific way we call for breadcrumbs, and you'll know exactly what we tested with.

When we specify **fine, dry breadcrumbs**, we're referring to the commercial ones. You can purchase them plain or seasoned; our recipes indicate if you should use one of the seasoned types.

If we simply say **dry breadcrumbs**, we mean homemade ones. First toast the bread (day-old bread works well); then crumb the toast in a blender or food processor. Include the crust if you wish.

Soft breadcrumbs refer to homemade breadcrumbs made from left-over rolls or sandwich bread. Do not toast the bread.

If you use breadcrumbs regularly, you can stockpile bits of leftover bread in the freezer until you have the amount you need. Then make the leftovers into crumbs all at once. Place breadcrumbs in freezer bags, label, and return to the freezer until needed. The breadcrumbs will remain free-flowing in the freezer; you can measure just the amount you need and return the rest to the freezer. Don't let breadcrumbs thaw before returning them to the freezer, or they will get soggy.

CHOCOLATE

Our recipes use **unsweetened, semisweet, sweet baking,** and **milk chocolate.** The first three come in 1-ounce squares, so they're easy to measure. Semisweet chocolate comes in morsel form, too. You can substitute morsels for squares ounce for ounce. One cup of morsels equals 6 ounces. Milk chocolate comes in morsel and candy bar form; check the label to make sure you're using pure milk chocolate.

You can often substitute **cocoa** for unsweetened chocolate for baking purposes. Use 3 tablespoons cocoa plus 1 tablespoon melted butter or margarine for each 1-ounce square of unsweetened chocolate.

Chocolate-flavored candy coating is not chocolate at all, but a product made to look and taste similar to chocolate. It is often used as a dipping chocolate in place of semisweet chocolate because it's not as sticky after it firms back up.

CREAM

Whipping cream (heavy cream) is the richest cream you can buy; it contains 30% to 40% milk fat and is used for making whipped cream.

Half-and-half (light cream) contains about half the amount of fat as whipping cream and is more like milk than cream. It will not whip.

Sour cream is a commercially cultured product that is thick and has a slightly sour taste. In testing our recipes, we use dairy sour cream rather than cream soured at home.

FATS

Fats can be divided into two groups: fats and oils. Those that are solid at room temperature—such as **butter, margarine, shortening,** and **lard**—are called fats. **Corn, vegetable, peanut, sesame seed, olive,** and **safflower oils** are liquid at room temperature.

Butter and **margarine** are two fats widely used in cooking and flavoring. While butter and margarine are often used interchangeably, they are different products. Butter has milk fat or cream as a base, while most margarines are made from vegetable oil, with some made from a combination of vegetable oil and animal fat. (Read the list of ingredients on the label to determine what's in your brand of margarine.)

Both butter and margarine are available in salted, unsalted, and whipped form. The whipped products have air incorporated to make them more spreadable. Don't substitute whipped for regular butter or margarine without making necessary adjustments. Usually 1½ cups whipped margarine equals 1 cup margarine.

Diet or **imitation margarine** is a soft margarine with about half the fat and more than three times the water of plain margarine. It is used primarily as a spread and isn't suitable for baking because of the high water content.

Shortening is composed of vegetable or animal fat or a combination of the two. It is solid at room temperature and has a long shelf life. It is tasteless, but is commonly used for baking because it adds moisture and tenderness. Butter-flavored shortening is simply shortening processed to give more of a butter flavor to the food in which it is used.

Lard is rendered pork fat. Years ago it was used almost exclusively for making pastry and biscuits. Its use has declined in recent years.

Since **oils** are liquid at room temperature, do not substitute oil for shortening in baked products, even when the shortening is to be melted. Olive oil, one of the most expensive oils, is used for salad dressings and other recipes where the taste will be noticed. Vegetable oil is a good all-purpose cooking oil. Corn oil and peanut oil are excellent for frying because they can be brought to high temperatures without smoking.

FLOUR

Flour is milled from all kinds of grains—wheat, corn, rye, oats, and barley—each resulting in one or more kinds of flour. The differences lie in the particular grain used and how it's processed.

Wheat flours are divided into two basic groups: whole grain and white. **Whole-grain wheat flours** include whole wheat, graham, and cracked wheat. Among the **white flours** are bread, unbleached, all-purpose, and cake; these are often enriched with iron and the B-vitamins to replace nutrients lost when the germ was removed.

Wheat flours also vary in protein content. Protein is important when it comes to how a flour performs during baking. When mixed with a liquid, protein forms a substance called gluten, which gives elasticity to batters and doughs, as well as provides the structure or framework for whatever you're baking. In addition, gluten affects the tenderness and volume of baked products. The white flours have more protein (more gluten) than whole-grains.

Bread flour is a hard-wheat flour milled especially for breadmaking. It can be hard to find, but all-purpose flour can be substituted.

All-purpose flour is a combination of hard- and soft-wheat flour and is commonly used for all types of baked products. If an all-purpose flour is labeled "higher protein," it's better suited for yeast breads. All-purpose flours with a lower protein content give better results when used for cakes, quick breads, and sweet rolls. **Unbleached flour** is an all-purpose flour that has no bleaching agents added during processing and is often used interchangeably with all-purpose.

Self-rising flour is an all-purpose flour to which leavening and salt have been added; it is not suitable for yeast breads. It is best not to substitute self-rising for all-purpose flour; however, all-purpose can be substituted for self-rising by making the following adjustments: For 1 cup self-rising flour, use 1 cup all-purpose flour plus 1 teaspoon baking powder and ½ teaspoon salt.

Cake flour is a soft-wheat type and has a much lower protein content than all-purpose flour. Products made with cake flour have a tender, delicate texture. Substitute all-purpose flour for cake flour by using 2 tablespoons less per cup.

GELATIN
You can purchase gelatin either unflavored or sweetened and flavored; the two are not interchangeable. **Unflavored gelatin** is sold in packages containing slightly less than 1 tablespoon. Each package will gel 2 cups of liquid. **Flavored gelatin** is sold in 3- or 6-ounce packages and contains sugar, flavoring, and coloring. Flavored and unflavored gelatin require different softening procedures. For more about using each type, refer to the congealed salad section in the salad chapter.

LIQUEURS AND BRANDIES
Our recipes sometimes call for liqueurs and brandies by names with which you might not be familiar.

Amaretto—Almond liqueur
Cointreau—Orange liqueur
Crème de cacao—Vanilla-chocolate liqueur
Crème de cassis—Black currant liqueur
Crème de menthe—Mint liqueur; green or white
Kahlúa—Coffee liqueur
Kirsch—Cherry brandy
Tia Maria—Spiced coffee liqueur
Triple Sec—Orange liqueur

MILK
We test our recipes using **whole milk** unless otherwise stated. This milk has at least 3.25% fat content. **Skim milk** has most of the fat removed; it has less than .5% fat. **Low-fat milk** is available from .5% to 2% fat content; it tastes and looks more like whole milk than skim milk.

Evaporated milk has had 60% of the water removed. Available in cans only, evaporated milk can be substituted for fresh milk; mix it equally with water.

Sweetened condensed milk is made by removing half the water from whole milk and adding a lot of sugar. It's available in cans; it can't be substituted for fresh milk.

Nonfat dry milk powder is what remains after all the water and fat have been removed from whole milk. It rehydrates easily with water or another liquid.

Buttermilk is the liquid that remains after butter is made from whole milk. Cultured buttermilk is the product left after skim milk is treated with a lactic acid bacteria.

Yogurt is simply fermented milk. Available plain or flavored, the plain can often be used as a lower calorie substitute for sour cream.

SUGAR
Granulated sugar is the most common form of sugar; it's what we mean when we specify "sugar." Sometimes we call for **super-fine sugar**, which is granulated sugar with smaller crystals resulting from extra processing. It's used when making meringues or other products where quick mixing or dissolving is important. If you can't find super-fine sugar, make it by processing regular granulated sugar in the blender until you have finer crystals.

Powdered sugar (confectioner's sugar) is granulated sugar that has been crushed and screened until the grains are like powder. It's used for frostings and for sprinkling over baked products. You can tell the degree of fineness of powdered sugar by the number of x's indicated on the package—the fine powdered is 4x, the very fine powdered is 6x, and the ultra-fine powdered is 10x. The 10x type is what we use in our test kitchens when a recipe calls for powdered sugar.

Brown sugar is less refined than granulated sugar, and comes in a light and dark form. Dark brown sugar has a stronger flavor. Our recipes specify which one to use when it makes a difference; otherwise, use your choice.

Brown sugar will dry out easily after opening because it's more moist than granulated sugar. After a package is opened, we transfer the unused part to an airtight container; this keeps it soft and moist. You can soften hardened brown sugar by putting it in an airtight container and adding a slice of apple or bread.

Caramelized sugar is sugar that

has been cooked long enough to take it to the caramelization stage. It will be colored and flavored like caramel. The Flan Almendra Step-By-Step sequence on page 185 gives directions on caramelizing sugar.

SYRUPS

Molasses is the syrup left after making granulated sugar from sugar cane. It is most commonly sold as light or dark molasses. **Unsulfured** and **blackstrap molasses** are less-refined forms that have a stronger flavor. Use them only when they are specified in a recipe.

Honey is a thick syrup made by bees from the nectar of flowers. It's sweeter than sugar and has a characteristic flavor.

Corn syrup is available in light or dark form, the lighter being lighter in flavor as well as color. Our recipes specify which form to use.

Cane syrup comes from sugar cane that has been boiled down to the consistency of syrup.

Sorghum comes from a coarse grass by the same name. It is processed to obtain a juice, which is then boiled down to a syrup.

Maple syrup comes from the sap of the sugar maple tree. Like sugar cane, it's boiled down to the consistency of syrup.

THICKENING AGENTS

All-purpose flour is the most common thickener. It is used for gravies, sauces, and puddings and gives an opaque appearance. Two tablespoons of flour will thicken one cup of liquid.

Use **cornstarch** to thicken puddings and sauces when you want a more translucent look. One tablespoon of cornstarch will thicken one cup of liquid.

Arrowroot is not used as often now as in the past, but it will thicken fillings and sauces, leaving them sparkling and clear. One tablespoon of arrowroot will thicken one cup of liquid.

Instant blending flour is a commercially developed mixture that will dissolve in hot liquids without lumping and can be added directly to sauces and gravies without first being dissolved in water. Do not use this kind of flour for baking.

Use **tapioca** for thickening pie fillings and puddings. It gives a characteristic granular texture to foods. Use about 1½ tablespoons tapioca per cup of liquid.

Thickening agents must be handled correctly during cooking so they'll thicken without lumping. Refer to page 435 and 436 in our chapter on sauces for specifics.

VINEGAR

White or **all-purpose vinegar** has the sharpest flavor of all vinegars. Use it when our recipes simply specify vinegar. **Red** and **white wine vinegar** are milder in flavor and make a nice addition to salads.

Cider vinegar is a strong type of vinegar commonly used for pickling. Whether you use cider or regular vinegar for canning, make sure the label says it has 5% acidity.

Commercial availability of specially flavored **herb vinegars** is growing, and you can also make them at home. See page 265 for recipes. Use mild **Japanese rice vinegar** on delicate salads and vegetables.

Food Shopping

When and how you plan your trips to the supermarket have a direct relationship to how much time and money you spend for groceries. Keep these things in mind before you shop.

● Plan weekly menus to fit your budget. Then make out a grocery list from your meal plans. By doing this, you'll never end up without an ingredient you need when you start to prepare a meal, and you can also check your pantry for ingredients you already have on hand. Never go to the store without a list. You'll end up buying a little of this and that — and spending more money than you planned.

● Look through your newspaper for coupons and advertised specials. You'll probably find many items you want to stock up on as well as ideas for menus.

● When writing out your grocery list, try grouping the items under the following headings: Canned Vegetables and Soups, Canned Fruits, Baking Items, Imported or Specialty Items, Produce, Meats, Dairy Products, Frozen Foods, Cleaning Supplies, and Miscellaneous. We use these headings on our lists and have found that they reduce the time we spend in the grocery store.

● Organize your list so that it corresponds to the layout of the grocery store. For example, if the produce section is located at the front of the store, start your list with produce.

● Be sure to read labels as you select your purchases. Labels help you compare nutrition information, grades of the product, and the forms in which you can buy the product.

● Consider the cost per serving or per unit of different sizes of a particular product. Buying in quantity is a good idea only if you have a place to store the excess properly and you can use it before it spoils.

● Never go shopping when you're hungry. Everything looks appetizing, and you'll end up spending more money than you planned.

Storing Food

REFRIGERATOR STORAGE

Often there's a fine line between refrigerated items that are safe to eat and those that need to be thrown out. The refrigerator storage chart on this page will show you how long you can safely keep products such as milk, cottage cheese, and meats.

FRESH FRUITS AND VEGETABLES

Most fresh fruit is best used within three to five days. Apples maintain their best quality about three weeks, and citrus fruits ten days to two weeks. Try to use fresh vegetables as soon as possible after purchasing or after picking from the garden. Corn in the husk will only hold up one day in the refrigerator. Carrots and radishes will last two to three weeks; most other vegetables should be eaten within three to seven days.

PANTRY STORAGE

Store food in the coolest area of your kitchen, away from the oven and cook surface. Hot, humid air decreases the storage life of most products. Keep all dry foods in their original containers or in airtight ones. Date your purchases and always use the oldest items first.

If you need to know the shelf life of unopened canned goods or staples

SAFE STORAGE IN REFRIGERATOR

Canned goods (opened)		Fresh fish	1 to 2 days
Fruit	5 to 7 days		
Jams and jellies	6 months		
Mayonnaise	1 to 2 months	Poultry	1 to 2 days
Meats	1 to 2 days		
Pickles	2 to 3 months		
Vegetables	2 to 3 days	**Dairy**	
		Butter and margarine	1 month
Meats		Buttermilk	1 to 2 weeks
Fresh beef, lamb, pork, and veal:		Cheese (opened):	
Roasts	2 to 4 days	Hard; Cheddar,	
Steaks, chops	3 days	Swiss	3 to 4 weeks
Ribs	2 days	Parmesan, grated	1 year
Stew meat	2 days	Soft; cream,	
Ground meat	1 to 2 days	Neufchâtel	2 weeks
Processed meats, after package		Cottage cheese	5 to 7 days or pkg. date
is opened:			
Ham, whole and		Eggs	1 month
half	7 days	Half-and-half	7 to 10 days
Bacon	5 to 7 days	Milk: Whole and	
Frankfurters	4 to 5 days	skimmed	1 week
Luncheon meats,		Sour cream	3 to 4 weeks
sliced	3 days	Whipping cream	10 days

then check the pantry storage chart on the next page. We compiled this information after consulting various sources in the food industry.

FREEZER STORAGE

Use your freezer for long-term storage of foods. Set at 0° or lower, your freezer will keep these products in good quality for the length of time specified in the freezer storage chart on the next page.

IF YOUR FREEZER GOES OFF

If your freezer has ever stopped running due to a power failure or mechanical problem, then you know the panicky feeling you have when you think about losing a freezer full of food.

The most important thing to remember is that if the freezer door is kept closed, a fully loaded freezer will keep foods frozen for two days; a freezer partially filled will keep

SAFE STORAGE IN PANTRY

Canned foods

Fruits	1 year
Vegetables	1 year
Soups	1 year
Meat, fish, and poultry	1 year

Packaged mixes

Cake mix	1 year
Casserole mix	18 months
Frosting mix	8 months
Pancake mix	6 months

Staples

Baking powder and soda	1 year
Breakfast cereal:	
Ready to eat	Check pkg. date
Uncooked	1 year
Coffee (opened and refrigerated)	6 to 8 weeks
Cornmeal: Regular and self-rising	10 months
Dried beans and peas	18 months
Flour: All-purpose	10 to 15 months
Whole wheat, refrigerated	3 months
Grits: Regular	10 months
Instant, flavored	9 months
Milk: Evaporated and sweetened condensed	1 year
Pasta	10 to 15 months
Peanut butter	6 months
Salt, pepper, sugar	18 months
Shortening	8 months
Spices: Ground	6 months
Whole	1 year
(Discard if aroma fades)	
Tea bags	1 year
Vegetable oil	3 months
Worcestershire sauce	2 years

SAFE STORAGE IN FREEZER

Baked goods

Bread	3 months
Cakes	3 to 5 months
Cookies	6 months
Pies and pastry	2 months

Dairy

Butter	6 months
Cheese	4 months
Ice Cream	1 to 3 months
Eggs: Whites	6 months
Yolks	8 months

Fish and shellfish

Fat fish	3 months
Lean fish	6 months
Shellfish	3 months

Poultry

Chicken, whole	3 to 6 months
Chicken, pieces	3 months
Chicken, cooked	1 month
Turkey	6 months

Meat

Beef	6 to 12 months
Pork	3 to 6 months
Lamb	6 to 9 months
Veal	6 to 9 months
Ground meats	3 to 4 months
Ham	1 to 2 months
Bacon	1 month
Frankfurters	1 month
Sausage	2 months
Variety meats	3 to 4 months
Leftover cooked meat	3 months

Vegetables and fruits

Vegetables, commercially frozen	8 months
Vegetables, home frozen	12 months
Fruits, commercially frozen	12 months
Fruits, home frozen	12 months

food cold for only about a day.

If the power will be off for several days or if your freezer can't be repaired quickly, you may want to check with neighbors or a food locker plant in your area to see if your food can be stored there.

(When transporting food, wrap in newspapers and pack in cardboard boxes to help prevent thawing.)

If neither of these options is available, use dry ice. Place ice in the freezer as soon as possible; 25 pounds will keep the temperature below freezing for three to four days in a full 10-cubic-foot freezer and about two to three days in a half-full freezer the same size. (Locate dry ice by checking the Yellow Pages.)

Never touch dry ice with bare hands, as it will burn; always wear gloves. Wrap the ice block in several thicknesses of heavy paper, and place wrapped block on heavy cardboard or small boards over the food packages but not directly on them.

Once the power is restored or your freezer is repaired, check foods carefully to determine the extent of thawing. Get rid of any food that is off-color or has a strange odor.

You may safely refreeze food if it still has ice crystals or if the freezer temperature is below 40°F. and has not been at that temperature longer than one or two days. Foods warmed to 40°F. or higher are probably unfit for refreezing.

You can refreeze thawed fruit that still smells and tastes good. Or use it immediately for cooking and making jam, jelly, and preserves.

Meats and poultry should be examined carefully. If they still have ice crystals, they may be safe to refreeze. Look carefully at the color, and check the odor. If there is any question, get rid of them.

Shellfish, vegetables, and cooked foods such as TV dinners, leftovers, pies, and ice cream spoil quickly. Once thawed, don't refreeze — throw them away.

Basic Preparations

MEASURING INGREDIENTS

For your recipes to turn out the way you want, you must measure ingredients accurately. Not all ingredients are measured the same way or in the same type of measuring utensil. Learn to measure the right way with the proper equipment.

*To measure
liquid ingredients*

Measure liquids in glass or clear plastic measuring cups with a rim above the last cup level to prevent spilling. Liquid measuring cups are available in 1-cup, 2-cup, and 4-cup sizes. To correctly measure liquids, put the cup on a level surface. Then get eye level with the marking you want to read, and fill the cup to that line. Don't pick the cup up and bring it to your eye level, because chances are you won't hold it perfectly level.

*To measure
dry ingredients*

Measure dry ingredients in metal or plastic measuring cups that come in graduated sets of 1-cup, ½-cup,

⅓-cup, and ¼-cup sizes. To measure accurately, use the cup that holds the exact amount called for in the recipe. Lightly spoon the dry ingredient into the cup, letting it mound slightly; then level the top of the dry ingredient with a flat edge or knife.

*To measure
brown sugar*

Measure brown sugar in the same dry measuring cups in which you measure other dry ingredients, but be sure to pack it firmly into the cup instead of spooning it in as you do other dry ingredients. It needs to be packed firmly enough so that the sugar keeps the shape of the cup when it's turned out. All lumps are pressed out as it is packed into the measuring cup.

*To measure
grated cheese*

Lightly spoon or place shredded or grated cheese, nuts, coconut, soft breadcrumbs, or chopped fruit and vegetables into a dry measuring cup until the ingredients are even with the rim of the cup; do not pack.

MEASURING SOLID SHORTENING OR BUTTER

Shortening, like brown sugar, should be packed into the right-size dry measuring cup. To be sure all air bubbles are out, cut through the shortening in the cup with a metal spatula, pack it again, and then level off the top.

Butter or margarine is often already measured. For ½ cup, use a stick (quarter of a pound); for ¼ cup, use a half stick. If a different amount is needed, each stick is usually marked on the wrapper to help you measure accurately. Remember, whipped margarine is not an equal substitute for regular margarine; do not use it in a recipe unless it is specified.

TO SIFT OR NOT

Most brands of flour today are pre-sifted, making it no longer necessary to sift them as you measure them. Just stir the flour gently, and spoon it lightly into the proper size measuring cup.

Both powdered sugar and cake flour are very light and have a tendency to pack down easily. You will need to sift these ingredients before measuring; then lightly spoon them into the measuring cup.

MEASURING SPOONS

When measuring liquid or dry ingredients in amounts less than ¼ cup, use measuring spoons (¼ cup equals 4 tablespoons). Pour thin liquids into the appropriate spoon until full. Pour or scoop thick liquids or dry ingredients into the appropriate spoon until full; then level the spoon with a straight edge or knife.

ADD JUST A DASH

Some recipes call for a dash of an ingredient—especially when using a potent seasoning or when the exact amount is not critical. A dash is a measure of less than ⅛ teaspoon, which is the smallest amount that you can accurately measure using standard measuring spoons. A dash is considered to be about half of a standard ⅛ teaspoon.

PREPARATION TERMS

Knowing the difference between similar food preparation tasks is important to the success of a recipe. To help you identify these tasks, we have described and pictured them below.

Slice foods into pieces of the desired thickness using a sharp slicing knife. Use a knife with a serrated edge when slicing breads or cakes.

Diagonally slice vegetables and fruits by holding the knife at an angle to the food. This technique gives food more surface area and a more interesting look.

Cut julienne strips by first cutting the food into equal lengths, then cutting it into matchstick strips. Many food processors also have blades that help you cut julienne strips.

Dice food by cutting it into pieces ⅛ to ¼ inch on each side. First cut the food into strips the desired width. Then arrange the strips into a pile, and cut them crosswise into cubes. Use the same technique for cubing, but make the pieces ½ inch or larger on each side.

Shred foods by cutting food into long narrow strips. Foods like cabbage that grow in concentric layers can be shredded by slicing with a sharp knife. To shred other types of food, rub them against a metal grating surface.

Chop food by cutting it into irregular pieces about ¼ inch in size. Food is minced when you chop it into still finer, irregular pieces. Use a chef knife, an electric blender, or food processor.

Slice

Diagonally Slice

Julienne

Dice/Cube

Shred

Chop/Mince

Meal Planning

The ultimate compliment for the cook is for someone to ask for a recipe. When you've been rewarded with a request of this nature, chances are it's because you're particular about the food you serve. You probably spend a few extra minutes when planning your menu to ensure that your food tastes good, looks good, and is good for you.

To help you plans meals that are nutritious and tasty, whether for family or friends, be sure you take into consideration these important aspects of meal planning.

BASIC FOUR FOOD GROUPS

Nutrition experts have grouped the majority of foods we eat into the Basic Four Food Groups. Eating the proper amount of foods from each group each day will help ensure that you have a well-balanced diet.

Recipes that represent more than one food group can short cut your meal preparation. For example, a meat casserole may include meat, one or two vegetables, as well as rice, pasta, or bread. Determine which foods are in the prepared dish, and what food groups they come from to calculate your servings from the food groups. The food groups include:

Meat Group: Protein is provided by the meat group, which includes meat, poultry, fish and seafood, eggs, as well as legumes, nuts, and cheese. Include two servings from the meat group in your meals each day. One serving equals 2 to 3 ounces of cooked fish, poultry, or meat, 2 eggs, or 1 cup cooked dried beans or peas.

Milk Group: Dairy products, including milk, are the main sources of calcium in the diet. They also provide protein, vitamins, and minerals. This group includes milk, buttermilk, yogurt, cheese, cottage cheese, and ice milk. Servings recommended per day range from two for an adult, three for children up to 12 years of age, and four for teenagers. One serving from this group equals 1 cup milk, 1 cup yogurt, 2 cups ice milk, 1½ ounces of most hard cheeses, or 2 cups cottage cheese. Although these amounts will provide equal amounts of calcium, calories per serving are not always the same.

Fruit and Vegetable Group: These foods are generally high in vitamins, minerals, and fiber, contain little if any fat, no cholesterol, and are relatively low in calories. A balanced diet includes four servings from the fruit and vegetable group daily. Include at least one vitamin C-rich food (oranges, grapefruit, melons, strawberries, green peppers, potatoes, cabbage, and broccoli are all high in vitamin C). Also include at least one vitamin A-rich food every other day, such as deep yellow, orange, and dark green vegetables, as well as tomatoes, apricots, and cantaloupe.

One serving of this food group equals ½ cup sliced or cooked fruit or fruit juice, 1 small apple, ½ grapefruit, 1 medium orange, ½ cup cooked vegetable, or 1 small baked potato. When you have a choice, eat bulkier, higher fiber food, such as an apple instead of apple juice.

Bread and Cereal Group: Bread,

Meat Group: Select 2 servings daily.

Milk Group: Select 2 servings daily.

cereal, pasta, and rice are rich in complex carbohydrates and, if whole grain, are high in fiber. Enriched or whole grain breads and cereals are sources of iron and the B vitamins thiamine, riboflavin, and niacin. You should include four servings from the bread and cereal group each day. One serving equals 1 slice whole grain or enriched bread, 1 ounce ready-to-eat cereal, or ½ cup cooked cereal, rice, or pasta.

Extra Foods: Those foods that are not listed under the above four categories include fats, alcohol, and sweets (including soft drinks, jams, jellies, honey, cakes, pies, and sweet breads) and contain few nutrients. They primarily provide calories in the diet. Limiting the amount of these foods is a good idea if you're trying to lose weight.

PLAN MEALS FOR LOOKS AND TASTE

Nutrition is not the only factor to consider when meal planning. The foods selected should also look and taste good together. To start planning a menu, choose a focus for the meal. Center the menu around a sandwich, meat, main-dish salad, or casserole. Then plan accompaniments carefully. Don't match fried chicken with French-fried potatoes or stuffed pork chops with stuffed baked potatoes. As a rule, let variety be your guide. By serving a variety of foods prepared in a variety of ways, chances are you'll be providing nutritious as well as attractive meals.

Consider the color, flavor, texture, shape, and size of each part of a meal. Foods come in a multitude of colors, so be sure to include contrasting ones. Instead of serving fried chicken, creamed potatoes, and cauliflower, all white or beige, substitute broccoli or carrots for the cauliflower. Colorful garnishes also help. Simple extras such as orange twists, parsley sprigs, or lemon wedges add sparkle to your dinner plates. Several garnishing ideas are pictured and described on page 25.

Don't repeat flavors. If you've put tomatoes in a salad, avoid serving a broiled tomato as a side dish. Be sure to introduce milder flavors before strong ones. So if you want your entrée to be fully appreciated, don't serve a spicy, full-flavored appetizer—it tends to overpower the taste buds. Remember, plan only one highly seasoned or strong-flavored item for each meal. Also, plan only one starchy food for each meal.

Temperature variations of foods in a meal are especially pleasing to the palate. Cold soups, chilled fruit, and vegetable salads provide welcome contrasts to hot entrées. Always serve food at the proper temperature—serve hot foods hot and cold foods cold.

Vary the shapes of food just as you would the color and texture. For example, meatballs, new potatoes, and brussels sprouts create a poor menu because of the repetitious shapes. Sliced meat loaf and green beans would make better partners for new potatoes. Don't include too many mixtures. For instance, don't serve beef stew, Waldorf salad, and peas and carrots.

When planning menus, remember not to overextend yourself. If time is limited, plan quick and easy dishes that can be prepared in minutes instead of hours. Plan to use leftovers, convenience foods, and the neighborhood deli.

On the following pages, you will find suggested menus using recipes from this book. You can use the menus as presented or use them as models to create your own. You can also experiment by mixing and matching recipes within the menus.

Fruit and Vegetable Group: Select 4 servings daily.

Bread and Cereal Group: Select 4 servings daily.

Menus

DINNER FOR THE FAMILY

Chicken With a Flair
(Serves 4)
Skillet Chicken With Vegetables
Browned New Potatoes
Spinach-Mushroom Salad
Old-Fashioned Buttermilk Pound Cake

Quick and Easy Fare
(Serves 6)
Spicy Broiled Fish
*Skillet Snow Peas
Lemon Vermicelli
Commercial Rolls
Vanilla Ice Cream With
*Hot Fudge Sauce

Seafood Special
(Serves 6 to 8)
Charleston-Style Shrimp Curry
Hot Cooked Rice
Marinated Asparagus
Braided White Bread
*Pots de Crème

Make-Ahead Dinner
(Serves 4)
Grilled Chicken With
Tarragon Mayonnaise
Vegetable-Pasta Salad
Sour Cream Rolls
Black Bottom Ice Cream Pie

Dinner From the Microwave
(Serves 4 to 6)
Wild Rice-Stuffed Chicken
Asparagus With Orange Sauce
Commercial Rolls
Vanilla Ice Cream With
Praline Sauce

Just for the Two of You
(Serves 2)
Broiled Lobster
Mixed Vegetable Stir-Fry
Baked Potatoes
Commercial Rolls
Blueberries and Cointreau

Dieter's Delight
(Serves 6)
Grilled Flank Steak
Stir-Fried Squash Medley
Carrot Sticks
Celery Sticks
Fresh Fruit

Sunday Dinner
(Serves 8)
Standing Rib Roast
Yorkshire Pudding
or *Onion Rice
Green Bean Casserole
Carrot-Ambrosia Salad
Whipping Cream Biscuits
Apple Cider Pie

Patio Picnic
(Serves 6)
Beef and Vegetable Kabobs
Vegetable-Rice Salad
Potato Rolls
Crusty Peach Cobbler

MENUS FOR SPECIAL OCCASIONS

Lunch for New Year's Day
(Serves 6)
Spicy Hot Black-eyed Peas
Green-and-White Vegetable Salad
Beefed-Up Cornbread
Lemon Chess Pie

Easter Dinner
(Serves 8)
Roast Leg of Lamb
Mint Sauce
*Orange-Raisin Carrots
*Herbed Rice
*Watercress Salad
Sour Cream Rolls
Elegant Lemon Cake Roll

Celebration for the 4th of July
(Serves 8)
Smoked Pork Shoulder
Southern Baked Beans
Crispy Coleslaw
Hard Rolls
Peach Ice Cream

A Thanksgiving Feast
(Serves 8)
Roast Turkey
Giblet Gravy
Green Beans Amandine
Old-Fashioned Cornbread Dressing
Cranberry Fruit Salad Mold
Sour Cream Yeast Crescents
Pumpkin Pie

Christmas Dinner
(Serves 12)
Cranberry-Orange Glazed Ham
Steamed Broccoli
*Mousseline Sauce
*Stuffed Sweet Potatoes
Spiced Cranberries
Cloverleaf Rolls
Stately Coconut Layer Cake
Light Fruitcake

A Birthday Celebration
(Serves 6)
Individual Beef Wellingtons
Dressed-Up Potatoes
Salad Composée
Commercial Dinner Rolls
Chocolate Mousse Baked Alaska

Tailgate Special
(Serves 6)
Beer-Cheese Soup
London Broil
Mustard Spread
Vegetable-Pasta Salad
Hard Rolls
Filled Lemon Cookies

Bridal Tea
(Serves 48)
****Chicken Salad in
*****Two-Inch Cream Puffs
Mixed Nuts
*Mint Twists
*Petit Fours
**Bunch of Punch

Dessert Party
(Serves 16)
Champagne
Strawberries to dip in
*Chocolate Sauce Supreme
Heavenly Dessert Cheese Molds
Coffee Chiffon Cake
**Spiced Coffee

Holiday Open House
(Serves 24)
Pecan-Cheese Ring
*Southern Ham 'n Biscuits
Fruitcake Cookies
Jam Kolaches
Cherry Divinity
Mocha Fudge
*Holiday Eggnog Deluxe

Recipe Key *Double recipe **Triple recipe ***Quadruple recipe ****Five times recipe *****Six times recipe

An Appetizer Buffet
(Serves 50)
Chicken Liver Pâté
**Marinated Shrimp
**Spiced Meatballs
**Tomatoes Tapenade
**Marinated Mushrooms
**Individual Spinach Tarts
Cheese Straws
***Chocolate Truffles
**Sparkling Champagne Punch

SOUPS, SANDWICHES, AND SIMPLE MENUS

Packed for a Picnic
(Serves 6 to 8)
*Seasoned Country-Fried Chicken
Marinated Vegetable Salad
Pimiento-Cheese Spread Sandwiches
Best Deviled Eggs
Frosted Fudge Brownies
Fresh Lemonade

TV Tray Dining
(Serves 4)
Monte Cristo Sandwich
Dressed-Up Tomato Soup
Commercial Pound Cake With Brandied
Strawberry Sauce

Simple Menu for a Crowd
(Serves 20)
Brunswick Stew
**Crispy Coleslaw
Cracker Bread
or Commercial Rolls
Favorite Oatmeal Cookies

Quick Lunch for the Kids
(Serves 6)
Muffin Pizzas
Carrot Sticks
Celery Sticks
*Rich Vanilla Milkshake

30-Minute Special
(Serves 6)
*Speedy Chili
Mixed Green Salad
Zippy Italian Dressing
Sherbet Refresher

Microwave Magic
(Serves 6)
Cream Cheese Lasagna
Mixed Green Salad
Herb Vinaigrette
Commercial Pound Cake With Fresh
Lemon Sauce

Kids Lunchbox Special
(Serves 6)
Quick Vegetable Soup
Soft Breadsticks
Fruited Granola

Sunday Night Capers
(Serves 4 to 6)
Sour Cream-Ham Omelet
Summertime Melon Salad
Quick Monkey Bread

For Breakfast or Brunch
(Serves 4)
Overnight Orange French Toast
Bacon or Sausage
Fresh Fruit

WHEN COMPANY IS COMING

After-Work Entertaining
(Serves 6)
Spinach-Cheese Phyllo Triangles
Spicy Shrimp Creole
Mixed Green Salad
Buttermilk Dressing
Commercial French Bread
Garlic Butter
Lemon Soufflé

Luncheon for the Ladies
(Serves 8)
*Rosy Berry Soup
Chicken Crêpes
*Crispy Marinated Carrots
Chocolate Triangle Cake

A Cajun Feast
(Serves 6)
Southern Seafood Gumbo
**Orange-Rum Roast Duckling
Green Peas and Pearl Onions
Carrots Madeira
No-Knead French Bread
Southern Pralines

From South of the Border
(Serves 8 to 10)
*Chiles Rellenos
*Fajitas
*Great Guacamole
Picante Sauce
Shredded Lettuce
*Spanish Rice
Nacho Chips
*Flan Almendra

Springtime Feast
(Serves 8)
*Shrimp Cocktail
*Lemon-Veal Piccata
*Vegetable Rice
*Fresh Asparagus Salad
Shredded Wheat Feather Rolls
*Strawberry-Champagne Sherbet

Dinner From the Sea
(Serves 8)
*Clams or Oysters Casino
Low-Country Seafood Boil
Mixed Green Salad
Blue Cheese Dressing
Sourdough Country Crust Bread
Raspberry Dream

Supper Club Gourmet
(Serves 10)
**Escargots Provençal
Stuffed Turkey Roll
**Saffron Rice Mold
Summer Fruit Salad
*Cheese Crescents
Chocolate-Glazed
Triple-Layer Cheesecake

For Men Only
(Serves 10)
*Oysters Rockefeller
Grilled Venison Steaks
*Pecan Wild Rice
*Caesar Salad
Whole Wheat Rolls
Deluxe Cheesecake

Invite the Whole Family
(Serves 12)
Brie Appetizer Round
Spicy Rib-Eye Roast
*Plantation Squash
Angel Biscuits
Chocolate Marble Pound Cake

Elegant Entertaining
(Serves 6)
Endive Boats
Stuffed Crown Pork Flambé
Steamed Fresh Broccoli
Cheddar Cheese Sauce
Carrots Madeira
Sachertorte

Simple but Sensational
(Serves 12)
Marinated Mushrooms
Crab-Stuffed Flounder
*Romano-Topped Tomatoes
*Orange Walnut Salad
Commercial French Bread
*French Silk Pie

Entertaining

Cooking for a Crowd

When you're cooking for more people than you're used to cooking for, meal planning, preparation, and serving get a little more complicated. But don't panic—if you'll organize early, according to the following considerations, you can dazzle your friends and still be cool and confident enough to enjoy the party festivities yourself.

GEARING UP FOR THE PARTY

Get your date on the calendar and invitations in the mail at least three weeks ahead of time—earlier if you suspect others are planning events around the same date. Always put an RSVP on the invitation and don't hesitate to include the date by which you'd like those invited to respond. You'll want to know approximately how many guests to count on before you buy groceries.

If your invitation list is large and your house is small, you might stagger the hours on the invitations. That way, everybody won't arrive at the same time.

Two weeks ahead, plan your menu and make out the grocery lists and timetable. After deciding on the menu, make the grocery list in two parts: things that can be bought and prepared ahead of time or stored, and perishables that have to be purchased a day or two before the day of the party.

Regardless of the informality of your party, make two time schedules. The first schedule should include any preparation that can be done ahead, such as preparing some food, checking linens, polishing silver, or ordering items that must be rented. The second schedule organizes the time for all preparation to be done the day of the party. Allow extra time in your schedule to relax and get yourself ready in time to greet early arrivals.

PLAN A MENU THAT'S EASY

Planning the menu is one of the most important things you'll do. As you plan, don't make every dish complicated and demanding, or you'll end up frustrated. Eliminate dishes that require last-minute cooking—the more you can do ahead of time, the better. Cakes, pies, cookies, breads, and some casseroles and sauces can often be prepared in advance and frozen until needed. Salad dressings, gelatin salads, and desserts can generally be made one or two days in advance. And don't be afraid to pick up items from the bakery. Your guests probably won't know unless you tell them.

Plan foods that you think will appeal to the majority of your guests. Pick recipes that will give a variety of colors, tastes, textures, and temperatures in the overall menu. Make sure all food is simple to serve so that guests can help themselves, leaving you free to circulate. If you don't have room to seat everyone, it's probably best to offer "finger food" or "fork food."

TAKE STOCK OF EQUIPMENT

As you add each recipe to your menu, determine what equipment it will require. Do you have the right size soufflé dish or enough refrigerator and oven space? Portable toaster ovens can expand your oven space, and insulated ice chests come in handy for keeping beverages or other items cold. Also, many people make arrangements to store several items in a neighbor's refrigerator as they prepare recipes in advance.

Most people don't own enough of one china, crystal, or silver pattern to serve everyone at a large party, and there's nothing wrong with mixing and matching the different patterns that you have (or that you borrow or rent). You can help unify them with the color of linens or accessories that you use.

KEEP THE CROWD MOVING

When you give a party, there are always congested areas around the food. Scatter the placement of food, and you'll scatter the crowd. They'll see and meet more people and enjoy themselves more if you subtly motivate them to move from room to room. If food is "pick-up at your leisure," set each course in a different room, and scatter individual snacks or appetizers throughout the house. The living room, dining room, den, and even a large bedroom can be used as serving areas.

To serve in other rooms, use the furniture that's already there—the desk, a chest, coffee tables—and bring in moveable carts or folding tables, if necessary. Set the food on trays to protect wood furniture you're serving from.

SETTING UP A BUFFET

The way you set up a buffet table can help guests serve themselves quickly and easily. Equipment should be placed on the table in logical serving order to avoid the necessity of backtracking. For example, plates are always placed where the line begins. But since guests won't need the flatware and napkins as they go through the serving line, place them where the line ends.

Food should be placed on the table in logical serving order: main dish, vegetables, salad, bread, condiments. If the main dish is to be served over rice, the rice should come first in line. Salad dressings and sauces should be placed close to the dish they complement. Desserts may be served at one end of the buffet or placed on a serving cart and served after the guests have completed the main course. Beverages can be placed on a side table or served from a tray after the guests are seated.

If the dining table is used as the serving table, it may be left in the center of the room or placed against the wall to provide additional space in a small room. For a large crowd, the serving table is best placed in the center of the room with a serving line on each side of the table.

As for the buffet table itself, proximity to the kitchen is important so that dishes may be replenished with ease. If food is to be kept in electric warmers, sufficient outlets must be close at hand.

To double-check your serving plan, have a trial run a couple of days before the party. Set out the trays and serving pieces, and label each with the food it will hold. Then imagine going through the buffet line. Does everything seem to flow smoothly? Will you need any additional serving pieces? Mark the location of each item to recreate your plan the day of the party.

A Festive Look for the Table

When you're planning a seated dinner, pay attention to those special details for the table that will set the mood you want. The centerpiece and your use of china and linens can give your table a unique appearance that reflects your personal style.

JUST THE RIGHT CENTERPIECE

Many hostesses no longer routinely telephone the florist to order a formal flower arrangement when they entertain. Flowers or greenery arrangements may often be created from your own yard or by arranging cut flowers purchased from a favorite flower shop.

Today's informal entertaining provides a wonderful opportunity for displaying originality by using whatever is on hand. First look around your house for a decorative object that might become the basis for a centerpiece. It may be a prized collectible or even a dessert or other featured dish. With an eye-catcher at the core of your centerpiece, the remainder of the arrangement can quickly be filled in with seasonal greenery, seed pods, nuts, and other natural materials. Shells, rocks, and driftwood all make creative accessories. Just remember that for a table centerpiece, the arrangement should not be above eye level.

Candles can also set a festive mood for the table. You can scatter them as singles or arrange in groups throughout the house as well, dimming supplemental lighting as the evening progresses.

MIX AND MATCH YOUR CHINA

Give your special dinners a flair by mixing china patterns. Soup bowls or salad plates that are not in your dinnerware pattern, but which have a similar feeling, can give your table setting a lively new look. Color, repetition (of, for instance, a floral motif), and a similar feeling of formality or casualness will unify unmatched patterns.

Start by investigating what you already have. Perhaps the color or design of a breakfast set of pottery or stoneware goes well with your formal china. Or perhaps you have a set of dessert plates which would add interest to your setting. Take a dinner plate, salad plate, and cup and saucer from each pattern, and try different combinations of pieces to see if you can achieve a pleasing mix. If nothing seems to work, or if you have only one pattern, purchasing a few pieces of a different pattern may be all you need to do.

Often, you'll find that the best bargains at antique stores or flea markets are sets of salad or dessert plates and soup bowls, priced reasonably because the dinner plates are not available.

The past decade has produced a wide choice of intermediate-priced dinnerware that is usually more trendy—in popular new colors and fashionable patterns. These provide an inexpensive and easy way to update the timeless pattern of your fine china. If your new arrangement appeals to you, have confidence in your judgment.

LINENS FOR THE TABLE

Formally set tables are traditionally covered with a damask cloth, although linens and lace can also be used. Napkins are usually of the same fabric. When the setting is informal, colors, prints, and checks may be added, as well as place mats.

Varieties of Napkin Folds

The napkin should be folded as desired and placed directly on the plate, unless the first course is served before the diners are seated. In that case, the napkin is placed to the left of the forks, not under them. The Traditional Fold is used for most formal dinners. The V-Fold and Butterfly Fold are for more casual dinners.

THE TRADITIONAL FOLD

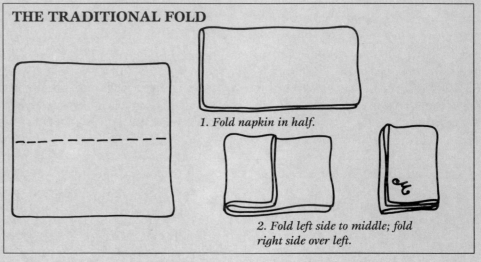

1. Fold napkin in half.

2. Fold left side to middle; fold right side over left.

THE V-FOLD

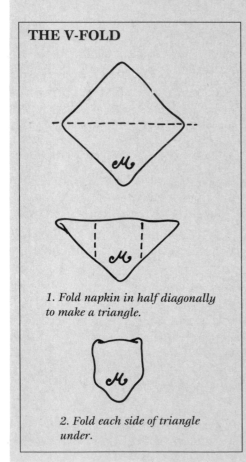

1. Fold napkin in half diagonally to make a triangle.

2. Fold each side of triangle under.

THE BUTTERFLY FOLD

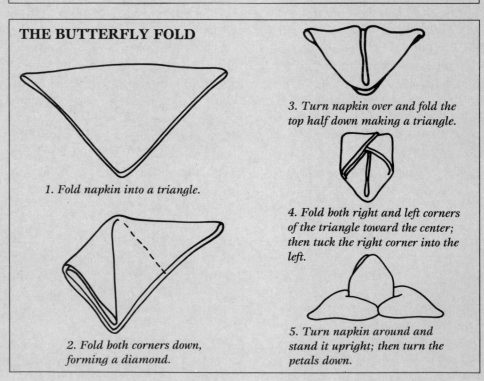

1. Fold napkin into a triangle.

2. Fold both corners down, forming a diamond.

3. Turn napkin over and fold the top half down making a triangle.

4. Fold both right and left corners of the triangle toward the center; then tuck the right corner into the left.

5. Turn napkin around and stand it upright; then turn the petals down.

What Goes Where . . . and When

Don't be embarrassed if you have several questions about the proper ways to set the table and serve the meal. It's not uncommon at all for even a frequent diner or hostess to be unsure of what to do. These guidelines may help.

SETTING THE TABLE

Whether you're planning a simple family meal or you're polishing the silver for company, there are simple rules about the placement of the utensils on the table. The biggest difference between the formal and the informal place setting is that the more formal the dining, the more utensils and accessories there are.

Place the silver 1 inch from the edge of the table, arranging it so that the pieces used first are farthest from the plate. Place the knife, sharp edge inward, and then the spoon to the right of the plate. The fork or forks go to the left. When a salad is served as the first course, place the salad fork on the far left. If the salad is served with the entrée, place the salad fork on the inside, next to the plate. If soup is to be served, place the soup spoon to the right of the teaspoon. If serving an appetizer, place an appetizer fork to the outside of the teaspoon or soup spoon.

Set bread and butter plates at the tip of the forks. Place the butter spreader on the plate parallel to the edge of the table, with the handle to the right.

Set glasses above the knife, with the wine glass to the right of the water glass. When there is more than one wine glass, order them by height, so that shorter ones are not hidden behind taller ones.

The dessert fork or spoon is usually brought in with dessert; it is acceptable, however, to place dessert silver at the top of the place setting, parallel to the edge of the table, with the handle of the spoon to the right, and the handle of the fork to the left.

If coffee and tea are to be served with the meal, the cup and saucer go slightly above and to the right of the spoons. If served only with dessert, bring in the cup and saucer with dessert.

SERVING THE MEAL

Before guests are seated, place the butter on the table, fill the water glasses, and have the wine beside or in front of the host. The salad or appetizer may already be at the table as the guests are seated, unless it's something that would get cold. When all guests are finished with the appetizer, remove the appetizer dishes before serving dinner.

There are several ways to serve a seated dinner. The host can serve the meat from his place, and pass the plate left to the hostess, who serves the vegetables. She passes the plate left, where it stops at the guest seated to the right of the host. After everyone is served, the hostess is served. She then takes a bite of food to signal for all to eat. If the party is large, however, she may signal for guests to begin eating as they are served.

Another serving option is for the host to serve the meat as well as the vegetables from his place, still passing the plates to the left. Or, the plates may be served in the kitchen and then distributed to guests. If hired help is serving, the hostess is served first, then the person to the hostess' left, and on around. Diners are served a plate from the left; the plate is removed from the right.

When everyone is finished dining, clear the table of all items relating to the main meal before bringing dessert and dessert accessories. Service patterns for dessert are the same as for the main meal.

TABLE ETIQUETTE

A general rule for table manners is to follow the lead of the hostess. Wait until the hostess has her napkin placed in her lap before placing your napkin in your lap. After dinner, leave your napkin on your lap until the hostess has removed hers. Then place the napkin loosely on the table to the left of the plate. Don't refold it neatly.

The hostess will begin the meal by taking the first bite. If you're in doubt about what piece of silverware to use, watch to see what the hostess uses. Silverware is usually placed so that you'll use the outer pieces first.

Generally, pass food to the right. Offer the food with your left hand, turning the handle of the dish toward the person receiving it.

When eating soup, dip the spoon away from you and sip the soup from the side of the spoon. If tipping the bowl to get the last bit of soup is common in your area, tip it away from you.

When your knife is not in use, leave it on the upper edge of your plate with the cutting edge toward the center. Leave the fork with its bowl centered on the plate. When you're not using the spoon, rest it on the saucer or dessert plate. When there is no plate of this nature, just lay the spoon on the dinner plate — never place it back on the tablecloth.

Don't Forget the Garnish

However attractive the food is, you'll probably want to add garnishes for special occasions. Garnishes can be as simple as a lining of leafy greens under a salad or a few sprigs of parsley or other fresh herb to crown the top of a casserole. For more elaborate garnishes, try some of these specialty shaped garnishes to place atop all types of food.

FROSTED GRAPES

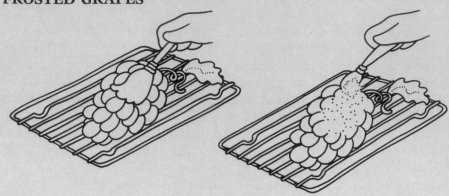

Place purple, blue, or green grapes on a wire rack (individually or in bunches). Beat an egg white just until frothy. Paint grapes with egg white, using a soft pastry brush. While grapes are still wet, sprinkle with granulated sugar to create a frosted look, and allow to dry in a cool place.

Don't refrigerate the frosted grapes because the moisture in the refrigerator will melt the sugar.

FROSTED CRANBERRIES

Follow directions for Frosted Grapes to make Frosted Cranberries.

CARROT CURLS

Scrape carrot. Cut off ½ inch from each end; discard. Using a vegetable peeler, cut thin lengthwise strips from carrot. Roll strips jellyroll fashion; secure with wooden picks. Drop in ice water, and refrigerate at least 1 hour for curls to set. Remove picks before serving.

CARROT FLOWERS

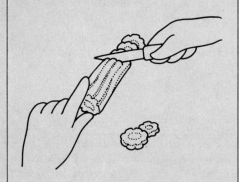

Scrape carrot. Using a sharp knife, cut 4 or 5 grooves, evenly spaced, down the length of carrot; then slice the carrot to produce flowers.

TOMATO ROSE

Cut a thin slice from bottom of tomato, using a sharp paring knife; discard. Beginning at top, peel a continuous paper-thin strip (about ¾-inch wide for regular tomato and about ¼-inch wide for cherry tomato) from entire tomato.

Beginning with first portion cut, shape the strip like a rose. With flesh side inward, coil the strip tightly at first to form the center of the rose, gradually letting it become looser to form the outer petals.

LEMON OR ORANGE ROSE

Follow directions for Tomato Rose to make a Lemon or Orange Rose, cutting strip about ½- to ¾-inch wide.

FLUTED MUSHROOMS

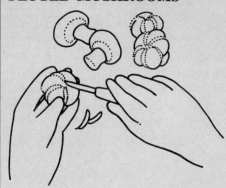

Select firm white mushrooms. Cut several slits at even intervals around each mushroom cap, cutting from the center of the cap to the edge, using a curving motion with the knife. Make another set of slits parallel to the first slits, allowing about 1/16 inch between them. Remove and discard the thin strips of mushroom between the slits.

CELERY FANS

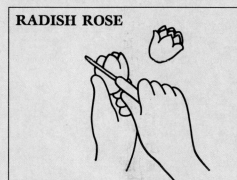

Slice celery stalks into 3- or 4-inch lengths, and place on a cutting board. Using a sharp knife, cut several slits at one or both ends of each piece of celery, cutting almost to, but not through, the center. Place in ice water, and refrigerate until fans curl.

GREEN ONION FANS

Follow directions for Celery Fans to make Green Onion Fans, slicing off root and most of onion's top portion before beginning.

RADISH ROSE

Slice stem end and root tip from radish. Hold radish with root tip up, and slice 4 or 5 petals around the radish by slicing from top to, but not through, bottom. Leave a little red between each petal. Drop radish in ice water, and refrigerate at least 1 hour for rose to open.

ONION MUM

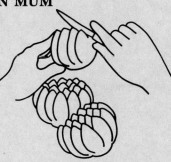

Select a firm white or red onion; peel onion. Set onion on cutting board, root end down. Cut onion almost into quarters, slicing to within ¼ inch of bottom. Continue slicing onion into smaller divisions, slicing to, but not through, bottom. Hold onion under warm running water, and gently separate sections. Place onion in ice water, and refrigerate at least 1 hour for onion to open. Drain well.

CITRUS CUPS

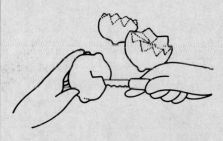

Cut a thin slice from each end of the fruit so that the cups will set level. Insert the blade of a small knife at a downward angle into the middle of the fruit; remove the blade. Insert knife again at an upward angle to make a zigzag pattern. Continue cutting in this fashion all the way around fruit.

Separate the halves by twisting slightly and carefully pulling them apart. Scoop out the pulp if the cups will be used as a container.

TOMATO OR GREEN PEPPER CUPS

Follow directions for Citrus Cups to make Tomato or Green Pepper Cups.

CHOCOLATE CURLS

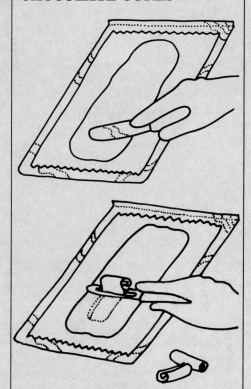

Melt squares or morsels of semisweet chocolate in top of a double boiler. Let chocolate cool slightly.

Pour chocolate out in a stream onto a wax paper-lined baking sheet. Spread chocolate with a spatula into a 2- or 3-inch wide strip. (The width of strip determines the length of curls.) Smooth top of strip with spatula.

Let stand at room temperature until chocolate cools and feels slightly tacky, but is not firm. (If chocolate is too hard, curls will break; if too soft, chocolate will not curl.)

Gently pull a vegetable peeler across length of chocolate until curl forms, letting chocolate curl up on top of peeler. Insert wooden pick in curl to transfer. Chill until ready to use.

APPETIZERS & SANDWICHES

From dainty dinner appetizers to meal-in-one sandwiches, the assortment of recipes in this chapter is varied enough to satisfy any craving. When serving pre-dinner snacks, offer just enough to stimulate, not satisfy, the appetite. With sandwiches, you'll usually want something a little heartier.

EQUIPMENT

When making appetizers and sandwiches, you'll probably need more equipment for serving than for preparing the recipes. The most helpful tools in the kitchen are as basic as sharp knives and large baking sheets to help you cut and cook efficiently when a crowd is expected.

As for serving appetizers, you'll find a large assortment of trays, bowls, and spreaders handy for setting up buffets. Concentrate on variation in the size, shape, and height of containers to add interest to the arrangement. Don't overlook baskets and china novelties you normally decorate with—they'll often double as interesting containers.

You'll also need to have access to warming trays and containers to keep hot appetizers at the right temperature. If you don't have a chafing dish, a fondue pot or slow cooker will do the job well.

RECEPTION APPETIZERS

If the party or reception crowd is too large to provide each guest a seat,

Oysters Rockefeller (page 46) will surely cause a crowd to gather.

you'll want to serve strictly finger foods. Plan your menu so it contains both hot and cold appetizers, as well as items easy for guests to serve themselves if you have no one to help serve. Set up one or two main appetizer buffets, and also scatter a few individual nibbles around the

house, such as seasoned nuts, popcorn, or dips and dippers. Remember to provide plenty of napkins for sticky fingers, and try to avoid messy foods that are apt to drip as guests eat them.

FIRST COURSE APPETIZERS

Choose one special appetizer as the first course to dinner, and make servings a little more substantial than those offered as part of an appetizer buffet. First courses are usually served at the dining table, but nothing should stop you from serving them in the den or living room for variety. Many first course appetizers are offered within this chapter, such as Oysters Rockefeller, Jalapeño-Tomato Seviche and Swiss-Stuffed Mushrooms. You'll find many other delightful first course appetizers if you flip through the soups and salads chapters.

FREEZING APPETIZERS

Many appetizers are appropriate for freezing, especially those made with meat or bread. Avoid freezing appetizers that contain fresh vegetables, mayonnaise, and hard-cooked eggs. The secret to keeping appetizers fresh in the freezer is proper wrapping. No matter what kind of wrapping you use, be sure it is airtight to avoid freezer burn. Usually, you can let appetizers thaw overnight in the refrigerator (if they require refrigeration). Some of our appetizer recipes give specific directions for baking them straight from the freezer.

MICROWAVING APPETIZERS

Any hostess will tell you that serving hot appetizers to a crowd takes a lot of advance planning and preparation. But with the help of a microwave oven, it's easier than you might think. Appetizers can often be made ahead, refrigerated on microwave-safe serving platters, and microwaved as needed. Directions are given for each of our recipes suitable for microwave cooking.

Arrange individual appetizers about ¼ inch apart in a ring on the microwave dish. Microwaves will then enter on every side of the appetizers, allowing more even heating.

The amount of food being microwaved affects the cooking time. Our recipes recommend cooking a specific number of appetizers at a time. If the number is increased, the time required will increase, and cooking may be uneven. If fewer appetizers are microwaved, decrease cooking time slightly.

Snacks

Snacks are those tempting little nibbles that you'd swear you weren't eating many of—until the bowl is empty. When stored in an airtight container, they'll give you days of enjoyment.

Recipes like Raisin-Nut Party Mix and Granola yield fairly large amounts and make attractive and welcome gifts for friends and neighbors. And popcorn, easily made in generous amounts, can be seasoned in many different ways. Tuck some away for your family, and package the rest in airtight containers to share.

Although these recipes are simple to make, there may be times when company unexpectedly drops in and you can't take the time to prepare a recipe to serve them. If you have any of the following common foodstuffs on hand, you can present them on a silver tray at a moment's notice: cheese and crackers, commercial picante sauce and taco chips, sliced fresh fruit, and commercially seasoned nuts and crackers.

RAISIN-NUT PARTY MIX

1 (8-ounce) jar dry roasted peanuts
1 (7-ounce) jar dry roasted cashews
1 (6-ounce) can roasted almonds
2 cups bite-size crispy wheat squares
¼ cup plus 2 tablespoons butter or margarine, melted
1½ tablespoons soy sauce
1½ tablespoons Worcestershire sauce
3 dashes of hot sauce
1 cup raisins

Combine first 4 ingredients in a large bowl; stir well. Combine butter, soy sauce, Worcestershire sauce, and hot sauce; mix well and pour over nut mixture, tossing to coat.

Spread half of mixture in a 15- x 10- x 1-inch jellyroll pan. Bake at 325° for 15 minutes; cool and place in a large bowl. Repeat with remaining mixture. Add raisins, and stir well. Store in an airtight container. Yield: 9 cups.

CURRIED ALMONDS

3 cups blanched whole almonds
1 tablespoon butter or margarine, melted
1¼ teaspoons seasoned salt
¾ teaspoon curry powder

Place almonds in a shallow roasting pan; brush with butter, and stir well. Roast almonds at 350° for 10 minutes or until golden brown.

Combine salt and curry powder; sprinkle over almonds, and stir until coated. Return to oven, and bake an additional 10 minutes. Drain on paper towels; cool. Store in an airtight container. Yield: 3 cups.

Curried Pecans: Three cups raw pecan halves may be substituted for almonds, if desired.

Curried Nut Mix: Three cups raw mixed nuts may be substituted for almonds, such as pecans, peanuts, cashews, walnuts, Brazil nuts, or filberts.

GRANOLA

You'll enjoy Granola as a snack or as a cereal with milk. Vary it each time you make it by the addition of different nuts and dried fruits.

3 cups regular oats, uncooked
½ cup flaked coconut
½ cup sliced almonds
¼ cup wheat germ
¼ cup sunflower kernels
¼ cup plus 2 tablespoons honey
¼ cup vegetable oil
2½ tablespoons water
2 tablespoons brown sugar
¾ teaspoon vanilla extract
¼ teaspoon salt
¾ cup raisins

Combine first 5 ingredients in a large bowl; stir well and set aside.

Combine honey, oil, water, brown sugar, vanilla, and salt; pour over oat mixture, and stir well. Spread mixture evenly in a lightly greased 15- x 10- x 1-inch jellyroll pan. Bake at 350° for 25 minutes or until golden brown, stirring every 5 minutes. Cool. Stir in raisins. Store mixture in an airtight container in a cool, dry place up to 1½ months. Serve as a snack or as a cereal with milk. Yield: 5½ cups.

Nutty Granola: Stir 2 cups mixed raw nuts (pecans, walnuts, pine nuts, almonds) into oat mixture before baking mixture.

Fruited Granola: Stir 2 cups mixed chopped dried fruit (banana chips, dried apricots, apples, peaches, pineapple) into granola with raisins.

BARBECUED PECANS

2 tablespoons butter or margarine
¼ cup Worcestershire sauce
1 tablespoon catsup
⅛ teaspoon hot sauce
4 cups pecan halves
Salt to taste

Melt butter in a Dutch oven. Remove butter from heat; add Worcestershire sauce, catsup, and hot sauce, stirring well. Add pecan halves to mixture, stirring to coat.

Spread pecans evenly in a 15- x 10- x 1-inch jellyroll pan. Bake at 350° for 13 to 15 minutes, stirring every 5 minutes. Place pecans on paper towels; sprinkle lightly with salt, and cool completely. Yield: 4 cups.

CANDIED POPCORN

5 quarts freshly popped popcorn
1½ cups raw peanuts (optional)
1 cup butter or margarine
2 cups firmly packed brown sugar
½ cup dark corn syrup
½ teaspoon baking soda
½ teaspoon salt
½ teaspoon vanilla extract

Place popcorn and peanuts, if desired, in a lightly greased roasting pan; set mixture aside.

Melt butter in a large saucepan; stir in sugar and corn syrup. Bring to a boil; boil 5 minutes, stirring often. Remove from heat; stir in soda, salt, and vanilla.

Pour sugar mixture over popcorn; stir well. Bake at 250° for 1 hour, stirring every 15 minutes. Cool; store in an airtight container. Yield: 5 quarts.

Everyone Loves Popcorn

Popcorn is the delight of small children, late-night staple for collegians, and whole-grain snack for nutrition-conscious adults. But people seldom venture from salt and butter when it comes to dressing this favorite snack. Consider making these popcorn variations next time you get the munchies.

To make flavored popcorn, start with freshly popped corn. For every 4 cups of popped corn, stir in 2 tablespoons melted butter or margarine and ¼ teaspoon salt. Then add additional seasonings as indicated for each type of popcorn described below.

Chippercorn: Toss ¾ to 1 cup semisweet chocolate mini-morsels per 4 cups cooled buttered, salted popcorn. For variations, try substituting an equal amount of peanut butter or butterscotch morsels.

Currycorn: Add an Indian dimension with a light sprinkling of curry powder; add ½ to ¾ teaspoon per 4 cups buttered, salted popcorn. This is a concoction you'll want to serve with beverages!

Hotcorn: For true fire-eaters, shake ½ teaspoon chili powder and ¼ teaspoon dried crushed red pepper over 4 cups buttered, salted popcorn. Make sure you have plenty of liquid refreshments on hand.

Italian Popcorn: Add 2 tablespoons melted butter per 4 cups popped corn, but omit salt. Stir in ¼ cup grated Parmesan cheese, 1 tablespoon dried whole oregano, and ½ teaspoon garlic salt. Mix well, and be prepared for cries of "Bravo!"

Nutcorn: Toss about 1 cup of your favorite unsalted nuts into 4 cups buttered, salted popcorn. A variety of nuts to equal 1 cup works well, too. If salted nuts are used, omit salt in popcorn.

CHEESE CRACKERS

1 cup all-purpose flour
⅛ teaspoon red pepper
⅔ cup grated Parmesan cheese
½ cup butter or margarine, softened

Combine flour and red pepper in a mixing bowl; add cheese, stirring well. Cut in butter until mixture resembles coarse meal. Mix with hands until dough is smooth; shape into a ball.

Roll dough on a lightly floured surface to about ¼-inch thickness. Cut into desired shapes with 1-inch cookie or canapé cutters. (Crackers are fragile; do not use a larger cutter.) Place crackers on ungreased baking sheets; bake at 350° for 12 minutes or until lightly browned. Yield: 6 dozen.

CHEESE STRAWS

2 cups (8 ounces) shredded sharp Cheddar cheese
½ cup butter or margarine, softened
1½ cups all-purpose flour
1 teaspoon paprika
½ teaspoon salt
¼ to ½ teaspoon red pepper

Combine cheese and butter in a large mixing bowl; beat well at medium speed of an electric mixer. Combine remaining ingredients, stirring well. Gradually add flour mixture to cheese mixture, mixing until dough is no longer crumbly. Shape mixture into a ball.

Use a cookie gun to shape dough into straws, following manufacturer's instructions, or use the following procedure: Divide dough into fourths; on wax paper, roll each piece into a rectangle ⅓-inch thick. Use a pastry wheel to cut dough into 2- x ½-inch strips.

Place strips on ungreased baking sheets; bake at 375° for 10 to 12 minutes or until lightly browned. Store in airtight containers, placing wax paper between layers. Yield: about 8 dozen.

Dips and Spreads

Dips and spreads are usually in great demand for parties or family enjoyment because they're so easy to make ahead. Store them in airtight containers; those without meat or other perishable foodstuff will last for days.

At a party, guests can easily serve dips and spreads for themselves. Just set out an assortment of crackers, chips, and other accompaniments.

Dippers that Surprise

Ordinary crackers and chips make tasty and convenient dippers, but a little imagination can add new dimensions to your favorite dips. Cocktail sausages, cold shrimp, or spears of scallops or ham make good meat choices. Also, take advantage of less-used vegetable dippers, like snow peas, turnip strips, brussels sprouts, and steamed asparagus.

VEGETABLE DIP

1 cup mayonnaise
½ cup whipping cream, whipped
½ cup chopped fresh parsley
2 tablespoons minced fresh chives
1 tablespoon grated onion
1½ teaspoons lemon juice
¼ teaspoon salt
¼ teaspoon paprika
⅛ teaspoon curry powder
1 small clove garlic, minced

Combine all ingredients; stir well. Chill 3 hours. Serve with fresh vegetables. Yield: 2 cups.

CURRIED DIP

1 (8-ounce) carton commercial sour cream
1 cup mayonnaise
2 teaspoons curry powder
2 teaspoons instant minced onion
2 teaspoons prepared horseradish
2 teaspoons vinegar

Combine all ingredients; stir well. Store in refrigerator. Serve with fresh vegetables. Yield: 1⅔ cups.

Dilled Dip: Substitute 2 teaspoons dried dillweed for curry powder.

SAN ANTONIO CHILE DIP

1 (28-ounce) can whole tomatoes, drained and chopped
1 medium onion, finely chopped
2 (4-ounce) cans chopped green chiles, drained
3 cloves garlic, crushed
2 tablespoons vegetable oil
1 tablespoon vinegar
2 teaspoons crushed red pepper
1 teaspoon salt
1 teaspoon dried whole oregano
¼ teaspoon ground cumin

Combine all ingredients; stir well. Chill 2 to 3 hours. Serve with taco chips. Yield: 3 cups.

GREAT GUACAMOLE

Guacamole is commonly thought of as a dip for corn or taco chips, but you can also serve it as a salad dressing. Just spoon the tasty concoction over shredded lettuce, and top with chopped tomatoes.

1 medium avocado, peeled and
   mashed
¼ cup finely chopped onion
¼ cup chopped tomato
1 tablespoon lemon juice
½ teaspoon salt
¼ teaspoon hot sauce
2 cloves garlic, minced
1 jalapeño pepper, seeded and
   chopped (optional)

Combine all ingredients, stirring until blended. Yield: 1½ cups.

Creative Dip Containers

Firm-textured raw fruits and vegetables make excellent containers for dips. Try pineapple, grapefruit, cantaloupe, green pepper, turnip, or a large cucumber. First, cut a narrow slice from bottom so container sits flat; then, carve out center and fill cavity.

FESTIVE EGG DIP

1 (8-ounce) package cream cheese,
   softened
½ cup milk
3 hard-cooked eggs, finely chopped
2 tablespoons mayonnaise
1 tablespoon chopped chives
1 teaspoon prepared mustard
¼ teaspoon salt
⅛ teaspoon pepper

Combine cream cheese and milk in a small mixing bowl; beat at medium speed of an electric mixer until creamy. Add remaining ingredients, mixing until light and fluffy. Serve with fresh vegetables. Yield: 2 cups.

SMOKED OYSTER DIP

1 (8-ounce) package cream cheese,
   softened
1½ cups mayonnaise
1 tablespoon lemon juice
⅛ teaspoon hot sauce
⅓ cup chopped ripe olives
1 (3.66-ounce) can smoked oysters,
   drained and chopped

Combine first 4 ingredients, mixing well. Stir in olives and oysters. Serve with fresh vegetables or crackers. Yield: about 3 cups.

Shrimp Dip: One (4¼-ounce) can medium shrimp, rinsed, drained, and chopped, may be substituted for oysters, if desired.

HOT CHILE-CHEESE DIP

1 small onion, finely chopped
3 slices bacon, chopped
1 pound process American cheese,
   cubed
1 (15-ounce) can chili without beans
1 (10-ounce) can tomatoes with
   chiles, chopped and undrained

Sauté onion and bacon in a saucepan until onion is tender. Stir in cheese cubes, chili, and tomatoes; cook until bubbly, stirring well. Serve warm with chips. Yield: 4 cups.

FRESH PINEAPPLE DIP

1 medium pineapple
1 egg, well beaten
2 to 4 tablespoons sugar
1 teaspoon all-purpose flour
1 cup whipping cream, whipped

Cut a lengthwise slice from pineapple, removing about one-third of pineapple. Scoop pulp from slice; discard rind.

Scoop pulp from remaining portion of pineapple, leaving shell ½-inch thick; set aside.

Cut pineapple pulp into bite-size pieces, discarding core. Crush 1 cup of pineapple pieces, reserving remaining pineapple pieces for dipping.

Combine crushed pineapple (and juice that accumulates), egg, sugar, and flour in a large saucepan. Cook over low heat until thickened, stirring constantly; cool. Fold in whipped cream, and spoon into pineapple shell.

Serve dip with reserved pineapple pieces and other fresh fruit cut into pieces. Yield: 2½ cups.

SPINACH DIP IN CABBAGE

(pictured on page 34)

1 (10-ounce) package frozen chopped
   spinach
⅔ cup commercial sour cream
⅔ cup mayonnaise
¼ cup chopped green onions
½ teaspoon herb-seasoned salt
½ teaspoon dried whole oregano
¼ teaspoon dried whole
   dillweed
1 teaspoon lemon juice
1 large cabbage

Cook spinach according to package directions; drain well, and stir in all remaining ingredients except cabbage. Chill mixture.

Trim core end of cabbage to form a flat base. Fold back several outer leaves of cabbage, if desired. Cut a crosswise slice from the top, making it wide enough to remove about one-fourth of the head; then lift out enough inner leaves from the cabbage to form a shell about 1 inch thick. (Reserve slice and inner leaves of cabbage for other uses.)

Spoon dip into cabbage cavity, and serve with an assortment of fresh vegetables. Yield: 2 cups.

Spread Sandwiches for a Party

You can transform many of our sandwich spreads into fancy sandwiches by following these stacking and slicing techniques.

Just arrange and slice the bread; then spread with your choice of fillings according to the individual sandwich diagrams below, working on one pattern at a time to ensure maximum freshness of bread.

If your sandwiches will be chilled more than 2 hours before serving, spread the bread with butter before adding fillings, to prevent the filling from soaking into the bread.

As individual sandwiches are assembled, place them in a shallow pan lined with a damp towel and wax paper. Cover with another layer of wax paper and a damp towel; store in refrigerator until ready to serve.

RIBBON SANDWICHES

Stack 3 slices whole wheat and 2 slices white bread alternately, filling with 1 or more spreads. Press each stack together firmly, and trim crusts.

Wrap each stack in plastic wrap, and chill at least 2 hours. Cut into 6 (½-inch) slices. Cut each slice into halves and place on serving tray. (About 1½ cups filling will spread approximately 5 dozen sandwiches.)

CHECKERBOARD SANDWICHES

Follow first step for ribbon sandwiches, except stack 2 slices whole wheat and 2 slices white bread alternately. Cut into 6 (½-inch) slices. Stack 3 slices together so that whole wheat and white slices alternate, filling with 1 or more spreads. Repeat process with remaining 3 slices.

Wrap in plastic wrap, and chill several hours. Remove from refrigerator; cut each of two stacks into 6 (½-inch) slices. (About 2⅓ cups filling will spread approximately 5 dozen sandwiches.)

PINWHEEL SANDWICHES

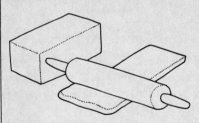 

Trim crust off a 1-pound loaf of unsliced bread. Slice loaf lengthwise into ¼-inch-thick slices, and roll each slice with a rolling pin to flatten. Spread with softened butter and a filling.

If desired, place olives, pickles, Vienna sausage, or a frankfurter across the short end of slice; roll up tightly. Wrap in plastic wrap, and chill 8 hours. Cut chilled rolls into ½-inch slices, and place on serving trays. (About 1½ cups filling will spread approximately 3 dozen sandwiches.)

CUTOUT SANDWICHES

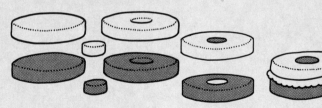

Cut 2 rounds white and 2 rounds whole wheat bread with desired cutter. Remove center of 1 whole wheat and 1 white round with smaller cutter.

Insert small rounds of whole wheat into holes of large white rounds, and small rounds of white into large whole wheat rounds. Spread filling on whole rounds; top with opposite-colored cutout rounds. (About 1½ cups filling will spread 3½ dozen sandwiches.)

PIMIENTO CHEESE SPREAD

2 cups (8 ounces) shredded
  extra-sharp Cheddar cheese
1 (2-ounce) jar diced pimiento,
  drained
¼ cup plus 2 tablespoons chopped
  pecans
¼ cup mayonnaise
6 pimiento-stuffed olives, diced
1 tablespoon dry sherry
¼ teaspoon hot sauce
⅛ to ¼ teaspoon pepper

Combine all ingredients, stirring well.
Chill. Yield: about 2 cups.

EDAM-SHERRY SPREAD

(pictured on page 34)

1 (2-pound) whole Edam or Gouda
  cheese
¼ cup butter or margarine,
  softened
½ teaspoon dry mustard
½ cup finely chopped
  pimiento-stuffed olives
¼ cup finely chopped onion
1 clove garlic, minced
2 tablespoons dry sherry

Allow Edam cheese to come to room
temperature before preparing. Carefully
cut off top quarter of cheese; cut out
cheese from both sections, leaving a ½-
inch shell in bottom section. Discard top
shell of wax.
  Cut cheese into small pieces. Position
knife blade in processor bowl, and add
cheese. Process until cheese is smooth
and forms a ball. Add butter and mustard. Process until blended. Knead in
olives, onion, garlic, and sherry until
blended. Pack cheese spread into cavity
of cheese. Serve with crackers. Yield:
about 5 cups.

PARTY CUCUMBER SPREAD

1 medium cucumber
1 (3-ounce) package cream cheese,
  softened
¼ cup minced onion
2 teaspoons lemon juice
⅛ teaspoon salt
⅛ teaspoon white pepper
⅛ teaspoon hot sauce

Coarsely shred enough cucumber to
make 1 cup. Press shredded cucumber
between paper towels to remove excess
moisture. Beat cream cheese until fluffy.
Stir prepared cucumber and remaining
ingredients into cream cheese. Serve
spread on party rye bread. Yield: 1 cup.

HORSERADISH HAM SPREAD

1½ cups coarsely ground cooked
  ham
1 (8-ounce) can crushed pineapple,
  well drained
¼ cup mayonnaise
1 tablespoon prepared horseradish
1 teaspoon prepared mustard

Combine all ingredients, stirring well.
Store in refrigerator. Serve spread with
assorted crackers or party rye bread.
Yield: about 2 cups.

CORNED BEEF SPREAD

1 (12-ounce) can corned beef
1 (8-ounce) package braunschweiger
½ cup mayonnaise
3 tablespoons instant minced onion
3 tablespoons vinegar
1½ teaspoons dry mustard

Combine all ingredients, stirring well.
Serve with crackers or party rye bread.
Yield: 3 cups.

CHICKEN SALAD SPREAD

1½ cups coarsely ground chicken
¼ cup sweet pickle relish
3 to 4 tablespoons mayonnaise
2 tablespoons finely chopped onion
¾ teaspoon salt
½ teaspoon celery seeds
¼ teaspoon pepper

Combine all ingredients, stirring well.
Store in refrigerator. Yield: 1½ cups.

BAKED ARTICHOKE SPREAD

2 (14-ounce) cans artichoke hearts,
  drained and chopped
1 cup grated Parmesan cheese
1 cup mayonnaise
⅛ teaspoon garlic powder
Dash of Worcestershire sauce
Dash of hot sauce
Fresh parsley sprigs (optional)

Combine first 6 ingredients, stirring
well. Spoon into a lightly greased 1-
quart casserole or soufflé dish. Bake at
350° for 20 minutes. Garnish with parsley, if desired; serve with toast points or
melba rounds. Yield: 3 cups.

PINEAPPLE-CHEESE BALL

2 (8-ounce) packages cream cheese,
  softened
1 (8-ounce) can crushed pineapple,
  drained
¼ cup finely chopped green pepper
2 tablespoons chopped onion
1 teaspoon seasoned salt
1 cup chopped pecans

Combine cream cheese, pineapple,
green pepper, onion, and salt; mix well.
Chill; shape into a 4-inch ball, and roll
in pecans. Yield: about 2½ cups.

SALMON-CHEESE BALL

1 (7¾-ounce) can red salmon, drained and flaked
1 (8-ounce) package cream cheese, softened
1 tablespoon lemon juice
1 tablespoon grated onion
1 teaspoon prepared horseradish
¼ teaspoon liquid smoke
Chopped fresh parsley

Combine all ingredients except the chopped parsley; chill. Shape mixture into a 4-inch ball, and roll in parsley. Serve with crackers. Yield: 2 cups.

TANGY CHEESE BALL

2 (8-ounce) packages cream cheese, softened
4 cups (16 ounces) shredded sharp Cheddar cheese
¼ cup milk
¼ cup chopped pimiento-stuffed olives
1 (.06-ounce) envelope Italian salad dressing mix
1 cup chopped pecans or walnuts

Combine all ingredients except nuts, mixing well. Shape into 2 balls, and coat with pecans. Chill 8 hours. Serve at room temperature. Yield: 4¼ cups.

CHUTNEY CHEESE

2 (8-ounce) packages cream cheese, softened
1 (8-ounce) jar chutney
½ cup chopped green onions
½ cup coarsely chopped, dry roasted peanuts
½ cup flaked coconut

Spread cream cheese into a 7½-inch diameter circle on a serving plate. Spread chutney over cream cheese; top with rings of green onions and peanuts, and sprinkle coconut in center. Serve immediately, or refrigerate up to 1 hour. Serve with crackers. Yield: about 3 cups.

HERBED CHEESE ROUND

2 (8-ounce) packages cream cheese, softened
2 teaspoons chopped fresh chives
1 teaspoon dried whole basil
1 teaspoon caraway seeds
1 teaspoon dillseeds
Freshly ground pepper
Sliced lemon wedges (optional)

Combine cream cheese, fresh chives, basil, caraway seeds, and dillseeds. Shape into a 5- x 1-inch patty; lightly coat top and sides with pepper.

Cover patty, and chill several hours; garnish top with lemon wedges, if desired. Serve with crackers. Yield: 2 cups.

Plan your party menu to include dips and spreads in an assortment of flavors, shapes, and textures. From top, Spinach Dip in Cabbage (page 31), Edam-Sherry Spread (page 33), and Herbed Cheese Round (page 34).

BRIE APPETIZER ROUND

Brie, like Camembert, belongs to the family of soft-ripened cheeses that are so popular now. Characteristic of these cheeses, they ripen from the outside in, forming a thin tender snow-white rind. It is a natural covering that can be eaten with the cheese.

1 (2½-pound) round fully ripened Brie
⅔ cup coarsely chopped pecans
2 tablespoons brown sugar

Remove rind from top of cheese, cutting to within ¼ inch of outside edges. Place cheese on an ungreased baking sheet, and arrange pecans over top. Sprinkle with sugar.

Broil 8 inches from heat for 3 to 5 minutes or until sugar and cheese are bubbly. Serve hot with crackers. Yield: one 8-inch cheese round.

PECAN-CHEESE RING

4 cups (16 ounces) shredded extra sharp Cheddar cheese
4 cups (16 ounces) shredded medium Cheddar cheese
1 small onion, grated
1 cup mayonnaise
1 teaspoon red pepper
1 cup chopped pecans
Fresh parsley sprigs
Round buttery crackers
Strawberry preserves (optional)

Combine first 5 ingredients, mixing well. Sprinkle about ¼ cup pecans in an oiled 7-cup ring mold, and press cheese mixture into mold. Chill until firm.

Unmold on platter, and pat remaining pecans onto cheese ring. Garnish with parsley sprigs. Serve on crackers with strawberry preserves on top, if desired. Yield: about 6 cups.

CHICKEN LIVER PÂTÉ

Many people who say they don't care for pâté have enjoyed this particular version. The brandy is the secret ingredient that smooths out the flavor of this traditional spread.

¼ cup finely minced green onions
2 pounds chicken livers (about 4 cups)
¼ cup butter or margarine, melted
⅔ cup brandy
½ cup whipping cream
¾ teaspoon salt
¼ teaspoon ground allspice
¼ teaspoon pepper
Pinch of ground thyme
1 cup butter or margarine, melted
Green onion stems
Carrot curls
Fresh parsley sprigs

Sauté minced green onions and livers in ¼ cup butter until livers are done; spoon liver mixture into container of an electric blender or food processor.

Place brandy in a small saucepan; simmer over medium-low heat until reduced to 6 tablespoons. Add brandy, whipping cream, and seasonings to liver mixture; blend 1 minute or until smooth. Add 1 cup butter to mixture; blend well.

Spoon pâté into a lightly oiled 5-cup mold; chill at least 3 hours. Unmold, and wrap green onion stems around pâté as ribbon, and place carrot curls on pâté as bow. Garnish with parsley. Serve with crackers. Yield: about 5 cups.

GARLIC-CHIVE CHEESE MOLD

1 recipe Cream-Style Cheese (page 225)
2 cloves garlic, crushed
2 tablespoons chopped fresh chives

Combine Cream-Style Cheese, garlic, and chives, stirring until blended.

Line a smooth-sided 1½-cup mold with 4 thicknesses of dampened cheesecloth large enough to extend over edges. Spoon cheese mixture into mold, pressing firmly with the back of a spoon. Gather edges of cheesecloth, and tie securely. Invert mold on a wire rack in a shallow pan. Cover pan with enough plastic wrap to make an airtight seal. Refrigerate 1 to 2 days or until mixture is firm and well drained. Unmold cheese, and remove cheesecloth before serving. Serve cheese with crackers. Yield: 1½ cups.

Note: Two 8-ounce packages commercial cream cheese, softened, can be substituted for 1 recipe Cream-Style Cheese. If using commercial cream cheese, add 2 tablespoons plus 2 teaspoons milk to mixture. Then mold as directed. No drainage is necessary.

THREE-CHEESE MOLD

1 envelope unflavored gelatin
¼ cup cold water
2 cups (8 ounces) shredded sharp Cheddar cheese
1 cup whipping cream
¾ cup mayonnaise
½ cup grated Parmesan cheese
¼ cup chopped pecans
¼ cup crumbled blue cheese
1½ teaspoons prepared mustard
⅛ teaspoon salt
Dash of hot sauce
Mayonnaise
Chopped fresh parsley (optional)
Cherry tomatoes (optional)

Soften gelatin in water in a small saucepan; place over low heat, stirring until dissolved. Combine Cheddar cheese and next 8 ingredients in a medium bowl, stirring well; stir in gelatin mixture. Lightly coat a 4-cup mold with mayonnaise; pour cheese mixture into mold; chill overnight or until firm. Unmold on serving plate; garnish with parsley and tomatoes, if desired. Serve with crackers. Yield: about 3¼ cups.

BLUE CHEESE MOLD

½ recipe Cream-Style Cheese
  (page 225)
6 to 8 ounces blue cheese, crumbled
¼ cup plus 2 tablespoons butter or
  margarine, softened
1 tablespoon coarsely chopped onion
1 small clove garlic, cut in half
Dash of coarsely ground pepper
1 tablespoon diced, drained pimiento

Position knife blade in food processor
bowl; add Cream-Style Cheese, blue cheese, butter, onion, garlic, and pepper. Top with cover, and process until smooth. Remove knife blade, and gently stir in pimiento.

Line a 3-cup smooth-sided mold with 4 thicknesses of dampened cheesecloth large enough to extend over edges. Spoon cheese mixture into mold, pressing firmly with the back of a spoon. Gather edges of cheesecloth, and tie securely. Invert mold on a wire rack in a shallow pan. Cover pan with enough plastic wrap to make an airtight seal. Refrigerate 1 to 2 days or until mixture is firm and well drained. Unmold cheese, and remove cheesecloth before serving. Yield: 2 cups.

Note: One 8-ounce package commercial cream cheese, softened, can be substituted for ½ recipe Cream-Style Cheese. If using commercial cream cheese, add 1 tablespoon plus 1 teaspoon milk. Then mold as directed. No drainage is necessary.

Cold Appetizers

Usually served straight from the refrigerator, cold appetizers have that convenient make-ahead quality that smart party-planners look for. Most of these cold appetizers are equally good after they come to room temperature, too, making them a good choice to sit out on a buffet for a while.

CAVIAR POTATOES

7 small new potatoes
2½ cups boiling water
½ cup plus 1 tablespoon commercial
  sour cream
About 2½ teaspoons black caviar,
  drained
About 2½ teaspoons gold caviar,
  drained

Cook potatoes in boiling water for 15 minutes or until tender; drain. Chill.

Slice potatoes crosswise into ¼-inch slices. Place potato slices on a serving platter. Top each slice with about ¾ teaspoon sour cream and about ⅛ teaspoon caviar. Yield: about 3 dozen.

DILLY CARROTS

¾ cup white wine vinegar
¼ cup water
¼ cup honey
½ teaspoon dried whole dillweed
½ teaspoon mixed pickling spices
Dash of salt
1 (12-ounce) package baby carrots,
  scraped
Fresh dill sprigs (optional)

Combine first 6 ingredients in a large saucepan; bring to a boil. Add carrots; cover, reduce heat, and simmer 10 to 12 minutes or until crisp-tender. Remove from heat, and chill. Serve with a slotted spoon. Garnish with dill sprigs, if desired. Yield: 15 appetizer servings.

□*Microwave Directions:* Combine first 7 ingredients in a 1½-quart baking dish; cover with lid. Microwave at HIGH for 5 to 7 minutes or until carrots are crisp-tender. Chill. Serve with a slotted spoon. Garnish with dill sprigs, if desired.

Note: Three-fourths pound large carrots cut into julienne strips may be substituted for baby carrots, if desired.

MARINATED MUSHROOMS

1 (2-ounce) can anchovies,
  drained
1 clove garlic, minced
1 (2-ounce) jar diced pimiento,
  drained
1⅓ cups vegetable oil
1 cup lemon juice
½ teaspoon dried whole
  tarragon
½ teaspoon dried whole basil
¼ teaspoon dried whole
  oregano
⅛ teaspoon pepper
2 pounds small fresh
  mushrooms
Lettuce leaves (optional)

Mash anchovies in a shallow container. Add minced garlic and next 7 ingredients; stir mixture well. Add mushrooms, and toss gently to coat. Cover and refrigerate 8 hours, stirring occasionally.

Drain marinated mixture well, and serve on lettuce leaves, if desired. Yield: 20 appetizer servings.

JALAPEÑO-STUFFED CELERY

1½ cups (6 ounces) shredded
   Cheddar cheese
2 tablespoons mayonnaise
1½ tablespoons coarsely chopped
   onion
2½ tablespoons jalapeño relish or
   salsa jalapeño
8 celery stalks, cut into 3-inch pieces
Ripe olive slices (optional)
Chili powder

Position knife blade in food processor bowl; add cheese, mayonnaise, and onion. Top with cover, and process until smooth. Spoon mixture into a bowl; stir in jalapeño relish. Stuff celery pieces with cheese mixture. Top with olive slices, if desired. Sprinkle with chili powder. Yield: about 20 celery sticks.

STUFFED SNOW PEAS

2 dozen fresh or frozen snow pea
   pods
¾ cup whipped cream cheese,
   softened
2 tablespoons orange juice
1½ teaspoons prepared horseradish
⅛ teaspoon freshly ground pepper
Finely grated orange rind

Thaw snow pea pods, if frozen. Trim ends from snow peas; place in a steaming basket. Plunge basket into boiling water, and remove immediately. Place snow peas in a ice water to cool quickly. Remove from water, and refrigerate.

Combine cream cheese, orange juice, horseradish, and pepper; stir until smooth. Chill at least 1 hour.

Using a sharp knife, carefully slit one side of each snow pea. Spoon cream cheese mixture into decorating bag fitted with tip No. 18. Pipe about 1½ teaspoons cream cheese mixture into each snow pea. Sprinkle with grated orange rind. Refrigerate until ready to serve.

ENDIVE BOATS

2 small heads Belgian endive
¾ cup whipped cream cheese,
   softened
¼ cup crumbled blue cheese
½ teaspoon dried whole dillweed
Few drops of milk
Pimiento strips

Peel leaves from core of endive. Wash leaves, and pat dry with paper towels. Place in a plastic food storage bag, and refrigerate.

Combine cream cheese, blue cheese, and dillweed; stir with a fork until blended. Stir a few drops of milk into cheese mixture, if necessary, to make cheese a piping consistency. Spoon cheese mixture into decorating bag fitted with large tip No. 4B. Pipe about 1 teaspoon cheese mixture down inside spine of each endive leaf. Top with a pimiento strip. Refrigerate until ready to serve. Yield: about 1½ dozen.

TOMATOES TAPENADE

1 pint small cherry tomatoes
Salt
¾ cup pitted ripe olives
4 anchovy fillets, rinsed and drained
1 clove garlic, cut in half
2 tablespoons lemon juice
1 tablespoon capers
⅛ teaspoon pepper
2 tablespoons olive oil
Fresh parsley sprigs

Cut top off each tomato; scoop out pulp, reserving pulp for other uses. Sprinkle inside of tomatoes lightly with salt, and invert on paper towels to drain.

Position knife blade in food processor bowl. Combine olives, anchovies, garlic, lemon juice, capers, and pepper in processor bowl. Top with cover; process 5 seconds or until minced.

Combine olive mixture and olive oil, stirring well. Refrigerate olive mixture if

not serving immediately.

No more than 1 hour before serving, spoon about 1½ teaspoons olive mixture into each tomato shell; insert a small sprig of parsley in top side of each tomato. Serve at room temperature. Yield: about 2 dozen.

FRUIT-TOPPED CANAPÉS

This recipe suggests particular fruits to adorn the simple cracker bases, but other fresh fruits, as well as steamed asparagus pieces, broccoli flowerets, and carrot slices could be substituted.

1 (8-ounce) package cream cheese,
   softened
1 teaspoon grated orange rind
2 tablespoons orange juice
½ teaspoon ground ginger
4 dozen multi-shaped crackers, lightly
   toasted
¼ medium honeydew melon
8 fresh strawberries
1 or 2 kiwifruit
1½ cups fresh pineapple wedges,
   drained
¾ cup seedless red grapes
¾ cup seedless green grapes
½ cup mandarin orange sections,
   drained
½ cup fresh blueberries
Small fresh mint leaves

Beat cream cheese at medium speed of an electric mixer until smooth; add orange rind, orange juice, and ground ginger, mixing well. Spoon mixture into a decorating bag fitted with tip No. 18, and pipe mixture onto crackers; set aside. Cut fruit into various shapes, and decorate crackers as desired with fruit and mint leaves. Yield: 4 dozen.

PARTY ANTIPASTO TRAY

Antipasto means "before the meal" in Italian, and it refers to a variety of foods served as a first course. Present this feast of appetizers with small plates and forks and tangy Antipasto Dressing on the side.

½ medium-size head iceberg lettuce
1 small head curly endive
1 (3½-ounce) package thinly sliced pepperoni
1 (4-ounce) package thinly sliced Genoa salami, quartered
1 (6-ounce) package thinly sliced Italian ham
1 (11½-ounce) jar peperoncini, drained
1 (2-ounce) can anchovies with capers, drained
1 (15-ounce) can garbanzo beans, drained
1 pint cherry tomatoes
1 cup radishes
1 cup carrot sticks
½ cup ripe olives
½ cup green olives
8 ounces provolone cheese, cubed
Antipasto Dressing

Shred lettuce, and spread on a tray.
Make a border of endive leaves around edge of tray. Arrange meats, vegetables, olives, and cheese on top of shredded salad greens. Serve with Antipasto Dressing. Yield: 10 to 12 servings.

Antipasto Dressing

¾ cup olive or vegetable oil
¼ cup white wine vinegar
1 tablespoon dried whole oregano
1 teaspoon dried whole basil
¼ teaspoon dried whole thyme
⅛ teaspoon pepper
2 tablespoons water
1 clove garlic, crushed

Combine all ingredients in a jar; cover tightly, and shake vigorously. Let stand several hours at room temperature. Yield: 1¼ cups.

Serving Party Antipasto Tray is like serving several appetizers at once.

OYSTERS ON THE HALF SHELL

2 large lemons, halved
1 cup Zippy Cocktail Sauce, chilled (page 441)
2 dozen oysters on the half shell
Lemon wedges
Saltine crackers

Cut a thin slice from the bottom of each lemon half so that it sits flat. Gently remove pulp, leaving shell intact. Reserve pulp for other uses. Fill lemon shells with Zippy Cocktail Sauce, and place a lemon shell in center of 4 deep dishes filled with crushed ice. Arrange 6 oysters on the half shell around each bowl of sauce, and serve immediately with lemon wedges and crackers. Yield: 4 appetizer servings.

SHRIMP COCKTAIL

2 cups shredded lettuce
1 pound Boiled Shrimp, peeled and
  chilled (page 234)
¾ cup Zippy Cocktail Sauce
  (page 441)
Lemon wedges

Arrange lettuce on individual serving plates. Top with chilled Boiled Shrimp; drizzle with Zippy Cocktail Sauce before serving. Garnish with lemon wedges. Yield: 4 to 6 appetizer servings.

SHRIMP REMOULADE

1 cup mayonnaise
1½ tablespoons dry mustard
2 tablespoons vegetable oil
1 tablespoon vinegar
1 tablespoon prepared horseradish
1 teaspoon paprika
½ teaspoon salt
¼ teaspoon white pepper
Dash of hot sauce
2 green onions, cut into 1-inch
  lengths
½ stalk celery, cut into 1-inch
  lengths
2 tablespoons coarsely chopped fresh
  parsley
1 clove garlic, cut in half
2 pounds medium shrimp, cooked,
  peeled, and deveined
Leaf lettuce

Combine all ingredients except shrimp and lettuce in container of an electric blender or food processor; process at high speed until blended and smooth. Chill thoroughly.

To serve, arrange shrimp on lettuce leaves, and pour dressing over shrimp. Yield: 10 appetizer servings.

Note: Shrimp Remoulade serves 6 as a salad over shredded lettuce.

ICY MARINATED SHRIMP

3 pounds unpeeled fresh shrimp
1 (3-ounce) package crab and shrimp
  boil
1 teaspoon salt
1 cup vegetable oil
⅓ cup catsup
⅓ cup vinegar
2 cloves garlic, crushed
1 tablespoon Worcestershire sauce
1½ teaspoons dry mustard
¼ teaspoon freshly ground pepper
⅛ teaspoon hot sauce
1 cup chopped green onions
4 bay leaves
Fresh parsley sprigs

Prepare shrimp according to package directions on crab boil, adding 1 teaspoon salt. Drain well; cool completely. Peel and devein shrimp.

Combine oil and next 7 ingredients in container of an electric blender; process marinade until smooth. Layer half each of shrimp, green onions, and bay leaves in a large bowl; pour half of marinade over shrimp mixture. Repeat procedure with remaining shrimp, green onions, bay leaves, and marinade. Cover and chill mixture at least 8 hours.

Arrange seashells in the bottom of a 6-cup ring mold; fill with water, and freeze at least 8 hours.

To serve, unmold ice ring onto a large, 2-inch deep waterproof platter. Remove bay leaves from shrimp mixture. Using a slotted spoon, fill ice ring with marinated shrimp; pile remaining shrimp around ice ring. Garnish Icy Marinated Shrimp with fresh parsley sprigs. Yield: 12 appetizer servings.

JALAPEÑO-TOMATO SEVICHE

Seviche is a Spanish dish of uncooked fish marinated in lemon or lime juice. Other ingredients traditionally added are olive oil, onion, and tomatoes.

½ pound trout, boned, skinned,
  and diced
½ cup lemon or lime juice
1½ tablespoons olive oil
1 small onion, chopped
1 small jalapeño pepper, seeded
  and minced
1 small tomato, chopped
⅛ teaspoon salt
⅛ teaspoon pepper
Pinch of dried whole oregano
2 ripe avocados (optional)
Shredded lettuce (optional)
Lemon juice (optional)

Place fish in a glass or earthenware bowl (do not use metal); pour lemon juice over fish. Cover and refrigerate at least 1 hour. Drain fish. Stir in oil, onion, pepper, tomato, and seasonings.

Serve in avocado shells or on a bed of shredded lettuce. To make avocado shells, cut avocados in half lengthwise; remove seed. Scoop out some of avocado to form deeper shells; chop avocado pulp, and add to fish mixture. Rub cut surfaces of avocado shells with lemon juice; fill shells with fish mixture. Yield: 4 servings.

LAYERED SALMON-SPINACH TERRINE

1 pound fresh spinach
6 green onions, finely chopped
3 tablespoons butter or margarine, melted
½ pound lightly smoked salmon (pink salmon preferred)
2 cups finely crumbled, lightly packed French bread
2 cups whipping cream
¼ cup lemon juice
1 teaspoon salt
¼ teaspoon white pepper
¼ teaspoon ground nutmeg
2 eggs
1½ pounds sole fillets or any other mild-flavored lean white fish
Sour Cream Sauce

Remove stems from spinach; wash leaves thoroughly, and pat dry. Finely chop leaves. Sauté spinach and green onions in butter 1 to 2 minutes or until vegetables are limp. Set aside.

Carefully remove bones from salmon; set salmon aside.

Combine remaining ingredients except sole and Sour Cream Sauce; set mixture aside.

Cut sole into 2-inch pieces. Position knife blade in food processor bowl; add half of sole, and top with cover. Process 45 seconds or until smooth. Add half of bread mixture to processor bowl; replace cover, and process 30 seconds or until mixture is smooth. (Mixture should hold shape softly.) Spoon sole mixture into a large bowl. Repeat with remaining half of same ingredients. Stir sole mixtures together.

Spread 1¼ cups of pureed sole mixture in a buttered 9- x 5- x 3-inch loafpan. Smooth sole mixture layer with the back of a spoon.

Place salmon and 1½ cups sole mixture in bowl of food processor; process 30 seconds or just until mixture is smooth. Carefully spread salmon mixture over pureed sole mixture; smooth with the back of a spoon. Spread 1¼ cups sole mixture over second layer. Combine spinach mixture and 2 cups pureed sole mixture; spread spinach mixture over third layer. Smooth with the back of a spoon.

Cover loafpan with buttered wax paper cut just larger than the top of pan. Fit aluminum foil over wax paper and top of pan, and crimp tightly to top of pan. (Do not cover sides of pan with foil.) Carefully prick holes through foil and wax paper in several places to allow steam to escape.

Place loafpan in a 13- x 9- x 2-inch baking pan. Fill baking pan with hot water to reach halfway up sides of loafpan. Bake at 350° for 1 hour and 15 minutes to 1 hour and 25 minutes or until terrine starts to rise above the rim of loafpan and top is firm and springy to the touch.

Remove wax paper and foil; allow terrine to cool. When warm to the touch, pour off excess liquid. Cool terrine completely; cover and refrigerate at least 8 hours.

Invert terrine onto a platter; let stand at room temperature 30 minutes. Slice with an electric knife. To serve, spoon about 2 tablespoons Sour Cream Sauce on each serving plate; place Layered Salmon-Spinach Terrine slices over sauce. Yield: 15 to 18 servings.

Sour Cream Sauce

1 (16-ounce) carton commercial sour cream
2 tablespoons Dijon mustard
2 teaspoons lemon juice
½ teaspoon salt
Dash of white pepper

Combine all ingredients, stirring well. Yield: 2 cups.

Hot Appetizers

Many of your favorite baked meat and cheese appetizers are found within this section. Because most of these appetizers will be cooked at the last minute, they do require prior planning and scheduling to coordinate the serving easily, especially for large crowds. The end result is worth the effort, however.

If the thought of serving hot appetizers still intimidates you, look for the recipes that specify they can be made ahead and baked straight from the freezer. You'll appreciate their convenience at party time or when unexpected guests drop in.

While many of these appetizers are equally good at room temperature, such as Miniature Cheese Quiches and Spinach-Cheese Phyllo Triangles, some you'll want to keep hot for serving, such as Hot Swiss Canapés and Chestnut Meatballs. Depend on chafing dishes and warming trays to keep them at the proper serving temperature. Make sure there's an electrical outlet near where you plan to set up the buffet.

To microwave small appetizers: Arrange them in a ring on a microwave-safe plate to help them cook evenly.

Fried Cheese Step-By-Step

1. The breading is important when making Fried Cheese. First dip cheese cubes in beaten egg, dredge in flour, and dip again in egg.

2. Roll cheese cubes in breadcrumbs, pressing firmly so crumbs adhere; chill 30 minutes.

3. Fry breaded and chilled cheese cubes in hot oil until golden brown; drain well.

4. Offer Fried Cheese by itself or with your favorite dipping sauce. Serve the cheese immediately after cooking so it will be warm and soft.

EASY NACHOS

1 (11-ounce) package tortilla chips
1 (16-ounce) can refried beans
½ cup chopped green onions
1 cup (4 ounces) shredded Cheddar cheese
1 (12-ounce) jar pickled hot jalapeño pepper slices

Place about 3 dozen tortilla chips on an ungreased baking sheet. Spread about 2 teaspoons refried beans on each chip; sprinkle with green onions and cheese. Top each with a slice of jalapeño pepper. (Reserve remaining tortilla chips and jalapeño slices for other uses.) Bake at 350° for 5 minutes or until cheese melts. Yield: 3 dozen.

⬤*Microwave Directions:* Spread about 2 teaspoons refried beans on each of 3 dozen tortilla chips; sprinkle with green onions and cheese. Top each with a slice of jalapeño pepper. (Reserve remaining tortilla chips and jalapeño slices for other uses.) Arrange 1 dozen tortilla chips at a time on a glass pizza plate; microwave at HIGH for 35 to 55 seconds or until cheese melts.

FRIED CHEESE

Fried Cheese sounds difficult to make, but it won't be if you simply remember to chill the cheese after breading and before frying. This will prevent the cheese from melting before the nuggets turn brown. That's the trick restaurants use!

6 ounces Gruyère cheese, cut into 1-inch cubes
2 eggs, well beaten
½ cup all-purpose flour
¾ cup fine, dry breadcrumbs
Vegetable oil
Curly endive
Picante sauce (optional)

Dip cheese cubes into egg. Dredge in flour; dip again in egg. Roll in breadcrumbs; press firmly so crumbs adhere. Place on wax paper; chill 30 minutes.

Deep fry cubes in hot oil (375°) until golden brown. Drain. Arrange endive and Fried Cheese on platter; serve immediately with picante sauce, if desired. Yield: about 1½ dozen.

CHEESY POTATO SKINS

3 medium baking potatoes
Vegetable oil
Seasoned salt
1 cup (4 ounces) shredded Cheddar cheese
6 slices bacon, cooked and crumbled
Commercial sour cream

Scrub potatoes thoroughly, and rub skins with oil; bake at 400° for 1 hour or until done.

Allow potatoes to cool to touch. Cut in half lengthwise; carefully scoop out pulp, leaving ¼- to ⅛-inch shell. (Pulp may be reserved for mashed potatoes or other uses.) Cut shells in half crosswise, and deep fry in hot oil (375°) 2 minutes or until lightly browned. Drain on paper towels. Place skins on a baking sheet; sprinkle with salt, cheese, and bacon. Place under broiler until cheese melts. Serve with sour cream. Yield: 1 dozen.

APPETIZER SPARERIBS

1½ pounds spareribs
1 (10-ounce) jar plum jelly
⅓ cup soy sauce
¼ cup dark corn syrup
3 tablespoons minced onion
2 teaspoons ground ginger
2 cloves garlic, minced

Instruct butcher to cut rib section lengthwise into individual ribs, and crosswise, through bone, into 2- to 2½-inch long pieces.

Combine remaining ingredients in a saucepan; bring to a boil. Remove from heat, and pour over ribs. Cover and chill 2 hours. Place ribs in a greased 13- x 9- x 2-inch baking pan. Bake, uncovered, at 375° for 1 hour. Yield: 6 to 8 appetizer servings.

SHRIMP CANAPÉS

9 slices white bread
¼ pound frozen cooked shrimp, thawed and minced
½ cup (2 ounces) shredded Swiss cheese
⅓ cup mayonnaise
½ teaspoon dried whole thyme
¼ teaspoon salt
Small sprigs of fresh dillweed, pimiento strips, or olive slices (optional)

Cut each slice of bread into four 1½-inch circles. (Make breadcrumbs from leftover bread pieces, and reserve for other uses.) Place cutouts on baking sheets, and broil 6 inches from heat for 1 minute or until lightly browned.

Combine shrimp, cheese, mayonnaise, thyme, and salt; stir well and spread on bread cutouts. Bake at 425° for 7 minutes. Garnish each canapé with dillweed, pimiento, or olive slices, if desired. Yield: 3 dozen.

HOT SWISS CANAPÉS

3 egg whites
3 slices uncooked bacon, chopped
1½ cups (6 ounces) shredded Swiss cheese
½ cup chopped green pepper
¼ cup chopped green onions
⅛ teaspoon salt
⅛ teaspoon pepper
24 slices party rye bread

Beat egg whites (at room temperature) until stiff peaks form; fold in chopped bacon, Swiss cheese, green pepper, onions, salt, and pepper. Spread about 1 tablespoon mixture on each bread slice. Place on baking sheets, and broil 4 to 5 inches from heat about 5 minutes or until bacon cooks. Serve immediately. Yield: 2 dozen.

MINIATURE CHEESE QUICHES

Pastry for 9-inch pie
2 eggs, beaten
½ cup milk
1½ tablespoons butter or margarine, melted
1 cup (4 ounces) shredded Cheddar cheese
Red pepper or paprika (optional)

Shape pastry into 24 (1-inch) balls. Place in lightly greased 1¾-inch muffin pans, shaping each into a shell. Bake at 350° for 5 minutes.

Combine eggs, milk, butter, and cheese; stir well, and pour into pastry shells. Sprinkle with red pepper, if desired. Bake at 350° for 25 minutes or until set. Yield: 2 dozen.

Miniature Quiche Lorraines: Stir 3 slices cooked and crumbled bacon into egg mixture before pouring into pastry shells.

Miniature Herb Quiches: Stir 2 tablespoons chopped chives, 1 tablespoon chopped fresh or 1 teaspoon dried whole tarragon, and ⅛ teaspoon ground nutmeg into egg mixture before pouring into pastry shells.

TASTY LITTLE PIZZA SNACKS

1 pound Italian sausage
1 pound hot bulk pork sausage
1 cup chopped onion
½ green pepper, chopped
1 tablespoon dried whole oregano
1 tablespoon fennel seeds
⅛ teaspoon garlic powder
1 (16-ounce) package process American cheese, cut into small cubes
2 (8-ounce) packages mozzarella cheese, cut into small cubes
3 (8-ounce) loaves party rye bread

Remove casing from Italian sausage; crumble into a large skillet. Add hot sausage, onion, and green pepper; cook until meat is browned. Drain well on paper towels.

Return meat mixture to skillet, and add oregano, fennel seeds, and garlic powder; heat gently over low heat. Stir in cheeses; cook until melted, and remove from heat.

Spread a scant tablespoon of meat mixture on each bread slice. Place slices in a single layer on large baking sheets; freeze. When slices are frozen, place in plastic bags and keep frozen until slices are needed.

To serve, thaw and place on lightly greased baking sheets. Bake at 425° for 8 to 10 minutes. Yield: about 11 dozen.

INDIVIDUAL SPINACH TARTS

1 (10-ounce) package frozen chopped spinach, thawed and drained
1 egg, beaten
1 cup crumbled feta or grated Romano cheese
¼ cup butter or margarine, melted
2 tablespoons chopped onion
¼ teaspoon salt
⅛ teaspoon pepper
Cream Cheese Patty Shells
2 tablespoons grated Romano cheese
Diced pimiento (optional)

Place spinach on paper towels, and squeeze until barely moist. Combine spinach and next 6 ingredients; stir well. Fill Cream Cheese Patty Shell with 1 heaping teaspoonful of spinach mixture; sprinkle with cheese. Bake at 350° for 30 to 35 minutes. Garnish tarts with pimiento, if desired. Yield: 2½ dozen.

Cream Cheese Patty Shells

1 (3-ounce) package cream cheese, softened
½ cup butter or margarine, softened
1½ cups all-purpose flour

Combine cream cheese and butter; beat at medium speed of an electric mixer until mixture is smooth. Add flour, and mix well.

Shape dough into 30 (1-inch) balls. Place in ungreased 1¾-inch muffin pans, and shape each ball into a shell. Yield: 2½ dozen.

TEMPTING CHEESE TORTE

½ recipe Basic Puff Pastry (page 376)
1 egg yolk
1 teaspoon water
1 cup (4 ounces) shredded mozzarella cheese
¾ cup (3 ounces) shredded Swiss cheese
⅓ cup minced green onion tops
½ teaspoon dried whole oregano
¼ cup grated Parmesan cheese

Roll dough into a 14½- x 7½-inch rectangle on a lightly floured surface. Sprinkle a baking sheet with water, and shake off excess water. Place dough on baking sheet.

Working quickly, cut a ¾-inch wide strip from each long side of pastry. Brush strips with water, and lay them, moist side down, on top of each long side of pastry rectangle, edges flush together. To complete pastry border, repeat procedure on short sides of rectangle, trimming away excess at corners. Prick pastry shell generously with a fork, excluding the border.

Combine egg yolk and 1 teaspoon water; brush border of pastry with egg mixture. Freeze 10 minutes. Bake at 425° for 12 minutes or until puffed and golden brown.

Combine remaining ingredients except Parmesan, tossing lightly. Spread cheese mixture over pastry. Sprinkle with Parmesan. Bake at 350° for 3 minutes or until cheese melts. Let stand 5 minutes before slicing. Cut into squares and serve hot. Yield: 1 dozen squares.

Note: One-half (17¼-ounce) package frozen puff pastry may be substituted for ½ recipe Basic Puff Pastry.

SPINACH-CHEESE PHYLLO TRIANGLES

1 (10-ounce) package frozen chopped spinach
⅓ cup minced onion
3 tablespoons butter or margarine, melted
¼ pound fresh Parmesan cheese, grated
2 eggs, beaten
¾ cup (3 ounces) shredded Monterey Jack or mozzarella cheese
3 tablespoons crumbled blue cheese or feta cheese
2 tablespoons soft breadcrumbs
¼ teaspoon salt
¼ teaspoon pepper
¼ teaspoon ground nutmeg
About ½ (16-ounce) package frozen phyllo pastry, thawed
Melted butter or margarine
Fresh spinach leaves

Thaw spinach; place between paper towels, and squeeze until barely moist.

Sauté onion in 3 tablespoons butter in a large skillet; add spinach, and cook 5 minutes. Remove vegetables from skillet; cool. Add Parmesan and next 7 ingredients to spinach mixture; stir well.

Cut sheets of phyllo lengthwise into 3½-inch strips. Working with one at a time, brush each phyllo strip with melted butter. Keep remaining strips covered, according to package directions. Place 2 teaspoons spinach mixture at base of phyllo strip, folding the right bottom corner over it into a triangle. Continue folding back and forth into a triangle to end of strip. Repeat process with remaining phyllo. Keep finished triangles covered before baking.

Place triangles, seam side down, on ungreased baking sheets. Brush with melted butter; bake at 450° for 10 to 15 minutes. Drain on paper towels. Serve on spinach leaves. Yield: 3 dozen.

Note: Spinach-Cheese Phyllo Triangles may be frozen before baking. To bake, follow instructions above.

SWISS-STUFFED MUSHROOMS

1 pound medium mushrooms
Salt
2 tablespoons butter or margarine, melted
½ cup fine, dry breadcrumbs
½ cup (2 ounces) shredded Swiss cheese
1 egg, beaten
1 teaspoon dried parsley flakes
1 teaspoon crushed dried whole dillweed
¼ to ½ teaspoon grated lemon rind
2 tablespoons lemon juice

Clean mushrooms with damp paper towels. Remove stems, and set aside. Sprinkle inside of caps with salt.

Chop stems finely; sauté in butter over medium heat 3 to 4 minutes. Add remaining ingredients except mushroom caps, mixing well. Spoon mixture into mushroom caps.

Place stuffed mushrooms on ungreased baking sheet; bake at 350° for 5 to 8 minutes or until thoroughly heated. Serve hot. (These may be made ahead of time and refrigerated until ready to bake.) Yield: 1½ dozen.

◻ *Microwave Directions:* Clean mushrooms with damp paper towels. Remove stems, and set aside. Sprinkle inside of caps with salt.

Chop stems finely; combine stems and butter in a 1-quart microwave-safe bowl. Cover with heavy-duty plastic wrap, and microwave at HIGH for 2 to 3 minutes or until tender. Add remaining ingredients except mushroom caps, mixing well. Spoon mixture into caps.

Arrange 9 stuffed mushrooms at a time on a glass pizza plate. Microwave at HIGH for 3 to 4 minutes or until stuffed mushrooms are thoroughly heated.

CRAB-STUFFED MUSHROOMS

20 to 24 large fresh mushrooms (about 1 pound)
1 cup commercial Italian salad dressing
¾ cup soft breadcrumbs, divided
1 (6-ounce) can crabmeat, drained and flaked
2 eggs, beaten
¼ cup mayonnaise
¼ cup minced onion
1 teaspoon lemon juice

Clean mushrooms with damp paper towels. Remove stems, and reserve for other uses. Combine mushroom caps and Italian dressing; cover and refrigerate 1 to 2 hours. Drain well.

Combine ½ cup breadcrumbs and remaining ingredients; stir well. Spoon crabmeat mixture into mushroom caps, and sprinkle with remaining ¼ cup breadcrumbs. Place in an large baking dish; bake at 375° for 15 minutes. Yield: about 2 dozen.

◻ *Microwave Directions:* Clean mushrooms with damp paper towels. Remove stems, and reserve for other uses. Combine mushroom caps and Italian dressing; cover and refrigerate 1 to 2 hours. Drain well.

Combine ½ cup breadcrumbs and remaining ingredients; stir well. Spoon crabmeat mixture into mushroom caps, and sprinkle with remaining ¼ cup breadcrumbs. Arrange 10 to 12 stuffed mushrooms at a time on a glass pizza plate. Microwave at HIGH for 2 to 4 minutes or until hot.

GOLDEN CHICKEN NUGGETS

6 chicken breast halves, skinned and boned
½ cup all-purpose flour
2 teaspoons sesame seeds
¾ teaspoon salt
1 egg, slightly beaten
½ cup water
Vegetable oil

Cut chicken into 1½- x 1-inch pieces; set aside. Combine remaining ingredients except oil. Dip chicken into batter, and fry in hot oil (375°) until golden brown. Drain on paper towels. Yield: 12 to 15 appetizer servings.

Chestnut Meatballs and Spiced Meatballs make good make-ahead choices. Cook the meatballs a day ahead, and just reheat them in the sauce at the last minute. Serve with wooden picks for easy handling.

CHESTNUT MEATBALLS

1½ cups soft breadcrumbs
½ pound bulk pork sausage
½ pound ground beef
1 (8-ounce) can water chestnuts, drained and chopped
1 tablespoon soy sauce
½ teaspoon garlic salt
¼ teaspoon onion powder
½ cup milk
2 (9-ounce) jars commercial sweet-and-sour sauce

Combine all ingredients except sweet-and-sour sauce; mix well and shape into 1-inch balls. Place in a lightly greased 13- x 9- x 2-inch baking dish; bake at 350° for 25 to 30 minutes. Drain meatballs, and return to baking dish. Add sauce; stir lightly to coat meatballs. Bake meatballs and sauce an additional 15 minutes. Yield: 3 dozen.

SPICED MEATBALLS

1 pound ground beef
2 eggs, well beaten
¾ cup Italian breadcrumbs
2 tablespoons finely chopped onion
½ teaspoon salt
½ teaspoon prepared horseradish
¼ teaspoon pepper
⅛ teaspoon hot sauce
2 to 3 tablespoons butter or
  margarine, melted
½ cup catsup
½ cup chili sauce
⅓ cup firmly packed brown sugar
3 tablespoons cider vinegar
2 tablespoons finely chopped onion
1 tablespoon Worcestershire sauce
½ teaspoon dry mustard
¼ teaspoon pepper
4 drops of hot sauce
Chopped green onions (optional)

Combine first 8 ingredients; mix well, and shape into 1-inch balls. Sauté meatballs in butter until browned; drain and set aside.

Combine remaining ingredients ex-cept green onions in a large saucepan; bring to a boil. Reduce heat, and simmer 5 minutes. Add meatballs, and simmer an additional 10 minutes. Transfer to chafing dish, and keep warm. Garnish with chopped green onions, if desired. Yield: 3 dozen.

○*Microwave Directions:* Combine first 8 ingredients; mix well, and shape into 1-inch balls. Arrange meatballs in a 12- x 8- x 2-inch baking dish. Cover loosely with heavy-duty plastic wrap, and microwave at HIGH for 4 minutes. Rearrange meatballs, putting less cooked ones to outside of dish. Cover and micro-wave at MEDIUM LOW (30% power) for 3 to 4 minutes or until done. Drain meatballs, and return to baking dish.

Combine remaining ingredients ex-cept green onions. Pour over meatballs, and stir well. Cover and microwave at HIGH for 3 to 4 minutes or until heated thoroughly, stirring once. Transfer to chafing dish, and keep warm. Garnish with chopped green onions, if desired.

SAUSAGE PINWHEELS

2 cups all-purpose flour
1 tablespoon baking powder
½ teaspoon salt
2 tablespoons cornmeal
¾ cup milk
¼ cup vegetable oil
1 pound bulk pork sausage, softened
1 cup (4 ounces) shredded Cheddar
  cheese

Combine flour, baking powder, salt, and cornmeal; stir in milk and oil. Di-vide dough into 3 equal portions. Roll each into a 12- x 9-inch rectangle. Spread one-third of sausage over dough, and top with ⅓ cup cheese. Roll up jellyroll fashion, beginning with long side; pinch seam and ends to seal. Wrap in wax paper, and chill until firm. Re-peat with remaining ingredients.

Cut rolls into ¼-inch slices; place on ungreased mesh wire racks or baking sheets. Bake at 400° for 15 to 20 min-utes. Yield: 5 dozen.

Note: Sausage Pinwheels may be placed on a baking sheet and frozen. After slices are frozen, transfer to an airtight container, and freeze up to 1 month. Thaw slightly, and bake as directed above.

RUMAKI

About ½ pound chicken livers
¼ cup soy sauce
1½ tablespoons dry white wine
⅛ teaspoon ground ginger
2 cloves garlic, minced
1 (6-ounce) can water chestnuts,
  drained
12 slices bacon, cut into thirds

Cut chicken livers into about 1-inch pieces. Combine soy sauce, wine, ginger, and garlic in an 8-inch square baking dish; stir well. Place chicken livers in soy sauce mixture. Cover and marinate in refrigerator 2 to 3 hours.

Cut water chestnuts in half. Place a water chestnut half and a piece of chicken liver on each piece of bacon. Roll up, and secure with a wooden pick. Arrange on baking sheets, and broil 4 inches from heat 3 minutes on each side or until bacon is done. Yield: about 3 dozen.

○*Microwave Directions:* Cut chicken livers into about 1-inch pieces. Combine soy sauce, wine, ginger, and garlic in an 8-inch square baking dish; stir well. Place chicken livers in soy sauce mixture. Cover and marinate in refrigerator 2 to 3 hours.

Cut water chestnuts in half. Place a water chestnut half and a piece of chicken liver on each piece of bacon. Roll up, and secure with a wooden pick. Arrange on paper towel-lined glass pizza plates or microwave-safe platters, plac-ing about a dozen appetizers on each. Cover appetizers, and refrigerate up to 2 hours.

When ready to microwave, cover plat-ters with paper towel. Microwave each platter of appetizers on HIGH for 4½ to 7 minutes or until bacon is crisp and liver is done, giving each platter one half-turn.

Note: Rumaki may be microwaved without final chilling. Microwaving time will not be changed.

CRISPY SAUSAGE WONTONS

1 tablespoon cornstarch
2 tablespoons water
½ pound hot bulk pork sausage
3 tablespoons chopped green onions
1 (1-pound) package frozen wonton wrappers, thawed
Peanut or vegetable oil
Sweet-and-Sour Sauce (page 442)
Chinese Hot Mustard (page 438)

Combine cornstarch and water; stir until smooth, and set aside.

Brown sausage in a large skillet, stirring to crumble; drain well. Combine sausage and green onions. Working with one at a time, spoon 1 teaspoonful sausage mixture in center of wonton wrapper. Brush edges of wonton wrapper lightly with cornstarch mixture. Fold wrapper once to form a triangle, pressing edges together to seal.

On long side of triangle, fold opposite sides together, overlapping them; brush ends with cornstarch mixture, and press to seal. Fold point of triangle backwards, away from overlapping edges. Repeat procedure with remaining wrappers.

Keep covered to prevent drying out.

Drop wontons into a small amount of hot oil (375°); cook until golden brown, turning once. Drain on paper towels. Serve with Sweet-and-Sour Sauce or Chinese Hot Mustard. Yield: about 3 dozen.

To make wonton or egg roll wrappers hold together: Always dampen the wrappers during the shaping process.

OYSTERS ROCKEFELLER

When the term Rockefeller is part of a recipe title, it usually means the dish contains spinach, although some sources say that watercress was the key ingredient in the original oyster dish that carries the famous name.

(pictured on page 26)

Rock salt
⅓ cup finely chopped green onions
¼ cup butter or margarine, melted
1 (10-ounce) package frozen chopped spinach, thawed and well drained
¼ teaspoon salt
⅛ teaspoon pepper
⅛ teaspoon garlic powder
3 tablespoons fine, dry breadcrumbs
1½ dozen oysters on the half shell, drained
2 tablespoons dry sherry (optional)
Lemon juice
Hot sauce
3 slices bacon, cooked and crumbled
18 strips pimiento

Sprinkle a thin layer of rock salt in a large shallow pan.

Sauté green onions in butter until tender. Stir in spinach, salt, pepper, and garlic powder. Cook, uncovered, 5 minutes, stirring occasionally. Remove from heat, and stir in breadcrumbs.

Arrange oysters (in shells) over salt. Brush each oyster with sherry, if desired, and sprinkle with a few drops of lemon juice and hot sauce. Top with spinach mixture, and sprinkle with crumbled bacon.

Bake at 350° for 15 minutes. Place under broiler (about 5 inches from heat source) about 1 minute. Garnish with pimiento strips. Yield: 1½ dozen.

CLAMS CASINO

1 dozen clams in shells
¼ cup chopped onion
¼ cup chopped green pepper
1 tablespoon butter or margarine, melted
¼ cup chopped pimiento
3 slices bacon, cut into fourths
Lemon wedges
Fresh parsley sprigs

Wash clams, discarding any open (dead) clams. Pry open shells; discard top shells, and loosen meat from bottom shells. Place shells and meat on paper towels to drain thoroughly.

Sauté onion and green pepper in butter; stir in chopped pimiento. Return clams to shells, and arrange shells in a shallow baking pan. Spoon 1 tablespoon vegetable mixture onto each clam; top with bacon. Bake at 375° for 15 to 20 minutes or until bacon is browned. Garnish with lemon wedges and parsley sprigs. Yield: 1 dozen.

Note: Oysters may be substituted for clams. Follow directions above.

ESCARGOTS PROVENÇAL

Serve these tasty little appetizers on a snail plate or a salad plate lined with rock salt.

1 (7-ounce) can snails, drained and rinsed
½ cup Chablis or other dry white wine
½ cup canned beef broth
⅛ teaspoon pepper
Dash of ground nutmeg
13 snail shells, rinsed and drained
½ cup butter or margarine, softened
1 cup coarsely chopped fresh parsley
4 cloves garlic, cut in half
Rock salt (optional)
Fresh parsley sprigs (optional)

Combine first 5 ingredients; stir well. Cover and chill at least 3 hours. Drain; insert each marinated snail into a shell.

Combine butter, parsley, and garlic in container of a food processor or electric blender; process well. Pack about 2 teaspoons butter mixture into each shell.

Place filled shells in a snail pan, or pour rock salt into an 8-inch square baking dish to cover bottom; arrange filled shells, open end up, on salt. Bake at 400° for 15 minutes. Garnish with parsley sprigs, if desired; serve immediately. Yield: 3 or 4 servings.

EGG ROLLS

1½ cups shredded cabbage
1¼ cups fresh bean sprouts, chopped
¼ pound fresh mushrooms, thinly sliced
¼ cup finely chopped celery
2 tablespoons peanut or vegetable oil
1 (8-ounce) package frozen cooked shrimp, thawed and drained
½ cup bamboo shoots, drained and finely chopped
⅛ teaspoon salt
⅛ teaspoon pepper
1 tablespoon soy sauce
1½ teaspoons cornstarch
1 egg, beaten
1½ teaspoons water
1 (1-pound) package egg roll wrappers
Peanut or vegetable oil
Sweet-and-Sour Sauce (page 442)
Chinese Hot Mustard (page 438)

Stir-fry cabbage, bean sprouts, mushrooms, and celery in 2 tablespoons hot oil 2 minutes or until vegetables are crisp-tender. Add shrimp, bamboo shoots, salt, and pepper.

Combine soy sauce and cornstarch, stirring well. Stir into vegetable mixture, and cook 1 minute, stirring constantly. Remove from heat, and chill.

Combine egg and water; mix well, and set aside.

Mound about ⅓ cup of chilled filling in center of each egg roll wrapper. Fold top corner of wrapper over filling; then fold left and right corners over filling. Lightly brush exposed corner of wrapper with egg mixture. Tightly roll the filled end of the wrapper toward the exposed corner; gently press the corner to seal securely.

Heat 1½ inches peanut oil to 375° in a Dutch oven. Place 2 egg rolls in hot oil, and fry for 35 to 45 seconds on each side or until golden brown; drain on paper towels. Repeat with remaining egg rolls. Serve with Sweet-and-Sour Sauce and Chinese Hot Mustard. Yield: about 10 egg rolls.

Note: Remaining egg roll wrappers may be frozen and reserved for later use.

Sandwiches

You can have a sandwich every day for lunch and still not fall into a boring routine when armed with these recipes. Some are open-faced; others are traditional. Some use regular sandwich bread; others suggest the use of buns, pocket bread, English muffins, whole grain breads, and loaves of French bread. One sandwich is even made between two frozen pizzas; it's filled, wrapped in foil, baked, and then sliced into wedges to serve.

For convenience, especially when you pack sandwiches in lunch boxes every day, you might like to make some sandwiches ahead and freeze them. Spread sandwiches to be frozen with mustard, sour cream, peanut butter, or butter; avoid spreads of mayonnaise, salad dressing, and jelly because they make sandwiches soggy when thawed.

Avoid freezing sandwiches with hard-cooked eggs, salad greens, and vegetables in the filling; these do not freeze well. Omit those items, or add them after removing the sandwiches from the freezer. When you're packaging sandwiches to travel, wrap juicy fillings like tomatoes or coleslaw separately; these items can be added just before eating.

MUFFIN PIZZAS

1 (8-ounce) can tomato sauce with onions
1 (6-ounce) can tomato paste
1 clove garlic, minced
1 teaspoon dried whole basil
⅛ teaspoon pepper
6 English muffins, split and toasted
1 (3½-ounce) package sliced pepperoni
1½ cups (6 ounces) shredded Provolone cheese
¼ cup chopped green pepper

Combine tomato sauce, tomato paste, garlic, basil, and pepper, mixing well. Spread sauce evenly over cut surface of toasted muffins. Arrange pepperoni slices over sauce; sprinkle with shredded Provolone cheese, and top with green pepper. Bake at 400° for 5 minutes or until thoroughly heated. Yield: 1 dozen.

OPEN-FACED CRAB AND TOMATO SANDWICHES

1 egg, slightly beaten
1 (3-ounce) package cream cheese, softened
1 teaspoon lemon juice
2 tablespoons grated Parmesan cheese
2 tablespoons chopped fresh parsley
3 tablespoons mayonnaise
½ cup (3 ounces) cooked crabmeat
6 slices sandwich bread, crusts removed, or 3 English muffins, split
6 (½-inch) tomato slices

Combine egg, cream cheese, lemon juice, cheese, parsley, and mayonnaise; mix well. Stir in crabmeat; set aside. Toast one side of bread; turn. Place a tomato slice on each untoasted side of bread.
Spread crab mixture evenly over tomato slices. Broil sandwiches about 6 inches from heat until golden brown. Yield: 6 servings.

SOUTHERN HAM 'N BISCUITS

2 cups all-purpose flour
1 tablespoon baking powder
½ teaspoon baking soda
⅛ teaspoon salt
⅓ cup butter or margarine
1 cup buttermilk
2 tablespoons butter or margarine, melted
1 (8-ounce) package cooked country or regular ham slices
Mustard spread (recipe follows)

Combine flour, baking powder, soda, and salt; cut in butter with a pastry blender until mixture resembles coarse meal. Add buttermilk, stirring just until dry ingredients are moistened. Turn dough out onto a lightly floured surface, and knead lightly 4 or 5 times.
Roll dough to ½-inch thickness; cut with a 1½-inch cutter. Place biscuits on an ungreased baking sheet; bake at 450° for 10 to 12 minutes or until golden brown. Brush with melted butter. Serve with country ham and mustard spread. Yield: 2 dozen.

Mustard Spread

¼ cup plus 2 tablespoons mayonnaise
3 tablespoons Dijon mustard
1½ tablespoons sweet pickle relish

Combine all ingredients, stirring well. Chill until ready to use. Yield: ½ cup.

Build a Sandwich for Eye Appeal

Next time you're layering several items into a sandwich, don't stack things so neatly that they're all hidden beneath the bun. Let a little of the lettuce, tomato slices, and bacon strips peek out from the bread; the sandwich will look more colorful, hearty, and appealing.

To keep hefty sandwiches intact: Use decorative wooden picks to spear bread and fillings together.

OPEN-FACED CHICKEN SANDWICHES

2 tablespoons butter or margarine
2 tablespoons all-purpose flour
1 cup milk
½ teaspoon salt
⅛ teaspoon white pepper
½ cup (2 ounces) shredded Cheddar cheese
1 pound sliced cooked chicken or turkey
4 slices sandwich bread, toasted
8 slices bacon, cooked, drained, and crumbled
¼ cup grated Parmesan cheese

Melt butter in a heavy saucepan over low heat; add flour, stirring until smooth. Cook 1 minute, stirring constantly. Gradually add milk; cook over medium heat, stirring constantly, until thickened and bubbly. Add salt, pepper, and Cheddar cheese, stirring until cheese melts.
Place chicken on toast, and cover with sauce. Sprinkle wtih crumbled bacon and grated Parmesan cheese. Bake at 400° for 10 minutes. Yield: 4 servings.

MEXICALI HOT DOGS

Vegetable cooking spray
8 frankfurters
1 (8-ounce) can tomato sauce
½ cup water
¾ cup chopped onion
½ cup chopped green pepper
2 tablespoons prepared mustard
2 teaspoons chopped hot pepper
1 teaspoon chili powder
⅛ teaspoon salt
8 hot dog buns

Spray a large skillet with cooking spray. Pierce frankfurters with a fork in several places, and cook in skillet until lightly browned.

Combine tomato sauce and next 7 ingredients in a large saucepan; bring mixture to a boil. Add frankfurters; reduce heat, and simmer 10 minutes or until sauce is thickened. Serve on warm buns. Yield: 8 servings.

❑*Microwave Directions:* Delete vegetable cooking spray. Pierce frankfurters with a fork in several places, and place in an 8-inch square baking dish.

Combine tomato sauce and next 7 ingredients, stirring well. Spoon over frankfurters. Cover with heavy-duty plastic wrap, and microwave at HIGH for 5 to 6 minutes, rearranging frankfurters and rotating the baking dish after 3 minutes. Serve on warm buns.

CLASSY CLUB SANDWICHES

1 (3-ounce) package cream cheese, softened
1 (2-ounce) package blue cheese, crumbled
1 teaspoon instant minced onion
Dash of Worcestershire sauce
Mayonnaise
12 slices sandwich bread, toasted
8 slices tomato
8 slices cooked turkey or chicken
4 slices Swiss cheese
Salt and pepper
8 slices bacon, cooked and drained
Lettuce leaves

Combine cream cheese, blue cheese, onion, Worcestershire sauce, and 1 tablespoon mayonnaise; stir well.

Spread cheese mixture on 4 slices of toast. Top each with 2 slices tomato, 2 slices turkey, and 1 slice Swiss cheese; sprinkle with salt and pepper. Add second slice of toast; top with 2 slices bacon and lettuce.

Spread remaining toast with mayonnaise, and place over lettuce leaves. Secure each sandwich with wooden picks; cut each sandwich into 4 triangles to serve. Yield: 4 servings.

TASTY TURKEY SANDWICHES

¼ cup mayonnaise
¼ cup Dijon mustard
12 slices pumpernickel bread
1 pound thinly sliced smoked turkey
½ pound mozzarella cheese, sliced
1 large tomato, sliced
1½ cups shredded lettuce

Combine mayonnaise and mustard. Spread mayonnaise mixture on 1 side of each slice of bread. Arrange turkey on 6 slices of bread, sauced side up. Top with cheese, a tomato slice, shredded lettuce, and remaining bread slices, sauced side down. Cut in half. Yield: 6 servings.

EGGSCLUSIVE SANDWICHES

4 hard-cooked eggs, chopped
½ cup finely chopped celery
1½ teaspoons diced pimiento
¼ teaspoon salt
⅛ teaspoon pepper
1 tablespoon chopped fresh parsley (optional)
⅓ cup mayonnaise or salad dressing
12 slices buttered toast
2 tomatoes, sliced
8 slices bacon, cooked and drained
4 lettuce leaves

Combine eggs, celery, pimiento, salt, pepper, and parsley, if desired; add mayonnaise, and stir well. Spread egg mixture on 4 slices of toast; top each with another slice of toast. Arrange tomato slices, bacon, and lettuce on top of toast. Top with remaining toast. Cut each sandwich into quarters to serve, using wooden picks to hold layers together. Yield: 4 servings.

BEEF SALAD POCKET SANDWICHES

1¼ cups shredded lettuce
½ cup shredded fresh spinach
6 Greek olives, pitted and sliced
1 green onion, chopped
1 radish, sliced
3 tablespoons commercial Italian salad dressing
1 (3-ounce) package cream cheese, softened
3 (6-inch) pita bread rounds, cut in half
6 ounces thinly sliced cooked roast beef, chopped

Combine first 6 ingredients; toss gently. Let stand 5 minutes.

Spread about 1½ tablespoons cream cheese inside each bread half; fill each with equal portions of roast beef and salad mixture. Yield: 6 servings.

HEARTY ROAST BEEF SANDWICHES

1/3 cup commercial sour cream
2 tablespoons Dijon mustard
2 teaspoons prepared horseradish
4 individual French loaves
4 slices Provolone cheese, cut in half
1 pound thinly sliced cooked roast beef
1 cup alfalfa sprouts

Combine sour cream, mustard, and horseradish. Split bread loaves in half horizontally, and spread sour cream mixture on cut surfaces. Top bread bottoms with cheese and roast beef. Replace bread tops, and wrap sandwiches in aluminum foil. Bake sandwiches at 350° for 25 minutes.

Remove bread tops, and place alfalfa sprouts on top of roast beef. Replace bread tops. Cut each sandwich in half to serve. Yield: 4 servings.

SWISS-TUNA GRILL

1 (6½-ounce) can tuna, drained and flaked
½ cup (2 ounces) shredded Swiss cheese
½ cup finely chopped celery
2 tablespoons finely chopped onion
¼ cup mayonnaise
¼ cup commercial sour cream
Dash of pepper
12 slices rye bread
Butter or margarine, softened

Combine tuna, cheese, celery, onion, mayonnaise, sour cream, and pepper, stirring well. Spread mixture on 6 slices of bread, and top with remaining bread slices. Spread butter on outer sides of bread, and grill over medium heat in a large skillet until browned, turning once. Yield: 6 sandwiches.

SLOPPY JOE POCKET SANDWICHES

1 pound ground beef
1 small onion, chopped
½ cup chopped celery or green pepper
1 (8-ounce) can tomato sauce
½ cup catsup
1 tablespoon vinegar
1 tablespoon Worcestershire sauce
1 teaspoon dry mustard
⅛ teaspoon pepper
2 (6-inch) pita bread rounds
Lettuce leaves (optional)

Combine ground beef, onion, and celery in a large skillet; cook until meat is browned. Drain off pan drippings. Add tomato sauce, catsup, vinegar, Worcestershire sauce, mustard, and pepper; bring to a boil. Cover sauce, reduce heat, and simmer 15 to 20 minutes, stirring occasionally.

Cut pita bread rounds in half; line each pocket with lettuce leaves, if desired, and fill each half with meat sauce. Yield: 4 servings.

GRILLED REUBEN SANDWICHES

1 cup commercial Thousand Island dressing, divided
18 slices rye bread
12 slices Swiss cheese
½ cup canned sauerkraut, drained
24 slices thinly sliced corned beef (about 1 pound)
Butter or margarine, softened

Spread ⅔ cup Thousand Island dressing on one side of 12 slices of bread; arrange 1 slice cheese, 2 teaspoons sauerkraut, and 2 slices corned beef evenly over each slice. Stack to make six (2-layer) sandwiches; spread remaining ⅓ cup dressing on remaining 6 bread slices, and invert on top of sandwiches.

Spread butter on outside of top slice of bread; invert sandwiches onto a hot skillet or griddle. Cook until bread is golden. Spread butter on ungrilled side of sandwiches; carefully turn, and cook until bread is golden and cheese is slightly melted. Secure sandwiches with wooden picks; cut crosswise into thirds. Serve hot. Yield: 6 servings.

ITALIAN SAUSAGE SANDWICHES

1 pound Italian sausage, sliced ¼ inch thick
½ Spanish onion, sliced and separated into rings
¾ cup thinly sliced green pepper strips
2 tomatoes, peeled and cut into wedges
½ teaspoon dried whole oregano
6 large French rolls
1 cup (4 ounces) shredded mozzarella cheese
1 cup shredded lettuce

Brown sausage over medium heat, and drain well; add onion, green pepper, and tomato. Cook over low heat, stirring constantly, about 7 minutes or until vegetables are tender. Remove from heat, and stir in oregano.

Heat rolls according to package directions; split in half, and set aside.

Spoon meat mixture on bottom half of each roll; sprinkle with cheese. Bake at 400° for 2 minutes or until cheese melts. Top each with lettuce and roll top. Yield: 6 servings.

No one will say sandwiches are boring when you serve Big Wheel Sandwich Loaf. This packed sandwich is large enough to satisfy eight hungry people.

BIG WHEEL SANDWICH LOAF

1 (8-inch) round loaf sourdough
  bread
2 teaspoons prepared horseradish
¼ pound thinly sliced roast beef
2 tablespoons mayonnaise
4 slices Swiss cheese
2 tablespoons prepared mustard
¼ pound thinly sliced cooked ham
1 medium tomato, thinly sliced
4 slices bacon, cooked and drained
4 slices American cheese
½ medium-size red onion, thinly
  sliced
¼ cup butter or margarine, softened
1 tablespoon sesame seeds, toasted
⅛ teaspoon onion powder

Slice bread horizontally into 6 equal layers using an electric or serrated knife. Spread horseradish on first layer, and top with roast beef and second bread layer. Spread mayonnaise on second layer, and top with Swiss cheese and third bread layer. Spread mustard on third layer, and top with ham and fourth bread layer. Cover fourth layer with tomato slices, bacon, and fifth bread layer. Top fifth layer with American cheese, onion, and remaining bread layer.

Combine remaining 3 ingredients; spread over top and sides of loaf. Place loaf on a baking sheet; bake, uncovered, at 400° for 15 minutes. Slice into wedges with an electric knife. Yield: 8 servings.

MUFFALETTA-STYLE PO-BOYS

2 (10-ounce) packages club rolls
½ cup mayonnaise
2½ tablespoons pimiento-stuffed
  olive juice
12 (4-inch square) ham slices
½ cup chopped pimiento-stuffed
  olives
12 slices salami
¼ cup chopped ripe olives
12 slices mozzarella cheese

Heat club rolls according to package directions. Split rolls; place cut-side up on baking sheets. Combine mayonnaise and olive juice, stirring well; spread on each roll half.

Fold each ham slice in half, and place 2 folded slices on bottom half of each roll. Top ham evenly with pimiento-stuffed olives. Fold salami slices, and place 2 slices on top of olives. Top each evenly with ripe olives. Fold cheese slices, and place 2 slices on each remaining roll half.

Place roll halves under broiler, and broil until cheese is melted and bubbly. Place cheese halves on top of meat halves; slice to serve. Yield: 6 servings.

HOT HAM SANDWICHES

¼ cup butter or margarine, softened
2 tablespoons finely chopped onion
2 tablespoons mustard with
  horseradish
2 teaspoons poppy seeds or sesame
  seeds
6 hamburger buns
6 slices cooked ham
6 slices Swiss cheese

Combine butter, onion, mustard, and poppy seeds; stir well. Spread on both sides of hamburger buns.

Place 1 cooked ham slice and 1 Swiss cheese slice on bottom of each bun; cover with top bun. Wrap each sandwich in aluminum foil, and bake Hot Ham Sandwiches at 350° for 25 minutes. Yield: 6 servings.

POLYNESIAN CHICKEN SANDWICHES

1 (8-ounce) can pineapple slices,
  undrained
¼ cup plus 1 tablespoon
  mayonnaise
¼ teaspoon ground ginger
¼ cup teriyaki sauce
2 chicken breast halves, skinned
  and boned
4 slices Swiss cheese
4 (¾-inch thick) diagonally cut
  slices French bread
1 cup alfalfa sprouts

Drain pineapple, reserving juice; set aside. Combine 2 teaspoons reserved pineapple juice, mayonnaise, and ginger; stir well. Cover and chill.

Combine remaining pineapple juice and teriyaki sauce in a shallow dish; set aside. Place each chicken breast between 2 sheets of wax paper, and flatten to ¼-inch thickness using a meat mallet or rolling pin. Cut each breast in half; add to teriyaki sauce mixture, turning once to coat. Cover and marinate 2 to 4 hours in the refrigerator.

Remove chicken; reserve marinade. Broil chicken 5 inches from heat, 2 minutes on each side, basting once with reserved marinade. Top each chicken piece with a slice of cheese and pineapple; broil until cheese melts. Place chicken on bread; spread each open-faced sandwich with seasoned mayonnaise mixture, and top each with ¼ cup sprouts. Yield: 4 servings.

GIANT PIZZA SANDWICH

½ pound Italian sausage
¼ cup chopped onion
¼ cup chopped green pepper
1 (4½-ounce) can sliced mushrooms,
  drained
2 tablespoons sliced pimiento-stuffed
  olives
½ teaspoon dried whole oregano
1 cup (4 ounces) shredded
  mozzarella cheese, divided
2 (10.1-ounce) frozen cheese pizzas
Sliced pimiento-stuffed olives

Remove casings from sausage, and crumble sausage into a large skillet; add onion, green pepper, sliced mushrooms, 2 tablespoons sliced olives, and oregano. Cook over medium heat until meat is browned; drain well, and stir in ½ cup cheese.

Place 1 pizza on a lightly greased baking sheet, cheese side up. Spoon sausage mixture over pizza; top with second pizza, cheese side down. Wrap sandwich securely in aluminum foil. Bake at 375° for 15 minutes. Remove foil, and bake an additional 10 minutes.

Sprinkle remaining mozzarella cheese on top of sandwich; bake an additional 5 minutes. Garnish sandwich with sliced olives. Cut into wedges to serve. Yield: 4 to 6 servings.

THE GARDEN SANDWICH

2 (10-ounce) packages frozen
  chopped spinach, thawed
½ cup minced green onions
¼ cup plus 2 tablespoons
  mayonnaise
1 tablespoon minced green
  pepper
1 tablespoon lemon juice
¼ teaspoon salt
1 tablespoon butter or margarine
½ pound fresh mushrooms, sliced
¼ cup butter or margarine,
  softened
12 slices pumpernickel bread
¾ cup alfalfa sprouts
2 tablespoons salted sunflower
  kernels
6 slices Provolone cheese
6 slices Cheddar cheese
6 slices Swiss cheese

Squeeze spinach to remove excess liquid. Combine spinach, green onions, mayonnaise, minced green pepper, lemon juice, and salt; stir mixture well, and set aside.

Melt 1 tablespoon butter in a skillet; add sliced mushrooms, and sauté until tender; set aside.

Spread about 1 teaspoon softened butter on one side of each bread slice. Lightly brown 6 bread slices, buttered side down, on a hot griddle; remove from heat.

Spread spinach mixture evenly on unbuttered sides of toasted bread; sprinkle with alfalfa sprouts, sautéed mushrooms, and sunflower kernels. Set aside.

Place 1 slice each of Provolone, Cheddar, and Swiss cheese on unbuttered side of remaining 6 bread slices. Place bread, buttered side down, on hot griddle; cook over medium heat, just until cheese softens and bread lightly browns. To serve, put cheese-topped bread slices and spinach-topped bread slices together. Yield: 6 servings.

MONTE CRISTO SANDWICHES

¼ cup mayonnaise
2 teaspoons prepared mustard
8 slices sandwich bread
4 slices cooked turkey
4 slices cooked ham
4 slices Swiss cheese
2 egg whites
3 eggs
½ cup commercial sour cream
2 tablespoons milk
About 1 cup fine, dry breadcrumbs
Vegetable oil

Combine mayonnaise and mustard, stirring well; spread on one side of each bread slice. Place one slice each of turkey, ham, and cheese on top of 4 bread slices. Top with remaining bread. Cut each sandwich in half diagonally; secure with wooden picks.

Beat egg whites (at room temperature) until stiff; set aside. Beat eggs; add sour cream and milk, stirring well. Fold in egg whites. Dip sandwich halves in batter; coat with breadcrumbs. Carefully lower sandwich halves, one at a time, into deep hot oil (375°); fry until golden brown, turning once. Drain; remove wooden picks. Serve sandwiches immediately. Yield: 4 servings.

FRIED OYSTER SANDWICH

1 (1-pound) loaf French bread
¼ cup butter or margarine, softened
2 (12-ounce) containers Standard oysters, drained
1 cup cornmeal mix
Vegetable oil
⅓ cup mayonnaise
2½ tablespoons sweet pickle relish
1 tablespoon lemon juice
⅛ teaspoon hot sauce
1 cup shredded lettuce
1 large tomato, thinly sliced

Slice off top third of loaf; hollow out bottom section, reserving crumbs for other uses. Spread inside surfaces of bread with butter. Place bread on baking sheet, and broil until lightly browned; set aside.

Dredge oysters in cornmeal mix. Fry oysters in deep hot oil (375°) until oysters float to the top and are golden brown. Drain oysters well on paper towels; keep warm.

Combine mayonnaise, pickle relish, lemon juice, and hot sauce, stirring well. Stir in lettuce. Spread lettuce mixture in hollowed bread. Top with tomato slices, oysters, and top half of loaf. Cut filled loaf into serving-size portions. Yield: 4 to 6 servings.

SUPERB SUBMARINE SANDWICHES

Try substituting your family's favorite sandwich meats and toppings for the ingredients called for in Superb Submarine Sandwiches, and serve sandwiches tailored to individual tastes!

2 (1-pound) loaves French bread
1 (3-ounce) package cream cheese, softened
⅔ cup mayonnaise
2 tablespoons chopped chives
8 slices cooked ham
8 slices salami
8 slices pickle and pimiento loaf
8 slices summer sausage
4 cups torn romaine or iceberg lettuce
1 medium tomato, chopped and drained
⅓ cup sliced pimiento-stuffed olives
2 tablespoons commercial Italian salad dressing

Cut bread loaves into quarters crosswise; split each quarter horizontally. Set bread aside.

Combine cream cheese, mayonnaise, and chives; stir well. Spread about 1 tablespoon mayonnaise mixture on inside cut surface of each piece of bread. Fold the meat slices in half; arrange 1 folded slice of each type of meat on bread bottoms; set aside.

Combine lettuce, tomato, olives, and Italian dressing; toss gently. Spoon salad mixture over meat slices; cover with bread tops. Serve immediately. Yield: 8 servings.

BEVERAGES

Beverages have a remarkable way of hitting the spot when you're thirsty, whether you want fresh lemonade on a hot summer day or hot buttered rum when it's nippy outside. Regardless of the temperature outside or time of day, the beverage most requested in the South might be iced tea. Most folks in this area still favor it sweetened like their mother used to make it.

EQUIPMENT

You can make a wide variety of beverages without a lot of special equipment. Most basic of all beverage equipment might be a teapot or glass or ceramic saucepan for steeping tea. If you make tea using loose tea leaves, you'll need a strainer or teaball to hold the leaves.

To make coffee other than the instant variety, you'll need a percolator, drip coffeepot, or vacuum coffeepot, and any paper filters your type coffee maker requires.

For the freshest tasting coffee, grind your own fresh coffee beans just before brewing. Choose from hand grinders, which come in novelty shapes and sizes, or electric grinders, which offer the quickest and most efficient way to grind the fresh beans.

You'll also need an electric blender on hand for making bar-type drinks, milk shakes, and other ice cream beverages.

MAKING BEVERAGES AHEAD

Many beverages, especially fruit drinks and punches, can be made a

Remove Citrus Cooler (page 62) from the freezer several hours before you need it so it will be the right slushy consistency for serving. Garnish rims of glasses with assorted cut fruit.

day or two before you need them and chilled until ready to serve. But if the recipe calls for a carbonated beverage or alcohol, wait until just before serving to add them to the recipe. Make sure any last-minute additions are thoroughly chilled, though, so they won't warm up the previously chilled portion of your punch recipe.

MICROWAVING BEVERAGES

Few beverages actually cook faster in the microwave than they do on the cook surface, but your microwave oven can be a great tool for reheating one or two cups of a leftover beverage.

Leftovers can be reheated in microwave-safe mugs, bowls, or casseroles. Just be sure there is no metallic trim on the mugs or other containers. When reheating two mugs, arrange them about 2 inches apart in the center of the oven. When microwaving more than two mugs, arrange them in a circular pattern. Microwave times for individual mugs of leftover beverages may vary, depending on the size of the mug, the ingredients that make up the beverage, and the initial temperature of the beverage. Times usually range from 1½ to 2½ minutes for one 10-ounce mug of a water-based or juice-based beverage.

Coffee, Tea, and Cocoa

There's something magnetizing about beverages brewed from the aromatic leaves and beans of the coffee, tea, and cocoa plants. Whether for breakfast, lunch, dinner, or in between, it's hard to beat those distinctive, invigorating flavors.

BREW THE BEST COFFEE

Hardly anyone agrees on how strong coffee should be or the best way to make it; variances depend on the type of coffee chosen, the proportion of water to coffee, the brewing method used, and the equipment used. Once you arrive at a good combination, don't change it!

You can choose from regular, instant, or freeze-dried coffee on your supermarket shelf, all of which are also available in a decaffeinated form. If regular coffee is chosen, the grind should be determined by the method used to make the coffee. Purchase regular or percolator grind coffee for percolators, drip grind for drip coffeepots, and fine grind for vacuum coffeepots. Purchase coffee in small quantities, because it loses its freshness quickly. Coffee will keep its flavor best when stored in an airtight container in the refrigerator or freezer.

Your coffee will taste better if you clean the coffee maker well after each use; that keeps oils and residue from building up and causing a bitter taste. Occasionally clean hard-to-reach places with a small brush.

Freshly drawn cold water usually makes better tasting coffee than hot tap water.

Coffee is best when freshly brewed. If it must be held before serving, it's better to keep it hot for up to one hour than to cool and reheat it. If your pot is not automatic, set it over low heat or in a pan of hot water.

IT'S TIME FOR TEA

Hot or cold, plain or spiced, anytime is teatime in the South. If you're a true tea connoisseur, you'll know that there are literally hundreds of varieties of tea. Most tea in your supermarket is a blend of 20 or more varieties, carefully teamed by professional tea tasters to yield the best quality.

Black, green, and oolong are the three main types of tea. All these tea leaves come from the same plant, but the processing time varies, giving each a distinct taste and color.

Black tea results from partially drying the tea leaves and then crushing them in a roller machine to release their juices. Then the leaves ferment and dry in a controlled environment until they turn a brownish black. The fermentation time determines the strength of the tea. Black tea is hearty and strong and is the most popular. Darjeeling, Keemun, and Ceylon are all varieties of black tea.

The leaves of *green tea* are steamed, preventing them from fermenting and changing colors. Then the leaves are crushed and dried for packaging. Green tea is usually a light color when brewed. When the leaves are rolled into tiny pellets after steaming, the result is called gunpowder tea.

Oolong tea is the king of the teas. It's semi-fermented, so it's between a black and green tea. After processing, oolong leaves turn greenish brown and brew light in color.

When brewing tea, start with cold tap water; hot water has lost most of its oxygen and will make tea taste flat and stale. Bring the water to a full rolling boil, and make your tea immediately, according to our recipe. If the water is not hot enough, the tea will not fully brew. If you boil the water too long, it will become flat and lose its freshness. Don't brew the tea any longer than the recipe directs or it will be bitter. After brewing, remove the tea bag or tea ball immediately. If using tea bags, squeeze them just enough to remove the excess water, not enough to extract bitter tannins.

DON'T FORGET ABOUT COCOA

The most concentrated form of chocolate available, cocoa is used to make steaming beverages of the same name, as well as to flavor a host of desserts. Store cocoa, tightly covered, in a cool, dry place. It can become lumpy and lose its brown color if exposed to moisture or high temperatures.

Flame Coffee for Dessert

Dazzle your guests by serving a flaming, spirited coffee for dessert. Brandies, liqueurs, and liquors with a high alcoholic content are best for flaming. When flaming coffee, follow these directions. Warm the spirit in a small saucepan just long enough to produce flames (do not boil); remove the spirit from heat, ignite, and pour the flames into the mugs. The flames will go out when the coffee is poured over them.

Offer Café Brûlot as an elegant dinner finale. Dainty cookies make a nice accompaniment.

COFFEE

¾ cup cold water
2 tablespoons ground
  coffee

Select the particular grind of coffee that your coffee maker requires.

Drip: Assemble drip coffee maker according to manufacturer's directions. Place ground coffee in the coffee filter or filter basket. Add water to coffee maker, and brew.

Percolator: Pour water into percolator; assemble stem and basket in the pot. Add coffee. Replace lid on pot. Plug in coffee pot if using an electric percolator. If using a non-automatic model, bring to a boil over high heat; reduce heat, and perk gently 5 to 7 minutes.

Vacuum: Heat water to a boil in lower bowl. Place a filter in the upper bowl, and fill with ground coffee. Reduce heat. Stir water when it rises into the upper bowl. Brew 1 to 3 minutes. Remove from heat and allow coffee to return to lower bowl.

Serve coffee immediately with cream and sugar. Yield: ¾ cup.

Espresso-style Coffee: Espresso is strongly brewed coffee made specifically in a steam-pressured espresso machine. A close substitute can be made in your own coffee maker by using 3 to 4 tablespoons ground dark-roast coffee beans to ¾ cup water. Serve in demitasse cups.

Café au Lait: Brew coffee using 3 to 4 tablespoons ground coffee beans per ¾ cup water. Add ¾ cup warmed milk.

SPICED COFFEE

½ cup whole Colombian coffee
  beans or ⅓ cup plus 3 tablespoons
  ground coffee beans
½ teaspoon ground nutmeg
½ teaspoon almond extract
1 teaspoon vanilla extract
4½ cups water

Place whole coffee beans in coffee grinder; process to a medium grind.

Assemble drip coffee maker according to manufacturer's directions. Place ground coffee beans in the coffee filter or filter basket; sprinkle with nutmeg and flavorings.

Add water to coffee maker, and brew. Serve immediately with cream and sugar to taste. Yield: 1 quart.

CAFÉ BRÛLOT

Rind of 1 orange, cut into strips
3 (3-inch) sticks cinnamon
6 to 8 sugar cubes
⅔ cup brandy
4 cups hot coffee
Cinnamon sticks (optional)

Combine orange rind, 3 sticks cinnamon, and sugar in a silver bowl. Heat brandy in a small saucepan with a long handle just long enough to produce fumes (do not boil). Remove mixture from heat, ignite, and pour over ingredients in bowl. Ladle brandy over ingredients until sugar dissolves. Add coffee. Ladle into demitasse cups. Serve with cinnamon stick stirrers, if desired. Yield: 4⅔ cups.

FLAMING CAPPUCCINO

Lemon juice
Sugar
¾ cup Galliano liqueur, divided
6 cups hot coffee, divided
2 tablespoons chocolate syrup,
   divided
½ cup whipping cream, whipped
6 (4½-inch) sticks cinnamon

Rinse glass with hot water; dry. Dip rim of glass in lemon juice, then in sugar, making a ¼-inch band of sugar around top of glass. Rotate glass over flame of an Irish coffee burner or alcohol burner until sugar crystallizes on glass.

Pour 2 tablespoons Galliano in glass. Rotate over flame until liqueur ignites. Fill with coffee to ½ inch from top of glass; stir in 1 teaspoon chocolate syrup. Top Flaming Cappuccino with whipped cream; garnish with a cinnamon stick. Repeat procedure for each serving. Yield: 6 servings.

KAHLÚA COFFEE

6 cups hot coffee
1 cup chocolate syrup
¼ cup Kahlúa or other
   coffee-flavored liqueur
⅛ teaspoon ground cinnamon
Whipped cream

Combine coffee, chocolate syrup, Kahlúa, and cinnamon in a large container; stir well. Serve immediately. Top servings with a dollop of whipped cream. Yield: 7¼ cups.

Flaming Cappuccino Step-By-Step

1. To make Flaming Cappuccino, dip rim of glass in lemon juice and then in sugar, making a band of sugar across top.

2. Rotate glass over flame until the sugar crystallizes.

Garnish Flaming Cappuccino with whipped cream and a cinnamon stick stirrer.

3. Pour 2 tablespoons Galliano in glass. Place over flame, and rotate until liqueur ignites.

4. Fill each glass with hot coffee to ½ inch from top.

FLAMING IRISH COFFEE

When you make Flaming Irish Coffee or other beverages in which liqueur is heated in the container, select containers that are strong enough to withstand the heat. You'll find several styles made specifically for Irish coffee; many include burners as well.

¾ cup Irish Mist liqueur, divided
6 cups hot coffee, divided
2 tablespoons sugar, divided
½ cup whipping cream, whipped
Ground nutmeg

Rinse glass with hot water; dry. Pour 2 tablespoons Irish Mist into glass. Rotate over flame of Irish coffee burner or alcohol burner until liqueur ignites.

Fill with coffee; stir in 1 teaspoon sugar. Top with whipped cream; dust with nutmeg. Repeat for each serving. Yield: 6 servings.

HOT TEA

1 regular-size tea bag
¾ cup boiling water

Warm teapot, mug, or cup by rinsing with boiling water. Place tea bag in teapot. Immediately pour boiling water over tea bag. Cover and steep 5 minutes. Remove tea bag; serve with sugar and lemon, if desired. Yield: ¾ cup.

HOT FRUITED TEA

4 (3-inch) sticks cinnamon, halved
1 teaspoon whole cloves
½ teaspoon whole allspice
1 quart hot tea
½ cup sugar
3 cups orange juice
3 cups unsweetened pineapple juice
Orange wedges (optional)

Combine first 3 ingredients in a tea ball or cheesecloth bag; set aside.

Combine hot tea and sugar in a large Dutch oven; stir in fruit juices. Add spice mixture, and bring to a boil. Cover, reduce heat, and simmer 30 minutes; remove spice mixture. Garnish each serving with orange wedges, if desired. Serve hot. Yield: 2 quarts.

Tea may become cloudy if refrigerated after it's brewed. Add a little boiling water to clear up the cloudiness.

ICED TEA

1 tablespoon loose tea, or 3 regular-size tea bags, or 1 family-size tea bag
2 cups boiling water
2 cups water

Warm teapot or glass or ceramic saucepan by rinsing with boiling water. Place loose tea in a tea ball. Place tea ball in teapot. Pour boiling water over tea. Cover and steep 3 to 5 minutes. Remove tea ball, and stir in 2 cups water. Serve tea over ice. Yield: 1 quart.

Southern Sweetened Iced Tea: After removing tea ball, add ¼ to ½ cup sugar, stirring until sugar dissolves. Then add water as directed.

MINT TEA

2 quarts boiling water
10 regular-size tea bags
1½ cups sugar
Fresh mint sprigs
3 tablespoons lemon juice

Pour boiling water over tea bags; cover and steep 5 minutes. Remove tea bags, squeezing gently. Stir in sugar, 10 mint sprigs, and lemon juice; cover and steep 25 minutes. Strain and cool. Serve over ice. Garnish each glass with a sprig of mint, if desired. Yield: 7½ cups.

CITRUS TEA

2 cups water
6 whole cloves
1½ quarts water
8 regular-size tea bags
⅔ cup orange juice
½ cup lemon juice
1½ cups sugar

Combine 2 cups water and cloves in a saucepan; bring to a boil. Remove from heat, and let stand 1 hour.

Bring 1½ quarts water to a boil in a large saucepan; add tea bags. Remove from heat; cover and let stand 5 minutes. Remove tea bags.

Strain clove mixture; add to tea. Stir in fruit juices and sugar, stirring until sugar dissolves. Serve beverage hot or cold. Yield: 9 cups.

INSTANT SPICED TEA MIX

Keep Instant Spiced Tea Mix on hand to stir up when guests drop in during the winter. It's a tasty warmer-upper, and it makes your kitchen smell good, too. For a thoughtful gift, package Instant Spiced Tea Mix in an attractive container labeled with mixing instructions.

1¼ cups instant orange-flavored breakfast drink
⅔ cup instant tea with sugar and lemon
1 teaspoon ground cloves
1 teaspoon ground cinnamon
1 teaspoon ground allspice
¼ teaspoon grated lemon rind
¼ teaspoon grated orange rind

Combine all ingredients, stirring well. Store mix in an airtight container. To serve, place 3 to 4 teaspoons mix in a cup. Add 1 cup boiling water, and stir well. Yield: about 25 servings.

HOT COCOA

Serve Hot Cocoa immediately after it's prepared. Otherwise, a skin will form on top of the beverage. If this skin does form, just spoon it off before serving.

⅓ cup sugar
¼ cup cocoa
Pinch of salt
½ cup water
4 cups milk
¼ teaspoon vanilla extract
Marshmallows (optional)

Combine sugar, cocoa, and salt in a heavy saucepan. Add water, and bring to a boil over medium heat, stirring constantly. Stir in milk, and heat thoroughly (do not boil). Stir in vanilla. Serve Hot Cocoa immediately with marshmallows, if desired. Yield: 4½ cups.

Hot Cinnamon Cocoa: Prepare as above, but stir 1 teaspoon ground cinnamon into cocoa mixture before cooking. Serve hot cocoa with cinnamon stick stirrers, if desired.

Hot Mocha Cocoa: Prepare as above, but stir 2 tablespoons instant coffee granules into cocoa mixture before cooking.

HOT COCOA MIX

2 cups sugar
4 cups instant nonfat dry milk powder
1 cup cocoa

Combine sugar, dry milk powder, and cocoa in a large bowl, stirring well. Store mix in an airtight container. To serve, place ¼ cup mix in a cup. Add 1 cup boiling water, and stir well. Yield: about 28 servings.

Hot Mocha Mix: Add 1 (2-ounce) jar instant coffee granules (¾ cup plus 2 tablespoons) to other ingredients, stirring well.

Beverages With a Punch

Turn to these refreshing punches and fruit beverages when company is coming. When you expect a large crowd, select a punch with a yield to accommodate the crowd. Calculate how much beverage you'll need by the size of your punch cups; most cups hold about four ounces.

ICED TEA PUNCH

3 quarts boiling water
8 regular-size tea bags
½ cup sugar
1 (12-ounce) can frozen lemonade concentrate, thawed and undiluted
1 (33.8-ounce) bottle ginger ale, chilled

Pour boiling water over tea bags; cover and steep 5 minutes. Remove tea bags, squeezing gently; stir in sugar and lemonade concentrate. Set tea aside to cool; stir in ginger ale just before serving. Serve tea over ice. Yield: 4¼ quarts.

BUNCH OF PUNCH

Bunch of Punch is an economical way to serve punch for a large crowd. Citric acid is its magic ingredient; it is a flavoring substance in powder form that can be found in most drugstores.

2 ounces (¼ cup) citric acid
2 quarts boiling water
5 cups sugar
5 quarts cold water
1 (46-ounce) can pineapple juice, chilled
1 (6-ounce) can frozen orange juice concentrate, thawed and undiluted

Combine citric acid and boiling water in a ceramic heatproof container; stir until citric acid dissolves. Let mixture stand 24 hours.

Combine sugar and 5 quarts cold water; stir until sugar dissolves. Add citric acid mixture, chilled pineapple juice, and orange juice concentrate; stir mixture well. Serve over ice. Yield: about 8½ quarts.

Bunch of Punch serves a lot of people inexpensively. Dress it up with a colorful ice ring.

TROPICAL SLUSH

2 cups mashed bananas
1 (20-ounce) can crushed pineapple, undrained
1 (6-ounce) jar maraschino cherries, drained and chopped
2 cups orange juice
1 tablespoon lemon juice
1 cup sugar
1 (33.8-ounce) bottle ginger ale, chilled

Combine all ingredients, except ginger ale; stir well, and freeze until firm.

To serve, partially thaw fruit mixture. Place in punch bowl, and break into chunks. Add ginger ale; stir until slushy. Yield: about 3 quarts.

QUICK SHERBET PUNCH

If making Quick Sherbet Punch for a shower, tea, or reception, choose flavors of sherbet that coordinate with the color scheme of the occasion.

½ gallon pineapple, lime, or orange sherbet
10½ cups ginger ale, chilled

Just before serving, spoon sherbet into punch bowl by heaping tablespoonfuls. Slowly pour chilled ginger ale over sherbet, stirring gently. Serve immediately. Yield: 4½ quarts.

COFFEE PUNCH

2 quarts strong coffee, cooled
2 cups milk
½ cup sugar
2 teaspoons vanilla extract
1 quart vanilla ice cream, softened
1 cup whipping cream, whipped
Ground nutmeg

Combine coffee, milk, sugar, and vanilla, stirring well.

Place ice cream in a punch bowl; add coffee mixture. Top the punch with whipped cream, and sprinkle with nutmeg. Yield: 4 quarts.

For slushy beverages: Break frozen mixture into large pieces, and add remaining liquid ingredients. Stir gently until mixture becomes slushy, breaking up frozen pieces with a spoon.

ANYTIME WINE PUNCH

2 quarts Burgundy or rosé
1 (6-ounce) can frozen lemonade or limeade concentrate, thawed and undiluted
¾ cup apricot nectar or orange juice
1 (32-ounce) bottle lemon-lime carbonated beverage, chilled
Orange or lemon slices

Combine first 3 ingredients; chill. To serve, pour chilled mixture into an ice-filled punch bowl. Pour in carbonated beverage; stir gently. Float fruit slices on top. Yield: about 3½ quarts.

Note: A blend of 1 quart Burgundy and 1 quart rosé may be substituted for 2 quarts of the same kind of wine, if desired.

NEW ORLEANS MILK PUNCH

1½ cups milk
1½ cups half-and-half
½ cup white crème de cacao
⅓ to ½ cup bourbon
2 tablespoons powdered sugar
2 egg whites
Ground cinnamon or nutmeg (optional)

Combine all ingredients, except cinnamon, in container of an electric blender; blend until frothy. If desired, serve over cracked ice and sprinkle with cinnamon. Yield: 5 cups.

SYLLABUB

4 cups whipping cream
1 cup milk
¼ cup sherry or whiskey
1 cup sugar
1 teaspoon vanilla extract

Combine all ingredients in a mixing bowl; beat at medium speed of an electric mixer until frothy. Serve immediately. Yield: 1½ quarts.

ORANGE BREAKFAST DRINK

⅓ cup frozen orange juice concentrate, thawed and undiluted
½ cup milk
½ cup water
¼ cup sugar
½ teaspoon vanilla extract
5 to 6 ice cubes

Combine all ingredients in container of an electric blender; process mixture until frothy. Serve beverage immediately. Yield: 2 cups.

To make an ice ring: Arrange cut fruit in bottom of a ring mold, and add just enough water to cover fruit but not float it; freeze until firm. Fill remainder of mold with water, and freeze.

FRESH LEMONADE

1½ cups sugar
½ cup boiling water
2 to 3 teaspoons grated lemon
   rind
1½ cups fresh lemon juice
5 cups cold water
Lemon slices
Fresh mint sprigs

Combine sugar and boiling water, stirring until sugar dissolves. Add lemon rind, lemon juice, and cold water; mix well. Chill.

Serve over ice. Garnish with lemon slices and mint sprigs. Yield: 2 quarts.

Fresh Limeade: Substitute equal amounts of lime rind and juice for that of lemons.

TOMATO JUICE COCKTAIL

7 medium-size ripe tomatoes (about 3
   pounds)
2 medium onions, quartered
2 large bay leaves
7 whole cloves
¼ teaspoon red pepper
1 cup water
2 tablespoons sugar
2 tablespoons vinegar
2 tablespoons lemon juice
1 teaspoon salt

Wash tomatoes thoroughly. Remove blemishes and stem ends; cut tomatoes into quarters. Place 5 tomato quarters in a Dutch oven; cook over high heat until thoroughly heated; mash tomatoes. Repeat procedure, adding raw tomatoes to tomatoes in Dutch oven, cooking and mashing, until all tomato quarters have been added. Add onions, bay leaves, cloves, red pepper, and water. Bring to a boil; cover, reduce heat, and simmer 20 minutes. Remove from heat. Discard bay leaves, and put vegetables through a food mill or sieve.

Combine tomato juice and remaining ingredients. Bring to a boil; cover, reduce heat, and simmer 20 minutes. Chill. Yield: 5 cups.

Note: Five cups commercial tomato juice may be substituted for homemade tomato juice; add sugar, vinegar, and lemon juice to tomato juice, omitting salt. Bring to a boil; cover, reduce heat, and simmer 20 minutes.

SPARKLING CHAMPAGNE PUNCH

4 (6-ounce) cans frozen lemonade
   concentrate, thawed and
   undiluted
4 (6-ounce) cans frozen pineapple
   juice concentrate, thawed and
   undiluted
6 cups water
Ice cubes or ice ring
2 (33.8-ounce) bottles ginger ale,
   chilled
1 (28-ounce) bottle tonic water,
   chilled
1 (25.4-ounce) bottle champagne,
   chilled

Combine first 3 ingredients; chill well. To serve punch, pour juice mixture over ice in a large punch bowl. Gently stir in ginger ale, tonic water, and champagne. Yield: 7 quarts.

CITRUS COOLER

(pictured on page 54)

¾ cup sugar
1¼ cups water
3 cups pineapple juice
3 cups orange juice
¾ cup lemon juice
1 (33.8-ounce) bottle ginger ale,
   chilled
Assorted cut fruit (optional)

Combine sugar and water in a medium saucepan; bring to a boil, stirring until sugar dissolves. Pour sugar mixture into a 4½-quart freezer container. Stir in fruit juices; freeze until firm.

Remove from freezer several hours before serving (mixture should be slushy). Stir in ginger ale. Garnish with cut fruit, if desired. Yield: 3 quarts.

Slip a Fruit Garnish onto the Glass

When adding fruit garnishes to a beverage, select a fruit already in the drink or one that will complement the drink. Arrange the garnish, whole or sliced, right on the glass. Just slice from one edge to the center of the fruit, and slip it over the rim.

HOLIDAY EGGNOG DELUXE

6 eggs, separated
¾ cup sugar
½ teaspoon vanilla extract
¼ teaspoon ground nutmeg
¾ cup brandy
¼ cup plus 2 tablespoons rum
3 cups whipping cream
2 cups milk
¼ cup sugar
Ground nutmeg

Beat egg yolks until thick and lemon colored; gradually add ¾ cup sugar, vanilla, and ¼ teaspoon nutmeg, beating well at medium speed of an electric mixer. Slowly stir in brandy and rum; cover and chill 8 hours.

Place chilled mixture in a punch bowl; gradually stir in cream and milk. Beat egg whites (at room temperature) in a large mixing bowl until soft peaks form. Gradually add ¼ cup sugar, and beat until stiff. Fold whites into chilled mixture. Sprinkle with nutmeg. Yield: about 3 quarts.

WASSAIL

2 quarts apple juice
2¼ cups pineapple juice
2 cups orange juice
1 cup lemon juice
½ cup sugar
1 (3-inch) stick cinnamon
1 teaspoon whole cloves

Combine all ingredients in a Dutch oven; bring to a boil. Cover, reduce heat, and simmer 20 minutes. Uncover and simmer an additional 20 minutes. Strain and discard cinnamon and cloves. Serve hot. Yield: 3 quarts.

HOT PERCOLATOR PUNCH

If you brew Hot Percolator Punch for a party, the blend of spices will send a wonderful aroma throughout several rooms. Consider serving the tasty blend during the winter holidays.

3 cups unsweetened pineapple juice
3 cups cranberry juice cocktail
1½ cups water
⅓ cup firmly packed brown sugar
2 lemon slices
1 or 2 (4-inch) sticks cinnamon, broken
1½ teaspoons whole cloves
Cinnamon sticks (optional)

Pour first 3 ingredients into a 12-cup percolator. Place remaining ingredients, except whole cinnamon sticks, in percolator basket. Perk through complete cycle of electric percolator. Serve with cinnamon stick stirrers, if desired. Yield: about 7 cups.

HOT CRANBERRY TEA

4 cups fresh cranberries
3 quarts water
Juice of 3 oranges, strained
Juice of 3 lemons, strained
2 cups sugar
1 (3-inch) stick cinnamon (optional)
1 teaspoon whole cloves (optional)

Combine cranberries and water in a large Dutch oven; bring to a boil. Reduce heat, and cook until cranberry skins pop (about 5 minutes). Remove from heat; cover and allow to cool completely. Strain cranberry juice; add remaining ingredients to juice, and bring to a boil. Strain mixture, and serve hot. Yield: 14 cups.

BEETLE CIDER MIX

Beetle Cider Mix makes 12 cute little beetles from ingredients typically used to spice apple cider and Burgundy wine. Take them to holiday parties as hostess gifts, or give them as favors to guests in your home. Be sure to attach a recipe for using them.

6 oranges
About 2¼ cups firmly packed brown sugar
12 (1½-inch) sticks cinnamon
12 small whole nutmegs
24 large whole allspices
96 (about 1½ tablespoons) whole cloves

Slice oranges in half crosswise; scoop out pulp leaving ⅛-inch thick rind, and reserve pulp for other uses. Place orange halves, cut side up, on a wire rack on a baking sheet. Bake at 250° about 2 hours or until dry and hard. Let cool.

Pack brown sugar firmly into each orange half, mounding it slightly. Arrange spices in brown sugar to resemble a beetle, pressing slightly into brown sugar. Use cinnamon sticks for bodies, nutmegs for heads, allspices for eyes, and cloves for feet. Cover filled orange halves tightly with plastic wrap; store in refrigerator. Yield: 12 servings.

Note: To use in apple cider, combine 1 beetle and 1½ quarts apple cider in a saucepan; simmer 30 minutes. Add 1 cup brandy, if desired; heat well. Remove orange rind and spices to serve.

To use in Burgundy, combine 1 beetle and 1 (25.4-ounce) bottle of Burgundy in a saucepan; heat almost to boiling point. Cover, remove from heat, and let steep 30 minutes. Serve hot or cold. Remove orange rind and spices to serve.

Ice Cream Beverages

It's hard to go wrong with a beverage that contains ice cream, especially when it's teamed with fruit, chocolate, or a splash of spirits. Just add a straw, and start sipping!

For several of these beverages, an electric blender is a necessity. You simply won't get the same texture if you try to blend these beverages without one.

RICH VANILLA MILKSHAKE

3 cups vanilla ice cream
1 cup milk
½ teaspoon vanilla extract
1 egg (optional)

Combine all ingredients in container of an electric blender; blend mixture until smooth. Serve immediately. Yield: 2½ cups.

Strawberry Milkshake: Substitute strawberry ice cream for vanilla ice cream, or add 1 (10-ounce) package frozen strawberries, thawed, or 1 cup fresh strawberries to ingredients in blender.

Chocolate Milkshake: Substitute chocolate ice cream for vanilla ice cream, or add ¼ cup chocolate syrup to ingredients in blender.

Peach Milkshake: Add 1 (16-ounce) can sliced peaches, drained, to ingredients in blender.

Banana Milkshake: Add 1 large banana, sliced, to ingredients in blender.

Coffee Milkshake: Substitute coffee ice cream for vanilla ice cream, or add 1 tablespoon instant coffee granules to ingredients in blender.

ROOT BEER FLOAT

¾ cup root beer or other cola, divided
2 scoops vanilla ice cream (about ¾ cup)

Pour ½ cup root beer into a 16-ounce soda glass, and spoon ice cream into glass. Top with remaining root beer. Yield: about 2 cups.

Garnish with a Fruit Boat

For an unusual garnish, make a fruit boat to float atop a thick or icy beverage. Cut two crosswise slices from a lemon or lime, one with a little larger diameter than the other. Cut the fruit away from the rind on the smaller slice, leaving the rind intact. Fold the large slice, and slide it through the smaller rind, folded side down. Place a cherry in the boat, and set it afloat.

OLD-FASHIONED STRAWBERRY SODAS

1 (10-ounce) package frozen strawberries in syrup, thawed
3 cups strawberry ice cream, divided
2 (12-ounce) cans creme soda, divided
Whipped cream
4 whole strawberries

Mash thawed strawberries with a fork until strawberries are well blended with syrup. Add 1 cup ice cream and ½ cup creme soda; stir well.

Spoon an equal amount of strawberry mixture into 4 (14-ounce) soda glasses; top with remaining ice cream, and fill glasses with remaining soda. Garnish each serving with whipped cream and a strawberry. Yield: 4 servings.

KAHLÚA VELVET FROSTY

1 cup Kahlúa
1 cup half-and-half
1 pint vanilla ice cream
⅛ teaspoon almond extract
Ice cubes

Combine all ingredients, except ice cubes, in container of an electric blender. Add enough ice cubes to make mixture measure 5 cups in blender. Blend mixture until smooth. Serve immediately. Yield: 5 cups.

FRENCH VANILLA FROSTY

1 pint French vanilla ice cream
3 tablespoons crème de cacao
3 tablespoons Drambuie
2 tablespoons chocolate-flavored syrup
1½ cups milk

Combine all ingredients in container of an electric blender; blend mixture until smooth. Serve immediately. Yield: 3½ cups.

BRANDY ALEXANDER

1 quart vanilla ice cream
¼ cup brandy
¼ cup crème de cacao

Combine all ingredients in container of an electric blender; blend mixture until smooth. Serve immediately. Yield: 3 cups.

Favorites From the Bar

You can blend a batch of daiquiris and margaritas like a pro with these recipes. And don't forget the garnish! Cut fruit garnishes work especially well with most of these spirited beverages.

WINE SPRITZERS

2 (25.4-ounce) bottles white wine
1 (33.8-ounce) bottle club soda
Lemon slices
Lime slices

Combine wine and club soda; stir gently. Pour into ice-filled glasses; garnish with lemon or lime slices. Yield: 2½ quarts.

Wine Cooler: Substitute 1 (32-ounce) bottle lemon-lime carbonated beverage for club soda.

RASPBERRY KIR

2⅔ cups Chablis or other dry white wine, chilled
1 tablespoon Chambord or other raspberry liqueur

Pour ⅔ cup wine in each wine glass. Add ¾ teaspoon Chambord to each one, and stir well. Yield: 4 servings.

MIMOSAS

2 (12-ounce) cans frozen orange juice concentrate, thawed and divided
1 (16-ounce) jar maraschino cherries with stems, drained
6 cups extra dry champagne, chilled
Mint sprigs

Prepare 1 can orange juice concentrate according to can directions. Pour into ice cube trays. Place a cherry in each cube; freeze 8 hours or overnight.

Prepare remaining orange juice concentrate acording to can directions. Stir in the champagne just before serving. Add ice cubes, and garnish with mint. Yield: 3 quarts.

WHITE SANGRÍA

1 (25.4-ounce) bottle Riesling wine
1 (6-ounce) can frozen lemonade concentrate, thawed and undiluted
1 (10-ounce) bottle club soda
Lime slices

Combine wine and lemonade concentrate; stir well. Stir in club soda. Serve over ice cubes, and garnish with lime slices. Yield: 5 cups.

RED SANGRÍA

1 (25.4-ounce) bottle Burgundy or other dry red wine, chilled
½ cup sugar
1 orange, thinly sliced
1 lemon, thinly sliced
1 (10-ounce) bottle club soda, chilled

Combine first 4 ingredients in a large pitcher, stirring to dissolve sugar. Add club soda just before serving. Serve over ice. Yield: 1½ quarts.

SCREWDRIVERS

1½ quarts orange juice
1 to 1½ cups vodka
2 tablespoons lime juice (optional)
Lime slices (optional)

Combine orange juice, vodka, and lime juice, if desired; mix well, and pour into punch bowl. Float lime slices on top, if desired. To serve, pour into ice-filled glasses. Yield: 7½ cups.

BLOODY MARYS

4 cups tomato juice
⅓ cup lemon juice
3 tablespoons Worcestershire sauce
1 teaspoon seasoned salt
1 teaspoon celery salt
½ teaspoon freshly ground pepper
½ teaspoon lemon-pepper seasoning
⅛ teaspoon hot sauce
1 cup vodka
Celery stalks

Combine all ingredients, except vodka and celery; stir well, and chill until ready to serve. Stir in vodka just before serving. Serve over ice cubes, and garnish each serving with a stalk of celery. Yield: 5½ cups.

MINT JULEPS

½ cup sugar
1 cup water
8 fresh mint sprigs, finely
    chopped
1 quart bourbon
10 fresh mint sprigs

Combine sugar, water, chopped mint, and bourbon in a glass container; stir until sugar dissolves. Cover and let stand 4 to 6 hours.

Strain mixture into a large pitcher, discarding chopped mint. To serve, fill glasses with cracked ice; add bourbon mixture, and garnish with mint sprigs. Yield: 5½ cups.

OLD-FASHIONEDS

2 cups Sweet Citrus Syrup (recipe
    follows)
6 cups lemon-lime carbonated
    beverage
3 cups Canadian whiskey
½ teaspoon aromatic bitters
Crushed ice
Orange, lemon, and lime slices
Maraschino cherries

Combine all ingredients except crushed ice, fruit slices, and cherries. Fill glasses with crushed ice; pour mixture over ice. Garnish with fruit. Yield: 11 cups.

Sweet Citrus Syrup

1 (12-ounce) can frozen five-fruit
    citrus beverage concentrate
½ cup grenadine syrup or maraschino
    cherry juice
1 tablespoon sugar

Combine all ingredients in a saucepan; bring to a boil. Remove from heat, and let cool. Pour into a container; cover and refrigerate up to two weeks. Yield: 2 cups.

Note: For each individual serving, place 2 tablespoons Sweet Citrus Syrup, ¼ cup plus 1 tablespoon lemon-lime carbonated beverage, 3 tablespoons whiskey, and a dash of aromatic bitters in a glass. Mix well. Add enough finely crushed ice to fill glass; stir gently. Garnish with citrus slices and a cherry.

To process icy blender beverages: Add enough ice to make mixture in blender measure a designated amount. Process mixture until blended but still icy.

FROSTY PIÑA COLADAS

1 (9-ounce) can cream of coconut
1 (8-ounce) can crushed pineapple,
    undrained
¼ cup light rum
¼ cup milk
1 tablespoon powdered sugar
Ice cubes

Combine all ingredients, except ice cubes, in container of an electric blender; process until smooth. Gradually add enough ice to make mixture measure 4 to 5 cups in blender; process until mixture is smooth and thickened. Yield: 4 to 5 cups.

FROZEN STRAWBERRY DAIQUIRIS

1 (6-ounce) can frozen limeade
    concentrate, thawed and
    undiluted
1 cup light rum
1 cup water
¼ cup sifted powdered sugar
1 cup sliced fresh strawberries
Lime slices
Maraschino cherries

Combine all ingredients, except lime slices and cherries, in a large bowl. Cover and freeze 8 hours.

To serve, place frozen mixture in container of an electric blender; blend mixture until smooth. Garnish with lime slices and cherries, and serve immediately. Yield: 3 cups.

Frozen Banana Daiquiris: Substitute 1 large banana, sliced, for strawberries.

Frozen Peach Daiquiris: Substitute 1 fresh peach or 2 canned peach halves, chopped, for strawberries.

Frozen Pineapple Daiquiris: Substitute 1 (15¼-ounce) can unsweetened pineapple tidbits, drained, for strawberries.

BLENDER DAIQUIRIS

1 (6-ounce) can frozen limeade
    concentrate, thawed and
    undiluted
1 cup light rum
Ice cubes

Combine limeade concentrate and rum in container of an electric blender. Add enough ice cubes to make mixture measure 3 cups. Blend to desired consistency. Yield: 3 cups.

ICY MARGARITAS

Lime wedge
Salt
1 (6-ounce) can frozen limeade concentrate, thawed and undilutcd
¾ cup tequila
¼ cup Triple Sec or other orange-flavored liqueur
Ice cubes
Lime slices (optional)

Rub rim of cocktail glasses with wedge of lime. Place salt in saucer; spin rim of each glass in salt. Set prepared glasses aside.

Combine limeade concentrate, tequila, and Triple Sec in container of an electric blender; blend well. Add enough ice cubes to make mixture measure 3½ cups in blender; blend well.

Pour beverage into prepared glasses; garnish with a slice of lime, if desired. Yield: 3½ cups.

HOT MULLED WINE

2 cups apple juice
¾ cup sugar
1 lemon, sliced
1 orange, sliced
12 whole allspices
12 whole cloves
2 (3-inch) sticks cinnamon
3 cups Burgundy or other dry red wine
Cinnamon sticks (optional)

Combine apple juice, sugar, and fruit slices in a Dutch oven.

Tie whole allspices, whole cloves, and 2 cinnamon sticks in a cheesecloth bag; add spice bag to juice mixture, and bring mixture to a boil. Reduce heat and simmer 5 minutes.

Add wine to juice mixture, and simmer an additional 10 minutes. Remove and discard spice bag. Serve juice mixture hot, with cinnamon stick stirrers, if desired. Yield: 5½ cups.

HOT BUTTERED RUM

2 cups butter, softened
1 (16-ounce) package light brown sugar
1 (16-ounce) package powdered sugar
2 teaspoons ground cinnamon
2 teaspoons ground nutmeg
1 quart vanilla ice cream, softened
Light rum
Whipped cream
Cinnamon sticks

Combine butter, sugars, and spices; beat well at medium speed of an electric mixer. Add ice cream, stirring until blended. Spoon mixture into a 2-quart freezer container; freeze.

To serve, thaw slightly. Place 3 tablespoons butter mixture and 1 jigger rum in a large mug; fill with boiling water. Stir well. (Any unused butter mixture can be refrozen.) Top with whipped cream, and serve with cinnamon stick stirrers. Yield: about 25 servings.

Your Own Liqueurs

These homemade liqueurs taste amazingly like the bottled brands when stirred into recipes for beverages and desserts.

ALMOND LIQUEUR

3 cups sugar
2¼ cups water
Finely grated rind of 3 lemons
1 quart vodka
3 tablespoons almond extract
2 tablespoons vanilla extract

Combine first 3 ingredients in a Dutch oven; bring to a boil. Reduce heat and simmer 5 minutes, stirring occasionally; cool completely. Stir in remaining ingredients; store in airtight containers. Yield: about 6½ cups.

COFFEE LIQUEUR

3 cups sugar
3 cups water
3½ tablespoons instant coffee granules
1 quart vodka
1 tablespoon vanilla extract

Combine sugar, water, and coffee granules in a heavy saucepan. Bring to a boil; cover, reduce heat, and simmer 10 minutes. Remove from heat and cool. Stir in vodka and vanilla; pour into bottles, and cover with plastic wrap. Punch holes in plastic wrap, and store in a cool, dark place 4 weeks. For later use, store in airtight containers. Yield: 6½ cups.

ORANGE LIQUEUR

3 medium-size oranges
3 cups brandy
1 cup honey

Peel oranges, leaving inner white skin on fruit. Cut orange rind into 2- x ¼-inch strips. Reserve orange pulp for other uses.

Combine brandy and orange rind in a jar. Cover tightly, and let stand at room temperature 3 weeks.

Remove orange rind; stir in honey. Let stand 3 days. Strain off clear portion, and store in airtight containers; reserve cloudy portion for cooking. Yield: about 3 cups.

BREADS

Nothing quite compares to the aroma of a quick or yeast bread baking in the oven. The freshness and flavor of homemade bread is special too. Once you're hooked on your own bread, it's hard to settle for anything less.

It doesn't take long to make your own bread when working with quick breads. They're leavened by baking powder or baking soda; they're quick to stir together, and they're baked immediately.

Making yeast bread is somewhat more involved but definitely worth the effort. Kneading the dough takes extra time as does the rising process. And it's a bit more technical, too. Yeast is a living organism which requires mixing with liquid at a critical temperature to activate its growth process; liquid that's too hot or too cold can ruin the end product. Be sure to use the temperature specified in the recipe. Once you've mastered the technique, the process of baking your own yeast bread won't seem intimidating at all.

One recipe of Sourdough Country Crust Bread (page 92) bakes into two perfect loaves—one to spread with butter and eat yourself, and one to share.

EQUIPMENT

If you're a serious bread baker, you can't have too many sizes and types of baking sheets, loafpans, and speciality baking pans. Select good, heavy grade pans and baking sheets for long-term use. Choose shiny pans because they reflect heat best and produce baked goods with nicely browned and tender crusts.

We tested all our muffin recipes in standard 2½-inch muffin pans. The loafpan called for most often is 9 x 5 x 3 inches, although some bread recipes specify pans 8½ x 4½ x 3 inches or smaller. It's best to use the size pan called for in the recipe, otherwise, expect breads that are shallower or deeper and baking times that vary.

FLOUR FOR BREADS

The texture of bread depends largely on the type of flour you use and the amount of gluten it contains. Flour made predominately from "hard wheat" is richer in gluten than that made predominately from "soft wheat." Hard wheat flour absorbs liquids differently and yields a better textured loaf. Our bread recipes were tested with flour that is a combination of hard and soft wheat, which is considered a good flour for home bread baking.

Whole wheat flour has less gluten than all-purpose flour, so breads baked with only whole wheat flour are dense and compact. Most recipes add all-purpose flour to whole wheat for good volume and texture. Rye flour is usually teamed with whole wheat or all-purpose flour because rye gluten lacks elasticity.

Since flour is sifted during milling, there's no need to sift before measuring. To measure all-purpose or whole-grain flour, stir it lightly; then spoon it into a dry measuring cup (don't pack it). Level using the straight edge of a spatula. Don't shake the cup level, as this packs the flour. You do need to sift cake flour.

STORING AND FREEZING BREADS

Both quick breads and yeast breads turn stale quickly. Contrary to popular belief, bread will get stale faster in the refrigerator than at room temperature (although it will mold faster at room temperature than when in the refrigerator). If you want to keep bread for several days, cover it with an airtight wrap, and store it at room temperature.

For longer storage, let bread cool completely after baking, wrap tightly in aluminum foil, place in a freezer bag, and freeze up to 3 months. To serve, partially unwrap, and let stand at room temperature until thawed. Place thawed bread on a baking sheet, and bake, uncovered, at 350° for 5 to 15 minutes or until heated thoroughly, depending on the size and density of the bread.

MICROWAVING BREADS

While some breads developed especially for the microwave oven produce good results, most breads simply are not suited for baking in the microwave. Breads will not brown in the microwave, and they sometimes cook unevenly and have wet spots. Most conventional recipes require substantial changes in the ingredients or procedure before they'll work in the microwave, so we've not included microwave conversions for our breads.

However, you will appreciate the time you save in letting yeast dough rise in the microwave. Refer to our section on yeast breads for specifics.

Quick Breads

This type of bread is aptly named — it's quick and easy to make. The batter is usually stirred together just until the dry ingredients are moistened, and it's baked immediately. Once in the oven, it rises quickly, leavened by steam, eggs, and the gases formed by baking powder or baking soda.

Baking powder is sold in three forms. *Tartrate* baking powder produces the gases to make bread rise as soon as it's mixed with liquid. *Phosphate* baking powder is activated equally by the liquid and the heat of the oven. The *double-acting* type reacts more from the heat of the oven, but somewhat by the liquid in the batter. While you should bake all quick breads as soon as possible after mixing, recipes made with double-acting powder will rise better than those made with other types of baking powder even if they stand at room temperature a few minutes before baking. All of our recipes were tested with the double-acting type of baking powder.

Baking soda starts reacting as soon as it is combined with a liquid, so recipes calling for it should be baked immediately. Baking soda is usually used only in recipes that contain an acid to help the soda act, such as buttermilk, lemon juice, sour cream, molasses, or chocolate.

Biscuits

You'll find tender flaky biscuits gracing breakfast, lunch, or dinner tables in the South, accounting for their broad appeal as well as debates about which type of biscuit is better.

The tenderest biscuits contain solid fat, such as shortening or butter. Cut the butter into the dry ingredients using a pastry blender until the mixture resembles coarse meal. (Two knives or a fork work almost as well.) Add the liquid ingredients, and stir just until the dry ingredients are moistened. Too much mixing makes biscuits heavy. Knead the biscuits on a lightly floured surface only three or four times — just until the dough feels soft and not sticky. Quickly roll, cut, and bake as the recipe directs.

A good biscuit should be level and golden brown on top. It should have straight sides and should be tender and slightly moist inside.

1. You can mix up Quick Buttermilk Biscuits in minutes. Cut butter into flour with a pastry blender until mixture resembles coarse meal.

2. Add buttermilk to the flour mixture, and stir just until dry ingredients are moistened.

3. Turn dough out onto a floured surface, and knead lightly 3 or 4 times.

4. Roll dough to ¾-inch thickness, and cut with a 2-inch biscuit cutter. Bake.

Quick Buttermilk Biscuits bake up deliciously tender and flaky every time.

Biscuits for More Than Serving on the Side

Many meat pies and thick stews are teamed with a biscuit topping. You can also slice biscuits in half and serve them shortcake fashion with creamed meat, eggs, and vegetables. With a tiny bit of sugar added, the traditional biscuit can stand in as dessert with mild cheese and sweet spreads.

QUICK BUTTERMILK BISCUITS

½ cup butter or margarine
2 cups self-rising flour
¾ cup buttermilk
Butter or margarine, melted

Cut ½ cup butter into flour with a pastry blender until mixture resembles coarse meal. Add buttermilk, stirring until dry ingredients are moistened. Turn dough out onto a lightly floured surface, and knead lightly 3 or 4 times.

Roll dough to ¾-inch thickness; cut with a 2-inch biscuit cutter. Place on a lightly greased baking sheet. Bake at 425° for 13 to 15 minutes. Brush with melted butter. Yield: 1 dozen.

WHIPPING CREAM BISCUITS

The recipe for Whipping Cream Biscuits is so simple you can remember it by heart. You'll probably make it often once you try it.

2 cups self-rising flour
1 cup whipping cream

Combine ingredients, stirring with a fork until blended. (Dough will be stiff.) Turn dough out onto a lightly floured surface, and knead 10 to 12 times.

Roll dough to ½-inch thickness; cut with a 2-inch biscuit cutter. Place on a lightly greased baking sheet. Bake at 450° for 10 to 12 minutes. Yield: 1 dozen.

BAKING POWDER BISCUITS

By increasing the milk a little in Baking Powder Biscuits, you can make Drop Biscuits. They aren't quite as shapely, but they're quicker to make and they taste just as good.

2 cups all-purpose flour
1 tablespoon baking powder
½ teaspoon salt
⅓ cup shortening
⅔ cup milk

Combine flour, baking powder, and salt; cut in shortening with a pastry blender until mixture resembles coarse meal. Add milk, stirring until dry ingredients are moistened. Turn dough out onto a lightly floured surface, and knead lightly 4 or 5 times.

Roll dough to ½-inch thickness; cut with a 2-inch biscuit cutter. Place on a lightly greased baking sheet. Bake at 425° for 12 minutes or until lightly browned. Yield: 1 dozen.

Drop Biscuits: Increase milk to 1 cup. Drop dough by heaping tablespoonfuls onto a lightly greased baking sheet, and bake as directed.

CHEESE BISCUITS

2 cups self-rising flour
½ cup shortening
½ cup (2 ounces) shredded Cheddar cheese
¾ cup milk

Combine flour and shortening; cut in shortening with a pastry blender until mixture resembles coarse meal. Add cheese and milk, stirring until dry ingredients are moistened. Turn dough out onto a lightly floured surface, and knead lightly 4 or 5 times.

Roll dough to ½-inch thickness; cut with a 2-inch biscuit cutter. Place on an ungreased baking sheet. Bake at 450° for 10 to 12 minutes. Yield: about 1 dozen.

Bacon Cheese Biscuits: Increase milk to ¾ cup plus 2 tablespoons. Stir ¼ cup chopped green onions and 4 slices bacon, cooked and crumbled, into biscuit dough as milk is added. Makes about 1½ dozen.

Zippy Cheese Biscuits: Increase milk to ¾ cup plus 2 tablespoons. Stir ½ cup chopped pecans and ¼ to ½ teaspoon red pepper into biscuit dough as milk is added. Makes about 1½ dozen.

SWEET POTATO BISCUITS

1 cup all-purpose flour
1½ teaspoons baking powder
¼ teaspoon salt
Pinch of ground nutmeg
½ cup cooked, mashed sweet potatoes
⅓ cup milk
3 tablespoons vegetable oil

Combine flour, baking powder, salt, and ground nutmeg, stirring well; set mixture aside. Combine remaining ingredients; pour over flour mixture, and stir until dry ingredients are moistened. (Dough will be soft.)

Turn dough out onto a heavily floured surface, and knead 4 or 5 times, adding more flour as needed.

Roll dough to ½-inch thickness; cut with a 2-inch biscuit cutter. Place on a lightly greased baking sheet. Bake at 425° for 15 minutes or until lightly browned. Yield: 10 biscuits.

CURRANT SCONES

Hailing from Scotland, scones are similar to biscuits, but they're slightly sweet and often contain currants or raisins.

2 cups all-purpose flour
2 tablespoons sugar
2 teaspoons baking powder
½ teaspoon salt
¾ cup butter or margarine
1½ cups currants
⅓ to ½ cup milk

Combine flour, sugar, baking powder, and salt; cut in butter with a pastry blender until mixture resembles coarse meal. Stir in currants. Gradually add enough milk to the mixture to form a soft dough, stirring just until dry ingredients are moistened. Turn dough out onto a lightly floured surface, and knead lightly 4 or 5 times.

Roll dough to ½-inch thickness; cut with a 2-inch biscuit cutter. Place on lightly greased baking sheets. Bake at 450° for 8 to 10 minutes or until lightly browned. Serve warm. Yield: 2 dozen.

RYE BISCUITS

Try Rye Biscuits sandwiched with ham for a party. We think you'll like the new flavor twist to the traditional ham and biscuit.

1½ cups all-purpose flour
1½ cups rye flour
2 tablespoons baking powder
1 teaspoon caraway seeds
½ teaspoon salt
¾ cup shortening
1 cup plus 2 tablespoons milk

Combine flours, baking powder, caraway seeds, and salt, and stir mixture well. Cut in shortening with a pastry blender until mixture resembles coarse meal. Add milk, stirring until dry ingredients are moistened. Turn dough out onto a lightly floured surface, and knead lightly 8 to 10 times.

Roll biscuit dough to ½-inch thickness; cut dough with a 2-inch biscuit cutter. Placc on ungreased baking sheets. Bake at 450° for 10 to 12 minutes. Yield: 2 dozen.

Whole Wheat Biscuits: Substitute whole wheat flour for rye flour. Delete caraway seeds.

Note: Biscuits may be frozen. To freeze, place uncooked biscuits on an ungreased baking sheet; cover and freeze until firm. Transfer frozen biscuits to plastic bags. To bake, place frozen biscuits on an ungreased baking sheet; bake at 400° for 20 to 23 minutes.

ANGEL BISCUITS

Angel Biscuits are so named because they rise more than the traditional biscuit due to the addition of yeast. They're lighter and airier—like a roll.

2 packages dry yeast
¼ cup warm water (105° to 115°)
2 cups buttermilk
5 cups all-purpose flour
¼ cup sugar
1 tablespoon baking powder
1 teaspoon baking soda
1 teaspoon salt
1 cup shortening

Combine yeast and warm water; let stand 5 minutes. Add buttermilk to yeast mixture, and set aside.

Combine all remaining ingredients except shortening in a large bowl; cut in shortening with a pastry blender until mixture resembles coarse meal. Add buttermilk mixture, stirring with a fork until dry ingredients are moistened. Turn biscuit dough out onto a lightly floured surface, and knead lightly 4 or 5 times.

Roll dough to ½-inch thickness; cut with a 2½-inch biscuit cutter. Place on lightly greased baking sheets. Cover and let rise in a warm place (85°), free from drafts, for 1 hour. Bake at 450° for 10 to 12 minutes or until browned. Yield: 2 dozen.

Note: Biscuits can be made ahead and frozen. Before freezing biscuits, bake 10 minutes; cool. Place biscuits in freezer bags, and freeze. To prepare biscuits for serving, remove from freezer; place biscuits on lightly greased baking sheets, and let thaw. Bake at 450° for 5 minutes or until thoroughly heated.

Muffins

Muffins are popular choices of bread bakers because there are so many variations. You can make them big or little, sweet or savory. Some are just right for home-style dining, while others seem more appropriate for the party table.

When making muffins, just remember that it's important to use the right mixing technique. Combine the dry ingredients, making a well in the center. Combine the liquid ingredients, and pour them into the well; stir just until dry ingredients are moistened. Spoon them into muffin pans, and bake as directed. If over-mixed, your muffins will be peaked, and will have tunnels and a coarse, tough texture. The perfect muffin has a pebbly brown top and a rounded even shape.

Muffins that call for beating with an electric mixer contain more sugar than the traditional muffin and have a texture more like cake. This additional mixing works well for them. Do not use a mixer unless your recipe calls for it.

Remove muffins from pans as soon as they are baked to keep condensation from forming and making them too moist on the bottom.

For well-shaped muffins: Make a well in center of dry ingredients; add liquid and stir just until dry ingredients are moistened. Overmixing causes peaks and tunnels.

SLIGHTLY SWEET MUFFINS

1½ cups all-purpose flour
⅓ to ½ cup sugar
2 teaspoons baking powder
½ teaspoon salt
1 egg, lightly beaten
½ cup milk
¼ cup vegetable oil

Combine first 4 ingredients in a large bowl; make a well in center of mixture. Combine egg, milk, and oil; add liquid mixture to dry ingredients, stirring just until moistened. Spoon into greased muffin pans filling two-thirds full. Bake at 400° for 20 to 25 minutes. Remove muffins from pans immediately. Yield: 10 muffins.

Apple Muffins: Stir ¾ cup peeled, chopped apple, ¼ teaspoon ground cinnamon, and ¼ teaspoon ground nutmeg into the dry ingredients.

Blueberry Muffins: Fold ¾ cup fresh blueberries (or ½ cup canned drained blueberries) into muffin batter.

Cranberry Muffins: Fold ¾ cup fresh cranberries into muffin batter.

Date-Nut Muffins: Fold ½ cup chopped dates and ½ cup chopped pecans into muffin batter.

Jam Muffins: Fill muffin pans one-third full, top with ½ teaspoon jam or preserves, and spoon remaining batter on top.

Oat Muffins: Reduce flour by ½ cup, and stir ½ cup quick-cooking oats in with flour.

Pecan Muffins: Stir ½ cup chopped pecans into dry ingredients.

Mix up the batter for Refrigerator Bran Muffins or Last-Minute Gingerbread Muffins to keep in the refrigerator, and bake the muffins as you need them.

REFRIGERATOR BRAN MUFFINS

1 (15-ounce) package wheat bran flakes cereal with raisins
5 cups all-purpose flour
3 cups sugar
1 tablespoon plus 2 teaspoons baking soda
1 teaspoon salt
4 eggs, beaten
1 quart buttermilk
1 cup shortening, melted

Combine first 5 ingredients in a large bowl; make a well in center of mixture. Combine eggs, buttermilk, and shortening; add to dry ingredients, stirring just until moistened. Cover batter and store in refrigerator up to 6 weeks.

When ready to bake, spoon batter into greased muffin pans, filling two-thirds full. Bake at 350° for 20 minutes. Remove from pans immediately. Yield: about 5½ dozen.

EASY CHEESE MUFFINS

3¾ cups biscuit mix
2 cups (8 ounces) shredded sharp Cheddar cheese
2 tablespoons poppy seeds
⅛ teaspoon red pepper
1 egg, beaten
1½ cups milk

Combine first 4 ingredients in a large bowl; make a well in center of mixture. Combine egg and milk; add mixture to dry ingredients, stirring just until moistened. Spoon into greased miniature (1¾-inch) muffin pans. Bake at 350° for 20 to 25 minutes. Remove muffins from pans immediately, and let cool slightly on wire racks. Yield: 4½ dozen.

Dilly Cheese Muffins: Delete poppy seeds and red pepper. Add ½ to ¾ teaspoon dried whole dillweed with biscuit mix.

HONEY-WHEAT MUFFINS

1 cup whole wheat flour
1 cup all-purpose flour
2 teaspoons baking powder
½ teaspoon salt
⅛ teaspoon ground cinnamon
1 egg, beaten
¾ cup milk
¼ cup vegetable oil
¼ cup honey

Combine flours, baking powder, salt, and cinnamon in a large bowl; make a well in center of mixture. Combine egg, milk, oil, and honey; add liquid ingredients to dry ingredients, stirring just until moistened. Spoon into greased muffin pans, filling two-thirds full. Bake at 400° for 20 minutes. Remove from pans immediately. Yield: 1 dozen.

LAST-MINUTE GINGERBREAD MUFFINS

1 cup shortening
1 cup sugar
1 cup molasses
4 eggs
2 teaspoons baking soda
1 cup buttermilk
4 cups all-purpose flour
1 tablespoon plus 1 teaspoon ground ginger
1 teaspoon ground allspice
½ teaspoon ground nutmeg
½ cup raisins (optional)
½ cup chopped pecans (optional)

Cream shortening; gradually add sugar, beating at medium speed of an electric mixer until light and fluffy. Add molasses. Add eggs, one at a time, beating well after each addition. Dissolve soda in buttermilk.

Combine flour and spices; add to creamed mixture alternately with buttermilk, beating after each addition. Stir in raisins and pecans, if desired. Cover batter and store in refrigerator up to 2 weeks.

When ready to bake, spoon batter into greased muffin pans, filling two-thirds full. Bake at 350° for 20 minutes. Remove from pans immediately. Yield: about 3 dozen.

CHEESE-AND-PEPPER MUFFINS

2½ cups all-purpose flour
¼ cup yellow cornmeal
¼ cup sugar
2 tablespoons baking powder
½ teaspoon salt
¼ teaspoon red pepper
¾ cup (3 ounces) shredded sharp Cheddar cheese
¼ cup finely chopped onion
3 tablespoons finely chopped green pepper
1 (2-ounce) jar diced pimiento, drained
2 eggs, beaten
1½ cups milk
¼ cup vegetable oil

Combine first 10 ingredients in a large bowl; make a well in center of mixture. Combine eggs, milk, and oil; add to dry ingredients, stirring just until moistened. Spoon into greased muffin pans, filling two-thirds full. Bake at 400° for 20 to 25 minutes. Remove from pans immediately. Yield: 1½ dozen.

GOOD-FOR-YOU MUFFINS

1½ cups unbleached all-purpose flour
½ cup sugar
¼ cup cornmeal
¼ cup wheat germ
2 tablespoons baking powder
½ teaspoon salt
1½ cups unprocessed bran
½ cup granola cereal
2 cups buttermilk
2½ tablespoons vegetable oil
2 tablespoons peanut butter
2 eggs, beaten

Combine first 6 ingredients in a large bowl; make a well in center of mixture, and set aside.

Combine bran, granola cereal, and buttermilk; stir well, and let stand 5 minutes. Add oil, peanut butter, and eggs, stirring well. Add to dry ingredients, stirring just until moistened.

Spoon into greased muffin pans, filling two-thirds full. Bake at 400° for 25 minutes. Remove from pans immediately. Yield: 1½ dozen.

PINEAPPLE MUFFINS

1 (8-ounce) can crushed pineapple
½ cup all-purpose flour
⅓ cup firmly packed brown sugar
¼ teaspoon ground cinnamon
¼ cup plus 2 tablespoons butter or margarine, melted and divided
2 cups all-purpose flour
½ cup sugar
1 tablespoon baking powder
½ teaspoon salt
1 egg, beaten
¾ cup milk

Drain pineapple, reserving ¼ cup juice. Set aside. Combine ½ cup flour, brown sugar, cinnamon, and 2 tablespoons butter; stir well. Set aside.

Combine 2 cups flour, sugar, baking powder, and salt in a large bowl; make a well in center of mixture. Combine egg, milk, remaining ¼ cup butter, and reserved ¼ cup pineapple juice; add to dry mixture, stirring just until moistened.

Spoon into greased and floured muffin pans, filling half full. Spoon pineapple over batter, and sprinkle with cinnamon mixture. Bake at 375° for 30 minutes. Remove from pans immediately. Yield: 16 muffins.

MINIATURE ORANGE TEA MUFFINS

½ cup orange juice
1 cup plus 2 tablespoons sugar
1 cup butter or margarine, softened
¾ cup sugar
2 eggs
1 teaspoon baking soda
¾ cup buttermilk
3 cups all-purpose flour
1 tablespoon grated orange rind
¼ cup orange juice
1 teaspoon lemon extract
1 cup currants

Combine first 2 ingredients in a small saucepan; bring to a boil, stirring until sugar dissolves. Chill.

Cream butter; gradually add ¾ cup sugar, beating at medium speed of an electric mixer until light and fluffy. Add eggs, one at a time, beating after each.

Combine soda and buttermilk, stirring well; add to creamed mixture alternately with flour. Stir in orange rind, ¼ cup orange juice, lemon extract, and currants. Fill greased miniature (1¾-inch) muffin pans three-fourths full. Bake at 400° for 10 to 12 minutes or until lightly browned. Remove from pans; dip top and sides of warm muffins in chilled sauce mixture. Place on wire racks to drain. Yield: 5 dozen.

Miniature Lemon Tea Muffins: Substitute lemon juice and rind for that of orange, and substitute orange extract for lemon extract.

The crunchy topping on Blueberry Streusel Muffins makes these breakfast breads extra tempting.

BLUEBERRY STREUSEL MUFFINS

¼ cup butter or margarine, softened
⅓ cup sugar
1 egg
2⅓ cups all-purpose flour
1 tablespoon plus 1 teaspoon baking powder
½ teaspoon salt
1 cup milk
1 teaspoon vanilla extract
1½ cups fresh or frozen blueberries, thawed
½ cup sugar
⅓ cup all-purpose flour
½ teaspoon ground cinnamon
¼ cup butter or margarine, softened

Cream butter; gradually add ⅓ cup sugar, beating at medium speed of an electric mixer until light and fluffy. Add egg, beating well.

Combine 2⅓ cups flour, baking powder, and salt; add to creamed mixture alternately with milk, stirring well after each addition. Stir in vanilla extract, and fold in blueberries.

Spoon batter into greased muffin pans, filling two-thirds full. Combine ½ cup sugar, ⅓ cup flour, and cinnamon; cut in ¼ cup butter with a pastry blender until mixture resembles crumbs. Sprinkle on top of muffin batter. Bake at 375° for 25 to 30 minutes or until golden brown. Remove from pans immediately. Yield: 1½ dozen.

Note: If using frozen blueberries, rinse and drain thawed berries; pat dry with paper towels. This will prevent discoloration of batter.

Quick Bread Loaves

Many of these classic sweet and savory loaves also benefit from the same quick mixing procedure as muffins. Some recipes make two loaves—perfect for eating one and freezing or sharing the other with a neighbor.

Many quick bread loaves have a crack down the top center. This is simply a characteristic of this type of bread; it does not mean there is something wrong with your bread.

MOIST PUMPKIN BREAD

⅔ cup shortening
2 cups sugar
4 eggs
2 cups cooked, mashed pumpkin
⅔ cup water
3⅓ cups all-purpose flour
2 teaspoons baking soda
¾ teaspoon salt
½ teaspoon baking powder
1 teaspoon ground cinnamon
1 teaspoon ground cloves
⅔ cup pecans or walnuts, chopped
⅔ cup raisins

Cream shortening; gradually add sugar, beating well at medium speed of an electric mixer. Add eggs, one at a time, beating after each addition. Stir in pumpkin and water.

Combine flour, and next five ingredients; add to creamed mixture, mixing well. Fold in pecans and raisins. Spoon into 2 greased and floured 9- x 5- x 3-inch loafpans; bake at 350° for 1 hour or until a wooden pick inserted in center comes out clean. Cool in pans 10 minutes; remove from pans, and let cool on wire racks. Yield: 2 loaves.

BANANA LOAF

1¾ cups all-purpose flour
¾ teaspoon baking soda
½ teaspoon salt
¾ cup sugar
1¼ teaspoons cream of tartar
2 eggs, beaten
½ cup vegetable oil
2 ripe bananas, mashed

Combine first 5 ingredients in a large bowl; make a well in center of mixture. Combine remaining ingredients; add to dry mixture, stirring until moistened.

Pour batter into a greased 9- x 5- x 3-inch loafpan. Bake at 350° for 45 minutes or until a wooden pick inserted in center comes out clean. Cool in pan 10 minutes; remove from pan, and let cool on wire rack. Yield: 1 loaf.

Banana Muffins: Spoon batter into greased muffin pans, filling three-fourths full. Bake at 400° for 18 minutes or until golden brown. Remove from pans immediately. Yield: 1½ dozen.

DATE-NUT BREAD

1 (8-ounce) package chopped dates
½ cup chopped pecans or walnuts
1 teaspoon baking soda
1 cup hot water
¼ cup shortening
⅔ cup sugar
1 egg
2 cups all-purpose flour
½ teaspoon salt
1 teaspoon vanilla extract

Stir dates, pecans, and soda into hot water; set aside to cool.

Cream shortening; gradually add sugar, beating at medium speed of an electric mixer. Add egg, and beat well.

Combine flour and salt; add to creamed mixture alternately with fruit-nut mixture, beginning and ending with flour mixture. Stir in vanilla.

Pour batter into 2 greased and floured 28-ounce fruit cans. Bake at 350° for 1 hour or until a wooden pick inserted in center comes out clean. Cool in cans 10 minutes; remove from pans, and let cool on wire racks. Yield: 2 loaves.

LEMON TEA BREAD

½ cup shortening
1 cup sugar
2 eggs
1½ cups all-purpose flour
1½ teaspoons baking powder
¼ teaspoon salt
½ cup milk
Grated rind of 1 lemon
½ cup chopped pecans (optional)
Glaze (recipe follows)

Cream shortening; gradually add sugar, beating well at medium speed of an electric mixer. Add eggs, one at a time, beating after each addition.

Combine flour, baking powder, and salt; add to creamed mixture alternately with milk, beginning and ending with flour mixture. Stir in lemon rind and pecans, if desired.

Pour batter into a greased and floured 9- x 5- x 3-inch loafpan. Bake at 350° for 50 to 55 minutes or until a wooden pick inserted in center comes out clean. Cool in pan 10 to 15 minutes; remove from pan and let cool on wire rack. Pour glaze over bread. Yield: 1 loaf.

Glaze

1 cup sifted powdered sugar
2 tablespoons lemon juice

Combine sugar and lemon juice, stirring well. Yield: about ⅓ cup.

HAWAIIAN BANANA NUT BREAD

3 cups all-purpose flour
¾ teaspoon salt
1 teaspoon baking soda
2 cups sugar
1 teaspoon ground cinnamon
1 cup chopped pecans or walnuts
3 eggs, beaten
1 cup vegetable oil
2 cups mashed ripe bananas
1 (8-ounce) can crushed pineapple, drained
2 teaspoons vanilla extract

Combine first 5 ingredients; stir in pecans. Combine remaining ingredients; add to flour mixture, stirring just until dry ingredients are moistened.

Spoon batter into 2 greased and floured 8½- x 4½- x 3-inch loafpans. Bake at 350° for 1 hour and 10 minutes or until a wooden pick inserted in center comes out clean. Cool in pans 10 minutes; remove from pans, and let cool on wire racks. Yield: 2 loaves.

Carrot Nut Bread: Substitute 2 cups grated carrots for 2 cups mashed bananas. Bake at 350° for 1 hour or until a wooden pick inserted in center comes out clean.

Zucchini Nut Bread: Substitute 2 cups coarsely shredded zucchini for 2 cups mashed bananas. Bake at 350° for 1 hour and 10 minutes or until a wooden pick inserted in center comes out clean.

BOSTON BROWN BREAD

1½ cups whole wheat flour
1 cup all-purpose flour
1½ teaspoons baking powder
½ teaspoon baking soda
½ teaspoon salt
½ cup cornmeal
2 eggs, slightly beaten
2 egg yolks
⅔ cup molasses
3 tablespoons sugar
2 tablespoons vegetable oil
1½ cups buttermilk

Combine first 6 ingredients; set aside.
Combine eggs, egg yolks, molasses, sugar, and oil in a large bowl. Add flour mixture to molasses mixture alternately with buttermilk, beating at medium speed of an electric mixer until blended.

Spoon mixture into 2 greased and floured 1-pound coffee cans. Bake at 350° for 45 to 50 minutes. Remove from cans, and let cool on wire racks. Yield: 2 loaves.

APRICOT NUT BREAD

½ cup dried apricots
1 cup water
1 egg
1 cup sugar
2 tablespoons butter or margarine, melted
2 cups all-purpose flour
1 tablespoon baking powder
½ teaspoon salt
¼ teaspoon baking soda
½ cup orange juice
¼ cup water
1 cup chopped walnuts or pecans

Combine apricots and 1 cup water in a small saucepan; bring to a boil. Remove from heat; cover and let stand 30 minutes. Drain well; finely chop apricots, and set aside.

Beat egg until thick and lemon colored; stir in sugar and butter.

Combine flour, baking powder, salt, and soda; add to creamed mixture alternately with orange juice and ¼ cup water, stirring after each addition. Stir in apricots and walnuts.

Spoon mixture into a greased 9- x 5- x 3-inch loafpan. Bake at 350° for 1 hour or until a wooden pick inserted in center comes out clean. Cool in pan 10 minutes; remove from pan, and let cool on wire rack. Yield: 1 loaf.

Cornbreads

Only in a Southern cookbook are cornbreads grouped as a separate category. Cornbread in any form carries a loyal following in our region.

You can buy cornmeal plain or in the self-rising or mix form. It is made from either yellow or white corn, and the two can be used interchangeably. However, cornbread made with yellow meal tends to be slightly coarser.

SKILLET CORNBREAD

2 cups cornmeal
2 teaspoons baking powder
1 teaspoon baking soda
¾ teaspoon salt
2 eggs, beaten
2 cups buttermilk
2 tablespoons vegetable oil

Combine cornmeal, baking powder, soda, and salt in a large bowl; add eggs, buttermilk, and oil, stirring just until dry ingredients are moistened.

Place a well-greased 10-inch cast-iron skillet in a 450° oven for 4 minutes or until hot. Remove from oven; spoon batter into skillet. Bake at 450° for 25 minutes or until lightly browned. Yield: 8 servings.

Crackling Cornbread: Stir in 1 cup cracklings with buttermilk.

BEEFED-UP CORNBREAD

Serve Beefed-Up Cornbread with a vegetable salad or soup. It's a hearty version of cornbread that's teamed with ground beef and cheese.

1 tablespoon yellow cornmeal
½ pound ground beef
1 cup yellow cornmeal
½ teaspoon salt
½ teaspoon baking soda
2 eggs, well beaten
1 cup milk
1 (17-ounce) can cream-style corn
¼ cup vegetable oil
2 cups (8 ounces) shredded hoop cheese
1 large onion, finely chopped
2 to 4 jalapeño peppers, seeded and chopped

Sprinkle 1 tablespoon cornmeal in a well-greased 10-inch cast-iron skillet. Cook over medium heat until cornmeal is lightly browned; set skillet aside.

Cook ground beef until browned, stirring to crumble meat; drain well, and set meat aside.

Combine 1 cup cornmeal, salt, and soda; add eggs, milk, corn, and oil. Stir just until dry ingredients are moistened. Pour half of batter into prepared skillet; sprinkle with cheese, onion, peppers, and ground beef. Top with remaining batter. Bake at 350° for 50 to 55 minutes. Yield: 6 servings.

CORNMEAL MUFFINS

1 cup yellow cornmeal
1 cup all-purpose flour
2 teaspoons baking powder
1 teaspoon baking soda
¾ teaspoon salt
2 to 4 tablespoons sugar
1 egg, beaten
1¼ cups commercial sour cream
¼ cup shortening, melted

Combine first 6 ingredients in a large bowl; make a well in center of mixture. Combine egg, sour cream, and shortening; add to dry ingredients, stirring just until moistened. Spoon into greased muffin pans, filling two-thirds full. Bake at 425° for 15 minutes or until golden brown. Remove from pans immediately. Yield: 1½ dozen.

CHEESY CORNBREAD

1 cup self-rising cornmeal
½ teaspoon baking soda
¼ teaspoon salt
1½ cups (6 ounces) shredded Cheddar cheese
½ cup chopped onion
1 cup milk
3 tablespoons bacon drippings
1 teaspoon garlic powder
3 eggs, beaten
1 (7-ounce) can whole kernel corn, drained
1 (2-ounce) jar diced pimiento, drained

Combine cornmeal, soda, and salt; add remaining ingredients, stirring just until dry ingredients are moistened. Spoon into a greased 10-inch cast-iron skillet. Bake at 350° for 45 minutes or until golden brown. Yield: 10 servings.

Bacon Cornbread: Add 6 slices bacon, cooked and crumbled, with onion.

Chile Cornbread: Add 1 (4-ounce) can chopped green chiles, drained, with onion.

Jalapeño Cornbread: Add 3 jalapeño peppers, seeded and chopped, with onion.

HUSH PUPPIES

1 cup cornmeal
½ cup self-rising flour
1 teaspoon baking powder
¾ teaspoon salt
¼ to ½ cup chopped onion
1 egg, beaten
⅔ cup milk
Vegetable oil

Combine first 5 ingredients in a large bowl. Add egg and milk, stirring just until dry ingredients are moistened. Let batter stand 5 minutes.

Carefully drop batter by rounded tablespoonfuls into deep hot oil (375°). Fry, turning once, 3 to 5 minutes or until hush puppies are golden brown. Drain well on paper towels. Yield: about 1½ dozen.

PEPPY HUSH PUPPIES

1¼ cups commercial hush puppy mix
1 (7½-ounce) can whole tomatoes, drained and chopped
1 small onion, chopped
¼ cup chopped green pepper
¼ teaspoon pepper
¼ teaspoon crushed red pepper
⅛ teaspoon garlic powder
Pinch of baking powder
1 egg, beaten
⅓ cup beer
Vegetable oil

Combine first 8 ingredients; make a well in center of mixture. Combine egg and beer; add to dry ingredients, stirring just until moistened. Drop batter by tablespoonfuls into deep hot oil (375°); fry only a few at a time, turning once, 3 to 5 minutes or until hush puppies are golden brown. Drain on paper towels. Yield: about 1½ dozen.

Bake Quick Corn Sticks to go with homemade soups and traditional Southern dinners.

QUICK CORN STICKS

1¼ cups cornmeal
¾ cup all-purpose flour
1 tablespoon plus 1 teaspoon baking
  powder
¾ teaspoon salt
1 tablespoon sugar
2 eggs, lightly beaten
1 cup milk
¼ cup vegetable oil

Combine first 5 ingredients, mixing well. Combine remaining ingredients; add to dry ingredients, stirring just until moistened.

Place a well-greased cast-iron corn stick pan in a 425° oven for 3 minutes or until hot. Remove pan from oven; spoon batter into pan, filling two-thirds full. Bake at 425° for 12 minutes or until lightly browned. Yield: 1½ dozen.

Quick Corn Muffins: Season muffin pans as for corn sticks. Spoon batter into pans, filling two-thirds full. Bake as for corn sticks. Makes 15 muffins.

At first taste, you might confuse spoonbread with a grits casserole. The texture is similar, but spoonbread is made from cornmeal instead of grits.

SOUTHERN SPOONBREAD

2 cups milk
1 cup water
1 cup yellow cornmeal
2 tablespoons butter or margarine
1 teaspoon salt
3 eggs

Combine first 5 ingredients; cook over medium heat until thickened, stirring constantly. Remove from heat.

Beat eggs at medium speed of an electric mixer until thick and lemon colored. Gradually stir about one-fourth of hot mixture into eggs; add to remaining hot mixture, stirring constantly. Pour into a lightly greased 1½-quart casserole.

Bake at 350° for 35 minutes or until a knife inserted in center comes out clean. Yield: 6 servings.

Cheddar Spoonbread: Stir 1½ cups (6 ounces) shredded Cheddar cheese into mixture after adding eggs.

CORN AND BACON SPOONBREAD

¾ cup yellow cornmeal
1½ cups water
2 cups (8 ounces) shredded Cheddar
  cheese
1½ cups cooked fresh cut corn
¼ cup butter or margarine
1 or 2 cloves garlic, minced
¾ teaspoon salt
1 cup milk
4 eggs, separated
10 slices bacon, cooked and crumbled

Combine cornmeal and water; bring to a boil, and boil 1 minute or until thickened, stirring constantly. Remove from heat. Add cheese, corn, butter, garlic, and salt; stir until cheese melts. Stir in milk.

Beat egg yolks at medium speed of an electric mixer until thick and lemon colored; add bacon. Stir into cornmeal mixture. Beat egg whites (at room temperature) until stiff but not dry; gently fold into cornmeal mixture.

Pour into a lightly greased 2½-quart casserole. Bake at 325° for 1 hour or until a knife inserted in center comes out clean. Yield: 10 servings.

Quick Breakfast Breads and Coffee Cakes

Those packaged mixes for pancakes and waffles make breakfast breads easy to make, but with just a few extra minutes, you can make them from scratch. The flavor and texture of the homemade versions are well worth the effort, especially when you have overnight guests for breakfast.

Grease the griddle or waffle iron lightly to keep these breads as fat-free as possible. It takes very little fat to keep them from sticking; any extra will just be absorbed into the breads.

Pancakes have a built-in indicator to tell you when to turn them. As soon as the top surface is full of bubbles and the edges begin to look cooked, they're ready to turn. The second side will take only a minute or two to brown. Most waffle irons have a signal light to tell you when they're ready. Follow the directions that come with your iron for specific information.

French toast is probably the easiest of all our breakfast breads to make, especially the version that sits overnight and is ready to cook as soon as you hop out of the shower.

Our coffee cakes aren't difficult to make for early morning enjoyment either. Several of them make use of convenience products, such as biscuit mix or refrigerated biscuits, to speed you along during preparation.

You can also make these coffee cakes the night before if you like. Most are equally good warm or at room temperature. Reheat them briefly in a microwave oven, or place them in the conventional oven at the temperature at which they originally baked just long enough to reheat them.

Turning pancakes: Pancakes are ready to be turned when the tops are covered with bubbles and when the edges start to look cooked.

BUTTERMILK PANCAKES

1 egg
1 cup all-purpose flour
1 tablespoon baking powder
½ teaspoon baking soda
½ teaspoon salt
1 tablespoon sugar
1 cup buttermilk
2 tablespoons vegetable oil
Homemade Maple Syrup

Beat egg. Combine flour, baking powder, soda, salt, and sugar; add to egg. Add buttermilk and oil, beating until mixture is smooth.

For each pancake, pour about ¼ cup batter onto a hot, lightly greased griddle. Turn pancakes when tops are covered with bubbles and edges look cooked. Serve with Homemade Maple Syrup. Yield: 8 (4-inch) pancakes.

Homemade Maple Syrup

1 cup water
2 cups sugar
½ teaspoon maple flavoring

Bring water to a boil in a 1-quart saucepan; add sugar and maple flavoring, stirring to dissolve. Cook 1 to 2 minutes, stirring constantly. Remove from heat. Leftover syrup may be stored in refrigerator. Yield: 2 cups.

Blueberry Pancakes: Fold ½ cup fresh or frozen blueberries into batter just before cooking.

SOUR CREAM PANCAKES

3 eggs, separated
1½ cups commercial sour cream
1 teaspoon baking soda
1¼ cups all-purpose flour
1 teaspoon baking powder
½ teaspoon salt
1 tablespoon sugar
3 tablespoons butter or margarine, softened

Beat egg yolks. Combine sour cream and soda; stir into egg yolks. Combine flour, baking powder, salt, and sugar; stir into sour cream mixture. Add butter, and beat at medium speed of an electric mixer 30 seconds. Beat egg whites (at room temperature) until stiff peaks form; fold egg whites into batter.

For each pancake, pour ¼ cup batter onto a hot, lightly greased griddle. Turn pancakes when tops are covered with bubbles and edges look cooked. Yield: 14 (4-inch) pancakes.

PANCAKE-SAUSAGE ROLLUPS

1 (12-ounce) package blueberry
  pancake mix (canned blueberries
  included)
1¾ cups milk
¼ cup vegetable oil
1 egg
Vegetable oil
1 pound mild bulk pork
  sausage
1 (8-ounce) carton commercial
  sour cream
Commercial blueberry syrup

Combine dry ingredients of pancake mix, milk, ¼ cup vegetable oil, and egg in a large bowl; stir with a wire whisk until fairly smooth. Rinse blueberries packaged with pancake mix, and drain well on paper towels. Fold blueberries into batter.

Brush the bottom of a 10-inch crêpe pan or heavy skillet with vegetable oil; place over medium heat until just hot, not smoking.

Pour ¼ cup batter into pan; quickly tilt pan in all directions so batter covers pan, making a 7-inch pancake. Turn pancake when top is covered with bubbles and edges look cooked. Repeat to make about 11 additional pancakes. Set pancakes aside; keep warm.

Cook sausage in a skillet until browned, stirring to crumble meat; drain well.

Spoon about 2 tablespoons sausage and about 1 tablespoon sour cream into center of each pancake; roll up and place, seam side down, in a 13- x 9- x 2-inch baking dish. Bake at 400° for 10 minutes. Serve hot with blueberry syrup. Yield: 6 servings.

Waffles and Pancakes for Desserts

For a refreshing variation in desserts, top waffles or pancakes with fruit and whipped cream.

Save Leftover Waffles

Use leftover waffles when you're serving creamed meat or vegetable sauces. Just spoon the sauce over the top of waffles. Or top them with fruit sauces or ice cream for dessert.

Make waffles fresh or freeze leftovers in a freezer bag for up to 1 month. Toast them on both sides straight from the freezer.

WAFFLES

2 cups all-purpose flour
1 teaspoon baking soda
½ teaspoon salt
2 eggs, separated
2 cups buttermilk
¼ cup butter or margarine, melted

Combine flour, soda, and salt; set aside. Combine egg yolks, buttermilk, and butter; add to flour mixture, stirring briskly until blended.

Beat egg whites (at room temperature) until stiff peaks form; carefully fold into batter. Bake in preheated oiled waffle iron. Yield: 3 (8-inch) waffles.

Ham Waffles: Stir 1¼ cups cooked ground ham into batter just before folding in egg whites.

Sausage Waffles: Cook and drain ½ pound mild bulk pork sausage. Stir sausage into batter just before folding in egg whites.

ORANGE PRALINE TOAST

6 (¾-inch thick) slices French bread
3 tablespoons butter or margarine,
  softened
⅓ cup firmly packed brown sugar
¼ cup finely chopped pecans
1 tablespoon grated orange rind
2 tablespoons orange juice

Toast bread on both sides, and spread one side with butter.

Combine remaining ingredients, stirring well. Spread about 1 tablespoon sugar mixture on buttered side of each slice of toast. Bake toast slices at 350° about 5 to 8 minutes or until sugar melts. Yield: 6 servings.

OVERNIGHT ORANGE FRENCH TOAST

8 (¾-inch thick) slices French
  bread
4 eggs
1 cup milk
2 tablespoons orange juice
½ teaspoon vanilla extract
⅛ teaspoon salt
2 tablespoons butter or margarine,
  divided
Powdered sugar
Orange Sauce

Place bread in a 13- x 9- x 2-inch baking dish. Combine eggs, milk, orange juice, vanilla, and salt; beat well. Pour mixture over bread slices; turn slices over to coat evenly. Cover and refrigerate overnight.

Melt 1 tablespoon butter in a large skillet; remove 4 slices bread from dish, and sauté in butter 4 minutes on each side or until browned. Repeat procedure with remaining butter and bread slices. Sprinkle toast with powdered sugar; serve immediately with Orange Sauce. Yield: 4 servings.

Orange Sauce

1 cup firmly packed brown sugar
2 teaspoons grated orange rind
½ cup orange juice

Combine all ingredients in a small saucepan, stirring well. Bring to a boil; reduce heat, and simmer until thickened (about 5 minutes), stirring frequently. Yield: 1¼ cups.

ALMOND FRENCH TOAST

¾ cup milk
2 eggs
1 tablespoon butter or margarine, melted
6 slices day-old bread
2 tablespoons butter or margarine
Powdered sugar
Almond Syrup

Combine first 3 ingredients in a shallow bowl, beating well. Dip each bread slice into egg mixture, coating each well.

Melt 2 tablespoons butter on a large griddle; arrange 3 slices bread on griddle, and cook 3 minutes on each side or until browned. Repeat procedure with remaining bread slices, adding additional butter, if needed. Sprinkle with powdered sugar. Serve with Almond Syrup. Yield 3 servings.

Almond Syrup

2 tablespoons butter or margarine
½ cup sliced almonds
1½ cups liquid brown sugar
½ teaspoon almond extract

Melt butter in a small saucepan; add almonds, and sauté over medium heat until golden. Stir in sugar and almond extract; serve warm. Yield: 1⅔ cups.

Waffled French Toast: Bake French toast in preheated oiled waffle iron 2 minutes or until browned.

QUICK MONKEY BREAD

½ cup chopped pecans
½ cup sugar
1 teaspoon ground cinnamon
3 (10-ounce) cans refrigerated buttermilk biscuits
1 cup firmly packed brown sugar
½ cup butter or margarine, melted

Sprinkle pecans evenly in bottom of a well-greased 10-inch Bundt pan. Set pan aside.

Combine sugar and cinnamon. Cut biscuits into quarters; roll each piece in sugar mixture, and layer in pan.

Combine brown sugar and butter; pour over dough. Bake at 350° for 30 to 40 minutes. Cool bread 10 minutes in pan; invert onto serving platter. Yield: one 10-inch coffee cake.

CRANBERRY-ORANGE COFFEE CAKE

¼ cup firmly packed brown sugar
½ cup chopped pecans
¼ teaspoon ground cinnamon
2 cups biscuit mix
2 tablespoons sugar
⅔ cup milk
1 egg, beaten
½ (14-ounce) jar cranberry-orange relish
Glaze (recipe follows)

Combine brown sugar, pecans, and cinnamon; stir well, and set aside.

Combine biscuit mix, sugar, milk, and egg; beat 30 seconds at medium speed of an electric mixer. Pour batter into a greased 9-inch square pan. Sprinkle batter with pecan mixture, and spoon relish evenly over top.

Bake at 400° for 25 minutes or until a wooden pick inserted in center comes out clean. Drizzle glaze over warm cake. Yield: one 9-inch coffee cake.

Glaze

1 cup sifted powdered sugar
2 tablespoons milk
½ teaspoon vanilla extract

Combine all ingredients; stir well. Yield: about ⅓ cup.

Add a tasty touch to breads with powdered sugar glaze: If glaze seems too thin, thicken with additional powdered sugar; if it is too thick, add more milk or water.

ORANGE BREAKFAST RING

1 cup sugar
3 tablespoons grated orange rind
2 (12-ounce) cans refrigerated buttermilk biscuits
⅓ cup butter or margarine, melted
1 (3-ounce) package cream cheese, softened
½ cup sifted powdered sugar
2 tablespoons orange juice

Combine sugar and orange rind. Separate biscuits; dip each in butter, and coat with sugar mixture. Stand biscuits on sides, overlapping edges, in a lightly greased 10-inch tube pan. Bake at 350° for 30 minutes or until golden brown.

Invert bread onto serving platter. Combine cream cheese and powdered sugar, beating until smooth. Add orange juice, stirring well; spoon mixture over top while ring is hot. Serve warm. Yield: one 10-inch coffee cake.

FRESH BLUEBERRY COFFEE CAKE

1¼ cups fresh blueberries
⅓ cup sugar
2 tablespoons cornstarch
½ cup butter or margarine, softened
1 cup sugar
2 eggs
2 cups all-purpose flour
1 teaspoon baking powder
1 teaspoon baking soda
½ teaspoon salt
1 (8-ounce) carton commercial sour cream
¾ teaspoon almond extract
½ cup finely chopped pecans
Glaze (recipe follows)

Combine blueberries, ⅓ cup sugar, and cornstarch in a small saucepan; cook over medium heat 2 to 3 minutes or until sauce is thickened, stirring constantly. Set sauce aside.

Cream butter; gradually add 1 cup sugar, beating at medium speed of an electric mixer. Add eggs, one at a time, beating after each addition.

Combine flour, baking powder, soda, and salt; add to creamed mixture alternately with sour cream, beginning and ending with flour mixture. Stir in almond extract.

Spoon half of batter into a greased 10-inch Bundt or tube pan; spoon on half the blueberry sauce, swirling partially through batter with a knife. Repeat with remaining batter and blueberry sauce. Sprinkle with pecans. Bake at 350° for 50 minutes or until done. Let stand 5 minutes before removing from pan. Invert onto serving plate, and drizzle with glaze. Yield: one 10-inch coffee cake.

Glaze

¾ cup sifted powdered sugar
1 tablespoon warm water
½ teaspoon almond extract

Combine all ingredients, stirring well. Yield: ¼ cup.

Cinnamon-Nut Coffee Cake: Delete blueberries, ⅓ cup sugar, and 2 tablespoons cornstarch. Combine ¾ cup firmly packed brown sugar, ½ cup chopped pecans, and 1 teaspoon ground cinnamon; replace blueberry mixture with brown sugar mixture.

Cranberry Coffee Cake: Delete blueberries, ⅓ cup sugar, and 2 tablespoons cornstarch. Replace blueberry mixture with 1 (16-ounce) can whole-berry cranberry sauce.

CHOCOLATE CHIP COFFEE CAKE

2 cups all-purpose flour
2 teaspoons baking powder
1½ cups sugar
½ cup butter or margarine, softened
2 eggs
¾ cup milk
1 teaspoon vanilla or almond extract
1 (6-ounce) package semisweet chocolate mini-morsels
Powdered sugar

Combine first 4 ingredients in a small mixing bowl; beat at low speed of an electric mixer until mixture resembles fine crumbs. Remove 1 cup crumb mixture, and set aside.

Add eggs, milk, and vanilla to remaining crumb mixture; mix until blended. Pour batter into a greased 11- x 7- x 1½-inch pan; sprinkle with chocolate morsels. Top with reserved 1 cup crumb mixture.

Bake at 350° for 35 to 40 minutes or until a wooden pick inserted in center comes out clean. Cool slightly; dust top with powdered sugar. Yield: 1 coffee cake.

Note: To freeze coffee cake, bake and let cool completely; remove from pan, wrap in foil, and freeze. To serve, thaw and heat in foil package at 300° for 20 minutes or until warmed. Remove from package; dust top with powdered sugar.

RASPBERRY-NUT STRUDEL

1 cup butter or margarine, softened
1 (8-ounce) package cream cheese, softened
3 cups all-purpose flour
Powdered sugar
1 cup raisins
1 cup raspberry preserves
1 cup finely chopped walnuts
1 cup firmly packed brown sugar
1 cup flaked coconut
¾ cup sifted powdered sugar
1 to 1½ tablespoons warm water

Cream butter and cream cheese at medium speed of an electric mixer; add flour, beating well. Divide dough into 4 equal portions. Wrap each in plastic wrap, and chill.

Work with 1 portion of dough at a time; keep remaining dough chilled. Sift powdered sugar lightly over work surface. Roll dough into a 12- x 8-inch rectangle.

Combine raisins, preserves, walnuts, brown sugar, and coconut; spread one-fourth of raisin mixture over dough. Roll up jellyroll fashion, starting at short side. Pinch seams and ends together.

Place roll, seam side down, on an ungreased baking sheet. Repeat procedure with remaining dough and filling mixture.

Bake at 325° for 55 minutes. Combine ¾ cup powdered sugar and water, stirring until blended. Drizzle powdered sugar glaze over warm strudels. Serve warm or at room temperature. Yield: four 8-inch rolls.

Note: Other flavors of preserves can be substituted for raspberry preserves.

Specialty Quick Breads

These breads don't fall under any particular category, but they're too important to neglect. Each plays a significant role in a menu.

GARLIC BREAD

1 (16-ounce) loaf unsliced French bread
½ cup butter or margarine, softened
2 cloves garlic, minced
¼ teaspoon dried parsley flakes

Slice French bread into 1-inch slices. Combine remaining ingredients, stirring well; spread butter mixture between bread slices and on top and sides of loaf. Bake at 350° for 15 minutes or until thoroughly heated. Yield: 1 loaf.

Cheesy Garlic Bread: Stir 1 cup (4 ounces) shredded Swiss cheese into butter mixture.

BREAKAWAY VEGETABLE BREAD

3 (10-ounce) cans refrigerated buttermilk biscuits
½ cup butter or margarine, melted
½ pound bacon, cooked and crumbled
½ cup grated Parmesan cheese
1 small onion, finely chopped
1 small green pepper, finely chopped

Cut biscuits into quarters; dip each piece in butter, and layer one-third in a lightly greased 10-inch Bundt pan. Sprinkle with half each of bacon, cheese, onion, and green pepper. Repeat layers until all ingredients are used, ending with biscuits. Bake at 350° for 40 to 45 minutes or until done. Yield: one 10-inch ring.

PINEAPPLE FRITTERS

3 cups all-purpose flour
2 tablespoons baking powder
½ teaspoon salt
¾ cup sugar
3 eggs, beaten
1 cup milk
1 (20-ounce) can crushed pineapple, drained
Vegetable oil
Powdered sugar

Combine first 4 ingredients; stir well. Add eggs, milk, and pineapple; stir until smooth. Heat 3 to 4 inches oil to 375°; carefully drop batter by heaping tablespoonfuls into hot oil, cooking 5 to 6 fritters at a time. Cook about 1 minute or until golden on one side; turn and cook other side about 1 minute. Drain well on paper towels; sprinkle with powdered sugar. Yield: 3 dozen.

POPOVERS

Popovers bake into crusty, hollow shells that you can eat alone or fill with sweet or savory sauces. Once in the oven, they'll rise high over the muffin pans. They're leavened by eggs and the steam created by the initial high oven temperature. Resist the temptation to open the oven door as they bake, or they won't rise as high.

1 cup all-purpose flour
¼ teaspoon salt
1 cup milk
2 eggs, slightly beaten

Combine all ingredients; beat at low speed of an electric mixer just until smooth.

Place well-greased muffin pans in a 425° oven for 3 minutes or until a drop of water sizzles when dropped in them. Remove pans from oven; fill half full with batter. Bake at 425° for 15 minutes. Reduce heat to 350°, and bake an additional 18 to 20 minutes. Serve immediately. Yield: 1 dozen.

Cheese Popovers: Stir ¼ cup (1 ounce) shredded Cheddar cheese into batter.

Vegetable Popovers: Sauté 2 teaspoons minced onion, 2 teaspoons minced green pepper, and 1 teaspoon diced pimiento in 1 tablespoon butter or margarine. Stir vegetables into batter.

Yorkshire Pudding: Do not grease or preheat muffin pans. Spoon 1 teaspoon beef drippings into each muffin pan; tilt to coat pan evenly. Add batter, and bake as for popovers.

PARMESAN TWISTS

¼ cup butter or margarine, softened
1 cup grated Parmesan cheese
½ cup commercial sour cream
1 cup all-purpose flour
½ teaspoon dried Italian seasoning
1 egg yolk, slightly beaten
1 tablespoon water
Caraway seeds or poppy seeds

Cream butter; add cheese and sour cream, beating well at medium speed of an electric mixer. Combine flour and Italian seasoning. Gradually add to creamed mixture, blending until smooth.

Turn dough out onto a lightly floured surface; divide in half. Roll out half of dough to a 12- x 7-inch rectangle and cut into 6- x ½-inch strips. Twist each strip 2 or 3 times, and place on greased baking sheets. Repeat procedure with remaining dough.

Combine egg yolk and water. Brush strips with egg mixture; sprinkle with seeds. Bake at 350° for 10 to 12 minutes or until browned. Yield: 4½ dozen.

1. *It's easy to make Basic Crêpes for use in all our recipes that call for the thin pancakes. Beat flour, salt, and milk at medium speed of an electric mixer until smooth.*

2. *Brush crêpe pan with oil, and place over medium heat just until hot.*

3. *Pour batter into pan; tilt pan in all directions so batter covers pan with a thin film.*

4. *To make Florentine Crêpe Pie, spread Spinach Filling over a crêpe, top with a crêpe, and spread with Mushroom Filling; repeat procedure using all filling and crêpes.*

NEVER-FAIL FLOUR TORTILLAS

In Mexico, almost everyone makes tortillas, but on this side of the border, folks think the process is difficult. Not so.

Many stores now carry tortilla presses, but even without one, you can roll the dough with a regular rolling pin.

3½ cups all-purpose flour
1 teaspoon salt
¾ teaspoon baking powder
⅓ cup shortening
1 cup warm milk (105° to 115°)

Combine first 3 ingredients; stir well. Cut in shortening with pastry blender until mixture resembles coarse meal. Stir in milk, mixing well. Turn dough out onto a smooth surface; knead about 3 minutes.

Divide dough into 10 equal portions. Roll each with a rolling pin into a very thin circle, about 8 inches in diameter, turning dough and rolling on both sides.

Heat an ungreased skillet over me-dium heat; cook tortillas about 2 min-utes on each side or until lightly browned, being careful not to let tor-tillas wrinkle. Pat tortillas lightly with spatula while browning the second side. Serve hot. Yield: 10 tortillas.

Use this Basic Crêpe recipe to make Florentine Crêpe Pie or any other recipe that calls for crêpes. When you have crêpes left over, stack them between layers of wax paper, place in a freezer bag, and freeze up to 1 month. Take out just what you need for an impromptu entrée or dessert.

BASIC CRÊPES

1 cup all-purpose flour
¼ teaspoon salt
1¼ cups milk
2 eggs
2 tablespoons butter or margarine, melted
Vegetable oil

Combine all-purpose flour, salt, and milk, beating at medium speed of an electric mixer until smooth. Add eggs, and beat well; stir in melted butter. Re-frigerate batter 1 hour. (This allows flour particles to swell and soften so crêpes will be light in texture.)

Brush bottom of a 6-inch crêpe pan or heavy skillet lightly with oil; place crêpe pan over medium heat until just hot, but not smoking.

Pour 2 tablespoons batter into pan; quickly tilt pan in all directions so batter covers pan with a thin film. Cook about 1 minute.

Lift edge of crêpe to test for doneness. Crêpe is ready for flipping when it can be shaken loose from pan. Flip crêpe, and cook about 30 seconds on other side. (This side of the crêpe is usually spotty brown and is the side on which the filling is placed.)

Place crêpes on a towel, and allow to cool. Repeat until all batter is used. Stack crepes between layers of wax paper to prevent sticking. Yield: 16 to 18 (6-inch) crêpes.

5. *Spoon Swiss Cheese Sauce over stack of crêpes; top with shredded cheese and paprika. Bake as directed.*

Slice Florentine Crêpe Pie into wedges to serve. It's a tasty and unique dish for brunch.

FLORENTINE CRÊPE PIE

1 recipe Basic Crêpes
Spinach Filling
Mushroom Filling
Swiss Cheese Sauce
¼ cup (1 ounce) shredded Swiss cheese
1 teaspoon paprika
Fresh parsley sprigs (optional)
Tomato roses (optional)

Place 1 crêpe in a lightly greased 10-inch quiche dish or pieplate. Spoon about 2 tablespoons Spinach Filling over crêpe, spreading evenly. Top with another crêpe; then spoon about 2 tablespoons Mushroom Filling over top, and spread evenly.

Repeat procedure with remaining crêpes, Spinach Filling, and Mushroom Filling, ending with a crêpe.

Spoon Swiss Cheese Sauce over stack of crêpes. Top with shredded Swiss cheese and paprika.

Bake at 375° for 20 to 25 minutes or until sauce is bubbly and top is lightly browned. Garnish with parsley sprigs and tomato roses, if desired. Cut into wedges to serve. Yield: 6 servings.

Spinach Filling

1 (10-ounce) package frozen chopped spinach
¼ cup Swiss Cheese Sauce

Cook spinach according to package directions; drain well. Combine spinach and Swiss Cheese Sauce, stirring well. Yield: 1½ cups.

Note: 1½ cups cooked fresh spinach may be substituted for frozen spinach.

Mushroom Filling

1 cup diced fresh mushrooms
2 tablespoons minced green onions
1 tablespoon butter or margarine, melted
1 (8-ounce) package cream cheese, softened
1 egg, beaten
½ cup Swiss Cheese Sauce

Sauté mushrooms and green onions in butter until tender.

Combine cream cheese and egg; beat at medium speed of an electric mixer until blended. Add mushroom mixture and Swiss Cheese Sauce; stir well. Yield: 2 cups.

Swiss Cheese Sauce

¼ cup butter or margarine
⅓ cup all-purpose flour
2¾ cups milk
½ teaspoon salt
⅛ teaspoon pepper
¼ teaspoon ground nutmeg
¼ cup whipping cream
1 cup (4 ounces) shredded Swiss cheese
2 tablespoons grated Parmesan cheese

Melt butter in a heavy saucepan over low heat; add flour, stirring until smooth. Cook 1 minute, stirring constantly. Gradually add milk; cook over medium heat, stirring constantly, until thickened and bubbly. Add seasonings and cream, stirring constantly. Add cheese, stirring until cheese melts. Yield: 3½ cups.

Yeast Breads

Yeast bread was probably discovered by accident, the result of a microorganism falling into a batch of dough and causing it to rise dramatically—surprising an ancient baker. A mystique still surrounds leavened bread and gives it a reputation for being difficult to bake. But there's no mystery to making beautiful yeast bread once you learn the basics.

TYPES OF YEAST

Yeast is a living organism that produces bubbles of carbon dioxide that cause bread to rise. It is available in several forms: active dry yeast, quick-acting active dry yeast, and compressed, cake form. One package of active dry yeast equals .6-ounce cake of compressed yeast. All of our recipes were tested with active dry yeast, so you'll get the best results by using it in these recipes. If you want to substitute the quick-acting kind of yeast, follow the package directions for necessary changes.

DISSOLVING THE YEAST

In most of our yeast recipes, we dissolve the yeast in warm water (105° to 115°) before adding any other ingredients. Water that is too hot will kill the yeast, while water that is too cool will make the bread slow to rise.

Some breads follow the rapid-mix method of making bread in which the yeast is mixed with some of the dry ingredients before adding the liquids. This method eliminates the need to dissolve the yeast first. When using this method, the liquid should be 120° to 130° when you add it to the dry ingredients unless otherwise specified.

KNEADING THE DOUGH

Turn the dough out onto a lightly floured surface. With lightly floured hands, lift the edge of the dough farthest from you and fold it toward you. Using the heels of both hands, press down into the dough and away from you. Give the dough a quarter turn. Fold the dough towards you again, and repeat the kneading procedure until the dough begins to feel smooth and elastic.

Continue adding flour in small amounts until the dough loses its stickiness; on humid days it will take more. Kneading usually takes about 8 to 10 minutes.

LETTING THE DOUGH RISE

The ideal rising temperature for yeast bread is 85°. A gas oven with a pilot light or an electric oven with the oven light on or containing a large pan of hot water should provide this temperature as well as a draft-free environment.

Place the dough in a greased bowl, turning it to coat the top surface. Cover the bowl with plastic wrap.

Rising is complete when the dough has doubled in bulk, unless your recipe specifies otherwise. To test the dough for doubled bulk, lightly press a finger ½ inch into the dough. If the indention remains, the dough is ready to shape for a second rising.

Punch the dough down in the center with your fist, and fold the edges to the center. Turn the dough over, and place it on a lightly floured breadboard or other surface.

To make the dough ahead of time, let it rise in the refrigerator. It will take about eight hours to rise at this cooler temperature, and it will keep there up to five days if the dough is made with water or three days if made with milk. Punch the dough down each day.

SHAPING THE DOUGH

Divide the dough according to your particular recipe, and form the portion you will be using into a ball. (Cover and store excess dough in the refrigerator until needed.) Cover and let rest 5 to 10 minutes. This allows the gluten in the dough to relax, making the dough less elastic and easier to handle.

Specific directions for shaping the dough are given in individual recipes. After shaping the dough, and placing it in a properly prepared loafpan or on a baking sheet, allow it to rise again, according to directions. When the shaped dough is double in size, lightly press a finger against the edge of the loaf. If the indention remains, it has risen enough.

BAKING THE BREAD

Unless the recipe specifies otherwise, bake the bread in a preheated oven. To be sure your bread bakes evenly, place the pan in the center of the oven. If you are putting more than one pan in the same oven, leave some space around each pan so heat can circulate freely.

The outward appearance is not always an accurate indication of doneness. You also need to tap the crust lightly with your knuckles and listen for a hollow sound. The more you use the tapping test, the more accustomed you'll become to recognizing this hollow sound. Aluminum foil may be used to cover the bread if it starts to get too brown before it sounds hollow.

Remove bread from pans immediately after baking. Cool baked loaves on a wire rack before wrapping in aluminum foil or plastic wrap.

YEAST BREAD AND THE MICROWAVE

Breads don't bake well in the microwave oven, but you can let many doughs rise in the microwave.

To let dough rise in the microwave oven, place dough in a greased bowl, turning to grease all sides. Set the bowl in a larger, shallow dish, and pour about 1 inch of water into the bottom dish. Cover dough loosely with wax paper, and place in oven. Microwave at MEDIUM-LOW (30% power) for 1 to 2 minutes; let stand in oven 5 minutes. Repeat microwaving and standing 2 to 4 times or until dough has doubled in bulk.

If surface of dough appears to be drying out during rising, turn dough over in bowl. When rising is complete, punch dough down and proceed as directed in recipe.

Two Versatile Yeast Doughs

We've developed a basic dough recipe and a sourdough recipe that you can use to make bread in many shapes and flavors.

The basic dough recipe is quick to mix, simple to work with, requires little kneading, and will keep in the refrigerator up to five days. First make the dough, and chill it. Then use part or all of it to shape the type of bread you want. Choose from loaves, rolls, and sweet breads. Bread baking was never so versatile.

To shape the perfect yeast loaf: Roll the dough jellyroll fashion according to dimensions in recipe. Let it rise in the pan.

BASIC YEAST DOUGH

1 package dry yeast
1 cup warm water (105° to 115°)
3 tablespoons sugar
2 tablespoons shortening
1 egg
½ teaspoon salt
3 to 3½ cups all-purpose flour

Dissolve yeast in warm water in a large mixing bowl; let stand 5 minutes. Add sugar, shortening, egg, salt, and half of flour; beat at low speed of an electric mixer until smooth. Gradually stir in enough remaining flour to make a soft dough.

Place dough in a well-greased bowl, turning to grease top. Cover and let rise in a warm place (85°), free from drafts, 1 hour or until doubled in bulk, or cover and refrigerate up to 5 days. (If refrigerated, let return to room temperature before proceeding.)

Punch dough down; turn out onto a lightly floured surface, and knead 4 or 5 times. Shape and bake as directed.

CLOVERLEAF ROLLS

1 recipe Basic Yeast Dough
¼ cup butter or margarine, melted

Lightly grease muffin pans. Shape dough into 1-inch balls; place 3 balls in each muffin cup. Cover and let rise in a warm place (85°), free from drafts, 40 minutes or until doubled in bulk. Bake at 400° for 10 to 12 minutes or until golden. Brush rolls with melted butter. Yield: 2 dozen.

SESAME BUNS

1 recipe Basic Yeast Dough
1 egg white
1 tablespoon water
1½ tablespoons sesame seeds

Divide dough into 8 equal pieces. Roll each into a ball, and place on greased baking sheets; press down lightly with fingertips to resemble a bun.

Cover and let rise in a warm place (85°), free from drafts, about 30 minutes or until doubled in bulk. Combine egg white and water, beating until frothy; brush over buns. Sprinkle buns with sesame seeds. Bake at 400° for 15 to 20 minutes or until browned. Yield: 8 buns.

CHEESE CRESCENTS

½ recipe Basic Yeast Dough
2 tablespoons butter or margarine, melted
¼ cup grated Parmesan cheese
Butter or margarine, melted

Roll dough into a 12-inch circle on a lightly floured surface. Brush with 2 tablespoons melted butter, and sprinkle with Parmesan cheese. Cut into 12 wedges; roll each wedge tightly, beginning at wide end. Seal points, and place rolls on a greased baking sheet.

Cover and let rise in a warm place (85°), free from drafts, about 30 minutes or until doubled in bulk. Bake at 400° for 8 to 10 minutes or until browned. Brush rolls with melted butter. Yield: 1 dozen.

CINNAMON LOAF

½ recipe Basic Yeast Dough
2 tablespoons butter or margarine, melted
1 tablespoon sugar
1 teaspoon ground cinnamon
⅓ cup raisins
1 cup sifted powdered sugar
1 to 1½ tablespoons milk
¼ cup chopped pecans

Roll dough into a 15- x 7-inch rectangle on a lightly floured surface; brush with melted butter. Combine 1 tablespoon sugar and cinnamon; sprinkle over dough. Sprinkle raisins over dough. Roll up jellyroll fashion, starting at narrow edge. Pinch seams and ends together. Place loaf, seam side down, in a greased 8½- x 4½- x 3-inch loafpan.

Cover and let rise in a warm place (85°), free from drafts, 40 minutes or until doubled in bulk. Bake at 350° for 30 to 35 minutes or until loaf sounds hollow when tapped. Remove from pan, and let cool on wire rack.

Combine powdered sugar and milk, stirring until smooth. Drizzle over loaf, and sprinkle with pecans. Yield: 1 loaf.

Basic Yeast Dough (page 89) can be shaped any way you desire. The bread will be equally moist and tender in any form.

ORANGE ROLLS

1 recipe Basic Yeast Dough
¼ cup butter or margarine, softened
2 tablespoons sugar
2 tablespoons grated orange rind
¾ cup sugar
½ cup butter or margarine
½ cup commercial sour cream
2 tablespoons orange juice

Roll dough into a 14- x 9-inch rectangle on a lightly floured surface. Combine ¼ cup softened butter, 2 tablespoons sugar, and orange rind; spread over dough, leaving a ½-inch margin at edges. Roll dough up jellyroll fashion, starting at long side; pinch long edge of roll (do not seal ends). Cut roll into ¾-inch slices. Place slices, cut side down, in a greased 13- x 9- x 2-inch pan.

Cover and let rise in a warm place (85°), free from drafts, about 40 minutes or until doubled in bulk. Bake at 400° for 20 to 25 minutes or until browned. Remove rolls from pan while hot.

Combine ¾ cup sugar, ½ cup butter, sour cream, and orange juice in a saucepan; cook over medium heat, stirring constantly, until thoroughly heated. (Do not boil.) Pour over warm rolls. Yield: 1½ dozen.

FILLED COFFEE RING

1 recipe Basic Yeast Dough
2 tablespoons butter or margarine, melted
½ cup raisins
½ cup chopped pecans
⅓ cup sugar
1 teaspoon ground cinnamon
1 cup sifted powdered sugar
1½ tablespoons milk

Roll dough into a 21- x 7-inch rectangle on a lightly floured surface. Brush butter evenly over dough, leaving a 1-inch margin at sides. Combine raisins, pecans, ⅓ cup sugar, and cinnamon; sprinkle mixture evenly over dough, leaving a 1-inch margin.

Roll up dough, jellyroll fashion, starting at long side; pinch seam to seal. Place roll on a large greased baking sheet, seam side down; shape into a ring, and pinch ends together to seal.

Using kitchen shears, make cuts in dough every inch around ring, cutting two-thirds of the way through roll at each cut. Gently turn each piece of dough on its side, slightly overlapping slices.

Cover dough and let rise in a warm place (85°), free from drafts, 45 minutes or until doubled in bulk. Bake ring at 375° for 20 to 25 minutes or until golden brown. Transfer to a wire rack. Combine powdered sugar and milk; drizzle over coffee ring while warm. Yield: 1 coffee cake.

SOURDOUGH BREAD

Sourdough bread has been around for centuries. Before the birth of Christ, ancient Egyptians reportedly captured wild yeast from the air and mixed it into their dough because it made their bread rise. With commercial yeast now so readily available, we no longer depend on sourdough for leavening, but still love it for its characteristic flavor and the novelty of its fermentation process. As the starter ages, its flavors mellow, imparting progressively more sourdough flavor each time it's used.

To make this bread, follow the recipe carefully. Let the starter stand in a warm place for 72 hours, so that it will bubble up and ferment. Stir it two or three times a day; then refrigerate it, and stir once a day.

Use the starter or share it with a friend within 14 days. Each time you remove a cup, replenish or "feed" the starter with Starter Food as directed in the recipe below; this maintains the volume and nourishes the yeast. If the starter sits too long without new Starter Food, it will become overly sour and will lose its leavening quality. If you don't use it within 14 days, pour off or give away one cup of the starter and feed the remaining part as if you had used it.

One cup of starter is a good amount to give to friends. Tell them to feed it immediately, then to chill it for a couple of days before using; this allows the flavor to develop.

If properly cared for, the starter should last indefinitely. But if it becomes too sour for your taste preferences, discard it and make a new batch. Below are other tips for the use and care of your starter.

● Mix and store the starter in glass, stoneware, or plastic. Metal can cause a chemical reaction with the starter.

● Place the starter in a bowl large enough to allow it to double in bulk as it ferments.

● Never cover the container too tightly, as gas needs to escape and air needs to get in to react with the yeast. Punch a small hole in a plastic wrap cover or leave the lid ajar.

● If a clear liquid forms on top of the mixture, just stir it back in.

● Allow the starter to come to room temperature before using it.

SOURDOUGH STARTER

1 package dry yeast
½ cup warm water
(105° to 115°)
2 cups all-purpose flour
3 tablespoons sugar
1 teaspoon salt
2 cups warm water
(105° to 115°)

Dissolve yeast in ½ cup warm water; let stand 5 minutes. Combine flour, sugar, and salt in a medium-size nonmetal bowl, and stir well. Gradually stir in 2 cups warm water. Add yeast mixture, and mix well.

Cover starter loosely with plastic wrap or cheesecloth; let stand in a warm place (85°) for 72 hours, stirring 2 or 3 times daily. Place fermented mixture in refrigerator, and stir once a day. Use within 11 days.

To use, remove sourdough starter from refrigerator; let stand at room temperature at least 1 hour.

Stir starter well, and measure amount of starter needed for recipe. Replenish remaining starter with starter food (recipe follows), and return to refrigerator; use starter within 2 to 14 days, stirring daily.

When Sourdough Starter is used again, repeat above procedure for using starter and replenishing with Starter Food. Yield: 3 cups.

Starter Food

½ cup sugar
1 cup all-purpose flour
1 cup milk

Stir all ingredients into remaining Sourdough Starter.

SOURDOUGH BISCUITS

2 cups self-rising flour
¼ teaspoon baking soda
¼ cup shortening
¾ cup Sourdough Starter (at room temperature)
½ cup buttermilk
1 tablespoon butter or margarine, melted

Combine flour and baking soda in a nonmetal bowl; stir well. Cut in shortening with a pastry blender until mixture resembles coarse meal. Add Sourdough Starter and buttermilk, stirring until dry ingredients are moistened. Turn dough out onto a floured surface; knead lightly 10 to 12 times.

Roll dough to ½-inch thickness; cut with a 2¾-inch biscuit cutter. Place on a lightly greased baking sheet, and brush tops with butter. Bake at 425° for 12 to 15 minutes. Yield: 10 biscuits.

SOURDOUGH-BUTTERMILK PANCAKES

2 cups all-purpose flour
1½ teaspoons baking powder
½ teaspoon baking soda
½ teaspoon salt
2 tablespoons sugar
1⅓ cups buttermilk
1 cup Sourdough Starter (at room temperature)
1 egg, beaten
2 tablespoons vegetable oil

Combine first 5 ingredients in a nonmetal bowl; stir well. Add buttermilk, Sourdough Starter, and egg; beat just until large lumps disappear. Stir in oil.

For each pancake, pour about ¼ cup batter onto a hot, lightly greased griddle. Turn pancakes when tops are covered with bubbles and edges look cooked. Yield: 12 (4-inch) pancakes.

SOURDOUGH COUNTRY CRUST BREAD

(pictured on page 68)

2 packages dry yeast
1¼ cups warm water (105° to 115°)
1 cup Sourdough Starter (at room temperature)
¼ cup vegetable oil
¼ cup sugar
2 teaspoons salt
2 eggs, beaten
5½ to 6 cups unbleached flour
Vegetable oil
Butter or margarine, melted

Dissolve yeast in warm water in a large nonmetal bowl; let stand 5 minutes. Stir in Sourdough Starter, ¼ cup oil, sugar, salt, eggs, and 3 cups flour. Gradually stir in enough remaining flour to make a soft dough.

Turn dough out onto a floured surface, and knead until smooth and elastic (about 8 to 10 minutes). Place in a well-greased bowl, turning to grease top. Cover and let rise in a warm place (85°), free from drafts, 1 to 1½ hours or until doubled in bulk.

Punch dough down, and divide in half; place on a floured surface. Roll each half into an 18- x 9-inch rectangle. Tightly roll up dough, starting at narrow edge; pinch seam and ends together to seal. Place loaves, seam side down, in two greased 9- x 5- x 3-inch loafpans. Brush tops with oil.

Cover and let rise in a warm place, free from drafts, about 1 hour or until doubled in bulk. Bake at 375° for 30 to 35 minutes or until loaves sound hollow when lightly tapped. Remove loaves from pans; brush with melted butter. Yield: 2 loaves.

Yeast Bread Loaves

Whether baked freeform or in a loafpan, you'll enjoy the satisfaction of baking loaves of homemade bread. If baking in a loafpan, be sure to use the size pan specified in the recipe; otherwise your loaf will not be shaped as pretty, and the baking time may not be right.

In general, remove the loaf of bread from the pan immediately after removal from the oven, and place it on a wire rack to cool. This is a good time to brush the hot loaf with melted butter, if you desire.

After the loaf has cooled, it is ready to slice. Slice loaf with a bread knife (a long, slender knife with serrated edges) to give you a neater cut.

BASIC WHITE BREAD

About 6 cups all-purpose flour, divided
3 tablespoons sugar
2½ teaspoons salt
1 package dry yeast
1½ cups water
½ cup milk
3 tablespoons butter or margarine

Combine 2 cups flour, sugar, salt, and yeast in a large mixing bowl; stir well. Combine water, milk, and butter; heat until butter melts, stirring occasionally. Cool to 120° to 130°.

Gradually add liquid mixture to flour mixture, beating well at high speed of an electric mixer. Beat an additional 2 minutes at medium speed. Gradually add ¾ cup flour, beating 2 minutes at medium speed. Gradually stir in enough remaining flour to make a soft dough.

Turn dough out onto a floured surface, and knead until smooth and elastic (about 10 minutes). Shape into a ball, and place in a well-greased bowl, turning to grease top. Cover and let rise in a warm place (85°), free from drafts, 1 hour or until doubled in bulk.

Punch dough down; turn out onto a lightly floured surface, and knead lightly 4 or 5 times. Divide dough in half. Roll one portion of dough into a 14- x 7-inch rectangle. Roll up dough, starting at narrow edge, pressing firmly to eliminate all pockets; pinch ends to seal. Place dough, seam side down, in a well-greased 9- x 5- x 3-inch loafpan. Repeat procedure with remaining portion of dough.

Cover and let rise in a warm place, free from drafts, 1 hour or until doubled in bulk. Bake at 375° for 45 to 50 minutes or until loaves sound hollow when tapped. Remove bread from pans immediately; cool on wire racks. Yield: 2 loaves.

Braided White Bread: Punch dough down after first rising. Turn dough out onto a lightly floured surface; knead lightly 4 or 5 times. Divide dough into thirds. Shape each third into a 20-inch rope. Place ropes on a greased baking sheet (do not stretch); pinch ends together at one end to seal. Braid ropes; pinch loose ends to seal.

Cover and let rise in a warm place, free from drafts, about 30 minutes or until doubled in bulk. Gently brush dough with one slightly beaten egg white. Bake at 350° for 25 to 30 minutes or until loaf sounds hollow when tapped; cool on wire rack. Yield: 1 loaf.

WHOLE WHEAT BREAD

7 to 8 cups whole wheat flour,
  divided
2 packages dry yeast
1 tablespoon salt
1½ cups milk
1½ cups water
¼ cup plus 2 tablespoons butter or
  margarine
¼ cup honey
Butter or margarine, melted

Combine 3 cups flour, yeast, and salt in a mixing bowl; stir and set aside.

Combine milk, water, butter, and honey in a medium saucepan; place over low heat, stirring constantly, until mixture reaches 120° to 130°. Stir milk mixture into flour mixture, and beat at medium speed of an electric mixer 2 minutes or until smooth. Stir in enough remaining flour to make a stiff dough.

Turn dough out onto a lightly floured surface; let dough rest 10 minutes. Knead dough until smooth and elastic (about 3 minutes). Place in a well-greased bowl, turning to grease top. Cover and let rise in a warm place (85°), free from drafts, for 50 minutes or until

dough has doubled in bulk.

Punch dough down, and divide in half; shape each portion into a loaf. Place in 2 well-greased 9- x 5- x 3-inch loafpans. Cover and let rise in a warm place, free from drafts, 50 minutes or until doubled in bulk. Bake at 375° for 35 to 45 minutes or until loaves sound hollow when tapped. Brush loaves with melted butter; remove from pans, and let cool on wire racks. Yield: 2 loaves.

Whole Wheat Rolls: Punch dough down after first rising, and divide dough into thirds. Working with one third, divide into 8 pieces; shape each into a ball. Place 8 balls in a lightly greased 9-inch round cakepan. Repeat procedure with remaining dough. Cover and let rise in a warm place, free from drafts, 40 minutes or until doubled in bulk. Bake at 375° for 20 to 25 minutes or until golden brown. Brush rolls with melted butter. Yield: 2 dozen.

MONKEY BREAD

1 cup milk
½ cup butter or margarine
¼ cup sugar
1 teaspoon salt
1 package dry yeast
3½ cups all-purpose flour
½ cup butter or margarine, melted

Combine first 4 ingredients in a saucepan; heat until butter melts. Cool to 105° to 115°. Add yeast; stir until dissolved. Let stand 5 minutes. Combine flour and milk mixture in a large bowl; stir until blended. Cover and let rise in a warm place (85°), free from drafts, 1 hour and 20 minutes or until doubled in bulk.

Punch dough down, and shape into 1½-inch balls; dip each in melted butter. Layer balls in a greased 10-inch one-piece tube pan or Bundt pan. Cover and repeat rising procedure 45 minutes or until doubled. Bake at 375° for 35 minutes. Cool in pan 5 minutes; then invert. Yield: one 10-inch ring.

Recipes that don't require kneading are called no-knead or batter breads. You just stir up the dough (it will be moister than most doughs), spoon it into the pan, and let it rise.

The texture of these breads will be slightly coarser than kneaded bread, and the surface will not be as smooth. The taste is excellent, however, and batter breads are quicker and easier to make than traditional yeast breads.

NO-KNEAD HERB BREAD

2 packages dry yeast
2 cups warm water (105° to 115°)
2 teaspoons salt
½ cup sugar
2 cups whole wheat flour, divided
4 to 5 cups all-purpose flour,
  divided
1 egg
¼ cup vegetable oil
¾ teaspoon dried whole basil
½ teaspoon rubbed sage

Dissolve yeast in warm water; let stand 5 minutes. Combine yeast mixture, salt, sugar, 1 cup whole wheat flour, and 2 cups all-purpose flour in a mixing bowl. Beat at medium speed of electric mixer 2 minutes. Add egg, oil, herbs, and ½ cup all-purpose flour; beat at medium speed 2 minutes.

Combine remaining flours; gradually stir in enough to form a moderately stiff dough. Divide dough in half; place each portion in a well-greased bowl, turning to grease top. Cover and let rise in a warm place (85°), free from drafts, one hour or until doubled in bulk.

Punch dough down; shape each portion into a loaf. Place in two greased 9- x 5- x 3-inch loafpans. Cover and let rise in a warm place, free from drafts, 40 minutes or until doubled in bulk. Bake at 375° for 25 to 35 minutes or until loaves sound hollow when tapped. Remove from pans, and let cool on wire racks. Yield: 2 loaves.

SALLY LUNN

1 package dry yeast
¼ cup warm water (105° to 115°)
¾ cup warm milk (105° to 115°)
½ cup butter or margarine, softened
⅓ cup sugar
3 eggs, well beaten
4 cups all-purpose flour
1 teaspoon salt

Dissolve yeast in warm water in a medium bowl; let stand 5 minutes. Stir in milk. Cream butter and sugar in a large bowl at medium speed of an electric mixer until light and fluffy; add eggs, beating well.

Combine flour and salt; add to creamed mixture alternately with milk mixture, beginning and ending with flour. Mix well after each addition. (Batter will be stiff.)

Cover batter, and let rise in a warm place (85°), free from drafts, 2 hours or until doubled in bulk.

Spoon batter into a well-greased 10-inch tube pan or Bundt pan. Cover and let rise in a warm place, free from drafts, until doubled in bulk. Bake at 350° for 50 to 60 minutes. Remove bread from pan, and let cool on wire rack. Yield: one 10-inch ring.

HONEY OATMEAL BREAD

2¼ cups milk
⅓ cup honey
¼ cup shortening
2½ teaspoons salt
2 packages dry yeast
½ cup warm water
  (105° to 115°)
2 cups regular oats, uncooked
6 to 6½ cups all-purpose flour
Butter or margarine, melted
  (optional)

Combine milk, honey, shortening, and salt in a saucepan; heat until shortening melts. Cool to 105° to 115°.

Dissolve yeast in warm water in a large bowl; let stand 5 minutes. Add milk mixture, oats, and 2 cups flour; mix well. Stir in enough remaining flour to make a soft dough.

Turn dough out onto a lightly floured surface, and knead until smooth and elastic (about 8 to 10 minutes). Place in a well-greased bowl, turning to grease top. Cover and let rise in a warm place (85°), free from drafts, 1 hour or until doubled in bulk.

Punch dough down; cover and let stand 10 minutes. Divide dough in half, and place on a lightly floured surface. Roll each half into a 15- x 9-inch rectangle. Roll up dough jellyroll fashion, starting with narrow end; pinch seams and ends to seal. Place loaves, seam side down, in two well-greased 9- x 5- x 3-inch loafpans. Brush with melted butter, if desired.

Cover and let rise in a warm place, free from drafts, 40 minutes or until doubled in bulk. Bake at 375° for 45 minutes or until loaves sound hollow when tapped. Cover with aluminum foil the last 15 minutes of baking, if necessary, to prevent excessive browning. Remove loaves from pans, and let cool on wire racks. Yield: 2 loaves.

DARK PUMPERNICKEL BREAD

3 packages dry yeast
1½ cups warm water
  (105° to 115°)
½ cup molasses
1 tablespoon caraway seeds
2 teaspoons salt
2 tablespoons shortening
2½ cups rye flour
¼ cup cornmeal
¼ cup cocoa
2 to 2½ cups all-purpose
  flour
Cornmeal

Dissolve yeast in warm water in a large mixing bowl. Stir in molasses, caraway seeds, salt, shortening, rye flour, ¼ cup cornmeal, and cocoa. Beat at medium speed of an electric mixer until smooth. Stir in enough all-purpose flour to make a stiff dough.

Turn dough out onto a lightly floured surface. Cover and let rest 10 to 15 minutes. Knead until smooth and elastic (5 to 10 minutes). Shape dough into a ball, and place in a well-greased bowl, turning to grease top. Cover and let rise in a warm place (85°), free from drafts, 1 hour or until doubled in bulk.

Punch dough down; shape into a ball. Cover and let rise in a warm place, free from drafts, about 40 minutes or until doubled in bulk.

Grease a baking sheet, and sprinkle with cornmeal. Punch dough down, and divide in half. Shape each half into a round, slightly flat loaf. Place loaves on opposite corners of baking sheet. Cover and let rise in a warm place, free from drafts, 1 hour.

Bake at 375° for 25 to 30 minutes or until loaves sound hollow when tapped. Remove from baking sheet, and let cool on wire racks. Yield: 2 loaves.

WHOLE WHEAT-RYE BREAD

2 packages dry yeast
½ cup warm water (105° to 115°)
⅓ cup molasses
1 tablespoon salt
1 tablespoon caraway seeds
¼ cup shortening
1¾ cups lukewarm water
1½ cups rye flour
1½ cups whole wheat flour
3 to 4 cups all-purpose flour
1 egg white, slightly beaten

Dissolve yeast in ½ cup warm water in a large mixing bowl; let stand 5 minutes. Stir in molasses, salt, caraway seeds, shortening, 1¾ cups water, rye flour, and whole wheat flour. Beat at medium speed of an electric mixer until smooth. Gradually stir in enough all-purpose flour to make a soft dough.

Turn dough out onto a floured surface, and knead until smooth and elastic (about 8 to 10 minutes). Place in a well-greased bowl, turning to grease top. Cover and let rise in a warm place (85°), free from drafts, 1 hour or until doubled in bulk.

Punch dough down; roll dough into a 19- x 16-inch rectangle. Roll dough jellyroll fashion, starting at long side; pinch seam and ends to seal. Place loaf, seam side down, on a greased baking sheet. Cover and let rise in a warm place, free from drafts, 1 hour or until doubled in bulk.

Brush loaf with egg white. Bake at 400° for 35 to 40 minutes or until loaf sounds hollow when tapped. Let cool on wire rack. Yield: 1 loaf.

Marble Bread: Prepare dough for Whole Wheat-Rye Bread and for Basic White Bread (page 92), letting both doughs rise the first time.

Punch whole wheat-rye dough down; divide into 2 equal portions. Place each portion onto a lightly floured surface. Cover and let rest 15 minutes.

Repeat procedure with white dough.

Combine 1 portion whole wheat-rye dough and 1 portion white dough; lightly knead 12 to 15 times.

Roll combined dough into a 19- x 16-inch rectangle. Roll dough jellyroll fashion, starting at long side; pinch seam and ends to seal. Place loaf, seam side down, on a greased baking sheet. Repeat procedure with remaining dough. Cover and let rise in a warm place, free from drafts, 1 hour or until doubled in bulk.

Brush each loaf with half of a slightly beaten egg white. Bake at 400° for 35 to 40 minutes or until loaves sound hollow when tapped. Let cool on wire racks. Yield: 2 loaves.

RYE BREAD

1½ to 1¾ cups all-purpose flour,
    divided
1½ cups rye flour, divided
1 package dry yeast
¾ teaspoon salt
1 cup water
¼ cup molasses
1 tablespoon vegetable oil
Butter or margarine, melted

Combine 1 cup all-purpose flour, 1 cup rye flour, yeast, and salt in a large mixing bowl; stir well. Combine water, molasses, and oil in a small saucepan. Heat mixture to 120°, stirring occasionally; remove from heat.

Gradually add hot liquid mixture to dry ingredients, beating at low speed of an electric mixer 30 seconds. Beat an additional 3 minutes at high speed. Gradually add remaining rye flour and enough remaining all-purpose flour to form a moderately stiff dough, stirring well after each addition.

Turn dough out onto a lightly floured surface, and knead until smooth and elastic (about 8 minutes). Shape dough into a ball, and place in a well-greased bowl, turning to grease top. Cover dough, and let rise in a warm place (85°), free from drafts, 1½ hours or until dough is doubled in bulk.

Punch dough down; let dough rest 10 minutes. Shape dough into a ball, and place in a well-greased 1½-quart ovenproof bowl. Let rise about 1 hour or until doubled in bulk.

Brush top with melted butter. Bake at 350° for 35 to 40 minutes or until loaf sounds hollow when tapped. Remove from bowl, and let cool on wire rack. Yield: 1 loaf.

CHEESE BREAD

2 packages dry yeast
1 cup warm water (105° to 115°)
1 cup milk
2 tablespoons sugar
2 tablespoons shortening
2 teaspoons salt
1 egg, slightly beaten
6 to 7 cups all-purpose flour,
    divided
2 cups (8 ounces) shredded
    Cheddar cheese

Dissolve yeast in warm water in a large bowl; let stand 5 minutes. Combine milk, sugar, shortening, and salt in a saucepan; heat until shortening melts. Cool mixture to 105° to 115°. Add milk mixture, egg, and 2 cups flour to yeast mixture; stir until smooth. Stir in cheese; gradually stir in enough remaining flour to make a soft dough.

Turn dough out onto a floured surface; cover and let rest 10 to 15 minutes. Knead dough until smooth and elastic (about 8 to 10 minutes). Place in a well-greased bowl, turning to grease top. Cover and let rise in a warm place (85°), free from drafts, 1 hour or until doubled in bulk.

Punch dough down, and divide in half; shape each portion into a loaf. Place in two greased 9- x 5- x 3-inch loafpans. Cover and let rise in a warm place, free from drafts, 45 minutes or until doubled in bulk. Bake at 375° for 30 minutes or until loaves sound hollow when tapped. Remove from pans, and let cool on wire racks. Yield: 2 loaves.

NO-KNEAD FRENCH BREAD

½ cup warm water (105° to 115°)
2½ teaspoons sugar
2 packages dry yeast
1 cup boiling water
2 tablespoons sugar
2 tablespoons butter or margarine
2 teaspoons salt
1 cup cold water
6½ to 7 cups all-purpose flour
1 egg, beaten
2 tablespoons milk
Poppy seeds or sesame seeds

Combine warm water, 2½ teaspoons sugar, and yeast in a small bowl; let stand 5 minutes. Combine boiling water, 2 tablespoons sugar, butter, and salt in a large mixing bowl. Stir until butter melts. Add cold water; cool to lukewarm (105° to 115°). Stir yeast mixture into water mixture. Add 2½ cups flour. Beat at medium speed of an electric mixer until blended. Gradually stir in enough remaining flour to make a soft dough.

Let dough stand in mixing bowl 10 minutes. Stir gently for a few seconds; cover. Repeat gentle stirring every 10 minutes for the next 40 minutes.

Turn dough out onto a lightly floured surface; divide into 3 equal portions. Roll each portion into a 13- x 8-inch rectangle on a lightly floured surface. Roll up jellyroll fashion, starting with long side; pinch ends and seam to seal.

Place each loaf, seam side down, on a separate greased baking sheet. Cover and let rise in a warm place (85°), free from drafts, about 40 minutes or until doubled in bulk. Make diagonal slits about ¼-inch deep down the length of loaves using a sharp knife. Combine egg and milk in a small bowl, beating until blended. Brush gently over loaves after rising. Sprinkle each loaf with poppy seeds. Bake at 400° for 20 to 25 minutes or until loaves sound hollow when tapped. (This bread freezes well.) Yield: 3 loaves.

For freestanding yeast breads: With a sharp knife, make several slashes across the top of the loaf after rising and before baking. The slashes are decorative and help prevent cracks during baking.

CHOCOLATE PINWHEEL LOAF

½ cup milk
¼ cup butter or margarine
¼ cup sugar
¾ teaspoon salt
1 package dry yeast
¼ cup warm water
  (105° to 115°)
2 eggs, beaten
3 to 3¼ cups all-purpose flour
1 (1-ounce) square unsweetened
  chocolate, melted and cooled
Glaze (recipe follows)

Combine milk, butter, sugar, and salt in a saucepan; heat until butter melts. Cool to 105° to 115°.

Dissolve yeast in warm water in a large mixing bowl. Stir in milk mixture, eggs, and 2 cups flour; beat at medium speed of an electric mixer until smooth.

Stir in enough remaining flour to make a soft dough.

Divide dough in half, and set one half aside. Turn one portion of dough out onto a floured surface, and knead until smooth and elastic (about 8 to 10 minutes). Place in a well-greased bowl, turning to grease top. Cover and let rise in a warm place (85°), free from drafts, 1 hour or until doubled in bulk.

Pour melted chocolate over remaining dough; knead dough until blended (about 8 to 10 minutes). Place in a well-greased bowl, turning to grease top. Cover and let rise in a warm place, free from drafts, 1 hour or until dough is doubled in bulk.

Punch each dough down, and turn out onto a floured surface; roll each into an 18- x 10-inch rectangle. Position chocolate dough on top of plain dough. Roll halves together, jellyroll fashion, starting at short end. Fold ends under, and place, seam side down, in a greased 9- x 5- x 3-inch loafpan. Cover and let rise in a warm place, free from drafts, 50 to 60 minutes or until doubled in bulk.

Bake at 350° for 30 minutes or until golden brown. Remove from pan, and let cool on wire rack. Drizzle powdered sugar glaze over warm loaf. Serve warm or cool. Yield: 1 loaf.

Glaze

1 cup sifted powdered sugar
1½ tablespoons milk
½ teaspoon vanilla extract

Combine all ingredients, stirring well. Yield: about ⅓ cup.

Rolls

Freshly baked rolls not only smell wonderful as they bake, but they assume a prized position on the dinner menu as well. There's just no substitute for that fresh-from-the-oven texture of tender rolls.

If you've mastered the art of making yeast breads, you'll have no problem making dinner rolls. They take a little more time to hand-shape, but they'll bake and be ready to serve faster than large loaves.

SHREDDED WHEAT FEATHER ROLLS

⅔ cup milk
½ cup butter or margarine
2 tablespoons sugar
1¼ teaspoons salt
2 packages dry yeast
½ cup warm water (105° to 115°)
2 eggs, beaten
4 cups all-purpose flour
4 shredded whole wheat cereal biscuits, crumbled (about 1½ cups)

Combine milk, butter, sugar, and salt in a saucepan; heat until butter melts. Cool to 105° to 115°. Dissolve yeast in warm water in a large mixing bowl; let stand 5 minutes. Stir in milk mixture, eggs, and 2 cups flour; beat at medium speed of an electric mixer until blended. Add remaining 2 cups flour and shredded wheat; beat at medium speed 1 minute, scraping sides of bowl with a spatula. Cover and let rise in a warm place (85°), free from drafts, 1 hour or until doubled in bulk.

Punch dough down, and shape into ¾-inch balls; place 3 balls in each cup of well-greased muffin pans. Cover and let rise in a warm place, free from drafts, 45 minutes or until doubled in bulk. Bake at 375° for 18 to 20 minutes. Yield: about 1½ dozen.

HURRY-UP CHEESE BUNS

1 package dry yeast
2 cups all-purpose flour, divided
1 (5-ounce) jar sharp process cheese spread
½ cup water
¼ cup shortening
2 tablespoons sugar
½ teaspoon salt
1 egg, beaten

Combine yeast and 1 cup flour in a medium mixing bowl; set aside. Combine cheese spread, water, shortening, sugar, and salt in a small saucepan; heat to 105° to 115°, stirring constantly. Add cheese mixture and egg to yeast mixture; beat ½ minute at low speed of an electric mixer, scraping sides of bowl. Beat 3 minutes at high speed. Stir in remaining 1 cup flour.

Turn dough out onto a lightly floured surface, and knead 1 to 2 minutes. Shape dough into 12 balls. Place in well-greased muffin pans. Cover and let rise in a warm place (85°), free from drafts, 1½ hours or until doubled in bulk. Bake at 350° for 15 to 18 minutes. Yield: 1 dozen.

Cheesy Onion Buns: Add 2 tablespoons minced onion with egg.

SOUR CREAM CRESCENT ROLLS

½ cup butter or margarine
1 (8-ounce) carton commercial sour cream
½ cup sugar
2 packages dry yeast
½ cup warm water (105° to 115°)
2 eggs, beaten
4 cups all-purpose flour
1 teaspoon salt
Butter or margarine, melted

Place butter in a small saucepan, and bring to a boil. Remove from heat; stir in sour cream and sugar. Cool mixture to 105° to 115°.

Dissolve yeast in warm water in a large mixing bowl; let yeast mixture stand 5 minutes. Stir in sour cream mixture and eggs. Combine flour and salt; gradually add flour mixture to yeast mixture, mixing well. Cover and refrigerate at least 8 hours.

Punch dough down, and divide into 4 equal parts. Roll each into a 10-inch circle on a floured surface; brush with butter. Cut each circle into 12 wedges; roll up each wedge, beginning at wide end. Place on greased baking sheets, point side down.

Cover and let rise in a warm place (85°), free from drafts, 1 hour or until doubled in bulk. Bake at 375° for 10 to 12 minutes or until golden brown. Yield: 4 dozen.

Note: Dough for Sour Cream Crescent Rolls may be baked in other shapes. For ideas, refer to the shaping information on the following page.

Make Your Rolls Shapely

Don't be tempted to stop by the bakery to pick up dinner rolls for your special meals. Just look up your favorite yeast roll recipe and create those butter-rich and irresistible treats yourself. As you make them, try some of these shapes, glazes, and toppings. With a few twists, turns, and sprinkles, your rolls will take on a professionally made look—yet have the aroma and goodness of home-baked bread.

We've included directions and illustrations for bow ties, butterfans, and other shapes of rolls. The shapes will be easy to adapt for most any yeast roll recipe; just make sure the recipe makes a rather firm dough. If the dough is too soft, the rolls won't hold their shape.

After the rolls are shaped and have risen, brush the rolls very gently but thoroughly with one of the following glazes:

- A whole egg or egg yolk beaten with a little water will make the rolls shiny and give them a golden color.
- A glaze made with egg white and water can be used to hold toppings such as poppy seeds and sesame seeds in place. Try sprinkling some rolls with poppy seeds and others with sesame seeds; this makes for an eye-catching bread basket.
- Melted butter is often brushed on rolls before baking, but you can add more butter after baking for extra flavor and shine.

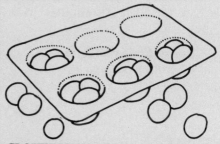

CLOVERLEAF ROLLS: *Lightly grease muffin pans. Shape dough into 1-inch balls; place 3 dough balls in each muffin cup. Cover and let rise until doubled in bulk. Bake.*

S ROLLS: *Divide dough into several small portions. Roll each portion into a 9-inch rope about ¾ to 1 inch thick. Place on greased baking sheets; curl ends in opposite directions, forming an S shape. Cover and let rise until doubled in bulk. Bake.*

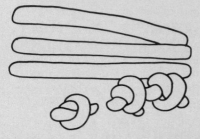

BOW TIES: *Roll dough into several long ropes about ½ inch in diameter. Cut ropes into 8-inch strips. Carefully tie each dough strip into a knot. Place bow ties on a lightly greased baking sheet. Cover and let rise until doubled in bulk. Bake.*

BUTTERFANS: *Roll dough into a large rectangle about ¼ inch thick. Spread softened butter over dough. Cut lengthwise into 1-inch strips. Stack 5 or 6 strips, buttered side up, on top of one another. Cut each stack into 1-inch sections. Place each stacked section, cut side down, into lightly greased muffin pans. Cover and let rise until doubled in bulk. Bake.*

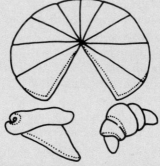

CRESCENTS: *If using a recipe with 3 to 4 cups of flour, you'll need to divide dough in half. Roll one portion of dough into a 12-inch circle on a lightly floured surface. Spread softened butter over dough. Cut into 12 wedges; roll each wedge tightly, beginning at wide end. Seal points, and place rolls, point side down, on a greased baking sheet, curving into a half-moon shape. Cover and let rise until doubled in bulk. Bake.*

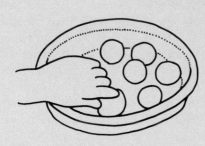

EASY PAN ROLLS: *Lightly grease one or two 9-inch round cakepans. Shape dough into 1½-inch balls. Place dough balls in pan, leaving about ½ inch space between them. Cover and let rise until doubled in bulk. Bake.*

HARD ROLLS

2 packages dry yeast
2 cups warm water
   (105° to 115°)
2 teaspoons sugar
1 teaspoon salt
4½ to 4¾ cups all-purpose flour
¼ cup butter or margarine,
   melted and divided

Dissolve yeast in warm water in a large mixing bowl; let stand 5 minutes. Add sugar and salt; stir well. Gradually stir enough flour into the yeast mixture to make a soft dough.

Turn dough out onto a floured surface, and knead until smooth and elastic (about 8 to 10 minutes). Place in a well-greased bowl, turning to grease top. Cover and let rise in a warm place (85°), free from drafts, 45 minutes or until doubled in bulk.

Punch dough down, and shape into 18 (3½- x 1½-inch) loaf-shaped rolls. Place on greased baking sheets. Score tops of rolls with scissors, making ¼-inch deep slashes; brush with 2 tablespoons butter. Cover and let rise in a warm place, free from drafts, 30 minutes or until doubled in bulk. Bake at 400° for 25 to 30 minutes or until golden brown. Brush warm rolls with remaining butter. Yield: 1½ dozen.

BRIOCHE

Brioche is a shapely and buttery French yeast roll typically served by itself for breakfast, or as a lunch or dinner accompaniment. But twist off the top-knot, scoop out a little of the center bread, and you'll find an area just the right size for a meat or salad filling. Make larger ones for entrées, and smaller ones to serve as appetizers. Then tear up the centers, and stir up a tasty bread pudding.

The classic brioche features fluted edges that are achieved by baking in brioche pans. The pans are available in a variety of sizes in kitchen specialty shops and department stores. Our recipe specifies individual 3½-inch brioche pans. If you use larger or smaller pans, adjust the size of the rolls and the baking time. The rolls can be baked in muffin pans, however, with no adjustments necessary.

1 package dry yeast
¼ cup warm water (105° to 115°)
1 cup butter or margarine,
   softened
5 eggs
2 tablespoons sugar
1 teaspoon salt
3½ cups all-purpose flour
1 egg yolk
1 tablespoon milk

Dissolve yeast in warm water in a large mixing bowl; let stand 5 minutes. Add butter, eggs, sugar, salt, and 2 cups flour. Beat at medium speed of an electric mixer 3 to 4 minutes, scraping sides of bowl occasionally. Add remaining flour, and beat until smooth.

Place dough in a well-greased bowl, turning to grease top. Cover and let rise in a warm place (85°), free from drafts, 1½ hours or until doubled in bulk. Punch dough down; cover and refrigerate at least 8 hours.

Punch dough down, and divide into 4 equal portions; set one portion aside. Divide each of the 3 portions into 8 pieces; shape each piece into a ball. Place in well-greased 3½-inch brioche or muffin pans. Make a deep indention in center of each using a floured finger.

Divide reserved portion of dough into 24 pieces, and shape into balls. Press one ball in each indention. Cover and let rise in a warm place, free from drafts, 45 minutes or until doubled in bulk.

Combine egg yolk and milk; mix well, and lightly brush on top of each brioche. Bake at 375° for 15 minutes or until golden brown. Yield: 2 dozen.

POTATO ROLLS

2 medium potatoes, peeled and
   quartered
2 packages dry yeast
1 teaspoon sugar
½ cup butter or margarine, melted
¼ cup shortening, melted
½ cup honey
2 eggs, beaten
2 teaspoons salt
About 6½ cups all-purpose flour

Cook potatoes in boiling water to cover 15 minutes or until tender. Drain, reserving 1 cup water; set potatoes aside. Cool water to 105° to 115°. Stir yeast and sugar into water; let stand 5 minutes.

Mash enough potatoes to measure 1 cup; place in a large mixing bowl. Add butter, shortening, honey, eggs, salt, yeast mixture, and 2½ cups flour. Beat at medium speed of an electric mixer 2 minutes. Gradually stir in enough remaining flour to make a soft dough.

Turn dough out onto a floured surface, and knead until smooth and elastic (about 8 to 10 minutes). Place in a well-greased bowl, turning to grease top. Cover and let rise in a warm place (85°), free from drafts, 1 hour or until doubled in bulk.

Punch dough down, and divide into thirds. Shape each third into 15 balls. Place in three greased 9-inch round cakepans. Cover and let rise in a warm place, free from drafts, 40 to 50 minutes or until doubled in bulk. Bake at 400° for 20 to 25 minutes. Yield: 45 rolls.

Note: Potato Rolls may be wrapped in aluminum foil, then placed in a freezer bag, and frozen up to 2 months. To reheat, let thaw almost to room temperature, place in cakepans, cover with foil, and bake at 400° for 10 minutes or until thoroughly heated.

Coffee Cakes and Sweet Rolls

A continental breakfast will seem much more special when you serve sweet breads fresh from the oven. Some of these recipes direct you to chill the dough overnight. For most of the other recipes you can cover and chill the dough overnight for the first rising, as discussed in the text about working with yeast bread. Then you'll be a step ahead in the morning.

FRUIT-FILLED COFFEE CAKE

1 package dry yeast
¼ cup warm water (105° to 115°)
2 cups all-purpose flour
2 tablespoons sugar
½ teaspoon salt
1 cup butter or margarine
1 egg, beaten
1 teaspoon vanilla extract
Fruit Filling
1½ teaspoons sugar (optional)

Dissolve yeast in warm water; let stand 5 minutes. Combine flour, 2 tablespoons sugar, and salt in a large mixing bowl; cut butter into flour mixture with pastry blender. Combine yeast mixture, egg, and vanilla; stir into flour mixture, blending until smooth. Turn dough out onto a lightly floured surface; roll into a 14- x 10-inch rectangle. Place in a lightly greased 11- x 7- x 2-inch baking pan, allowing extra dough to hang over sides of pan. Spread Fruit Filling over dough; fold overhanging dough over fruit. Sprinkle dough with 1½ teaspoons sugar, if desired. (Do not allow dough to rise.) Bake at 375° for 30 minutes; reduce heat to 300° and bake 15 to 20 minutes or until lightly browned. Yield: 8 servings.

Fruit Filling

⅔ cup chopped prunes
⅔ cup chopped dried apricots
1 (8-ounce) can crushed pineapple, undrained
½ cup sugar
1½ tablespoons quick-cooking tapioca

Cook prunes and apricots in a small amount of water 5 to 10 minutes or until tender. Drain. Combine fruit mixture and remaining ingredients, stirring well. Yield: about 2⅓ cups.

CREAM CHEESE BRAIDS

1 (8-ounce) carton commercial sour cream
½ cup sugar
½ cup butter or margarine
1 teaspoon salt
2 packages dry yeast
½ cup warm water (105° to 115°)
2 eggs, beaten
4 cups all-purpose flour
Filling (recipe follows)
Glaze (recipe follows)

Combine sour cream, sugar, butter, and salt in a saucepan; heat until butter melts. Cool to 105° to 115°. Dissolve yeast in warm water in a large bowl; let stand 5 minutes. Stir in sour cream mixture and eggs. Gradually stir in flour (dough will be soft). Cover dough tightly, and chill at least 8 hours.

Divide dough into 4 equal portions. Turn each portion out onto a heavily floured surface, and knead 4 or 5 times. Roll each portion into a 12- x 8-inch rectangle. Spread one-fourth of filling over each rectangle, leaving a ½-inch margin around edges. Carefully roll up dough jellyroll fashion, starting at long side; pinch the seam and ends to seal.

Carefully place loaves, seam side down, on greased baking sheets.

Make 6 equally spaced X-shaped cuts across top of each loaf. Cover and let rise in a warm place (85°), free from drafts, about 1 hour or until doubled in bulk. Bake at 375° for 15 to 20 minutes. Spread loaves with glaze while warm. Yield: four 12-inch loaves.

Filling

2 (8-ounce) packages cream cheese, softened
¾ cup sugar
1 egg, beaten
2 teaspoons vanilla extract

Combine all ingredients. Process in food processor or electric mixer until blended. Yield: about 2 cups.

Glaze

2 cups sifted powdered sugar
¼ cup milk
2 teaspoons vanilla extract

Combine all ingredients, stirring well. Yield: about ¾ cup.

Cream Cheese Rolls: After dough for Cream Cheese Braids is rolled jellyroll fashion, cut each roll into 1½-inch slices. Place slices, cut side down, 2 inches apart on greased baking sheets.

Cover and let rise in a warm place (85°), free from drafts, 1½ hours or until doubled in bulk. Bake at 375° for 12 minutes or until rolls are golden brown. Drizzle glaze over each roll. Makes about 2½ dozen.

Cherry Blossom Braids: Prepare dough and roll into a 12- x 8-inch rectangle as directed for Cream Cheese Braids. Spread one-fourth of a (21-ounce) can of cherry pie filling evenly over each rectangle instead of the cream cheese filling. Complete recipe as directed for Cream Cheese Braids.

CINNAMON TWIST COFFEE CAKE

2 packages dry yeast
½ cup warm water (105° to 115°)
1 cup boiling water
¾ cup instant potato flakes
1 teaspoon salt
½ cup sugar
½ cup instant nonfat dry milk powder
½ cup butter or margarine, softened
3 eggs
About 5 cups all-purpose flour
¼ cup butter or margarine, softened and divided
⅔ cup sugar
1½ teaspoons ground cinnamon
½ cup chopped almonds, divided
2 cups sifted powdered sugar
3 tablespoons milk
Candied cherries (optional)
Toasted slivered almonds (optional)

Dissolve yeast in warm water; let stand 5 minutes. Combine boiling water, potato flakes, and salt in a large mixing bowl; beat well at medium speed of an electric mixer. Add ½ cup sugar, dry milk powder, and ½ cup butter; beat well. Add eggs and yeast mixture, beating well. Gradually beat in 3 cups flour; add remaining flour, ½ cup at a time, beating well after each addition.

Turn dough out onto a heavily floured surface, and knead until smooth and elastic. Place in a well-greased bowl, turning to grease top. Cover and let rise in a warm place (85°), free from drafts, 1 hour or until doubled in bulk.

Punch dough down, and divide into 6 equal portions. Roll each portion into a 12-inch circle.

Place one circle on a lightly greased 12-inch pizza pan. Spread 2 tablespoons butter over top of dough, leaving a ½-inch margin. Combine ⅔ cup sugar and cinnamon; sprinkle about 2½ tablespoons cinnamon mixture and 2 tablespoons almonds over dough. Place a second circle of dough on top of first. Repeat process with butter, cinnamon

Serve Cinnamon Twist Coffee Cake for breakfast or brunch. A sprinkling of cinnamon, sugar, and almonds hides between the three layers of bread.

mixture, and almonds. Top with a third circle of dough. Moisten outer edge of circle, and seal.

Repeat process with remaining 3 portions of dough to make a second cake.

Place a 2½-inch cookie cutter in center of 1 loaf (do not cut through dough). Cut dough into 8 wedges, cutting from cookie cutter to outside edge of dough. Gently lift each wedge, and twist several times to form a spiral pattern.

Remove cookie cutter. Repeat process with second coffee cake. Cover cakes, and let rise in a warm place, free from drafts, 45 minutes or until dough is doubled in bulk. Bake at 350° for 20 to 25 minutes or until golden brown. Cool 10 minutes.

Combine powdered sugar and milk; drizzle over bread. Decorate with candied cherries and almonds, if desired. Yield: two 12-inch coffee cakes.

SAVARIN

1 package dry yeast
¼ cup warm milk (105° to 115°)
2 cups all-purpose flour
¼ cup plus 2 tablespoons sugar
1 teaspoon salt
4 eggs
½ cup butter or margarine, softened
Rum syrup (recipe follows)
About 2 tablespoons light rum
About ½ cup apricot jam, melted
Whole fresh cherries, pitted
Sliced fresh peaches
Fresh blueberries, raspberries, and
    strawberries
Sweetened whipped cream
Mint sprigs

Dissolve yeast in warm milk in a large mixing bowl; let stand 5 minutes.

Add flour to yeast mixture, stirring gently. Add sugar, salt, and eggs; beat at low speed of an electric mixer until smooth. Add butter, 1 tablespoon at a time, beating well after each addition.

Spoon batter into a greased 10-inch tube pan. Cover and let rise in a warm place (85°), free from drafts, 2½ to 3 hours or until doubled in bulk. Place pan in a 500° oven; immediately reduce heat to 350°, and bake 15 to 20 minutes.

Invert onto a serving plate. Spoon rum syrup over hot cake. Sprinkle lightly with rum. Brush apricot jam over cake; arrange fruit on top. Brush additional apricot jam over fruit to prevent darkening. Pipe or spoon whipped cream around base. Garnish with mint sprigs. Yield: one 10-inch coffee cake.

Rum Syrup

¾ cup water
½ cup sugar
2 tablespoons light rum

Combine water and sugar in a small saucepan; bring to a boil, and cook until sugar dissolves. Cool and stir in rum. Yield: about 1 cup.

SPIRAL CINNAMON ROLLS

¼ cup milk
¼ cup sugar
½ teaspoon salt
3 tablespoons butter or margarine
1 package dry yeast
¼ cup warm water (105° to 115°)
2¼ cups all-purpose flour, divided
1 egg
2 tablespoons butter or margarine,
    softened
¼ cup firmly packed brown sugar
½ teaspoon ground cinnamon
½ cup raisins (optional)
1 tablespoon butter or margarine,
    melted
1 cup sifted powdered sugar
2 tablespoons milk

Combine ¼ cup milk, sugar, salt, and 3 tablespoons butter in a saucepan; heat until butter melts. Cool to 105° to 115°.

Dissolve yeast in warm water in a large mixing bowl; let stand 5 minutes. Stir in milk mixture, 1½ cups flour, and egg; beat at medium speed of an electric mixer until smooth. Stir in remaining ¾ cup flour.

Turn dough out onto a lightly floured surface, and knead until smooth and elastic (about 8 minutes). Place in a well-greased bowl, turning to grease top. Cover and let rise in a warm place (85°), free from drafts, 1 hour (dough will not quite double in bulk).

Punch dough down; turn dough out onto a lightly floured surface. Roll dough into a 12- x 8-inch rectangle; spread with 2 tablespoons butter. Combine brown sugar and cinnamon; sprinkle mixture over rectangle. Sprinkle with raisins, if desired. Roll dough jellyroll fashion, starting at long side. Pinch seam to seal (do not seal ends). Cut roll into 1-inch slices; place slices, cut side down, in greased 8-inch square pan. Brush tops with 1 tablespoon melted butter. Using a fork, gently lift center of rolls to form a peak.

Cover and let rise in a warm place, free from drafts, about 40 minutes (rolls will not double in bulk). Bake at 350° for 35 minutes. Combine powdered sugar and 2 tablespoons milk, stirring well. Drizzle over warm rolls. Yield: 1 dozen.

Blueberry Cinnamon Rolls: Sprinkle with ½ cup fresh or frozen blueberries instead of raisins.

AUSTRIAN TWISTS

1 package dry yeast
3 cups all-purpose flour
1 cup butter, softened
3 egg yolks
1 (8-ounce) carton commercial sour
    cream
½ cup sugar
½ cup chopped pecans
¾ teaspoon ground cinnamon
Glaze (recipe follows)

Combine yeast and flour; add butter; mix well. Stir in yolks and sour cream. Shape dough into 4 balls; wrap each in wax paper, and refrigerate 8 hours.

Combine sugar, pecans, and cinnamon; set aside.

Working with 1 portion of dough at a time, place onto a lightly floured surface, and roll into a ¼-inch-thick circle. Spread one-fourth of sugar mixture evenly over each circle, and cut into 16 wedges. Roll up each wedge, beginning at wide end. Pinch points to seal. Place on greased baking sheets, point side down. Do not allow to rise.

Bake at 350° for 18 minutes or until lightly browned. Transfer to wire racks; drizzle with glaze. Yield: 64 twists.

Glaze

2 cups sifted powdered sugar
3 tablespoons milk

Combine sugar and milk, stirring until smooth. Yield: about ⅔ cup.

Spiral Cinnamon Rolls Step-By-Step

1. Bake Spiral Cinnamon Rolls for a breakfast treat. Dissolve yeast in warm water in a large mixing bowl.

2. Stir in milk mixture, flour, and egg; beat until mixture is smooth.

3. Turn dough out onto a floured surface, and knead until smooth and elastic.

4. Place in a greased bowl, turning to grease top. Cover and let rise in a warm place.

5. Dough is risen when you can punch a hole in dough with your finger and the indention stays there.

6. Roll dough on a floured surface into a 12- x 8-inch rectangle. Spread with butter, and sprinkle with cinnamon mixture.

7. Sprinkle with raisins, and roll jellyroll fashion, starting at long side.

8. Cut roll into 1-inch slices, and place slices, cut side down, in greased pan. Let rise and bake as directed.

Drizzle glaze over the top of Spiral Cinnamon Rolls, and expect them to disappear quickly.

GLAZED DOUGHNUTS

1 package dry yeast
2 tablespoons warm water (105° to 115°)
¾ cup warm milk (105° to 115°)
¼ cup sugar
3 tablespoons shortening
½ teaspoon salt
½ teaspoon ground nutmeg
⅛ teaspoon ground cinnamon
1 egg
2½ cups bread flour
Vegetable oil
Glaze

Dissolve yeast in warm water in a large mixing bowl; let stand 5 minutes. Add milk, next 6 ingredients, and 1 cup flour; beat at medium speed of an electric mixer until blended, about 2 minutes. Stir in remaining 1½ cups flour. Cover and let rise in a warm place (85°), free from drafts, 1 hour or until doubled in bulk.

Punch dough down; turn dough out onto a well-floured surface, and knead several times. Roll dough to ½-inch thickness, and cut with a 2½-inch doughnut cutter. Place doughnuts on a lightly floured surface. Cover and let rise in a warm place, free from drafts, 30 minutes or until doubled in bulk.

Heat 2 to 3 inches of oil to 375°; drop in 4 or 5 doughnuts at a time. Cook about 1 minute or until golden on one side; turn and cook other side about 1 minute. Drain well. Dip each doughnut, while warm, in glaze, letting excess glaze drip off. Let cool on wire racks. Yield: about 1½ dozen.

Glaze

2 cups sifted powdered sugar
¼ cup milk

Combine ingredients, and stir until smooth. Yield: ⅔ cup.

HOT CROSS BUNS

¾ cup milk
2 packages dry yeast
¼ cup warm water (105° to 115°)
4 to 4½ cups bread flour, divided
¾ cup unseasoned mashed potatoes
⅔ cup currants
½ cup chopped citron
½ cup butter or margarine, softened
⅓ cup sugar
¾ teaspoon ground cinnamon
½ teaspoon salt
¼ teaspoon ground nutmeg
2 eggs
1 egg white, lightly beaten
1 cup sifted powdered sugar
1 tablespoon milk
½ teaspoon vanilla extract

Heat milk; cool to 105° to 115°. Dissolve yeast in warm water; let stand 5 minutes. Add milk, 2 cups flour, and next 9 ingredients; beat at medium speed of an electric mixer until smooth. Stir in enough flour to make a soft dough.

Turn dough out onto a floured surface; knead until smooth (about 5 minutes). Place in a well-greased bowl, turning to grease top. Cover and let rise in a warm place (85°), free from drafts, 1½ hours or until doubled in bulk.

Punch dough down; divide into fourths. Divide each fourth into 8 equal parts. Shape each part into a smooth ball, tucking edge under so it resembles a mushroom cap. Place about 2 inches apart on greased baking sheets. With scissors, snip a cross in top of each ball. Cover and let rise in a warm place (85°), free from drafts, 40 minutes or until doubled in bulk. Brush with egg white. Bake at 375° for 15 to 18 minutes or until golden; let cool on wire racks.

Combine remaining ingredients; stir well. Pipe a cross with glaze into indentions on buns. Yield: 32 buns.

The next three recipes are Christmas breads; their flavoring and fruit adornment make them similar in taste, but each remains unique with its traditional shape.

STOLLEN

1 package dry yeast
¾ cup warm water (105° to 115°)
½ cup sugar
½ teaspoon salt
3 eggs
1 egg yolk
½ cup butter or margarine, softened
3½ cups all-purpose flour, divided
½ cup chopped almonds
½ cup chopped mixed candied fruit
¼ cup raisins
Butter or margarine, softened
1 cup sifted powdered sugar
1½ tablespoons hot water
Sliced almonds
Chopped candied fruit

Dissolve yeast in ¾ cup warm water in a large mixing bowl; let stand 5 minutes. Add sugar, salt, eggs, egg yolk, ½ cup butter, and 1¾ cups flour; beat at medium speed of an electric mixer 10 minutes. Stir in remaining 1¾ cups flour, chopped almonds, ½ cup candied fruit, and raisins. Cover and let rise in a warm place (85°), free from drafts, 1½ to 2 hours. (Dough will not double in bulk.) Stir batter well; cover and refrigerate at least 8 hours.

Turn dough out onto a lightly floured surface, turning to coat with flour. Divide in half; shape each half into a 10- x 7-inch oval. Spread with butter, and fold lengthwise in half, firmly pressing folded edge. Place on lightly greased baking sheets. Cover and let rise in a warm place, free from drafts, 45 minutes or until doubled in bulk. Bake at 375° for 20 minutes or until golden brown.

Combine powdered sugar and hot water, stirring well. Drizzle over each loaf. Garnish with sliced almonds and candied fruit. Yield: 2 loaves.

SWEDISH LUCIA BUNS

2 packages dry yeast
2¼ cups milk
⅔ cup butter or margarine
1½ cups sugar
½ teaspoon ground saffron
½ teaspoon salt
1 egg
7 to 7½ cups all-purpose flour
Raisins
1 egg, beaten

Place yeast in a large mixing bowl. Combine milk and butter in a saucepan; heat until butter melts. Cool to luke-warm (105° to 115°). Add to yeast; let stand 5 minutes. Add sugar, saffron, salt, 1 egg, and 3½ cups flour; beat at medium speed of an electric mixer until blended. Gradually stir in enough remaining flour to make a soft dough.

Turn dough out onto a floured surface; knead until smooth (about 8 to 10 minutes). Place in a well-greased bowl, turning to grease top. Cover and let rise in a warm place (85°), free from drafts, 1 hour or until doubled in bulk.

Punch dough down; turn out onto a floured surface, and knead 1 minute. Divide dough into thirds. Roll each into a 10-inch rope. Cut each rope into 10 pieces; roll each into a 9-inch rope. Place on greased baking sheets; curl ends in opposite directions, forming "S" shapes. Cover and let rise in a warm place, free from drafts, 30 minutes or until doubled. Press raisin gently into center of each curl. Brush with egg. Bake at 450° for 10 minutes or until browned; cool on wire racks. Yield: 2½ dozen.

DANISH PASTRY WREATH

1½ cups butter or margarine, softened
¼ cup all-purpose flour
¾ cup milk
⅓ cup sugar
1 teaspoon salt
2 packages dry yeast
½ cup warm water (105° to 115°)
1 egg
About 3¾ cups all-purpose flour
Almond Filling
Glaze (recipe follows)
Candied cherries (optional)

Beat butter and ¼ cup flour until smooth and fluffy. Place wax paper on a large, wet baking sheet. Spread butter mixture evenly into a 12- x 8-inch rectangle on wax paper. Chill well.

Combine milk, sugar, and salt in a saucepan; heat until sugar dissolves. Cool to 105° to 115°.

Dissolve yeast in warm water in a large mixing bowl; let stand 5 minutes. Stir in milk mixture, egg, and 3¾ cups flour; beat at medium speed of an electric mixer until mixture is smooth and leaves side of bowl (dough will be soft). Cover and chill 30 minutes.

Turn dough out onto a floured surface. Place stockinette cover on rolling pin; flour well. Roll dough into a 16- x 12-inch rectangle. Fit cold butter mixture over half of dough, leaving a margin at edges; remove wax paper. Fold dough over butter; pinch edges to seal.

Place fold of dough to the right; roll dough into a 16- x 8-inch rectangle. (If butter breaks through dough, flour heavily and continue rolling.) Fold rectangle into thirds; pinch edges to seal. Wrap dough in wax paper; chill 1 hour. Repeat rolling, folding, and sealing process; chill 30 minutes. Repeat rolling, folding, and sealing process; wrap dough in aluminum foil, and chill 8 hours.

Divide dough into 2 equal portions; chill half of dough. Roll remaining dough into a 22- x 8-inch rectangle. Cut dough into 3 equal lengthwise strips. Spread ⅓ cup Almond Filling down center of each strip, leaving a 1-inch margin at each end.

Fold edges of dough over filling, pinching edges and ends to seal; turn ropes seam side down. Firmly pinch loose ends of the three ropes at one end to seal. Braid ropes; firmly pinch loose ends to seal.

Place brown paper on a baking sheet (do not use recycled paper). Carefully transfer braid to baking sheet; form into a wreath with a 6-inch-diameter hole. Join ends of braid; pinch ends to seal.

Cover and let rise in a warm place (85°), free from drafts, until doubled in bulk. Bake at 375° for 30 minutes or until golden brown. Carefully transfer to wire rack to cool (pastry is very fragile, so move gently).

Repeat process with remaining dough. Spread half of glaze over each wreath. Garnish each with candied cherries, if desired. Yield: 2 coffee cakes.

Almond Filling

¾ cup zwieback crumbs
½ cup butter, melted
1 egg, beaten
½ teaspoon almond extract
1 (8-ounce) can almond paste

Combine all ingredients except almond paste; stir well. Cut almond paste in with pastry blender until blended. Yield: about 2 cups.

Glaze

3 to 4 tablespoons milk
2 cups sifted powdered sugar

Combine milk and powdered sugar; stir until smooth. Yield: about ⅔ cup.

Specialty Yeast Breads

These breads don't fit any particular category; in a sense each is a category unto itself. Most of them are commercially available, but they're not difficult to make, and you'll enjoy the freshness of their flavor when baked at home. They'll also make handsome and tasty offerings to share with neighbors.

SOFT BREADSTICKS

2¾ to 3 cups all-purpose flour, divided
1 package dry yeast
1 tablespoon sugar
1 teaspoon salt
1¼ cups warm water (105° to 115°)
1 tablespoon vegetable oil
1 cup grated Parmesan cheese
1 clove garlic, minced
Butter or margarine, melted
Additional grated Parmesan cheese or sesame seeds

Combine 1½ cups flour, yeast, sugar, and salt in a large bowl. Add water and oil; beat at medium speed of an electric mixer 3 to 4 minutes or until smooth. Stir in 1 cup Parmesan cheese, garlic, and enough flour to make a stiff dough.

Turn dough out onto a lightly floured surface, and knead until smooth and elastic (about 1 minute).

Divide dough into fourths; shape each into a ball. Cut each ball into 10 pieces. Shape each piece into an 8-inch rope. (Cover remaining dough while working to prevent drying.) Dip rope in butter, and roll in Parmesan cheese.

Place 2 inches apart on greased baking sheets. Cover and let rise in a warm place (85°), free from drafts, 50 minutes. (Dough will not double in bulk.) Bake at 400° for 12 to 15 minutes or until lightly browned. Yield: 40 breadsticks.

Herbed Breadsticks: Stir in 1 teaspoon dried whole basil and 1 teaspoon dried whole oregano with salt.

CRACKER BREAD

Cracker bread, a thin, crisp flatbread, is popping up on menus all across the country. You might see individual-sized rounds sprinkled with dried herbs and served with hot soup, or giant sesame seed versions tucked into large baskets on appetizer tables, intended for breaking into bite-size pieces and serving with dips or spreads.

Sprinkled with cinnamon and sugar, this bread becomes a tea time treat, while grated Parmesan cheese or chopped nuts dress it for snack time. You just can't beat cracker bread whenever you want something to munch on—serve it fresh from the oven, plain or slathered with butter.

Don't worry if your cracker bread doesn't bake perfectly round, perfectly flat, or evenly browned. Irregularity in its look is what gives each round its individual character.

5½ to 6 cups all-purpose flour, divided
1 package dry yeast
1 teaspoon salt
2 cups warm water (105° to 115°)
⅓ cup butter or margarine, melted
2 tablespoons sesame seeds, toasted

Combine 4 cups flour, yeast, and salt in a large mixing bowl; stir well. Gradually add water to flour mixture, stirring well. Add butter; beat at medium speed of an electric mixer until blended. Gradually stir in enough remaining flour to make a stiff dough.

Turn dough out onto a floured surface, and knead until smooth and elastic (about 4 minutes). Place in a well-greased bowl, turning to grease top. Cover and let rise in a warm place (85°), free from drafts, 1 hour or until doubled in bulk.

Punch dough down, and divide into 10 equal portions. Shape each portion into a ball, and place on a lightly floured surface; let rest 10 minutes.

Roll each ball to a 10-inch round on a lightly floured surface, rolling only enough to bake at one time. Chill extra dough to slow down the rising process as you await oven space. Place rolled rounds on lightly greased baking sheets. Brush lightly with cold water, and sprinkle lightly with sesame seeds. Prick entire surface with fork. (Do not allow to rise). Bake at 350° for 25 minutes or until lightly browned and crisp. Remove from pans, and let cool on wire racks. Repeat with remaining balls of dough. Yield: 10 cracker rounds.

Note: Cinnamon sugar, seasoned salt, or grated Parmesan cheese may be substituted for sesame seeds.

BAGELS

2 packages dry yeast
2 cups warm water (105° to 115°)
2 tablespoons honey
5 to 5½ cups all-purpose flour, divided
1½ teaspoons salt
3½ quarts water
1 teaspoon salt
Sesame seeds

Dissolve yeast in warm water in a large bowl; let stand 5 minutes. Add honey, stirring well. Stir in 2 cups flour and 1½ teaspoons salt; mix well. Gradually stir in enough remaining flour to make a soft dough.

Turn dough out onto a heavily floured surface (dough will be sticky), and knead until smooth and elastic (8 to 10 minutes). Place dough in a well-greased bowl, turning to grease top. Cover dough, and let rise in a warm place (85°), free from drafts, 1½ hours or until doubled in bulk.

Punch dough down, and divide dough into 12 equal pieces. Roll each into a smooth ball. Cut with 1-inch cutter or punch a hole in the center of each ball with a floured finger. Gently pull dough away from center to make a 1- to 1½-inch hole. Place shaped bagels on lightly greased baking sheets. Cover and let rise 15 minutes. Broil bagels 5 inches from heat 2 minutes on each side or until lightly browned.

Bring water and 1 teaspoon salt to a boil in a large Dutch oven. Reduce heat, and simmer bagels 3 minutes on each side.

Place bagels on lightly greased baking sheets. Sprinkle with sesame seeds; lightly press seeds into bagels. Bake at 425° for 20 to 25 minutes or until golden brown. Yield: 1 dozen.

Whole Wheat Bagels: Substitute 2 cups whole wheat flour for 2 cups of the all-purpose flour.

RAISIN ENGLISH MUFFINS

1 package dry yeast
1 cup warm water (105° to 115°)
1 cup milk
2 tablespoons sugar
1 teaspoon salt
3 tablespoons butter or margarine, softened
1 cup raisins
5½ to 6 cups all-purpose flour
Cornmeal

Dissolve yeast in warm water in a large bowl; let stand 5 minutes. Combine milk, sugar, salt, and butter in a saucepan; heat until butter melts. Cool to 105° to 115°. Stir milk mixture, raisins, and 3 cups flour into yeast mixture; beat until smooth. Stir in enough remaining flour to form a stiff dough.

Turn dough out onto a floured surface, and knead 2 minutes or until dough can be shaped into a ball (dough will be slightly sticky). Place in a well-greased bowl, turning to grease top. Cover and let rise in a warm place (85°), free from drafts, 1 hour or until doubled in bulk.

Punch dough down, and divide in half. Turn each half out onto a smooth surface heavily sprinkled with cornmeal. Pat dough into a circle, ½-inch thick, using palms of hands; cut dough into rounds with a 2¾-inch cutter. (Cut carefully, as leftover dough should not be reused.)

Sprinkle 2 baking sheets with cornmeal. Transfer dough rounds to baking sheets, placing 2 inches apart with cornmeal side down (one side of dough should remain free of cornmeal). Repeat process with remaining half of dough. Cover and let rise in a warm place, free from drafts, 30 minutes or until doubled in bulk.

Using a wide spatula, transfer rounds to a preheated, lightly greased electric skillet (360°). Place rounds, cornmeal side down, in skillet; cook 6 minutes. Turn and cook an additional 6 minutes. Cool on wire racks. To serve, split muffins and toast until lightly browned. Store muffins in an airtight container. Yield: 16 muffins.

Note: Muffins may be cooked over direct medium-high heat in a skillet.

POCKET BREAD

1 package dry yeast
1 tablespoon sugar
3 cups warm water (105° to 115°)
9 cups all-purpose flour
2 teaspoons salt
1 tablespoon vegetable oil

Combine yeast, sugar, and water; let stand 5 minutes.

Make a well in center of flour in a large mixing bowl; add salt, oil, and half of yeast mixture. Stir well. Add remaining yeast mixture, beating well.

Turn dough out onto a well-floured surface. Divide dough in half; cover half, and set aside.

Divide one portion of dough into 10 equal pieces; knead each piece 2 minutes or until smooth and elastic. Shape each piece into a ball, and place seam side down on towel. Cover with another towel; place a damp towel on top. Repeat process with remaining half of dough.

Let dough rise in a warm place (85°), free from drafts, 1 to 1½ hours or until slightly puffy.

Place each ball of dough onto a well-floured surface; roll into a 6-inch circle. Shake off excess flour, and place on dry towels; cover again with dry towels, then with damp towels. Place plastic wrap on top. Let dough rise in a warm place, free from drafts, 1 hour or until slightly puffy.

Lift circles carefully, and place ½ inch apart on lightly greased baking sheets; do not stretch dough. Place oven rack 2 inches from bottom heating element. Bake at 475° for 4 to 6 minutes or until bottom is lightly browned (it will puff, forming a pocket). Immediately turn oven to broil. Broil 4 inches from broiler element 30 to 60 seconds or until lightly browned (watch carefully to prevent overbrowning). Place on towels. When cool to touch, flatten each piece by gently pressing down with fingertips.

Repeat baking process with remaining bread. Store bread in airtight containers. Yield: 20 bread rounds.

Note: Bread may be frozen. Thaw and reheat at 300° for 5 minutes.

CAKES & FROSTINGS

Moist and feathery light, cakes have been a favorite dessert for as long as Southerners have been baking. You'll rarely go to a covered dish supper without seeing at least one or two on the buffet, and those pretty glass-domed cake plates at home usually don't sit empty very often either.

Baking cakes is not more difficult than other types of cooking, but it does require that you be more exact. Throwing in a little more of one ingredient, or substituting another usually doesn't work for cakes. Cake baking requires skill, accuracy, and precise measuring of ingredients.

EQUIPMENT

Standard cakepans come in both 8- and 9-inch diameters, and you'll probably want to have three of each. Shiny metal pans are apt to produce the lightest, tenderest crust. Avoid darkened metal or enamel pans as they can cause uneven and excessive browning.

You'll probably also want a 10-inch tube pan and a 10-inch Bundt pan. You can often substitute a tube pan when the recipe calls for a Bundt pan, but be careful using a Bundt pan when a tube pan is called for; most Bundt pans hold slightly less batter than tube pans.

Make sure you have several wire cooling racks. Cakes that cool on a solid surface often become soggy.

Chocolate, cherries, and whipped cream team up to make Black Forest Cake (page 120) a rich and satisfying treat.

TIPS FOR PERFECT CAKES

A perfect cake results not from luck but from accurate measuring and proper mixing and baking. To ensure your success, use the tips and techniques that follow, unless your recipe specifies something different.

● Position oven rack in the center of the oven. Always preheat the oven when baking cakes.

● Be sure to use the correct pan size.

● Grease cakepans with shortening; do not use oil, butter, or margarine. Lightly dust pans with flour. Do not grease pans for sponge-type cakes.

● Let eggs, butter, and milk reach room temperature before mixing.

● Do not sift all-purpose flour unless specified. Always sift cake flour before measuring.

● Cream shortening thoroughly. Gradually add sugar, and beat until light and fluffy. (Beating will take about 7 minutes with a standard mixer, longer with a portable type.)

● Add only one egg at a time, and beat after each addition.

● Add dry and liquid ingredients alternately to creamed mixture, beginning and ending with the dry ingredients. Beat after each addition, but only until the batter is smooth; do not overbeat. Using a rubber spatula, scrape sides and bottom of bowl often during beating.

● Stagger cakepans so they do not touch each other or the sides of the

To grease cakepans: Use a pastry brush to lightly grease sides and bottom of cakepans with shortening.

To flour cakepans: Dust greased cakepans with flour, shaking pans to coat bottom and sides. Invert pans and shake out excess flour.

To bake cakes: Place pans on center rack of a preheated oven, 1 inch from edge of oven. Do not let pans touch.

To test cake for doneness: Insert a wooden pick in center of cake; if it comes out clean, the cake is done.

oven. If placed on separate racks, stagger the pans so air can circulate.
● Keep the oven door closed until minimum baking time has elapsed.
● Test the cake for doneness before removing it from the oven (underbaking can cause a cake to fall). The cake is done when a wooden pick inserted in the center comes out clean or if the cake springs back when lightly touched.
● Let cakes cool in pans 10 minutes for layer cakes and 15 minutes for tube cakes. Then invert cakes onto wire racks to cool completely.
● Let the layers cool completely before adding filling and frosting. Lightly brush the cake to remove loose crumbs.

STORAGE FOR CAKES

Cool cakes thoroughly before storing, even the unfrosted ones. If covered while warm, the cake may become sticky. Store unfrosted cakes and those with a creamy-type frosting under a cake dome or a large inverted bowl. Covering it well with plastic wrap will also work, but will mar the frosted surface if you don't first insert wooden picks into the cake in several places to hold the wrap away from the frosting.

Cakes with a frosting of fluffy meringue are best eaten the day they are made. That type frosting gradually disintegrates when stored. If you have leftovers, store under a cake dome with a knife under the edge to keep the dome slightly ajar so air can circulate.

Store cakes with cream in the frosting or filling in the refrigerator.

CAN I FREEZE MY CAKE?

That's one of the most commonly asked questions we receive from readers, especially as the holidays draw near. Unfrosted cakes freeze better than frosted ones. Let the cake cool completely; wrap it in alumi-

HIGH ALTITUDE ADJUSTMENTS

More than any other type of baked good, cake is affected by the lower air pressure at high altitudes. When baked above 3,000 feet, cakes will not rise properly and may be dry and tough. Use this chart as a guide when baking cakes at high altitudes.

In addition, when baking a cake above 3,000 feet in altitude, increase the baking temperature by 25°.

Ingredients	3,000 ft.	5,000 ft.	7,000 ft.	10,000 ft.
Sugar: for each cup, decrease	1 to 3 teaspoons	1 to 2 tablespoons	1½ to 3 tablespoons	2 to 3½ tablespoons
Liquid: for each cup, add	1 to 2 tablespoons	2 to 4 tablespoons	3 to 4 tablespoons	3 to 4 tablespoons
Baking Powder: for each teaspoon, decrease	⅛ teaspoon	⅛ to ¼ teaspoon	¼ teaspoon	¼ to ½ teaspoon

To cool cakes: Cool in pans 10 minutes; then invert onto wire racks to cool completely.

wrap frosted cakes as soon as you remove them from the freezer, and let them stand at room temperature until thawed.

CAKES IN THE MICROWAVE ARE TRICKY

Some cakes bake well in the microwave oven, but they require special pans and adjustments in ingredient proportions. For that reason we have not given microwave directions for our cakes. The manual that came with your particular microwave oven is your best guide to cake recipes that will work well in your oven.

WHAT WENT WRONG

Since cakes require such exact measurements and baking and mixing procedures, there are a number of things that can go wrong when baking a cake. Use the following chart to help you diagnose and correct problems with your cakes.

num foil, and then in plastic wrap. The quality will stay good up to five months when frozen.

Frosted cakes are trickier to freeze. Those with creamy-type frostings freeze better. Do not freeze those with meringue-type frostings. When freezing a frosted cake, place it in the freezer uncovered for several hours or until it is frozen. Then loosely but thoroughly wrap it in plastic wrap, and return it to the freezer. It should keep up to three months.

Let unfrosted cakes thaw in their wrapper at room temperature. Un-

CAKE PROBLEM CHART
Problems and Possible Causes

If cake falls:
Oven not hot enough
Undermixing
Insufficient baking
Opening oven door during baking
Too much leavening, liquid, or sugar

If cake peaks in center:
Oven too hot at start of baking
Too much flour
Not enough liquid

If cake sticks to pan:
Cake cooled in pan too long
Pan not greased and floured properly

If cake cracks and falls apart:
Removed from pan too soon
Too much shortening, leavening, or sugar

If crust is sticky:
Insufficient baking
Oven not hot enough
Too much sugar

If texture is heavy:
Overmixing when flour and liquid added
Oven temperature too low
Too much shortening, sugar, or liquid

If texture is coarse:
Inadequate mixing or creaming
Oven temperature too low
Too much leavening

If texture is dry:
Overbaking
Overbeaten egg whites
Too much flour or leavening
Not enough shortening or sugar

Shortening Cakes

There are two basic kinds of cakes. Most are classified as shortening or butter cakes; the others are sponge-type cakes, discussed later in the chapter.

Shortening cakes are the type you probably bake most often. They include the basic white, yellow, and chocolate cakes, pound cakes, fruitcakes, and any others that are made with shortening, butter, or margarine (use only stick-type margarine, not whipped). They usually depend on baking powder or baking soda for leavening. Sometimes eggs are added whole; sometimes they're separated and the whites beaten until fluffy before adding. Unless the recipe specifies otherwise, use the standard mixing procedure discussed earlier.

BASIC YELLOW CAKE

1 cup shortening
2 cups sugar
4 eggs
3 cups sifted cake flour
2½ teaspoons baking powder
½ teaspoon salt
1 cup milk
1 teaspoon almond extract
1 teaspoon vanilla extract

Cream shortening; gradually add sugar, beating well at medium speed of an electric mixer. Add eggs, one at a time, beating well after each addition.

Combine flour, baking powder, and salt; add to creamed mixture alternately with milk, beginning and ending with flour mixture. Mix after each addition. Stir in flavorings.

Pour batter into 3 greased and floured 9-inch round cakepans. Bake at 375° for 20 to 25 minutes or until a wooden pick inserted in center comes out clean. Cool in pans 10 minutes; remove from pans, and let cool completely on wire racks. Frost as desired. Yield: one 3-layer cake.

Yellow Cupcakes: Spoon batter into paper-lined muffin pans, filling each cup half full. Bake at 375° for 20 minutes. Remove from pans, and let cool on wire racks. Frost as desired. Yield: 3 dozen.

WHITE CAKE SUPREME

¾ cup shortening
1½ cups sugar
2¼ cups sifted cake flour
1 tablespoon baking powder
¾ teaspoon salt
1 cup milk
1½ teaspoons vanilla extract
5 egg whites

Cream shortening; gradually add sugar, beating well at medium speed of an electric mixer.

Combine flour, baking powder, and salt; add to creamed mixture alternately with milk, beginning and ending with flour mixture. Mix after each addition. Stir in vanilla.

Beat egg whites (at room temperature) until stiff peaks form. Gently fold into batter.

Pour batter into 2 greased and floured 9-inch round cakepans. Bake at 350° for 25 to 30 minutes or until a wooden pick inserted in center comes out clean. Cool in pans 10 minutes; remove from pans, and let cool completely on wire racks. Frost as desired. Yield: one 2-layer cake.

White Cupcakes: Spoon batter into paper-lined muffin pans, filling each cup two-thirds full. Bake at 350° for 20 minutes. Remove from pans, and let cool on wire racks. Frost as desired. Yield: 26 cupcakes.

BASIC CHOCOLATE CAKE

4 (1-ounce) squares unsweetened chocolate
½ cup shortening
2 cups sugar
2 eggs
2 cups sifted cake flour
½ teaspoon baking powder
1 teaspoon baking soda
¾ teaspoon salt
¾ cup buttermilk
¾ cup water
1 teaspoon vanilla extract

Place chocolate in top of a double boiler; bring water to a boil. Reduce heat to low; cook until chocolate melts.

Cream shortening; gradually add sugar, beating well at medium speed of an electric mixer. Add eggs, one at a time, beating well after each addition. Add chocolate, mixing well.

Combine flour, baking powder, soda, and salt; add to chocolate mixture alternately with buttermilk, beginning and ending with flour mixture. Mix after each addition. Add water, mixing well. Stir in vanilla.

Pour batter into 2 greased and floured 9-inch round cakepans. Bake at 350° for 30 minutes or until a wooden pick inserted in center comes out clean. Cool in pans 10 minutes; remove from pans, and let cool completely on wire racks. Frost as desired. Yield: one 2-layer cake.

Chocolate Cupcakes: Spoon batter into paper-lined muffin pans, filling each cup half full. Bake at 350° for 15 to 18 minutes. Remove from pans, and let cool on wire racks. Frost as desired. Yield: 3 dozen.

GOLD CAKE

½ cup butter or margarine, softened
1 tablespoon grated lemon rind (optional)
1¾ cups sugar
6 egg yolks
2½ cups sifted cake flour
1 tablespoon baking powder
½ teaspoon salt
1 cup plus 3 tablespoons milk
Seven-Minute Frosting (page 135)
1 (3½-ounce) can flaked coconut

Cream butter; add lemon rind, if desired. Gradually add sugar, beating well at medium speed of an electric mixer. Add egg yolks, one at a time, beating well after each addition.

Combine flour, baking powder, and salt; add to creamed mixture alternately with milk, beginning and ending with flour mixture. Mix after each addition.

Pour batter into 2 greased and floured 9-inch round cakepans. Bake at 350° for 25 to 30 minutes or until a wooden pick inserted in center comes out clean. Cool in pans 10 minutes; remove from pans, and let cool completely on wire racks.

Spread Seven-Minute Frosting between layers and on top and sides of cake. Lightly sprinkle top and sides with coconut. Yield: one 2-layer cake.

CARROT CAKE

3 cups grated carrots
2 cups all-purpose flour
1 teaspoon baking powder
2 teaspoons baking soda
½ teaspoon salt
2 cups sugar
1 teaspoon ground cinnamon
4 eggs, well beaten
1¼ cups vegetable oil
1 teaspoon vanilla extract
Cream Cheese Frosting (page 135)

Combine first 7 ingredients; stir in eggs, oil, and vanilla, mixing well. Pour batter into 3 greased and floured 9-inch round cakepans. Bake at 350° for 30 minutes or until a wooden pick inserted in center comes out clean. Cool in pans 10 minutes; remove from pans, and let cool completely on wire racks. Spread Cream Cheese Frosting between layers and on top of cake. Yield: one 3-layer cake.

Carrot Cupcakes: Spoon batter into paper-lined muffin pans, filling each cup half full. Bake at 350° for 20 minutes. Remove from pans, and let cool on wire racks. Frost with Cream Cheese Frosting. Yield: 3 dozen.

OLD-FASHIONED GINGERBREAD

½ cup butter or margarine, softened
½ cup sugar
1 egg
1 cup molasses
2½ cups all-purpose flour
1½ teaspoons baking soda
½ teaspoon salt
1 teaspoon ground cinnamon
1 teaspoon ground cloves
1 teaspoon ground ginger
1 cup hot water
Sweetened whipped cream

Cream butter; gradually add sugar, beating at medium speed of an electric mixer until light and fluffy. Add egg and molasses, mixing well.

Combine flour and next 5 ingredients; add to creamed mixture alternately with water, beginning and ending with flour mixture. Mix after each addition.

Pour batter into a lightly greased and floured 9-inch square pan. Bake at 350° for 35 to 40 minutes or until a wooden pick inserted in center comes out clean. Serve with a dollop of whipped cream. Yield: 9 servings.

COLA CAKE

2 cups all-purpose flour
1 teaspoon baking soda
2 cups sugar
1 cup cola-flavored carbonated beverage
1 cup butter or margarine
2 tablespoons cocoa
½ cup buttermilk
2 eggs, beaten
1 teaspoon vanilla extract
1½ cups miniature marshmallows
Cola Frosting (page 137)
½ cup finely chopped pecans

Combine flour, soda, and sugar; stir well, and set aside.

Combine cola, butter, and cocoa in a heavy saucepan; bring to a boil, stirring constantly. Gradually stir into flour mixture. Stir in buttermilk, eggs, vanilla, and marshmallows. Pour into a greased and floured 13- x 9- x 2-inch pan. Bake at 350° for 30 to 35 minutes or until a wooden pick inserted in center comes out clean. Spread Cola Frosting over warm cake; sprinkle with pecans. Yield: 15 servings.

PEANUT BUTTER CAKE

¾ cup butter, softened
¾ cup creamy peanut butter
2 cups firmly packed brown sugar
3 eggs
2 cups all-purpose flour
1 tablespoon baking powder
½ teaspoon salt
1 cup milk
1 teaspoon vanilla extract
½ recipe Rich Chocolate Frosting (page 137)
½ cup chopped peanuts

Cream butter and peanut butter; gradually add sugar, beating well at medium speed of an electric mixer. Add eggs, one at a time; beat well after each addition.

Combine flour, baking powder, and salt; add to creamed mixture alternately with milk, beginning and ending with flour mixture. Mix after each addition. Stir in vanilla.

Pour batter into a greased and floured 13- x 9- x 2-inch pan. Bake at 350° for 45 to 50 minutes or until a wooden pick inserted in center comes out clean. Let cool completely on a wire rack.

Spread Rich Chocolate Frosting on top of cake, and sprinkle with peanuts. Cut into squares. Yield: 15 servings.

PINEAPPLE UPSIDE-DOWN CAKE

¼ cup butter or margarine
1 cup firmly packed brown sugar
½ cup chopped pecans
1 (15¼-ounce) can pineapple slices, undrained
3 eggs, separated
1 cup sugar
1 cup all-purpose flour
1 teaspoon baking powder
½ teaspoon salt
6 to 8 maraschino cherries

Melt butter in a 9-inch cast-iron skillet. Add brown sugar and pecans; stir well. Drain pineapple, reserving ¼ cup plus 1 tablespoon pineapple juice; set juice aside. Arrange pineapple slices in a single layer over brown sugar mixture; set skillet aside.

Beat egg yolks at medium speed of an electric mixer until thick and lemon colored; gradually add sugar, beating well. Combine flour, baking powder, and salt; add dry mixture to yolk mixture. Stir in reserved pineapple juice.

Beat egg whites (at room temperature) until stiff peaks form; fold egg whites into batter. Spoon batter evenly over pineapple slices. Bake at 350° for 40 to 45 minutes. Remove cake from oven. Cool cake in skillet 30 minutes; invert cake onto a serving plate. Place cherries in centers of pineapple rings. Yield: one 9-inch cake.

Pineapple Upside-Down Cake Step-By-Step

1. Use a cast-iron skillet to make this cake. Melt butter in the skillet. Add brown sugar and pecans; stir well

2. Arrange pineapple slices in a single layer over brown sugar mixture.

3. Pour cake batter evenly over pineapple slices, and bake as directed.

4. Cool cake in skillet 30 minutes, and invert onto serving plate. Place cherry in center of each pineapple ring.

The crunchy topping and old-fashioned goodness of Pineapple Upside-Down Cake will earn raves from family and friends.

MARVELOUS BANANA CAKE

1 cup butter or margarine, softened
3 cups sugar
2 cups mashed bananas
4 eggs, beaten
3¾ cups all-purpose flour
2 teaspoons baking soda
1 cup buttermilk
1 teaspoon vanilla extract
2 tablespoons bourbon or orange juice
1 cup chopped pecans
Banana-Nut Frosting (page 139)

Cream butter; gradually add sugar, beating well at medium speed of an electric mixer. Add bananas; mix until smooth. Stir in eggs.

Combine flour and soda. Add to banana mixture alternately with buttermilk, beginning and ending with flour mixture. Mix after each addition. Stir in vanilla, bourbon, and pecans.

Pour batter into 3 greased and floured 9-inch round cakepans. Bake at 350° for 35 to 40 minutes or until a wooden pick inserted in center comes out clean. Cool in pans 10 minutes; remove from pans, and let cool completely on wire racks. Spread Banana-Nut Frosting between layers and on top of cake. Yield: one 3-layer cake.

LANE CAKE

1 cup butter or margarine, softened
2 cups sugar
3¼ cups all-purpose flour
1 tablespoon baking powder
¾ teaspoon salt
1 cup milk
1 teaspoon vanilla extract
8 egg whites, stiffly beaten
Lane Cake Filling (page 144)
½ recipe Seven-Minute Frosting (page 135)
Pecan halves (optional)

Cream butter; gradually add sugar, beating well at medium speed of an electric mixer. Combine flour, baking powder, and salt; add to creamed mixture alternately with milk, beginning and ending with flour mixture. Mix after each addition. Stir in vanilla. Fold in egg whites.

Pour batter into 3 greased and floured 9-inch round cakepans. Bake at 325° for 25 minutes or until a wooden pick inserted in center comes out clean. Cool in pans 10 minutes; remove from pans, and let cool completely on wire racks.

Spread Lane Cake Filling between layers and on top of cake; spread Seven-Minute Frosting on sides. Garnish with pecan halves, if desired. Yield: one 3-layer cake.

COCONUT-FILLED LAYER CAKE

1 cup shortening
2 cups sugar
5 eggs
2 cups all-purpose flour
1 teaspoon baking powder
½ teaspoon salt
1 cup milk
2 teaspoons vanilla extract
Coconut Filling (page 144)
Easy Cocoa Frosting (page 137)

Cream shortening; gradually add sugar, beating well at medium speed of an electric mixer. Add eggs, one at a time, beating well after each addition.

Combine flour, baking powder, and salt; add to creamed mixture alternately with milk, beginning and ending with flour mixture. Mix after each addition. Stir in vanilla.

Pour batter into 2 greased and floured 9-inch round cakepans. Bake at 350° for 30 to 35 minutes or until a wooden pick inserted in center comes out clean. Cool in pans 10 minutes; remove from pans, and let cool completely on wire racks.

Split cake layers in half horizontally. Place half of one cake layer, cut side up, on a cake plate; spread one-third Coconut Filling on layer. Repeat procedure with second and third layers. Place remaining layer, cut side down, on top of cake. Spread Easy Cocoa Frosting on top and sides of cake. Yield: one 4-layer cake.

HUMMINGBIRD CAKE

3 cups all-purpose flour
1 teaspoon baking soda
1 teaspoon salt
2 cups sugar
1 teaspoon ground cinnamon
3 eggs, beaten
1 cup vegetable oil
1½ teaspoons vanilla extract
1 (8-ounce) can crushed pineapple, undrained
1 cup chopped pecans
2 cups chopped bananas
Cream Cheese Frosting (page 135)
½ cup chopped pecans

Combine first 5 ingredients in a large bowl; add eggs and oil, stirring until dry ingredients are moistened. Do not beat. Stir in vanilla, pineapple, 1 cup pecans, and bananas.

Pour batter into 3 greased and floured 9-inch round cakepans. Bake at 350° for 25 to 30 minutes or until a wooden pick inserted in center comes out clean. Cool in pans 10 minutes; remove from pans, and let cool completely on wire racks.

Spread Cream Cheese Frosting between layers and on top and sides of cake; then sprinkle ½ cup chopped pecans on top. Yield: one 3-layer cake.

APPLE COCONUT CAKE

3 cups all-purpose flour
1 teaspoon baking soda
½ teaspoon salt
1 cup vegetable oil
3 eggs
2¼ cups sugar
2 teaspoons vanilla extract
2 cups chopped pecans
3 cups peeled, chopped cooking
  apples
½ cup flaked coconut
Brown Sugar Glaze (page 145)

Combine flour, soda, and salt; stir well, and set aside.

Combine oil, eggs, sugar, and vanilla; beat at medium speed of an electric mixer 2 minutes. Add flour mixture; beat at low speed just until blended. Fold in pecans, apples, and coconut. (Batter will be stiff.)

Spoon batter into a greased and floured 10-inch tube pan. Bake at 350° for 1 hour and 25 to 30 minutes or until a wooden pick inserted in center comes out clean. Cool in pan 10 minutes; remove from pan and place on serving plate. Immediately drizzle Brown Sugar Glaze over cake while both are still warm. Yield: one 10-inch cake.

PERFECT CHOCOLATE CAKE

1 cup cocoa
2 cups boiling water
1 cup butter or margarine, softened
2½ cups sugar
4 eggs
1½ teaspoons vanilla extract
2¾ cups all-purpose flour
2 teaspoons baking soda
½ teaspoon baking powder
½ teaspoon salt
Whipped Cream Filling (page 144)
Rich Chocolate Frosting (page 137)

Combine cocoa and boiling water, stirring until smooth. Set aside to cool.

Cream butter, sugar, eggs, and vanilla at high speed of an electric mixer until light and fluffy, about 5 minutes.

Combine flour, soda, baking powder, and salt; add to creamed mixture alternately with cocoa mixture, beating at low speed of an electric mixer, beginning and ending with flour mixture. Do not overbeat.

Pour batter into 3 greased and floured 9-inch round cakepans. Bake at 350° for 25 to 30 minutes. Cool in pans 10 minutes; remove from pans, and let cool completely on wire racks.

Spread Whipped Cream Filling between layers; spread Rich Chocolate Frosting on top and sides of cake. Yield: one 3-layer cake.

SUGAR 'N SPICE CAKE

¾ cup shortening
1 cup sugar
¾ cup firmly packed brown sugar
3 eggs
2¼ cups all-purpose flour
1 teaspoon baking powder
¾ teaspoon baking soda
½ teaspoon salt
¾ teaspoon ground cinnamon
¾ teaspoon ground cloves
1 cup buttermilk
1 teaspoon vanilla extract
Spiced Buttercream Frosting
  (page 141)

Cream shortening; gradually add sugars, beating well at medium speed of an electric mixer. Add eggs, one at a time, beating well after each addition.

Combine flour and next 5 ingredients. Add flour mixture to creamed mixture alternately with buttermilk, beginning and ending with flour mixture. Mix just until blended after each addition. Stir in vanilla.

Grease two 9-inch round cakepans, and line with wax paper; grease wax paper. Pour batter into prepared pans; bake at 350° for 30 to 35 minutes or until a wooden pick inserted in center comes out clean. Cool in pans 10 minutes; remove from pans, and let cool completely on wire racks. Spread frosting between layers and on top and sides of cake. Yield: one 2-layer cake.

Sugar 'n Spice Cupcakes: Spoon batter into paper-lined muffin pans, filling each cup half full. Bake at 350° for 20 minutes. Remove from pans, and let cool on wire racks. Frost with Spiced Buttercream Frosting. Yield: 3 dozen.

STATELY COCONUT LAYER CAKE

1 cup shortening
2 cups sugar
4 eggs
3 cups sifted cake flour
2½ teaspoons baking powder
½ teaspoon salt
1 cup milk
1 teaspoon almond extract
1 teaspoon vanilla extract
Lemon-Orange Filling (page 144) or
  Pineapple Filling (page 144)
Boiled Frosting (page 137)
1 small fresh coconut, grated, or ½
  cup flaked coconut

Cream shortening; gradually add sugar, beating well at medium speed of an electric mixer. Add eggs, one at a time, beating well after each addition.

Combine flour, baking powder, and salt; add to creamed mixture alternately with milk, beginning and ending with flour mixture. Mix after each addition. Stir in flavorings.

Pour batter into 3 greased and floured 9-inch round cakepans. Bake at 375° for 20 to 25 minutes or until a wooden pick inserted in center comes out clean. Cool in pans 10 minutes; remove from pans, and let cool completely on wire racks.

Spread Lemon-Orange Filling between layers; spread Boiled Frosting on top and sides, and sprinkle with coconut. Yield: one 3-layer cake.

FIG PRESERVE CAKE

1½ cups sugar
2 cups all-purpose flour
1 teaspoon baking soda
½ teaspoon salt
1 teaspoon ground nutmeg
1 teaspoon ground cinnamon
½ teaspoon ground allspice
½ teaspoon ground cloves
1 cup vegetable oil
3 eggs
1 cup buttermilk
1 tablespoon vanilla extract
1 cup fig preserves
½ cup chopped pecans or walnuts
Buttermilk Glaze (page 145)

Combine first 8 ingredients in a large mixing bowl; add oil and eggs, beating well at medium speed of an electric mixer. Add buttermilk and vanilla, beating well. Stir in preserves and pecans.

Pour batter into a greased and floured 10-inch tube pan. Bake at 350° for 1 hour and 15 minutes or until a wooden pick inserted in center comes out clean. Cool in pan 10 minutes; remove from pan and place on serving plate. Pour Buttermilk Glaze over cake while both are still warm. Yield: one 10-inch cake.

Prune Cake: Substitute 1 cup diced prunes for fig preserves.

GERMAN CHOCOLATE CAKE

1 (4-ounce) package sweet baking
  chocolate
½ cup water
1 teaspoon vanilla extract
1 cup butter or margarine, softened
2 cups sugar
4 eggs, separated
3 cups sifted cake flour
1 teaspoon baking soda
½ teaspoon salt
1 cup buttermilk
Coconut-Pecan Frosting (page 139)

Combine chocolate and water; bring to a boil, and stir until chocolate melts. Cool; stir in vanilla, and set aside.

Cream butter; gradually add sugar, beating well at medium speed of an electric mixer. Add egg yolks, one at a time, beating well after each addition. Add chocolate mixture; beat until blended.

Combine flour, soda, and salt; add to creamed mixture alternately with buttermilk, beginning and ending with flour mixture. Beat egg whites (at room temperature) until stiff peaks form; fold into batter.

Pour batter into 3 greased and floured 9-inch round cakepans. Bake at 350° for 30 to 35 minutes or until a wooden pick inserted in center comes out clean. Cool in pans 10 minutes; remove from pans, and let cool completely on wire racks.

Spread Coconut-Pecan Frosting between layers and on top and sides of cake. Yield: one 3-layer cake.

LADY BALTIMORE CAKE

1 cup butter or margarine, softened
2 cups sugar
4 eggs, separated
3 cups all-purpose flour
1 tablespoon baking powder
½ teaspoon salt
1 cup milk
½ teaspoon vanilla extract
½ teaspoon almond extract
Boiled Frosting (page 137)
1¼ cups chopped walnuts
1 cup currants
1 (8-ounce) package dried figs,
  chopped

Cream butter; gradually add sugar, beating well at medium speed of an electric mixer. Add egg yolks, one at a time, beating well after each addition.

Combine flour, baking powder, and salt; add to creamed mixture alternately with milk, beginning and ending with flour mixture. Mix just until blended after each addition. Stir in flavorings.

Beat egg whites (at room temperature) until stiff peaks form; fold into batter.

Pour batter into 2 greased and floured 9-inch round cakepans. Bake at 350° for 30 to 35 minutes or until a wooden pick inserted in center comes out clean. Cool in pans 10 minutes; remove from pans, and let cool completely on wire racks.

Combine Boiled Frosting, walnuts, currants, and figs, stirring well. Spread frosting between layers and on top and sides of cake. Yield: one 2-layer cake.

APPLESAUCE STACK CAKE

¾ cup shortening
1 cup sugar
1 cup molasses
3 eggs
4 cups all-purpose flour
½ teaspoon baking soda
1 teaspoon salt
1 teaspoon ground ginger
1 cup milk
3 cups applesauce
Ground cinnamon

Cream shortening; gradually add sugar and molasses, beating until smooth. Add eggs, one at a time, beating well after each addition.

Combine flour, soda, salt, and ginger; add to creamed mixture alternately with milk, beginning and ending with flour mixture. Mix after each addition.

Pour batter evenly into 6 greased and floured 9-inch round cakepans. Bake at 375° for 18 to 20 minutes or until a wooden pick inserted in center comes out clean. Remove layers from pans, and let cool completely on wire racks.

Spread about ½ cup applesauce between each layer, and stack layers. Spoon remaining applesauce on top of cake. Sprinkle top of cake with cinnamon. Let stand at least 8 hours before serving. Store in refrigerator. Yield: one 9-inch stack cake.

Note: Flavor of stack cake is enhanced when stored for up to 3 days.

Whipped cream and sliced fresh strawberries crown each layer of Strawberry Shortcake.

STRAWBERRY SHORTCAKE

1 quart strawberries, sliced
¼ to ½ cup sugar
½ cup butter or margarine, softened and divided
2 cups all-purpose flour
1 tablespoon plus 1 teaspoon baking powder
¼ teaspoon salt
¼ cup sugar
Dash of ground nutmeg
½ cup milk
2 eggs, separated
¼ cup sugar
1 cup whipping cream
¼ cup sifted powdered sugar
Whole strawberries

Combine sliced strawberries and ¼ to ½ cup sugar; stir gently, and chill 1 to 2 hours. Drain.

Butter two 9-inch round cakepans with ½ tablespoon butter each; set aside.

Combine flour, baking powder, salt, ¼ cup sugar, and nutmeg in a large mixing bowl; cut in remaining butter with pastry blender until mixture resembles coarse meal.

Combine milk and egg yolks; beat well. Add to flour mixture; stir with a fork until a soft dough forms. Pat dough out evenly into cakepans. (Dough will be sticky; moisten fingers with water as necessary.)

Beat egg whites (at room temperature) until stiff but not dry. Brush surface of dough with beaten egg whites; sprinkle evenly with ¼ cup sugar. Bake at 450° for 8 to 10 minutes or until layers are golden brown. Remove from pans, and let cool completely on wire racks. (Layers will be thin.)

Beat whipping cream until foamy; gradually add powdered sugar, beating until soft peaks form.

Place 1 cake layer on serving plate. Spread half of whipped cream over layer, and arrange half of sliced strawberries on top. Repeat procedure with remaining layer, whipped cream, and strawberries, reserving a small amount of whipped cream. Garnish top of cake with remaining whipped cream and whole berries. Yield: one 2-layer cake.

BEST FUDGE CAKE

3 (1-ounce) squares unsweetened
  chocolate
½ cup butter or margarine, softened
2¼ cups firmly packed brown sugar
3 eggs
1½ teaspoons vanilla extract
2¼ cups sifted cake flour
2 teaspoons baking soda
½ teaspoon salt
1 (8-ounce) carton commercial sour
  cream
1 cup boiling water
Whipped Cream Filling (page 144)
Chocolate Mocha Frosting (page 137)

Place chocolate in top of a double boiler; bring water to a boil. Reduce heat to low; cook until chocolate melts. Set aside to cool.

Cream softened butter; gradually add sugar, beating well at medium speed of an electric mixer. Add eggs, one at a time, beating well after each addition. Add chocolate and vanilla; mix just until blended.

Combine flour, soda, and salt; add to creamed mixture alternately with sour cream, beginning and ending with flour mixure. Stir in boiling water. (Batter will be thin.)

Pour batter into 2 greased and floured 9-inch round cakepans. Bake at 350° for 30 to 35 minutes or until a wooden pick inserted in center comes out clean. Cool in pans 10 minutes; remove from pans, and let cool completely on wire racks.

Split cake layers in half horizontally to make 4 layers. Spread Whipped Cream Filling between layers; spread Chocolate Mocha Frosting on top and sides of cake. Refrigerate until ready to serve. Yield: one 4-layer cake.

DOUBLE-CHOCOLATE TORTE

4 (1-ounce) squares unsweetened
  chocolate
1¾ cups all-purpose flour
¼ teaspoon baking powder
1¼ teaspoons baking soda
1 teaspoon salt
1¾ cups sugar
⅔ cup butter or margarine,
  softened
1¼ cups water
1 teaspoon vanilla extract
3 eggs
Chocolate Filling (page 144)
Whipped Cream Frosting (page 137)
Grated sweet chocolate (optional)

Place chocolate in top of a double boiler; bring water to a boil. Reduce heat to low; cook until chocolate melts. Cool.

Combine chocolate, flour, baking powder, soda, salt, sugar, butter, water, and vanilla. Beat 2 minutes at medium speed of an electric mixer. Add eggs, and beat an additional 2 minutes.

Pour batter into 4 greased and floured 9-inch round cakepans. Bake at 350° for 15 to 18 minutes or until a wooden pick inserted in center comes out clean. Cool cake layers in pans 10 minutes; remove from pans, and let cool completely on wire racks.

Place 1 layer on cake platter. Spread with half the Chocolate Filling. Place another cake layer on top, and spread with half the Whipped Cream Frosting. Repeat layers, and garnish with grated chocolate, if desired. Refrigerate. Yield: one 4-layer torte.

LIGHT CHOCOLATE CAKE

2½ cups sugar, divided
3 tablespoons water
2 (1-ounce) squares
  unsweetened chocolate
¾ cup butter or margarine,
  softened
4 eggs, separated
1 teaspoon vanilla extract
2¼ cups sifted cake flour
½ teaspoon baking soda
½ teaspoon salt
1 cup milk
1 teaspoon cream of tartar
Mocha Frosting (page 139)

Grease three 9-inch round cakepans, and line with wax paper. Grease and flour wax paper. Set aside.

Combine ½ cup sugar, water, and chocolate in a small saucepan; cook over low heat, stirring constantly, until chocolate melts. Cool.

Cream butter; gradually add remaining 2 cups sugar, beating well at medium speed of an electric mixer. Add egg yolks, one at a time, beating after each addition. Stir in vanilla and chocolate mixture.

Combine flour, soda, and salt; add to creamed mixture alternately with milk, beginning and ending with flour mixture. Mix after each addition.

Beat egg whites (at room temperature) until frothy; add cream of tartar, and beat until stiff peaks form. Gently fold into batter.

Pour batter into prepared cakepans. Bake at 350° for 25 to 30 minutes or until a wooden pick inserted in center comes out clean. Cool in pans 10 minutes; remove from pans, and let cool completely on wire racks.

Spread Mocha Frosting between layers and on top and sides of cake. Yield: one 3-layer cake.

BLACK FOREST CAKE

(pictured on page 108)

2 cups plus 2 tablespoons
  all-purpose flour
1½ teaspoons baking powder
¾ teaspoon baking soda
¾ teaspoon salt
2 cups sugar
¾ cup cocoa
½ cup shortening
3 eggs
1 cup milk
1 tablespoon vanilla extract
3 cups whipping cream
⅓ cup sifted powdered sugar
1 (25-ounce) jar cherry pie
  filling

Combine first 6 ingredients in a large mixing bowl; stir until well mixed. Add shortening, eggs, milk, and vanilla; beat mixture 3 minutes at low speed of an electric mixer, scraping sides of bowl occasionally.

Grease two 9-inch round cakepans; line bottoms with wax paper. Pour batter into pans. Bake at 350° for 30 to 35 minutes or until a wooden pick inserted in center comes out clean. Cool in pans 10 minutes; remove from pans, and let cool completely on wire racks.

Split cake layers in half horizontally to make 4 layers. Make fine crumbs using 1 cake layer; set crumbs aside.

Beat whipping cream until foamy; gradually add powdered sugar, beating until soft peaks form. Place 1 cake layer on cake platter; spread with 1 cup whipped cream, and top with ¾ cup cherry pie filling. Repeat with second layer, and then top with third cake layer. Frost sides and top with whipped cream, reserving a small amount for garnish. Pat cake crumbs generously around sides of cake. (There may be leftover cake crumbs.) Spoon or pipe whipped cream around top of cake; spoon remaining pie filling on center of top. Chill well. Yield: one 3-layer cake.

ALMOND LEGEND CAKE

Make Almond Legend Cake every New Year's Eve for a fun tradition at your house. Somewhere hidden in the baked cake will be a single whole almond. Whoever gets the almond in their slice of cake, according to legend, will enjoy good fortune during the year.

1 (2-ounce) package slivered
  almonds, chopped
⅓ cup butter or margarine,
  softened
⅓ cup shortening
1¼ cups sugar
3 eggs, separated
1 teaspoon grated lemon rind
2 tablespoons lemon juice
1 teaspoon vanilla extract
1 teaspoon almond extract
2⅓ cups sifted all-purpose flour
2 teaspoons baking powder
¼ teaspoon baking soda
¾ teaspoon salt
¾ cup milk
½ teaspoon cream of tartar
¼ cup sugar
1 whole almond
Apricot Glaze (page 145)

Sprinkle chopped almonds into a well-greased 10-inch Bundt pan; set aside.

Cream butter and shortening; gradually add 1¼ cups sugar, beating well at medium speed of an electric mixer. Add egg yolks, and beat well. Add lemon rind, juice, and flavorings; beat well.

Combine flour, baking powder, soda, and salt. Add to creamed mixture alternately with milk, beginning and ending with flour mixture. Mix after each addition; set batter aside.

Beat egg whites (at room temperature) and cream of tartar until foamy. Gradually add ¼ cup sugar, beating until stiff peaks form; fold egg white mixture into batter.

Pour batter into prepared pan. Press whole almond just below surface of batter. Bake at 350° for 50 to 55 minutes or until a wooden pick inserted in center comes out clean. Cool in pan 10 minutes; remove from pan, and let cool completely on a wire rack. Drizzle Apricot Glaze over cake. Yield: one 10-inch cake.

Note: Cake texture and taste is very similar to a batter bread.

SACHERTORTE

5 (1-ounce) squares semisweet
  chocolate
1 cup butter
6 eggs, separated
1 cup sugar
1¼ cups sifted cake flour
⅔ cup apricot preserves
Chocolate Glaze (page 145)

Place chocolate in top of a double boiler; bring water to a boil. Reduce heat to low; cook until chocolate melts. Remove from heat; add butter, stirring until butter melts.

Beat egg yolks until thick and lemon colored. Gradually add chocolate mixture to egg yolks, beating continuously at medium speed of an electric mixer. Add sugar, beating until blended. Let chocolate mixture cool 10 minutes.

Beat egg whites (at room temperature) at high speed of an electric mixer until stiff peaks form. Gently fold in flour alternately with chocolate mixture. Pour into a greased and floured 9-inch round cakepan. Bake at 325° for 40 to 45 minutes or until a wooden pick inserted in center comes out clean. Cool in pan 10 minutes; remove from pan, and let cool completely on a wire rack.

Carefully split cake in half horizontally to make 2 layers. Heat apricot preserves in a small saucepan; press preserves through a sieve. Spread preserves between layers and on top of cake. Let stand 20 minutes. Pour Chocolate Glaze over cake; spread evenly over top and sides. Yield: one 9-inch cake.

PETITS FOURS

1 cup shortening
2 cups sugar
3 cups all-purpose flour
2 teaspoons baking powder
¼ teaspoon salt
1 cup ice water
1½ teaspoons imitation butter
   flavoring
1 teaspoon vanilla or almond
   extract
6 egg whites
1 egg white
1 tablespoon powdered sugar
Petits Fours Frosting (page 141)
Decorator Frosting (page 141)

Cream shortening; gradually add sugar, beating well at medium speed of an electric mixer.

Combine flour, baking powder, and salt; add to creamed mixture alternately with water, beginning and ending with flour mixture. Mix after each addition. Stir in flavorings.

Beat 6 egg whites (at room temperature) until soft peaks form. Gently fold into batter.

Pour batter into 2 greased and floured 8-inch square pans. Bake at 325° for 40 minutes or until a wooden pick inserted in center comes out clean. Cool in pans 10 minutes; remove from pans, and let cool completely on wire racks.

Wrap cakes tightly in aluminum foil; freeze for several hours or until firm.

Remove cakes from foil, and carefully trim crust from all surfaces, making sure top of cake is flat. Cut each cake into 16 squares, or cut into circles using a 1½-inch cutter.

Beat 1 egg white (at room temperature) until frothy and slightly thickened. Add powdered sugar, mixing well. Brush egg white mixture lightly over top of cakes; allow glaze to dry.

Arrange cakes 2 inches apart on a wire rack; place rack in a large shallow pan. Quickly pour warm Petits Fours Frosting over cakes, completely covering top and sides.

Spoon up all frosting that drips through rack, and reheat to 110°. Continue pouring and reheating until cakes are smoothly and evenly coated.

Place cakes on a cutting board, and trim away any surplus frosting from bottom edge of each cake using a sharp knife. Decorate cakes as desired using Decorator Frosting. Yield: 32 petits fours.

Pound Cakes

Pound cakes take their name from the original recipe—a pound each of butter, sugar, eggs, and flour. Today's pound cakes include more ingredients than the original recipe, but the rich flavor still prevails.

CREAM CHEESE POUND CAKE

1½ cups chopped pecans, divided
1 cup butter, softened
1 (8-ounce) package cream cheese,
   softened
2½ cups sugar
6 eggs
3 cups sifted cake flour
Dash of salt
1½ teaspoons vanilla extract

Sprinkle ½ cup pecans in a greased and floured 10-inch tube pan; set aside.

Cream butter and cream cheese; grad-ually add sugar, beating at medium speed of an electric mixer until light and fluffy. Add eggs, one at a time, beating after each addition. Add flour and salt, stirring until combined. Stir in vanilla and remaining 1 cup pecans.

Pour batter into prepared pan. Bake at 325° for 1½ hours or until a wooden pick inserted in center comes out clean. Cool in pan 10 minutes; remove from pan, and let cool completely on a wire rack. Yield: one 10-inch cake.

Pound Cakes Make Versatile Desserts

You're never at a loss for a dessert with a pound cake in your pantry—or freezer. Serve it plain or toasted with a topping. Top with a fruit glaze from this chapter or a dessert sauce from the sauce chapter.

MILLION DOLLAR POUND CAKE

1 pound butter, softened
3 cups sugar
6 eggs
4 cups all-purpose flour
¾ cup milk
1 teaspoon almond extract
1 teaspoon vanilla extract

Cream butter; gradually add sugar, beating at medium speed of an electric mixer until light and fluffy. Add eggs, one at a time, beating after each addition. Add flour to creamed mixture alternately with milk, beginning and ending with flour mixture. Mix after each addition. Stir in flavorings.

Pour batter into a greased and floured 10-inch tube pan. Bake at 300° for 1 hour and 40 minutes or until a wooden pick inserted in center comes out clean. Cool in pan 10 to 15 minutes; remove to wire rack. Cool. Yield: one 10-inch cake.

ANGEL POUND CAKE

1 cup butter, softened
½ cup shortening
3 cups sugar
5 eggs
3 cups all-purpose flour
1 teaspoon baking powder
1 cup milk
1 teaspoon vanilla extract
1 teaspoon lemon extract

Cream butter and shortening; gradually add sugar, beating well at medium speed of an electric mixer. Add eggs, one at a time, beating after each addition.

Combine flour and baking powder; add to creamed mixture alternately with milk, beginning and ending with flour mixture. Mix just until blended after each addition. Stir in flavorings.

Pour batter into a greased and floured 10-inch tube pan. Bake at 350° for 1 hour and 15 minutes or until a wooden pick inserted in center comes out clean. Cool in pan 10 to 15 minutes; remove from pan, and let cool completely on a wire rack. Yield: one 10-inch cake.

CINNAMON-LACED SOUR CREAM POUND CAKE

½ cup chopped pecans
2 tablespoons sugar
1 teaspoon ground cinnamon
1 cup butter or margarine, softened
2 cups sugar
2 eggs
2 cups sifted cake flour
1 teaspoon baking powder
⅛ teaspoon salt
1 teaspoon vanilla extract
1 (8-ounce) carton commercial sour cream

Combine pecans, 2 tablespoons sugar, and cinnamon, stirring well. Set aside.

Cream butter; gradually add 2 cups sugar, beating well at medium speed of an electric mixer. Add eggs, one at a time, beating after each addition.

Combine flour, baking powder, and salt; add to creamed mixture, mixing just until blended. Stir in vanilla. Gently fold sour cream into batter.

Pour half of batter into a greased and floured 10-inch Bundt pan. Sprinkle half of the pecan mixture over batter. Repeat procedure. Bake at 350° for 55 to 60 minutes or until a wooden pick inserted in center comes out clean. Cool in pan 10 minutes; remove from pan, and let cool completely on a wire rack. Yield: one 10-inch cake.

BUTTERED RUM POUND CAKE

1 cup butter, softened
2½ cups sugar
6 eggs, separated
3 cups all-purpose flour
¼ teaspoon baking soda
1 (8-ounce) carton commercial sour cream
1 teaspoon vanilla extract
1 teaspoon lemon extract
½ cup sugar
Buttered Rum Glaze (page 145)

Cream butter; gradually add 2½ cups sugar, beating well at medium speed of an electric mixer. Add egg yolks, one at a time, beating after each addition.

Combine flour and soda; add to creamed mixture alternately with sour cream, beginning and ending with flour mixture. Mix just until blended after each addition. Stir in flavorings.

Beat egg whites (at room temperature) until foamy; gradually add ½ cup sugar, 1 tablespoon at a time, beating until stiff peaks form. Gently fold into batter.

Pour batter into a greased and floured 10-inch tube pan. Bake at 325° for 1 hour and 30 minutes or until a wooden pick inserted in center comes out clean. Cool in pan 10 to 15 minutes; remove from pan, and place on a serving plate. While warm, prick cake surface at 1-inch intervals with a wooden pick; pour Buttered Rum Glaze over cake. Yield: one 10-inch cake.

CHOCOLATE POUND CAKE

½ cup shortening
1 cup butter or margarine, softened
3 cups sugar
5 eggs
3 cups all-purpose flour
½ teaspoon baking powder
½ teaspoon salt
½ cup cocoa
1¼ cups milk
1 teaspoon vanilla extract
Chocolate Glaze (page 145, optional)
Chopped pecans (optional)

Cream shortening and butter; gradually add sugar, beating well at medium speed of an electric mixer. Add eggs, one at a time, beating after each addition.

Sift flour, baking powder, salt, and cocoa together. Add to creamed mixture alternately with milk, beginning and ending with flour mixture. Mix just until blended after each addition. Stir in vanilla.

Pour batter into a greased and floured 10-inch tube pan. Bake at 350° for 1 hour and 15 minutes or until a wooden pick inserted in center comes out clean. Cool in pan 10 to 15 minutes; remove from pan, and let cool completely on a wire rack.

Spoon Chocolate Glaze over top of cake, if desired, allowing it to drizzle down sides. Sprinkle top of cake with chopped pecans, if desired. Yield: one 10-inch cake.

1. Cream butter and shortening; gradually add sugar, beating well with an electric mixer.

2. Add eggs, one at a time, beating after each addition.

3. Add flour mixture to creamed mixture alternately with buttermilk.

4. Pour batter into prepared tube pan, and bake as directed.

Old-Fashioned Buttermilk Pound Cake has a smooth even texture inside and a tender, golden crust.

OLD-FASHIONED BUTTERMILK POUND CAKE

½ cup butter or margarine, softened
½ cup shortening
2 cups sugar
4 eggs
½ teaspoon baking soda
1 cup buttermilk
3 cups all-purpose flour
⅛ teaspoon salt
2 teaspoons lemon extract
1 teaspoon almond extract

Cream butter and shortening; gradually add sugar, beating well at medium speed of an electric mixer. Add eggs, one at a time, beating after each addition.

Dissolve soda in buttermilk. Combine flour and salt; add to creamed mixture alternately with buttermilk, beginning and ending with flour mixture. Mix just until blended after each addition. Stir in flavorings.

Pour batter into a greased and floured 10-inch tube pan. Bake at 350° for 1 hour and 5 to 10 minutes or until a wooden pick inserted in center comes out clean. Cool in pan 10 to 15 minutes; remove from pan, and let cool completely on a wire rack. Yield: one 10-inch cake.

Note: Cake may also be baked in two 9- x 5- x 3-inch loafpans. Bake at 350° for 45 to 50 minutes.

Chocolate Marble Pound Cake:
Melt 1 tablespoon shortening and 1 (1-ounce) square unsweetened chocolate in a small saucepan, stirring until smooth. Set aside.

Prepare batter for Old-Fashioned Buttermilk Pound Cake using vanilla extract in place of lemon extract. Remove 2 cups of batter, and add chocolate mixture, stirring until blended. Spoon one-third of remaining plain batter into a greased and floured 10-inch tube pan; top with half of chocolate batter. Repeat layers, ending with plain batter. Gently swirl batter with a knife to create marble effect. Bake as directed above.

Fruit and Nut Cakes

Especially around holiday time, many Southerners look for those chunky fruit and nut cakes that typify the season. The most popular kind of holiday fruitcake, our version of which is called Light Fruitcake, can be baked up to three weeks in advance. Soak the cake in brandy to keep it moist and flavorful until its Christmas debut.

RAISIN-NUT CAKE WITH BROWN SUGAR GLAZE

1 cup raisins
½ cup bourbon
1 cup butter or margarine, softened
2¼ cups sugar
5 eggs
3¼ cups all-purpose flour
1 teaspoon baking powder
½ teaspoon baking soda
1½ teaspoons ground nutmeg
1 cup buttermilk
2 cups coarsely chopped pecans
Brown Sugar Glaze (page 145)

Combine raisins and bourbon, stirring well. Cover and refrigerate at least 1 hour. Cream butter; gradually add sugar, beating well at medium speed of an electric mixer. Add eggs, one at a time, beating well after each addition.

Combine flour, baking powder, soda, and nutmeg; add to creamed mixture alternately with buttermilk, beginning and ending with flour mixture. Mix after each addition. Fold in pecans and reserved raisin mixture.

Pour batter into a greased and floured 10-inch tube pan. Bake at 325° for 1 hour and 30 minutes or until a wooden pick inserted in center comes out clean. Cool in pan 10 minutes; remove from pan, and place on serving plate. Drizzle Brown Sugar Glaze over cake. Cool completely. Yield: one 10-inch cake.

DATE-NUT LOAF

2 (8-ounce) packages pitted dates, chopped
2 cups chopped walnuts
1 cup chopped pecans
1 cup chopped maraschino cherries
¾ cup all-purpose flour
½ teaspoon baking powder
½ teaspoon salt
¾ cup sugar
4 eggs, beaten
1 teaspoon vanilla extract

Combine first 4 ingredients; stir well. Combine flour, baking powder, salt, and sugar; stir into fruit mixture. Add eggs and vanilla; stir well.

Spoon batter into a greased and wax paper-lined 8½- x 4½- x 3-inch loafpan. Bake at 300° for 2 hours and 30 minutes or until a wooden pick inserted in center comes out clean. Cool in pan 10 minutes; remove from pan, and let cool completely on a wire rack. Yield: 1 loaf.

LIGHT FRUITCAKE

1½ cups butter, softened
1½ cups sugar
1 tablespoon vanilla extract
1 tablespoon lemon extract
7 eggs, separated
3 cups all-purpose flour
1½ pounds (about 3 cups) yellow, green, and red candied pineapple
1 pound (about 2 cups) red and green candied cherries
¼ pound (about ½ cup) candied citron
½ pound (about 1½ cups) golden raisins
3 cups pecan halves
1 cup black walnuts, coarsely chopped
½ cup all-purpose flour
Additional candied fruit and nuts
¼ cup brandy
Additional brandy

Make a liner for a 10-inch tube pan by drawing a circle with an 18-inch diameter on a piece of brown paper. (Do not use recycled paper.) Cut out circle; set pan in center, and draw around base of pan and inside tube. Fold circle into eighths, having the drawn lines on the outside.

Cut off tip end of circle along inside drawn line. Unfold paper; cut along folds to the outside drawn line. From another piece of brown paper, cut another circle with a 10-inch diameter; grease and set aside. Place the 18-inch liner in pan; grease and set aside.

Cream butter and sugar at medium speed of an electric mixer until light and fluffy. Stir in flavorings. Beat egg yolks. Alternately add egg yolks and 3 cups flour to creamed mixture.

Combine candied fruit, raisins, and nuts. Dredge with ½ cup flour. Stir to coat well. Stir mixture into batter. Beat egg whites until stiff; fold into batter.

Spoon batter into prepared pan. Arrange additional fruit and nuts on top, if desired. Cover pan with greased 10-inch brown paper circle, placing greased side down. Bake at 250° for 4 hours or until cake tests done. Remove from oven. Take off paper cover, and slowly pour ¼ cup brandy evenly over cake; let cool completely on a wire rack.

Remove cake from pan; peel paper liner from cake. Wrap cake in brandy-soaked cheesecloth. Store in an airtight container in a cool place 3 weeks. Pour a small amount of brandy over cake each week. Yield: one 10-inch cake.

Note: Refrigerate Light Fuitcake for longer storage. Refrigeration also makes the cake slice neater and easier.

JAPANESE FRUITCAKE

1 cup butter or margarine, softened
2 cups sugar
4 eggs
3¼ cups sifted cake flour
1 tablespoon baking powder
¾ cup milk
1 teaspoon vanilla extract
1 teaspoon ground cinnamon
1 teaspoon ground allspice
¼ teaspoon ground cloves
1 cup raisins
Japanese Fruitcake Filling (page 144)
Seven-Minute Frosting (page 135)

Cream butter; gradually add sugar, beating well at medium speed of an electric mixer. Add eggs, one at a time, beating well after each addition.

Combine flour and baking powder; add to creamed mixture alternately with milk, beginning and ending with flour mixture. Mix after each addition. Stir in vanilla.

Divide batter in half; stir spices and raisins into one half. Pour plain batter into 2 greased and floured 9-inch round cakepans; pour spiced batter into 2 greased and floured 9-inch round cakepans. Bake at 350° for 20 to 25 minutes or until a wooden pick inserted in center comes out clean. Cool in pans 10 minutes; remove from pans, and let cool completely on wire racks.

Spread filling between layers. Spread frosting on top and sides of cake. Yield: one 4-layer cake.

To add fruit or nuts to cake batter: Dredge pieces in a small portion of the flour before folding them into cake. This keeps pieces from settling to the bottom.

Start With a Mix

Keep a few packages of cake mix on hand for occasions when you're short on time and ingredients. These recipes add just a few extras to the mix that will win you compliments every time. In fact you'll probably find yourself making these recipes even when you have enough time to bake from scratch.

Examine the label of the cake mix closely before you buy it. Different brands of the same flavor of cake mix can vary greatly, and it can make a big difference in the end product if you don't use the intended brand. Make sure to choose the exact ounce size specified in the recipe, and check to see whether or not pudding is included in the mix.

CHOCOLATE DREAM CAKE

1 (18.5-ounce) package fudge cake mix without pudding
1 (1.4-ounce) envelope whipped topping mix
4 eggs
1 cup water
1 teaspoon vanilla extract
1 teaspoon butter flavoring
Sour Cream-Chocolate Frosting (page 137)

Combine all ingredients except Sour Cream-Chocolate Frosting in a large mixing bowl; beat 4 minutes at medium speed of an electric mixer. Pour batter into 2 greased and floured 9-inch round cakepans. Bake at 325° for 35 minutes or until a wooden pick inserted in center comes out clean. Cool in pans 10 minutes; remove from pans, and let cool completely on wire racks.

Spread Sour Cream-Chocolate Frosting between layers and on top and sides of cake. Yield: one 2-layer cake.

CHOCOLATE-CARAMEL NUT CAKE

1 (18.25-ounce) package German chocolate cake mix with pudding
1 (14-ounce) package caramels
½ cup butter or margarine
⅓ cup milk
1 cup chopped dry roasted peanuts
¾ cup milk chocolate morsels

Prepare cake mix according to package; pour half of batter into a greased and floured 13- x 9- x 2-inch pan. Bake at 350° for 10 minutes. (Cake will not test done.) Cool cake 10 minutes.

Combine caramels, butter, and milk in a saucepan; cook over low heat, stirring constantly, until caramels melt. Spread over cake.

Sprinkle peanuts and chocolate morsels over caramel mixture. Pour remaining cake batter evenly over top. Bake at 350° for 20 to 25 minutes. Let cake cool in pan on a wire rack. Cut cake into squares to serve. Yield: 15 servings.

PIÑA COLADA CAKE

1 (18.5-ounce) package white cake mix without pudding
1 (3½-ounce) can flaked coconut, divided
1⅓ cups water
2 egg whites
1 (9-ounce) can cream of coconut
1 (8-ounce) container frozen whipped topping, thawed

Combine cake mix, 1 cup coconut, water, and egg whites; beat 2 minutes at high speed of an electric mixer. Reduce speed to low; beat 1 minute. Pour batter into a greased and floured 13- x 9- x 2-inch pan. Bake at 350° for 25 to 30 minutes or until a wooden pick inserted in center comes out clean. Cool in pan 10 minutes.

Punch holes in top of cake with a wooden pick. Pour cream of coconut over cake while still warm. Let cake cool completely in pan on a wire rack. Spread whipped topping over cake; sprinkle with remaining coconut. Cover and chill at least 4 hours. Cut into squares to serve. Yield: 15 servings.

ICE CREAM ANGEL CAKE

1 (14.5-ounce) package white angel food cake mix
1 quart strawberry ice cream, softened and divided
1 pint chocolate ice cream, softened
Whipped Cream Frosting (page 137)
¼ cup slivered almonds, toasted
Chocolate leaves (optional)

Prepare and bake cake mix according to package directions, using a 10-inch tube pan. Invert pan on funnel or bottle until cake is completely cooled (approximately 2 hours).

Loosen cake from sides of pan using a narrow metal spatula. Remove from pan; then split cake horizontally into 4 layers.

Place bottom layer of cake on a cake plate and spread with half of strawberry ice cream; freeze. Add second cake layer, and spread with chocolate ice cream; freeze. Add third cake layer, and spread with remaining strawberry ice cream; freeze. Place remaining layer, cut side down, on top of cake. Cover and freeze cake several hours.

Spread Whipped Cream Frosting on top and sides of cake. Sprinkle with almonds. Garnish with chocolate leaves, if desired. Yield: one 10-inch cake.

SELF-FILLED CUPCAKES

1 (18.5-ounce) package devil's food cake mix without pudding
1 (8-ounce) package cream cheese, softened
⅓ cup sugar
1 egg
1 (6-ounce) package semisweet chocolate morsels

Prepare cake mix according to package directions. Spoon batter into paper-lined muffin pans, filling two-thirds full.

Combine cream cheese and sugar, creaming until light and fluffy. Add egg, beating well; stir in chocolate morsels. Spoon 1 heaping teaspoon cream cheese mixture into center of each cupcake. Bake at 350° for 25 minutes. Remove from pans, and let cool on wire racks. Yield: 2½ dozen.

Angel, Sponge, and Chiffon Cakes

Often grouped together in food textbooks under the label of "foam" cakes, these desserts are noted for their lightness and delicacy. They all depend on beaten egg whites for their characteristic texture, while subtle differences distinguish the three types of cakes.

Angel food cakes are the purest. They contain no leavening, no egg yolks, and no shortening. Sponge cakes contain yolks as well as beaten whites, and sometimes leavening; they never contain shortening. Sponge cake batters are often used for jellyroll-type cakes. Chiffon cakes contain qualities of both foam and shortening cakes. Their lightness comes from beaten egg whites, but they do contain egg yolks, leavening, and shortening or oil.

Egg whites play an important role in foam cakes, so handle them so they'll yield the best volume. Separate the eggs as soon as they are removed from the refrigerator, but allow the whites to come to room temperature before beating. Always beat the whites just before adding them to the batter; they'll lose volume even if beaten and set aside for a few minutes.

Foam cakes are commonly baked in tube pans, but make sure the pans are not greased. The batter will cling to the sides and rise higher in ungreased pans.

Cool foam cakes upside-down to prevent shrinking and falling. To cool, invert the hot cakepan. If the pan has feet, let it cool on the feet. If not, set the pan over the neck of a bottle so air can circulate beneath it. When cool, gently loosen the sides with a knife.

ANGEL FOOD CAKE

12 egg whites
1½ teaspoons cream of tartar
¼ teaspoon salt
1½ cups sugar
1 cup sifted cake flour
1½ teaspoons vanilla extract

Beat egg whites (at room temperature) until foamy. Add cream of tartar and salt; beat until soft peaks form. Add sugar, 2 tablespoons at a time, beating until stiff peaks form. Sprinkle flour over egg white mixture, ¼ cup at a time; fold in carefully. Fold in vanilla.

Pour batter into an ungreased 10-inch tube pan, spreading evenly. Bake at 375° for 30 to 35 minutes or until cake springs back when lightly touched. Invert pan; cool 40 minutes. Loosen cake from sides of pan using a narrow metal spatula; remove from pan. Yield: one 10-inch cake.

Chocolate Angel Food Cake: For a chocolate version, sift ¼ cup cocoa with flour.

DAFFODIL SPONGE CAKE

1 cup sifted cake flour
½ cup sugar, divided
4 egg yolks
½ teaspoon lemon extract
10 egg whites
1 teaspoon cream of tartar
½ teaspoon salt
¾ cup sugar
½ teaspoon vanilla extract

Sift flour and ½ cup sugar together 3 times; set aside.

Beat egg yolks at high speed of an electric mixer 4 minutes or until thick and lemon colored. Add lemon extract; beat at medium speed an additional 5 minutes or until thick. Set aside.

Beat egg whites (at room temperature) until foamy. Add cream of tartar and salt; beat until soft peaks form. Add ¾ cup sugar, 2 tablespoons at a time; continue beating until stiff peaks form.

Sprinkle one-fourth of flour mixture over egg whites; gently fold it in. Repeat procedure with remaining flour, adding one-fourth of the mixture at a time. Divide egg white mixture in half.

Fold vanilla into half of egg white mixture. Gently fold beaten egg yolks into remaining egg white mixture.

Pour half of yellow mixture into an ungreased 10-inch tube pan; then gently add half of white mixture. Repeat procedure with remaining mixtures. Gently swirl batters with a knife to create marble effect.

Bake at 350° for 45 to 50 minutes or until cake springs back when lightly touched. Invert pan carefully. Let cake cool in pan 40 minutes. Loosen cake from sides of pan using a narrow metal spatula; remove from pan. Yield: one 10-inch cake.

Vanilla Sponge Cake: For a plain sponge cake, do not divide egg white mixture in half. Substitute vanilla extract for lemon extract.

What About All the Egg Yolks Left?

After making a foam cake, many cooks are puzzled about what to do with all the egg yolks that remain. You can beat them and brush them over homemade yeast bread before baking to add a nice glaze to the bread, or you can toss a few extra yolks into your regular scrambled egg mixture for breakfast. Another alternative is to make the Gold Cake (page 112); it uses six egg yolks and no whites.

CHIFFON CAKE

1 cup sifted all-purpose flour
1 cup sugar, divided
1½ teaspoons baking powder
¼ teaspoon salt
¼ cup vegetable oil
4 eggs, separated
¼ cup water
1 teaspoon vanilla extract
½ teaspoon cream of tartar

Sift together flour, ½ cup sugar, baking powder, and salt in a mixing bowl. Make a well in center; add oil, egg yolks, water, and vanilla. Beat at high speed of an electric mixer about 5 minutes or until satiny smooth.

Beat egg whites (at room temperature) and cream of tartar in a large mixing bowl until soft peaks form. Add remaining ½ cup sugar, 2 tablespoons at a time, and beat until stiff peaks form.

Pour egg yolk mixture in a thin, steady stream over entire surface of egg whites; then gently fold whites into yolk mixture.

Pour batter into an ungreased 10-inch tube pan, spreading evenly with a spatula. Bake at 325° for 1 hour or until cake springs back when lightly touched. Invert pan; cool 40 minutes. Loosen cake from sides of pan using a narrow metal spatula; remove from pan. Yield: one 10-inch cake.

Coffee Chiffon Cake: Dissolve 1 teaspoon instant coffee powder in ¼ cup water specified in original recipe. Frost cake with Kahlúa Cream Frosting (page 137).

Cakes From a Jellyroll Pan

Many cakes have their beginnings in a jellyroll pan. From there, most are rolled into the traditional jellyroll shape, but two of our cakes take on more novel shapes that you might enjoy serving for company.

When baking cakes in jellyroll pans, grease the pans and line them with wax paper. This helps keep the thin layers from sticking and will help you invert the layers without tearing them.

Most jellyroll cake recipes have a sponge-type cake base. Since they bake in very thin layers, watch them very carefully to make sure they don't overbake; always check them at the lower end of the range in cooking time. When overbaked, these cakes can be tough.

For most jellyroll cakes, roll the cake on a powdered sugar-sprinkled cloth towel while they're still hot to help prevent tearing. Roll the towel and cake together, and set aside on a wire rack until cool. The towel keeps the cake from sticking together as it cools. Your recipe will specify if another cooling technique is used. Gently unroll the cake and remove the towel.

Lightly tinted coconut adds just the right garnish to Elegant Lemon Cake Roll.

ELEGANT LEMON CAKE ROLL

4 eggs, separated
¼ cup sugar
1 tablespoon vegetable oil
1 teaspoon lemon extract
½ cup sugar
⅔ cup sifted cake flour
1 teaspoon baking powder
¼ teaspoon salt
1 to 2 tablespoons powdered sugar
Creamy Lemon Filling
½ cup flaked coconut
½ teaspoon water
1 or 2 drops of yellow food coloring
Sprigs of fresh mint

Grease bottom and sides of a 15- x 10- x 1-inch jellyroll pan with vegetable oil; line with wax paper, and grease and flour wax paper. Set aside.

Beat egg yolks in a large bowl at high speed of an electric mixer until thick and lemon colored; gradually add ¼ cup sugar, beating constantly. Stir in vegetable oil and lemon extract; set aside.

Beat egg whites (at room temperature) until foamy; gradually add ½ cup sugar, beating until stiff but not dry. Fold egg whites into yolks. Combine flour, baking powder, and salt; gradually fold into egg mixture. Spread batter evenly into prepared pan. Bake at 350° for 8 to 10 minutes.

Sift powdered sugar in a 15- x 10-inch rectangle on a towel. When cake is done, immediately loosen from sides of pan, and turn out on sugared towel. Carefully peel off wax paper. Starting at narrow end, roll up cake and towel together; let cake cool completely on a wire rack, seam side down.

Unroll cake. Spread cake with half of Creamy Lemon Filling, and carefully reroll cake, without towel. Place cake on serving plate, seam side down; spread remaining filling on all sides.

Combine coconut, water, and food coloring in a plastic bag; close securely, and shake well. Sprinkle colored coconut over cake roll. Refrigerate cake roll 1 to 2 hours before serving. Garnish cake platter with sprigs of fresh mint. Yield: 8 to 10 servings.

Creamy Lemon Filling

1 (14-ounce) can sweetened condensed milk
1 to 2 teaspoons grated lemon rind
⅓ cup lemon juice
5 drops of yellow food coloring
1½ cups frozen whipped topping, thawed

Combine sweetened condensed milk, lemon rind, lemon juice, and food coloring; stir well. Fold in whipped topping. Yield: about 3 cups.

STRAWBERRIES 'N CREAM SPONGE CAKE ROLL

3 egg yolks
1 teaspoon vanilla extract
5 egg whites
½ teaspoon cream of tartar
¼ teaspoon salt
¾ cup sifted powdered sugar
½ cup all-purpose flour
1 to 2 tablespoons powdered sugar
2 cups sliced strawberries
2 tablespoons sugar
2 cups whipping cream
3 tablespoons sugar
Whole strawberries (optional)

Grease bottom and sides of a 15- x 10- x 1-inch jellyroll pan with vegetable oil; line with wax paper, and grease wax paper with oil. Set pan aside.

Beat egg yolks in a large bowl at high speed of an electric mixer until thick and lemon colored; stir in vanilla, and set aside.

Beat egg whites (at room temperature) until foamy; add cream of tartar and salt, beating until stiff but not dry. Fold in ¾ cup powdered sugar. Fold whites into yolk mixture. Gradually fold flour into egg mixture. Spread batter evenly into prepared pan. Bake at 350° for 10 to 12 minutes.

Sift 1 to 2 tablespoon powdered sugar in a 15- x 10-inch rectangle on a cloth towel. When cake is done, immediately loosen from sides of pan, and turn out onto sugared towel. Peel off wax paper. Starting at narrow end, roll up cake and towel together; let cool completely on a wire rack, seam side down.

Combine sliced strawberries and 2 tablespoons sugar; set aside.

Beat whipping cream until foamy; gradually add 3 tablespoons sugar, beating until soft peaks form.

Unroll cake. Spread cake with sliced strawberries and half of whipped cream; reroll cake, without towel. Place on serving plate, seam side down; spread remaining whipped cream on all sides. Garnish with whole strawberries, if desired. Chill until serving time. Yield: 8 to 10 servings.

CHOCOLATE ROULAGE

1 (6-ounce) package semisweet
　chocolate morsels
5 eggs, separated
1¼ cups sugar, divided
1 teaspoon vanilla extract
2 teaspoons cocoa
1 cup whipping cream
1 tablespoon powdered sugar
2 tablespoons green crème de
　menthe or Kahlúa
Additional powdered sugar
Whole strawberries

Grease bottom and sides of a 15- x 10-
x 1-inch jellyroll pan with vegetable oil;
line with wax paper, and grease wax
paper with oil. Set aside.

Place chocolate morsels in top of a
double boiler; bring water to a boil. Reduce heat to low; cook, stirring occasionally, until chocolate melts.

Beat egg yolks in a large bowl at high
speed of an electric mixer until foamy.
Gradually add ¾ cup sugar, beating
until mixture is thick and lemon colored. (The mixture will look much like
cake batter.)

Gradually stir about one-fourth of
melted chocolate into yolk mixture; fold
in remaining chocolate.

Beat egg whites (at room temperature) until foamy. Gradually add remaining ½ cup sugar, 2 tablespoons at a
time; continue beating until stiff peaks
form. Fold egg whites into chocolate
mixture; gently fold in vanilla.

Pour chocolate mixture into prepared
pan, spreading evenly. Bake at 350° for
15 to 18 minutes in middle of oven; do
not overbake (surface will shine when
done). Immediately cover top with a
damp cloth towel or 2 layers of very
damp paper towels; place on a wire
rack, and let cool 20 minutes. Carefully
remove towel. Loosen edges with a
metal spatula, and sift cocoa over top.

Place 2 lengths of wax paper (longer
than jellyroll pan) on a smooth, slightly
damp surface; overlap edge of paper
nearest you over second sheet. Quickly
invert jellyroll pan onto wax paper, with
long side nearest you; remove pan, and
carefully peel paper from chocolate roll.

Beat whipping cream until foamy;
gradually add 1 tablespoon powdered
sugar and crème de menthe, beating
until soft peaks form.

Spoon whipped cream over chocolate
roll, spreading it so that there is more on
the side facing you (mixture will spread
out as you roll); leave a 1-inch margin
on all sides.

Starting at long side, carefully roll jellyroll fashion; use the wax paper to help
support the roulage as you roll. Secure
wax paper around roulage; smooth and
shape it with your hands.

Carefully slide roulage onto a large
baking sheet, seam side down; store in
refrigerator until serving time. Before
serving, sift additional powdered sugar
over roulage; carefully transfer to serving dish, using the wax paper to lift and
slide it. Trim away excess wax paper.
Garnish with whole strawberries. Yield:
10 servings.

Note: Roulage is very fragile and may
crack or break during rolling.

JELLYROLL LAYER
CAKE

*On the outside, Jellyroll Layer Cake
looks like any other cake, but slicing
reveals vertical, not horizontal layers.
The layers are baked in a jellyroll pan,
sliced, then rolled in the traditional
manner, adding a new strip where the
rolled strip ends.*

6 eggs
1⅔ cups sugar
2 cups self-rising flour
1 teaspoon ground cinnamon
½ teaspoon ground nutmeg
¼ teaspoon ground allspice
⅔ cup water
2 teaspoons vanilla extract
2 to 4 tablespoons powdered sugar
English Toffee Frosting (page 137)
Chocolate curls (optional)

Grease bottom and sides of two 15- x
10- x 1-inch jellyroll pans with vegetable
oil; line with wax paper, and grease and
flour wax paper. Set aside.

Beat eggs at high speed of an electric
mixer until foamy. Gradually add 1⅔
cups sugar, beating until mixture is
thick and lemon colored (about 5 to 6
minutes). Sift flour and spices together.
Gradually fold flour mixture, water, and
vanilla into egg mixture. Spread batter
evenly into prepared pans. Bake at 375°
for 8 to 10 minutes.

Sift powdered sugar in a 15- x 10-inch
rectangle on each of 2 towels. When
cakes are done, immediately loosen from
sides of pan, and turn each out on a
sugared towel. Peel off wax paper. Trim
⅛ inch from edges of cake, using a long
serrated knife. Starting at narrow end,
roll up cake and towel together; chill.

Carefully unroll chilled cakes. Cut
each cake lengthwise into 3 equal strips.
Spread each cake strip with about ⅓ cup
English Toffee Frosting; set aside remaining frosting. Gently roll up one
cake strip jellyroll fashion starting at
narrow end. Set roll upright in center of
serving plate. Starting where roll ends,
wind second cake strip around first roll.
Repeat until all 6 strips are used.

Spread top and sides of cake with
remaining frosting. Arrange chocolate
curls in a pattern on top, if desired. Chill
cake several hours before serving. Yield:
one 8-inch cake.

CHOCOLATE TRIANGLE
CAKE

*The slicing technique for Chocolate
Triangle Cake is tricky but we think
you'll be proud of the end result. Two
layers are stacked on top of each other;
then they're sliced into seven strips of
varied widths. The strips are frosted and
stacked by graduated sizes into two
halves of a triangle. The stacks are
weighted down to compress the layers*

and make them adhere; then they're joined into a triangle and frosted. A garnish of crystallized violets finishes the cake beautifully.

4 eggs, separated
¾ cup sugar, divided
1 teaspoon vanilla extract
¾ cup all-purpose flour
¾ teaspoon baking powder
¼ teaspoon salt
Satiny Chocolate Frosting (page 137)
Crystallized violets (optional)

Grease bottom and sides of two 15- x 10- x 1-inch jellyroll pans with vegetable oil, and line with wax paper; grease and flour wax paper. Set aside.

Beat egg yolks in a large bowl at high speed of an electric mixer until thick and lemon colored. Gradually add ¼ cup sugar to egg yolks, beating constantly. Beat in vanilla.

Beat egg whites (at room temperature) until foamy. Gradually add remaining ½ cup sugar, 1 tablespoon at a time, beating until stiff peaks form. Fold egg whites into yolk mixture. Combine flour, baking powder, and salt; gently fold flour mixture, one-third at a time, into egg mixture. Spread batter evenly into prepared pans; bake at 400° for 5 minutes. When cake is done, turn out onto wire racks to cool completely. Peel off wax paper.

Stack the two layers on top of each other to allow even slicing. Using a long serrated knife, slice layers crosswise into strips of the following widths: 3½ inches, 3 inches, 2½ inches, 2 inches, 1½ inches, 1 inch, and ½ inch.

Spread one side of both of the 3½-inch strips with a thin layer of Satiny Chocolate Frosting. Top each strip with a 3-inch strip, keeping edges even on one lengthwise side. Forming two stacks of strips, repeat spreading thin layers of frosting, and topping with successively smaller cake strips, keeping edges even, until all cake strips are used. (Stacks will be slanted on one side, with layers running horizontal; each stack of cake strips represents half the triangle.)

Turn stacks onto jellyroll pan, even edges down (layers now run vertical). Cover cake stacks with aluminum foil, and place a weight (packages of cake or pancake mix) on the slanted side of each stack. Refrigerate about 1 hour.

Remove weights and foil. Spread a thin layer of frosting against the 3½-inch side of one of the stacks, and join stacks to make a triangle.

Carefully transfer cake to serving platter using wide spatulas. Spread remaining frosting over the cake. Arrange crystallized violets down sides and peak of cake, if desired. Slice with an electric knife. Yield: 12 to 15 servings.

CHOCOLATE YULE LOG

1 cup sifted cake flour
1 teaspoon baking powder
⅛ teaspoon salt
3 eggs
1 cup sugar
¼ cup plus 1 tablespoon water
1 teaspoon vanilla extract
1 to 2 tablespoons powdered
 sugar
Yule Log Frosting
¼ cup sifted powdered sugar
2 tablespoons cocoa

Grease bottom and sides of a 15- x 10- x 1-inch jellyroll pan with vegetable oil; line with wax paper, and grease and flour wax paper. Set aside.

Combine flour, baking powder, and salt; set aside.

Beat eggs at high speed of an electric mixer until foamy. Gradually add 1 cup sugar, beating until mixture is thick and lemon colored (about 5 to 6 minutes). Stir in water and vanilla. Gradually fold in flour mixture. Spread batter evenly into prepared pan. Bake at 375° for 10 to 12 minutes.

Sift 1 to 2 tablespoon powdered sugar in a 15- x 10-inch rectangle on a towel. When cake is done, immediately loosen from sides of pan, and turn out on sugared towel. Peel off wax paper. Starting at narrow end, roll up cake and towel together; let cool completely on a wire rack, seam side down.

Unroll cake. Thinly spread Yule Log Frosting over cake; set aside remaining frosting. Reroll cake, without towel, and place on serving plate, seam side down.

Diagonally cut a 1-inch piece from one end of cake. Position cut edge of short piece against side of longer piece, to resemble a knot.

Combine remaining Yule Log Frosting with ¼ cup powdered sugar and cocoa; beat at medium speed of an electric mixer until blended. Thinly spread frosting over cake roll. Score frosting with fork tines to resemble bark. Yield: 8 to 10 servings.

Yule Log Frosting

2 (1-ounce) squares unsweetened
 chocolate
1 (1-ounce) square semisweet
 chocolate
1½ teaspoons instant coffee granules
½ cup sugar
¼ cup water
3 egg yolks
1 cup unsalted butter, softened
1 tablespoon Kahlúa

Place unsweetened and semisweet chocolate in top of a double boiler; bring water to a boil. Reduce heat to low; cook until chocolate melts, stirring occasionally. Remove from heat.

Combine coffee granules, sugar, and water in a large saucepan. Bring to a boil; cook over medium heat until mixture reaches soft ball stage (240°).

Beat egg yolks at high speed of an electric mixer until thick and lemon colored; continue beating, slowly adding hot syrup. Continue beating until mixture thickens and cools. Add butter, 2 tablespoons at a time, beating until smooth. Stir in chocolate and Kahlúa. Chill 30 minutes. Yield: 1½ cups.

Cheesecakes

Smart hostesses choose cheesecake often for dessert, not only because of its rich and extravagant look and taste, but also because it's easy to make several cheesecakes days ahead and chill until party time. Just cover cheesecake well with plastic wrap, and leave it in the springform pan until ready to unmold.

DELUXE CHEESECAKE

Recipe for 1 (9-inch) Graham
 Cracker Crust (page 357)
3 (8-ounce) packages cream cheese,
 softened
1 cup sugar
3 eggs
½ teaspoon vanilla extract
1 (16-ounce) carton commercial sour
 cream
3 tablespoons sugar
½ teaspoon vanilla extract

Press Graham Cracker Crust mixture into a 10-inch springform pan; set aside.

Beat cream cheese at high speed of an electric mixer until light and fluffy; gradually add 1 cup sugar, beating well. Add eggs, one at a time, beating well after each addition. Stir in ½ teaspoon vanilla. Pour into prepared pan. Bake at 375° for 35 minutes or until cheesecake is set.

Beat sour cream at medium speed of an electric mixer 2 minutes. Add 3 tablespoons sugar and ½ teaspoon vanilla; beat an additional 1 minute. Spread over cheesecake. Bake at 500° for 5 minutes. Let cool to room temperature on a wire rack; chill at least 8 hours. Yield: 8 to 10 servings.

Dress Amaretto Cheesecake for company; it tastes as delicious as it looks.

MINIATURE CHEESECAKES

½ cup graham cracker crumbs
2 tablespoons butter or margarine,
 melted
1 (8-ounce) package cream cheese,
 softened
¼ cup sugar
1 egg
½ teaspoon vanilla extract
2 tablespoons strawberry preserves

Combine graham cracker crumbs and butter, stirring well. Line 1¾-inch muffin pans with miniature paper liners. Spoon 1 teaspoon crumb mixture into each liner; gently press into bottom.

Beat cream cheese at high speed of an electric mixer until light and fluffy; gradually add sugar, and mix well. Add egg and vanilla, beating well. Spoon mixture into liners. Bake at 350° for 10 minutes.

Spoon about ¼ teaspoon strawberry preserves over each cheesecake. Chill thoroughly. Yield: 2 dozen.

AMARETTO CHEESECAKE

Recipe for 1 (9-inch) Graham
Cracker Crust (page 357)
3 (8-ounce) packages cream cheese,
softened
1 cup sugar
4 eggs
⅓ cup amaretto
1½ cups commercial sour cream
2 tablespoons sugar
2 tablespoons amaretto
¼ cup sliced almonds, toasted
Grated chocolate
Chocolate leaves
Strawberry halves

Press Graham Cracker Crust mixture firmly on bottom and ½ inch up the sides of a 9-inch springform pan.

Beat cream cheese at high speed of an electric mixer until light and fluffy; gradually add 1 cup sugar, beating well. Add eggs, one at a time, beating well after each addition. Stir in ⅓ cup amaretto; pour mixture into prepared pan. Bake at 375° for 45 to 50 minutes or until mixture is set.

Combine sour cream, 2 tablespoons sugar, and 2 tablespoons amaretto; stir well, and spoon over cheesecake. Bake at 500° for 5 minutes. Let cool to room temperature on a wire rack; chill. Garnish with almonds, grated chocolate, chocolate leaves, and strawberry halves. Yield: 12 servings.

RICH CHOCOLATE CHEESECAKE

Recipe for 1 (9-inch) Chocolate
Wafer Crust (page 357)
1 (12-ounce) package semisweet
chocolate morsels
4 (8-ounce) packages cream cheese,
softened
2 cups sugar
4 eggs
1 tablespoon cocoa
2 teaspoons vanilla extract
1 (16-ounce) carton commercial sour
cream
Whipped cream

Press Chocolate Wafer Crust mixture on bottom and ½ inch up the sides of a 10-inch springform pan. Pre-bake as crust recipe directs.

Place chocolate morsels in top of a double boiler; bring water to a boil. Reduce heat to low; cook until chocolate melts.

Beat cream cheese at high speed of an electric mixer until light and fluffy; gradually add sugar, mixing well. Add eggs, one at a time, beating well after each addition. Stir in melted chocolate, cocoa, and vanilla; beat until blended. Stir in sour cream, blending well. Pour into prepared pan. Bake at 300° for 1 hour and 40 minutes (center may be soft but will firm when chilled). Let cool to room temperature on a wire rack; chill at least 8 hours. Garnish each serving with whipped cream. Yield: 10 to 12 servings.

ORANGE CHEESECAKE

Recipe for 1 (9-inch) Graham
Cracker Crust (page 357)
1 (11-ounce) can mandarin
oranges
¼ cup Cointreau or other
orange-flavored liqueur
4 (8-ounce) packages cream cheese,
softened
2 tablespoons finely grated orange
rind
2 teaspoons orange extract
1 teaspoon vanilla extract
1⅓ cups sugar
4 eggs
½ cup orange juice
1 tablespoon plus 1 teaspoon
cornstarch

Press Graham Cracker Crust mixture into a 10-inch springform pan. Bake at 375° for 8 minutes; cool.

Drain mandarin oranges, reserving ½ cup liquid. Combine mandarin oranges and Cointreau; stir gently. Set aside, stirring occasionally.

Combine cream cheese, orange rind, and flavorings in a large mixing bowl; beat at high speed of an electric mixer until fluffy; gradually add sugar, beating well. Add eggs, one at a time, beating well after each addition. Pour filling into prepared pan. Bake at 350° for 50 minutes or until cheesecake is almost set. Turn oven off, and partially open oven door; leave cake in oven 30 minutes. Let cool to room temperature on a wire rack; chill at least 8 hours.

Drain mandarin orange mixture, reserving Cointreau. Arrange mandarin oranges on top of cheesecake.

Combine reserved mandarin orange liquid, reserved Cointreau, orange juice, and cornstarch in a saucepan; stir well. Cook over medium heat 5 minutes or until thickened; cool slightly. Spoon glaze over top of cheesecake; chill. Yield: 10 to 12 servings.

CHOCOLATE-GLAZED TRIPLE-LAYER CHEESECAKE

1 (8½-ounce) package chocolate wafer cookies, crushed (about 2 cups)
¾ cup sugar, divided
¼ cup plus 1 tablespoon butter or margarine, melted
2 (8-ounce) packages cream cheese, softened and divided
3 eggs
1 teaspoon vanilla extract, divided
2 (1-ounce) squares semisweet chocolate, melted
1⅓ cups commercial sour cream, divided
⅓ cup firmly packed dark brown sugar
1 tablespoon all-purpose flour
¼ cup chopped pecans
5 ounces cream cheese, softened
¼ teaspoon almond extract
Chocolate glaze (recipe follows)
Chocolate leaves (optional)

Combine cookie crumbs, ¼ cup sugar, and butter in a bowl; blend well. Press on bottom and 2 inches up sides of a 9-inch springform pan. Set aside.

Combine 1 (8-ounce) package cream cheese and ¼ cup sugar; beat until fluffy. Add 1 egg and ¼ teaspoon vanilla; blend well. Stir in melted chocolate and ⅓ cup sour cream. Spoon over chocolate crust.

Combine remaining (8-ounce) package cream cheese, brown sugar, and flour; beat until fluffy. Add 1 egg and ½ teaspoon vanilla; blend well. Stir in pecans. Spoon gently over chocolate layer.

Combine 5 ounces cream cheese and remaining ¼ cup sugar; beat until fluffy. Add remaining egg, and blend well. Stir in remaining 1 cup sour cream, ¼ teaspoon vanilla, and almond extract. Spoon gently over pecan layer.

Bake at 325° for 1 hour; turn off oven, and leave cheesecake in oven 30 minutes; partially open door of oven, and

leave cheesecake in oven an additional 30 minutes. Let cool to room temperature on a wire rack. Chill at least 8 hours. Remove from pan. Spread warm chocolate glaze over cheesecake. Garnish with chocolate leaves, if desired. Yield: 10 to 12 servings.

Chocolate Glaze

6 (1-ounce) squares semisweet chocolate
¼ cup butter or margarine
¾ cup sifted powdered sugar
2 tablespoons water
1 teaspoon vanilla extract

Combine chocolate and butter in top of a double boiler; bring water to a boil. Reduce heat to low; cook, stirring occasionally, until chocolate melts. Remove from heat; add remaining ingredients, stirring until smooth. Spread over cheesecake while glaze is warm. Yield: enough for one 9-inch cheesecake.

FRUIT-GLAZED CHEESECAKE

2 tablespoons graham cracker crumbs
1 (16-ounce) carton cream-style cottage cheese
2 (8-ounce) packages cream cheese, softened
1½ cups sugar
4 eggs, slightly beaten
1 (16-ounce) carton commercial sour cream
½ cup butter or margarine, melted
⅓ cup cornstarch
2 tablespoons lemon juice
1 teaspoon vanilla extract
About 2 cups whole strawberries, washed and hulled
Strawberry Glaze

Grease a 9-inch springform pan; dust with graham cracker crumbs.

Combine cheeses; beat at high speed of an electric mixer until smooth. Gradually add sugar, beating well. Add eggs,

one at a time, beating well after each addition. Add sour cream, butter, cornstarch, lemon juice, and vanilla; beat at low speed until mixture is smooth.

Pour batter into prepared pan. Bake at 325° for 1 hour and 10 minutes. Turn oven off; leave cheesecake in oven 2 hours. Let cool to room temperature on a wire rack; cover and chill at least 8 hours. Arrange whole strawberries on top of cheesecake; drizzle with Strawberry Glaze. Chill thoroughly. Yield: 10 to 12 servings.

Strawberry Glaze

1 cup strawberries, washed and hulled
½ cup sugar
1½ tablespoons cornstarch
2 tablespoons Grand Marnier or other orange-flavored liqueur

Mash strawberries. Combine strawberries, sugar, and cornstarch in a heavy saucepan; stir well. Cook over medium heat until thick, stirring constantly. Stir in Grand Marnier; cover and chill. Yield: ¾ cup.

Note: If desired, Blueberry Glaze may be substituted for the whole strawberries and Strawberry Glaze.

Blueberry Glaze

½ cup fresh blueberries, washed and drained
¼ cup water
¼ cup sugar
¼ cup kirsch
1½ tablespoons cornstarch
3 tablespoons water

Combine blueberries and ¼ cup water in a heavy saucepan; cook over medium heat, stirring constantly, 15 minutes or until berries are very soft. Press through a sieve, and return to saucepan. Stir in sugar and kirsch; cook over medium heat 10 minutes, stirring often, or until slightly thickened. Dissolve cornstarch in 3 tablespoons water; add to blueberry mixture. Cook, stirring constantly, until thickened. Cover and chill. Yield: 1 cup.

Frostings

When two slices of the same cake sit side-by-side on a cafeteria line, the first chosen is usually the one with the most frosting. Sweet and creamy frostings indeed make plain cakes worth the calories.

Although most of our cake recipes suggest one or two frostings to use, we separated the frosting section from the cake section to encourage you to mix and match the two. No one frosting is exclusive for any one cake, and we hope you'll create some new combinations.

Before frosting a cake, make sure the layers are completely cool. Brush the excess crumbs from the top and sides of the layers before you begin. To keep frosting off the serving plate, arrange several strips of wax paper around the edges of the plate before stacking the layers.

Place the bottom cake layer upside-down on the serving plate. Spread about one-fifth to one-fourth of frosting on top of the bottom layer, and smooth to the sides of the cake with a metal spatula. (If there are three or more layers to the cake, invert subsequent layers in this same direction, and frost them.) Place the top layer of the cake right side up.

Spread the sides of the cake with a liberal amount of frosting, making decorative swirls, if desired. Always keep the frosting just ahead of the spatula; do not backstroke until the entire area is frosted, or spatula will drag up crumbs from the unfrosted area. Spread remaining frosting on top of the cake, joining the frosting at the top and sides, and making decorative swirls. Carefully pull the wax paper strips from under the frosted cake.

You'll get neater slices from your cake if you use a knife with a serrated blade. If crumbs and frosting adhere to the knife, wipe the blade with a paper towel before cutting the next slice.

To keep frosting free of crumbs: Keep frosting just ahead of spatula as you spread. Do not backstroke until entire surface is frosted.

To keep frosting off serving plate: Before frosting, place strips of wax paper under cake on all sides; once cake is frosted, gently pull out wax paper.

CREAM CHEESE FROSTING

1 (8-ounce) package cream cheese, softened
½ cup butter or margarine, softened
1 (16-ounce) package powdered sugar, sifted
1 teaspoon vanilla extract

Combine cream cheese and butter, beating until smooth. Add powdered sugar and vanilla; beat until light and fluffy. Yield: about 3 cups.

Cream Cheese-Pecan Frosting: Stir 1 cup finely chopped pecans into frosting.

SEVEN-MINUTE FROSTING

1½ cups sugar
¼ cup plus 1 tablespoon cold water
2 egg whites
1 tablespoon light corn syrup
Dash of salt
1 teaspoon vanilla extract

Combine all ingredients except vanilla in top of a large double boiler. Beat at low speed of an electric mixer 30 seconds or just until blended.

Place over boiling water; beat constantly on high speed 7 minutes or until stiff peaks form. Remove from heat. Add vanilla; beat 2 minutes or until frosting is thick enough to spread. Yield: 4¼ cups.

1. Boiled Frosting sounds intimidating, but it's easy to make if you use an accurate thermometer. Combine sugar, cream of tartar, salt, and water in a heavy saucepan.

2. Cook over medium heat, stirring constantly, until mixture is clear. Cook, without stirring, to soft ball stage (240°).

3. Beat egg whites (at room temperature) until soft peaks form.

4. Continue to beat egg whites while slowly adding hot syrup mixture.

5. Add flavorings, and beat mixture until frosting is thick enough to spread.

Boiled Frosting spreads into pretty swirls on Stately Coconut Layer Cake. (page 116)

BOILED FROSTING

1½ cups sugar
½ teaspoon cream of tartar
⅛ teaspoon salt
½ cup hot water
4 egg whites
½ teaspoon almond extract
½ teaspoon coconut extract
   (optional)

Combine sugar, cream of tartar, salt, and water in a heavy saucepan. Cook over medium heat, stirring constantly, until clear. Cook, without stirring, to soft ball stage (240°).
Beat egg whites (at room temperature) until soft peaks form; continue to beat, slowly adding syrup mixture. Add flavorings; continue beating until stiff peaks form and frosting is thick enough to spread. Yield: 7 cups.

WHIPPED CREAM FROSTING

2 cups whipping cream
2 tablespoons powdered sugar
1 teaspoon vanilla extract

Combine all ingredients in a medium mixing bowl; beat until firm peaks form. Yield: 4 cups.

Kahlúa Cream Frosting: Combine 2 tablespoons Kahlúa, 1 teaspoon instant coffee powder, and 1 teaspoon water, stirring until smooth.
Beat whipping cream, sugar, and vanilla until foamy; add coffee mixture, beating until firm peaks form.

RICH CHOCOLATE FROSTING

1 cup semisweet chocolate morsels
½ cup half-and-half
1 cup butter or margarine
2½ cups sifted powdered sugar

Combine chocolate morsels, half-and-half, and butter in a saucepan; cook over medium heat, stirring until melted and smooth. Remove from heat; blend in powdered sugar. Set saucepan in ice; beat at medium speed of an electric mixer until frosting holds its shape. Yield: about 3 cups.

SOUR CREAM-CHOCOLATE FROSTING

1 (12-ounce) package semisweet
   chocolate morsels
½ cup commercial sour cream
1½ cups sifted powdered sugar
4 to 5 tablespoons milk

Place chocolate in top of a double boiler; bring water to a boil. Reduce heat to low; cook until chocolate melts. Cool.
Combine chocolate and sour cream. Add sugar alternately with milk, beating at medium speed of an electric mixer until smooth. Yield: 2⅓ cups.

CHOCOLATE MOCHA FROSTING

½ cup butter or margarine, softened
5 cups sifted powdered sugar
¼ cup cocoa
¼ cup strong coffee
2 teaspoons vanilla extract
About 2 tablespoons whipping cream
   (optional)

Cream butter at medium speed of an electric mixer; add sugar, cocoa, coffee, and vanilla, beating until fluffy. Add enough whipping cream, if necessary, to make frosting a spreading consistency, beating well. Yield: 2½ cups.

Easy Cocoa Frosting: Substitute ¼ cup whipping cream for coffee.

COLA FROSTING

½ cup butter or margarine
¼ cup cola-flavored carbonated
   beverage
3 tablespoons cocoa
3 cups sifted powdered sugar
1 teaspoon vanilla extract

Combine butter, cola, and cocoa in a heavy saucepan; bring to a boil, stirring constantly. Remove from heat; stir in sugar and vanilla. Yield: 1¼ cups.

SATINY CHOCOLATE FROSTING

4½ (1-ounce) squares unsweetened
   chocolate
½ cup plus 1 tablespoon butter or
   margarine
5⅔ cups sifted powdered sugar
½ cup plus 1 tablespoon milk
1 teaspoon vanilla extract

Combine chocolate and butter in top of a double boiler; bring water to a boil. Reduce heat to low; cook until chocolate melts. Remove from heat, and cool.
Add powdered sugar and milk to chocolate mixture; beat at low speed of an electric mixer until smooth. Stir in vanilla. Yield: 3 cups.

ENGLISH TOFFEE FROSTING

5 (1⅛-ounce) English toffee-flavored
   candy bars, crushed
1½ tablespoons amaretto or other
   almond-flavored liqueur
3 tablespoons flaked coconut, toasted
1 (12-ounce) container frozen
   whipped topping, thawed

Gently fold first 3 ingredients into whipped topping. Yield: about 4½ cups.

1. Sprinkle ½ cup sugar in a heavy saucepan, and place over medium heat to begin Favorite Caramel Frosting.

2. You'll think you've messed up when the sugar starts to clump; just keep stirring and cooking.

3. Continue cooking the sugar until it melts and turns light golden brown.

4. Stir butter mixture into hot caramelized sugar; the mixture will again lump. Don't panic!

5. Cook over medium heat, stirring frequently, until a candy thermometer registers 230°. Let mixture cool about 5 minutes.

6. Beat mixture with a wooden spoon to almost spreading consistency. Mixture cools and thickens quickly at this point. Test a small portion on the cake when you think it's ready.

Spread Favorite Caramel Frosting on plain cake layers. It is guaranteed to turn a plain cake into something special. It's a frosting that's also good on spice cakes.

FAVORITE CARAMEL FROSTING

3 cups sugar, divided
¾ cup milk
1 egg, beaten
Pinch of salt
½ cup butter or margarine, cut up

Sprinkle ½ cup sugar in a heavy saucepan; place over medium heat. Cook, stirring constantly, until sugar melts and syrup is light golden brown.

Combine remaining 2½ cups sugar, milk, beaten egg, and salt, stirring well; stir in butter. Stir butter mixture into hot caramelized sugar. (The mixture will tend to lump, becoming smooth with further cooking.)

Cook over medium heat, stirring frequently, until a candy thermometer registers 230° (about 15 to 20 minutes). Cool 5 minutes. Beat with a wooden spoon to almost spreading consistency (about 5 minutes), and spread on cooled cake. Yield: about 2½ cups.

ROYAL ICING

Royal Icing dries to a smooth, hard finish as opposed to our other frostings. Use it to make cake decorations or to frost cookies when this type of hard finish is desired.

3 large egg whites
½ teaspoon cream of tartar
1 (16-ounce) package powdered sugar, sifted
Paste food coloring

Combine egg whites and cream of tartar in a large mixing bowl. Beat at medium speed of an electric mixer until frothy. Add half of powdered sugar, mixing well. Add remaining sugar, and beat at high speed 5 to 7 minutes.

Color as desired with food coloring. Yield: about 2 cups.

Note: Icing dries very quickly; keep covered with a damp cloth at all times.

BANANA-NUT FROSTING

½ cup mashed banana
1 teaspoon lemon juice
⅓ cup butter or margarine, softened
1 (16-ounce) package plus 3 cups powdered sugar, sifted
3 to 4 tablespoons milk
1 cup flaked coconut, toasted
⅔ cup finely chopped pecans

Combine banana and lemon juice; set mixture aside.

Cream softened butter at medium speed of an electric mixer; add powdered sugar, and milk, mixing well. Add banana mixture, beating until fluffy. Stir in toasted coconut and chopped pecans. Yield: 3½ cups.

LEMON FLUFF FROSTING

½ cup butter or margarine, softened
4 cups sifted powdered sugar
2 teaspoons grated lemon rind
2 to 2½ tablespoons lemon juice

Cream butter at medium speed of an electric mixer; gradually add sugar, beating until light and fluffy. Add lemon rind and lemon juice; beat until smooth. Yield: 2 cups.

Orange Fluff Frosting: Substitute orange rind and orange juice for lemon rind and lemon juice.

COCONUT-PECAN FROSTING

1⅓ cups evaporated milk
1⅓ cups sugar
4 egg yolks, beaten
⅔ cup butter or margarine
1½ teaspoons vanilla extract
1⅓ cups flaked coconut
1⅓ cups chopped pecans

Combine milk, sugar, egg yolks, and butter in a heavy saucepan; bring to a boil, and cook over medium heat 12 minutes, stirring constantly. Add vanilla, coconut, and pecans; stir until frosting is cool and of spreading consistency. Yield: 3½ cups.

MOCHA FROSTING

1½ cups butter or margarine, softened
3 cups sifted powdered sugar, divided
1 tablespoon plus 1 teaspoon instant coffee powder
1 tablespoon plus 1 teaspoon cocoa
2¼ teaspoons hot water
3 egg yolks
2 teaspoons almond extract
3 tablespoons rum

Cream butter at medium speed of an electric mixer; gradually add 2 cups powdered sugar, beating until mixture is light and fluffy.

Combine coffee powder, cocoa, and hot water, stirring until smooth; add to creamed mixture.

Add egg yolks, and beat 5 minutes. Add remaining powdered sugar, beating until smooth. Stir in almond extract and rum. Yield: 3¾ cups.

If you're tired of plain frosted cakes that taste great but look like any other, give these easy decorating ideas a try. They're simple to do, and can give your cake a unique, more professional look. These techniques work on any type of frosting.

Pipe, Then Pull Webbed Chocolate

Perk up frosted cakes or cheesecakes with either a linear or round webbed design. To make either pattern across the top of a cake, melt 2 ounces of semisweet chocolate, and let it stand until cooled and thickened, but not set. Spoon melted chocolate into a decorating bag fitted with No. 2 round tip. For a linear pattern, pipe chocolate in parallel lines ½ inch apart across the top of cake. Pull the point of a wooden pick back and forth perpendicular to the lines to create the webbed pattern. Let the cake stand until chocolate hardens; chill briefly to set the chocolate, if necessary.

For a round webbed design, pipe chocolate in concentric circles ½-inch apart on the top of the cake. Pull the point of a wooden pick across the chocolate circles from the center to the outer edge.

Drizzle a Chocolate Border

Make any cake or cheesecake more tempting by drizzling its edge with chocolate. Simply melt 3 ounces semisweet chocolate, and let it cool slightly. Drizzle the chocolate from a spoon around the edge of the cake, a small amount at a time, letting some of the chocolate drip down the side. Let stand until the chocolate hardens; if necessary, chill briefly to set the chocolate.

Coat the Cake with Nuts

You can easily jazz up cakes with nuts by just patting them onto the frosting. Coat the entire cake with nuts or coat just the sides or top.

When choosing what type of nut, consider the form in which you'll use it. Pecans, peanuts, walnuts, macadamias, and almost any other nut work well coarsely chopped. (Don't chop the nuts too finely, or they won't look as pretty and may not adhere to the frosting as well.) Halves of pecans and sliced or slivered almonds add even more visual interest than the chopped form.

Toast the nuts lightly before patting them onto the cake; this will bring out their full flavor and color.

Comb the Frosting

The process is done just like it sounds—comb the frosting into either straight, curvy, or zigzag lines using an inexpensive gadget known as a frosting comb. The tool is available in most kitchen specialty shops. If you can't locate one in your area, you can comb with the tines of a fork (although the process will take longer and a little more care) or a regular wide-toothed hair comb (buy a new one to use just for cake decorating purposes).

Before combing, spread the frosting smoothly using a metal spatula. Comb the sides of the cake first, then the top. Periodically wipe off any excess frosting that accumulates on the comb.

This design is especially pretty used in combination with other simple designs, such as an arrangement of nuts.

Shape Some Chocolate Leaves

For chocolate leaves, select such nonpoisonous leaves as mint or rose leaves. Wash leaves and pat dry with paper towels. Melt 1 or 2 ounces semisweet chocolate or chocolate-flavored candy coating over hot water in a double boiler; let cool slightly.

Using a small spatula, spread a ⅛-inch layer of chocolate on the back of each leaf, spreading to the edges. Place leaves on a wax paper-lined cookie sheet, chocolate side up; freeze until chocolate is firm, about 10 minutes.

Grasp leaf at stem end, and carefully peel leaf from chocolate. Chill chocolate leaves until ready to use. (Handle carefully since chocolate leaves are thin and will melt quickly from the heat of your hand.)

Decorator Frosting and Buttercream Frosting are the choices of most professional cake decorators who decorate with metal tips. Novices should begin with Decorator Frosting. It is easier to use because the shortening stays firm when you work with it. The butter or margarine in Buttercream Frosting can soften from the heat of your hand as you pipe it if you pipe too slowly. Both frostings can be spread with a spatula as usual, omitting any specialty work with the decorating bag.

DECORATOR FROSTING

8 cups sifted powdered sugar
2 cups shortening
¾ cup milk
2 teaspoons vanilla extract
1 teaspoon almond extract
Paste food coloring

Combine all ingredients except food coloring in a mixing bowl; beat at low speed of an electric mixer until blended. Then beat at high speed 5 minutes or until light and fluffy. Color as desired with food coloring. Yield: 8 cups.

VANILLA BUTTERCREAM FROSTING

1½ cups butter or margarine, softened
4 cups sifted powdered sugar
2 tablespoons milk
1 teaspoon vanilla or almond extract

Cream butter at medium speed of an electric mixer; gradually add sugar, beating until light and fluffy. Add milk; beat until spreading consistency. Stir in vanilla. Yield: 3 cups.

Spiced Buttercream Frosting: Substitute 2 tablespoons orange juice for milk, and stir in 1 teaspoon ground cinnamon and ¼ teaspoon ground cloves in place of 1 teaspoon vanilla extract.

Chocolate Buttercream Frosting: Add ¼ cup cocoa with sugar.

Mocha Buttercream Frosting: Dissolve 2 tablespoons instant coffee powder in the 2 tablespoons milk. Add as directed for milk.

PETITS FOURS FROSTING

Petits Fours Frosting pours onto cakes and dries to a smooth, thin coating typical of the dainty little desserts often served at receptions and showers. It is not appropriate for frosting cakes in the traditional manner.

½ cup plus 3 tablespoons water
7 cups sifted powdered sugar
3 tablespoons light corn syrup
1 teaspoon vanilla or almond extract

Combine all ingredients in a medium saucepan; cook over low heat, stirring constantly, until frosting reaches 110°. Quickly pour warm frosting over cakes. Yield: 3 cups.

Some occasions call for a decorated cake—a special birthday, an anniversary, a wedding or baby shower. If you want a beautiful cake that is perfectly tailored to the occasion and is not bakery-expensive, learn the craft of cake decorating.

These directions will teach the beginning cake decorator all the basics—from baking the cake to decorating it.

Baking The Cake: A cake that is to be decorated needs special care during baking. Use any favorite cake recipe, or substitute a commercial cake mix as many professional decorators do.

Generously grease the inside of pans with shortening, using a pastry brush to spread the shortening evenly. Sprinkle flour inside pans, and shake pans so that flour covers all the greased surfaces. Tap out excess flour, and touch up shiny spots with more shortening and flour. To make cake layers rise higher and have a level top and moist edges, wrap the sides of pans with damp strips cut from a bath towel.

Bake the layers in a preheated oven according to the time and temperature specified in the recipe or on package instructions. Do not overbake.

Remove layers from oven and cool in pan 10 minutes on a wire rack. Invert layers onto wire rack. Lift off pans carefully. Cool layers completely, and brush off loose crumbs.

If the crown is too high or one side of cake is higher than the other, trim off excess using a sharp, serrated knife. If you freeze the layers first, they will be easier to trim.

If you bake layers the day before, allow them to cool thoroughly on wire racks; then cover with wax paper and towels overnight. When you remove the wax paper the next day, excess crumbs will go with it leaving a smooth cake to frost.

Frosting The Cake: There are two main types of frostings used for cake decorating: Decorator Frosting (page 141) and Royal Icing (page 139). Decorator Frosting stays soft and moist and is the most frequently used recipe for frosting and decorating.

Royal Icing is a near-permanent frosting that dries hard and is used for decorations that last indefinitely or for making flowers or other decorations in advance. It is ideal for decorating cookies. Professionals also use Royal Icing for making display cakes or crafts like sugar molds. It is an edible icing that is crunchy like hard candy.

When making decorations in advance with Royal Icing, pipe the decoration onto wax paper; let dry several hours or until firm, and then peel from paper, and attach to cake with a small amount of Decorator Frosting or Royal Icing. You can also make decorations in advance with Decorator Frosting. Pipe them on wax paper; then freeze until firm, and transfer to cake.

The proper consistency in frosting is the key to decorating an eye-catching cake. The frosting must be firm enough to hold swirls and designs, yet pliable enough to mold. If the frosting seems too thin, stir in a small amount of sifted powdered sugar; if it's too thick add a little water.

Color the frosting with paste food coloring, adding a very small amount at a time; a little goes a long way. Remember also that the frosting will darken in color slightly as it dries. Always mix enough of each color in the beginning, because it is difficult to duplicate any tint exactly.

To assemble the cake, use about ½ cup frosting between cake layers. Many professionals suggest stacking the layers with top sides together to make the finished cake more level. Others recommend placing bottom sides together to reduce the chance of crumbs getting into the frosting and marring the top frosting surface.

For successful decorating, make sure the cake is frosted to a smooth even surface. Spread frosting on sides, then top of cake using a long metal spatula. To keep frosting free of crumbs, keep frosting ahead of spatula; do not backstroke until entire surface is frosted.

Dip spatula into glass of warm water and let excess drip off. Smooth sides by gently rotating cake (a turntable makes process easier) while holding spatula against side of cake. Lift spatula and remove excess frosting. Smooth top of cake by placing spatula flat on one edge of cake top and sweeping it across to center of cake. Lift off, remove excess frosting, and repeat procedure until entire top surface of cake is smooth.

To smooth the center of cake, apply even pressure to spatula as you turn cake stand around in a full circle. Lift off spatula and any excess frosting.

Choosing And Using Equipment: For decorating a cake you'll need bags to hold frosting, metal decorating tips to define the frosting shapes you'll make, and couplers to allow you to change tips without refilling bags.

You can purchase reusable plastic bags, disposable bags, or you can make your own disposable bags from parchment paper. (See diagram below.)

To assemble the decorating bag, drop coupler into bag and push as far down into bag as possible. Insert metal tip over tip of coupler, and screw coupler ring over metal tip. Spoon frosting into decorating bag, filling it about half full; fold corners of bag over and crease until all air is pressed out. To change tips, simply unscrew the coupler ring and replace the tip.

Metal decorating tips come in five

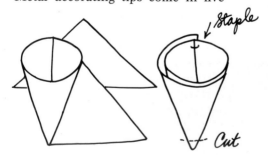

basic groups that determine the type of decorations they produce. The size and shape of the opening on a decorating tip determines the group to which it belongs. Refer to the photographs on this page for the five types of tips and their functions. The tips photographed represent only a few of the sizes and shapes of tips in each basic group.

Decorating The Cake: As with any craft, cake decorating requires practice to perfect skills. Before decorating the cake, mix up a batch of frosting to practice borders and decorations. Pipe them right on the pan just as if it were the real cake. Practice piping the frosting until you develop the pressure control necessary to make the decorations you'll use.

The amount of pressure and the steadiness with which it is applied to the decorating bag will determine the size and uniformity of any design. Some decorations require even pressure, others a varying application of light, medium, or heavy pressure. The more pressure is controlled, the more exact the decoration will be. If the frosting ripples, you are squeezing the bag too hard. If frosting breaks, you are moving the bag too quickly or frosting is too thick.

When piping frosting, left-handed people need special instructions. If you are left-handed, hold decorating bag in your left hand and guide decorating tip with the fingers of your right hand. If instructions say to hold decorating bag to the right, you should hold it to the left. A right-handed person should always decorate from left to right. A left-handed person should always decorate from right to left, except when writing. When decorating a cake on a turntable, rotate the stand counterclockwise as you decorate.

There are six decorating techniques that require different pressure and tip positions. Follow these basic instructions for each technique, and you can make almost any type decoration.

Dots, stars, and drop flowers: Hold bag at a 90° angle with tip almost touching the surface. Steadily squeeze out frosting. Lift bag slightly as frosting builds up in desired design. Keep tip buried in frosting; then stop pressure and pull tip away.

Straight lines: To pipe a straight line, touch the tip to the cake at a 45° angle, letting a small amount of frosting flow. Continue squeezing bag, and draw tip across cake about ½ inch from surface. Touch cake with tip and release pressure to end line. Literally pulling the line of frosting through the air rather than against the cake keeps line straight.

Leaves: Hold bag at a 45° angle to surface. Squeeze bag to build up a base; then pull bag away as you relax pressure, stop squeezing, and lift tip away.

Borders: For most borders, hold bag at a 45° angle. Touch tip to cake and squeeze out frosting as you pull tip in desired border design such as zigzag, push-pull, interlooping "e" shape, etc.

Writing: Use a small round tip, holding tip at a 45° angle to cake; move tip with motion of arm, not wrist, to form desired letters. The tip should lightly touch the cake as you write.

Shaped flowers: Flowers more intricate than drop flowers are generally shaped on a flower nail and transferred to the cake. Specific directions vary for each flower design.

Round Tip: No. 2, top; No. 8, bottom. Smooth, round tips produce dots, lines, stems, lattice, figure piping, stringwork, and writing.

Leaf Tip: No. 67, top; No. 65, bottom. Leaf tips produce plain or ruffled leaves of all sizes. They also produce ferns as well as decorative borders.

Rose Tip: No. 101, top; No. 104, bottom. Rose tips produce pansies, daffodils, daisies, as well as roses and many other flowers. They also make bows and ruffled borders.

Drop Flower Tip: No. 199, top; No. 136, bottom left; No. 193, bottom right. Drop flower tips produce flowers of all sizes and shapes. Round tips make dot centers.

Star Tip: No. 20, top; No. 14, bottom. Star tips produce many decorations, such as stars, shells, drop flowers as well as zigzag and other borders.

Fillings

Add a filling to a cake, and you'll add a new flavor dimension separate from the cake and frosting. Anywhere from one-half to one cup of filling is appropriate for spreading between each cake layer.

WHIPPED CREAM FILLING

1 cup whipping cream
1 teaspoon vanilla extract
2 to 4 tablespoons powdered sugar

Beat whipping cream and vanilla extract until foamy; gradually add powdered sugar, beating until soft peaks form. Yield: 2 cups.

CHOCOLATE FILLING

2 tablespoons cornstarch
½ cup sugar
½ cup water
1 tablespoon butter or margarine
2 (1-ounce) squares semisweet chocolate

Combine cornstarch, sugar, and water in a small saucepan, stirring well; cook over medium heat, stirring constantly, until thickened. Remove from heat; add butter and chocolate, stirring until melted. Let cool. Yield: 1 cup.

PINEAPPLE FILLING

3 tablespoons all-purpose flour
½ cup sugar
1 (20-ounce) can crushed pineapple, undrained
2 tablespoons butter or margarine

Combine flour and sugar in a small saucepan; add pineapple and butter. Cook over medium heat, stirring constantly, until thickened. Cool. Yield: 2⅔ cups.

COCONUT FILLING

1 cup sugar
1 cup milk
1 (12-ounce) plus 1 (6-ounce) package frozen coconut, thawed
12 large marshmallows
1 teaspoon vanilla extract

Combine sugar and milk in a saucepan; bring to a boil. Add coconut and marshmallows; boil over medium heat 5 minutes. Remove from heat, and stir in vanilla. Yield: about 3 cups.
Note: Filling is very moist, and absorbs into cake.

LEMON-ORANGE FILLING

1 cup sugar
⅓ cup all-purpose flour
¼ teaspoon salt
¼ cup water
2 tablespoons grated orange rind
1 tablespoon grated lemon rind
1¼ cups orange juice
¼ cup lemon juice
4 egg yolks, well beaten

Combine sugar, flour, salt, and water in a heavy saucepan; stir well. Stir in fruit rind and juices. Cook over medium heat, stirring constantly, until mixture thickens and boils.

Gradually stir about one-fourth of hot mixture into egg yolks; add to remaining hot mixture, stirring constantly. Return to a boil; cook 1 to 2 minutes, stirring constantly. Remove from heat, and let cool completely. (Mixture will be thick.) Yield: 2¼ cups.

JAPANESE FRUITCAKE FILLING

1½ cups flaked coconut
1 cup sugar
2 tablespoons cornstarch
1 cup water
1 (8-ounce) can crushed pineapple, undrained
2 oranges, peeled, sectioned, and finely chopped

Combine all ingredients in a medium saucepan, stirring until cornstarch dissolves. Cook over medium heat, stirring constantly, 1 minute or until thickened and bubbly. Cool completely before spreading on cake. Yield: 3⅓ cups.

LANE CAKE FILLING

8 egg yolks
1½ cups sugar
½ cup butter or margarine
1 cup chopped pecans
1 cup raisins
1 cup flaked coconut
½ cup bourbon
½ cup sliced maraschino cherries

Combine egg yolks, sugar, and butter in a heavy saucepan. Cook over medium heat, stirring constantly, until thickened (about 20 minutes).

Remove from heat, and stir in remaining ingredients. Cool completely. Yield: 3½ cups.

Glazes

Choose a glaze to add just a touch of flavor atop unfrosted cakes baked in Bundt or tube pans. Glazes look prettiest when spread or drizzled over the cake so that a little runs down the sides of the cake. If a glaze seems too thin, stirring a little sifted powdered sugar into it will usually help. If too thick, heat it, or stir in a very small amount of the liquid ingredient already used in the recipe. Some cooks like to punch holes in the top of the cake before adding a glaze, so the glaze will seep into the cake as it sits. This makes the cake moister.

POWDERED SUGAR GLAZE

1 cup sifted powdered sugar
1½ tablespoons milk
½ teaspoon vanilla extract

Combine all ingredients, stirring well. Yield: ⅓ cup.

Lemon Glaze: Substitute lemon juice for milk.

APRICOT GLAZE

½ cup apricot preserves
1 tablespoon rum or orange juice

Heat preserves, and strain through a sieve. Add rum; stir well. Yield: about ½ cup.

BROWN SUGAR GLAZE

½ cup firmly packed light brown sugar
½ cup butter or margarine
¼ cup milk

Combine all ingredients in a heavy saucepan; bring to a full boil and cook, stirring constantly, 2 minutes. Let cool to lukewarm. Yield: ⅔ cup.

BUTTERED RUM GLAZE

¼ cup plus 2 tablespoons butter or margarine
¾ cup sugar
3 tablespoons rum
3 tablespoons water
½ cup chopped walnuts

Combine all ingredients except walnuts in a small saucepan; bring to a boil. Boil mixture, stirring constantly, 3 minutes. Remove from heat, and stir in chopped walnuts. Pour over cake while glaze is warm. Yield: 1¼ cups.

BUTTERMILK GLAZE

2 tablespoons buttermilk
¼ cup sugar
2 tablespoons butter or margarine
¾ teaspoon cornstarch
⅛ teaspoon baking soda
¾ teaspoon vanilla extract

Combine buttermilk, sugar, butter, cornstarch, and baking soda in a small saucepan. Bring mixture to a boil. Cool slightly, and stir in vanilla extract. Pour over cake while both are still warm. Yield: ½ cup.

CHOCOLATE GLAZE

3 (1-ounce) squares unsweetened chocolate
¾ cup sifted powdered sugar
2 tablespoons hot water
1 egg
1 egg yolk
¼ cup plus 1 tablespoon butter or margarine, softened

Place chocolate in top of a double boiler; bring water to a boil. Reduce heat to low; cook until chocolate melts. Remove from heat; add sugar and water, beating at medium speed of an electric mixer until blended. Add egg, and beat until blended. Add egg yolk, and beat until mixture cools. Add butter, one tablespoon at a time, beating until blended. Yield: 1⅓ cups.

COOKIES & CANDIES

Southerners think of cookies and candies more fondly than just as a way to satisfy a craving for something sweet. These bite-size confections bring back many a childhood memory—like Christmas buffets laden with gaily colored cookies and candies, and pulling a chair up to the counter to help Mom roll and cut a batch of cookies.

Cookies

It's always a challenge to keep the cookie jar filled—not that it's difficult to make the cookies, they just disappear quickly once made. Whether you want a chunky chocolate chip cookie with a glass of milk before bed or a dainty tea cookie for a gathering of the ladies, you'll likely find the style and flavor of a cookie here to suit your needs.

Cookies are classified by the way they're shaped. You'll find drop, bar, refrigerator, rolled, hand-shaped, and specially-shaped cookies categorized in this chapter. Hints to help you with each type of shaping are included within each section.

EQUIPMENT

Have several sturdy, shiny metal cookie sheets if you plan to bake a lot of cookies. Select cookie sheets that are at least 2 inches narrower and

A variety of cookies to dazzle everyone: (from front, the first time each is shown) Date Pinwheel Cookies (page 157), Melt-Away Butter Cookies (page 164), Dainty Sandwich Cookies (page 161), Molasses Sugar Cookies (page 162), and Easy Frosted Brownies (page 152).

shorter than your oven to allow heat to circulate evenly around them. Don't use pans with high sides for baking cookies, as they deflect the heat causing the cookies to bake unevenly. If you have cookie sheets with a nonstick coating, watch the cookies carefully as they bake; dark surfaced pans of this type tend to make cookies brown quicker. You'll also need a sturdy spatula and a couple of wire cooling racks.

BAKING THE COOKIES

Always bake cookies in a preheated oven unless specified otherwise. Grease the cookie sheet only if directed. Many cookie recipes contain enough fat that greasing the sheet isn't necessary. If you do grease the sheet, don't worry about washing or regreasing between batches; just wipe away excess

...mbs. Place dough on a cool cookie sheet; dough spreads on a hot one.

For best results, bake only one pan of cookies at a time, placing the pan in the center of the oven. If you have to bake two pans at a time, stagger the oven racks so they divide the oven into thirds, and stagger the pans on the racks. If the cookies begin to brown unevenly, you may need to switch the pans halfway through the baking time. Don't ever bake cookies with one pan directly over the other one. One batch would invariably have tops that are too light and bottoms that are too dark, while the other batch would have the opposite problem.

Cookies are often difficult to test for doneness. Since personal preference varies as to soft or crisp cookies, we give a range in our baking times. If you like soft and chewy cookies, take them from the oven at the lower end of the time. Leaving them in one or two minutes longer will make the cookies crispier. We often use the phrase "until lightly browned" to help in determining doneness, too. Unless your recipe states otherwise, remove the cookies from the pan immediately after removal from the oven. Transfer them, usually with a spatula, to a wire rack to cool completely, being careful not to stack cookies or let the sides touch as they cool.

STORING AND FREEZING

Let the cookies cool completely before storing. Store soft, chewy cookies in an airtight container to keep them from drying out. A small slice of apple or bread placed in the container will help keep them fresh. Place crisp cookies in a container with a loose-fitting lid. Store bar cookies directly in their baking pan. Seal tightly with plastic wrap or aluminum foil.

Most baked cookies and cookie dough can be frozen successfully up to 6 months. Thaw baked cookies at room temperature about 10 minutes. Thaw cookie dough in the refrigerator or at room temperature until it's a good consistency to shape as the recipe directs.

MICROWAVING COOKIES

We tested the majority of these cookie recipes in a microwave oven on the same day we tested them conventionally. In almost every case, the end product simply didn't compare favorably enough to the conventional product for us to offer microwave directions. The only exceptions are several recipes in the section on bar cookies. With only minor adjustments, some bar cookies work well in the microwave.

Since corners of bar cookies cook faster than the center, you'll need to shield the corners with aluminum foil to reduce energy received and slow the cooking process. But before doing this, check your manufacturer's directions; some older models of microwave ovens can be damaged by the use of foil. If your oven doesn't allow shielding, bake cookies in a round dish.

To shield bar cookies, cut triangles of foil and place over the top corners of the dish, keeping foil smooth, close to the dish, and at least 1 inch from the walls of the oven. If foil is not smooth or touches oven walls, it may cause an arc (spark of electricity). If an arc does occur, flatten the foil and continue microwaving.

For most bar cookies, shields should be left in place during the entire microwave cycle. However, you'll need to remove the shields earlier if the cycle is almost complete and the corners are not cooking as rapidly as the center.

Other types of cookies will work in your microwave if significant changes are made in your recipe. You'll need a stiffer dough than most conventional ones. Since the cookies won't brown in the microwave, your recipe should use ingredients that contain natural color, such as chocolate, brown sugar, or dark spices.

Drop Cookies

You'll find drop cookies easy to make—they're literally dropped from a teaspoon with no further shaping necessary. Drop cookies have somewhat rounded tops and are slightly irregular in shape. If your drop cookies are too irregular, however, you probably haven't dropped them correctly. Pick up the desired amount of cookie dough with the tip of one teaspoon (not a measuring spoon), and use another teaspoon to push the dough onto the cookie sheet, patting it into a relatively smooth mound. Take care to scoop equal amounts of dough each time so the cookies will all be approximately the same size. Allow at least 2 inches between each cookie on the cookie sheet so they won't run together as they bake.

COCONUT MACAROONS

1⅓ cups flaked coconut
⅓ cup sugar
2 egg whites
2 tablespoons all-purpose flour
½ teaspoon vanilla extract
⅛ teaspoon salt

Combine ingredients; stir well. Drop by level tablespoonfuls onto a greased cookie sheet. Bake at 350° for 20 minutes; cool on wire racks. Yield: 1 dozen.

NO-BAKE PEANUT BUTTER-OATMEAL COOKIES

2 cups sugar
¼ cup cocoa
¼ cup butter or margarine
½ cup milk
2½ cups regular oats, uncooked
¾ cup crunchy peanut butter
2 teaspoons vanilla extract

Combine sugar, cocoa, butter, and milk in a heavy saucepan; stir well. Cook over medium heat until mixture comes to a boil; boil 1 minute. Stir in oats, peanut butter, and vanilla. Drop dough by heaping teaspoonfuls onto lightly greased wax paper; cool thoroughly. Yield: about 4 dozen.

MINCEMEAT DROP COOKIES

½ cup shortening
½ cup sugar
1 egg
1 cup prepared mincemeat
1½ cups all-purpose flour
½ teaspoon baking soda
¼ teaspoon salt

Cream shortening; gradually add sugar, beating at medium speed of an electric mixer until light and fluffy. Add egg, and beat well. Add mincemeat, mixing well. Combine flour, soda, and salt; stir into creamed mixture.

Drop dough by teaspoonfuls onto greased cookie sheets. Bake at 350° for 16 to 18 minutes. Cool on wire racks. Yield: 4½ dozen.

To bake cookies all the same size: Spoon cookie dough in equal amounts onto cookie sheet.

SWEET DREAM MERINGUE COOKIES

2 egg whites
¼ teaspoon cream of tartar
½ cup sugar
½ teaspoon vanilla extract
1 cup chopped pecans
1 (6-ounce) package semisweet chocolate morsels

Preheat oven to 350°. Beat egg whites (at room temperature) and cream of tartar at high speed of an electric mixer 1 minute. Gradually add sugar, 1 tablespoon at a time, beating until stiff peaks form and sugar dissolves (about 2 to 4

minutes). Stir in remaining ingredients.

Drop by teaspoonfuls onto cookie sheets lined with aluminum foil. Place in oven, and immediately turn off heat. Do not open oven door for at least 8 hours. Carefully peel cookies from foil. Yield: 4 dozen.

BEST-EVER CHOCOLATE CHIP COOKIES

¾ cup butter or margarine, softened
¼ cup shortening
¾ cup sugar
¾ cup firmly packed brown sugar
2 eggs
1 teaspoon vanilla extract
2¼ cups all-purpose flour
1 teaspoon baking soda
¼ teaspoon salt
1 (12-ounce) package semisweet chocolate morsels

Cream butter and shortening; gradually add sugars, beating well at medium speed of an electric mixer. Add eggs and vanilla, beating well. Combine flour, soda, and salt; add to creamed mixture, mixing well. Stir in chocolate morsels.

Drop dough by heaping teaspoonfuls onto ungreased cookie sheets. Bake at 375° for 9 to 11 minutes. Cool slightly on cookie sheets; remove to wire racks to cool completely. Yield: about 6½ dozen.

Double Chip Cookies: Prepare Best-Ever Chocolate Chip Cookies, using 1 cup peanut butter morsels or butterscotch morsels and 1 (6-ounce) package semisweet chocolate morsels instead of 1 (12-ounce) package semisweet chocolate morsels.

Jumbo Chocolate Chip Cookies: Prepare Best-Ever Chocolate Chip Cookies, dropping them onto ungreased cookie sheets by ¼ cupfuls. Lightly press each cookie into a 3-inch circle with fingertips. Bake at 350° for 15 to 17 minutes. Yield: 1½ dozen.

Keep Chocolate Oatmeal Chippers on hand for after school treats with a glass of milk.

FAVORITE OATMEAL COOKIES

1 cup butter or margarine, softened
1½ cups sugar
1 egg
¼ cup water
1 teaspoon vanilla extract
1½ cups all-purpose flour
½ teaspoon baking soda
½ teaspoon salt
½ teaspoon ground cinnamon
½ teaspoon ground nutmeg
3 cups quick-cooking oats, uncooked
1 cup chopped pecans (optional)

Cream butter; gradually add sugar, beating at medium speed of an electric mixer until light and fluffy. Add egg, and beat well; add water and vanilla, mixing well.

Combine flour, soda, salt, cinnamon, and nutmeg; add to creamed mixture, mixing well. Stir in oats and pecans, if desired.

Drop dough by rounded teaspoonfuls onto ungreased cookie sheets. Bake at 350° for 10 to 12 minutes or until lightly browned. Cool slightly on cookie sheets; remove to wire racks to cool completely. Yield: about 8 dozen.

Chocolate Oatmeal Chippers: Prepare Favorite Oatmeal Cookies, adding 1 (6-ounce) package semisweet chocolate morsels to dough.

Raisin Oatmeal Cookies: Prepare Favorite Oatmeal Cookies, adding 1 cup raisins to dough.

Peanut Butter Oatmeal Chippers: Prepare Favorite Oatmeal Cookies, adding 1 cup peanut butter morsels to dough.

MONSTER COOKIES

Make Monster Cookies and you'll be famous. They contain almost all the ingredients reputed to make a good cookie—oats, peanut butter, and chocolate. More stunning than that is their size—they're dropped from ¼-cup measures rather than teaspoons. The recipe makes only 2½ dozen, but they're big!

½ cup butter or margarine, softened
1 cup sugar
1 cup plus 2 tablespoons firmly packed brown sugar
3 eggs
2 cups peanut butter
¾ teaspoon light corn syrup
¼ teaspoon vanilla extract
4½ cups regular oats, uncooked
2 teaspoons baking soda
¼ teaspoon salt
1 cup candy-coated milk chocolate pieces
1 (6-ounce) package semisweet chocolate morsels

Cream butter; gradually add sugars. Beat well at medium speed of an electric mixer. Add eggs, peanut butter, syrup, and vanilla; beat well. Add oats, soda, and salt; stir well. Stir in remaining ingredients. (Dough will be stiff.)

Pack dough into a ¼-cup measure. Drop dough 4 inches apart, onto lightly greased cookie sheets. Lightly press each cookie into a 3½-inch circle with fingertips. Bake at 350° for 12 to 15 minutes (centers of cookies will be slightly soft). Cool slightly on cookie sheets; remove to wire racks, and cool completely. Yield: 2½ dozen.

CHOCOLATE-CHOCOLATE CHIPPERS

1 (6-ounce) package semisweet
  chocolate morsels, divided
1½ cups all-purpose flour
1 teaspoon baking powder
¼ teaspoon salt
½ cup shortening
1 cup sugar
1 egg
1 teaspoon vanilla extract
2 tablespoons milk
¾ cup coarsely chopped walnuts

Place ½ cup chocolate morsels in top of a double boiler; bring water to a boil. Reduce heat to low; cook until chocolate melts. Set aside to cool.

Combine flour, baking powder, and salt; set aside.

Cream shortening; gradually add sugar, beating well at medium speed of an electric mixer. Add cooled chocolate, egg, and vanilla; beat well. Add milk, mixing well. Add dry ingredients, and mix well. Stir in remaining ½ cup chocolate morsels and walnuts.

Drop dough by heaping teaspoonfuls onto lightly greased cookie sheets. Bake at 350° for 10 minutes or until done. Carefully transfer cookies to wire racks to cool (cookies will be soft). Yield: about 5½ dozen.

RAISIN COOKIES

2 cups raisins
1 cup water
1 cup shortening
1¾ cups sugar
2 eggs
1 teaspoon vanilla extract
3½ cups all-purpose flour
1 teaspoon baking powder
1 teaspoon baking soda
½ teaspoon salt
½ teaspoon ground cinnamon
½ teaspoon ground nutmeg
1 cup chopped pecans or walnuts

Combine raisins and water in a medium saucepan; bring to a boil, and boil about 3 minutes. Cool. (Do not drain.)

Cream shortening; gradually add sugar, beating at medium speed of an electric mixer until light and fluffy. Add eggs; beat well. Stir in raisins (with liquid) and vanilla.

Combine remaining ingredients except pecans; gradually add to raisin mixture, stirring after each addition. Stir in pecans.

Drop dough by teaspoonfuls 2 inches apart onto well-greased cookie sheets. Bake at 375° for 10 to 12 minutes or until browned. Cool on wire racks. (Cookies will be soft.) Yield: 5 dozen.

FRUITCAKE COOKIES

2 (8-ounce) packages yellow candied
  pineapple, chopped
1 (8-ounce) package red candied
  cherries, chopped
1 (8-ounce) package green candied
  cherries, chopped
2 cups golden raisins
4 cups chopped pecans or walnuts
3½ cups all-purpose flour, divided
½ cup butter or margarine, softened
1 cup firmly packed brown sugar
4 eggs, separated
1 tablespoon baking soda
3 tablespoons milk
¼ cup brandy
1 teaspoon ground cinnamon
1 teaspoon ground nutmeg

Combine first 5 ingredients; dredge with 1 cup flour, stirring well. Set aside.

Cream butter; gradually add sugar, beating well at medium speed of an electric mixer. Add egg yolks, mixing well.

Dissolve soda in milk; add to creamed mixture. Add brandy, spices, and remaining 2½ cups flour, mixing well.

Beat egg whites (at room temperature) until stiff; fold into batter. Fold in fruit mixture.

Drop dough by rounded teaspoonfuls onto greased cookie sheets. Bake at 325° for 12 to 15 minutes. Cool on wire racks. Yield: about 10 dozen.

FROSTED PUMPKIN-WALNUT COOKIES

½ cup butter or margarine, softened
1½ cups firmly packed brown sugar
2 eggs
1 cup cooked, mashed pumpkin
½ teaspoon lemon extract
½ teaspoon vanilla extract
2½ cups all-purpose flour
1 tablespoon baking powder
½ teaspoon salt
2 teaspoons pumpkin pie spice
1 cup chopped walnuts
Maple Frosting

Cream butter; gradually add brown sugar, beating well at medium speed of an electric mixer. Add eggs, one at a time, beating after each addition. Stir in pumpkin and flavorings.

Combine flour, baking powder, salt, and pumpkin pie spice. Gradually add to creamed mixture, mixing well. Stir in walnuts.

Drop dough by teaspoonfuls 2 inches apart onto greased cookie sheets. Bake at 375° for 12 minutes. Cool on wire racks. Frost with Maple Frosting. Yield: 7½ dozen.

Maple Frosting

¼ cup butter or margarine, softened
2¼ cups sifted powdered sugar
2 tablespoons milk
¾ teaspoon maple extract

Cream butter; gradually add 1 cup powdered sugar, beating well at medium speed of an electric mixer. Add remaining sugar alternately with milk, beating until smooth enough to spread. Add maple extract, and beat well. Yield: about 1 cup.

Bar Cookies

You'll find bar cookies easy to make. After the dough is mixed, it's simply spread in the pan and baked. Once cool, cut cookies into bars, squares, or triangles. Be sure to bake them in the size pan indicated; otherwise, the baking time and texture of the cookie may be affected.

Bar cookies can have either a cake-like or a fudge-like texture, depending on the proportion of shortening to flour used. The most famous of all bar cookies, brownies, leads this section. The most familiar plain chocolate type is here, but so too are many interesting variations.

BROWNIE MIX

7 cups sugar
4 cups all-purpose flour
2½ cups cocoa
1 tablespoon plus 1 teaspoon baking powder
1 tablespoon salt
2 cups shortening

Combine first 5 ingredients; stir well. Cut in shortening with pastry blender until mixture resembles coarse meal. Place in an airtight container; store in a cool, dry place or in refrigerator up to 6 weeks. Yield: 14 cups.

Quick and Easy Brownies

3 cups Brownie Mix
½ cup chopped pecans
3 eggs, beaten
1½ teaspoons vanilla extract

Combine all ingredients, stirring until blended. Spoon into a greased and floured 8-inch square pan. Bake at 350° for 35 to 40 minutes. Cool and cut into squares. Yield: 16 brownies.

EASY FROSTED BROWNIES

(pictured on page 146)

½ cup sugar
⅓ cup butter or margarine
2 tablespoons water
1 (6-ounce) package semisweet chocolate morsels
1 teaspoon vanilla extract
2 eggs
¾ cup all-purpose flour
¼ teaspoon baking soda
¼ teaspoon salt
1 cup chopped pecans or walnuts
1 (6-ounce) package semisweet chocolate morsels (optional)
½ cup chopped pecans or walnuts (optional)

Combine sugar, butter, and water in a medium saucepan; cook over high heat, stirring frequently, until mixture comes to a boil. Remove from heat. Add 1 package chocolate morsels and vanilla, stirring until chocolate melts. Add eggs, one at a time, beating well after each addition. Combine flour, soda, and salt; stir dry ingredients and 1 cup pecans into chocolate mixture.

Pour batter into a greased and floured 9-inch square pan. Bake at 325° for 30 minutes. Cool on wire rack. Cut into squares and serve plain, or sprinkle 1 package chocolate morsels over hot brownies, if desired. Let stand until morsels are softened; then spread evenly over brownies with a spatula. Sprinkle ½ cup pecans on top, if desired. Let cool, and cut into squares. Yield: 3 dozen.

FROSTED FUDGE BROWNIES

1 cup shortening
4 (1-ounce) squares unsweetened chocolate
2 cups sugar
4 eggs, beaten
1 teaspoon vanilla extract
1½ cups all-purpose flour
½ teaspoon salt
1 cup chopped pecans
Frosting (recipe follows)

Combine shortening and chocolate in top of a double boiler; bring water to a boil. Reduce heat to low; cook until chocolate melts. Add sugar, stirring well. Add eggs and vanilla; stir well. Stir in flour and salt, and mix thoroughly. Remove chocolate mixture from heat, and stir in pecans.

Spread batter into a well-greased 13- x 9- x 2-inch pan. Bake at 400° for 20 minutes. Cool; spread with frosting. Cut into squares. Store in refrigerator. Yield: about 3 dozen.

Frosting

2 (1-ounce) squares unsweetened chocolate
3 tablespoons boiling water
1 tablespoon butter or margarine
3½ cups sifted powdered sugar
½ teaspoon vanilla extract
1 egg

Combine chocolate and boiling water, stirring until chocolate melts. Blend in butter. Stir powdered sugar and vanilla into mixture; add egg, and beat until blended. Yield: enough for 3 dozen brownies.

1. *Melt unsweetened chocolate and butter in a small, heavy saucepan.*

2. *Add chocolate mixture to brownie batter, and bake as directed.*

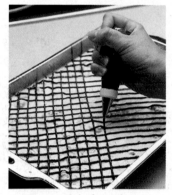

3. *Spread Crème de Menthe Frosting over brownie layer.*

4. *Pipe or drizzle melted chocolate across the top, and cut into bars.*

Brownies aren't just for kids. Crème de Menthe Brownie Bars dress plain brownies for an elegant party.

CRÈME DE MENTHE BROWNIE BARS

4 (1-ounce) squares unsweetened chocolate
1 cup butter or margarine
4 eggs
2 cups sugar
1 cup all-purpose flour
½ teaspoon salt
1 teaspoon vanilla extract
Crème de Menthe Frosting
½ cup semisweet chocolate morsels, melted

Combine unsweetened chocolate and butter in a small, heavy saucepan; cook over low heat, stirring constantly, until melted. Let stand 10 minutes.

Beat eggs at medium speed of an electric mixer until thick and lemon colored; gradually add sugar, beating well. Add flour, salt, vanilla, and chocolate mixture; beat at low speed 1 minute.

Spoon mixture into a lightly greased and floured 13- x 9- x 2-inch pan. Bake at 350° for 25 to 30 minutes or until a wooden pick inserted in center comes out clean. Cool 10 minutes; spread Crème de Menthe Frosting over top. Chill at least 4 hours.

Drizzle melted chocolate over frosting, or pipe in desired design using metal tip No. 3 or 4. Cut into bars immediately. Remove from pan, and chill at least 1 hour. Store in an airtight container in refrigerator. Yield: 4 dozen.

Crème de Menthe Frosting

4 cups sifted powdered sugar
½ cup butter or margarine, softened
¼ cup half-and-half
¼ cup green crème de menthe
1 cup finely chopped walnuts

Combine all ingredients except walnuts in a mixing bowl; beat at high speed of an electric mixer until smooth. Stir in walnuts. Yield: enough for 4 dozen bars.

CREAM CHEESE SWIRL BROWNIES

1 (4-ounce) package sweet baking chocolate
3 tablespoons butter or margarine
2 tablespoons butter or margarine, softened
1 (3-ounce) package cream cheese, softened
¼ cup sugar
1 egg
1 tablespoon all-purpose flour
½ teaspoon vanilla extract
2 eggs
¾ cup sugar
½ cup all-purpose flour
½ teaspoon baking powder
¼ teaspoon salt
1 teaspoon vanilla extract
¼ teaspoon almond extract
½ cup chopped pecans or walnuts

Combine chocolate and 3 tablespoons butter in top of a double boiler; bring water to a boil. Reduce heat to low; cook until chocolate melts. Set aside to cool.

Combine 2 tablespoons butter and cream cheese, creaming until light and fluffy. Gradually add ¼ cup sugar, beating until light and fluffy. Stir in 1 egg, 1 tablespoon flour, and ½ teaspoon vanilla. Set aside.

Beat 2 eggs at medium speed of an electric mixer until thick and lemon colored. Gradually add ¾ cup sugar, beating well. Combine ½ cup flour, baking powder, and salt; add to egg mixture, mixing well. Stir in cooled chocolate, flavorings, and pecans.

Pour half of chocolate batter into a greased 8-inch square pan. Spread with cheese mixture; top with remaining chocolate batter. Cut through mixture in pan with a knife to create a marbled effect. Bake at 350° for 35 to 40 minutes. Cool on wire rack; cut into squares. Yield: 16 brownies.

BLONDE CHOCOLATE CHIP BROWNIES

⅓ cup butter or margarine, softened
1 cup firmly packed brown sugar
1 egg
1 teaspoon vanilla extract
1 cup all-purpose flour
¼ teaspoon baking soda
¼ teaspoon salt
½ cup semisweet chocolate morsels
½ cup chopped pecans

Cream butter; gradually add brown sugar, beating well at medium speed of an electric mixer. Add egg and vanilla; beat well.

Combine flour, soda, and salt; add to creamed mixture, and mix well. Stir in chocolate morsels and pecans. Spread mixture into a greased 8-inch square pan. Bake at 350° for 25 to 30 minutes. Cool and cut into squares. Yield: 16 brownies.

CHOCO-CRUMBLE SQUARES

1½ cups all-purpose flour
¾ cup firmly packed brown sugar
¼ teaspoon salt
½ cup butter or margarine, softened
1 (6-ounce) package semisweet chocolate morsels
1 cup peanut butter

Combine flour, sugar, and salt; cut in butter with a pastry blender until mixture resembles coarse meal. Pat mixture into an ungreased 13- x 9- x 2-inch pan. Bake at 375° for 10 minutes.

Combine chocolate morsels and peanut butter in a small saucepan; cook over low heat, stirring constantly, until chocolate melts. Spread over crust; chill until firm. Cut into squares. Store in refrigerator, and serve chilled. Yield: about 2½ dozen.

DATE SQUARES

1½ cups regular oats, uncooked
1½ cups all-purpose flour
¼ teaspoon baking soda
¼ teaspoon salt
1 cup firmly packed brown sugar
¾ cup shortening
2 (8-ounce) packages whole pitted dates
1 cup water
½ cup sugar

Combine first 5 ingredients in a medium bowl. Cut in shortening with pastry blender until mixture resembles coarse meal. Reserve 1 cup crumb mixture for topping. Press remaining mixture into an ungreased 13- x 9- x 2-inch pan.

Chop dates. Combine dates, water, and sugar in a saucepan. Bring to a boil; reduce heat, and simmer 1 minute, stirring constantly. Spread date mixture over crumb mixture. Sprinkle with reserved 1 cup crumb mixture. Bake at 350° for 25 to 30 minutes. Cool and cut into squares. Yield: 4 dozen.

SHORTBREAD

1 cup butter, softened
½ cup sifted powdered sugar
2 cups all-purpose flour
Sugar

Cream butter; gradually add powdered sugar, beating until light and fluffy. Stir in flour. (Mixture will be stiff.) Press into a 15- x 10- x 1-inch jellyroll pan; prick all over with a fork. Chill 30 minutes.

Bake at 375° for 5 minutes; reduce heat to 300°, and bake an additional 20 minutes or until golden brown.

Cut into squares or diamond shapes while warm, and sprinkle with sugar. Yield: 6 dozen.

BLACKBERRY JAM BARS

¼ cup plus 3 tablespoons butter
  or margarine, softened
½ cup firmly packed brown
  sugar
1 cup all-purpose flour
¼ teaspoon baking soda
¼ teaspoon salt
1 cup quick-cooking oats,
  uncooked
¾ cup blackberry jam

Cream butter; gradually add sugar, beating well at medium speed of an electric mixer. Combine flour, soda, and salt; add to creamed mixture, mixing well. Stir in oats.

Press half of mixture into a lightly greased 8-inch square pan. Top mixture with jam, spreading to within ¼-inch of edge. Press remaining crumb mixture firmly on top. Bake at 400° for 30 minutes. Cool and cut into bars. Yield: about 2 dozen.

□ *Microwave Directions:* Cream butter; gradually add sugar, beating well at medium speed of an electric mixer. Combine flour, soda, and salt; add flour mixture to creamed mixture, mixing well. Stir in oats.

Press half of mixture into a lightly greased 8-inch square baking dish. Shield corners of dish with triangles of foil, keeping foil smooth and close to dish. Microwave at MEDIUM (50% power) for 5 to 7 minutes or until firm, rotating dish a quarter-turn at 2-minute intervals. Top with jam, spreading to within ¼-inch of edge. Press remaining crumb mixture firmly on top.

Microwave, with edges shielded, at MEDIUM for 11 to 13 minutes or until firm, rotating dish a quarter-turn at 2-minute intervals. (Do not overcook; mixture will firm up as it cools.) Cool and cut into bars.

PECAN BARS

1¾ cups all-purpose flour
⅓ cup firmly packed brown sugar
¾ cup butter or margarine
1 cup firmly packed brown sugar
4 eggs
1 cup dark corn syrup
¼ cup butter or margarine, melted
⅛ teaspoon salt
1¼ cups chopped pecans

Combine flour and ⅓ cup brown sugar. Cut in ¾ cup butter with pastry blender until mixture resembles coarse meal. Press mixture evenly into a greased 13- x 9- x 2-inch pan. Bake at 350° for 15 to 17 minutes.

Combine 1 cup brown sugar and remaining ingredients except pecans, beating well. Stir in pecans. Pour filling over prepared crust. Bake at 350° for 35 to 40 minutes or until firm. Let cool, and cut into bars. Yield: about 2½ dozen.

NUTTY APRICOT BARS

2 (6-ounce) packages dried apricots
¾ cup sugar
¾ cup butter or margarine, softened
1 cup sugar
2 cups all-purpose flour
½ teaspoon baking soda
¼ teaspoon salt
1 (3-ounce) can flaked coconut
½ cup chopped pecans or walnuts

Cover apricots with water, and bring to a boil; reduce heat, and simmer, uncovered, 15 minutes or until tender. Drain, reserving ¼ cup liquid. Coarsely chop apricots, and set aside. Combine reserved apricot liquid and ¾ cup sugar in a saucepan; simmer 5 minutes. Stir in chopped apricots.

Cream butter; gradually add 1 cup sugar, beating at medium speed of an electric mixer until light and fluffy. Combine flour, baking soda, and salt;

add floured mixture to creamed mixture, mixing well (mixture will be crumbly). Stir in coconut and pecans. Pat about three-fourths of coconut mixture into an ungreased 13- x 9- x 2-inch pan. Bake at 350° for 10 minutes.

Spread apricot mixture evenly over crust, spreading to within ¼ inch from edge of pan. Sprinkle with remaining coconut mixture. Bake an additional 30 minutes. Let cool in pan; chill. Cut into bars. Store in refrigerator. Yield: about 4 dozen.

COCONUT GRANOLA BARS

2¼ cups quick-cooking oats,
  uncooked
1 cup flaked coconut
¼ cup wheat germ
¼ cup plus 2 tablespoons butter or
  margarine
¼ cup firmly packed brown sugar
½ cup honey
½ cup peanut butter
1½ teaspoons vanilla extract
½ cup chopped unsalted peanuts
½ cup raisins

Combine oats, coconut, and wheat germ in a greased 9-inch square pan. Bake at 325° for 25 minutes, stirring occasionally. Set aside.

Combine butter, sugar, and honey in a medium saucepan; cook over medium heat, stirring occasionally, until butter melts and sugar dissolves. Remove from heat, and add peanut butter and vanilla, stirring until peanut butter melts. Pour over oat mixture. Add peanuts and raisins, and stir well. (Mixture will seem dry at first; continue stirring until moist.)

Press mixture firmly into pan with greased fingertips. Bake at 350° for 12 minutes. Cool on a wire rack. Cut into bars. Yield: 2 dozen.

LEMON BARS

2½ cups all-purpose flour, divided
½ cup sifted powdered sugar
¾ cup butter or margarine
½ teaspoon baking powder
4 eggs, beaten
2 cups sugar
½ teaspoon grated lemon rind
   (optional)
⅓ cup lemon juice
Powdered sugar

Combine 2 cups flour and ½ cup powdered sugar. Cut butter into flour mixture with a pastry blender until mixture resembles coarse meal.

Spoon flour mixture into an ungreased 13- x 9- x 2-inch pan; press firmly and evenly into pan using fingertips. Bake at 350° for 20 to 25 minutes or until crust is lightly browned.

Combine remaining ½ cup flour and baking powder; set aside. Combine eggs, 2 cups sugar, lemon rind, if desired, and lemon juice; stir well. Stir dry ingredients into egg mixture, and pour over baked crust.

Bake at 350° for 25 minutes or until lightly browned and set. Cool on a wire rack. Dust lightly with powdered sugar,

and cut into bars. Yield: about 2 dozen.

Lime Bars: Substitute lime juice and rind for lemon juice and rind.

PEANUT BUTTER AND FUDGE CRUNCH BARS

1 cup peanut butter morsels
½ cup light corn syrup
2 tablespoons butter or margarine
4 cups crisp rice cereal
1 (12-ounce) package semisweet
   chocolate morsels
¼ cup butter or margarine
1 cup sifted powdered sugar
2 tablespoons milk
½ teaspoon vanilla extract

Combine peanut butter morsels, corn syrup, and 2 tablespoons butter in top of a double boiler; bring water to a boil. Cook over hot water until morsels melt; stir well. Add cereal, and stir well. Press half the mixture into a buttered 12- x 8- x 2-inch baking dish, and chill while preparing chocolate layer. Set remaining cereal mixture aside.

Combine chocolate morsels and ¼

cup butter in top of a double boiler; bring water to a boil. Cook mixture over hot water until chocolate melts; stir well. Add powdered sugar, milk, and vanilla extract, stirring until well blended. Spread chocolate mixture over chilled layer. Spread remaining cereal mixture over chocolate layer; press layered mixture firmly. Chill until set. Cut into bars. Yield: 2 dozen.

☐ *Microwave Directions:* Combine peanut butter morsels, corn syrup, and 2 tablespoons butter in a large bowl. Microwave at HIGH for 1½ to 2 minutes or until morsels begin to melt. Stir until morsels melt. Add cereal, and stir well. Press half the mixture into a buttered 12- x 8- x 2-inch baking dish, and chill while preparing chocolate layer. Set remaining cereal mixture aside.

Place chocolate morsels and ¼ cup butter in a 1-quart casserole. Microwave at HIGH for 1½ to 2 minutes or until morsels begin to melt. Stir until morsels melt. Add powdered sugar, milk, and vanilla, stirring until well blended. Spread chocolate mixture over chilled layer. Spread remaining cereal mixture over chocolate layer; press firmly. Chill until set. Cut into bars.

Refrigerator Cookies

Crisp and thin, almost like rolled cookies in texture, refrigerator cookies are often classified as a make-ahead cookie. The dough is rolled into a log and chilled for up to 7 days. When it's baking time, just slice the dough directly from the refrigerator, and bake only the number of cookies you want. Return the remaining dough to the refrigerator or freezer for future use. See each recipe for specific directions.

CHOCOLATE-PEANUT BUTTER CUPS

1 (15-ounce) roll refrigerated
   ready-to-slice peanut butter cookie
   dough
48 miniature peanut butter cup
   candies

Slice cookie dough into ¾-inch slices. Cut each slice into quarters. Place each quarter into a lightly greased 1¾-inch

muffin cup. No shaping is necessary. Bake at 350° for 8 to 10 minutes (dough will rise during baking).

Remove muffin pan from oven, and immediately press a miniature peanut butter cup gently and evenly into each cookie. Cool cookies before removing from pans. Refrigerate cookie cups until firm. Yield: 4 dozen.

VANILLA SLICE-AND-BAKE COOKIES

½ cup butter or margarine, softened
1 cup sugar
1 egg
2 teaspoons vanilla extract
1¾ cups all-purpose flour
½ teaspoon baking soda
¼ teaspoon salt
½ cup chopped pecans

Cream butter; gradually add sugar, beating well at medium speed of an electric mixer. Add egg and vanilla; beat well. Combine flour, soda, and salt; add to creamed mixture, beating well. Stir in pecans. Shape dough into two 12-inch rolls; wrap in wax paper, and chill at least 2 hours.

Unwrap rolls, and cut into ¼-inch slices; place on ungreased cookie sheets. Bake at 350° for 10 to 12 minutes. Cool slightly on cookie sheets; remove to wire racks to cool completely. Yield: about 7 dozen.

Slice of Spice Cookies: Prepare Vanilla Slice-And-Bake Cookies, substituting firmly packed brown sugar for granulated sugar. Combine ¼ cup granulated sugar and 2 teaspoons ground cinnamon; dip each cookie slice (on both sides) in mixture before baking.

Note: Dough may be frozen up to 3 months. Slice dough while frozen, and bake as directed.

DOUBLE PEANUT BUTTER COOKIES

1¾ cups all-purpose flour
½ teaspoon baking soda
¼ teaspoon salt
½ cup sugar
½ cup shortening
½ cup creamy peanut butter
¼ cup light corn syrup
1 tablespoon milk
¼ cup creamy peanut butter

Combine flour, soda, salt, and sugar; cut in shortening and ½ cup peanut butter with pastry blender until mixture resembles coarse meal. Stir in corn syrup and milk. Shape dough into a 12-inch roll; wrap in wax paper, and chill at least 2 hours.

Unwrap roll, and cut into ¼-inch slices; place half of slices on ungreased cookie sheets. Spread each with ½ teaspoon peanut butter. Top with remaining cookie slices, and seal edges with a fork. Bake at 350° for 10 to 12 minutes. Cool on wire racks. Yield: about 2 dozen.

Note: Dough may be frozen up to 3 months. Slice dough while frozen; let thaw slightly. Assemble and bake as directed.

SLICE-AND-BAKE OATMEAL COOKIES

1½ cups all-purpose flour
1 teaspoon baking soda
½ teaspoon salt
1 cup shortening
1 cup sugar
1 cup firmly packed brown sugar
2 eggs
1 teaspoon vanilla extract
3 cups quick-cooking oats, uncooked
½ cup chopped pecans

Combine flour, soda, and salt; stir well, and set aside.

Cream shortening; gradually add sugars, beating well at medium speed of an electric mixer; add eggs and vanilla, mixing well. Add flour mixture, mixing well. Stir in oats and pecans. Shape dough into two 12-inch rolls; wrap in wax paper, and chill at least 6 hours.

Unwrap rolls, and cut into ¼-inch slices; place on ungreased cookie sheets. Bake at 375° for 8 to 10 minutes or until lightly browned. Cool on wire racks. Yield: about 7 dozen.

Note: Dough may be frozen up to 3 months. Slice dough while frozen, and bake at 375° for 12 minutes.

DATE PINWHEEL COOKIES

(pictured on page 146)

½ cup shortening
1 cup firmly packed dark brown sugar
1 egg
2 cups all-purpose flour
½ teaspoon baking soda
¼ teaspoon salt
1 teaspoon ground cinnamon
Filling (recipe follows)

Cream shortening; gradually add sugar, beating well at medium speed of an electric mixer. Add egg, and beat well. Combine flour, soda, salt, and cinnamon; gradually add to creamed mixture, mixing well. Shape dough into a ball. (Dough will be stiff.)

Place dough on a lightly floured surface; roll into a 16- x 8-inch rectangle. Spread filling over dough, leaving a ½-inch margin on all sides. Starting at long side, carefully roll dough, jellyroll fashion; pinch seam and ends of roll to seal. Wrap dough in wax paper, and chill at least 1 hour.

Unwrap roll, and cut into ¼-inch slices. Place 1 inch apart on greased cookie sheets. Bake at 350° for 12 to 15 minutes. Cool on wire racks. Yield: about 4 dozen.

Filling

1 (8-ounce) package whole pitted dates, chopped
½ cup sugar
¼ cup water
1 cup finely chopped pecans

Combine dates, sugar, and water in a medium saucepan. Cook over medium heat 3 to 5 minutes or until thickened, stirring constantly. Remove filling from heat; stir in pecans. Let cool. Yield: about 1¾ cups.

FILLED LEMON COOKIES

2 cups butter or margarine, softened
1 cup sifted powdered sugar
4 cups all-purpose flour
¼ teaspoon salt
2 teaspoons lemon extract
Filling (recipe follows)
Additional powdered sugar

Cream butter; gradually add 1 cup powdered sugar, beating well at medium speed of an electric mixer.

Combine flour and salt; add to creamed mixture, beating well. Stir in lemon extract. Flour hands, and shape dough into two 16-inch rolls; wrap in wax paper, and chill several hours.

Unwrap rolls, and cut into ¼-inch slices; place on ungreased cookie sheets. Bake at 400° for 8 minutes or until browned. Cool on wire racks.

Spoon filling on bottom side of half the cookies, spreading evenly. Place a second cookie on top of filling, top side up, and sprinkle lightly with powdered sugar. Yield: 5 dozen.

Filling

1 egg, beaten
⅔ cup sugar
2 tablespoons butter or margarine, softened
1½ teaspoons grated lemon rind
3 tablespoons lemon juice
1 teaspoon cornstarch

Combine all ingredients in top of a double boiler, stirring until blended. Bring water to a boil. Reduce heat to low; cook, stirring constantly, until thickened and smooth. Chill about 1 hour. Yield: about ¾ cup.

CHOCOLATE SPIDERWEB SNAPS

1¼ cups shortening
2 cups sugar
4 (1-ounce) squares unsweetened chocolate, melted
2 eggs
⅓ cup light corn syrup
2½ tablespoons water
1 teaspoon vanilla extract
4 cups all-purpose flour
2 teaspoons baking soda
½ teaspoon salt
Frosting (recipe follows)
½ cup semisweet chocolate morsels

Cream shortening; gradually add sugar, beating at medium speed of an electric mixer until light and fluffy. Add melted chocolate, eggs, corn syrup, water, and vanilla; mix well. Combine flour, soda, and salt; add to creamed mixture, beating just until blended. Shape dough into two 12-inch rolls; wrap in wax paper. Chill several hours.

Unwrap rolls, and cut into ¼-inch slices; place on ungreased cookie sheets. Bake at 350° for 10 to 12 minutes. Cool on cookie sheets 5 minutes. Remove to wire racks to cool completely. Spread frosting over cookies to within ⅛ inch of edge; let stand until frosting sets.

Place chocolate morsels in top of a double boiler; bring water to a boil. Reduce heat to low; cook until chocolate melts. Let stand until almost cool but not set. Spoon melted chocolate into decorating bag fitted with metal tip No. 2.

For round pattern, pipe chocolate in 5 or 6 circles around top of cookie. Pull the point of a wooden pick across chocolate circles from the center to the outer edge. Repeat 8 or 10 times, spacing evenly across top of cookie.

For linear pattern, pipe chocolate in parallel lines, about ¼-inch apart, across top of cookie. Pull the point of a wooden pick diagonally across lines. Let stand at room temperature until chocolate is firm. Yield: 6 dozen.

Frosting

6 cups sifted powdered sugar
About 6 tablespoons warm water
Paste food coloring

Combine sugar and enough water to make frosting a spreading consistency, stirring well. Color as desired with a very small amount of paste food coloring. Yield: 1¾ cups.

Note: Dough may be frozen up to 3 months. Slice dough while frozen, and bake as directed.

Rolled Cookies

Rolled cookies are prepared from dough that has been rolled to a designated thickness and cut with cookie cutters. Cut and baked plain, sprinkled with decorator candies before baking, or spread with frosting afterward, rolled cookies are favorites any time of the year, but they're most popular around the holidays.

To be rolled and shaped properly, the dough needs to be firmer than most. To get a neat roll, many recipes call for chilling the dough before rolling. Large amounts of dough can be divided so you can work with one portion while the rest remains chilled. If your dough still seems too soft to roll after chilling, roll it directly onto the cookie sheet, cut with cutters, and peel away the scraps. This eliminates transferring cut cookies to cookie sheets, a task that can be virtually impossible when the dough is soft.

When you're in a hurry and don't have time to cut the dough with cookie cutters, cut the dough into squares or diamonds using a sharp knife or fluted pastry wheel. This eliminates most scraps, too. When you have a little extra time but lack the cutter shape you want, cut your own patterns from cardboard or sturdy construction paper. Lay the pattern on the rolled dough, and trim around it with a sharp knife.

ROLLED SUGAR COOKIES

3 cups all-purpose flour
2 teaspoons baking powder
¾ teaspoon baking soda
½ teaspoon ground nutmeg
1 cup shortening
2 eggs, beaten
1 cup sugar
¼ cup milk
1 teaspoon vanilla extract

Combine flour, baking powder, soda, and nutmeg; cut in shortening with a pastry blender until mixture resembles coarse meal.

Combine eggs, sugar, milk, and vanilla; stir well, and pour into crumb mixture. Stir with a fork until dry ingredients are moistened. Shape dough into a ball, and chill at least 1 hour.

Divide dough in half; store 1 portion in refrigerator. Roll dough to ⅛-inch thickness on a lightly floured surface. Cut with a 3-inch cookie cutter, and place on lightly greased cookie sheets.

Bake at 375° for 8 minutes or until edges are lightly browned. Cool on wire racks. Repeat procedure with remaining dough. Yield: 6 dozen.

JAM KOLACHES

½ cup butter or margarine, softened
1 (3-ounce) package cream cheese, softened
1¼ cups all-purpose flour
About ½ cup strawberry jam
¼ cup sifted powdered sugar

Cream butter and cream cheese, beating at medium speed of an electric mixer until light and fluffy. Add flour to creamed mixture, mixing well.

Roll dough to ⅛-inch thickness on a lightly floured surface; cut into rounds with a 2½-inch cookie cutter. Place on lightly greased cookie sheets. Spoon ¼ teaspoon jam on each cookie; fold opposite sides to center, slightly overlapping edges. Bake at 375° for 15 minutes. Cool on wire racks, and sprinkle with powdered sugar. Yield: about 3½ dozen.

SOUR CREAM COOKIES

1 cup shortening
1 cup sugar
1 egg
1 (8-ounce) carton commercial sour cream
1 teaspoon vanilla extract
½ teaspoon almond extract
4¾ cups all-purpose flour
1 teaspoon baking powder
1 teaspoon baking soda
¼ teaspoon salt
Red and green decorator sugar crystals (optional)

Cream shortening; gradually add sugar, beating at medium speed of an electric mixer until light and fluffy. Add egg, and beat well. Add sour cream and flavorings, mixing well. Combine flour, baking powder, soda, and salt; add to creamed mixture, beating well. Chill dough at least 1 hour.

Work with one-fourth of dough at a time, and store remainder in refrigerator. Roll dough to ⅛-inch thickness on a

lightly floured surface. Cut with a 3-inch cookie cutter, and place on ungreased cookie sheets. Sprinkle with sugar crystals, if desired.

Bake at 350° for 10 to 12 minutes or until lightly browned. Cool on wire racks. Repeat procedure with remaining dough. Yield: about 7 dozen.

MORAVIAN SUGAR COOKIES

½ cup butter, softened
1 cup sugar
1 egg
½ teaspoon vanilla extract
2¼ to 2½ cups all-purpose flour
½ teaspoon baking soda
½ teaspoon salt
¼ cup buttermilk
Superfine sugar

Cream butter; gradually add sugar, beating well at medium speed of an electric mixer. Add egg and vanilla; beat well. Combine 2¼ cups flour, soda, and salt; add to creamed mixture alternately with buttermilk, mixing well. Add remaining ¼ cup flour if dough seems very sticky. Cover and chill 8 hours.

Work with one-fourth of dough at a time, and store remainder in refrigerator. Place stockinette cover on rolling pin; flour well. Roll dough to 1/16-inch thickness on a lightly floured pastry cloth. Cut with a 3-inch round cutter, and carefully place on lightly greased cookie sheets.

Bake at 375° for 6 to 8 minutes or just until cookies begin to brown around edges. Cool slightly on cookie sheets, and sprinkle with superfine sugar. Remove cookies to wire racks, and cool completely. Repeat procedure with remaining dough. Store in airtight containers. Yield: about 9 dozen.

Old-Fashioned Teacakes: Roll dough to ¼-inch thickness. Cut as directed above. Bake at 375° for 8 to 10 minutes. Makes about 2 dozen.

PAINTED SUGAR COOKIES

Forego the usual sugar sprinkles to decorate the tops of rolled sugar cookies, and try painting them with Egg Yolk Paint. This cookie recipe works particularly well for the technique since it has no leavening added, and the cookies don't rise as much as some. Rising could alter the look of the design you paint before baking.

½ cup butter or margarine, softened
½ cup shortening
1 cup sifted powdered sugar
1 egg
1 teaspoon vanilla extract
2½ cups all-purpose flour
½ teaspoon salt
Egg Yolk Paint

Cream butter and shortening; gradually add sugar, beating well at medium speed of an electric mixer. Add egg and vanilla, beating well.

Combine flour and salt; stir into creamed mixture. Chill dough at least 1 hour.

Divide dough in half; store 1 portion in refrigerator. Roll dough to ⅛-inch thickness on a lightly floured surface. Cut with a 2-inch cookie cutter, and place on ungreased cookie sheets. Using a small paintbrush, paint assorted designs on cookies with Egg Yolk Paint.

Bake at 375° for 9 to 10 minutes or until cookies are lightly browned. Cool on a wire rack. Repeat procedure with remaining dough. Yield: about 5½ dozen.

Egg Yolk Paint

1 egg yolk, beaten
¼ teaspoon water
Assorted colors of paste or liquid food coloring

Combine egg yolk and water; stir well. Divide mixture into several custard cups; tint as desired with food coloring. Keep paint covered until ready to use. If paint thickens, add a few drops of water, and stir well. Yield: 1½ tablespoons.

EDIBLE CRAFT DOUGH COOKIES

You might label our Edible Craft Dough Cookies "For Kids Only"—the dough looks and shapes remarkably like the colored craft dough that children often play with, but it's totally edible. Children can hand shape the dough much like they do craft dough, or they can roll and cut it with cookie cutters.

1 cup butter or margarine, softened
1 cup shortening
2½ cups sifted powdered sugar
6 hard-cooked egg yolks, mashed
2 teaspoons baking soda
2 teaspoons cream of tartar
1 tablespoon vanilla extract
5 cups all-purpose flour
Red, yellow, and green paste food coloring

Cream butter and shortening; gradually add sugar, beating well at medium speed of an electric mixer. Add egg yolks, soda, cream of tartar, and vanilla, beating well. Gradually add flour, mixing well.

Divide dough into 4 equal portions. Color one portion red, one yellow, one green, and leave remaining dough plain. Wrap each separately in plastic wrap, and chill at least 1 hour.

Hand shape cookies into desired designs, or roll dough to ¼-inch thickness on a lightly floured surface and cut with 2½-inch cookie cutters. Place on ungreased cookie sheets. Bake at 350° for 8 to 10 minutes. Let cool on cookie sheets 1 to 2 minutes; remove to wire racks and cool completely. Yield: about 5½ dozen.

GINGERBREAD MEN COOKIES

⅓ cup water
½ cup shortening
¼ cup butter or margarine
4½ cups all-purpose flour
2 teaspoons baking soda
Pinch of salt
1½ teaspoons ground ginger
1 teaspoon ground cinnamon
1½ cups molasses
Currants

Combine first 3 ingredients in a small saucepan. Cook over medium heat, stirring constantly, until shortening melts.

Combine flour, soda, salt, ginger, and cinnamon; add shortening mixture, stirring well. Stir in molasses; chill 8 hours.

Divide dough in half; store 1 portion in refrigerator. Roll dough to ¼-inch thickness on a lightly floured surface. Cut with a 5-inch gingerbread man cutter, and place on lightly greased cookie sheets. Press currants into dough for eyes, nose, and mouth.

Bake at 350° for 10 minutes. Cool cookies 2 minutes on cookie sheets; remove to wire racks, and cool completely. (Cookies will be soft.) Repeat procedure with remaining dough. Store in airtight containers. Yield: about 4 dozen.

To cool cookies: *Place on wire racks to keep bottoms from becoming soggy.*

DAINTY SANDWICH COOKIES

(pictured on page 146)

1 cup butter, softened
⅔ cup sugar
2 egg yolks
2½ cups all-purpose flour
¼ teaspoon salt
1 to 2 tablespoons powdered sugar
½ cup sugar
½ cup ground blanched almonds
2 egg whites
About 1½ cups raspberry preserves
Powdered sugar (optional)
½ cup semisweet chocolate morsels, melted

Cream butter; gradually add ⅔ cup sugar, beating at medium speed of an electric mixer until light and fluffy. Add egg yolks, one at a time, beating well. Combine flour and salt; add to creamed mixture, beating well. Shape dough into a ball; cover and chill at least 2 hours.

Divide dough in half; store 1 portion in refrigerator. Sift powdered sugar lightly over work surface. Roll half of dough to ⅛-inch thickness; cut with a 2½-inch round cutter. Roll remaining dough as before; cut with a 2½-inch doughnut cutter, reserving centers. Chill dough, if necessary.

Combine ½ cup sugar and almonds; mix well. Beat egg whites until frothy. Brush one side of all cookie cutouts with egg white, and coat with almond mixture; place coated side up on lightly greased cookie sheets. Bake at 375° for 8 to 10 minutes or until lightly browned. Cool on wire racks. Repeat procedure with remaining dough.

Raspberry Sandwich Cookies: Spread uncoated side of each solid cookie with a thin layer of raspberry preserves. (Cookies are very delicate and must be handled carefully.) Lightly dust almond side of doughnut-shaped cookies with powdered sugar, if desired; place sugar side up on top of raspberry filling. Yield: 2 dozen.

Chocolate Sandwich Cookies: Using half of reserved cookie centers, spread a thin layer of melted chocolate on side without almonds. Top with remaining cookie centers, almond side up. Drizzle tops of cookies with remaining chocolate, if desired. Yield: 1 dozen.

Hand-Shaped Cookies

Dough for these cookies is rolled into balls in the palms of your hands. They're either baked as balls or are further shaped into more intricate designs.

The dough for this type of cookie needs to be firmer than regular cookie dough so you can shape it in your hands without making a mess. If your dough seems too soft to shape, chill it in the refrigerator for one hour or more until it's firm enough to shape.

When shaping the cookies, take care to roll all the balls the same size so cookies will be uniform after baking. Many of these cookies spread as they bake so allow at least 2 inches between the cookies so they won't run together. Grease the pan only if directed.

DATE-NUT BALLS

1 (8-ounce) package whole pitted dates
¾ cup sugar
½ cup butter or margarine
2½ cups crisp rice cereal
1 cup chopped pecans
Flaked coconut or powdered sugar

Chop dates; combine dates, sugar, and butter in a medium saucepan. Bring to a boil; cook, stirring constantly, 1 minute. Stir in cereal and pecans; cool mixture to touch. Shape into 1-inch balls, and roll balls in coconut or powdered sugar. Yield: 4 dozen.

BOURBON BALLS

1 (12-ounce) package vanilla wafers, finely crushed
1 cup chopped pecans or walnuts
¾ cup sifted powdered sugar
2 tablespoons cocoa
2½ tablespoons light corn syrup
½ cup bourbon
Additional sifted powdered sugar

Combine vanilla wafers, pecans, powdered sugar, and cocoa in a large bowl; stir well.

Combine corn syrup and bourbon, stirring well. Pour bourbon mixture over wafer mixture; stir until blended. Shape into 1-inch balls; roll in additional powdered sugar. Yield: 4 dozen.

WEDDING COOKIES

1 cup plus 2 tablespoons all-purpose
  flour
⅛ teaspoon ground cinnamon
½ cup butter or margarine, softened
½ cup finely chopped pecans
¼ cup sifted powdered sugar
½ teaspoon vanilla extract
Powdered sugar

Combine flour and cinnamon in a large bowl. Add butter, pecans, ¼ cup powdered sugar, and vanilla; stir until well blended (mixture will be stiff).

Shape dough into 1-inch balls. Place on ungreased cookie sheets. Bake at 400° for 10 to 12 minutes. Remove to wire racks to cool slightly. Roll cookies in powdered sugar, and cool completely on wire racks. Yield: 2 dozen.

ANGEL COOKIES

1 cup shortening
½ cup sugar
½ cup firmly packed brown sugar
1 egg
2 cups all-purpose flour
1 teaspoon baking soda
1 teaspoon cream of tartar
1 teaspoon vanilla extract
Powdered sugar

Cream shortening; gradually add sugars, beating well at medium speed of an electric mixer. Add egg, and beat well. Combine flour, soda, and cream of tartar; gradually add dry ingredients to creamed mixture, mixing well. Add vanilla, and mix well.

Shape dough into 1-inch balls; roll in powdered sugar. Place on lightly greased cookie sheets. Bake at 275° for 10 to 12 minutes. Cool on wire racks. Yield: 4 dozen.

PEANUT BUTTER SNAPS

1 cup butter or margarine,
  softened
1 cup sugar
1 cup firmly packed brown
  sugar
2 eggs
2⅔ cups all-purpose flour
2 teaspoons baking soda
¼ teaspoon salt
⅔ cup peanut butter
2 teaspoons vanilla extract

Cream butter; gradually add sugars, beating well at medium speed of an electric mixer. Add eggs, mixing well.

Combine flour, soda, and salt; add to creamed mixture, and beat until smooth. Stir in peanut butter and vanilla; chill dough at least 1 hour.

Shape dough into 1-inch balls. Place on ungreased cookie sheets. Bake at 375° for 10 to 12 minutes. Let cookies cool slightly before removing from cookie sheets. Cool on wire racks. Yield: about 7 dozen.

MOLASSES SUGAR COOKIES

(pictured on page 146)

¾ cup shortening
1 cup sugar
1 egg
¼ cup molasses
2 cups all-purpose flour
2 teaspoons baking soda
¼ teaspoon salt
½ teaspoon ground cinnamon
½ teaspoon ground ginger
½ teaspoon ground cloves
Sugar

Cream shortening; gradually add 1 cup sugar, beating at medium speed of an electric mixer until light and fluffy. Add egg and molasses; mix well.

Combine flour, soda, salt, and spices; mix well. Add about one-fourth of dry mixture at a time to creamed mixture, mixing until smooth after each addition. Chill dough at least 1 hour.

Shape dough into 1-inch balls, and roll in sugar. Place 2 inches apart on ungreased cookie sheets. Bake at 375° for 10 minutes. (Tops will crack.) Cool on wire racks. Yield: 4½ dozen.

Gingersnaps: Prepare Molasses Sugar Cookies, omitting cloves, and increasing ground ginger to 1 tablespoon.

CHERRY NUT NUGGETS

1 cup shortening
1 (3-ounce) package cream cheese,
  softened
1 cup sugar
1 egg
1 teaspoon almond extract
2½ cups all-purpose flour
¼ teaspoon baking soda
½ teaspoon salt
1⅓ cups finely chopped pecans
Maraschino cherries, drained and
  halved

Cream shortening and cream cheese; gradually add sugar, beating at medium speed of an electric mixer until light and fluffy. Add egg and almond extract, beating well.

Combine flour, soda, and salt; stir flour mixture into creamed mixture. Chill dough at least 1 hour.

Shape dough into 1-inch balls. Roll in pecans, and place on ungreased cookie sheets. Gently press a cherry half into center of each cookie. Bake at 350° for 16 to 18 minutes. Cool on wire racks. Yield: 4½ dozen.

Pecan Nuggets: Prepare dough for Cherry Nut Nuggets. Do not roll balls in pecans; press a pecan half instead of cherry in center of each cookie.

THUMBPRINT COOKIES

1 cup butter or margarine,
  softened
⅔ cup sugar
2 egg yolks
½ teaspoon vanilla extract
2¼ cups all-purpose flour
¼ teaspoon salt
Chocolate Frosting or Powdered
  Sugar Glaze

Cream butter; gradually add sugar, beating at medium speed of an electric mixer until light and fluffy. Add egg yolks, one at a time, beating well after each addition. Stir in vanilla.

Combine flour and salt; add to creamed mixture, mixing well. Chill dough at least 1 hour.

Shape dough into 1-inch balls; place about 2 inches apart on ungreased cookie sheets. Press thumb in each cookie leaving an indention. Bake at 300° for 20 to 25 minutes; do not brown. Cool on wire racks. Spoon about ½ teaspoon Chocolate Frosting or Powdered Sugar Glaze in each cookie indention. Yield: 3½ dozen.

Chocolate Frosting

1 cup sugar
¼ cup cocoa
¼ cup milk
¼ cup butter or margarine
½ teaspoon vanilla extract

Combine first 3 ingredients in a saucepan. Bring to a boil; boil 1½ to 2 minutes, stirring constantly. Remove from heat; stir in butter and vanilla. Beat until mixture cools slightly. Yield: 1 cup.

Powdered Sugar Glaze

2 cups sifted powdered sugar
3 to 4 tablespoons milk
½ teaspoon vanilla extract
Few drops of desired food coloring

Combine all ingredients, and stir until smooth. Yield: 1 cup.

Note: One cup strawberry preserves may be substituted for frosting or glaze. If so, bake cookies 15 minutes. Spoon preserves into indentions, and bake an additional 5 minutes.

DEVILISH MARSHMALLOW COOKIES

½ cup shortening
1 cup sugar
2 eggs
1¾ cups all-purpose flour
1 teaspoon baking soda
¼ salt
½ cup cocoa
1 teaspoon vanilla extract
1 teaspoon butter flavoring
About 21 large marshmallows, cut in
  half
Frosting (recipe follows)

Cream shortening; gradually add sugar, beating well at medium speed of an electric mixer. Add eggs, one at a time, beating well after each addition.

Combine flour, soda, salt, and cocoa; add to creamed mixture, mixing well. Stir in flavorings. (Dough will be stiff.) Chill dough at least 30 minutes.

Shape dough into 1-inch balls; place on greased cookie sheets. Bake at 350° for 7 minutes. Place a marshmallow half on top of each cookie; bake an additional 2 minutes. Cool on wire racks, and spread frosting over tops. Yield: about 3½ dozen.

Frosting

½ cup semisweet chocolate morsels
¼ cup milk
2 tablespoons butter or margarine
2 cups sifted powdered sugar
Milk (optional)

Combine first 3 ingredients in a saucepan. Cook over low heat, stirring constantly, until chocolate melts. Add powdered sugar, and beat until smooth. Add additional milk to frosting mixture, if needed, for proper spreading consistency. Yield: 1 cup.

CHOCO-SURPRISE COOKIES

1 cup all-purpose flour
1 teaspoon baking powder
¾ to 1 teaspoon ground cinnamon
1 cup peanut butter
½ cup butter or margarine, softened
1 cup firmly packed brown sugar
2 eggs
2 (4¾-ounce) packages milk
  chocolate stars
Powdered sugar

Combine flour, baking powder, and cinnamon; set aside.

Combine peanut butter, butter, and brown sugar in a large mixing bowl; beat well at medium speed of an electric mixer. Add eggs, beating well. Gradually add dry ingredients, mixing well. Chill dough at least 30 minutes.

Shape 1 rounded teaspoon dough around each chocolate star; place on lightly greased cookie sheets. Bake at 350° for 9 to 11 minutes or until lightly browned. Cool slightly on wire racks; then roll in powdered sugar. Cool completely before storing. Yield: 7 dozen.

SNAPPIN' TURTLE COOKIES

½ cup butter or margarine, softened
½ cup firmly packed brown sugar
1 egg
1 egg, separated
1 teaspoon vanilla extract
1½ cups all-purpose flour
¼ teaspoon baking soda
¼ teaspoon salt
12½ dozen pecan halves
Frosting (recipe follows)

Cream butter; gradually add brown sugar, beating at medium speed of an electric mixer until light and fluffy. Add

1 egg, 1 egg yolk, and vanilla, beating until well blended.

Combine flour, soda, and salt; add to creamed mixture, mixing well. Chill dough at least 1 hour. Arrange pecan halves in groups of 5 on ungreased cookie sheets, resembling head and legs of turtles.

Shape dough into 1-inch balls, and dip bottoms in remaining egg white. Press gently onto pecans to resemble turtle bodies. Bake at 350° for 10 to 12 minutes. Cool on wire racks. Spread frosting on tops of cookies. Yield: 2½ dozen.

Frosting

2 (1-ounce) squares unsweetened chocolate
¼ cup milk
1 tablespoon butter or margarine
About 1¾ cups sifted powdered sugar

Combine chocolate, milk, and butter in a small saucepan; cook over low heat, stirring constantly, until chocolate melts. Remove from heat. Add powdered sugar; beat until smooth. Yield: about 1 cup.

Specially-Shaped Cookies

Sometimes a creative person wants to make more than just an ordinary cookie. With cookie guns, imprinted rolling pins, and shaping irons on the market, you can make cookies so special you'll hardly want to eat them. But don't resist the temptation to indulge.

When making cookies that require special tools use only recipes developed with that tool in mind, so the type of leavening and the consistency of the cookie dough will be appropriate.

Similiary, check each individual recipe as to the particular type of equipment required to make the recipe. In most cases, substitutions won't do. The equipment you'll use to make these cookies includes cookie guns, madeleine molds, pizzelle and rosette irons, and Springerle rolling pins. All of this equipment is usually standard stock at kitchen specialty shops or large department stores. Some foods related mail-order catalogues market these items as well.

MELT-AWAY BUTTER COOKIES

(pictured on page 146)

Melt-Away Butter Cookies call for a cookie gun to shape the dough. With a cookie gun, you can stamp out a wide variety of perfectly shaped cookies in a minimum of time, making this piece of equipment a practical investment for someone who does a lot of baking and entertaining.

You'll find both electric and hand-pump models of cookie guns available in most kitchen shops or department stores. Most are constructed so that you can make mints, cheese straws, and canapés as well as cookies. Since the models differ in construction, follow the specific manufacturer's directions for assembling and loading the gun.

1¼ cups butter, softened
¾ cup sifted powdered sugar
2½ cups all-purpose flour
½ teaspoon vanilla extract
½ teaspoon almond extract
Few drops of liquid food coloring (optional)

Cream butter; gradually add sugar, beating at medium speed of an electric mixer until light and fluffy. Add flour, and mix well. Stir in flavorings and food coloring, if desired.

Use a cookie gun to shape dough as desired, following the manufacturer's instructions. Place cookies on ungreased cookie sheets. Bake at 325° for 15 minutes. Cool on wire racks. Store in airtight containers, placing wax paper between each layer. Yield: about 7 dozen (2-inch) cookies.

Chocolate-tipped Butter Cookies: Melt together 1 (12-ounce) package semisweet chocolate morsels and 1 tablespoon shortening. Dip half of each prepared butter cookie in chocolate mixture. Roll chocolate-dipped portion in ½ cup finely chopped pecans. Place cookies on wire racks until chocolate is firm.

MADELEINES

2 eggs
⅛ teaspoon salt
⅓ cup sugar
½ cup all-purpose flour
1 teaspoon grated lemon rind
½ cup butter, melted and cooled
Powdered sugar

Beat eggs and salt at high speed of an electric mixer until foamy. Gradually add sugar; beat at high speed 15 minutes or until thick. Combine flour and lemon rind; fold in 2 tablespoons at a time. Fold in butter, 1 tablespoon at a time. Spoon 1 tablespoon batter into greased and floured madeleine molds. Bake at 400° for 8 to 10 minutes or until lightly browned. Cool in molds about 3 minutes. Remove from molds, and cool on a wire rack, flat side down. Sprinkle with powdered sugar. Yield: 2 dozen.

PIZZELLES

3 eggs
¾ cup sugar
¾ cup butter or margarine, softened
1 teaspoon vanilla extract
¼ teaspoon anise oil
1½ cups all-purpose flour
1 teaspoon baking powder
Vegetable oil

Beat eggs at medium speed of an electric mixer until foamy; gradually add sugar, beating until thick and lemon colored. Add butter, vanilla, and anise oil; mix well. Add flour and baking powder; beat until smooth.

Brush pizzelle iron lightly with oil; preheat iron over medium heat 2 minutes. Place 1 tablespoon batter in center of iron; close iron and cook 30 seconds on each side or until pizzelle is lightly browned. Repeat with remaining batter; cool on wire racks. Yield: 2½ dozen.

SPRINGERLE COOKIES

Spingerle is a particular kind of cookie that originated in Europe and is made with a special rolling pin having a carved design embedded in the surface. By rolling over the dough with this special pin, the design motif becomes imprinted on the dough.

In addition to its distinctive design, the Spingerle has a firm texture and a strong anise flavor that distinguishes it from other cookies. It is traditionally served at holidays and other special occasions.

When shaping Spingerles, first roll the dough with a regular rolling pin, then with the carved pin, pressing firmly to imprint the design. Cut the cookies into squares following the imprinted lines.

Use this recipe to make Springerle Cookies. It contains very little leavening, so the cookies won't rise too much and will keep their design during baking.

3 eggs
1⅓ cups sugar
1¼ teaspoons grated lemon rind
⅛ teaspoon baking powder
2¼ to 2½ cups all-purpose flour, divided
1¼ teaspoons anise seeds, crushed

Beat eggs at medium speed of an electric mixer until thick and lemon colored; gradually add sugar, and continue beating 5 minutes. Add lemon rind, baking powder, and enough flour to make a soft dough, beating well. Chill dough at least 3 hours.

Let dough stand at room temperature 15 minutes. Turn dough out onto a floured surface; roll dough to ¼-inch thickness using a regular rolling pin. Roll with a floured springerle rolling pin, pressing firmly to imprint dough. Cut cookie squares apart. Place cookies on a wire rack; cover with a paper towel, and let stand in a cool, dry place about 12 hours to set the design.

Sprinkle anise seeds onto well-greased cookie sheets. Top with cookies, design side up. Bake at 300° for 15 minutes or until light yellow, but not golden. Cool on wire racks. Yield: 4 dozen.

FRENCH CURLED COOKIES

¼ cup plus 2 tablespoons butter or margarine, softened
1 cup sifted powdered sugar
⅔ cup all-purpose flour
4 egg whites
1 teaspoon vanilla extract

Cream butter; gradually add sugar, beating well at medium speed of an electric mixer. Add flour, egg whites, and vanilla; mix well.

Divide a well-greased cookie sheet into four sections. Spoon 1½ teaspoons batter in center of each section. Spread each portion of batter evenly with a spatula to make a 4- x 3-inch oval. Bake at 425° for 3 minutes or until edges are golden.

Loosen cookies with a metal spatula, but leave on cookie sheet. Place one cookie upside down on counter, and quickly roll it lengthwise around the handle of a wooden spoon. Remove cookie, and let cool on wire rack. Repeat procedure with remaining cookies as quickly as possible. (If cookies become too stiff before rolling, return cookie sheet to oven briefly to soften them.) Continue procedure with remaining cookie batter. Yield: 3 dozen.

ROSETTES

1 cup plus 1 tablespoon all-purpose
   flour
¼ teaspoon salt
1 cup milk
1 egg
1 tablespoon sugar
1 tablespoon vanilla extract
Vegetable oil
Powdered sugar

Combine flour, salt, milk, egg, sugar, and vanilla extract in a medium mixing bowl; beat at low speed of an electric mixer until blended and smooth. Cover and chill at least 30 minutes.

Pour about 2 inches of vegetable oil in a large skillet; heat oil to 370°. Heat rosette iron in hot oil about 1 minute. Drain excess oil from iron, and dip iron into batter, being careful not to coat top of iron with batter.

Dip iron into hot oil. As soon as ro-sette is formed (about 5 seconds), lift iron slowly up and down to release rosette from iron. (If necessary, push rosette gently with a fork to release.) Fry until golden, turning to brown other side. Drain upside-down on paper towels.

Reheat iron in oil for a few seconds, and repeat procedure for each shell. Dust lightly with powdered sugar. Yield: 1 dozen (3-inch) rosettes.

Candies

Many people who've never made candy before shy away from ever attempting to make the sweets, labeling them too difficult to make. It's true that many candies must be cooked to critical temperatures, and prepared according to other precise specifications as well, but if you follow the simple rules associated with candy making, you shouldn't have a problem.

EQUIPMENT

You'll need several sizes of heavy saucepans. Candy mixtures usually triple in volume as they cook, so you'll need large pans to allow large mixtures to boil without boiling over. For smaller batches of candy, you'll need smaller pans. If the pan is too large for the amount of candy you're making, the candy mixture won't be deep enough to allow you to insert a thermometer and get a good temperature reading.

Wooden spoons are preferable to metal ones, since you'll be stirring constantly at some points, and wooden ones won't heat up.

While you can test for the proper candy temperature by using the cold-water test alone, a candy thermometer is almost a necessity because it allows you to cook candy to precisely the right temperature and stage. Always test the accuracy of a thermometer by letting it stand in boiling water 10 minutes. If the thermometer doesn't register 212°, allow for that inaccuracy when cooking each batch. Always read the thermometer at eye level.

COOKING CANDY

In candy making, just as in any other cooking process, there are special rules that need to be followed. Ingredients must be measured accurately to keep them in proper proportions. Measure ingredients and assemble equipment before starting to cook, because you may not have time later.

The main goal of candy making is to control the formation of sugar crystals. Stir the candy mixture gently until it comes to a boil and the sugar dissolves, trying to prevent crystals from clustering on the sides of the pan. Then cover the pan, and

To keep candy from being grainy: Cook the sugar mixture until sugar dissolves, stirring gently. Then cover and cook 2 to 3 minutes to wash down sugar crystals from sides of pan.

cook over medium heat about 2 to 3 minutes to wash crystals from the sides of the pan. Remove the lid and complete cooking.

After this point, avoid stirring unless directed. Occasional stirring of candies made with milk or cream is necessary, however, to avoid sticking or scorching. Stir gently so sugar doesn't splash on the sides of the pan.

Avoid doubling a candy recipe. It's safer to make a second batch. During humid or rainy weather, cook candy until thermometer registers 1 to 2° higher than the recipe directions specify.

TESTING FOR DONENESS

The most accurate test for doneness is to use a candy thermometer.

When using a candy thermometer, make sure the thermometer bulb is in the boiling mixture but not touching the bottom of the pan. Watch the thermometer carefully, because the temperature rises quickly as the candy nears doneness.

If you do not have a candy thermometer, the cold-water test may be used to check all candy stages except the thread stage and caramel stage. Remove the syrup from the heat while testing. Drop a small amount of syrup into a cup of very cold water; then test with your fingers to determine consistency (see chart). Use fresh, cold water each time a sample is tested. For thread stage, syrup should spin a 2-inch thread when dropped from a metal spoon. For caramel stage, syrup will be honey-colored when spooned onto a white plate.

COOLING CANDY

Some recipes call for candy mixtures to cool in the pan until it is

TESTS FOR CANDY STAGES

Thread Stage - 230° to 234°
Syrup spins 2-inch thread when dropped from a spoon.

Soft Ball Stage - 234° to 240°
In cold water, syrup forms a soft ball that flattens when removed from water.

Firm Ball Stage - 242° to 248°
In cold water, syrup forms a firm ball that does not flatten when removed from water.

Hard Ball Stage - 250° to 268°
Syrup forms a hard, yet pliable ball when removed from cold water.

Soft Crack Stage - 270° to 290°
When dropped into cold water, syrup separates into threads that are hard but not brittle.

Hard Crack Stage - 300° to 310°
When dropped into cold water, syrup separates into threads that are hard and brittle.

Caramel Stage - 310° to 340°
Syrup will be honey colored when spooned onto a white plate. The longer it's cooked, the darker it will be.

lukewarm (110°). Let pan sit undisturbed during this cooling period; don't stir unless instructed to do so, or the candy might be grainy.

When the mixture is ready for pouring, do so quickly, and don't scrape the sides of the pan since this may add sugar crystals to the candy. Let candy cool completely before cutting or packaging.

STORING CANDY

Store all candies in airtight containers as soon as they are cooled; this prevents them from picking up moisture from the atmosphere. Most candies will stay fresh up to a week;

fudge-like candies will sometimes keep up to two weeks if properly stored. Your recipe will indicate if the candy needs storing in the refrigerator. In general, candy is not a good candidate for freezing.

MICROWAVING CANDY

Candy is considered good for microwave cooking, because it cooks quickly and requires minimum attention. Most suited for microwave cooking are those candies that only require melting commercial chocolates and caramels and call for only a small amount of cooking.

Candies that require cooking to a certain temperature are trickier in the microwave and often require substantial proportion changes of ingredients from those that work well conventionally. The best source for cooking this type candy in your particular microwave is the manual that came with your oven. It will contain candy recipes that were tested in your specific model and will take much of the guesswork out of cooking times.

When preparing recipes that require a specific end temperature, use either the cold-water test for doneness or a candy thermometer made especially for use in microwave ovens. Because a conventional candy thermometer is metal, you can't keep it in the candy mixture during the cooking procedure. If you remove the hot candy mixture from the microwave oven and then insert a conventional thermometer, it will take at least 2 minutes for the temperature to rise and stabilize enough to give you an accurate reading. In many cases, you'd have so many waiting periods to check the temperature that the consistency of the candy might be affected.

Easy Candies

These confections require either no cooking at all or just a little cooking to melt and blend ingredients. They're an excellent choice if you're a beginner or don't have much time to devote to candy making or when you're letting a youngster try his hand at the art.

APRICOT BALLS

3 (6-ounce) packages dried apricots, diced
1 (14-ounce) package flaked coconut
1 cup chopped pecans
1 (14-ounce) can sweetened condensed milk
½ cup sifted powdered sugar

Combine apricots, coconut, and pecans in a large bowl; add sweetened condensed milk, stirring well. Chill. Shape mixture into 1-inch balls, and roll each ball in powdered sugar. Store balls in an airtight container in refrigerator. Yield: 8 dozen.

Shape Marzipan Like Fruit

Marzipan is a colorful and tasty candy that is often tinted and shaped to look like little fruits. Serve them as a party food, arrange them as a holiday decoration, or give them to friends in gift packs. Best of all, marzipan can be mixed up ahead, sealed in an airtight container, and stored up to a month in the refrigerator. To shape it, remove it from the refrigerator; let it return to room temperature, and knead it a little.

Tint marzipan and shape fruit and leaves following the directions below.
- Leaves: Roll green dough to ⅛-inch thickness on wax paper. Cut dough into leaves using cookie or canapé cutter. Draw leaf indentations using a wooden pick or press with indented leaf mold.
- Apples: Shape about 1½ teaspoons red dough into ball for each apple; gently stretch balls, forming apple shapes. Indent stem ends slightly using a wooden stick with a pointed edge. Insert a clove in stem ends.
- Strawberries: Shape about 1 teaspoon red dough into ball for each strawberry. Shape a rounded point at one end; slightly flatten other end. Indent flattened end slightly using a wooden stick.

Combine 2 tablespoons granulated sugar and a few drops of red food coloring, stirring until color is blended thoroughly and desired shade is obtained. Brush strawberries with glaze, and roll in red sugar; place strawberries on wax paper. Shape point on stem end of an equal number of leaves; press point of a leaf into each strawberry indention.
- Cherries: Shape about ¼ teaspoon red dough into ball for each cherry. Push ¼-inch piece of licorice into each cherry for stem.
- Peaches: Shape about 1¼ teaspoons yellow dough into ball for each peach. Push clove into each peach for stem. Press a groove with wooden pick on one side of each peach. Combine 2 tablespoons water, 2 drops yellow, and 2 drops red food coloring, stirring well. Brush mixture on sides of each peach for blush.
- Bananas: Shape bananas using about 1 teaspoon yellow dough for each. Push clove into stem end of each banana. Combine 2 tablespoons water, 1 drop green, 4 drops yellow, and 3 drops red food coloring, stirring well. Brush streaks on each banana with colored mixture.
- Oranges: Shape about 1¼ teaspoons orange dough into ball for each orange. Roll each orange over grater to get rough skin. Insert clove in each orange for stem.
- Grapes: Shape about 2 teaspoons purple dough into small balls (about ⅛ teaspoon each) for each cluster. Brush balls with slightly beaten egg white, and shape balls into cluster.

For each cluster, brush egg white on stem end of 2 leaves. Attach to back of each cluster, pressing gently to make adhere. Allow to dry.

MARZIPAN

1 (8-ounce) can almond paste
1½ tablespoons light corn syrup
1⅓ cups sifted powdered sugar
Liquid food coloring
Glaze (recipe follows)

Knead almond paste by hand in a medium bowl. Add corn syrup, and knead into almond paste. Gradually knead in sugar. Cover almond paste mixture with plastic wrap, and store in airtight container in refrigerator until ready to shape.

Tint marzipan by kneading in food coloring; then shape as desired. Brush with glaze to achieve a shinier surface. Let dry 8 hours on wax paper; then refrigerate in an airtight container. Yield: about ¾ pound candy, or enough to shape approximately 3 dozen small pieces of fruit.

Glaze

2 tablespoons light corn syrup
¼ cup water

Combine corn syrup and water in a saucepan, mixing well. Bring to a boil, stirring until syrup dissolves. Yield: ¼ cup plus 2 tablespoons.

DATE-NUT LOGS

1 (8-ounce) package chopped dates
1 cup sugar
½ cup butter or margarine
1 teaspoon vanilla extract
1 egg
2 cups crisp rice cereal
2 cups chopped pecans
1 cup flaked coconut

Combine first 5 ingredients in a large saucepan; cook over low heat 10 minutes, stirring constantly. Remove mixture from heat; add rice cereal and pecans, stirring well.

Shape into two 11-inch logs, and roll each in coconut. Cool and slice thinly. Yield: two 11-inch logs.

CREAM CHEESE BUTTER MINTS

There are many decorative molds available in all shapes and sizes which you can use for shaping mints. Just be sure to use a mold made of soft, pliable rubber so the mints will be easier to mold. If you have trouble with the mixture sticking to the mint molds when making Cream Cheese Butter Mints, try dusting the molds lightly with cornstarch before using them.

1 (3-ounce) package cream cheese, softened
2 teaspoons butter flavoring
⅛ teaspoon oil of peppermint
1 (16-ounce) package powdered sugar, sifted
Paste food coloring

Combine cream cheese, butter flavoring, peppermint, and powdered sugar in a large mixing bowl; beat at low speed of an electric mixer until blended. Add a small amount of food coloring; beat at medium speed until blended. (Mixture will be dry. Knead mixture lightly to soften it.)

Press mixture into mint molds or roll into small balls and flatten slightly. Yield: about 1 pound or 8 dozen 1-inch wafer mints.

Chocolate Candies

Chocolate-laced and chocolate-dipped candies are so tempting to most people that we combined them into a section of their own. Recipes of this nature are usually easy to prepare, whether conventionally or in the microwave.

The most challenging recipes are those that require dipping candy in melted chocolate. Until you have a little experience with this technique, your candies probably won't be as smooth and symmetrical as those dipped commercially.

There are two mediums you can use for dipping—either real chocolate (usually the semisweet type) or a product called chocolate-flavored candy coating. Most people prefer real chocolate because it tastes like the chocolate that's most familiar; its biggest disadvantage is that after melting under home conditions, it does not harden back up completely and tends to be a little sticky. Many of our recipes add a little shortening (do not use oil) to the chocolate to help it firm back up more solidly. Some recipes call for keeping chocolates chilled so they'll be firmer.

Chocolate-flavored candy coating is not actually real chocolate at all but is flavored and colored to look like chocolate. It melts like real chocolate (only a little faster) and when the candy coating cools to room temperature, there's usually not a problem with stickiness.

When dipping candies in either medium, melt the chocolate according to recipe directions. You can use a candy dipper utensil as shown in our technique photograph, two forks, or a wooden pick to dip and remove candies from the chocolate. Let excess chocolate drip back into the pan; then transfer chocolates to wax paper to cool and harden.

ROCKY ROAD CANDY

1 (12-ounce) package semisweet chocolate morsels
½ cup butter or margarine
1 (10½-ounce) package regular miniature marshmallows
1 cup finely chopped pecans or walnuts

Combine chocolate and butter in top of a double boiler; bring water to a boil. Reduce heat to low; cook until chocolate melts. Cool to lukewarm. Stir in marshmallows and pecans. Shape into 2 rolls 2 inches in diameter. Chill. Slice into ½-inch slices. Yield: about 3 dozen.

☐*Microwave Directions:* Combine chocolate and butter in a 2-quart glass bowl. Microwave at MEDIUM (50% power) for 3½ to 4 minutes or until morsels are softened. Stir well; cool to lukewarm. Stir in marshmallows and pecans. Shape into 2 rolls 2 inches in diameter. Chill. Cut into ½-inch slices.

CHEWY CHOCOLATE-PEANUT CLUSTERS

2 tablespoons peanut butter
1 (6-ounce) package butterscotch morsels
1 (6-ounce) package semisweet chocolate morsels
2 cups salted Spanish peanuts

Combine peanut butter, butterscotch morsels, and chocolate morsels in a heavy saucepan; cook over low heat, stirring constantly, until melted. Stir in peanuts. Drop by rounded teaspoonfuls onto wax paper; chill until firm. Store in an airtight container in refrigerator. Yield: about 4 dozen.

▢*Microwave Directions:* Combine peanut butter, butterscotch morsels, and chocolate morsels in a 1½-quart glass bowl. Microwave at MEDIUM (50% power) for 3 to 4 minutes or until morsels are softened; stir well. Stir in peanuts. Drop by rounded teaspoonfuls onto wax paper; chill until firm. Store in an airtight container in refrigerator.

TOASTED PECAN CLUSTERS

3 tablespoons butter or margarine
3 cups pecan pieces
12 ounces chocolate-flavored candy coating

Melt butter in a 15- x 10- x 1-inch jellyroll pan. Spread pecans evenly in pan. Bake at 300° for 30 minutes, stirring every 10 minutes.

Place candy coating in top of a double boiler; bring water to a boil. Reduce heat to low; cook until coating melts. Cool 2 minutes; add pecans, and stir until coated. Drop by rounded teaspoonfuls onto wax paper. Cool completely. Yield: about 4 dozen.

▢*Microwave Directions:* Place butter in a 1-quart glass bowl; microwave at HIGH for 50 seconds or until melted. Add pecans; toss pecans to coat with butter. Spread pecans evenly on a glass pizza plate. Microwave at HIGH for 6 to 8 minutes or until lightly toasted, stirring at 3-minute intervals.

Place candy coating in a 1-quart glass bowl. Microwave at MEDIUM (50% power) for 2 to 3 minutes or until coating is softened; stir well. Cool 2 minutes; add pecans, and stir until coated. Drop by rounded teaspoonfuls onto wax paper. Cool completely.

CHOCOLATE TRUFFLES

1 (6-ounce) package semisweet chocolate morsels
3 tablespoons butter or margarine
3 tablespoons powdered sugar
2 egg yolks
Cocoa

Place chocolate morsels in top of a double boiler; bring water to a boil. Reduce heat to low; cook until chocolate melts. Add butter and powdered sugar, stirring until sugar dissolves. Remove from heat.

Add egg yolks, one at a time, beating with an electric mixer after each addition. Pour mixture into a bowl; cover and let sit 12 hours in a cool, dry place (do not refrigerate).

Shape mixture into 1-inch balls; roll lightly in cocoa. Yield: 2 dozen.

Chocolate Almond Truffles: Insert 1 whole toasted almond in center of each ball. Roll balls in ½ cup finely chopped almonds instead of cocoa.

Chocolate Rum Truffles: Stir in 1 tablespoon dark rum after adding egg yolks.

▢*Microwave Directions:* Place chocolate morsels in a 1-quart glass bowl. Microwave at MEDIUM (50% power) for 2 to 3 minutes or until chocolate is softened; stir well. Add butter and powdered sugar, stirring until powdered sugar dissolves.

Add egg yolks, one at a time, beating with an electric mixer after each addition. Pour mixture into a bowl; cover and let sit 12 hours in a cool, dry place (do not refrigerate).

Shape mixture into 1-inch balls; roll lightly in cocoa.

CHOCOLATE-COVERED CHERRIES

¼ cup plus 2 tablespoons butter, softened
2½ cups sifted powdered sugar
1½ teaspoons milk
¼ teaspoon vanilla extract
About 42 maraschino cherries with stems
1 (12-ounce) package semisweet chocolate morsels
1 tablespoon shortening

Cream butter; gradually add sugar, beating well. Blend in milk and vanilla. Chill mixture 2 hours or until firm.

Drain cherries, and dry thoroughly on paper towels. Place bowl of sugar mixture in a bowl of ice to keep mixture chilled. Shape a small amount of sugar mixture around each cherry. Place on wax paper-lined baking sheet; chill about 2 hours or until firm.

Combine chocolate morsels and shortening in top of a double boiler; bring water to a boil. Reduce heat to low; cook until chocolate melts. Dip each cherry by the stem into chocolate. Place on a wax paper-lined baking sheet; chill until firm. Store in a cool place. Yield: 3½ dozen.

CHOCOLATE-DIPPED STRAWBERRIES

2 pints fresh strawberries
1 (6-ounce) package semisweet
  chocolate morsels
1 tablespoon shortening

Rinse strawberries, and dry thoroughly on paper towels (chocolate will not stick to wet strawberries). Set aside.

Place chocolate morsels and shortening in top of a double boiler; bring water to a boil. Reduce heat to low, and cook until chocolate melts. Cool chocolate to lukewarm (110°).

Grasp strawberries by the stem, and dip in chocolate mixture; place on a wire rack sprayed with vegetable cooking spray, and chill until firm. Serve within 8 hours. Yield: 3 to 4 dozen.

MILLIONAIRES

1 (14-ounce) package caramels
1½ tablespoons milk
2 cups coarsely chopped
  pecans
12 ounces chocolate-flavored
  candy coating

Unwrap caramels; combine caramels and milk in a heavy saucepan. Cook over low heat until melted, stirring frequently. Stir in pecans. Drop by rounded teaspoonfuls onto buttered wax paper. Cool; cover and chill.

Place candy coating in top of a double boiler; bring water to a boil. Reduce heat to low, and cook until coating melts. Dip caramel centers into coating. Place on wax paper to cool. Yield: about 4 dozen.

◻*Microwave Directions:* Unwrap caramels, and place in a 2-quart casserole. Microwave at HIGH for 1 to 1¼ minutes; stir well.

Add milk to caramels, and microwave at HIGH for 1½ to 2 minutes, stirring

every 30 seconds. Stir until mixture is smooth; stir in pecans. Drop by rounded teaspoonfuls onto buttered wax paper. Cool; cover and chill.

Place candy coating in a 4-cup glass measure. Microwave at MEDIUM (50% power) for 2 to 3 minutes or until coating melts. Dip caramel centers into coating. Place on wax paper to cool.

To dip chocolates easily: Use a gadget called a candy dipper; let excess chocolate drip off.

BUTTER CREAMS

½ cup butter, softened
1 (16-ounce) package powdered
  sugar, sifted
2 tablespoons milk
1 teaspoon vanilla extract
¼ teaspoon salt
10 ounces chocolate-flavored candy
  coating

Cream butter; gradually add sugar, beating well. Stir in milk, vanilla, and salt. Chill several hours or until firm. Shape into ¾-inch balls.

Place candy coating in top of a double boiler; bring water to a boil. Reduce heat to low; cook until coating melts. Dip each ball of candy into coating. Place on wax paper to cool. Yield: 5 dozen.

◻*Microwave Directions:* Cream butter; gradually add sugar, beating well. Stir in milk, vanilla, and salt. Chill several hours or until firm. Shape into ¾-inch balls.

Place candy coating in a 1-quart glass bowl; microwave at MEDIUM (50% power) for 2 to 3 minutes or until coating is softened; stir well. Dip each ball of candy into coating. Place on wax paper to cool. Yield: about 5 dozen.

BOURBON BONBONS

½ cup butter, softened
⅓ cup plus 2 teaspoons bourbon
1½ tablespoons milk
7½ cups sifted powdered sugar
½ cup finely chopped pecans
2 (12-ounce) packages semisweet
  chocolate morsels
3 tablespoons shortening

Combine butter, bourbon, and milk; add sugar, and knead until mixture is blended and does not stick to hands. Knead in pecans. Refrigerate 1 hour. Shape into 1-inch balls; freeze.

Combine chocolate morsels and shortening in top of a double boiler; bring water to a boil. Reduce heat to low; cook until chocolate melts. Dip each ball of candy into chocolate mixture. Place on wax paper to cool. Store in refrigerator. Yield: 6 dozen.

◻*Microwave Directions:* Combine butter, bourbon, and milk; add sugar, and knead until mixture is blended and does not stick to hands. Knead in pecans. Refrigerate 1 hour. Shape into 1-inch balls; freeze.

Combine chocolate morsels and shortening in a 1½-quart bowl; microwave at MEDIUM (50% power) for 5 to 6 minutes or until chocolate is softened; stir well. Dip each ball of candy into chocolate mixture. Place on wax paper to cool. Store in refrigerator.

PEANUT BUTTER CHOCOLATE BALLS

1½ cups graham cracker crumbs
1½ cups flaked coconut
1½ cups chopped peanuts or pecans
1 cup butter or margarine, melted
1 (16-ounce) package powdered sugar, sifted
1 (12-ounce) jar crunchy peanut butter
1 teaspoon vanilla extract
2 (12-ounce) packages semisweet chocolate morsels
3 tablespoons shortening

Combine first 7 ingredients, stirring well. Shape mixture into 1-inch balls.

Combine chocolate morsels and shortening in top of a double boiler; bring water to a boil. Reduce heat to low; cook until chocolate melts. Dip each peanut butter ball into chocolate mixture. Place on wax paper to cool. Store in refrigerator. Yield: about 9 dozen.

◻ *Microwave Directions:* Combine first 7 ingredients, stirring well. Shape mixture into 1-inch balls.

Combine chocolate morsels and shortening in a 1½-quart bowl; microwave at MEDIUM (50% power) for 5 to 6 minutes or until chocolate is softened; stir well. Dip each peanut butter ball into chocolate mixture. Place on wax paper to cool. Store in refrigerator.

Note: Peanut Butter Chocolate Balls may be frozen in an airtight container for later use. Remove balls from freezer 1 hour before serving.

Fudge _____

There is enough variety with these recipes to turn your kitchen into a fudge factory—mocha, peanut butter, white chocolate, as well as the traditional dark chocolate. Because fudge has good keeping quality you can make a couple of batches at a time, and store it. Seal it in an airtight container, and keep at room temperature up to two weeks.

FAST FUDGE

2 cups sugar
⅔ cup evaporated skim milk
½ cup butter
12 large marshmallows
Few grains of salt
1 (6-ounce) package semisweet chocolate morsels
1 cup chopped pecans
1 teaspoon vanilla extract

Combine first 5 ingredients in a large saucepan. Cook over medium heat until mixture comes to a boil, stirring gently; boil 5 minutes, stirring constantly. Remove from heat.

Add chocolate morsels to marshmallow mixture, stirring until melted. Add pecans and vanilla, stirring well. Spread evenly in a buttered 8-inch square pan. Cool and cut into squares. Yield: 2 pounds.

Mocha Fudge: Add 1 tablespoon instant coffee granules with the salt.

FAMOUS FUDGE

2 cups sugar
⅔ cup half-and-half
¼ cup light corn syrup
1 (1-ounce) square unsweetened chocolate
¼ cup butter or margarine
2 teaspoons vanilla extract

Combine sugar, half-and-half, corn syrup, and unsweetened chocolate square in a Dutch oven; cook over low heat, stirring gently, until sugar dissolves. Cover chocolate mixture and cook over medium heat 2 to 3 minutes to wash down sugar crystals from sides of pan. Uncover and cook to soft ball stage (238°), stirring occasionally.

Remove chocolate mixture from heat. Add butter and vanilla. (Do not stir.) Cool to lukewarm (110°); beat with a wooden spoon until mixture thickens and begins to lose its gloss.

Pour mixture into a buttered 8-inch square pan, spreading with a spatula. Cool and cut into squares. Yield: about 1¼ pounds.

Double Good Fudge: Prepare Famous Fudge as directed above, but pour mixture into a buttered 9-inch square pan. Prepare Peanut Butter Fudge (page 173), and pour over chocolate layer. Yield: 3 pounds.

PEANUT BUTTER FUDGE

1 cup sugar
1 cup firmly packed light brown sugar
½ cup half-and-half
2 tablespoons light corn syrup
¼ cup butter or margarine
½ cup crunchy peanut butter
½ cup marshmallow cream
2 teaspoons vanilla extract

Combine sugars, half-and-half, and corn syrup in a Dutch oven. Cook over low heat, stirring gently, until sugar dissolves. Cover and cook over medium heat 2 to 3 minutes to wash down sugar crystals from sides of pan. Uncover and cook to soft ball stage (235°), stirring occasionally.

Remove from heat. Add butter, peanut butter, marshmallow cream, and vanilla; stir until smooth. Pour mixture into a buttered 8-inch square pan, spreading with a spatula. Cool and cut into squares. Yield: 1¾ pounds.

WHITE CHOCOLATE FUDGE

6 ounces white chocolate, grated
½ (8-ounce) package cream cheese, softened
3 cups sifted powdered sugar
½ teaspoon vanilla extract
1 cup chopped pecans or walnuts
16 pecan halves

Place chocolate in top of a double boiler; bring water to a boil. Reduce heat to low; cook until chocolate melts.

Combine cream cheese and sugar; beat at medium speed of an electric mixer until smooth. Add chocolate and vanilla, beating well. Stir in chopped pecans.

Press chocolate mixture into a lightly greased 8-inch square pan. Chill until firm, and cut into squares. Top each fudge square with a pecan half, pressing gently. Store in refrigerator. Yield: about 1½ pounds.

PENUCHE

1½ cups sugar
¾ cup firmly packed brown sugar
¾ cup milk
1 tablespoon light corn syrup
1 tablespoon butter or margarine
Pinch of salt
1 teaspoon vanilla extract
1 cup chopped pecans

Combine first 6 ingredients in a small Dutch oven. Cook over low heat, stirring gently, until sugar dissolves. Cover and cook over medium heat 2 to 3 minutes to wash down sugar from sides of pan. Uncover and cook to soft ball stage (234°), without stirring.

Remove from heat (do not stir). Cool to lukewarm (110°). Add vanilla and pecans; beat with a wooden spoon 2 to 3 minutes or until mixture thickens and begins to lose its gloss.

Working rapidly, spread mixture in a buttered 8-inch square pan. Mark top of warm candy into squares using a sharp knife. Cool completely before cutting. Yield: about 1½ pounds.

Traditional Candies

Traditional candies include the shiny sweet nuggets you remember from childhood—peanut brittle, taffy, divinity, lollipops. All are cooked to a critical temperature. You won't have any trouble with them if you follow the basic guidelines for minimizing sugar crystallization and checking for the specific end temperature. Avoid making these candies on a rainy or humid day, as they can pick up excess moisture from the atmosphere and become sticky.

ORANGE PECANS

1 cup sugar
1 teaspoon cream of tartar
⅓ cup orange juice
2¼ cups pecan halves
½ teaspoon grated orange rind

Combine sugar, cream of tartar, and orange juice in a saucepan. Cook over low heat, stirring gently, until sugar dissolves. Cover orange mixture, and cook over medium heat 2 to 3 minutes to wash down sugar crystals from sides of pan. Uncover and cook over medium heat to soft ball stage (240°).

Remove from heat, and beat with a wooden spoon just until mixture begins to thicken. Stir in pecans and orange rind. Working rapidly, drop by heaping teaspoonfuls onto wax paper; let cool. Yield: about 2 dozen.

SOUTHERN PRALINES

2 cups sugar
2 cups pecan halves
¾ cup buttermilk
2 tablespoons butter or margarine
⅛ teaspoon salt
¾ teaspoon baking soda

Combine all ingredients except baking soda in a large heavy saucepan. Cook over low heat, stirring gently, until sugar dissolves. Cover and cook over medium heat 2 to 3 minutes to wash down sugar crystals from sides of pan. Uncover and cook to soft ball stage (235°), stirring constantly. Remove from heat, and stir in soda. Beat with a wooden spoon just until mixture begins to thicken. Working rapidly, drop by tablespoonfuls onto greased wax paper; let stand until firm. Yield: 1½ to 2 dozen.

☐ *Microwave Directions:* Combine all ingredients except baking soda in a 4-quart casserole, stirring well. Microwave at HIGH for 12 to 13 minutes, stirring every 4 minutes. Stir in soda.

Microwave at HIGH for 1 to 1½ minutes. Beat with a wooden spoon just until mixture begins to thicken. Working rapidly, drop by tablespoonfuls onto greased wax paper; let stand until firm.

PEANUT BRITTLE

1½ cups raw peanuts
1 cup sugar
½ cup light corn syrup
¼ teaspoon salt
1 tablespoon butter or margarine
1 teaspoon baking soda
1 teaspoon vanilla extract

Combine peanuts, sugar, corn syrup, and salt in a Dutch oven. Cook over low heat, stirring gently, until sugar dissolves. Cover and cook over medium heat 2 to 3 minutes to wash down sugar crystals from sides of pan. Uncover and cook, stirring occasionally, to hard crack stage (300°). Stir in butter, soda, and vanilla. Pour into a buttered 15- x 10- x 1-inch jellyroll pan, spreading thinly. Let cool. Break into pieces. Yield: about 1 pound.

ENGLISH TOFFEE

2 cups sugar
⅔ cup butter or margarine
2 tablespoons water
1 tablespoon light corn syrup
1 teaspoon vanilla extract
1 (6-ounce) package semisweet chocolate morsels
1 cup finely chopped walnuts

Combine sugar, butter, water, and corn syrup in a 3-quart Dutch oven. Cook over low heat, stirring gently, until sugar dissolves. Cover and cook over medium heat 2 to 3 minutes to wash down sugar crystals from sides of pan. Uncover and cook to hard crack stage (300°). Remove from heat, and stir in vanilla. Pour into an ungreased 15- x 10- x 1-inch jellyroll pan, spreading to edges of pan.

Sprinkle chocolate morsels over toffee; let stand 1 minute or until chocolate begins to melt. Spread chocolate over entire candy layer; sprinkle with walnuts. Let stand until set. Break into pieces. Store in an airtight container in refrigerator. Yield: about 1½ pounds.

Southern Pralines Step-By-Step

1. Southern Pralines aren't difficult to make. Cook sugar, pecan halves, buttermilk, butter, and salt over low heat until sugar dissolves.

2. Then cover the saucepan and cook over medium heat to wash down sugar crystals from sides of pan.

3. Uncover the saucepan, and cook mixture to soft ball stage.

4. Remove from heat, add soda, and stir with a wooden spoon just until mixture begins to harden.

OLD-FASHIONED TAFFY

2½ cups sugar
½ cup water
¼ cup vinegar
1 tablespoon butter or margarine
⅛ teaspoon salt
1 teaspoon vanilla extract

Combine all ingredients except vanilla in a small Dutch oven; cook over low heat, stirring gently, until sugar dissolves. Cover and cook over medium heat 2 to 3 minutes to wash down sugar crystals from sides of pan. Uncover and cook over medium heat, without stirring, to soft crack stage (270°). Remove from heat. Stir in vanilla.

Pour candy onto a buttered 15- x 10- x 1-inch jellyroll pan or slab of marble. Let cool to touch; butter hands, and pull candy until light in color and difficult to pull. Divide candy in half, and pull into a rope, 1 inch in diameter. Cut into 1-inch pieces; wrap each in wax paper. Yield: about 40 (1-inch) pieces.

CARAMELS

1 cup butter or margarine
2 cups sugar
2 cups light corn syrup
2 cups whipping cream, divided
2 teaspoons vanilla extract

Combine butter, sugar, corn syrup, and 1 cup whipping cream in a large Dutch oven. Cook over low heat, stirring gently, until sugar dissolves. Cover and cook over medium heat 2 to 3 minutes to wash down sugar crystals from sides of pan. Uncover and cook, stirring occasionally, until candy thermometer registers 224°.

Stir in remaining 1 cup whipping cream. Continue to cook mixture over medium heat to firm ball stage (248°). Stir in vanilla.

Pour into a buttered 13- x 9- x 2-inch pan. Let cool about 5 hours. Cut into squares, and wrap individually in wax paper. Yield: 2¾ pounds.

CANDIED ORANGE PEEL

1 quart (¼-inch wide) orange peel strips (about 15 oranges)
½ teaspoon salt
2 cups sugar
1 cup water
Sugar

Place orange peel in water to cover in a Dutch oven; add salt. Bring to a boil, and boil 20 minutes. Drain. Repeat boiling procedure twice without salt, and set orange peel aside.

Combine 2 cups sugar and 1 cup water in a small saucepan; bring to a boil and cook, stirring often, until syrup spins a thread, about 7 minutes (234°). Add orange peel; simmer 30 minutes, stirring often. Drain orange peel well. Discard syrup.

Roll peel, a few pieces at a time, in sugar. Arrange in a single layer on wire racks; let dry 4 to 5 hours. Store in airtight container. Yield: about 1 pound.

5. Drop mixture by tablespoons onto wax paper, working rapidly before mixture cools too much and hardens.

You'll find a crunchy pecan half in every delicious bite of Southern Pralines.

DIVINITY

2½ cups sugar
½ cup water
½ cup light corn syrup
2 egg whites
1 teaspoon vanilla extract
1 cup chopped pecans

Combine sugar, water, and corn syrup in a 3-quart saucepan; cook over low heat, stirring gently, until sugar dissolves. Cover and cook over medium heat 2 to 3 minutes to wash down sugar crystals from sides of pan. Uncover and cook over medium heat, without stirring, to hard ball stage (260°). Remove from heat.

Beat egg whites (at room temperature) in a large mixing bowl until stiff peaks form. Pour hot sugar mixture in a very thin stream over egg whites while beating constantly at high speed of an electric mixer. Add vanilla, and continue beating just until mixture holds its shape (3 to 4 minutes). Stir in pecans.

Drop by rounded teaspoonfuls onto wax paper. Let cool. Yield: about 6 dozen.

Cherry Divinity: Substitute 1 cup chopped red candied cherries for pecans.

Peanut Ripple Divinity: Omit pecans, and stir in ½ cup peanut butter chips and ½ cup chopped roasted peanuts.

LOLLIPOPS

1 cup sugar
¼ cup water
¼ cup light corn syrup
1 to 2 drops of desired food coloring
¼ teaspoon oil of cinnamon or peppermint

Brush inside surfaces of metal lollipop molds with oil; set aside.

Combine sugar, water, and corn syrup in a medium saucepan. Cook over low heat, stirring gently, until sugar dissolves. Cover and cook mixture over medium heat 2 to 3 minutes to wash down sugar crystals from sides of pan. Uncover and cook, without stirring, to hard crack stage (300°). Remove mixture from heat, and stir in desired food coloring and oil of cinnamon.

Immediately pour hot mixture into prepared molds. Press sticks in indentions of molds, gently twirling sticks to embed. Cool completely; lift lollipops out of molds. Immediately wrap in plastic wrap. Store in a cool, dry place. Yield: about 8 (2-inch) lollipops.

MINT TWISTS

2 cups sugar
1 cup water
¼ cup butter or margarine
⅛ teaspoon oil of peppermint
4 drops of desired food coloring

Combine sugar and water in a large saucepan; bring to a boil, and add butter. Cook over low heat, stirring gently, until sugar dissolves. Cover and cook over medium heat 2 to 3 minutes to wash down sugar crystals from sides of pan. Uncover and cook to hard ball stage (260°). Remove from heat, and immediately pour syrup onto a buttered marble slab.

Sprinkle oil of peppermint and food coloring over surface of hot syrup; let rest 3 minutes or until edges begin to set. Begin scraping syrup with metal spatula into a central mass. Continue scraping and folding until color is evenly distributed.

Pull mixture with fingertips, allowing a spread of about 15 inches between hands; then fold mixture in half. Repeat pulling and folding until consistency of mixture changes from sticky to elastic.

Begin twisting while folding and pulling. Continue pulling until ridges on the twists begin to hold their shape. This takes 5 to 10 minutes, depending on the weather and your skill.

Shape mint mixture into a 1-inch thick rope. Using kitchen shears, cut the rope into 1-inch segments. Place mints on wax paper to cool, and cover with a towel. Let mints sit 8 hours or until they become creamy. Store in an airtight container. Yield: about 4 dozen.

Note: You can divide the mixture in half and make 2 colors of mints; the resting time will be shortened to about 1 minute. You may need someone to help knead and pull the second color so it doesn't harden too quickly.

Do not double recipe. If more mints are needed, make 2 batches.

OLD-FASHIONED POPCORN BALLS

2 cups firmly packed dark brown
  sugar
¾ cup light corn syrup
¾ cup water
½ teaspoon salt
½ cup butter or margarine
1 teaspoon vanilla extract
6 quarts popped corn

Combine sugar, corn syrup, water, and salt in a saucepan; cook over low heat, stirring gently, until sugar dissolves. Cook over medium heat, without stirring, to hard ball stage (254°). Remove from heat, and stir in butter and vanilla.

Place popped corn in a large pan. Pour hot syrup over top, stirring well with a wooden spoon. Grease hands with butter, and shape mixture into balls. Place on wax paper to dry. Wrap in plastic wrap, and store in a cool, dry place. Yield: about 2 dozen.

CANDIED APPLES

10 medium apples
3 cups sugar
⅔ cup water
1 teaspoon lemon juice
¼ teaspoon cream of tartar
15 whole cloves
2 to 3 drops of red food coloring

Wash and dry apples; remove stems. Insert a wooden skewer into stem end of each apple. Set aside.

Combine remaining ingredients in a heavy saucepan; stir well. Cook over low heat, stirring gently, until sugar dissolves. Cover and cook over medium heat 2 to 3 minutes to wash down sugar crystals from sides of pan. Uncover and cook over medium heat, without stirring, to hard crack stage (300°). Remove cloves.

Quickly dip apples in syrup; allow excess syrup to drip off. Place on lightly buttered baking sheets to cool. Wrap tightly in plastic wrap; store in a cool place. Yield: 10 servings.

DESSERTS

That old saying about saving the best for last is certainly true when you talk about the dessert course of the meal. While most everyone will enjoy a marinated tenderloin or a well-seasoned potato dish, the bulk of the praise usually goes to the last course. A really good dessert is probably the most anticipated part of the menu. And Southerners take their desserts very seriously. Look through the recipe file of a good cook, and usually the dessert category (including cakes and pies to which we devote separate chapters) will be the bulkiest. That may not be one of our healthiest habits, but it's certainly one of the most pleasurable!

EQUIPMENT

Because such emphasis is placed on desserts, we want them to look as pretty as they taste. Hence some of our recipes call for special molds, springform pans, and other equipment for specialty shaping and baking. Read through your selected recipe carefully before beginning to prepare it to make sure you have the piece of equipment called for or that you have a suitable substitute.

You'll need to make puddings and sauces for many of these recipes, and the trusty wire whisk and wooden spoons discussed in the chapter on sauces (page 435) will come in handy for these recipes, too. You might even want to review the information about sauces and thickeners before you tackle the puddings and custards in this chapter—many of the basic procedures are the same.

And no self-respecting Southerner would go for long without an ice

Present Raspberry Dream (page 187) on a serving plate with a lip around the edge; you'll want to save every drop of the sauce that's drizzled over the dessert.

cream freezer to make those creamy summer coolers. It doesn't matter whether yours is the electric or

hand-crank kind. They produce virtually indistinguishable end products. If you have kids around the house, they usually enjoy taking turns at the crank. After the kids are grown, many folks switch to electric models!

STORING AND FREEZING

Any of these desserts containing fresh fruit or cream bases will need storing in the refrigerator, both before serving if you make them ahead and afterward if you have leftovers. If the recipe doesn't specify freezing as part of the original recipe, it's probably not a good candidate for making ahead and freezing. Freezing would change the texture of most fruit dishes, and many of the pudding-based recipes would have a tendency to break down. Avoid freezing a dessert that contains gelatin unless you're instructed to do so; some of these desserts are good candidates for freezing, and some are not, depending on the ingredients.

One dessert that does freeze well is crêpes. You can make extras of the thin wrappers, stack them between wax paper, place the stack in a freezer bag, and freeze up to three months. They'll thaw in just a short time, ready to make into one of our recipes or to simply wrap around ice cream or fruit.

MICROWAVING DESSERTS

Some fruit or pudding-based desserts work well in the microwave oven. We've included microwave directions for those where the end product compared favorably to the version we tested conventionally and for those recipes that indeed cook faster in the microwave. (Some recipes that make a large volume actually take longer to cook in the microwave than they do when they are cooked conventionally.)

Refer to your recipe for specific times and temperatures to use in the microwave. Keep the following general concepts in mind as you make your desserts:

• It's important to stir fillings or custards occasionally to mix the cooked with the uncooked portions. This way you'll end up with a more evenly cooked product.

• Sometimes fillings or custards will not be thick enough after microwaving is complete; however, they will thicken more as they cool or stand.

• A glass measure or casserole dish is perfect for making custards or fillings in the microwave. Be sure the container is large enough to prevent the mixture from boiling over.

Custards and Puddings

In their simplest form, custards and puddings are nothing more than sweetened egg and milk mixtures. More elaborate versions may include other flavorings, such as chocolate, fruit, and liqueur. They're simple to make and are virtually foolproof if you follow directions.

Most of these recipes are thickened with flour or with cornstarch; usually eggs contribute to the thickening also. Most require frequent, if not constant, stirring to ensure a smooth base, so read the recipe carefully. Avoid using too high a heat or overcooking the mixture, as this can cause it to curdle.

As pudding cools, it sometimes forms a thin "skin" across the top. Prevent this skin by placing a piece of plastic wrap or wax paper directly on top of the hot pudding. Once the pudding has cooled, remove the covering, and spoon the pudding into dessert dishes.

OLD-FASHIONED STIRRED CUSTARD

Stirred Custard is very soft and fluid—almost sauce consistency. It can be served hot or cold; it will thicken slightly as it cools, but will still remain fluid enough to pour. Bake the same mixture in the oven, and you'll have a firmer custard. Baked Custard is done when a knife inserted in the center comes out clean. The mixture will still have a jiggly consistency, but will thicken slightly as it cools.

3 cups milk
2 eggs
⅔ cup sugar
1½ tablespoons all-purpose
    flour
1 teaspoon vanilla extract

Place milk in top of a double boiler; bring water to a boil. Cook until milk is thoroughly heated. Set aside.

Beat eggs at medium speed of an electric mixer until frothy. Add sugar and flour, beating until thick. Gradually stir about 1 cup hot milk into yolk mixture; add to remaining milk, stirring constantly. Cook custard mixture in double boiler over low heat, stirring occasionally, 30 minutes or until thickened. Stir in vanilla. Serve custard warm or cold. Yield: 6 servings.

Baked Custard: Pour custard mixture into 6 (6-ounce) custard cups. Set custard cups in a 13- x 9- x 2-inch custard pan; pour hot water to depth of 1 inch into pan.

Bake at 350° for 35 to 40 minutes or until knife inserted in center comes out clean. Remove custard cups from water. Serve warm or cold.

CREAMY VANILLA PUDDING

¼ cup sugar
1 tablespoon cornstarch
Pinch of salt
2 cups milk
2 egg yolks
1 tablespoon butter or margarine
1 teaspoon vanilla extract

Combine sugar, cornstarch, and salt in a small saucepan; gradually stir in milk. Cook over medium heat, stirring constantly, until mixture comes to a boil. Cook 1 additional minute, stirring constantly. Remove from heat.

Beat egg yolks at medium speed of an electric mixer until thick and lemon colored. Gradually stir about one-fourth of hot mixture into yolks; add to remaining hot mixture, stirring constantly. Bring mixture to a boil over medium heat and cook 1 minute, stirring constantly. Remove from heat; stir in butter and vanilla. Pour mixture into 4 (6-ounce) custard cups. Cover with plastic wrap, gently pressing directly on pudding. Chill. Yield: 4 servings.

Creamy Chocolate Pudding: Add ⅓ cup milk chocolate morsels to milk mixture after it comes to a boil. Cook 1 additional minute or until chocolate melts, stirring constantly.

POTS DE CRÈME

2 (4-ounce) packages sweet baking
  chocolate
1 cup whipping cream
4 egg yolks
1 teaspoon vanilla extract
Whipped cream
Chocolate curls (optional)

Place chocolate in top of a double boiler; bring water to a boil. Reduce heat to low; cook until chocolate melts. Gradually add whipping cream, stirring until smooth. Remove from heat.

Beat egg yolks with a wire whisk. Gradually stir about one-fourth of chocolate mixture into egg yolks; add to the remaining chocolate mixture, stirring constantly. Stir in vanilla.

Spoon mixture into small cordial glasses or demitasse cups. Refrigerate. Garnish with whipped cream and chocolate curls, if desired. Yield: 6 servings.

◻ *Microwave Directions:* Place chocolate in a 4-cup glass measure or a 1-quart glass bowl. Microwave at HIGH for 2½ to 3 minutes, stirring once. Gradually add the whipping cream, stirring until smooth.

Beat egg yolks with a wire whisk. Gradually stir about one-fourth of chocolate mixture into egg yolks; add to the remaining chocolate mixture, stirring constantly. Stir in vanilla.

Spoon mixture into small cordial glasses or demitasse cups. Refrigerate. Garnish with whipped cream and chocolate curls, if desired.

Lemon Cake Pudding and Chocolate Cake Pudding bake into two layers—one like a cake, and one like a pudding. Spoon some of both into serving dishes, drizzling the pudding part over the cake part. Top with whipped cream or ice cream, if desired. Serve hot or cold.

LEMON CAKE PUDDING

1 cup sugar
3 tablespoons all-purpose flour
Pinch of salt
2 teaspoons grated lemon rind
2 tablespoons lemon juice
1 egg yolk, beaten
1 cup milk
2 egg whites

Combine sugar, flour, salt, lemon rind, and juice in a large bowl; stir well. Stir in egg yolk and milk. Beat egg whites (at room temperature) until stiff but not dry. Fold beaten egg whites into lemon mixture. Pour pudding mixture into a greased 1½-quart casserole. Pour water to depth of 1 inch into a large pan; place casserole in pan. Bake mixture at 350° for 45 minutes or until edges are browned. Yield: 4 to 6 servings.

CHOCOLATE CAKE PUDDING

1 cup all-purpose flour
2 teaspoons baking
  powder
⅛ teaspoon salt
¾ cup sugar
2 tablespoons cocoa
½ cup milk
3 tablespoons butter or margarine,
  melted
1 teaspoon vanilla extract
½ cup sugar
½ cup firmly packed brown
  sugar
¼ cup cocoa
1½ cups water
Sweetened whipped cream or ice
  cream (optional)

Combine flour, baking powder, salt, sugar, and cocoa in a greased 9-inch square pan, stirring well. Stir in milk, butter, and vanilla, spreading mixture evenly in pan.

Combine ½ cup sugar, ½ cup brown sugar, and ¼ cup cocoa, and sprinkle mixture evenly over batter. Pour water over top. Bake pudding at 350° for 40 minutes. Serve with sweetened whipped cream or ice cream, if desired. Yield: 6 servings.

ORANGE-TAPIOCA PUDDING

1¾ cups milk
⅓ cup sugar
¼ cup quick-cooking tapioca
⅛ teaspoon salt
2 eggs, separated
2 tablespoons sugar
2 teaspoons grated orange rind
¼ cup orange juice

Combine milk, ⅓ cup sugar, tapioca, salt, and egg yolks; beat at low speed of an electric mixer until blended. Cook over medium heat 5 minutes or until mixture thickens, stirring constantly.

Beat egg whites (at room temperature) until frothy. Gradually add 2 tablespoons sugar, beating until stiff peaks form; fold in orange rind and juice. Fold egg white mixture into pudding mixture; spoon into dessert dishes. Chill until set. Yield: 4 servings.

❑*Microwave Directions:* Combine milk, ⅓ cup sugar, tapioca, salt, and egg yolks in a 2-quart glass bowl; beat at low speed of an electric mixer until blended. Microwave at HIGH, uncovered, for 7 to 7½ minutes or until thickened, stirring at 2-minute intervals.

Beat egg whites (at room temperature) until frothy. Gradually add 2 tablespoons sugar, beating until stiff peaks form; fold in orange rind and juice. Fold egg white mixture into pudding mixture; spoon into dessert dishes. Chill until set.

FROZEN VANILLA CUSTARD

4 egg yolks
1 cup sugar
1 cup milk
1 cup half-and-half
1½ teaspoons vanilla extract
⅛ teaspoon salt
2 cups whipping cream, whipped
Shaved chocolate (optional)

Beat egg yolks in a heavy saucepan until thick and lemon colored; gradually add sugar, beating well. Add milk, half-and-half, vanilla, and salt; beat well. Bring to a boil. Reduce heat to low; then cook, stirring constantly, until mixture thickens and coats a metal spoon. Let cool to room temperature.

Gently fold whipped cream into custard, and spoon into a 1½-quart dish; freeze until firm. Garnish with chocolate shavings, if desired. Yield: 8 servings.

BREAD PUDDING

1 (1-pound) loaf French bread or 6 cups broken bread slices
1 quart milk
3 eggs, beaten slightly
1½ cups sugar
1 cup raisins
2 tablespoons vanilla extract
3 tablespoons butter or margarine, melted
Whiskey Sauce

Break bread into small chunks, and put in a large bowl. Add milk, and let soak about 10 minutes; crush with hands until blended. Add eggs, sugar, raisins, and vanilla. Pour butter into a 13- x 9- x 2-inch pan. Spoon pudding mixture into pan; bake at 325° for 25 minutes or until pudding is very firm. Let mixture cool; then cut into squares. Place in dessert dishes, and spoon Whiskey Sauce over top of each serving. Yield: 12 to 15 servings.

Whiskey Sauce

½ cup butter
1 cup sugar
½ cup half-and-half
2 tablespoons whiskey

Combine butter, sugar, and half-and-half in a heavy saucepan; cook over medium heat until sugar dissolves. Bring to a boil; reduce heat and simmer 5 minutes. Remove from heat. Let cool, and add whiskey. Yield: 1½ cups.

RICE PUDDING WITH MARMALADE SAUCE

6 cups milk
1 cup uncooked medium-grain rice
⅛ teaspoon salt
1 cup sugar
3 eggs
¼ cup butter or margarine
1 teaspoon vanilla extract
Marmalade Sauce

Bring milk to a boil in a 3-quart saucepan; add rice and salt, stirring until mixture returns to a boil. Cover, reduce heat, and simmer mixture 40 minutes. Stir in sugar.

Beat eggs until thick and lemon colored. Gradually stir about one-fourth of hot mixture into eggs; add to remaining hot mixture, stirring constantly. Cook over low heat 5 minutes, stirring constantly. Remove from heat; stir in butter and vanilla.

Spoon cooked rice mixture into a lightly greased 1½-quart baking dish, and refrigerate at least 8 hours. Before serving pudding, drizzle Marmalade Sauce over the top. Yield: 8 to 10 servings.

Marmalade Sauce

1 teaspoon cornstarch
⅓ cup cream sherry
1 (10-ounce) jar orange marmalade
¼ cup chopped pecans
Pinch of ground cinnamon

Combine cornstarch and sherry in a small saucepan, stirring until cornstarch dissolves. Stir in marmalade, pecans, and cinnamon. Cook over low heat, stirring constantly, until thoroughly heated. Yield: about 1½ cups.

Southerners are particular about their Banana Pudding, but we think this version will please even the most discriminating palate.

BANANA PUDDING

3½ tablespoons all-purpose flour
1⅓ cups sugar
Dash of salt
3 eggs, separated
3 cups milk
1 teaspoon vanilla extract
1 (12-ounce) package vanilla wafers
6 medium bananas
¼ cup plus 2 tablespoons sugar
1 teaspoon vanilla extract

Combine flour, 1⅓ cups sugar, and salt in a heavy saucepan. Beat egg yolks; combine egg yolks and milk, mixing well. Stir into dry ingredients; cook over medium heat, stirring constantly, until smooth and thickened. Remove from heat; stir in 1 teaspoon vanilla.

Layer one-third of wafers in a 3-quart baking dish. Slice 2 bananas, and layer over wafers. Pour one-third of custard over bananas. Repeat layers twice.

Beat egg whites (at room temperature) until foamy. Gradually add ¼ cup plus 2 tablespoons sugar, 1 tablespoon at a time, beating until stiff peaks form. Add 1 teaspoon vanilla, and beat until blended. Spread meringue over custard, sealing to edge of dish. Bake at 425° for 10 to 12 minutes or until golden brown. Yield: 8 to 10 servings.

PEANUT-CHOCOLATE PUDDING DESSERT

½ cup butter or margarine, softened
1 cup all-purpose flour
⅔ cup finely chopped dry roasted peanuts
1 (8-ounce) package cream cheese, softened
⅓ cup peanut butter
1 cup sifted powdered sugar
1 (12-ounce) container frozen whipped topping, thawed and divided
1 (3½-ounce) package vanilla instant pudding mix
1 (4-ounce) package chocolate instant pudding mix
2¾ cups milk
1 (1.2-ounce) milk chocolate candy bar, shaved
⅓ cup chopped dry roasted peanuts

Cut butter into flour using a pastry blender until mixture resembles coarse meal; stir ⅔ cup peanuts into flour mixture. Press peanut mixture into a 13- x 9- x 2-inch pan. Bake at 350° for 20 minutes; cool completely.

Combine cream cheese, peanut butter, and powdered sugar in a mixing bowl; beat at medium speed of an electric mixer until fluffy. Stir 1 cup whipped topping into cream cheese mixture. Spread over crust; chill.

Combine pudding mixes and milk; beat 2 minutes at medium speed of an electric mixer. Spread pudding over cream cheese layer. Spread remaining whipped topping over pudding layer. Sprinkle with chocolate and ⅓ cup peanuts. Chill. Yield: 15 servings.

PLUM PUDDING

In England, a Plum Pudding is synonymous with holiday time. It began as a thick, boiled porridge containing plums. Gradually the plums were replaced by raisins. Plum Pudding is packed into a mold and steamed for several hours, resulting in a firm texture.

A traditional plum pudding calls for suet (hard, dry beef fat). The fat gives it a distinctive flavor and melts and moistens the pudding during steaming.

3 cups all-purpose flour
1 teaspoon baking soda
¼ teaspoon salt
2 teaspoons ground cinnamon
½ teaspoon ground allspice
½ teaspoon ground cloves
2 cups raisins
1 cup peeled, chopped cooking apple
1 cup currants
1 cup molasses
1 cup cold water
1 cup finely chopped suet
Hard Sauce (recipe follows)

Combine flour, soda, salt, and spices in a large bowl; stir well. Stir in raisins, apple, and currants.

Combine molasses, water, and suet; add to dry ingredients, stirring well.

Spoon mixture into a well-buttered 10-cup mold; cover tightly.

Place mold on shallow rack in a large, deep kettle with enough boiling water to come halfway up mold. Cover kettle; steam pudding 3 hours in continuously boiling water (replace water as needed). Unmold and serve with hard sauce. Yield: 10 to 12 servings.

Hard Sauce

½ cup butter or margarine, softened
1 cup sifted powdered sugar
2 to 4 tablespoons rum, sherry, or brandy

Combine butter and powdered sugar, beating until smooth. Add rum; beat until fluffy. Chill. Yield: ¾ cup.

FLAN ALMENDRA

½ cup sugar
1⅔ cups sweetened condensed milk
1 cup milk
3 eggs
3 egg yolks
1 teaspoon vanilla extract
1 cup slivered almonds
Strawberry halves

Sprinkle sugar in a 9-inch round cake-pan; place over medium heat. Using oven mitts, caramelize sugar by shaking pan occasionally until sugar melts and turns a light golden brown; cool. (Mixture may crack slightly as it cools.)

Combine next 6 ingredients in container of an electric blender; process at high speed 15 seconds. Pour over caramelized sugar; cover pan with aluminum foil, and place in a large shallow pan. Pour hot water to depth of 1 inch into larger pan. Bake at 350° for 55 minutes or until a knife inserted near center comes out clean.

Remove pan from water and uncover; let cool on wire rack at least 30 minutes. Loosen edges with a spatula. Invert flan onto plate; arrange strawberries around sides. Yield: 6 servings.

Individual Flans Almendra: Place 1 cup sugar in a heavy saucepan; place over medium heat. Using oven mitts, caramelize sugar by shaking pan occasionally until sugar melts and turns a light golden brown. Remove from heat. Pour hot caramel mixture into 6 (10-ounce) custard cups. Let cool. Pour flan mixture evenly into custard cups, making sure ground almond mixture is evenly divided; cover with aluminum foil. Place custard cups in a broiler pan; pour hot water to depth of 1 inch into pan. Bake at 350° for 35 to 40 minutes or until a knife inserted near center comes out clean. Remove cups from water, and cool. To serve, loosen edge of custard with a spatula; invert onto plates.

Note: A little stirring may be necessary when caramelizing the sugar if a gas burner is used.

Flan Almendra Step-By-Step

1. You'll need to caramelize sugar to make Flan Almendra. Sprinkle sugar directly into the cakepan, and shake pan over low heat.

2. The sugar will melt and lump as you cook it. Cook until all sugar melts, and set aside to cool.

3. Combine remaining ingredients in electric blender; blend and pour over cooled syrup in pan.

4. Cover pan with aluminum foil, and place in a larger baking dish. Pour hot water to depth of 1 inch into baking dish, and bake as directed.

Invert flan onto serving plate, letting syrup drizzle over top; garnish with strawberries.

Spoon deeply into English Trifle when serving. You'll want to savor each layer of pound cake, custard, strawberries, and whipped cream.

ENGLISH TRIFLE

1 recipe Angel Pound Cake (page 122)
¾ cup cream sherry, divided
1½ cups fresh strawberries, hulled and halved
Trifle Custard
1 cup strawberry preserves
1½ cups whipping cream
¼ cup plus 2 tablespoons sifted powdered sugar
Fresh cut strawberries
Mint leaves

Slice Angel Pound Cake into ¼-inch slices; trim and discard crust. Line bottom of a 16-cup trifle bowl with one-third of cake slices; sprinkle with ¼ cup sherry. Arrange strawberry halves, cut side out, around lower edge of bowl. Spoon 2 cups Trifle Custard over cake slices; place half of remaining cake slices over custard. Gently spread strawberry preserves over cake; top with remaining cake slices. Pour remaining ½ cup sherry over trifle. Spoon remaining custard on top. Cover and chill 3 to 4 hours.

Beat whipping cream until foamy; gradually add powdered sugar, beating until soft peaks form. Spread over trifle; garnish with strawberries and mint leaves. Serve immediately. Yield: 14 to 16 servings.

Trifle Custard

2 cups milk
⅔ cup whipping cream
4 eggs
⅔ cup sugar
½ teaspoon vanilla extract

Combine milk and whipping cream in a medium saucepan; cook over low heat until warm.

Combine eggs and sugar, beating well. Gradually stir about one-fourth of warm mixture into eggs; add to remaining warm mixture, stirring constantly.

Cook over low heat, stirring constantly, until mixture thickens and coats the spoon. Remove from heat; stir in vanilla. Cool to room temperature; chill. Yield: 3½ cups.

Mousses, Soufflés, and Gelatin Desserts

Light and airy from the egg whites or whipped cream folded into them, these desserts have almost universal appeal. They're also popular with hostesses, too, because they all instruct you to "chill until set." This can conveniently mean a night or two if you're looking for recipes to make ahead of time.

The consistency of these dishes is similar, but each has distinguishing characteristics.

The term *mousse* is used to define a light and airy chilled dessert that gets its frothiness from either beaten egg whites, whipped cream, or both.

A mousse does not contain gelatin.

Soufflés are similar in consistency, but are usually lighter in texture than mousses. They always have beaten egg whites and often contain whipped cream, too. Dinner soufflés are usually baked, whereas dessert soufflés are usually not baked. When they are not baked, soufflés often contain gelatin.

Bavarian creams always contain gelatin and whipped cream. They usually don't contain beaten egg whites. A Charlotte Russe is a Bavarian that is lined with sponge cake or ladyfingers.

CHOCOLATE-ORANGE MOUSSE

1 teaspoon grated orange rind
¼ cup firmly packed brown sugar
2 eggs yolks
2 eggs
6 (1-ounce) squares semisweet chocolate, melted and cooled
1 tablespoon orange juice
1 cup whipping cream, whipped
Additional whipped cream for garnish
Mandarin oranges

Combine orange rind, sugar, egg yolks, and eggs in container of an electric blender; process until frothy. Add chocolate and orange juice; process well. Fold in whipped cream.

Pour mixture into individual serving dishes, and chill until set. Garnish each serving with additional whipped cream and mandarin orange slices. Yield: 6 servings.

LEMON SOUFFLÉ

3 eggs, separated
1 envelope unflavored gelatin
½ cup sugar
⅛ teaspoon salt
1 cup water
Grated rind of 1 lemon
Juice of 1 lemon
⅓ cup sugar
1 cup whipping cream, whipped

Beat egg yolks at medium speed of an electric mixer until thick and lemon col-ored. Combine yolks, gelatin, sugar, salt, and water in a saucepan, stirring well. Cook over medium heat, stirring constantly, until mixture begins to boil. Remove from heat; stir in lemon rind and juice. Cool.

Beat egg whites (at room temperature) until foamy; gradually add ⅓ cup sugar, beating until stiff peaks form. Fold egg whites and whipped cream into yolk mixture. Spoon into a 1-quart dish; cover and chill. Yield: 6 servings.

RASPBERRY DREAM

(pictured on page 178)

1 envelope unflavored gelatin
¼ cup cold water
1 (8-ounce) package cream cheese, softened
½ cup sugar
½ teaspoon almond extract
Dash of salt
1 cup milk
1 cup whipping cream
Raspberry Sauce

Sprinkle gelatin over water in a small saucepan; let stand 1 minute. Cook over low heat, stirring until gelatin dissolves. Set aside.

Combine cream cheese, sugar, almond extract, and salt; beat at medium speed of an electric mixer until smooth and creamy. Gradually add milk and gelatin mixture to creamed mixture, mixing well. Beat whipping cream until soft peaks form (do not overbeat); fold into gelatin mixture.

Pour into a lightly oiled 4-cup mold; chill until set. Unmold dessert onto serving dish, and spoon Raspberry Sauce over dessert. Yield: 8 servings.

Raspberry Sauce

1 (10-ounce) package frozen raspberries, thawed
1 tablespoon cornstarch
2 tablespoons cream sherry

Drain raspberries, reserving juice. Put raspberries through a food mill, and discard seeds.

Combine raspberry puree, juice, cornstarch, and sherry in a small saucepan; stir well. Cook over low heat, stirring constantly, until smooth and slightly thickened. Cool. Yield: 1 cup.

To fold whipped cream or egg whites into fluffy desserts: With a rubber spatula, cut down through the center of the mixture, across the bottom, and up the sides of the bowl. Give the bowl a quarter turn, and repeat folding and turning until mixtures are blended.

BRANDY ALEXANDER SOUFFLÉ

2 envelopes unflavored gelatin
2 cups water
4 eggs, separated
¾ cup sugar
1 (8-ounce) package cream cheese, softened
3 tablespoons crème de cacao
3 tablespoons brandy
¼ cup sugar
1 cup whipping cream, whipped

Cut a piece of aluminum foil or wax paper long enough to fit around a 1½-quart soufflé dish, allowing a 1-inch overlap; fold lengthwise into thirds. Lightly oil one side of foil; wrap around outside of soufflé dish, oiled side against dish, allowing foil to extend 3 inches above rim to form a collar. Secure foil with freezer tape.

Combine gelatin and 1 cup water in top of a double boiler; bring water in bottom of double boiler to a boil. Cook, stirring constantly, until gelatin dissolves; stir in remaining 1 cup water.

Beat egg yolks at medium speed of an electric mixer until thick and lemon colored; gradually add ¾ cup sugar, beating well. Stir into gelatin mixture. Cook over low heat 20 to 25 minutes or until thickened, stirring constantly.

Beat cream cheese until smooth; gradually add yolk mixture, beating well. Stir in crème de cacao and brandy; chill until slightly thickened.

Beat egg whites (at room temperature) until foamy; gradually add ¼ cup sugar, beating until stiff peaks form. Gently fold whipped cream and beaten egg whites into cream cheese mixture.

Spoon into prepared soufflé dish or individual serving dishes, and chill until firm. Remove collar from dish. Yield: 8 to 10 servings.

Grasshopper Soufflé: Substitute ¼ cup plus 2 tablespoons green crème de menthe for crème de cacao and brandy.

Kahlúa Soufflé: Add 2 teaspoons instant coffee granules to gelatin and water in double boiler. Substitute ¼ cup plus 2 tablespoons Kahlúa for crème de cacao and brandy.

○*Microwave Directions:* Cut a piece of aluminum foil or wax paper long enough to fit around a 1½-quart soufflé dish, allowing a 1-inch overlap; fold lengthwise into thirds. Lightly oil one side of foil; wrap around outside of dish, oiled side against dish, allowing it to extend 3 inches above rim to form a collar. Secure foil with freezer tape.

Combine gelatin and ½ cup cold water, stirring well. In a 2½-quart casserole, microwave 1½ cups water at HIGH for 5 to 9 minutes or until boiling. Add gelatin mixture, stirring to dissolve.

Beat egg yolks at medium speed of an electric mixer until thick and lemon colored; gradually add ¾ cup sugar, beating well. Gradually stir in about one-fourth of hot gelatin mixture; then stir into remaining hot mixture. Microwave at HIGH for 2 to 4 minutes or until thickened, stirring at 2-minute intervals.

Beat cream cheese until smooth; gradually add yolk mixture, beating well. Stir in crème de cacao and brandy; chill until slightly thickened.

Beat egg whites (at room temperature) until foamy; gradually add ¼ cup sugar, beating until stiff peaks form. Gently fold whipped cream and beaten egg whites into cream cheese mixture.

Spoon into prepared soufflé dish or individual serving dishes, and chill until firm. Remove collar from dish.

CHARLOTTE RUSSE

4 eggs, separated
¼ cup sugar
1 envelope unflavored gelatin
½ cup cold water
1 teaspoon vanilla extract
¼ cup plus 2 tablespoons sugar
2 cups whipping cream, whipped and divided
12 to 18 ladyfingers

Beat egg yolks and ¼ cup sugar at medium speed of an electric mixer until thick and lemon colored. Set aside.

Sprinkle gelatin over cold water in a small saucepan; let stand 1 minute. Cook over low heat until gelatin dissolves; cool slightly. Add to yolk mixture, stirring well. Stir in vanilla.

Beat egg whites (at room temperature) until foamy. Gradually add ¼ cup plus 2 tablespoons sugar, one tablespoon at a time, beating until stiff peaks form.

Reserve ½ cup whipped cream. Fold remaining whipped cream and egg whites into yolk mixture.

Split ladyfingers in half lengthwise. Line a 2½-quart glass bowl with ladyfingers. Pour in filling; cover and chill at least 8 hours. Garnish with reserved whipped cream. Yield: 8 to 10 servings.

CHOCOLATE MOUSSE BAKED ALASKA

¼ cup all-purpose flour
¼ cup cocoa
3 eggs
½ cup sugar
¼ cup butter or margarine, melted
½ teaspoon vanilla extract
2 tablespoons sugar
¼ cup water
2 tablespoons Cognac or brandy
12 (1-ounce) squares semisweet
   chocolate
4 (1-ounce) squares unsweetened
   chocolate
6 eggs, separated
½ cup sugar
3 tablespoons Cognac
1½ tablespoons brewed strong coffee
1 cup whipping cream
5 egg whites
¼ teaspoon cream of tartar
¾ cup sugar
½ teaspoon vanilla extract
Pecan halves

Grease three 8-inch round cakepans; line bottoms with wax paper. Grease and flour wax paper; set aside.

Combine flour and cocoa; stir well, and set aside. Combine 3 eggs and ½ cup sugar in a medium mixing bowl; beat at medium speed of an electric mixer 5 minutes or until thick and lemon col-ored. Fold in cocoa mixture; then fold in butter and ½ teaspoon vanilla. Pour batter into prepared pans. Bake at 350° for 15 minutes or until a wooden pick inserted in center comes out clean. Remove from oven; immediately invert onto wire racks. Remove wax paper, and let cake cool completely.

Combine 2 tablespoons sugar and water in a small saucepan; cook over medium heat, stirring constantly, until mixture boils. Boil 3 minutes. Remove from heat; cool. Stir in 2 tablespoons Cognac; set aside.

Place chocolate in top of a double boiler; bring water to a boil. Reduce heat to low; cook until chocolate melts. Remove from heat.

Combine 6 egg yolks and ½ cup sugar in a large mixing bowl; beat at medium speed of electric mixer until yolks are thick and lemon colored and sugar dissolves. Stir in 3 tablespoons Cognac and coffee. Fold in melted chocolate. Beat 6 egg whites (at room temperature) until stiff peaks form; fold into chocolate mixture. Beat whipping cream until stiff peaks form; fold into chocolate mixture. Chill 30 minutes.

Line a 2½-quart mixing bowl (about 9 inches in diameter) with plastic wrap, leaving an overhang around the edges.

Cut 2 layers of the cake into pieces, and line bowl with cake completely.

Brush cake with about two-thirds of Cognac syrup; spoon in chocolate filling. Top with remaining cake layer; brush with remaining syrup. Pull edges of the plastic wrap over top to cover, and freeze for 24 hours.

Remove dessert from freezer; invert bowl of mousse onto an ovenproof wooden board or serving dish, leaving the plastic wrap intact. Remove bowl; place mousse in freezer while preparing the meringue.

Beat 5 egg whites (at room temperature) and cream of tartar until foamy. Gradually add ¾ cup sugar, 1 tablespoon at a time, beating until stiff peaks form and sugar dissolves. Add ½ teaspoon vanilla; beat until blended. Remove frozen mousse from freezer, and peel off plastic wrap. Quickly spread meringue over entire surface, making sure edges are sealed.

Bake at 450° for 5 minutes or until meringue peaks are browned. Garnish with pecan halves. Serve immediately. Yield: 14 to 16 servings.

Note: After meringue is sealed, the dessert can be returned to the freezer and baked just before serving. Keep in freezer up to 1 week.

Ice Cream and Frozen Desserts

No sound is more welcome on a warm summer day than the cranking of an ice cream freezer. From the moment the activity starts, family and friends gather around to share the fun and wait impatiently for the lid to be lifted.

In addition to those wonderful flavors that come from the ice cream freezer, there are a host of other desserts you can make from com-mercial ice cream—layering it with fruit, nuts, or chocolate into all types of freezer desserts. Don't wait for summer to enjoy them.

Before starting your ice cream, get acquainted with your freezer. Read the manufacturer's instructions carefully. Freezers are made of different materials, making a difference in the ice-salt ratio recommended. Most 1-gallon freezers will use three to four cups rock salt and 20 pounds crushed ice.

Don't skimp on the ice and salt; they're essential for proper freezing of the ice cream. The ice cream freezes because its heat is absorbed by the ice and salt. Ice alone is not cold enough to freeze the ice cream.

If too little salt is used, the brine will not get cold enough to thoroughly freeze the ice cream. If too much salt is used, the ice cream will freeze too quickly, causing large ice crystals to form. Rock salt is usually preferred over table salt because table salt dissolves rapidly. (Some freezer manufacturers do recommend using table salt for their models, however.)

Fill the freezer can only as full as recommended by the manufacturer. Most should be filled to no more than two-thirds or three-fourths of their capacity. For electric freezers, let the motor run about one minute before adding ice and salt in layers. Hand-turned freezers should be turned about one minute to stir the mixture before freezing.

When adding ice and salt, make four fairly thick layers of ice and four thin layers of salt, beginning with ice and ending with salt. You'll have some ice and salt left over to add as the ice melts and when ripening the ice cream.

After cranking, let the ice cream ripen in order to harden and blend flavors. First remove the dasher. Push the ice cream down from the top sides of the can, and blend soft portions with firm portions. Cover with aluminum foil, and replace lid. Pack the freezer bucket with ice and salt, using a higher ratio of salt to ice than for freezing. Wrap well, and let stand in a cool place for one to two hours. Drain off the brine and check the ice and salt frequently, adding more if needed. After ripening, the ice cream is ready to enjoy.

Spoon leftovers into small plastic foam cups. Cover tightly, and freeze. The plastic foam insulates the ice cream, and the small, serving-size amounts enable the ice cream to freeze quickly and solidly, making this a good storage method for leftover homemade ice cream.

New Shapes for Ice Cream

Dazzle your family and friends with ice cream molds in a rainbow of colors and flavors. For an added treat, spoon a sauce over them before serving.

There are molds designed specifically for ice cream, although just about any mold will work well. Molds with clean lines and simple designs are easier to unmold than those with intricate shapes and designs.

Molds made of metal are especially good because the metal conducts cold quickly, thus allowing for complete freezing and easy unmolding. If you use a mold made of another material, you will need to allow extra time for freezing and softening.

Molds made specifically for ice cream should be lightly oiled for easy unmolding. Line one-piece or non-metal molds with plastic wrap.

Let ice cream soften at room temperature a few minutes before unmolding. You can speed up the process by patting the mold with a warm, damp cloth or even blowing it with an electric hair dryer until the frost evaporates from the outside of the mold.

PEPPERMINT ICE CREAM

1 quart milk
1 pound soft peppermint candy sticks
2 cups half-and-half
2 cups whipping cream

Combine milk and candy; cover and refrigerate 12 hours. (Candy will dissolve.) Combine candy mixture, half-and-half, and whipping cream in freezer can of a 1-gallon hand-turned or electric freezer. Freeze according to manufacturer's instructions. Let ripen at least 1 hour. Yield: about 1 gallon.

LIGHTLY LEMON ICE CREAM

3 cups sugar
4 cups milk
2 cups whipping cream
1 cup half-and-half
½ cup grated lemon rind
¾ cup fresh lemon juice
2 egg whites, beaten

Combine sugar, milk, whipping cream, half-and-half, and lemon rind. Pour lemon juice over milk mixture; beat well. Fold in beaten egg whites. Pour mixture into freezer can of a 1-gallon hand-turned or electric freezer. Freeze according to manufacturer's instructions. Ice cream may be ripened for 1 hour, if desired. Yield: 1 gallon.

PEACH ICE CREAM

5 eggs
1½ cups sugar, divided
1 (14-ounce) can sweetened condensed milk
1 (12-ounce) can evaporated milk
1 tablespoon vanilla extract
5 cups milk
2 cups mashed fresh peaches

Beat eggs until frothy; add 1 cup sugar and beat well. Add condensed milk, evaporated milk, and vanilla, mixing well. Pour into freezer can of a 5-quart hand-turned or electric freezer; add milk. Turn about 5 minutes or until custard is thick.

Combine peaches and remaining ½ cup sugar. Remove dasher, and add peaches to cream mixture. Return dasher to freezer, and freeze mixture according to manufacturer's instructions. Let ice cream ripen about 1 hour. Yield: 1 gallon.

CHOCOLATE ICE CREAM

3 eggs
1 cup sugar
4 cups half-and-half
2 cups whipping cream
1 cup chocolate syrup
1 tablespoon vanilla extract
About 3 cups milk

Beat eggs at medium speed of an electric mixer until frothy. Gradually add sugar, beating until thick. Add next 4 ingredients; mix well. Pour mixture into freezer can of a 1-gallon hand-turned or electric freezer. Add enough milk to fill can about three-fourths full. Freeze according to manufacturer's instructions. Let ripen at least 1 hour before serving. Yield: about 1 gallon.

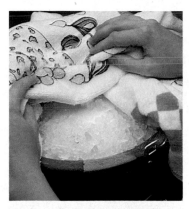

To firm the consistency of ice cream after freezing: Allow ice cream to ripen. Remove the dasher, and scrape ice cream back into the freezer can. Cover with foil, and replace the lid. Pack additional ice and salt around the can; cover freezer with heavy towels or newspaper. Let stand 1 to 2 hours.

VANILLA ICE CREAM SPECTACULAR

5 cups milk
2¼ cups sugar
¼ cup plus 2 tablespoons all-purpose flour
¼ teaspoon salt
5 eggs, beaten
4 cups half-and-half
1½ tablespoons vanilla extract

Heat milk in a 3-quart saucepan over low heat until hot. Combine sugar, flour, and salt; gradually add sugar mixture to milk, stirring until blended. Cook over medium heat 15 minutes or until thickened, stirring constantly.

Gradually stir about one-fourth of hot mixture into beaten eggs; add to remaining hot mixture, stirring constantly. Cook 1 minute; remove from heat, and let cool. Chill at least 2 hours.

Combine half-and-half and vanilla in a large bowl; add chilled custard, stirring with a wire whisk. Pour into freezer can of a 1-gallon hand-turned or electric freezer. Freeze according to manufacturer's instructions. Let ripen 1½ to 2 hours. Yield: 1 gallon.

STRAWBERRY ICE CREAM

2 cups sugar, divided
¼ cup all-purpose flour
Dash of salt
3 cups milk
4 eggs, slightly beaten
3 cups sieved or pureed fresh strawberries
3 cups whipping cream
1 tablespoon vanilla extract
2 teaspoons almond extract

Combine 1½ cups sugar, flour, and salt; set aside.

Heat milk in top of a double boiler until hot; add a small amount of milk to sugar mixture, stirring to make a smooth paste. Stir sugar mixture into remaining milk; cook, stirring constantly, until slightly thickened. Cover and cook 10 minutes.

Stir about one-fourth of hot mixture into beaten eggs; add to remaining hot mixture. Cook, stirring constantly, 1 minute. Let cool.

Combine strawberries, remaining ½ cup sugar, whipping cream, and flavorings; stir into custard. Pour into freezer can of a 1-gallon hand-turned or electric ice cream freezer; freeze according to manufacturer's instructions. Mixture does not need ripening. Yield: 3 quarts.

CARAMEL-VANILLA ICE CREAM

2 (14-ounce) cans sweetened condensed milk
4 eggs
2 cups sugar
4 cups half-and-half
2 cups whipping cream
4 cups milk

Pour sweetened condensed milk into two 8-inch pieplates. Cover with aluminum foil. Place each pieplate in a larger shallow pan filled with hot water to depth of ¼ inch. Bake at 425° for 1 hour and 20 minutes or until condensed milk is thick and caramel colored (add hot water to casseroles as needed). Remove foil; let caramelized milk cool.

Beat eggs in a large bowl at medium speed of an electric mixer until thick and lemon colored. Gradually add sugar, beating until light and fluffy. Add caramelized milk, half-and-half, and whipping cream, beating constantly until mixture is well blended.

Pour caramelized milk mixture into freezer can of a 1½-gallon hand-turned or electric ice cream freezer; add milk, stirring well. Freeze according to manufacturer's instructions. Let ripen 1 hour. Yield: about 1½ gallons.

Note: Recipe may be halved and prepared in a 1-gallon ice cream freezer.

PRALINES AND CREAM ICE CREAM

2 to 2½ cups chopped pecans
2 tablespoons butter or margarine, melted
6 eggs
1 (14-ounce) can sweetened condensed milk
1 (12-ounce) can evaporated milk
1 tablespoon vanilla extract
2 cups whipping cream, whipped
2 cups sugar, divided
1 (5-ounce) can evaporated milk
1⅓ cups milk

Sauté pecans in butter, stirring constantly, about 5 minutes or until toasted. Set aside to cool.

Beat eggs in a large bowl at medium speed of an electric mixer until frothy. Add next 3 ingredients, beating well. Fold in whipped cream.

Combine 1 cup sugar and remaining milk in a saucepan. Cook over low heat, stirring constantly, until mixture begins to boil; remove from heat.

Place remaining 1 cup sugar in a small saucepan; cook over medium heat, stirring mixture constantly, until sugar dissolves and forms a smooth liquid. Stir in the sautéed pecans. (Mixture may form lumps.)

Stir pecan mixture into sugar and milk mixture; break apart pecan lumps. Stir into egg mixture.

Pour into freezer can of a 5-quart hand-turned or electric freezer. Freeze according to manufacturer's instructions. Let ripen at least 1 hour. Yield: about 1 gallon.

Sherbets are made much like ice cream, but they're not as creamy. They are made of fruit juice and may contain added milk, egg white, or gelatin.

PINEAPPLE-ORANGE SHERBET

1 (8-ounce) can crushed pineapple, undrained
2 (14-ounce) cans sweetened condensed milk
6 (12-ounce) cans orange carbonated beverage

Combine pineapple and milk in freezer can of a 1-gallon hand-turned or electric freezer; stir well. Add orange beverage, stirring well. Freeze according to the manufacturer's instructions. Let ripen at least 1 hour. Yield: 1 gallon.

WATERMELON SHERBET

4 cups diced seeded watermelon
¾ to 1 cup sugar
3 tablespoons lemon juice
Dash of salt
1 envelope unflavored gelatin
¼ cup cold water
1 cup whipping cream

Combine watermelon, sugar, lemon juice, and salt in a large mixing bowl; refrigerate 30 minutes. Spoon mixture into container of an electric blender; process until smooth. Return to bowl.

Sprinkle gelatin over cold water in a saucepan; let stand 1 minute. Cook over low heat until gelatin dissolves; add to watermelon mixture, stirring well. Add whipping cream; beat at medium speed of electric mixer until fluffy. Pour into freezer can of a 1-gallon hand-turned or electric freezer. Freeze according to manufacturer's instructions. Mixture does not need ripening. Yield: 1 quart.

STRAWBERRY-CHAMPAGNE SHERBET

1 (10-ounce) package frozen strawberries, thawed
1 cup whipping cream
½ cup sugar
1½ cups champagne
2 egg whites
¼ teaspoon cream of tartar
¼ cup sugar

Mash strawberries; set aside. Combine whipping cream and ½ cup sugar in a medium saucepan; cook over low heat, stirring constantly, until sugar dissolves. Stir in strawberries and champagne. Pour mixture into a 13- x 9- x 2-inch pan; freeze until mixture is almost firm.

Beat egg whites (at room temperature) and cream of tartar until foamy. Gradually add ¼ cup sugar, 1 tablespoon at a time, beating until stiff peaks form; fold into champagne mixture. Freeze until firm. Yield: 1 quart.

Ices are similar to sherbets, but they're not as rich and fattening. They are generally made from a small amount of sugar, water, and juice, without any milk or cream. Occasional stirring during the freezing process breaks up the mixture and gives it an "icy" texture. When you serve ices, keep in mind that they melt fast. They'll stay frozen longer if you scoop them ahead of time, freeze them in the serving container (if it's freezerproof), and serve them straight from the freezer. If your container is not freezerproof, chill it in the refrigerator and freeze the scoops on a baking pan well ahead of serving time. Transfer the scoops to the container just at the moment you are ready to serve.

GRAPE ICE

3½ cups water
¾ cup sugar
1 tablespoon lemon juice
1 (12-ounce) can frozen grape juice concentrate, undiluted

Combine water and sugar in a large saucepan; cook over medium heat, stirring constantly, until sugar dissolves.

Add remaining ingredients, stirring until grape juice melts.

Pour mixture into freezer trays; freeze until firm, stirring several times during freezing process. Yield: 5½ cups.

Lemon Ice: Substitute 1 (12-ounce) can frozen lemonade concentrate, undiluted, for grape juice; omit lemon juice.

WINE ICE

1 cup water
1 cup sugar
2 teaspoons grated lemon rind
½ cup lemon juice
1 (25.6-ounce) bottle rosé

Combine water and sugar in a small saucepan; bring to a boil, stirring constantly until sugar dissolves. Let cool.

Combine sugar syrup and remaining ingredients; pour into freezer trays, and freeze until almost firm. Spoon mixture into a large bowl, and beat with an electric mixer until slushy. Return to freezer trays; freeze until firm. Yield: 4½ cups.

KIWIFRUIT ICE

4 kiwifruit, peeled and cubed
2 cups unsweetened apple juice
1 tablespoon lemon juice
½ teaspoon grated orange rind
Kiwifruit slices (optional)

Combine kiwifruit, apple juice, and lemon juice in container of an electric blender; process until smooth. Stir in orange rind. Pour mixture into an 8-inch square pan; freeze until almost firm.

Spoon frozen mixture into a mixing bowl; beat with an electric mixer until fluffy. Return mixture to pan, and freeze until firm. Let frozen mixture stand at room temperature 10 minutes before serving. Garnish with kiwifruit, if desired. Yield: about 4 cups.

SHERBET REFRESHER

12 scoops lemon or pineapple sherbet
1¼ cups fresh blueberries or raspberries
¾ cup lemon-lime carbonated beverage

Spoon 2 scoops sherbet into each individual compote. Sprinkle blueberries over sherbet. Spoon 2 tablespoons carbonated beverage over each serving. Serve immediately. Yield: 6 servings.

CHERRY CORDIAL DESSERT

4 (1-ounce) squares semisweet chocolate, finely grated
1 cup maraschino cherries, halved
½ cup coarsely chopped pecans
½ gallon vanilla ice cream, softened
¼ cup crème de cacao

Gently combine all ingredients except crème de cacao; spread into a 9-inch springform pan. Cover and freeze until mixture is firm.

To serve, slice dessert, and spoon about 1 teaspoon crème de cacao over each slice. Serve immediately. Yield: 10 to 12 servings.

DIXIE DESSERT CRÊPES

1 recipe Basic Crêpes (page 86)
3 to 4 cups vanilla ice cream
Chocolate Sauce Supreme (page 446)
⅓ cup chopped peanuts or pecans

Fill each crêpe with ¼ cup ice cream. Spoon Chocolate Sauce Supreme over each, and sprinkle with chopped peanuts. Yield: 6 to 8 servings.

Rainbow Sherbet Dessert is aptly named; each slice reveals three colorful layers of sherbet.

STRAWBERRY PARFAITS

1 pint strawberries, washed and hulled
⅓ cup sugar
1 tablespoon cornstarch
1 tablespoon lemon juice
⅛ teaspoon ground nutmeg
Dash of salt
¾ cup whipping cream, whipped and divided
2 tablespoons kirsch
Red food coloring (optional)
2 pints vanilla ice cream

Set aside 6 to 8 small strawberries; puree remaining berries.

Combine sugar, cornstarch, lemon juice, nutmeg, salt, and pureed strawberries in a saucepan; stir well. Cook over low heat, stirring constantly, until thickened. Let cool. Fold in 1 cup whipped cream, kirsch, and food coloring, if desired; chill.

Place a whole strawberry in each of 6 to 8 parfait glasses; top with a scoop of ice cream and about 2 tablespoons strawberry mixture. Repeat layers of ice cream and strawberry mixture. Top with remaining whipped cream. Yield: 6 to 8 servings.

RAINBOW SHERBET DESSERT

2 cups whipping cream
3 tablespoons powdered sugar
1 teaspoon vanilla extract
12 coconut macaroons, crushed and toasted
¾ cup chopped pecans, toasted
2½ cups raspberry sherbet, softened
2½ cups lime sherbet, softened
2½ cups orange sherbet, softened
Strawberry halves

Whip cream until frothy; add sugar and vanilla, beating until soft peaks form. Fold in macaroons and pecans. Spread half of mixture into a 9-inch springform pan; freeze. Spread a layer of each sherbet over whipped cream mixture, allowing each layer to freeze before spreading next layer. Top with remaining whipped cream mixture. Cover and freeze. Remove from pan, and place on serving plate. Garnish with strawberries. Yield: 12 servings.

Try a Flaming Dessert

Whipped cream and chocolate curls make a pretty garnish, but if you really want to impress your guests, try a flamed dessert. Assemble everything ahead of time, and do the flaming right at the table for a dazzling show.

There are two ways to flame desserts; the most common way is to use *liquors*. To flame desserts in this manner, heat the alcohol quickly just until fumes are produced; then remove it from heat, ignite, and pour evenly over the dessert. When heating the alcohol, remember that it's the fumes that ignite, not the alcohol. Don't overheat the alcohol, or the fumes will evaporate and the alcohol won't ignite.

In this method, the alcohol vanishes completely as it burns, and only the flavor remains. Those who do not care for alcohol may still enjoy this type of flamed dessert.

You can also use selected *extracts* to flame desserts. The higher the alcohol content of the extract, the better it will flame. Orange or lemon extract with 80% alcohol produces a very good flame, and peppermint extract with 65% alcohol produces a smaller yet good flame; vanilla extract with 35% alcohol produces no flame at all. Extracts flame without being heated, in contrast to alcoholic beverages that must be heated.

Because the flavor is so concentrated in extracts, you won't want to use the larger amounts used when flaming with alcoholic beverages. When using extracts, it's best to soak just a small portion of the dessert, such as the garnish, in the extract; then set the soaked portion in place, and ignite it.

One simple way to flame with extracts is to flame sugar cubes in maraschino cherry cups. Soak sugar cubes in extract for a couple of minutes; then tuck a sugar cube in a carved out maraschino cherry placed atop the dessert. Ignite the cube, and present dessert.

It's not dangerous to flame desserts if you use common sense and caution. Do remember that if you are heating the spirit over an open flame (gas or tabletop burner) prior to igniting, do not allow it to boil, as it can self-ignite. You only need to heat it long enough to begin producing fumes. And if you're nervous about igniting the dessert, you might be more comfortable using long-stemmed fireplace matches.

BANANAS FOSTER

¼ cup butter or margarine
¼ cup firmly packed brown sugar
½ teaspoon ground cinnamon
4 medium bananas, split and
 quartered
1 tablespoon imitation banana
 extract
¼ cup light rum
Vanilla ice cream

Melt butter in a large skillet; add brown sugar and cinnamon. Cook over medium heat until mixture is bubbly. Add bananas; heat 2 to 3 minutes, basting constantly with syrup. Stir in banana extract.

Place rum in a small, long-handled saucepan; heat just until warm (do not boil). Remove from heat. Ignite with a long match, and pour over bananas. Baste bananas with sauce until flames die down. Serve immediately over ice cream. Yield: 6 servings.

To flame desserts: Heat the spirit just until warm in a small saucepan; remove from heat, and ignite. Pour the flaming alcohol over the dessert, and serve after the flames die down.

CHERRIES JUBILEE

1 pound frozen sweet cherries
3 tablespoons sugar
1 tablespoon cornstarch
½ teaspoon grated orange rind
½ cup orange juice
½ cup water
¼ cup brandy
Vanilla ice cream

Partially thaw cherries; set aside.

Combine sugar, cornstarch, and orange rind in a saucepan. Stir in orange juice and water; bring to a boil, stirring constantly. Add cherries; reduce heat, and simmer 10 minutes, stirring gently. Transfer cherry sauce to a chafing dish or flambé pan, and keep warm.

Place brandy in a small, long-handled saucepan; heat until warm (do not boil). Remove from heat. Ignite with a long match; pour over cherries. Stir until flames die down. Serve immediately over ice cream. Yield: 4 to 6 servings.

1. Pack ice cream into a freezerproof bowl for Brownie Baked Alaska; freeze until very firm.

2. Prepare brownie batter, and bake as directed.

3. Place brownie layer on serving plate, and invert ice cream over top; freeze.

4. Remove dessert from freezer, and peel off the wax paper.

5. Immediately spread meringue over surface, sealing to edges. Bake just until meringue lightly browns.

Serve Brownie Baked Alaska immediately after baking, before the ice cream melts.

BROWNIE BAKED ALASKA

1 quart strawberry or vanilla ice
   cream
½ cup butter or margarine,
   softened
2 cups sugar, divided
2 eggs
1 cup all-purpose flour
½ teaspoon baking powder
¼ teaspoon salt
2 tablespoons cocoa
1 teaspoon vanilla extract
5 egg whites
Strawberry halves

Line a 1-quart freezerproof bowl (about 7 inches in diameter) with wax paper, leaving an overhang around the edges. Pack ice cream into bowl, and freeze until very firm.

Cream butter; gradually add 1 cup sugar, beating well at medium speed of an electric mixer. Add eggs, one at a time, beating after each addition. Combine flour, baking powder, salt, and cocoa; add to creamed mixture, mixing well. Stir in vanilla.

Pour batter into a greased and floured 8-inch round cakepan. Bake at 350° for 25 to 30 minutes or until a wooden pick inserted in center of cake comes out clean. Cool cake in pan 10 minutes. Remove cake from pan, and let cool completely on a wire rack.

Place cake on an ovenproof wooden board or serving dish. Invert bowl of ice cream onto cake layer, leaving wax paper intact; remove bowl. Place ice cream-topped cake in freezer.

Beat egg whites (at room temperature) until frothy; gradually add 1 cup sugar, 1 tablespoon at a time, beating until stiff peaks form and sugar dissolves (2 to 4 minutes). Remove ice cream-topped cake from freezer, and peel off wax paper. Quickly spread meringue over entire surface, making sure edges are sealed.

Bake at 500° for 2 to 3 minutes or until the meringue peaks are lightly browned. Arrange strawberry halves around edges, and serve immediately. Yield: 10 to 12 servings.

Note: After meringue is sealed, the dessert can be returned to the freezer and baked just before serving. Brownie Baked Alaska will keep in the freezer up to 1 week.

Baked Meringues

Southerners love to entertain with flair, and baked meringues will set Southern dessert tables in high style.

You're probably familiar with the soft and puffy type of meringue that typically tops pies, but baked meringues produce an entirely different dessert. The basic meringue mixture is piped or spread into freestanding shapes, then baked for a long time in a slow oven. This gives the shapes their characteristic crisp, melt-in-your-mouth texture.

For maximum volume in beaten egg whites, separate the eggs while cold, but let the whites come to room temperature before beating them.

Beat the meringue mixture just before you're ready to pipe, so it will be firm enough to hold peaks. After meringue sits a while, it will not be firm enough to hold its shape.

The baking temperatures range from 200° to 225°. (Temperatures are low to keep the meringue from browning during the time it takes to dry them out.) Meringues are baked until they are firm and almost dry; then the oven is turned off, and meringues are left in the oven to cool several hours or overnight.

Seal baked meringues in an airtight container, and store them at room temperature up to two days. For longer storage, freeze them up to a month in an airtight container. If the meringues feel soft or sticky after storage, crisp them in a 200° oven about 5 minutes. Then turn the oven off and let them cool in the oven until dry. Fill the meringues just before serving to keep them crisp.

Be sure not to make meringues in rainy or humid weather; extra moisture can make the end product soft and sticky.

BAKING MERINGUE

3 egg whites
¼ teaspoon cream of tartar
¼ teaspoon vanilla extract
¼ teaspoon almond extract
⅛ teaspoon salt
½ cup superfine sugar

Beat egg whites (at room temperature) in a large bowl at high speed of an electric mixer until foamy; sprinkle cream of tartar, flavorings, and salt over egg whites; continue beating until soft peaks form. Gradually add sugar, 1 tablespoon at a time, beating until stiff peaks form. Pipe or spread meringue into desired shapes; bake as directed.

Note: To make superfine sugar, place granulated sugar in a blender; process until finely ground.

LEMON CUSTARD IN MERINGUE CUPS

1 recipe Baking Meringue
Lemon Custard

Spoon meringue into 6 equal portions on baking sheet lined with unglazed brown paper. Using back of spoon, shape meringue into circles about 4 inches in diameter; then shape each circle into a shell. (Sides should be about 1½-inches high.)

Bake at 200° for 1 hour and 30 minutes to 1 hour and 45 minutes. Turn oven off. Cool in oven at least 2 hours or overnight. Spoon Lemon Custard into shells. Yield: 6 servings.

Lemon Custard

1 cup sugar
¼ cup plus 1 tablespoon cornstarch
Dash of salt
1½ cups boiling water
3 egg yolks
2 tablespoons grated lemon rind
¼ cup lemon juice

Combine sugar, cornstarch, and salt in a heavy saucepan; stir well. Add water, and cook over low heat, stirring constantly, until thickened.

Combine egg yolks, lemon rind, and juice; beat well. Gradually stir about one-fourth of hot mixture into yolks; add to remaining hot mixture, stirring constantly. Cook, stirring constantly, 10 minutes or until smooth and thickened. Chill. Yield: about 2½ cups.

MERINGUE FLOWERS

Make Meringue Flowers as edible garnishes to top cakes, pies, and other desserts, or to serve on the side as dainty little cookies. A whole recipe of Baking Meringue will make about 1 dozen meringue flowers, or you can make just a few flowers with meringue left from dessert meringue recipes.

1 recipe Baking Meringue
Small amount liquid food coloring (optional)

Prepare the Baking Meringue. (For colored flowers, add desired food coloring to meringue just before the sugar is added.) Pipe a dot of meringue onto a metal flower nail; place a 3-inch square of wax paper on flower nail.

Spoon meringue into a decorating bag fitted with large rose tip No. 126; holding wide end of tip down, pipe a flower onto wax paper, slowly rotating the nail as you pipe to form the flower. Transfer wax paper square to a baking sheet; repeat with remaining meringue. Bake at 225° for 1 hour and 45 minutes; turn off oven, and cool in oven 2 hours. Remove from oven; Cool on wire rack.

Peel the flowers from wax paper and use immediately, or carefully layer the flowers between wax paper in an airtight container. Store at room temperature up to 2 days, or freeze for several weeks. Yield: about 1 dozen.

Note: Soft or sticky flowers can be crisped in a 200° oven about 5 minutes. Turn off oven, and cool in oven 2 hours.

CHOCOLATE-ALMOND MERINGUE FINGERS

2 recipes Baking Meringue
1 tablespoon cornstarch
2 tablespoons cocoa
About 1 cup finely chopped almonds, toasted and divided
Chocolate Buttercream

Line 2 large baking sheets with unglazed brown paper; prepare Baking Meringue. Combine cornstarch and cocoa, stirring well; fold into meringue. Spoon mixture into a decorating bag fitted with No. 4B or 2D star tip; pipe about thirty-four 3- x 1½-inch rectangles using a zigzag motion. Sprinkle lightly with ⅔ cup almonds. Bake at 225° for 1½ hours. Turn off oven; cool in oven at least 2 hours or overnight. Carefully peel paper from meringue fingers. Store in an airtight container at room temperature up to 2 days.

Up to 2 hours before serving, pipe Chocolate Buttercream on flat sides of half the meringue fingers using No. 18, 19, or 20 star tip; sprinkle with remaining ⅓ cup almonds. Top with remaining meringue fingers. Refrigerate Chocolate-Almond Meringue Fingers until ready to serve. Yield: about 17 meringue fingers.

Chocolate Buttercream

1 cup butter or margarine, softened
2⅔ cups sifted powdered sugar
¼ cup cocoa
1 tablespoon plus 1 teaspoon milk
1 teaspoon vanilla extract

Cream butter at medium speed of an electric mixer; gradually add sugar, beating until light and fluffy. Add cocoa and milk; beat until spreading consistency. Stir in vanilla. Yield: 2 cups.

Design Your Own Meringues

Try our recipes for shaping meringues; then experiment with shapes on your own. Form simple shells with the back of a spoon, or pipe the mixture into elaborate designs. You can also make meringue cookies to serve with or without a filling.

When you experiment with your own creations, try folding extracts, finely chopped nuts, or a few drops of liquid food coloring into the prepared meringue before shaping and baking.

Always pipe meringue shapes on baking sheets lined with aluminum foil, unglazed brown paper, or wax paper underliners; without one of these underliners, the meringues will crack upon removal.

Fruit Desserts

Desserts made from fruit are often some of the simplest treats you can whip up, whether for the family or for company. It's hard to imagine that something as simple as fresh blueberries, liqueur, and whipping cream are just minutes away from a dessert as elegant as Blueberries and Cointreau. Layer the dessert in pretty stemmed glasses, and you're ready for company.

Fruit desserts also offer more nutrients and fiber than many other types of desserts. And without heavy sauces, creams, and a lot of sugar, fruit desserts are even better for you.

Thanks to modern transportation and storage, many fresh fruits are available year-round in most parts of the country and often at times of the year other than their peak season. For the best buys and fullest flavors, however, buy fruits in season.

Both frozen and canned fruits offer good alternatives to fresh fruit. Those fruits frozen whole without added syrup have flavors and textures most like those of the fresh product. You can also substitute fruits frozen and canned in syrup, but you may need to drain and pat them dry with paper towels before substituting them in recipes calling for fresh fruit. Study the recipe carefully before making substitutions.

When purchasing fresh fruit, evaluate its quality by the ripeness, texture, aroma, and appropriateness in color. Stay away from those fruits that show any signs of bumps or bruises—they'll deteriorate quickly. Whenever possible, choose loose fruit rather than that which is prepackaged. Place it in your own plastic bags, and store it in the refrigerator (except bananas).

BLUEBERRIES AND COINTREAU

2 cups fresh blueberries, rinsed and drained
¼ cup Cointreau or other orange-flavored liqueur
½ cup whipping cream
3 tablespoons powdered sugar

Place ½ cup blueberries in each of 4 stemmed glasses; pour 1 tablespoon Cointreau over each serving. Beat whipping cream until foamy; gradually add powdered sugar, beating until soft peaks form. Top each serving of blueberries with a dollop of whipped cream. Yield: 4 servings.

FRESH FRUIT COMPOTE

1 cup sugar
4 cups water
2 apples, peeled, cored, and quartered
2 peaches, peeled and quartered
2 pears, peeled, cored, and quartered
3 plums, pitted and quartered
¼ pound cherries, pitted
2 tablespoons lemon juice
2 or 3 (2-inch) sticks cinnamon
1 cup fresh strawberries, hulled
Whipped cream (optional)

Combine sugar and water in a large saucepan; bring to a boil. Add apples, peaches, pears, plums, cherries, lemon juice, and cinnamon sticks. Cook over medium heat 10 minutes, stirring occasionally; cool. Stir in strawberries, and chill. Serve with whipped cream, if desired. Yield: 8 servings.

BAKED APPLES

Since the texture, size, and ripeness of apples vary so greatly, cooking times for apples vary also. Be sure to check Baked Apples at the lower end of the range in cooking time to prevent overcooking, especially when baking them in a microwave oven.

4 large baking apples, peeled and cored
¼ cup firmly packed brown sugar
1 teaspoon ground cinnamon
1 teaspoon ground nutmeg
1 tablespoon plus 1 teaspoon butter or margarine
½ cup apple juice
Red food coloring (optional)

Place apples in an 8-inch square baking dish. Combine brown sugar, cinnamon, and nutmeg; spoon about 1 tablespoon sugar mixture into cavity of each apple. Top each with 1 teaspoon butter.

Bring apple juice to a boil; add food coloring, if desired. Pour juice into baking dish. Cover and bake at 400° for 25 to 35 minutes, basting occasionally with juice. Yield: 4 servings.

○*Microwave Directions:* Place apples in an 8-inch square baking dish. Combine brown sugar, cinnamon, and nutmeg; spoon about 1 tablespoon sugar mixture into cavity of each apple. Top each with 1 teaspoon butter.

Combine apple juice and food coloring, if desired. (Don't heat juice separately.) Pour juice into baking dish. Cover with heavy-duty plastic wrap; microwave at HIGH for 4 to 7 minutes or until almost tender, spooning juice over apples and giving dish a quarter turn at 2-minute intervals. Let stand 5 minutes before serving.

ORANGE-POACHED PEARS

1 cup sugar
½ cup water
½ cup orange juice
2 tablespoons lemon juice
6 pears
Twists of orange rind (optional)

Combine first 4 ingredients in a Dutch oven; bring to a boil over medium heat, stirring until sugar dissolves. Boil gently 5 minutes.

Peel pears and core just from the bottom, cutting to but not through the stem end. Add pears to Dutch oven. Cover, reduce heat, and simmer 15 minutes.

Transfer pears and syrup to a medium bowl; cover and chill thoroughly.

Spoon pears and syrup into dessert dishes; top each with a twist of orange rind, if desired. Yield: 6 servings.

FROZEN BANANA POPS

3 bananas
2 tablespoons orange juice
1 (6-ounce) package semisweet chocolate morsels
1 tablespoon shortening
1 cup finely chopped pecans or flaked coconut

Peel bananas, and slice in half crosswise; brush bananas with orange juice. Insert wooden skewers in cut end of bananas, and place on a wax paper-lined baking sheet. Freeze until firm.

Combine chocolate and shortening in top of a double boiler; bring water to a boil. Reduce heat to low; cook until chocolate melts. Then cool slightly. Spoon chocolate evenly over frozen bananas; immediately roll bananas in pecans. Serve at once, or wrap in plastic wrap and freeze. Yield: 6 servings.

To make pears and apples appear whole when serving: Core them just from the bottom, cutting to, but not through, the stem end.

SPICY COCONUT PEARS

1 (29-ounce) can pear halves
2 tablespoons cornstarch
¼ teaspoon ground cinnamon
¼ teaspoon ground nutmeg
⅛ teaspoon ground cloves
⅓ cup sugar
¼ cup lemon juice
2 tablespoons butter or margarine
½ cup flaked coconut, toasted

Drain pears, reserving 1 cup liquid. Combine ¼ cup reserved liquid, cornstarch, cinnamon, nutmeg, and cloves; stir until smooth. Set aside.

Combine remaining ¾ cup pear liquid, sugar, lemon juice, and butter in a small saucepan. Gradually stir in cornstarch mixture; cook over low heat, stirring constantly, until thickened.

Arrange pears in an 8-inch square baking dish. Pour sauce over pears; sprinkle with coconut. Bake at 350° for 15 minutes. Yield: 4 to 6 servings.

☐ *Microwave Directions:* Drain the pears, reserving 1 cup liquid. Combine ¼ cup reserved liquid, cornstarch, cinnamon, nutmeg, and cloves; stir until smooth. Set aside.

Combine remaining ¾ cup pear liquid, sugar, lemon juice, and butter in a 2-cup glass measure. Gradually stir in the cornstarch mixture; microwave at HIGH for 3 to 4 minutes or until mixture has thickened, stirring at 1-minute intervals.

Arrange pears in an 8-inch square baking dish. Pour sauce over pears; sprinkle with coconut. Microwave at HIGH for 4 to 5 minutes or until thoroughly heated.

PEACHY BLUEBERRY CRÊPES

2 cups fresh or frozen thawed blueberries
⅓ cup sugar
2½ cups cottage cheese, drained
1 cup sifted powdered sugar
1½ teaspoons vanilla extract
1 recipe Basic Crêpes (page 86)
1½ cups whipping cream
⅓ cup sifted powdered sugar
2 cups sliced canned peaches, drained

Combine blueberries and ⅓ cup sugar; stir gently, and set aside.

Combine next 3 ingredients in container of an electric blender; process until mixture is smooth.

Fill each crêpe with about 2 tablespoons cottage cheese mixture and 1 tablespoon blueberries. Roll up and place seam side up on serving dish.

Beat whipping cream until foamy; gradually add ⅓ cup powdered sugar, beating until soft peaks form. Top each crêpe with a dollop of whipped cream; garnish with peach slices and remaining blueberries. Yield: 8 to 9 servings.

CRÊPES SUZETTE

1 recipe Basic Crêpes (page 86)
½ teaspoon lemon, rum, or brandy
  extract
Orange Butter
Orange Sauce
3 tablespoons Grand Marnier or
  other orange-flavored liqueur

Prepare Basic Crêpes, adding flavoring (listed above) to batter with butter.

Spoon about 1 tablespoon Orange Butter on each crêpe, spreading to edges. Fold crêpe in half, then in quarters. Spoon half of Orange Sauce into chafing dish; arrange crêpes in sauce. Spoon remaining sauce over crêpes; place over low heat until thoroughly heated.

Place Grand Marnier in a small, long-handled saucepan; heat just until warm (do not boil). Pour over crêpes, and ignite with a long match. After flames die down, serve crêpes immediately. Yield: 8 servings.

Orange Butter

¾ cup unsalted butter, softened
¼ cup sifted powdered sugar
⅓ cup Grand Marnier or other
  orange-flavored liqueur
2 tablespoons grated orange rind

Cream butter and sugar until light and fluffy. Add Grand Marnier and orange rind, beating until well blended. Yield: 1¼ cups.

Orange Sauce

½ cup unsalted butter, melted
¾ cup sugar
2 tablespoons grated orange rind
⅔ cup orange juice
2 oranges, peeled and sectioned
¼ cup Grand Marnier or other
  orange-flavored liqueur

Combine butter, sugar, orange rind, and orange juice in a skillet or saucepan. Cook over low heat 10 minutes, stirring frequently. Add oranges and Grand Marnier. Keep warm. Yield: 2½ cups.

HEAVENLY DESSERT CHEESE MOLDS

We've placed Heavenly Dessert Cheese Molds with fruit desserts because it's intended to be served with sliced apple wedges and drizzled with a delightful orange sauce. It makes an attractive and not-so-sweet dinner finalé.

½ recipe Cream-Style Cheese
  (page 225)
⅔ cup sifted powdered sugar
½ teaspoon vanilla extract
1 cup whipping cream, whipped
Fresh Orange Sauce
Apple wedges or cookies

Combine Cream-Style Cheese, powdered sugar, and vanilla, mixing well. Fold whipped cream into cheese mixture.

Line six 3½-inch brioche pans, custard cups, or one 4-cup mold with 4 thicknesses of dampened cheesecloth large enough to extend over edges. Spoon cheese mixture evenly into molds, pressing firmly with the back of a spoon. Gather edges of cheesecloth, and tie securely. Invert molds on a wire rack set in a shallow pan. Cover pan with enough plastic wrap to make an airtight seal. Refrigerate 1 to 2 days or until firm and well drained. Unmold cheese and remove cheesecloth just before serving. Place each cheese mold on an individual dessert plate. Spoon Fresh Orange Sauce on plates around molds. Serve with apple wedges or cookies. Yield: six ½-cup cheese molds.

Fresh Orange Sauce

⅓ cup sugar
1 tablespoon cornstarch
1 cup orange juice
⅓ cup water
1 tablespoon butter or margarine
2 teaspoons grated orange rind

Combine first 4 ingredients in a small saucepan, stirring until smooth. Cook over medium heat, stirring constantly, until smooth and thickened. Add remaining ingredients; cook until butter melts. Chill. Yield: 1½ cups.

Note: One 8-ounce package commercial cream cheese, softened, can be substituted for ½ recipe Cream-Style Cheese. If using commercial cream cheese, add 1 tablespoon plus 1 teaspoon milk. Then mold as directed. No drainage is necessary.

STRAWBERRIES ZABAGLIONE

2 egg yolks
2 tablespoons sugar
2 tablespoons Marsala wine, sherry,
  or port
1 cup whipping cream
¼ cup sifted powdered sugar
2½ to 3 dozen large strawberries,
  washed and capped

Combine egg yolks, 2 tablespoons sugar, and wine in top of a double boiler; beat at medium speed of an electric mixer until blended. Place over boiling water. Reduce heat to low; cook about 5 minutes or until soft peaks form, beating constantly at medium speed of an electric mixer. Remove from heat.

Spoon mixture into a medium bowl; place in a larger bowl of ice. Beat about 2 minutes or until cool; refrigerate yolk mixture 30 minutes.

Combine whipping cream and powdered sugar; refrigerate 30 minutes. Add whipping cream to yolk mixture; beat until stiff.

Make two perpendicular slices down pointed end of each strawberry, cutting to within ½ inch of stem end. Carefully spread out quarter sections of each strawberry to form a cup. Using a pastry bag, fill each strawberry cup with the cream mixture. Refrigerate strawberries until ready to serve. Yield: 2½ to 3 dozen.

EGGS & CHEESE

Whether you are planning breakfast, lunch, or dinner, you can always rely on eggs and cheese as important parts of your menu—alone or in combination with other foods. In fact, if you stopped to add up just how often you do cook with eggs and cheese, you would agree that these are the most reliable and versatile foods in the kitchen.

Eggs

EQUIPMENT

Armed with a wire whisk, a spatula, and several sizes of nonstick skillets, you can cook almost every egg recipe in this chapter. For specialty dishes, such as soufflés and quiches, you might want to invest in cookware made especially for these purposes, although similarly shaped casserole dishes and pieplates make suitable substitutes.

And since both the egg and the cheese sections of this chapter include a lot of cheese, you might also like to invest in a good grater—so you'll have no more grated knuckles. There are some good hand-held graters, while food processors do the job especially quickly and neatly.

SELECTING EGGS

While mass production, labeling, and distribution take much of the guesswork out of buying eggs, sometimes the labels and categorizations

Huevos Rancheros (page 213) gives a Southwestern flair to brunch; it's based on tortillas and seasoned with regional herbs.

can be confusing. The U. S. Department of Agriculture lists six size categories of eggs: jumbo, extra large, large, medium, small, and peewee, although all markets don't always carry each size. The size doesn't matter much when cooking whole eggs, but for recipes with beaten eggs in specified numbers, the size can sometimes make a big difference in the end product. We always use large eggs in our recipe testing.

When considering the price difference in the sizes of eggs, if there is less than a 7-cent price spread per dozen eggs between one size and the next smaller size in the same grade, the larger size is the better buy.

Eggs are graded as either AA, A, and B. The higher quality grades are AA and A and are good for all egg cookery. They are especially desirable when appearance is important, such as in frying or poaching, because the white part of the egg is thick and the yolk is firm and stands high. When appearance is not important, grade B eggs are good for general cooking and baking. There is no difference in nutritional value among the grades of eggs.

Whether the egg is brown, white, or somewhere in between, there is no difference in the flavor, nutritive value, or cooking performance. Yolks can also vary in color, from almost orange to pale yellow. These color differences result from the chicken's feed and cause little difference in flavor.

STORING EGGS

Always store eggs in the refrigerator; there they'll keep up to five weeks without significant loss of quality. Store them with the large end up, preferably in the carton rather than in the refrigerator's egg tray. This allows the yolk to stay centered, which is important when deviling eggs or using sliced hard-cooked eggs as a garnish. Refrigerate hard-cooked eggs as soon after cooking as possible, and use them within a week.

If you have yolks or whites leftover from recipes, you can refrigerate them for several days, too. Place leftover whites in an airtight jar, and use within 10 days. Leftover yolks are more fragile. Store them in water in a tightly covered container, and use within two days.

WORKING WITH EGGS

You'll use some techniques dealing with eggs over and over in recipes. Following are some of the more common techniques, and how to perform them with skill.

Separating Eggs: You can purchase egg separators from kitchen shops to help you with this task, but separating eggs is really not hard to do without a separator. Eggs separate easiest when cold. Sharply tap the midpoint of the egg against a hard surface, such as the rim of a mixing bowl. Hold the egg over the bowl in which you want the whites, and gently pull the two halves apart holding one half like a cup to keep the yolk in that half, and letting the white part flow into the bowl underneath. Pass the yolk back and forth between the two shell halves until all the white has dripped into the bowl. It's safest to drop one white at a time

To separate an egg: Gently crack egg against edge of bowl; break shell into two halves, keeping yolk in one half and letting white drain into bowl. Transfer yolk back and forth between shells until all white has drained.

into a small bowl, then transfer it into a larger bowl with the other separated whites. This procedure avoids the problem of getting a little of the yolk into the whole bowl of whites; egg whites won't beat properly with even the slightest bit of yolk in them.

Perfectly Beaten Egg Whites Step-By-Step

1. When lightly beaten, egg whites will look bubbly and frothy.

2. At soft peak stage, egg whites mound, but no sharp tips form.

3. At stiff peak stage, sharp tips form when beaters are lifted.

4. At this stage, eggs are overbeaten. Better start over!

Beating Egg Yolks: Some recipes call for egg yolks to be beaten until thick and lemon colored. Beat the yolks at high speed of an electric mixer 3 to 5 minutes or until the yolks thicken and are a pale lemon-yellow color. At this stage, the yolks will have increased to their maximum volume.

Beating Egg Whites: Egg whites beat to the greatest volume when at room temperature. Place the whites in either a copper, glass, or stainless steel bowl, and let them stand about 45 minutes. (Be sure no yolk is contained within the whites, as the fatty composition of the yolks will prevent the whites from expanding properly. Make sure the mixing bowl and beaters are completely fat-free, too.) Beat the egg whites (and cream of tartar if your recipe calls for it) until foamy. If adding sugar to egg whites, do so at this point, adding one tablespoon at a time and beating until stiff peaks form.

When lightly beaten, egg whites will look foamy and bubbly. At this stage, the whites will easily separate back into liquid form. For recipes that call for soft peaks, beat the whites until they are moist and shiny; the whites will mound, but no sharp tips will form. For stiff peaks, the egg whites will be moist and glossy, and sharp peaks will form when the beaters are removed. When overbeaten, the egg whites will be dry and look almost curdled.

Folding in Egg Whites: Beat the egg whites at the very last minute before your recipe specifies to fold them in. To fold, use a rubber spatula and cut straight down through the center of the bowl, across the bottom, and up the sides. Give the bowl a quarter turn, and gently repeat the folding action just until egg whites are evenly dispersed. Be sure not to overwork the mixture or you'll lose the air incorporated into the beaten egg whites.

Tempering Eggs: This is a process used to combine uncooked eggs with a hot mixture. Beat the eggs until thick and lemon colored. Gradually stir about one-fourth of the hot mixture into the eggs; add that to the remaining hot mixture, stirring constantly. Using this process, the eggs should not curdle.

ABOUT FREEZING EGGS

If you have more eggs than you can use within four or five weeks, consider freezing them—not in the shell, of course. Whether freezing just yolks or whole eggs, they require special treatment to prevent the yolk from becoming gelatinous. Add either ⅛ teaspoon salt or 1½ teaspoons sugar per 4 egg yolks or 2 whole eggs. Label the container with the date, number of eggs, and whether you've added salt (for savory dishes) or sugar (for desserts). Freeze whole eggs or egg yolks up to six months. Thaw the container of eggs 8 hours in the refrigerator or run cold water over the container until eggs are thawed.

Egg whites can be frozen without any added ingredients. Just pour into freezer containers, label with the date and the number of whites, and freeze. For convenient freezer storage of individual egg whites, place egg whites separately into ice cube trays. When frozen, remove the cubes from trays, and store them in plastic bags up to eight months. Allow one cube for each egg white called for in a recipe. Thaw egg whites 8 hours in the refrigerator or run cold water over the plastic container until eggs are thawed.

Do not freeze hard-cooked eggs, as the white part becomes leathery when frozen. Most recipes that have a high proportion of eggs to other ingredients do not freeze well.

MICROWAVING EGGS

Eggs are a delicate food and demand special treatment when cooked in a microwave oven. Unless they are scrambled or mixed with several heartier ingredients, HIGH power is usually not used. The yolk, which is higher in fat, cooks faster than the white. HIGH power will overcook the yolk before the white is done. All eggs should be removed from the microwave oven before they are completely set and should be allowed to stand several minutes to complete cooking.

We tested most of our egg recipes in a microwave oven but omitted microwave directions for those recipes where we didn't feel the microwave results compared favorably to conventional cooking. When cooking basic eggs in a microwave, the following tips and techniques will ensure good results.

To remove egg shell: If a shell fragment has fallen into mixture, use another piece of egg shell to remove it.

Scrambled Eggs: Eggs scrambled in the microwave oven are fluffier than when conventionally cooked. It is not necessary to use butter or oil to prevent sticking; however, you can use it for added flavor, if desired. Scrambled eggs will cook first around the edges. Stir once or twice during the microwave cycle, breaking up set portions and pushing them to the center of the dish. After microwaving, let scrambled eggs stand 1 to 2 minutes to complete cooking; stir just before serving.

Poached Eggs: Microwaved poached eggs are slipped into boiling water much like conventionally poached eggs. The boiling water helps to set the white without overcooking the yolk. Pierce the egg yolks with a wooden pick before poaching; this prevents excess steam buildup, which will cause the yolks to burst. Let microwaved poached eggs stand 2 to 3 minutes before serving.

Puffy Omelets: Microwaved puffy omelets (egg whites beaten and folded into yolks) rise higher and don't collapse as readily as when conventionally cooked. After about half the cooking time has elapsed, lift edges of omelet with a spatula so uncooked portions can spread evenly. Continue microwaving until the center is almost set. The center will complete cooking while you add the filling and transfer the omelet to a serving dish.

Hard-Cooked Eggs: Eggs cannot be hard cooked in a microwave oven. Steam builds up inside the shell, causing the egg to burst. However, a product similar to hard-cooked eggs can be achieved by microwaving; see recipe for Hard-cooked Eggs on the next page.

WHAT WENT WRONG

The two most common problems that occur when working with eggs are lumpy sauces and whites that don't beat properly. Sauces become lumpy when the egg coagulates before it has a chance to thicken the mixture. Most of the time, you can avoid lumpy sauces by tempering the egg as you add it to a hot sauce. To rescue a lumpy sauce, try whisking it briskly with a wire whisk to remove or shrink the lumps; blending it in an electric blender will minimize the lumps as well.

If egg whites won't beat properly, they probably had a little egg yolk mixed with them before beating. There's no way to rescue the whites from this if you've already started beating them. For best results when beating eggs, make sure no yolk is mixed with the whites, and use fat-free beaters and bowls. Separate the eggs straight from the refrigerator, but allow whites to come to room temperature before beating them to attain maximum volume.

Soft- and Hard-Cooked Eggs

The simplest way to cook an egg is in its own shell in hot water. The length of cooking time determines whether the egg will be soft- or hard-cooked. Soft-cooked eggs may be served just as they are in eggcups, or they may be scooped from their shells into small bowls and topped with desired seasonings and condiments. When done, the white part of the egg is barely congealed, and the yolk is still somewhat runny.

Hard-cooked eggs may be peeled and eaten as they are, seasoned and stuffed, teamed with other ingredients in recipes, or used as an edible garnish for all types of foods. When done, both the yolk and the white will be set.

Whether making soft- or hard-cooked eggs, place the eggs in a saucepan of tap water, cover, and bring to a boil over medium heat. Then immediately remove from heat, and let stand as directed in the recipe. Never boil eggs, or cook them longer than directed, because the yolks may become hard and develop an unattractive green-gray ring. Serve soft-cooked eggs as soon as possible so they don't continue cooking. As soon as hard-cooked eggs are done, place them under running cold water until cooled. This stops the eggs from cooking and makes them easier to peel. If not preparing or serving the eggs right away, keep them refrigerated.

To peel a hard-cooked egg, gently tap it against the counter on all sides. Roll it between your hands, and gently peel away the shell under cold running water. Usually, the fresher the egg, the harder it will be to peel. Therefore, when hard-cooking a large number of eggs, it's a good idea to buy them several days before cooking them.

HARD-COOKED EGGS

Place desired number of eggs in a single layer in a saucepan. Add enough water to measure at least 1 inch over eggs. Cover and bring just to a boil. Remove from heat. Let stand, covered, in hot water 15 to 17 minutes for large eggs. (Adjust time up or down by about 3 minutes for each size larger or smaller.) Pour off water. Immediately run cold water over eggs until cool enough to handle.

To remove shell, gently tap egg all over, roll between hands to loosen egg shell, then hold egg under cold running water as you peel off shell.

○ *Microwave Directions:* Eggs cannot be hard-cooked in a microwave oven. Steam builds up inside the shell, causing the egg to burst from pressure. However, a product similar to hard-cooked eggs can be achieved by microwaving. Simply break eggs into lightly greased individual custard cups or microwave-safe coffee cups; pierce each yolk with a wooden pick. Cover with heavy-duty plastic wrap, and microwave at MEDIUM (50% power) for 1¼ to 1½ minutes for 1 egg, 1¾ to 2¼ minutes for 2 eggs, or 3¾ to 4¼ minutes for 3 eggs, or to desired degree of doneness, turning cups halfway through cooking time. Test eggs with a wooden pick (yolks should be just firm, and whites should be almost set). Let eggs stand, covered, for 1 to 2 minutes to complete cooking. (If eggs are not desired degree of doneness after standing, cover and continue microwaving briefly.) Let eggs cool.

While this product is not suitable for stuffing, it works well for creamed eggs, egg salad, or other dishes that use chopped eggs.

SOFT-COOKED EGGS

Prepare as for hard-cooked eggs, but let stand in hot water 1 to 4 minutes or to desired degree of doneness. Immediately run cold water over eggs until cool enough to handle.

To serve, slice each egg through the middle with a knife. Using a spoon, scoop egg from each shell half onto a serving plate. To serve in an egg cup, place egg in cup with the small end down. Slice off the large end of shell with a knife, and eat from shell.

BEST DEVILED EGGS

6 hard-cooked eggs
¼ cup mayonnaise
1½ tablespoons sweet pickle relish
1 teaspoon prepared mustard
⅛ teaspoon salt
Dash of pepper
Paprika

Slice eggs in half lengthwise, and carefully remove yolks. Mash yolks with mayonnaise. Add relish, mustard, salt, and pepper; stir well. Spoon yolk mixture into egg whites. Sprinkle with paprika. Yield: 6 servings.

PECAN-STUFFED EGGS

6 hard-cooked eggs
3 tablespoons mayonnaise
¼ cup chopped pecans
1 teaspoon grated onion
1 teaspoon vinegar
¼ to ½ teaspoon dry mustard
⅛ teaspoon salt
½ teaspoon minced fresh parsley
Fresh parsley sprigs (optional)

Slice eggs in half lengthwise, and carefully remove yolks. Mash yolks with a fork; add next 7 ingredients, mixing well. Spoon yolk mixture into egg whites. Garnish with parsley sprigs, if desired. Yield: 6 servings.

> ### *Invite Eggs to the Picnic*
>
> Transport deviled eggs by pressing two halves together, yolks touching, and wrap securely with plastic wrap. Be sure to keep the eggs on ice until ready to serve.

SAUCY DEVILED EGGS

6 hard-cooked eggs
¼ cup mayonnaise
2 tablespoons chopped onion
1 teaspoon vinegar
1 teaspoon prepared mustard
Dash of pepper
2 (8-ounce) cans tomato sauce
¼ cup water
¼ cup minced onion
⅛ teaspoon red pepper
6 slices bacon, cooked and crumbled
¼ cup round buttery cracker crumbs
Buttered toast points

Slice eggs in half lengthwise, and carefully remove yolks. Mash yolks, and add mayonnaise; stir well. Stir in chopped onion, vinegar, mustard, and pepper. Spoon yolk mixture into egg whites.

Combine tomato sauce, water, minced onion, and red pepper in a shallow 1-quart baking dish, stirring well. Arrange eggs in dish. Sprinkle eggs with bacon, and top with cracker crumbs. Bake at 450° for 15 minutes. Serve immediately over toast points. Yield: 6 servings

○ *Microwave Directions:* Slice eggs in half lengthwise, and carefully remove yolks. Mash yolks, and add mayonnaise; stir well. Stir in chopped onion, vinegar, mustard, and pepper. Spoon yolk mixture into egg whites.

Combine tomato sauce, water, minced onion, and red pepper in a shallow 1-quart baking dish, stirring well. Arrange eggs in dish. Sprinkle eggs with bacon, and top with cracker crumbs. Microwave at HIGH for 2 to 4 minutes or until sauce is thoroughly heated. Serve immediately over toast points.

SPICED PICKLED EGGS

12 hard-cooked eggs
2 cups vinegar
1 medium onion, sliced and separated
  into rings
2 tablespoons sugar
1½ teaspoons pickling spice
1 teaspoon salt

Peel eggs, and place loosely in a jar; set aside.

Combine remaining ingredients in a saucepan; bring to a boil. Reduce heat to low; simmer 5 minutes. Pour hot mixture over eggs; seal with airtight lid. Refrigerate 2 days before serving. Store in refrigerator up to 2 weeks. Yield: 12 servings.

COUNTRY CORNBREAD BRUNCH

3 tablespoons butter or margarine
3 tablespoons all-purpose flour
2 cups milk
¼ teaspoon salt
⅛ teaspoon pepper
6 hard-cooked eggs, chopped
½ cup mayonnaise
Skillet Cornbread (page 78)
Chopped green onions
Crumbled cooked bacon
Shredded Cheddar cheese

Melt butter in a heavy saucepan over low heat; add flour, stirring until smooth. Cook 1 minute, stirring constantly. Gradually add milk; cook until thickened and bubbly, stirring constantly. Add salt and next 3 ingredients; cook, stirring constantly, until thoroughly heated.

To serve, cut cornbread into wedges, and slice in half horizontally. Spoon egg mixture on cornbread wedges, and sprinkle with green onions, bacon, and cheese. Yield: 8 servings.

◻ *Microwave Directions:* Place butter in a 1½-quart glass bowl. Microwave at HIGH for 45 seconds or until melted. Add flour, stirring until smooth. Gradually add milk, stirring well. Microwave at HIGH for 5 to 6 minutes or until thickened and bubbly, stirring after 2 minutes, then at 1-minute intervals. Add salt and next 3 ingredients, stirring well. Microwave at HIGH for 1 minute or until thoroughly heated.

To serve, cut cornbread into wedges, and slice in half horizontally. Spoon egg mixture on wedges, and sprinkle with green onions, bacon, and cheese.

SHERRIED EGGS IN PATTY SHELLS

Serve Sherried Eggs in Patty Shells for a ladies lunch or brunch. You can cook the patty shells, eggs, and white sauce ahead of time; then combine everything and reheat at the last minute.

1 (10-ounce) package frozen patty
  shells
¼ cup plus 2 tablespoons butter or
  margarine, divided
¼ pound fresh mushrooms, sliced
1 tablespoon finely chopped onion
3 tablespoons all-purpose flour
1½ cups milk
¾ teaspoon salt
Pinch of red pepper
6 hard-cooked eggs
1 to 1½ tablespoons dry sherry
Fresh parsley sprigs

Bake patty shells according to package directions; set aside.

Melt 2 tablespoons butter in a heavy skillet. Add mushrooms and onion; sauté until tender. Set aside.

Melt remaining ¼ cup butter in a heavy saucepan over low heat; add flour, stirring until smooth. Cook 1 minute, stirring constantly. Gradually add milk; cook over medium heat, stirring constantly, until thickened and bubbly.

Stir in salt and red pepper.

Finely chop 5 eggs. Stir chopped eggs, sautéed vegetables, and sherry into sauce; cook, stirring constantly, until thoroughly heated. Spoon into patty shells. Cut remaining egg into 6 wedges. Garnish each serving with an egg wedge and a sprig of parsley. Yield: 6 servings.

◻ *Microwave Directions:* Bake patty shells according to package directions; set aside.

Place 2 tablespoons butter in a 1-quart glass measure. Microwave at HIGH for 45 seconds or until melted. Add mushrooms and onion; microwave at HIGH for 1 to 2 minutes or until tender; set vegetables aside.

Place remaining ¼ cup butter in a 1-quart glass measure. Microwave at HIGH for 55 seconds or until melted. Add flour, stirring until smooth. Gradually add milk, stirring well. Microwave at HIGH for 4 to 5 minutes or until thickened and bubbly, stirring after 2 minutes, then at 1-minute intervals. Stir in salt and red pepper.

Finely chop 5 eggs. Stir chopped eggs, sautéed vegetables, and sherry into sauce; microwave at HIGH for 1 minute or until thoroughly heated. Spoon into patty shells. Cut remaining egg into 6 wedges. Garnish each serving with an egg wedge and a sprig of parsley.

Garnish With Hard-Cooked Egg

Press the yolks and whites, singularly or together, through a fine sieve, to sprinkle over all types of foods. Or garnish with hard-cooked eggs slices or wedges. Use a sharp paring knife, and cut gently to avoid crumbling the yolk. You can purchase egg slicers and wedgers to help cut perfect shapes.

Fried Eggs

Some sources credit fried eggs as being the most popular breakfast egg. They're quick to cook and offer enough variations to please individual preferences.

Sunny-side-up (cooking the egg only on the bottom) is one way to fry an egg; be sure to cook it over low heat so the top of the egg is done before the bottom is overdone. Some cooks baste the top of the egg as it cooks with fat from the skillet to speed up the time it takes for the top to cook. Others flip the egg over once the bottom is set and cook it slightly (called over-easy) or until the yolk is firmly set (called over-well). Some like to break the yolk once the egg is flipped so the yolk is evenly done and distributed over the white.

When frying eggs, be sure your skillet is large enough that the eggs will stay separate as you cook them; once they join together and cook, you'll have to cut them apart.

SUNNY-SIDE-UP EGGS

1 tablespoon butter or margarine
2 eggs
Salt and pepper

Melt butter in a heavy skillet, and heat until hot enough to sizzle a drop of water. Break one egg into a saucer; carefully slip egg into skillet. Repeat procedure with remaining egg. Cook eggs over low heat until whites are firm and yolks are soft, or cook to desired degree of doneness; season with salt and pepper. Yield: 1 to 2 servings.

Save Those Egg Whites

Leftover egg whites will stay fresh in your refrigerator up to 10 days so don't throw them away. Here are some creative ways to use them.

● Frost fresh grapes for an elegant and edible garnish by lightly dipping them in unbeaten egg white and sprinkling with granulated sugar.
● When baking a pie with a juicy filling, brush the bottom and sides of the pastry shell with unbeaten egg white before adding the filling; this helps keep the pastry shell from being soggy after baking.
● Give homemade yeast bread a pretty shine by lightly brushing the top of the loaf with a small amount of unbeaten egg white before putting in the oven to bake.

EGG FOO YONG

For Egg Foo Yong, the eggs are scrambled with a few other ingredients, then fried into little patties. Serve them over a bed of rice for a light lunch or supper. The Green Pea Sauce looks pretty and binds the flavors.

4 eggs, beaten
1 (14-ounce) can chop suey vegetables, drained
1 (8-ounce) package frozen cooked shrimp
½ cup chopped green onions
2 teaspoons chicken-flavored bouillon granules
Vegetable oil
Hot cooked rice
Green Pea Sauce

Combine eggs, vegetables, shrimp, onions, and bouillon granules. Let stand 10 minutes; stir well.

Heat a small amount of vegetable oil in a large skillet. Spoon ¼ cup egg mixture into hot oil, shaping into a 3-inch circle with a spatula. Cook until browned on one side; turn and brown other side. Repeat until all egg mixture is used; add additional oil to skillet as necessary. Serve egg patties over rice; top patties with Green Pea Sauce. Yield: 4 to 6 servings.

Green Pea Sauce

1½ cups water
1 tablespoon soy sauce
2 teaspoons chicken-flavored bouillon granules
2 tablespoons cornstarch
½ cup water
½ cup frozen green peas

Combine first 3 ingredients in a medium saucepan. Cook over low heat until bouillon dissolves. Combine cornstarch and ½ cup water, stirring well; stir into bouillon mixture. Add peas. Cook over low heat until thickened, stirring constantly. Yield: 2 cups.

Scrambled Eggs

You'll have to beat eggs to scramble them, but take care not to stir them too much while they are cooking. Simply draw a spatula over the mixture as it begins to set on the bottom, making it form large curds. Continue until the eggs are thickened but still moist; do not stir constantly, or they will become dry and crumbly.

SCRAMBLED EGGS

4 eggs
2 tablespoons water or milk
¼ teaspoon salt
Dash of pepper
1 tablespoon butter or margarine

Combine eggs, water, salt, and pepper; stir briskly with a fork until uniformly blended. Melt butter in an 8-inch skillet over medium heat, tilting pan to coat bottom; pour in egg mixture. Cook without stirring until mixture begins to set on bottom. Draw a spatula across bottom of pan to form large curds. Continue until eggs are thickened, but still moist; do not stir constantly. Yield: 2 to 3 servings.

❑*Microwave Directions:* Combine eggs, water (do not use milk), salt, and pepper; stir briskly with a fork until uniformly blended. Place butter in a shallow 1-quart casserole. Microwave at HIGH for 45 seconds or until melted; rotate casserole to coat bottom of dish. Pour in egg mixture. Microwave at HIGH for 1 minute. Break up set portions of egg with a fork, and push toward center of dish. Microwave at HIGH for 1 to 2 minutes or until eggs are almost set (eggs will be soft and moist), stirring gently after 1 minute. Cover and let stand 1 to 2 minutes.

Cheese Scrambled Eggs: Sprinkle ½ cup (2 ounces) shredded Swiss or mild Cheddar cheese over egg mixture just before scraping with a spatula.

❑*Microwave Directions:* Sprinkle cheese on during standing time.

Herb Scrambled Eggs: Stir 1 tablespoon chopped fresh or 1 teaspoon dried whole oregano, basil, thyme, or parsley into egg mixture just before cooking.

❑*Microwave Directions:* Cut amount of herbs in half.

Bacon Scrambled Eggs: Reduce salt to ⅛ teaspoon, and stir 3 slices bacon, cooked and crumbled, into egg mixture just before cooking.

❑*Microwave Directions:* Reduce salt to ⅛ teaspoon, and sprinkle bacon on eggs after cooking.

Ham Scrambled Eggs: Reduce salt to ⅛ teaspoon, and stir ⅓ cup diced cooked ham into egg mixture just before cooking.

❑*Microwave Directions:* Reduce salt to ⅛ teaspoon, and sprinkle ham on eggs after cooking.

CREAMY EGG SCRAMBLE

6 eggs
½ cup milk
1 (3-ounce) package cream cheese, cubed
¼ teaspoon salt
⅛ teaspoon pepper
⅓ cup chopped green onions
3 tablespoons butter or margarine

Combine first 5 ingredients in container of an electric blender; cover and process at medium speed until frothy (7 to 10 seconds). Stir in onions.
Melt butter in a large nonstick skillet over medium heat, tilting pan to coat bottom; pour in egg mixture. Cook without stirring until mixture begins to set on bottom. Draw a spatula across bottom of pan to form large curds. Continue until eggs are thickened, but still moist; do not stir constantly. Yield: 3 to 4 servings.

❑*Microwave Directions:* Combine first 5 ingredients in container of an electric blender; cover and process at medium speed until frothy (7 to 10 seconds). Stir in onions.
Place butter in a 1½-quart casserole. Microwave at HIGH for 50 to 55 seconds or until melted; rotate casserole to coat bottom of dish. Pour in egg mixture. Microwave at HIGH for 1 to 2 minutes. Break up set portions of egg with a fork, and push toward center of dish. Microwave at HIGH for 3 to 4 minutes or until eggs are almost set (eggs will be soft and moist), stirring gently at 1-minute intervals. Stir gently again; cover and let stand 1 to 2 minutes.

COTTAGE-SCRAMBLED EGGS

3 tablespoons butter or margarine
3 tablespoons all-purpose flour
1 cup milk
10 eggs
1 cup cream-style cottage cheese
½ teaspoon salt
Dash of pepper

Melt butter in a heavy saucepan over low heat; add flour, stirring until smooth. Cook 1 minute, stirring constantly. Gradually add milk; cook over medium heat, stirring constantly, until thickened and bubbly.
Combine eggs, cottage cheese, salt, and pepper; beat well, and stir into white sauce. Cook in a large skillet, stirring often, until eggs are firm but still moist. Yield: 6 to 8 servings.

To scramble eggs: Don't scramble them to death! Beat them before cooking; then cook without stirring until mixture begins to set on bottom. Periodically draw a spatula across bottom of pan to form large curds until eggs are done.

SPANISH SCRAMBLED EGGS

12 eggs, beaten
3 tablespoons chopped green chiles, drained
1 (2-ounce) jar diced pimiento, drained
¼ cup butter or margarine
3 green onions, finely chopped
1 small tomato, chopped
1 (2-ounce) jar sliced mushrooms, drained
½ pound bacon, cooked and crumbled

Combine eggs, chiles, and pimiento; set aside. Melt butter in a large skillet. Add onions, tomato, and mushrooms; sauté until tender. Add egg mixture; cook over medium heat, stirring often, until eggs are firm but still moist. Sprinkle with bacon. Yield: 6 servings.

CHEDDAR EGG SCRAMBLE

¼ cup chopped onion
¼ cup chopped green pepper
1 tablespoon butter or margarine, melted
4 eggs, beaten
2 tablespoons milk
⅛ teaspoon seasoned salt
4 slices bacon, cooked and crumbled
¼ cup (1 ounce) shredded Cheddar cheese

Sauté chopped onion and green pepper in butter in a large skillet until tender. Combine eggs, milk, salt, and bacon; mix well. Pour egg mixture into hot skillet. Cook without stirring until egg mixture begins to set on bottom. Draw a spatula across bottom of pan to form large curds. Continue until eggs are thickened, but still moist; do not stir constantly.

Remove from heat. Sprinkle with cheese; cover and let stand 1 minute. Yield: 2 to 3 servings.

SCRAMBLED EGG CASSEROLE

1 cup cubed ham or Canadian bacon
¼ cup chopped green onions
3 tablespoons butter or margarine, melted
12 eggs, beaten
1 (4-ounce) can sliced mushrooms, drained
2 recipes Cheddar Cheese Sauce (page 437)
1 tablespoon butter or margarine, melted
¾ cup soft breadcrumbs
Paprika

Sauté ham and green onions in 3 tablespoons butter in a large skillet until onion is tender; add eggs. Cook without stirring until mixture begins to set on bottom. Draw a spatula across bottom of pan to form large curds. Continue until eggs are thickened but still moist; do not stir constantly. Gently stir in mushrooms and Cheddar Cheese Sauce. Spoon eggs into a greased 12- x 8- x 2-inch baking dish. Combine 1 tablespoon melted butter and breadcrumbs, stirring well; spread evenly over egg mixture. Sprinkle paprika over butter and breadcrumb topping. Cover and refrigerate 8 hours.

Remove from refrigerator; let stand 30 minutes. Bake, uncovered, at 350° for 30 minutes or until thoroughly heated. Yield: 8 servings.

BREAKFAST BURRITOS

1 cup hash brown potato mix with onions
2 cups hot water
6 (8-inch) flour tortillas
6 eggs, well beaten
½ pound bulk pork sausage, cooked, crumbled, and drained
½ teaspoon salt
Freshly ground pepper to taste
2 tablespoons butter or margarine
¾ cup (3 ounces) shredded Cheddar cheese (optional)
Picante sauce (optional)

Combine hash brown potato mix and water; stir well. Let stand, covered, 15 minutes. Drain.

Wrap tortillas securely in aluminum foil; bake at 350° for 10 minutes or until thoroughly heated.

Combine hash browns, eggs, sausage, salt, and pepper; stir well. Melt butter in a large skillet. Add egg mixture; cook over low heat, stirring gently, until eggs are set. Fill each tortilla with ½ cup egg mixture; sprinkle with 2 tablespoons cheese, if desired. Roll up, placing seam side down. Spoon picante sauce over tortillas, if desired. Yield: 6 servings.

Poached Eggs

For a fancier type of egg, try poaching. Poached eggs can be seasoned and eaten alone. For special occasions they are often served on English muffins and topped with a succulent sauce.

Poaching is tricky so follow the recipe carefully. Make sure the water is not more than 2 inches deep and that it stays at a gentle simmer.

To poach eggs in advance, immediately after cooking place eggs in ice water, and refrigerate until serving time. Drain eggs; place eggs in boiling water for 45 seconds, and drain again. Serve immediately.

POACHED EGGS

Lightly grease a large saucepan. Add water to depth of 2 inches in pan. Bring water to a boil; reduce heat, and maintain at a light simmer. Break eggs, one at a time, into a saucer; slip eggs, one at a time, into water, holding saucer as close as possible to surface of water. Simmer 3 to 5 minutes or to desired degree of doneness. Remove eggs with a slotted spoon. Trim edges, if desired.

Note: To cook eggs in poaching cups, first grease each cup. Place poacher in a pan of simmering water so water is below bottom of poacher. Break eggs into cups, and insert cups into poacher. Cover and cook 3 to 5 minutes or to desired degree of doneness.

☐ *Microwave Directions:* Microwave-poached eggs are best cooked in individual custard cups. Cooking directions and times are given here for 2 eggs (and for 4 eggs in parenthesis). Adjust cooking times accordingly for more or fewer eggs.

Place 2 tablespoons water in a 6-ounce custard cup for each egg. Add ¼ teaspoon vinegar to each. Microwave at HIGH for 1 to 2 (2 to 3) minutes or until water is boiling. Gently break 1 egg into each cup. Lightly pierce each yolk with a wooden pick. Cover cups with heavy-duty plastic wrap, and space evenly on a microwave-safe platter. Microwave at MEDIUM HIGH (70% power) for 1 to 1½ (2 to 2½) minutes or until almost all of white is opaque (eggs will not be completely set). Let eggs stand 2 to 3 minutes.

CRABMEAT AND EGGS NEW ORLEANS

1 pound fresh crabmeat, drained and flaked
¼ cup butter or margarine, melted
½ teaspoon salt
¼ teaspoon white pepper
6 English muffins, split and toasted
12 poached eggs
New Orleans Cream Sauce
Paprika

Sauté crabmeat in butter about 5 minutes. Stir in salt and pepper.

Spoon a small amount of crabmeat onto English muffins. Top each with a poached egg. Spoon New Orleans Cream Sauce over eggs. Sprinkle with paprika. Yield: 6 servings.

New Orleans Cream Sauce

¼ cup butter or margarine
3 tablespoons all-purpose flour
1½ cups milk
½ teaspoon salt
¼ teaspoon ground nutmeg
2 tablespoons brandy
⅛ teaspoon hot sauce

Melt butter in a heavy saucepan over low heat; add flour, stirring until smooth. Cook 1 minute, stirring constantly. Gradually add milk; cook over medium heat, stirring constantly, until thickened and bubbly. Stir in remaining ingredients. Yield: 1¾ cups.

EGGS BENEDICT

2 English muffins, split
Butter or margarine, softened
4 slices Canadian bacon, cooked
4 poached eggs
1 recipe Hollandaise Sauce (page 438)

Spread cut sides of muffins with butter. Broil until lightly browned.

Place a slice of Canadian bacon on each muffin half; top with poached egg, and cover with Hollandaise Sauce. Yield: 2 servings.

Serve Eggs Benedict for a leisurely breakfast or brunch. For color and appetite appeal, serve the eggs on a bed of spinach leaves garnished with a tomato rose.

Baked Eggs

If you need to prepare a lot of eggs at one time, baking is a good choice because eggs require little attention as they bake and they look attractive served in individual ramekins. The milk spooned over the eggs before cooking gives them a softer finish than fried or poached eggs. Serve baked eggs immediately, as the heat of the dish can make them continue to cook if set aside.

BAKED (SHIRRED) EGGS

4 eggs
Salt and pepper to taste
¼ cup half-and-half or milk (optional)

Grease 4 (6-ounce) custard cups. Break and slip 1 egg into each cup. Sprinkle with salt and pepper. Spoon 1 tablespoon half-and-half over each serving, if desired. Bake at 325° for 15 minutes or to desired degree of doneness. Yield: 2 to 4 servings.

BAKED EGGS IN SPINACH NESTS

1 tablespoon finely chopped onion
2 tablespoons butter or margarine
2 tablespoons all-purpose flour
1 teaspoon chicken-flavored bouillon granules
1 cup milk
⅛ teaspoon ground nutmeg
1 (10-ounce) package frozen chopped spinach, thawed and well drained
4 eggs
½ cup (2 ounces) shredded Cheddar cheese
Grated Parmesan cheese

Sauté onion in butter in a heavy saucepan until tender. Stir in flour and bouillon granules; cook 1 minute, stirring constantly. Gradually add milk, and cook over medium heat, stirring constantly, until thickened and bubbly. Stir in nutmeg and spinach.

Spoon equal portions of creamed spinach into 4 greased (6-ounce) custard cups or ramekins, spreading sides slightly higher than center. Break an egg into each cup. Bake at 350° for 30 minutes or until eggs are set. Sprinkle with Cheddar and Parmesan cheeses; bake an additional 3 to 5 minutes or until cheese melts. Yield: 4 servings.

BAKED EGG CRISPS

6 slices bread
1 tablespoon butter or margarine, softened
1 tablespoon grated Parmesan cheese
⅛ teaspoon salt
¼ teaspoon pepper
6 eggs
6 slices bacon, cooked and crumbled

Remove crust from bread, and spread butter lightly over one side. Using a 2½-inch biscuit cutter, cut a circle from center of each bread slice; then cut 4 equal triangles from remaining bread square.

Place each bread circle, buttered side up, in a buttered 6-ounce custard cup. Place triangles around edges of custard cups with points facing upward. Bake at 425° for 10 minutes.

Combine Parmesan cheese, salt, and pepper; stir well, and set aside.

Gently break 1 egg into each toast cup; sprinkle with cheese mixture. Bake at 350° for 12 to 15 minutes. Sprinkle bacon evenly over eggs. Serve immediately. Yield: 6 servings.

HUEVOS RANCHEROS

(pictured on page 202)

6 corn tortillas
Vegetable oil
2 (16-ounce) cans tomatoes
1 cup chopped onion
1 cup chopped green pepper
2 cloves garlic, minced
3 tablespoons olive oil
1 tablespoon all-purpose flour
½ teaspoon dried whole oregano
½ teaspoon ground cumin
½ teaspoon chili powder
¼ teaspoon salt
⅛ teaspoon pepper
6 eggs
½ cup (2 ounces) shredded sharp Cheddar cheese
¼ cup sliced ripe olives

Fry tortillas, one at a time, in ¼ cup hot oil 3 to 5 seconds on each side or just until softened. Add additional oil, if necessary. Drain tortillas thoroughly on paper towels. Line a 12- x 8- x 2-inch baking dish with tortillas, letting tortillas extend ½ inch up sides of dish. Set baking dish aside.

Drain canned tomatoes, reserving ¼ cup tomato juice. Chop tomatoes, and set aside.

Sauté onion, green pepper, and garlic in olive oil. Stir in flour, and cook 1 minute. Add ¼ cup reserved tomato juice, tomatoes, and seasonings; cook over medium heat 5 minutes. Pour mixture over corn tortillas. Make 6 indentations in tomato mixture, and break an egg into each. Cover and bake at 350° for 25 minutes.

Sprinkle with cheese and olives; bake, uncovered, an additional 5 minutes. Serve immediately. Yield: 6 servings.

Omelets

Many people shy away from making omelets because they think omelets are difficult to make. But omelets are nothing more than a beaten egg mixture cooked in a skillet and folded—often around a filling. Start with our recipes, which offer particular fillings; then use your imagination to dream up combinations of your own.

The most basic of all omelets is called a plain omelet; the egg is beaten with a few simple ingredients, then cooked as directed. Beating the egg yolks and whites separately results in what's called a puffy omelet, the most prized type. Puffy omelets require a short baking period to cook them evenly.

Whether making a plain or puffy omelet, you'll appreciate a nonstick omelet pan rather than a regular skillet. Just be sure the handle is ovenproof for making puffy omelets. If it's not, wrap the handle with aluminum foil to protect it from direct heat for the short baking time.

To cook an omelet evenly: As omelet starts to cook, gently lift edges with a spatula, and tilt pan so uncooked portion flows underneath.

PLAIN OMELET

2 eggs
⅛ teaspoon salt
Dash of white pepper
1 tablespoon water
1 tablespoon butter or margarine
Omelet fillings (optional)

Combine eggs, salt, white pepper, and water; whisk egg mixture just until blended.

Heat a 6- or 8-inch omelet pan or heavy skillet over medium heat until hot enough to sizzle a drop of water. Add butter, and rotate pan to coat bottom. Pour egg mixture into skillet. As mixture starts to cook, gently lift edges of omelet with a spatula, and tilt pan so uncooked portion flows underneath.

Sprinkle half of omelet with one or more of the following fillings, if desired: 2 slices bacon, cooked and crumbled; 2 tablespoons sautéed mushroom slices; 2 tablespoons shredded cheese; 2 tablespoons diced cooked ham; 1 tablespoon chopped fresh or 1 teaspoon dried whole herbs. Fold omelet in half, and transfer to plate. Yield: 1 serving.

Note: Recipe may be doubled and cooked in a 10-inch omelet pan or heavy skillet for 2 servings, if desired.

PUFFY OMELET

4 eggs, separated
2 tablespoons water
¼ teaspoon salt
1 tablespoon butter or margarine
½ recipe Cheddar Cheese Sauce
   (page 437)
Chopped fresh parsley

Beat egg whites (at room temperature) until foamy; add water and salt. Beat until stiff peaks form. Beat egg yolks in a large bowl until thick and lemon colored. Fold whites into yolks.

Heat an ovenproof 10-inch omelet pan or heavy skillet over medium heat until hot enough to sizzle a drop of water. Add butter, and rotate pan to coat bottom. Spread egg mixture in pan, leaving sides slightly higher. Cover, reduce heat, and cook 8 to 10 minutes or until puffed and set. Bake at 325° for 10 minutes or until a knife inserted in center comes out clean. Loosen omelet with a spatula; fold omelet in half. Gently slide omelet onto a serving plate; spoon cheese sauce over top. Sprinkle with chopped parsley. Yield: 2 servings.

▢ *Microwave Directions:* Beat egg whites (at room temperature) until foamy; add water and salt. Beat until stiff peaks form. Beat egg yolks in a large bowl until thick and lemon colored. Fold whites into yolks.

Place butter in a 10-inch pieplate. Microwave at HIGH for 35 seconds or until melted; tilt pieplate to coat bottom. Spread egg mixture in pieplate. Cover with heavy-duty plastic wrap; microwave at MEDIUM (50% power) for 2 to 3 minutes or until partially set. Gently lift cooked edges with a spatula, allowing uncooked portion to flow underneath. Cover and microwave at MEDIUM for 2 minutes or until center is almost set. Let stand, covered, 1 minute. Loosen omelet with a spatula; fold omelet in half. Gently slide omelet onto a serving plate; spoon cheese sauce over top. Sprinkle with chopped parsley.

SPANISH OMELET

¾ cup diced tomato
½ cup chopped green pepper
½ cup sliced fresh mushrooms
¼ cup butter or margarine, divided
6 eggs
¼ cup water
½ teaspoon salt
Dash of pepper
2 tablespoons picante sauce
4 slices bacon, cooked and crumbled
Picante sauce (optional)

Sauté tomato, green pepper, and mushrooms in 2 tablespoons butter until tender; drain.

Combine eggs, water, salt, and pepper; stir briskly with a fork until uniformly blended. Stir in vegetable mixture, 2 tablespoons picante sauce, and bacon.

Heat a 10-inch omelet pan or heavy skillet over medium heat until hot enough to sizzle a drop of water. Add 1 tablespoon butter, and rotate pan to coat bottom. Pour half of egg mixture into skillet. As mixture starts to cook, gently lift edges of omelet with a spatula, and tilt pan so uncooked portion flows underneath. Fold omelet in half, and place on a warm platter. Repeat procedure with remaining 1 tablespoon butter and egg mixture. Serve with additional picante sauce, if desired. Yield: 3 to 4 servings.

SOUR CREAM-HAM OMELET

5 eggs, separated
1½ cups chopped cooked ham
1 (8-ounce) carton commercial sour cream, divided
⅛ teaspoon pepper
Vegetable cooking spray

Beat egg whites (at room temperature) until stiff but not dry; set aside. Beat egg yolks until thick and lemon colored; stir in ham, ½ cup sour cream, and pepper. Fold whites into egg yolk mixture.

Coat an ovenproof 10-inch omelet pan or heavy skillet with cooking spray; heat over medium heat until hot enough to sizzle a drop of water. Pour egg mixture into skillet, and gently smooth surface. Reduce heat and cook about 5 minutes or until puffy and light brown on bottom, gently lifting omelet at edge to judge color.

Bake at 325° for 15 to 18 minutes or until a knife inserted in center comes out clean. Tip skillet and loosen omelet with a spatula; fold omelet in half, and place on a warm plate. To serve, slice in wedges and garnish with remaining sour cream. Yield: 4 to 6 servings.

VEGETABLE OMELET

1 small onion, sliced
½ cup broccoli flowerets (optional)
¼ cup chopped green pepper
1 tablespoon butter or margarine, melted
¼ cup sliced fresh mushrooms
¼ cup chopped tomatoes
3 slices bacon, cooked and crumbled
⅛ to ¼ teaspoon crushed red pepper
⅛ teaspoon salt
⅛ teaspoon pepper
⅛ teaspoon garlic powder
4 eggs, beaten
1 tablespoon milk
¼ teaspoon salt
Dash of pepper
1 tablespoon butter or margarine
½ cup (2 ounces) shredded Swiss cheese

Sauté first 3 ingredients in butter in a medium skillet until vegetables are tender. Add mushrooms and next 6 ingredients; cook an additional 5 minutes, stirring frequently. Set aside.

Combine eggs, milk, ¼ teaspoon salt, and dash of pepper; stir just until blended.

Heat a 10-inch omelet pan or heavy skillet over medium heat until hot enough to sizzle a drop of water. Add 1 tablespoon butter; rotate pan to coat bottom. Pour egg mixture into skillet. As mixture starts to cook, gently lift edges of omelet with a spatula, and tilt pan so uncooked portion flows underneath.

Spoon vegetable mixture over half of omelet. Loosen omelet with a spatula; fold omelet in half, and top with cheese. Cover until cheese melts. Gently slide omelet onto a warm serving plate. Yield: 2 servings.

Beefy Vegetable Omelet: Cook ¼ pound ground beef with onion mixture, omitting 1 tablespoon butter. Cook mixture until meat is browned; drain.

GERMAN APPLE PANCAKE

It's called a pancake, but this recipe is actually more like a cross between an omelet and a soufflé.

2 eggs
½ cup all-purpose flour
¼ teaspoon salt
½ cup milk
1 tablespoon butter or margarine
¾ cup firmly packed brown sugar
1½ tablespoons cornstarch
½ cup milk
¼ cup butter or margarine, melted
4 cups peeled and sliced apples

Combine eggs, flour, salt, and ½ cup milk; beat until smooth. Heat a 10-inch ovenproof nonstick skillet at 450° for 5 minutes or until hot. Add 1 tablespoon butter, stirring to coat skillet; pour in batter. Bake at 450° for 10 minutes. Reduce heat to 350°, and bake an additional 10 minutes or until golden brown.

Combine sugar and cornstarch in a saucepan; stir in ½ cup milk and ¼ cup melted butter. Cook over medium heat until thickened. Reduce heat; add apples, and cook until tender. Spoon half of mixture onto pancake. Cut into wedges, and serve with remaining apple mixture. Yield: 4 to 6 servings.

TART MILAN

Enjoy Tart Milan for special brunches and light luncheons. Make the omelets ahead of time, saving the assembly until the last minute. Let the dish cool 5 minutes after removal from the oven; then serve it immediately, so the pastry will maintain its puff.

1 pound fresh spinach
1 large sweet red pepper, chopped
2 cloves garlic, minced
1 tablespoon butter or margarine, melted
1 tablespoon vegetable oil
¼ to ½ teaspoon ground nutmeg
⅛ teaspoon salt
Pinch of pepper
1 (1-pound) package commercial puff pastry, thawed and divided
9 eggs
1 tablespoon chopped fresh chives
1 tablespoon chopped fresh parsley
¾ teaspoon dried whole tarragon
¼ teaspoon salt
2 tablespoons plus 2 teaspoons butter or margarine, divided
3 cups (12 ounces) shredded Swiss cheese, divided
12 ounces thinly sliced ham, divided
1 egg, beaten
Fresh spinach leaves
Pimiento cutouts
Fresh parsley sprigs

Remove stems from spinach; wash leaves in lukewarm water. Drain and set aside.

Sauté red pepper and garlic in 1 tablespoon butter and oil in a Dutch oven, remove red pepper and garlic, reserving drippings in pan. Add spinach, nutmeg, ⅛ teaspoon salt, and pepper, stirring gently. Cover and cook over high heat 3 to 5 minutes. Drain and press between paper towels to remove excess moisture.

Line a greased 8-inch springform pan with 1 sheet of puff pastry, leaving ½-inch overhang; set aside. Cut remaining sheet of puff pastry into a 9-inch circle; cover with a damp cloth and set aside.

Combine 9 eggs, chives, parsley, tarra-gon, and ¼ teaspoon salt; beat well. Heat an 8-inch omelet pan or heavy skillet over medium heat until it is hot enough to sizzle a drop of water. Add 2 teaspoons butter, and rotate pan to coat bottom. Pour about one-fourth of egg mixture into pan. As mixture starts to cook, gently lift edges of omelet with a spatula, and tilt pan so uncooked portion flows underneath. Cook until eggs are set and top is still moist and creamy. Loosen omelet with spatula; transfer to pastry-lined pan. Repeat procedure for second, third, and fourth omelet, transferring omelets to wax paper. Set aside.

Layer one-third of spinach, ½ cup cheese, one-third of ham, ½ cup cheese, and one-third red pepper over omelet in pan. Top with second omelet and the same amount of remaining layered ingredients. Top with third omelet and remaining layered ingredients; top with remaining omelet.

Top with pastry circle; seal well, crimping edges, if desired. Make indentations in pastry with a knife, dividing pie into 6 or 8 portions; brush top with beaten egg. Place springform pan in a shallow pan. Position oven rack in lower third of oven; bake at 350° for 60 to 65 minutes. Remove from oven; let stand 5 minutes before serving. Remove from springform pan, and place on serving platter lined with spinach leaves. Decorate top with pimiento cutouts and parsley sprigs. Yield: 6 to 8 servings.

Serve Tart Milan on spinach leaves, and garnish with parsley and pimiento cutouts.

BROCCOLI-CHEESE FRITTATA

A frittata is similar to an omelet, but it's not filled or folded. The egg mixture is often teamed with other ingredients before cooking, as in Broccoli-Cheese Frittata.

3 eggs
3 tablespoons milk
¼ teaspoon salt
⅛ teaspoon red pepper
1 (10-ounce) package frozen chopped broccoli, thawed and well drained
1 small onion, finely chopped
1 small clove garlic, crushed
2 tablespoons vegetable oil
1½ cups (6 ounces) shredded Swiss or Cheddar cheese

Combine eggs, milk, salt, and pepper; beat well, and set aside.

Sauté broccoli, onion, and garlic in oil in a 9-inch nonstick skillet until tender. Remove from heat; stir in egg mixture. Sprinkle with cheese; cover and cook over low heat about 10 minutes or until egg is set and cheese melts. Cut into wedges, and serve immediately. Yield: 4 servings.

☐*Microwave Directions:* Combine eggs, milk, salt, and pepper; beat well, and set aside.

Combine broccoli, onion, and garlic in a 9-inch pieplate coated with oil; cover with heavy-duty plastic wrap. Microwave at HIGH for 6 to 7 minutes or until tender. Stir in egg mixture. Cover with heavy-duty plastic wrap, and microwave at MEDIUM HIGH (70% power) for 2 minutes. Sprinkle with cheese, and give dish a half-turn. Cover and microwave at MEDIUM HIGH for 1 to 2 minutes or until almost set. Let stand, covered, 1 to 2 minutes.

Egg Pies and Quiches

Quiche, the savory, custard-like pie that was the rage of the seventies, is still a popular item for light luncheons and family meals today. You can serve it hot or cold and can make it from almost any handful of leftover meat and vegetables you might find in your refrigerator.

Making the pastry is the most time-consuming part of quiche recipes. You can use our Basic Pastry recipe in the Pies and Pastries chapter, or substitute any of the commercial pastry mixes or prepared pastries on the market. Just remember that when our recipe calls for a 9-inch pastry, those labeled 9 inches in the frozen food section of your grocery store will not work—they're actually shallower and narrower than pastries made in a standard 9-inch pieplate. If you want to use a frozen pastry, the kind labeled deep-dish will be a closer substitute.

MEXICANA BRUNCH PIE

5 eggs, beaten
2 tablespoons butter or margarine, melted
¼ cup all-purpose flour
½ teaspoon baking powder
1 (8-ounce) carton cream-style cottage cheese
2 cups (8 ounces) shredded Monterey Jack cheese
1 (4-ounce) can chopped green chiles, drained

Combine first 4 ingredients in a mixing bowl; beat well at medium speed of an electric mixer. Stir in remaining ingredients, and pour into a well-greased 9-inch pieplate.

Bake at 400° for 10 minutes; reduce heat to 350°, and bake about 20 minutes or until set. Cut into wedges to serve. Yield: 6 servings.

BREAKFAST POTATO PIE

1 (6-ounce) package hash brown potato mix with onions
1 quart hot water
5 eggs
½ cup cottage cheese
1 cup (4 ounces) shredded Swiss cheese
1 green onion, chopped
½ teaspoon salt
⅛ teaspoon pepper
4 drops of hot sauce
6 slices bacon, cooked and crumbled
Paprika

Cover hash browns with hot water; let stand 10 minutes. Drain well.

Beat eggs; add potatoes and remaining ingredients except bacon and paprika. Pour into a well-greased 10-inch piepan. Sprinkle with bacon and paprika. Cover and refrigerate at least 8 hours.

Place cold piepan, uncovered, in cold oven. Bake at 350° for 35 minutes or until potatoes are tender and eggs done. Yield: 6 to 8 servings.

QUICHE LORRAINE

Pastry for 9-inch pie
8 slices bacon, cut into ½-inch pieces
¼ cup chopped green onions
2 cups (8 ounces) shredded Swiss
  cheese, divided
6 eggs, beaten
1 cup whipping cream
½ teaspoon salt
Dash of red pepper
Dash of white pepper
⅛ teaspoon ground nutmeg
Ground nutmeg

Line a 9-inch quiche dish with pastry. Trim excess pastry around edges. Prick bottom and sides of pastry with a fork. Bake at 400° for 3 minutes; remove from oven, and gently prick with a fork. Bake an additional 5 minutes.

Sauté bacon and onions in a skillet until browned; drain well, and sprinkle evenly in pastry shell. Top with 1 cup cheese, and set aside.

Combine eggs, cream, salt, and pepper and ⅛ teaspoon ground nutmeg, stirring well. Pour mixture into pastry shell, and top with remaining 1 cup cheese. Sprinkle with nutmeg. Bake at 350° for 35 minutes or until set. Let stand 10 minutes. Yield: one 9-inch quiche.

SAUSAGE-CHEDDAR QUICHE

Pastry for 9-inch pie
1 pound bulk pork sausage
1 (4-ounce) can sliced mushrooms,
  drained
½ cup chopped onion
¼ cup chopped green pepper
½ teaspoon dried whole basil
⅛ teaspoon garlic powder
1½ cups (6 ounces) shredded
  Cheddar cheese
2 eggs, beaten
1 cup milk
Paprika

Line a 9-inch quiche dish with pastry. Trim excess pastry around edges. Prick bottom and sides of pastry with a fork. Bake at 400° for 3 minutes; remove from oven, and gently prick with a fork. Bake an additional 5 minutes.

Brown sausage in a heavy skillet; drain. Combine sausage, mushrooms, onion, green pepper, basil, and garlic powder, stirring well. Spoon into pastry shell, and top with cheese.

Combine eggs and milk; beat until foamy. Pour over cheese; sprinkle with paprika. Bake at 325° for 50 minutes or until set. Let stand 10 minutes before serving. Yield: one 9-inch quiche.

CRAB QUICHE

Pastry for 9-inch pie
2 eggs, beaten
½ cup mayonnaise
2 tablespoons all-purpose flour
½ cup milk
1 (6-ounce) package frozen crabmeat,
  thawed and drained
2 cups (8 ounces) shredded Swiss
  cheese
⅓ cup chopped green onions

Line a 9-inch quiche dish with pastry. Trim excess pastry around edges. Prick bottom and sides of pastry with a fork. Bake at 400° for 3 minutes; remove from oven, and gently prick with a fork. Bake an additional 5 minutes.

Combine eggs, mayonnaise, flour, and milk; mix thoroughly. Stir in crabmeat, cheese, and green onions. Spoon mixture into pastry shell. Bake at 350° for 30 minutes or until set. Let stand 10 minutes before serving. Yield: one 9-inch quiche.

INDIVIDUAL SPINACH QUICHES

1 (10-ounce) package frozen
  chopped spinach, thawed
1 cup (4 ounces) shredded Swiss
  cheese
1 cup (4 ounces) shredded
  mozzarella cheese
2 tablespoons all-purpose
  flour
3 eggs, beaten
1⅓ cups milk
¼ cup diced onion
¼ teaspoon salt
⅛ teaspoon pepper
¼ teaspoon dried whole
  thyme
¼ teaspoon dried whole
  rosemary, crushed
⅛ teaspoon hot sauce
Vegetable cooking spray
6 (6-inch) Basic Crêpes
  (page 86)

Drain spinach well, pressing between paper towels until barely moist. Set spinach aside.

Combine cheeses and flour; toss well, and set aside. Combine eggs and next 7 ingredients in a mixing bowl, stirring well. Stir in spinach and cheese mixture, mixing well.

Coat 6 (6-ounce) custard cups with cooking spray. Line each cup with a crêpe. Spoon spinach mixture into each crêpe-lined custard cup. Place cups on a baking sheet; bake at 325° for 45 to 50 minutes or until set. (Place a piece of aluminum foil over quiches after baking 15 minutes to prevent edges from getting too brown.) Let stand 5 minutes before serving. Yield: 6 servings.

HAM QUICHE

Pastry for 9-inch pie
1½ cups (6 ounces) shredded Swiss cheese
1 tablespoon all-purpose flour
½ cup diced cooked ham
4 eggs, beaten
2 cups half-and-half
½ teaspoon dry mustard
¼ teaspoon salt

Line a 9-inch pieplate with pastry. Trim excess pastry around edges; fold edges under, and flute. Prick bottom and sides of pastry with a fork. Bake at 400° for 3 minutes; remove from oven, and gently prick with a fork. Bake an additional 5 minutes.

Combine cheese and flour; sprinkle evenly into pastry shell. Top with ham. Set aside.

Combine eggs, half-and-half, dry mustard, and salt, stirring well. Pour mixture into pastry shell. Bake at 325° for 55 to 60 minutes or until set. Let stand 10 minutes before serving. Yield: one 9-inch quiche.

Summer Sausage Quiche: Substitute ½ cup diced summer sausage for ham.

Mushroom Quiche: Sauté ½ pound sliced mushrooms and 1 small onion, chopped, in 2 tablespoons vegetable oil; drain. Substitute mushrooms and onion for ham, and bake an additional 5 to 10 minutes.

Stratas & Soufflés

In French, soufflé literally means "puff," and that is a perfect description for soufflés and stratas. A large proportion of eggs makes the stratas rise. And the beaten egg whites folded into soufflés give them that extra lightness and height. Serve both immediately, as they deflate soon after removal from the oven.

A cream sauce usually forms the base for a soufflé; cheese or small pieces of meat or vegetables are added for flavor. Egg whites beaten to soft peaks are gently folded in at the last moment.

The traditional round soufflé dish is nice to use for soufflés, but any ovenproof, straight-sided casserole will work. High-rising soufflés are aided by the use of a removable collar. Directions for making a collar are given with each recipe.

Bake soufflés in the center of the oven; remove the rack above the dish in case the soufflé puffs more than you anticipate. Don't open the door before the end of the baking time, as the fast loss of heat could cause the soufflé to fall. At the end of the baking time, insert a knife into the center of the soufflé; it's done if the knife comes out clean. If you need to hold the soufflé a few minutes before serving it, just turn the oven off, and leave the soufflé in the oven, watching carefully through the window to make sure it doesn't overbrown.

HAM AND BROCCOLI STRATA

12 slices white bread, crusts removed
1 (10-ounce) package frozen chopped broccoli, thawed and drained
2 cups diced cooked ham
6 eggs, slightly beaten
3¼ cups milk
1 tablespoon instant minced onion
¼ teaspoon dry mustard
3 cups (12 ounces) shredded sharp Cheddar cheese

Cut bread into small cubes. Layer bread cubes, broccoli, and ham in a buttered 12- x 8- x 2-inch baking dish.

Combine eggs, milk, onion, mustard, and cheese; stir well. Pour into casserole; cover and refrigerate at least 8 hours. Remove from refrigerator; let stand 30 minutes. Bake, uncovered, at 325° for 55 to 60 minutes. Yield: 6 to 8 servings.

BREAKFAST SAUSAGE SANDWICHES

Softened butter or margarine
8 slices bread
1 pound bulk pork sausage, cooked, crumbled, and drained
1 cup (4 ounces) shredded Cheddar cheese
2 eggs, beaten
1½ cups milk
1½ teaspoons prepared mustard

Spread butter on one side of each bread slice. Place 4 slices, buttered side down, in a single layer in a lightly greased 8-inch square baking dish. Top each bread slice with sausage and remaining bread slices, buttered side up. Sprinkle with cheese. Combine remaining ingredients; pour over sandwiches. Cover and refrigerate at least 8 hours.

Remove from refrigerator; let stand 30 minutes. Bake, uncovered, at 350° for 45 minutes. Yield: 4 servings.

CLASSIC CHEESE SOUFFLÉ

2 tablespoons butter or margarine
¼ cup all-purpose flour
½ teaspoon salt
¼ teaspoon pepper
¼ teaspoon dry mustard
⅛ teaspoon hot sauce
1 cup milk
1½ cups (6 ounces) shredded sharp Cheddar cheese
6 eggs, separated

Lightly butter a 2-quart soufflé dish. Cut a piece of aluminum foil long enough to circle the dish, allowing a 1-inch overlap. Fold foil lengthwise into thirds, and lightly butter one side. Wrap foil, buttered side against the dish, so it extends 3 inches above the rim. Securely attach foil with string. Set aside.

Melt 2 tablespoons butter in a heavy saucepan over low heat; add flour, salt, pepper, mustard, and hot sauce, stirring until smooth. Cook 1 minute, stirring constantly. Gradually add milk; cook over medium heat, stirring constantly, until thickened and bubbly. Add cheese, stirring until melted; remove from heat, and cool slightly.

Beat egg yolks until thick and lemon colored. Gradually stir about one-fourth of hot cheese mixture into yolks; add to remaining hot mixture.

Beat egg whites (at room temperature) until stiff but not dry; fold into cheese mixture. Pour into prepared soufflé dish. Bake at 475° for 10 minutes. Reduce heat to 400°, and bake an additional 15 minutes or until puffed and golden brown. Remove collar and serve immediately. Yield: 6 servings.

Individual Cheese Soufflés: Spoon cheese mixture into 6 buttered (10-ounce) soufflé dishes or custard cups. Bake at 350° for 15 to 20 minutes or until puffed and golden brown.

Note: Individual Cheese Soufflés may be frozen before baking; cover with plastic wrap, and freeze. To bake, place frozen soufflés on baking sheet; bake at 350° for 40 minutes or until golden brown. Use only freezer-to-oven dishes.

SPINACH SOUFFLÉ ROLL

¼ cup plus 2 tablespoons all-purpose flour
¼ teaspoon salt
Dash of red pepper
⅓ cup butter or margarine
1¼ cups milk
¾ cup (3 ounces) shredded Cheddar cheese
¼ cup grated Parmesan cheese
7 eggs, separated
¼ teaspoon cream of tartar
¼ teaspoon salt
1 to 2 tablespoons grated Parmesan cheese
Spinach-Mushroom Filling
4 ounces sliced Cheddar cheese, cut diagonally
Fresh spinach (optional)

Grease bottom and sides of a 15- x 10- x 1-inch jellyroll pan with vegetable oil. Line with wax paper, allowing paper to extend beyond ends of pan; grease wax paper with oil.

Combine flour, ¼ teaspoon salt, and red pepper; stir well.

Classic Cheese Soufflé Step-By-Step

1. *To prepare soufflé dish, cut aluminum foil long enough to circle dish, plus overlap; fold into thirds. Butter soufflé dish and one side of foil.*

2. *Wrap aluminum foil, buttered side to dish, so foil extends 3 inches above rim. Tie with string.*

3. *Beat egg yolks until thick and lemon colored; gradually stir about one-fourth of hot cheese sauce into yolks. Add to remaining hot mixture.*

4. *Beat egg whites until stiff but not dry.*

Melt butter in a large, heavy saucepan over low heat; add flour mixture, stirring with a wire whisk until smooth. Cook 1 minute, stirring constantly with whisk. Gradually add milk; cook over medium heat, stirring constantly with whisk, until very thick and mixture leaves sides of pan. Remove from heat; beat in ¾ cup Cheddar and ¼ cup Parmesan cheese.

Place egg yolks in a large mixing bowl; beat at high speed of an electric mixer until thick and lemon colored. Gradually stir in one-fourth of hot cheese mixture; add to remaining cheese mixture, beating well.

Combine egg whites (at room temperature) and cream of tartar; beat at high speed of electric mixer until foamy. Add ¼ teaspoon salt, and beat until stiff peaks form. Fold one-third of egg whites into cheese mixture; then carefully fold in remaining egg whites.

Pour cheese mixture into prepared pan, spreading evenly. Bake on center rack of oven at 350° for 15 minutes or until puffed and firm to the touch (do not allow to overcook).

Loosen edges of soufflé with a metal spatula, but do not remove from pan; place on wire rack. Let cool 15 minutes.

Place 2 lengths of wax paper (longer than jellyroll pan) on a smooth, slightly damp surface; overlap edge of paper nearest you over second sheet. Sprinkle 1 to 2 tablespoons Parmesan cheese over the wax paper.

Quickly invert jellyroll pan onto wax paper, with long side nearest you; remove pan, and carefully peel wax paper from soufflé. Spoon Spinach-Mushroom Filling over surface, spreading to edges.

Starting at long side, carefully roll soufflé jellyroll fashion; use the wax paper to help support soufflé as you roll. Using your hands, gently smooth and shape the roll.

Carefully slide the roll, seam side down, onto a large ovenproof platter or baking sheet. Arrange cheese slices on top. Place 3 inches from broiler element, and broil until cheese melts and is lightly browned. Serve on a bed of fresh spinach, if desired. Yield: 8 servings.

Spinach-Mushroom Filling

2 (10-ounce) packages frozen chopped spinach
¼ cup finely chopped onion
¼ cup butter or margarine, melted
½ cup diced fresh mushrooms
¾ cup (3 ounces) shredded Cheddar cheese
½ cup commercial sour cream
¼ cup grated Parmesan cheese
¼ teaspoon salt
¼ teaspoon ground nutmeg

Cook spinach according to package directions; drain and press dry.

Sauté onion in butter until transparent. Add mushrooms, and sauté 3 minutes. Stir in remaining ingredients. Yield: about 1¾ cups.

Note: The soufflé is very fragile and may crack or break a little during the rolling process.

5. Fold beaten egg whites into cheese mixture.

Serve Classic Cheese Soufflé immediately. Soufflés fall minutes after removal from the oven.

Cheese

Whether served alone or stirred into a recipe, cheese is a popular item in most homes. And today's cheese market includes more kinds than ever before. With both foreign and domestic cheeses available, you have a wide choice among old favorites and new varieties.

Cheeses differ substantially in flavor, texture, and color, depending on how they're made and how long they're allowed to age. Classifications vary from soft, semisoft, firm, very hard, and blue-veined cheeses.

Cheese Identification Chart

1. Romano	10. Edam
2. Cheddar	11. Cottage
3. Parmesan	12. Swiss
4. Roulé	13. Chèvre (Goat)
5. Spiced Roulé	14. Brie
6. Port Salut	15. Roquefort
7. Gruyère	16. Fontina
8. Mozzarella	17. Cream
9. Provolone	18. Monterey Jack

Cheese comes in a multitude of colors, shapes, flavors, and textures. See diagram for identification.

WELSH RAREBIT

¾ cup milk
1½ cups (6 ounces) shredded mild
 Cheddar cheese
¾ teaspoon dry mustard
⅛ teaspoon red pepper
½ teaspoon Worcestershire sauce
1 egg, well beaten
4 large slices French bread, toasted
4 slices bacon, cooked and crumbled

Combine first 5 ingredients in top of a double boiler; bring water to a boil. Reduce heat to low; cook, stirring constantly, until cheese melts. Slowly stir about one-fourth of hot cheese mixture into beaten egg; add to remaining hot mixture, stirring constantly. Cook over low heat, stirring constantly, until mixture thickens and just begins to simmer. Serve over hot toast; sprinkle with bacon. Yield: 4 servings.

◯ *Microwave Directions:* Place milk in a 1-quart glass bowl; microwave at HIGH for 1½ to 2 minutes or until almost boiling. Gradually add cheese to hot milk, whisking well after each addition. Whisk in mustard, pepper, and Worcestershire sauce. Gradually stir about one-fourth of hot mixture into beaten egg; add to remaining hot mixture, stirring constantly. Microwave at HIGH for 1 to 1½ minutes or until cheese melts and mixture thickens, stirring at 30-second intervals. Serve over hot toast; sprinkle with bacon.

CREAM-STYLE CHEESE

You can experience some of the skill involved in cheesemaking by making this Cream-Style Cheese at home. It is a somewhat complicated and time-consuming process, but the wonderfully fresh flavor of the end product will be worth the occasional effort. This homemade cheese tastes a lot like commercial cream cheese, but it tastes a whole lot fresher. You can use the end product to flavor and shape your own cream cheese blends for appetizers or dessert. See Garlic-Chive Cheese Mold (page 35), Blue Cheese Mold (page 36), and Heavenly Dessert Cheese Molds (page 201).

3 cups half-and-half
¾ cup whipping cream
1½ tablespoons cultured buttermilk
¼ teaspoon plus ⅛ teaspoon salt

Combine half-and-half and whipping cream in a heavy saucepan. Cook over low heat until mixture is 90°. Stir in buttermilk. Pour mixture into a large glass or ceramic bowl; cover with plastic wrap. Wrap a large towel around entire bowl, and place bowl in an unheated oven with light on or in a warm place, about 85°, for 28 hours or until mixture is consistency of soft yogurt.

Cut several pieces of cheesecloth large enough to line a large colander and extend 4 inches over edges. Rinse cheesecloth, and squeeze out excess moisture; line colander with cheesecloth. Place colander in sink. Pour cream mixture into colander, and let drain 20 minutes.

Place colander in a container to drain completely. Cover colander and container tightly with enough plastic wrap to make an airtight seal. Refrigerate 12 hours or until well drained. Spoon cheese mixture into a bowl, and stir in salt. If the cheese is to be flavored and molded according to the recipes listed above, then do so at this point.

If cheese is to be molded unflavored, cut 4 (8-inch-square) pieces of cheesecloth; rinse cheesecloth, and squeeze out excess moisture. Smooth out wrinkles of cheesecloth, and stack layers on top of each other. Spoon cheese mixture in center of cheesecloth. Wrap cheesecloth around cheese mixture, and tie ends securely. Pat cheesecloth-wrapped cheese into an oval or round shape. (Cheese can also be shaped in desired mold. Line mold with cheesecloth, and spoon in cheese mixture, pressing with the back of a spoon to smoothly and firmly pack mixture.)

Place cheesecloth-wrapped cheese (or invert mold) over a wire rack in a shallow pan. Cover pan with enough plastic wrap to make an airtight seal. Refrigerate 1 to 2 days or until firm and well drained. Unmold cheese, and remove cheesecloth. Cheese will keep in refrigerator up to 5 days. Yield: about 2 cups.

FISH & SHELLFISH

This may sound like a fish story, but it's true! No area is more endowed with fresh fish and seafood than the South. Inland lakes and streams provide us with a multitude of freshwater fish, and from the Chesapeake Bay down the Atlantic to the Gulf of Mexico you'll find a limitless supply of saltwater fish and shellfish. Since fish and shellfish have such different characteristics, we've treated them separately within this chapter.

Fish

While fish has always been popular in the South, it's become an even more important part of the diet as people turn to more healthful eating. Fish is an excellent source of protein and other nutrients, and most fish is relatively low in fat. Served with simple seasonings and light sauces, fish has a lot to offer the health-conscious cook.

CHECK THE FISH FOR FRESHNESS

If you know the characteristics of good quality fish, you can easily judge it for freshness. The eyes should be very clear and bright with no signs of redness. The gills, however, should be bright red. The flesh needs to be firm and pliable with no signs of drying out. The skin should

Crispy Fried Catfish (page 231) packs a powerful punch after being marinated in commercial hot sauce before frying.

have no faded markings. Probably the best sign of freshness is the odor. The odor should always be mild with no offensive smell.

Use some of the same characteristics to judge freshness in fish that is dressed and cut. The flesh should be firm and elastic, and there should be no sign of browning or drying of the edges. The fish should have a mild, fresh odor.

When buying frozen fish, make sure the package is tightly wrapped and sealed. Be sure the fish is solidly frozen, and free of ice crystals. Ice crystals may indicate that the fish has been thawed and refrozen, which can ruin fish. Thaw frozen fish in the refrigerator, if possible. If you need it quicker than that, place the frozen fish wrapped in plastic

TIMETABLE FOR COOKING FISH AND SHELLFISH

Method of Cooking	Product	Market Form	Approximate Weight or Thickness	Cooking Temperature	Approximate Total Cooking Times Per Minute
Baking	Fish	Dressed	3 to 4 lbs.	350°F.	40 to 60
		Pan-dressed	½ to 1 lb.	350°F.	25 to 30
		Steaks	½ to 1 in.	350°F.	25 to 35
		Fillets	1 in.	350°F.	9 to 10 per inch
	Clams	Live		450°F.	15
	Lobster	Live	¾ to 1 lb.	400°F.	15 to 20
			1 to 1½ lbs.	400°F.	20 to 25
	Oysters	Live		450°F.	15
		Shucked		400°F.	10
	Scallops	Shucked		350°F.	25 to 30
	Shrimp	Headless		350°F.	20 to 25
	Spiny lobster	Headless	4 oz.	450°F.	20 to 25
	tails	Headless	8 oz.	450°F.	25 to 30
Broiling	Fish	Pan-dressed	½ to 1 lb.		10 to 15
		Steaks	½ to 1 in.		10 to 15
		Fillets	1 in.		9 to 10 per inch
	Clams	Live			5 to 8
	Lobster	Live	¾ to 1 lb.		10 to 12
			1 to 1½ lbs.		12 to 15
	Oysters	Live			5
		Shucked			5
	Scallops	Shucked			8 to 10
	Shrimp	Headless			8 to 10
	Spiny lobster	Headless	4 oz.		8 to 10
	tails		8 oz.		10 to 12
Cooking in Water	Fish	Pan-dressed	½ to 1 lb.	Simmer	10
		Steaks	½ to 1 in.	Simmer	10
		Fillets	1 in.	Simmer	9 per inch
	Crabs	Live		Simmer	15
	Lobster	Live	¾ to 1 lb.	Simmer	10 to 15
			1 to 1½ lbs.	Simmer	15 to 20
	Scallops	Shucked		Simmer	4 to 5
	Shrimp	Headless		Simmer	3 to 5
	Spiny lobster	Headless	4 oz.	Simmer	10
	tails		8 oz.	Simmer	15
Deep-Fat Frying	Fish	Pan-dressed	½ to 1 lb.	375°F.	2 to 4
		Steaks	½ to 1 in.	375°F.	2 to 4
		Fillets	½ to 1 in.	375°F.	1 to 5
	Clams	Shucked		375°F.	2 to 3
	Crabs	Soft-Shell	¼ lb.	375°F.	3 to 4
	Lobster	Live	¾ to 1 lb.	375°F.	3 to 4
			1 to 1½ lbs.	375°F.	4 to 5
	Oysters	Shucked		375°F.	2
	Scallops	Shucked		350°F.	3 to 4
	Shrimp	Headless		350°F.	2 to 3
	Spiny lobster	Headless	4 oz.	350°F.	3 to 4
	tails		8 oz.	350°F.	4 to 5

wrap under cold running water until thawed. Drain and blot thawed fish with paper towels before cooking.

KNOW WHAT YOU'RE BUYING

You can purchase fresh fish in a variety of market forms. Knowing these terms will help you pick the right type and amount of fish for your needs.

Whole fish are marketed just as they come from the ocean. Before cooking, the fish must be eviscerated (the internal organs removed) and scaled. Sometimes the head, tail, and fins are removed. Count on about 1 pound per serving.

A **drawn** fish is a whole fish that has been eviscerated. Allow 1 pound per serving.

A **dressed** fish is one that has been eviscerated and scaled. Usually, the head, fins, and tail have been removed also. Smaller fish are usually called **pan-dressed**. Allow ½ pound per serving.

Fish **steaks** are crosswise slices of whole dressed fish. They are usually cut about 1 inch thick. The only bone is a cross section of the backbone and ribs. Plan on about ⅓ to ½ pound per serving.

Fillets are the sides of the fish cut lengthwise away from the bone. They are usually skinned and are practically boneless. A **single fillet** is cut from only one side of the fish. For **butterfly fillets**, the fillets of the fish are held together by the uncut belly skin. Allow about ⅓ to ½ pound per serving.

FAT OR LEAN?

Fish is classified as either fat (having an oil content of more than 5%) or lean (having an oil content of less than 5%). Fat fish tends to be higher in calories and stronger in flavor.

The color of fat fish is usually darker, and the fish requires less basting during cooking to keep it moist and tender. When substituting one fish for another in a recipe, it's best to choose a substitute from within the same classification. Use the chart on this page as a guide.

COOKING FISH

Choose from baking, broiling, grilling, frying, steaming, and poaching for cooking fish. The dry heat methods are considered better for cooking fat fish, while lean fish remains more moist when cooked by moist heat methods. You can cook lean fish by a dry heat method, however, if it is basted often.

Overcooking and cooking at too high a temperature are the most common problems in cooking fish. These factors dry and toughen the fish and can destroy the flavor. Be sure to check the fish for doneness occasionally while cooking. To check for doneness, pierce the thickest part of the fish with a fork, and twist the fork; most fish will flake easily when done. It will also lose its transparency and become opaque.

STORING FISH

Fish is best if cooked the day of purchase, but it can be stored up to two days in the coldest part of the refrigerator, preferably on ice.

Frozen fish should be kept solidly frozen until you plan to thaw it. If it accidentally thaws, plan to use it within one day.

Leftover cooked fish will keep for two or three days in the refrigerator. Use the leftovers in salads, soups, omelets, and crêpes.

MICROWAVING FISH

Fish that is cooked in a microwave

FAT OR LEAN FISH CLASSIFICATIONS

Fat Fish	Lean Fish
amberjack	bluegill
butterfish	cod
carp	crappie
freshwater catfish	croaker
king mackerel	dolphin
lake trout	flounder
mullet	grouper
rainbow trout	haddock
sablefish	halibut
salmon	ocean catfish
sea herring	ocean perch
shad	orange roughy
Spanish mackerel	permit
tuna	pike
whitefish	plaice
	pollock
	pompano
	porgy
	red snapper
	redfish
	rockfish
	scamp
	scrod
	sea bass
	shark
	sheepshead
	sole
	speckled sea trout
	spot
	swordfish
	tilapia
	tilefish
	triggerfish
	turbot
	walleye
	white sea trout
	whiting

oven can be outstanding. With the natural tenderness and moisture of fish, the rapid cooking action of microwave ovens helps retain the delicate flavor and texture. Those fish recipes that adapt well to microwave cooking have microwave directions immediately following the conventional directions.

Generally, fish is microwaved at HIGH power to quickly seal in juices and flavor. Arrange the thicker portions to the outside of the dish so they will get done without overcooking the thinner areas.

When fish turns opaque, it's done. Sometimes, with thick fish fillets or steaks, the outer areas may be opaque, while the centers are still translucent. But the underdone parts will finish cooking after the fish is taken out of the oven. If after a few minutes the fish doesn't appear done, put it back in the microwave, but only for a few seconds.

Microwave ovens also work well for defrosting frozen fish. Fillets can be left in their original package for defrosting. Since fish defrosts rapidly, care must be taken not to toughen it by over-defrosting in the microwave oven. Remove the fish from the package while still slightly icy; hold under cold, running water to complete defrosting.

Weight and shape of the package affects defrosting time; thick packages take longer than flatter ones of the same weight. Use LOW or DEFROST setting, and allow 6 to 9 minutes per pound if fillets are solidly frozen. The package should be turned over and given a quarter-turn after half the defrosting time has elapsed. Check fillets after minimum time has elapsed. If necessary, continue to microwave, checking every 30 seconds.

FIRE UP THE GRILL FOR FISH

Southerners have long been grillers, but only recently have they begun grilling much fish. Since fish cooks so quickly and has such a different texture than most grilled meats, you'll need to keep a few pointers in mind.

Choosing the Right Fish. Almost any type of fish is suitable for the grill. Lean fish, such as scamp, snap-per, flounder, and grouper, need more basting during cooking to keep them moist and flavorful. You may want to baste fat fish, such as mackerel, salmon, and amberjack, for extra flavor, but it's not essential.

Also, choose fish—steaks, pan-dressed fish, or fillets—at least ¾ inch thick for grilling. Thinner pieces tend to dry out.

Starting the Fire. Use either a gas, electric, or charcoal grill. Prepare the grill as you would for anything else you would barbecue. Be sure to start the fire in advance so the grill will be hot by the time you're ready to cook. One method to use when lighting a charcoal fire is to mound the briquets into a cone shape. Lightly spray the briquets with a commercial lighter fluid. Let the fluid soak in about a minute before lighting. Remember, don't use gasoline.

The coals are ready for cooking when they're covered with a gray ash. Spread the coals evenly over an area slightly larger than the area the fish will cover.

Greasing the Grill. Before you put the fish on to cook, thoroughly grease the metal cooking grid. (Fish is so lean and fragile that it will stick to an ungreased grid during cooking.) In our test kitchens, we've found spraying the grid with vegetable cooking spray before placing grid over fire to be easy and quick. If you prefer, you could grease with shortening or vegetable oil.

A fish basket also comes in handy for grilling fish. The basket holds the fish and keeps it from sticking to the grill. Grease the part of the basket where fish will lie. Arrange the fish in the basket, and fasten shut. Place the basket flat on the grill. To turn the fish, simply flip the basket.

Grilling the Fish. Baste the fish often with melted butter or basting sauce during cooking to keep it moist and tender. Don't overcook the fish; it cooks so quickly that it's best not to leave fish when it's on the grill. The fish is ready when it flakes easily with a fork.

To fillet a fish: Run a boning knife lengthwise down the fish under the flesh as close to the backbone as possible. Repeat to fillet other side of the fish.

BAKED FISH

¼ cup butter or margarine, melted
2 tablespoons lemon or lime juice
2 pounds fish fillets
Salt and pepper
¼ cup chopped fresh parsley, basil, or oregano
1 lemon or lime, thinly sliced

Combine butter and lemon juice; dip each fish fillet in butter mixture, and arrange in a 13- x 9- x 2-inch baking dish. Sprinkle fillets with salt, pepper, and parsley. Arrange lemon slices over fillets. Bake at 350° for 30 minutes or until fish flakes easily when tested with a fork. Yield: about 6 servings.

GRILLED FISH FILLETS

6 (¾-inch-thick) fish fillets
½ cup butter or margarine
¼ cup lemon juice
1 tablespoon Worcestershire sauce
½ teaspoon seasoned salt
½ teaspoon paprika
¼ teaspoon red pepper

Place fillets in a large shallow dish.
Combine remaining ingredients in a saucepan; cook, stirring constantly, until butter melts. Pour marinade over fish. Cover; marinate 1 hour in refrigerator, turning once.
Drain fillets, reserving marinade; place fillets in a fish basket. Grill over hot coals 5 minutes on each side or until fish flakes easily when tested with a fork, basting often with marinade. Yield: 6 servings.

SMOKED FISH

5 pounds trout or mackerel, cut into 1½-inch-thick steaks (leave skin on)
1½ cups water
⅓ cup firmly packed brown sugar
3 tablespoons salt
¼ teaspoon red pepper

Soak hickory chips in water from 1 to 24 hours.
Place fish in a large shallow dish. Combine water, brown sugar, salt, and pepper; pour over fish. Cover and marinate at least 8 hours in refrigerator, turning fish occasionally.
Prepare charcoal fire in smoker, and let burn 10 to 15 minutes. Cover coals with soaked hickory chips. Place water pan in smoker. Add hot water to fill pan.
Place upper food rack on appropriate shelf in smoker. Arrange fish steaks on food rack. Cover with smoker lid, and cook 3 to 4 hours or to desired degree of doneness. Yield: 8 to 10 servings.

SPICY BROILED FISH

Although the seasoning and technique for Spicy Broiled Fish are different from those of the famous blackened redfish often served in restaurants, the taste and appearance are much the same.

6 (8- to 10-ounce) sea trout or other fish fillets
1 tablespoon Old Bay seasoning
2 teaspoons paprika
⅛ to ¼ teaspoon red pepper
¼ cup plus 2 tablespoons butter or margarine, melted
⅓ cup lemon juice
1 teaspoon dried parsley flakes

Place fish fillets in two lightly greased 13- x 9- x 2-inch baking dishes, skin side down. Sprinkle Old Bay seasoning, paprika, and red pepper evenly over the fish. Brush fish with butter; sprinkle with lemon juice, and top with parsley. Broil 10 to 12 minutes or until fish flakes easily when tested with a fork. Yield: 6 servings.

To cut steaks from a fish: First cut off the head. Then cut fish into 1-inch-wide slices, using a hammer to tap the knife through the backbone if necessary.

CRISPY FRIED CATFISH

(pictured on page 226)

6 medium catfish, cleaned and dressed
1 teaspoon salt
¼ teaspoon pepper
1 (2-ounce) bottle hot sauce
2 cups self-rising cornmeal
Vegetable oil
Watercress (optional)
Lemon slices (optional)

Sprinkle catfish with salt and pepper; place in a shallow dish. Add hot sauce; marinate 1 to 2 hours in refrigerator.
Place cornmeal in a plastic bag; drop in catfish, one at a time, and shake until completely coated. Fry in deep hot oil (375°) until fish float to the top and are golden brown; drain well. Garnish with watercress and lemon slices, if desired. Yield: 6 servings.

PAN-FRIED FISH AMANDINE

¼ cup sliced almonds
2 tablespoons butter or margarine, melted
6 large bass or trout fillets
Salt and pepper to taste
Dried whole thyme to taste
¼ cup milk
¾ cup all-purpose flour
½ cup vegetable oil
1 tablespoon chopped fresh parsley

Sauté almonds in butter until golden brown; set aside.
Sprinkle fillets with salt, pepper, and thyme; dip in milk, and dredge in flour. Fry fillets in hot oil (360°) over medium heat until golden brown, turning to brown both sides. Drain on paper towels. Remove to serving dish; sprinkle fish with almonds and parsley. Yield: 6 servings.

CRUNCHY FRIED FILLETS

1 pound frozen perch or other fish
fillets, thawed
¼ teaspoon salt
¾ cup all-purpose flour
1 egg, beaten
3 tablespoons water
25 to 30 saltine crackers, crushed
Vegetable oil

Sprinkle fillets with salt, and dredge
in flour. Combine egg and water, mixing
well. Dip floured fillets in egg mixture,
and coat with cracker crumbs. Fry in
hot oil (360°) over medium heat until
browned. Drain. Yield: 4 servings.

HERBED FISH FILLETS

¼ teaspoon onion salt
¼ teaspoon dried whole oregano
¼ teaspoon dried parsley flakes
¼ teaspoon dried whole tarragon
¼ teaspoon pepper
1 small clove garlic, minced
¼ cup plus 2 tablespoons butter or
margarine, melted
4 (4- to 6-ounce) perch or other fish
fillets
3 tablespoons dry sherry

Sauté seasonings and garlic in butter
in a large heavy skillet over medium
heat 1 minute. Reduce heat to low; add
fish. Cook fish 4 minutes; turn and cook
an additional 3 to 4 minutes or until fish
flakes easily when tested with a fork (do
not overcook). Remove fish with a slotted turner; place on a heated platter, and
keep warm.
Pour sherry into skillet; cook over
high heat 30 to 45 seconds. Pour sherry
mixture over fish; serve immediately.
Yield: 4 servings.

☐ *Microwave Directions:* Combine
seasonings, garlic, and butter in a 12- x
8- x 2-inch baking dish; microwave at
HIGH for 1 minute; stir well. Arrange
fish in butter mixture; cover with heavy-
duty plastic wrap, and microwave at
HIGH for 5 to 6 minutes. Turn fish over,
and rearrange in dish. Cover and microwave at HIGH for 5 to 6 minutes or until
fish flakes easily when tested with a fork
(do not overcook). Remove fish with a
slotted turner; place on a heated platter,
and keep warm.
Pour sherry into dish; microwave at
HIGH for 30 seconds. Pour sherry mixture over fish; serve immediately.

PERCH IN PAPILLOTE

*You'll find Perch in Papillote a unique
and tasty dish for company. Set up an
assembly line to put the packages
together; it's easy and fun! Cooking the
fish in the sealed parchment bags holds
in much of the moisture and flavor.*

Vegetable oil
4 (4- to 6-ounce) perch or other fish
fillets
Salt and pepper
⅓ cup diced tomato
⅓ cup chopped green onions
⅓ cup diced celery
3 tablespoons chopped fresh parsley
1 teaspoon dried whole tarragon
3 tablespoons lemon juice
1 lemon, thinly sliced and seeded

Cut four 15-inch squares of parchment paper or aluminum foil; fold
squares in half, and trim each into a
heart shape. Place parchment hearts on
2 large baking sheets. Brush top side of
each heart lightly with vegetable oil,
leaving edges ungreased. Set aside.
Arrange one fish fillet on one greased
half of each parchment heart, near the
crease. Sprinkle fillet lightly with salt
and pepper.
Combine tomato, green onions, celery, parsley, tarragon, ¼ teaspoon salt,
and ¼ teaspoon pepper, tossing gently.
Spoon vegetable mixture evenly over fillets. Sprinkle lemon juice evenly over
vegetables; top with lemon slices.
Fold over remaining halves of parchment hearts; pleat and crimp edges together to seal securely. Arrange
packages on a large baking sheet. Bake at
425° for 10 minutes or until bags are
puffed and lightly browned. Transfer
immediately to serving plates, and serve
in the bag. To serve, cut a cross in the
top of each package with scissors, and
fold paper back. Yield: 4 servings.

Sauce Up the Fish

Give a lift to fried, poached, or
grilled fish and seafood with a tasty
sauce from our Sauces chapter. Our
herb butters, Clarified or Lemon Butter, Herbed Yogurt Sauce, Cucumber
Sauce, or Zippy Cocktail Sauce add just
the right spark. Serve them from a
lemon cup or a cut green pepper.

POACHED SALMON WITH DILL SAUCE

1 (10¾-ounce) can chicken broth,
undiluted
½ cup dry white wine
½ cup chopped onion
4 (¾-inch thick) salmon steaks
½ cup commercial sour cream
½ cup chopped cucumber
¼ teaspoon dried whole dillweed

Combine first 3 ingredients in a fish
poacher or large skillet; bring to a boil,
and add salmon. Cover, reduce heat, and
simmer 8 to 10 minutes or until fish
flakes easily when tested with a fork.
Reserve 2 tablespoons poaching liquid;
set aside. Refrigerate salmon in remaining poaching liquid until chilled.
Combine 2 tablespoons reserved liquid, sour cream, cucumber, and dillweed, stirring well; chill.
Remove salmon from poaching liquid;
drain on paper towels. Serve salmon
with dill sauce. Yield: 4 servings.

Offer Vegetable-Fish Rolls when you want an unusual entrée. The flavor of dillweed is the perfect complement for the fish.

CRAB-STUFFED FLOUNDER

¾ cup minced celery
½ cup minced onion
½ cup minced fresh parsley
¼ cup minced shallots
¼ cup minced green pepper
1 clove garlic, minced
½ cup butter or margarine, melted
1 tablespoon all-purpose flour
½ cup milk
½ cup dry white wine
½ pound fresh lump crabmeat
1¼ cups seasoned dry breadcrumbs
¼ teaspoon salt
Dash of pepper
6 (8-ounce) flounder fillets, cut in
  half crosswise
Mornay Sauce (page 440)
Paprika
Minced fresh parsley (optional)

Sauté celery, onion, parsley, shallots, green pepper, and garlic in butter in a large skillet over medium heat; cook until vegetables are tender. Add flour, and cook 1 minute, stirring constantly. Gradually add milk and wine; cook over medium heat, stirring constantly, until mixture is slightly thickened. Remove from heat; stir in crabmeat, breadcrumbs, salt, and pepper.

Place 6 fillet halves in a greased jellyroll pan; spoon about ½ cup crabmeat stuffing on each fillet. Cut remaining fillet halves in half lengthwise; place a fillet fourth on each side of stuffed fillets in jellyroll pan, pressing gently into stuffing mixture. Top each portion with Mornay Sauce; sprinkle with paprika. Bake at 425° for 15 to 20 minutes or until fish flakes easily when tested with a fork. Garnish with parsley, if desired. Yield: 6 servings.

VEGETABLE-FISH ROLLS

1 large onion, finely chopped
1 clove garlic, minced
2 tablespoons vegetable oil
2 tablespoons butter or margarine
2 large carrots, scraped and cut into
  julienne strips
2 large stalks celery, cut into
  julienne strips
4 (4- to 6-ounce) sole or flounder
  fillets
¾ teaspoon dried whole dillweed
½ teaspoon salt
¼ teaspoon pepper
1 lemon, sliced
½ cup dry white wine
2 tablespoons lemon juice
Watercress

Sauté onion and garlic in hot oil until tender. Remove from skillet, and set aside. Melt butter in skillet; add carrots and celery, and sauté 3 minutes or until desired degree of doneness.

Place one-fourth of carrot and celery strips on short end of each fillet; roll up fillets, and place seam side down in an 8-inch square baking dish. Combine onion mixture, dillweed, salt, and pepper. Spoon mixture over and around rolls; top with lemon slices.

Combine wine and lemon juice; pour around fillets. Cover and bake at 375° for 15 to 20 minutes or until fish flakes easily when tested with a fork. Garnish with watercress. Yield: 4 servings.

TUNA STROGANOFF

1 (5-ounce) package medium egg
   noodles
1 (8-ounce) carton commercial sour
   cream
1 (10¾-ounce) can cream of
   mushroom soup, undiluted
¼ cup dry white wine
1 teaspoon dried whole thyme
½ cup sliced green onions
⅛ teaspoon pepper
2 (6½-ounce) cans tuna, drained and
   flaked
¼ cup soft breadcrumbs
Paprika

Cook noodles according to package directions; drain and set aside.

Combine sour cream, soup, wine, and thyme in a large bowl; stir well. Add onions, pepper, and tuna, stirring well. Stir in noodles.

Spoon mixture into a lightly greased shallow 2-quart casserole; sprinkle with breadcrumbs and paprika. Cover dish, and bake at 350° for 30 minutes. Yield: 4 to 6 servings.

SALMON CROQUETTES

1 (15½-ounce) can pink salmon
Milk
¼ cup butter or margarine
¼ cup finely chopped onion
¼ cup all-purpose flour
½ teaspoon salt
⅛ teaspoon red pepper
1 tablespoon lemon juice
1 cup dry breadcrumbs, divided
Vegetable oil
Cucumber or Herbed Yogurt Sauce
   (optional, page 438 or 439)

Drain salmon, reserving liquid; add enough milk to salmon liquid to measure 1 cup; set aside.

Melt butter in a heavy saucepan over low heat; add onion and cook until tender. Add flour, stirring until smooth. Cook mixture 1 minute, stirring constantly. Gradually add milk mixture, and cook over medium heat, stirring constantly, until sauce is thickened and bubbly. Stir in the salt and pepper, and set aside.

Remove skin and bones from salmon; flake salmon with a fork. Add lemon juice, ½ cup dry breadcrumbs, and white sauce, stirring well. Refrigerate mixture until thoroughly chilled; shape into croquettes. Roll croquettes in remaining ½ cup dry breadcrumbs. Fry in 3 inches of hot oil (375°) until golden brown. Serve croquettes with Cucumber Sauce or Herbed Yogurt Sauce, if desired. Yield: 4 servings.

Shellfish

Shrimp

Shrimp is probably the most frequently eaten shellfish. It's a treat simply boiled and served with spicy cocktail sauce as an appetizer, or teamed with other ingredients to make an elaborate entrée.

The shrimp you buy may be light gray, pink, or red. The color in no way reflects its freshness, only what type of water from which the shrimp were harvested. All turn pink upon cooking.

You'll have your choice of several sizes of fresh shrimp at the market. The smaller ones are a good choice for salad and casserole recipes. The larger ones work well stuffed, grilled, or in entrées suitable for more formal entertaining.

Shrimp should have a mild odor when you purchase it. Try another seafood market if the odor seems too strong. Store in the refrigerator, and use within a day or two after purchasing. Shrimp may be frozen raw in the shell or cooked and peeled for longer storage. Remember that 1 pound of shrimp in the shell will yield only about one-half pound after peeling. Allow one-fourth to one-third pound of peeled shrimp per serving.

BOILED SHRIMP

6 cups water
2 tablespoons salt
2 bay leaves
1 lemon, halved
1 stalk celery, cut into 3-inch pieces
2 pounds unpeeled fresh shrimp
Zippy Cocktail Sauce (optional,
   page 441)

Combine first 5 ingredients in a Dutch oven; bring to a boil. Add shrimp, and cook 3 to 5 minutes. Drain well; rinse with cold water. Chill. Peel and devein shrimp. Serve with Zippy Cocktail Sauce, if desired. Yield: 4 to 6 servings.

GRILLED SHRIMP

2 pounds unpeeled jumbo fresh
  shrimp
¾ cup butter or margarine, melted
¼ cup fresh lime juice

Peel and devein shrimp.

Combine butter and lime juice. Dip shrimp in butter mixture, and thread tail and neck of each shrimp on skewers so shrimp will lie flat. Grill over medium-hot coals 3 to 4 minutes on each side or until shrimp turn pink. Serve butter mixture with shrimp. Yield: 4 to 6 servings.

FRENCH FRIED SHRIMP

2 pounds unpeeled medium-size fresh
  shrimp
1 cup all-purpose flour
1½ teaspoons baking powder
½ teaspoon salt
⅔ cup water
2 tablespoons lemon juice
1 tablespoon vegetable oil
1 egg, beaten
Vegetable oil
Zippy Cocktail Sauce (page 441)

Peel and devein shrimp.

Combine flour, baking powder, and salt in a medium bowl; make a well in center. Combine water, lemon juice, 1 tablespoon oil, and egg; add to dry ingredients, and stir until batter is smooth. Dip shrimp in batter, and fry in hot oil (375°) until browned. Serve with Zippy Cocktail Sauce. Yield: 4 to 6 servings.

*French Fried Shrimp fries up puffy
and golden brown. Serve it
with Zippy Cocktail Sauce
for tasty dipping.*

SHRIMP SCAMPI

2 pounds unpeeled medium-size fresh
  shrimp
¼ cup chopped green onions
¼ cup chopped fresh parsley
4 cloves garlic, crushed
¾ cup butter or margarine, melted
¼ cup dry white wine
2 tablespoons lemon juice
¾ teaspoon salt
¼ teaspoon freshly ground pepper

Peel and devein shrimp.

Sauté green onions, parsley, and garlic in butter until onions are tender. Reduce heat to low; add shrimp. Cook, stirring frequently, 3 to 5 minutes. Remove shrimp with a slotted spoon to a serving dish; keep warm. Add remaining ingredients to butter mixture; simmer 2 minutes. Pour butter mixture over shrimp. Yield: 4 servings.

SPICY SHRIMP CREOLE

1½ pounds unpeeled fresh shrimp
1 small onion, chopped
1 small green pepper, chopped
½ cup chopped celery
2 medium cloves garlic, minced
2 tablespoons butter or margarine, melted
1 (16-ounce) can whole tomatoes, undrained and chopped
1 (8-ounce) can tomato sauce
2 teaspoons Worcestershire sauce
½ teaspoon dried whole oregano
½ teaspoon dried whole thyme
⅛ teaspoon red pepper
Hot cooked rice

Peel and devein shrimp.

Sauté onion, green pepper, celery, and garlic in butter in a Dutch oven until tender. Stir in tomatoes, tomato sauce, Worcestershire sauce, oregano, thyme, and red pepper. Cook over medium heat, stirring occasionally, about 15 minutes or until desired consistency. Stir in shrimp, and simmer over medium heat 5 to 10 minutes or until shrimp are done. Serve over rice. Yield: 4 to 6 servings.

GULF COAST SHRIMP AND VEGETABLES

2 quarts water
3 pounds unpeeled large fresh shrimp
1 cup sliced ripe olives
1 cup chopped green pepper
½ cup chopped celery
⅓ cup chopped sweet pickle
2 shallots, minced
1 tablespoon minced fresh parsley
2 cups commercial Italian salad dressing
¼ cup olive oil
1 tablespoon lemon juice
Leaf lettuce
4 medium tomatoes, cut in wedges

Bring water to a boil; add shrimp, and cook 3 to 5 minutes. Drain well, and rinse with cold water. Chill. Peel and devein shrimp.

Combine next 9 ingredients in a shallow airtight container. Add shrimp; cover and refrigerate at least 8 hours.

Line a serving platter with leaf lettuce; spoon on shrimp mixture using a slotted spoon. Garnish with tomato wedges. Yield: 8 to 10 servings.

Sauce Up the Shrimp

Whether they're crispy fried or plain and boiled, pair shrimp with sauces other than the traditional cocktail sauce. Flip through our chapter on sauces, and you'll find many that would make nice accompaniments, such as Horseradish Sauce (page 437), Dill Sauce (page 437), Curry Sauce (page 437), Béarnaise Sauce (page 438), Herbed Yogurt Sauce (page 439), Sweet-and-Sour Sauce (page 442), and any of our herbed butters (page 440).

CHARLESTON-STYLE SHRIMP CURRY

9 cups water
3 pounds unpeeled large fresh shrimp
1 large onion, finely chopped
½ cup finely chopped apple
½ cup finely chopped celery
¼ cup butter or margarine, melted
1 cup water
2 cups whipping cream
2 tablespoons curry powder
½ teaspoon salt
⅛ teaspoon pepper
Hot cooked rice

Bring water to a boil; add shrimp, and cook 3 to 5 minutes. Drain well, and rinse with cold water. Chill. Peel and devein shrimp.

Sauté onion, apple, and celery in butter 5 minutes; add water. Cook, uncovered, over low heat 30 minutes or until most of the liquid is absorbed. Stir in whipping cream, curry powder, salt, and pepper; simmer, uncovered, 10 minutes. Add shrimp, and simmer until thoroughly heated. Serve over rice.

Serve curry with several of the following condiments: flaked coconut, toasted almonds, fig preserves, chutney, crumbled bacon, sliced bananas, raisins, and chopped hard-cooked egg. Yield: 8 to 10 servings.

MARINATED SHRIMP

6 cups water
2 pounds unpeeled large fresh shrimp
Bay leaves
4 small onions, thinly sliced and separated into rings
1 cup vegetable oil
½ cup tarragon vinegar
2 tablespoons pickling spice
1 teaspoon salt
½ teaspoon dry mustard
Dash of red pepper
Fresh parsley sprigs

Bring water to a boil; add shrimp, and cook 3 to 5 minutes. Drain well; rinse with cold water. Chill. Peel and devein shrimp, leaving tails intact.

Place a layer of shrimp in a flat-bottomed container. Place 5 bay leaves on top of shrimp; cover shrimp with a layer of onion slices. Repeat layering until all shrimp are used.

Combine oil and next 5 ingredients, stirring well. Pour marinade over the shrimp. Cover; chill 24 hours, stirring mixture occasionally. Remove shrimp from marinade, and arrange in a serving dish. Garnish with parsley sprigs. Yield: 4 to 6 servings.

Sautéed with green onion, garlic, and wine, buttery Shrimp Destin can be served over toasted French rolls or hot cooked rice.

SHRIMP JAMBALAYA

1½ pounds unpeeled fresh
    shrimp
¼ cup chopped onion
¼ cup chopped green pepper
¼ cup butter or margarine,
    melted
1 tablespoon all-purpose flour
2 teaspoons chili powder
½ teaspoon salt
¼ teaspoon garlic powder
¼ teaspoon pepper
⅛ teaspoon red pepper
¼ cup Worcestershire sauce
1 tablespoon vinegar
2 cups peeled, chopped
    tomatoes
1 (10-ounce) package frozen
    sliced okra, thawed
2 cups hot cooked rice

Peel and devein shrimp.

Sauté onion and green pepper in butter until tender. Combine flour and dry seasonings; blend into onion mixture. Stir in Worcestershire sauce and vinegar until smooth. Add tomatoes and okra, stirring constantly until thickened. Add shrimp and simmer, uncovered, 15 minutes. Stir in rice. Yield: 6 servings.

SHRIMP DESTIN

2 pounds unpeeled large fresh shrimp
¼ cup chopped green onions
2 teaspoons minced garlic
1 cup butter or margarine, melted
1 tablespoon white wine
1 teaspoon lemon juice
⅛ teaspoon salt
⅛ teaspoon coarsely ground pepper
1 teaspoon dried whole dillweed
1 teaspoon chopped fresh parsley
2 French rolls, split lengthwise and toasted

Peel and devein shrimp.

Sauté green onions and garlic in butter until onions are tender. Add shrimp, wine, lemon juice, salt, and pepper; cook over medium heat about 5 minutes, stirring occasionally. Stir in dillweed and parsley. Spoon shrimp mixture over toasted rolls, and serve immediately. Yield: 4 servings.

Note: Shrimp Destin may also be served over hot cooked rice instead of rolls, if desired.

SEAFOOD PAELLA

Full of seafood and saffron-flavored rice, this version of paella is much like the original dish that originated in Spain. After all the ingredients are added, it is large, colorful, and impressive enough for company. To keep the rice fresh and fluffy, cook the dish just before you plan to serve it.

3 pounds chicken breasts, thighs, and legs
¼ cup olive oil
2 large onions, chopped
2 cloves garlic, minced
1 (28-ounce) can whole tomatoes, undrained and chopped
1 teaspoon salt
1 cup uncooked long-grain rice
1 teaspoon dried whole oregano
½ teaspoon dried whole saffron or ¼ teaspoon ground saffron
¼ cup boiling water
2¼ pounds unpeeled medium-size fresh shrimp
1 (15-ounce) can soft-shelled or steamer clams in shells, drained, or 6 fresh cherrystone clams
1 (10-ounce) package frozen green peas
1 (4-ounce) jar diced pimiento, drained

Brown chicken in hot oil in a large Dutch oven; remove chicken, and set aside. Add onion and garlic; sauté until tender. Add tomatoes and salt; return chicken to Dutch oven. Cover and simmer 30 minutes. Stir in rice and oregano. Dissolve saffron in boiling water; pour over chicken. Cover and simmer 25 minutes. Peel and devein shrimp. Add clams; cover and cook 10 minutes. Add shrimp; cover and cook 5 minutes. Spoon into center of a large serving dish.

Cook peas according to package directions; drain and stir in pimiento. Spoon peas around paella. Serve immediately. Yield: 6 servings.

CRAB-STUFFED SHRIMP

Enjoy Crab-Stuffed Shrimp next time you invite company for dinner. After the crab mixture is added, the shrimp are so large and rich that just two or three of them make an ample serving. To make them ahead, stuff the shrimp, cover, and chill several hours. Add paprika and butter just before baking.

1 dozen jumbo fresh shrimp
1 medium onion, finely chopped
½ medium-size green pepper, finely chopped
½ cup finely chopped celery
¼ cup butter or margarine, melted
1 pound lump crabmeat, drained and flaked
¾ cup saltine cracker crumbs
½ cup mayonnaise
1 tablespoon prepared mustard
2 teaspoons Worcestershire sauce
⅛ teaspoon red pepper
1 egg, beaten
Paprika
¼ cup butter or margarine, melted

Peel shrimp, leaving tails on; devein and butterfly shrimp. Cook shrimp in boiling water 1 minute. Drain and place in a shallow pan.

Sauté onion, green pepper, and celery in ¼ cup butter in a heavy skillet until tender. Set aside.

Combine crabmeat and next 6 ingredients, stirring lightly. Stir in sautéed vegetables.

Top each shrimp with 3 tablespoons crabmeat mixture. Sprinkle with paprika, and drizzle ¼ cup butter over shrimp.

Bake shrimp at 350° for 20 minutes. Broil 6 minutes, basting occasionally with butter in bottom of pan. Yield: 4 to 6 servings.

Note: To butterfly shrimp, make a slit down back of shrimp using a sharp paring knife, cutting almost through the shrimp. Open shrimp, and flatten.

Butterfly Shrimp— Step-By-Step

1. To butterfly shrimp, first devein it by slitting the shrimp down its back; then pull away the vein using the tip of a knife.

2. Make a deeper slit down the back of the shrimp, cutting almost through it.

3. Open the shrimp, and press the flat side of a knife across shrimp, cut side of shrimp down.

STIR-FRIED SHRIMP AND SNOW PEAS

1 pound unpeeled medium-size fresh shrimp
½ teaspoon salt
1 teaspoon sesame or vegetable oil
1½ teaspoons cornstarch
¼ cup water
3 tablespoons oyster sauce
½ teaspoon cornstarch
¼ teaspoon chicken bouillon granules
¼ cup peanut or vegetable oil
2 cloves garlic, crushed
2 teaspoons grated fresh gingerroot
½ pound fresh snow pea pods or 1 (6-ounce) package frozen snow pea pods, thawed
2 teaspoons rice wine or dry white wine

Peel and devein shrimp. Sprinkle shrimp with salt, and toss with sesame oil; dredge in 1½ teaspoons cornstarch. Set aside.

Combine water, oyster sauce, ½ teaspoon cornstarch, and bouillon granules; stir well. Set mixture aside.

Pour peanut oil around top of preheated wok, coating sides; allow to heat at medium high (325°) for 1 minute. Add garlic and gingerroot, and stir fry 30 seconds. Add shrimp, and stir-fry 1½ minutes. Remove and drain on paper towels.

Add snow peas to wok, and stir-fry 30 seconds. Add broth mixture, stirring constantly until slightly thickened. Stir in shrimp and rice wine. Serve immediately. Yield: 2 to 3 servings.

LEMON-GARLIC BROILED SHRIMP

2 pounds unpeeled large fresh shrimp
2 cloves garlic, minced
1 cup butter or margarine, melted
¼ cup lemon juice
½ teaspoon salt
¼ teaspoon pepper

Peel and devein shrimp.

Sauté garlic in butter until tender; remove from heat, and stir in lemon juice, salt, and pepper.

Arrange shrimp in a single layer in a large shallow baking pan; pour butter sauce over shrimp, and stir gently. Broil 6 inches from heat 5 to 6 minutes or until shrimp are done, basting once with sauce. Yield: 4 to 6 servings.

SWEET-AND-SOUR SHRIMP

1½ pounds unpeeled fresh shrimp
½ cup all-purpose flour
¼ cup cornstarch
½ teaspoon baking powder
1 egg, beaten
¼ teaspoon salt
½ cup water
1 teaspoon vegetable oil
Vegetable oil
Hot cooked rice
Sweet-and-Sour Sauce

Peel and devein shrimp.

Combine flour, cornstarch, baking powder, egg, salt, water, and 1 teaspoon vegetable oil; mix well. Dip shrimp into batter, and fry in hot oil (375°) until golden brown. Serve over rice, and top with Sweet-and-Sour Sauce. Yield: 6 servings.

Sweet-and-Sour Sauce

½ cup sliced carrots
½ cup chopped green pepper
½ cup sugar
⅓ cup catsup
1 tablespoon soy sauce
¼ teaspoon salt
1 cup water, divided
3½ tablespoons cornstarch
½ cup vinegar
1 (15¼-ounce) can unsweetened pineapple chunks, drained

Cook carrots in small amount of boiling water 1 to 2 minutes; add green pepper, and cook an additional 1 minute. Drain and rinse vegetables in cold water.

Combine sugar, catsup, soy sauce, salt, and ⅔ cup water in a saucepan; bring to a boil. Dissolve cornstarch in ⅓ cup water to make a paste. Gradually add cornstarch paste and vinegar to sauce mixture; cook, stirring constantly, until smooth and thickened. Stir in pineapple and vegetables. Yield: 3½ cups.

BROILED ROCK SHRIMP TAILS

Rock shrimp may not be as familiar to you as regular shrimp, but they're equally flavorful and tender, and are usually less expensive. Easily mistaken for a miniature lobster tail, the hard shell of the rock shrimp encloses a meat that tastes like a cross between lobster and shrimp. Rock shrimp are more perishable than either of these, however, and that's why they're often found marketed in the raw frozen state.

2½ pounds unpeeled, deveined split rock shrimp tails
½ cup butter or margarine, melted
¾ teaspoon salt
¼ teaspoon white pepper
⅛ teaspoon paprika
Lemon Butter (optional, page 440)

Place shrimp tails in a shallow pan, meat side up. Combine melted butter and seasonings, stirring well. Baste shrimp with butter mixture.

Broil 6 inches from source of heat 4 minutes (avoid overcooking) or until tails turn upward. Serve immediately with Lemon Butter, if desired. Yield: about 6 servings.

Scallops

You'll find great variety in the size of scallops available. The more common are large sea scallops; the smaller are bay scallops, which have a sweeter, more delicate flavor. Bay scallops are usually more tender. The two types can be used interchangeably in recipes, but cooking times may vary.

Fresh scallops should have little liquor around them and should have a slightly sweet odor. Rinse them well before cooking, as sand accumulates in the crevices. Store them loosely covered in the coldest part of the refrigerator, and use within a day or two.

Bay scallops are usually only available fresh. You'll find sea scallops in the frozen foods section of your supermarket; they're usually offered plain or breaded for frying.

BROILED SCALLOPS

1¾ cups vegetable oil
¼ cup catsup
1 small clove garlic, minced
1 teaspoon salt
1 teaspoon paprika
2 pounds fresh sea scallops

Combine first 5 ingredients in a large shallow dish; stir well. Add scallops, and refrigerate at least 2 hours.

Remove scallops from marinade; place in a 15- x 10- x 1-inch jellyroll pan. Pour enough marinade over scallops to coat but not cover (about 1 cup). Broil 2 minutes; turn scallops over, and broil 2 minutes or until done. Serve hot. Yield: 4 servings.

Broiled Shrimp: Substitute an equal amount of fresh shrimp, peeled and deveined. Broiling times will be about the same.

SCALLOPS PROVENÇAL

1 pound fresh bay scallops
3 tablespoons lemon juice
½ pound fresh mushrooms, sliced
½ cup sliced green onions
2 cloves garlic, minced
3 tablespoons olive oil
2 medium tomatoes, peeled and coarsely chopped
2 tablespoons chopped fresh parsley
½ teaspoon salt
½ teaspoon dried whole oregano
¼ teaspoon pepper

Toss scallops in lemon juice; set aside. Sauté mushrooms, green onions, garlic, and scallops in hot oil in a large skillet until scallops are almost done. Stir in remaining ingredients, and sauté until scallops are done. Serve with a slotted spoon. Yield: 4 servings.

☐*Microwave Directions:* Toss scallops and lemon juice in a shallow 2-quart casserole. Stir in mushrooms, green onions, garlic, and oil. Cover with heavy-duty plastic wrap; microwave at HIGH for 4 to 5 minutes or until scallops are almost done, stirring once. Stir in remaining ingredients. Cover and microwave at HIGH for 1 minute. Let stand 3 minutes. Serve scallops with a slotted spoon.

COQUILLES ST. JACQUES

Hailing from France, Coquilles St. Jacques is one of the most popular and elegant ways to serve scallops. Bake them in any type of small ramekin if you don't have individual baking shells.

¾ cup chopped fresh mushrooms
3 tablespoons chopped green onions
3 tablespoons butter or margarine, melted
1 pound fresh bay scallops
½ cup dry white wine
2 tablespoons chopped fresh parsley
1 tablespoon lemon juice
¾ teaspoon salt
Pinch of red pepper
3 tablespoons butter or margarine
¼ cup all-purpose flour
1 cup half-and-half
2 egg yolks
¼ cup soft breadcrumbs
1 tablespoon butter or margarine, melted

Sauté mushrooms and onions in 3 tablespoons butter in a large skillet until tender. Add scallops, wine, parsley, lemon juice, salt, and pepper; cover and cook over medium heat 3 minutes. Drain scallop mixture, reserving ¾ cup plus 2 tablespoons liquid. Set aside.

Melt 3 tablespoons butter in a heavy saucepan over low heat; add flour, stirring until smooth. Cook 1 minute, stirring constantly. Gradually add half-and-half; cook over medium heat, stirring constantly, until mixture is thickened and bubbly.

Beat egg yolks until thick and lemon colored. Gradually stir about one-fourth of hot mixture into yolks; add to remaining hot mixture, stirring constantly. Gradually stir in reserved scallop liquid (¾ cup plus 2 tablespoons); fold in scallop mixture. Spoon mixture into 6 greased individual baking shells.

Combine breadcrumbs and 1 tablespoon butter; sprinkle evenly over scallop mixture in shells. Place shells on a large baking sheet. Broil 3 to 5 minutes or until top is browned and bubbly. Yield: 6 servings.

SCALLOP KABOBS

1 (8-ounce) can pineapple
   chunks
2 tablespoons lemon juice
½ cup soy sauce
1 pound fresh sea scallops
½ pound bacon
1 green pepper, cut into 1-inch
   pieces

Drain pineapple, reserving juice. Combine pineapple juice, lemon juice, soy sauce, and scallops. Cover tightly; marinate in refrigerator at least 1 hour.

Cut bacon slices in half; cook until limp but not crisp. Drain and set aside.

Drain scallops; alternate pineapple chunks, scallops, bacon, and green pepper on skewers. Broil 3 minutes or until scallops are done. Yield: about 1 dozen appetizer or 4 main dish servings.

Shrimp Kabobs: Recipe may also be made substituting 2 pounds large fresh shrimp, peeled and deveined, for 1 pound scallops.

Crabs

Popular steamed and served with Lemon Butter, or stirred into entrées, appetizers, soups, and salads, crabmeat comes from several types of crabs. The most common is the blue crab, which weighs from ⅓ to ½ pound. Dungeness crabs range from 2 to 3 pounds each, while Alaskan king crabs range from 8 to 10 pounds. Usually only the legs of Alaskan king crabs are sold.

Soft-shell crabs are simply blue crabs that have shed their shells and are in the process of growing new ones. They are usually fried or broiled, and the entire crab, shell and all, can be eaten. To remove meat from the blue or Dungeness crab, refer to our step-by-step photographs that show the process on Steamed Blue Crabs (page 242).

Crabs are available live, cooked fresh or frozen in the shell, and cooked fresh, frozen, or canned out of the shell. When fresh, crabmeat will have little odor. Use crabmeat within a day of purchase.

STUFFED SOFT-SHELL CRABS

8 soft-shell crabs, fresh or frozen,
   thawed
½ pound backfin or lump crabmeat
¼ cup soft breadcrumbs
1 egg, beaten
2 tablespoons mayonnaise
½ teaspoon dry mustard
½ teaspoon Worcestershire sauce
¼ teaspoon salt
⅛ teaspoon pepper
All-purpose flour
Vegetable oil

To clean crabs, remove spongy substance (gills) that lies under the tapering points on either side of back shell. Place crabs on back, and remove the small piece at lower part of shell that terminates in a point (the apron). Wash crabs thoroughly; drain well.

Remove any cartilage or shell from crabmeat. Combine crabmeat and next 7 ingredients; mix well. Stuff crabmeat mixture evenly into cavity of each crab; dredge crabs in flour. Fry crabs in deep hot oil (375°) for 1 to 2 minutes. Drain on paper towels; serve immediately. Yield: 8 crabs.

DOWN EAST CRAB CAKES

1½ pounds fresh lump crabmeat,
   drained and flaked
1 cup soft breadcrumbs
2 eggs, beaten
2 tablespoons finely chopped
   onion
2 tablespoons finely chopped
   green pepper
1 teaspoon dry mustard
1 teaspoon Worcestershire sauce
¼ teaspoon ground thyme
⅛ teaspoon salt
¾ cup all-purpose flour
Vegetable oil
Hot sauce or cocktail sauce
   (optional)

Combine crabmeat, breadcrumbs, eggs, onion, green pepper, mustard, Worcestershire sauce, thyme, and salt, stirring well. Shape into 12 patties (2 inches in diameter); chill well (mixture will be slightly loose).

Dredge crab cakes in flour; fry in hot oil until golden brown, turning once. Drain on paper towels. Serve with hot sauce, if desired. Yield: 6 servings.

1. *Offer three Steamed Blue Crabs per serving. To get to the meat, first pry off the apron or tail flap.*

2. *Lift off the top shell, holding the crab in the space left by removing the apron.*

3. *Pull out and discard the feathery gills beneath the top shell.*

4. *Twist off claws where attached to body. Discard stomach mass. Twist off legs.*

5. *Crack claws and legs with a seafood cracker or nutcracker. Remove meat with a cocktail fork.*

STEAMED BLUE CRABS

¼ **cup plus 2 tablespoons Old Bay seasoning**
¼ **cup plus 2 tablespoons coarse salt**
3 **tablespoons red pepper**
3 **tablespoons pickling spice**
2 **tablespoons celery seeds**
1 **tablespoon crushed red pepper (optional)**
Vinegar
12 **live blue crabs**
Lemon Butter (page 440)

Serve Steamed Blue Crabs with Lemon Butter for dipping.

Combine first 6 ingredients; set aside.

Combine water and vinegar in equal amounts to a depth of 1 inch in a very large pot with a lid; bring to a boil. Place a rack in pot over boiling liquid; arrange half of crabs on rack. Sprinkle with half of seasoning mixture. Top with remaining crabs, and sprinkle with remaining seasoning mixture.

Cover tightly, and steam 20 to 25 minutes or until crabs turn bright red. Rinse with cold water, and drain well. Serve crabs hot or cold with Lemon Butter. Yield: 4 servings.

CRABMEAT AU GRATIN

2 tablespoons butter or margarine
2 tablespoons all-purpose flour
1⅓ cups milk
½ teaspoon salt
⅛ teaspoon white pepper
2 (6-ounce) packages frozen
  crabmeat, thawed and drained
¼ cup (1 ounce) shredded mozzarella
  cheese
¼ cup grated Parmesan cheese
¼ cup soft breadcrumbs
¼ teaspoon paprika
Hot cooked rice

Melt butter in a heavy saucepan over low heat; add flour, stirring until smooth. Cook 1 minute, stirring constantly. Gradually add milk; cook over medium heat, stirring constantly, until thickened and bubbly. Stir in salt and pepper; stir in crabmeat. Spoon seafood mixture into a lightly greased 1½-quart casserole. Bake at 350° for 15 minutes. Combine cheeses, breadcrumbs, and paprika, stirring well. Sprinkle over crabmeat mixture, and bake an additional 3 minutes or until cheeses melt. Serve over rice. Yield: 4 servings.

◻ *Microwave Directions:* Place butter in a 1-quart glass measure. Microwave at HIGH for 45 seconds or until melted. Add flour, stirring until smooth. Gradually add milk, stirring well. Microwave at HIGH for 4 to 5 minutes or until thickened and bubbly, stirring after 2 minutes, then at 1-minute intervals. Stir in salt and pepper; stir in crabmeat. Spoon seafood mixture into a lightly greased 1½-quart casserole. Microwave at HIGH for 4 to 5 minutes or until thoroughly heated. Combine cheeses, breadcrumbs, and paprika, stirring well. Sprinkle over crabmeat mixture; cover and let stand 2 minutes or until cheeses melt. Serve over rice.

CRABMEAT RAVIGOTE

1 frozen patty shell, thawed
  (optional)
6 egg yolks
1 cup butter or margarine
Juice of 1 lemon
Dash of hot sauce
¼ teaspoon salt
2 tablespoons butter or margarine
3 tablespoons all-purpose flour
1¾ cups milk
½ teaspoon salt
¼ teaspoon white pepper
1 pound cooked fresh lump crabmeat,
  drained and flaked
3 tablespoons chopped green onions
3 tablespoons finely chopped fresh
  parsley
Hot cooked rice (optional)
Fresh parsley sprigs

If pastry leaves are desired for garnish, roll patty shell to ⅛-inch thickness on a lightly floured surface. Cut into 12 leaf shapes. Place on a lightly greased baking sheet, and bake at 350° for 5 to 8 minutes or until browned. Set aside.

Combine egg yolks and 1 cup butter in top of a double boiler. Bring water to a boil (water in bottom of double boiler should not touch top pan). Reduce heat to low; cook, stirring constantly with a wire whisk, until butter melts. Remove pan from water, and stir rapidly 2 minutes. Stir in lemon juice, 1 teaspoonful at a time; add hot sauce and ¼ teaspoon salt. Place over boiling water; cook, stirring constantly, 2 to 3 minutes or until thickened. Remove from heat.

Melt 2 tablespoons butter in a heavy saucepan; add flour, and cook 1 minute, stirring constantly. Gradually add milk; cook over medium heat, stirring constantly, until thickened (5 minutes). Stir in ½ teaspoon salt and pepper.

Add cream sauce to mixture in double boiler. Gently fold in crabmeat, green onions, and chopped parsley. Spoon into individual serving dishes, or serve over hot cooked rice. Garnish with pastry leaves and parsley. Yield: 6 servings.

CRABMEAT OVER WILD RICE

½ cup chopped celery
¼ cup chopped green pepper
¼ cup butter or margarine, melted
¼ cup all-purpose flour
1½ cups milk
¾ teaspoon salt
¼ teaspoon freshly ground pepper
1 pound fresh lump crabmeat,
  drained
1 (2-ounce) jar diced pimiento
1 cup (4 ounces) shredded Swiss
  cheese, divided
Paprika
Wild Rice and Mushrooms

Sauté celery and green pepper in butter in a large skillet until tender. Add flour, stirring until smooth. Cook 1 minute, stirring constantly. Gradually add milk; cook over medium heat, stirring constantly, until thickened and bubbly. Stir in salt, pepper, crabmeat, pimiento, and ¾ cup cheese, and spoon into a lightly greased 1-quart casserole. Bake at 350°, uncovered, 15 minutes. Sprinkle with remaining ¼ cup cheese and paprika. Bake an additional 5 minutes. Serve over Wild Rice and Mushrooms. Yield: 4 to 6 servings.

Wild Rice and Mushrooms

1 (10¾-ounce) can chicken broth,
  undiluted
1 small onion, chopped
¼ cup uncooked wild rice
½ cup uncooked long-grain rice
1 cup sliced fresh mushrooms

Add enough water to broth to measure 2¼ cups. Combine broth and onion in a medium saucepan; bring to a boil, and add wild rice. Cover, reduce heat, and simmer 20 minutes. Add regular rice and mushrooms; bring to a boil. Cover, reduce heat, and simmer 15 minutes or until liquid is absorbed. Yield: 4 to 6 servings.

Offer Crabmeat Imperial for an appetizer or light lunch. It's full of fresh lump crabmeat.

CRABMEAT IMPERIAL

¼ cup chopped green pepper
¼ cup chopped celery
1 (2-ounce) jar diced pimiento, drained
2 tablespoons butter or margarine, melted
1 tablespoon chopped fresh parsley
1 teaspoon Old-Bay seasoning
½ teaspoon prepared mustard
Dash of hot sauce
Dash of red pepper
1 egg, beaten
3 tablespoons mayonnaise
1 pound fresh lump crabmeat, drained and flaked
Pimiento strips (optional)
Celery leaves (optional)

Sauté green pepper, celery, and pimiento in melted butter in a large skillet until tender. Stir in parsley, Old-Bay seasoning, mustard, hot sauce, and red pepper.

Combine egg and mayonnaise; stir in seasoned celery mixture. Gently stir in fresh lump crabmeat. Spoon into 4 baking shells. Bake at 375° for 15 minutes. Broil 2 to 3 minutes. Garnish with pimiento strips, and celery leaves, if desired. Yield: 4 servings.

Oysters, Mussels, and Clams

You can please a lot of folks just by giving them a tub full of these fresh shellfish accompanied with crackers, lemons, and cocktail sauce, and you won't even have to cook anything. There are lots of ways to cook them, too, plus you'll need to know some of the particulars about each type of shellfish beforehand.

You can purchase oysters, clams, and mussels live in the shell. The shells should be tightly closed and unbroken. If shells are open and don't close when you touch them, discard them.

Oysters and clams are also available fresh shucked or shucked and canned. If they are fresh shucked and in their liquor, don't discard the liquor; it contains a lot of flavor you could add to the recipe. The liquor should be more clear than milky.

Oysters are graded by their size. "Counts" and "Extra-Selects" are the largest. "Selects" are medium in size, and are commonly used for frying. Smaller "Standards" are often used for soups and stews.

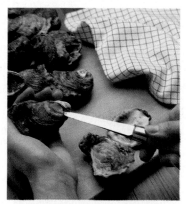

To open oyster shells: *Insert the tip of an oyster knife into the hinge, and twist the knife.*

To shuck oysters: *Scrape the knife between the oyster and the shell to free the meat.*

CRUSTY FRIED OYSTERS

1 egg, beaten
2 tablespoons cold water
1 (12-ounce) container fresh Select oysters, drained
1½ cups saltine cracker crumbs
Vegetable oil

Combine egg and water. Dip oysters in egg mixture, and roll each in cracker crumbs. Fry in hot oil (375°) about 2 minutes or until golden brown, turning to brown both sides. Drain on paper towels. Yield: 3 servings.

SCALLOPED OYSTERS

2 (12-ounce) containers fresh Standard oysters
2 cups saltine cracker crumbs
¾ teaspoon salt
¼ teaspoon pepper
½ cup butter or margarine, divided
2 eggs, beaten
1 cup half-and-half or milk
1 teaspoon Worcestershire sauce
¼ teaspoon hot sauce
2 tablespoons chopped fresh parsley (optional)

Drain oysters, reserving ⅓ cup oyster liquor. Set aside.

Sprinkle ½ cup cracker crumbs in a lightly greased 8-inch square baking dish. Layer half each of oysters, salt, pepper, butter, and cracker crumbs in dish. Repeat layers.

Combine eggs, half-and-half, Worcestershire sauce, hot sauce, and reserved oyster liquor; mix well. Pour over oyster mixture. Sprinkle with parsley, if desired. Bake at 350° for 35 minutes or until lightly browned. Yield: 6 servings.

WINE-POACHED MUSSELS

6 dozen mussels
1 cup dry white wine
3 green onions, chopped
¼ cup chopped fresh parsley
2 teaspoons fresh lemon juice
⅛ teaspoon freshly ground pepper
½ cup butter, cut into chunks

Remove beards on mussels, and scrub shells well with a brush. Discard opened or cracked mussels, or any heavy ones (they're filled with sand).

Bring wine to a boil in a large Dutch oven. Add mussels; cover and simmer 8 to 10 minutes or until shells open, shaking pot several times. When shells open, transfer to a bowl, reserving liquid in pan. Let mussels cool slightly. Discard halves of shells to which mussels are not attached. Loosen mussels remaining in shells, and arrange shells, open side up, on serving plates.

Strain reserved cooking liquid into a large skillet. Add green onions, parsley, lemon juice, and pepper. Cook over high heat until liquid is reduced to about ½ cup. Remove from heat, and whisk in butter until butter melts and sauce is thick. Spoon sauce over mussels, and serve immediately with French bread, if desired. Yield: 6 to 8 servings.

CLAM FRITTERS

1 (6½-ounce) can chopped clams
⅔ cup all-purpose flour
1 teaspoon baking powder
¼ teaspoon salt
⅛ teaspoon pepper
1 egg
3 tablespoons milk
⅓ cup chopped onion
Vegetable oil
Cocktail or tartar sauce

Drain clams, reserving 2 tablespoons juice. Set aside.

Combine flour, baking powder, salt, and pepper in a medium mixing bowl; stir well. Make a well in center of mixture, and set aside.

Combine egg, milk, and reserved clam juice, mixing well. Stir into dry ingredients. Stir in clams and onion.

Carefully drop mixture by tablespoonfuls into hot oil (375°). Fry until golden brown, turning once. Drain on paper towels. Serve hot with cocktail or tartar sauce. Yield: 1 dozen.

STEAMED CLAMS

Cherrystone clams are the best type to use for steaming. Serve them immediately after steaming, because they toughen as they cool. If all the clams don't open after steaming, use a clam or oyster knife to finish the job.

2 dozen cherrystone clams
½ cup water
¼ cup dry white wine
1 tablespoon Old Bay seasoning
½ teaspoon pepper
Melted butter
Lemon wedges

Scrub clams thoroughly, discarding any shells that are cracked or opened.

Combine water, wine, Old Bay seasoning, and pepper in a large Dutch oven. Bring mixture to a boil; add clams. Cover, reduce heat, and steam until shells open wide, about 10 to 12 minutes. Remove clams with a slotted spoon, reserving liquid.

Serve clams hot in shells with reserved clam liquid, melted butter, and lemon wedges. Yield: 2 main dish or 4 appetizer servings.

Before shucking clams: Scrub them under running water with a vegetable brush to remove dirt.

To open clam shells: Slide the blade of a clam or oyster knife between the shell halves opposite shell hinge. Twist knife to force shell apart. Cut meat loose as for oysters.

LOW COUNTRY SEAFOOD BOIL

The Atlantic Coast Indians originated the clambake, a seashore picnic still popular today. They cooked the clams over slow, but hot coals, and then settled down for a feast. The ingredients are similar today but potatoes and corn-on-the-cob are often cooked with the seafood. Our recipe for Low Country Seafood Boil will give you a spread much like the original clambake, although the ingredients are boiled instead of grilled over open coals.

2 dozen cherrystone clams
12 small red potatoes
12 small onions
1 tablespoon salt
1 dozen live blue crabs
1 (3-ounce) package crab boil
3 whole buds garlic
4 to 6 lemons, halved
1 cup vinegar
12 ears fresh corn
2½ pounds unpeeled large fresh
 shrimp
Melted butter
Cocktail sauce

Scrub clams, and set aside.

Fill a 5- or 6-gallon pot about two-thirds full with water; bring to a boil. Add potatoes, onions, and salt; cover and cook over high heat 20 minutes. Add clams, crabs, crab boil, garlic, lemons, and vinegar; cook an additional 10 minutes. Add corn, and cook 5 minutes. Remove from heat, and add shrimp; let stand in water 5 minutes. Drain off water.

Arrange boiled seafood and vegetables on a large serving platter. Serve with melted butter and cocktail sauce. Yield: 8 to 12 servings.

Lobsters

There are two types of lobsters. The American lobster is the meatiest variety, and the most popular. It contains a good bit of meat in the claws in addition to the tail meat. The claws of the spiny lobster contain very little meat; often only its tail section is marketed.

You can purchase lobster live; fresh or frozen cooked in the shell; or cooked, shelled, and canned.

Plain cooked lobster can be served hot and in its shell with Clarified, Lemon, or Herb Butter for dipping (page 440). Or, chill the lobster and team it with a cold sauce, such as Herbed Yogurt Sauce (page 439) or Cucumber Sauce (page 438). Count on about 1 serving from a 1-pound lobster.

LOBSTER NEWBERG

2 tablespoons chopped green
  onions
¼ cup butter or margarine, melted
3 tablespoons all-purpose flour
1½ cups half-and-half or milk
Dash of red pepper
3 tablespoons dry white wine
2 (7-ounce) cans lobster, drained
Patty shells
Chopped fresh parsley

Sauté green onions in butter in a large saucepan until tender. Add flour, stirring until smooth. Cook 1 minute, stirring constantly. Gradually add half-and-half; cook over medium heat, stirring constantly, until thickened and bubbly. Stir in red pepper, wine, and lobster. Cook 1 minute. Spoon lobster mixture into patty shells; sprinkle with parsley. Yield: 4 to 6 servings.

⬜ *Microwave Directions:* Combine onions and butter in a 2-quart casserole. Cover with heavy-duty plastic wrap, and microwave at HIGH for 3 minutes or until onion is tender. Add flour, stirring until smooth. Gradually add half-and-half, stirring well. Microwave at HIGH for 4 to 5 minutes or until thickened and bubbly, stirring after 2 minutes, then at 1-minute intervals. Stir in red pepper, wine, and lobster; microwave at HIGH for 1 minute. Spoon lobster mixture into patty shells; sprinkle with parsley.

Note: One pound fresh or frozen cooked lobster meat may be substituted for canned, if desired.

BROILED LOBSTER

2 (1-pound) live lobsters
1 tablespoon butter or margarine,
  melted
¼ teaspoon salt
⅛ teaspoon white pepper
⅛ teaspoon paprika
Lemon Butter (page 440)

Plunge lobsters headfirst into boiling water to cover; cook 2 minutes. Remove from water; cool.

Place lobster on its back. Cut lobster in half lengthwise. Remove the stomach (located just back of the head) and the intestinal vein (runs from the stomach to the tip of the tail). Crack claws.

Place lobster, shell side up, on a broiler pan. Broil 6 inches from heat 5 minutes. Turn lobster, and brush lobster meat with 1 tablespoon melted butter. Sprinkle with salt, pepper, and paprika. Broil 3 to 5 minutes. Serve with Lemon Butter. Yield: 2 servings.

LOBSTER THERMIDOR

2 quarts water
3 (10-ounce) lobster tails, fresh or
  frozen, thawed
1 cup sliced fresh mushrooms
¼ cup chopped onion
3 tablespoons butter or margarine,
  melted
3 tablespoons all-purpose flour
1¼ cups half-and-half or milk
2 tablespoons dry sherry
1 teaspoon dry mustard
¼ teaspoon salt
Dash of red pepper
⅓ cup grated Parmesan cheese
Paprika

Bring water to a boil; add lobster tails. Cover, reduce heat, and simmer 12 to 15 minutes. Drain. Rinse with cold water. Split and clean tails. Cut lobster tail meat (about 1 pound) into ½-inch pieces, and set aside.

Sauté sliced mushrooms and chopped onion in melted butter in a large skillet until tender. Add flour, stirring until smooth. Cook 1 minute, stirring constantly. Gradually add half-and-half; cook over medium heat, stirring constantly, until mixture is thickened and bubbly. Stir in sherry, mustard, salt, pepper, and lobster meat. Spoon mixture into 6 (6-ounce) well-greased baking shells or dishes; sprinkle each with Parmesan cheese and paprika. Bake at 400° for 10 minutes or until lightly browned. Yield: 6 servings.

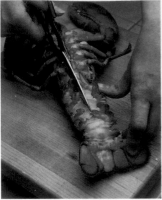

1. Start with a live lobster for boiling. Grasp lobster just behind the eyes using long tongs, and plunge into boiling water. Cover, reduce heat, and simmer 10 minutes.

2. Place lobster on its back. Cut the shell of the tail segment lengthwise.

3. Insert a sharp knife between the body shell and tail shell, cutting the two apart. Remove the stomach, intestinal vein, green liver, and coral roe (in female lobster only).

4. Pry open the tail section, and remove meat intact. Break off the large claws and legs. Crack the shell of the claws and legs using a seafood cracker or nutcracker, and extract the meat.

BOILED LOBSTER

2 (1-pound) live lobsters
3 quarts water
2 tablespoons salt
Clarified Butter (page 440)

Plunge lobsters headfirst into boiling salted water. Return water to a boil; cover, reduce heat, and simmer 10 minutes. Drain.

Place lobster on its back. Cut the shell of the tail segment lengthwise. Insert a sharp knife between the body shell and tail shell, cutting the two apart. Remove the stomach (located just back of the head) and the intestinal vein (runs from the stomach to the tip of the tail). Crack claws. Serve with Clarified Butter. Yield: 2 servings.

Slice the tail section of Boiled Lobster into medallions; serve medallions and claw meat with Clarified Butter.

Southern Surprises

Crazy about crawfish, Louisianans harvest 90% of the nation's supply, and they hold "crawfish boils" frequently. This is hands-on dining at its best; participants pick the crawfish apart with their fingers and suck the meat from the head, claws, and body. Beer is generally an essential part of the menu.

Frog legs are to Florida what crawfish are to Louisiana. Frog gigging is a favorite pastime, with the rewards of the hunt crisply fried for supper.

Crawfish and frog legs are available fresh in some parts of the South and frozen in other areas.

CRAWFISH ÉTOUFFÉE

2 pounds crawfish tails with fat
2 teaspoons hot sauce
¼ teaspoon red pepper
¼ cup vegetable oil
¼ cup all-purpose flour
2 stalks celery, chopped
2 large onions, chopped
2 large green peppers, chopped
½ cup chopped green onions
¼ cup water
½ teaspoon salt
¼ teaspoon black pepper
¼ teaspoon red pepper
¼ cup chopped fresh parsley
Hot cooked rice

Remove package of fat from crawfish tails, and set aside. Sprinkle crawfish with hot sauce and ¼ teaspoon red pepper; set aside.

Combine vegetable oil and flour in a 4-quart Dutch oven. Cook mixture over medium heat, stirring constantly, until roux is chocolate-colored (about 10 to 15 minutes).

Stir in celery and next 3 ingredients; cook until vegetables are tender, stirring often. Add crawfish tails and water; cook over low heat, uncovered, 15 minutes, stirring occasionally. Stir in 2 tablespoons crawfish fat (reserve the remaining fat for other uses), salt, and pepper; simmer 5 minutes. Stir in parsley. Serve over rice. Yield: 6 servings.

CRAWFISH BOIL

1 onion, quartered
1 lemon, quartered
1 clove garlic, halved
1 bay leaf
6 cups water
1 tablespoon salt
2 teaspoons red pepper
2 pounds whole crawfish

Tie onion, lemon, garlic, and bay leaf in a cheesecloth bag. Place cheesecloth bag in a large Dutch oven, and add water, salt, and red pepper; bring to a boil, and boil 5 minutes. Add crawfish, and cook 5 minutes. Drain crawfish; peel and serve warm or chilled. Yield: 2 to 3 servings.

CRISPY FROG LEGS

2½ pounds small frog legs
½ cup lemon juice or vinegar
Crushed ice
⅓ cup milk
2 eggs, separated
2 teaspoons olive or vegetable oil
Salt and pepper
2¼ cups all-purpose flour
Vegetable oil

Wash frog legs thoroughly. Place in a large Dutch oven; sprinkle with lemon juice, and cover with crushed ice. Refrigerate 1 to 3 hours.

Combine milk, egg yolks, and olive oil; mix well. Beat egg whites (at room temperature) until stiff; fold into batter.

Sprinkle frog legs with salt and pepper; dip each in batter, and dredge in flour. Fry until golden brown in deep hot oil (375°). Drain on paper towels. Yield: about 6 servings.

FOOD PRESERVATION

One of the advantages of a Southern summer has always been the abundance of fresh fruits and vegetables from our gardens. Over the years, jelly making, canning, pickling, freezing, and dehydrating have allowed us to preserve bounty for year-round enjoyment. Update your techniques by using the new processing and safety recommendations in this chapter. Whether you've been putting up food for years or are giving it your first try, you'll find this information helpful.

Canning

Your neighbor just brought over a bushel of corn and some of the prettiest tomatoes you've ever seen. If you're like many Southerners, you'll want to preserve what you can't use right away by canning.

Update your favorite recipes to the canning procedures listed below to ensure safety. Or, try some of our recipes for fruit, vegetable combos, and even vegetable soup.

EQUIPMENT

Before you start canning, be sure you have the proper equipment. For canning high-acid foods, such as fruits and tomatoes, you'll need a water-bath canner with a rack. For low-acid foods, such as meat, fish, poultry, and vegetables, you'll need a pressure canner with a rack. A jar filler or funnel, jar lifter, narrow rubber spatula, and timer are other essentials.

Stock your pickle pantry with this colorful collection of canned goods. From left, Pepper Relish (page 263), Kosher Dills (page 261), Mixed Vegetable Pickles (page 262), Pickled Beets (page 262), Brandy-Spiced Peaches (page 255), Bread-and-Butter Pickles (page 261), and Okra Pickles (page 261).

Use only standard canning jars and lids; leftover mayonnaise and peanut butter jars aren't safe for home canning. Use jars without any scratches, cracks, or chips.

Jars should be as clean as possible. Wash them in warm, soapy water, rinse, and keep hot. A dishwasher works well for this. If the required processing time in a water-bath canner is under 15 minutes, the jars need to be sterilized by boiling in water 15 minutes. Do not use a dishwasher for sterilizing jars.

You can reuse metal bands as long as they aren't rusted or dented, but be sure to buy new jar lids each time since the sealing compound only works once. Follow manufacturer's directions for heating them prior to use. Some types of jar lids need to be brought to a boil then left in hot water; others need boiling for a certain period of time.

To can safely: Use only standard canning jars and lids for home canning; leftover mayonnaise jars and the like aren't safe to use.

push all the air out and form a vacuum seal. Run a rubber spatula around the inside edge of jars to remove air bubbles. Don't use a metal utensil, since it may scratch the glass and cause the jar to break.

Wipe jar rims clean before putting the metal lids in place. Then screw on metal bands. Tightening the band onto the jar is an important step. If too loose, excess liquid will be lost during processing, and the seal will be weak. Bands screwed on too firmly may cause the lid to collapse, leaving a weak seal. The correct tightness can be achieved with the following method: Screw the band on with your fingertips until tight; then give another turn, just until the band is snug. Using a jar opener or continuing to turn the band with all your strength is probably too tight.

To fill jars: The amount of headspace to leave in the jar varies with the type of canning you're doing. Check your recipe for specifics.

PREPARING FRUITS AND VEGETABLES

Produce selected for canning should be perfect—firm, ripe, with no bruises or bad places. Wash the produce well and prepare as directed in the recipe. Meanwhile, heat water in the canner. The water-bath canner needs enough water to come 1 to 2 inches above jar tops; a pressure canner needs 2 to 3 inches in the bottom.

Place fruits or vegetables in hot jars following recipe directions for cold- or hot-pack methods. Fruit maintains better texture when packed in a sugar syrup rather than boiling water. See chart on page 254 for sugar syrup directions.

It's important to follow recipe directions for leaving headspace when filling jars. Too little headspace may cause the liquid to bubble up under the lid and prevent it from sealing. If too much headspace is allowed, processing time may be too short to

PROCESSING CANNED FOOD

Safety is the first word in canning,

To prepare produce: Carefully cut away all signs of bruised produce. Contrary to popular belief, canning is not a good use of produce undesirable to serve fresh.

so it's essential that canned goods be processed in a boiling-water bath or a pressure canner. The open-kettle method (placing cooked food in jars and sealing them without processing) is NOT considered a safe practice for any home-canned food.

Use the boiling-water bath method for high-acid foods, such as fruits and tomatoes. The water should be gently boiling when adding jars packed by the hot-pack method. If you use the cold-pack method, add jars while the water is warm to prevent jar breakage.

Place jars on the canner rack so water flows evenly around them. Add or remove water so that it levels 1 to 2 inches above the lids. Cover and set your timer for processing time when water returns to a boil.

Low-acid foods, such as vegetables, meat products, and vegetable-tomato combinations, must be processed in a pressure canner to make them safe. The 240° temperature obtained in this canner is necessary to kill harmful bacteria that thrive in low-acid conditions.

When using a pressure canner, be sure to allow steam to escape from the vent at least 10 minutes after closing the lid. Close the dial gauge vent, or set the weight in place on weighted-gauge models, then regulate the heat source to maintain 10 pounds pressure. The weight on a weighted-gauge model should jiggle or rock gently about three or four times a minute. Begin to count processing time after the canner reaches 10 pounds pressure.

After processing, remove the canner from heat and allow pressure to drop to 0. This will take 30 minutes to 1 hour. (Do not rush the cooling process by removing the weight, opening the vent pipe, or setting the canner in water.) Open the lid away from you, remove the jars, and allow to cool on a wire rack.

Once the jars processed by either method have cooled 12 to 24 hours, check to see that each sealed properly. You may hear them pop as they seal and feel a downward curve to the lids.

Another method of checking is to tap each lid with the back of a spoon. If the sound is a dull thud rather than a clear ring, turn the jar on its side for a few minutes to check for leakage. Leaky jars indicate a faulty seal and should be stored in the refrigerator and used right away.

If you're making several batches of the same product, it would be wise to mark each jar as to lot number. Then if you find a problem with one jar later, you can easily trace others processed at the same time.

After the jars have cooled, remove the metal bands, and store jars in a cool, dry, dark, well-ventilated place.

SERVING HOME-CANNED FOOD

Provided you've followed the recommended canning procedures and used clean equipment and surfaces, your canned goods should maintain good quality for at least one year if properly stored. However, spoiled

To add and remove jars from boiling water: Use a canning jar lifter; there will be less risk of a burn or jar breakage.

To check seals: Make sure lids have sealed properly before storing home-canned food. When sealed, you should feel a downward curve to the lid.

To label properly: Add a label to all your canned products, listing the name of the recipe and date.

home-canned products do account for some deaths each year, so it pays to be extra careful when canning. Some types of harmful spoilage, such as the one that causes botulism, show no normal signs of a bulging lid or leaking jar, mold, off-odor, cloudy liquid, or spurting liquid upon opening. Because of this, it's important to boil all home-canned food in a covered saucepan for 10 minutes, and corn, spinach, and meat for 20 minutes. Never taste the food before boiling.

If you notice any of the above-mentioned signs of spoilage, throw the food away. It's a good idea to burn the food or boil it before discarding to keep from spreading food toxins in any way to other people and animals.

Following are some general recipe directions for canning some of the most popular vegetables and fruits. They are followed by recipes for some tasty combinations you'll want to try.

Fruit

APPLES

Peel apples; cut in halves or quarters, and remove cores. Cut in slices, if desired. To prevent apples from darkening during preparation, use commercial ascorbic-citric powder according to manufacturer's directions, or immerse peeled apples in a sugar-syrup or lemon juice solution (¾ cup lemon juice to 1 gallon water).

Prepare a light or medium syrup. (See chart.) Use hot-pack method only.

Hot Pack: Simmer apples in hot syrup 5 minutes. Pack hot apples into hot jars, leaving ½-inch headspace. Cover apples with boiling syrup, leaving ½-inch headspace. Remove air bubbles; wipe jar rims. Cover at once with metal lids, and screw on bands. Process in boiling-water bath 20 minutes for pints and quarts.

BERRIES (EXCEPT STRAWBERRIES)

Select fully ripened berries. Handle as little as possible. Wash and cap berries; drain well.

Hot Pack: (Use for blackberries and others that hold their shape well.) Add ½ cup sugar to each 4 cups berries; cook until sugar dissolves and mixture comes to a boil, stirring gently to keep berries from sticking. Pack hot berries into hot jars, leaving ½-inch headspace. (If there is not enough syrup to cover berries, add boiling water, leaving ½-inch headspace.) Remove air bubbles; wipe jar rims. Cover at once with metal lids, and screw on bands. Process in boiling-water bath 10 minutes for pints; process 15 minutes for quarts.

Cold Pack: (Use for raspberries or others that do not hold their shape well.) Prepare a medium syrup. (See chart.) It usually takes 1 to 1½ cups syrup for

Type of Syrup	Sugar (Cups)	Liquid (Cups)	Yield (Cups)
Thin	2	4	5
Medium	3	4	5½
Heavy	4¾	4	6½

CANNING SYRUP FOR FRUIT

Directions: Combine sugar and water or fruit juice. Heat, stirring constantly, until sugar dissolves. Keep syrup hot.

each quart of fruit. Pack raw berries into hot jars, leaving ½-inch headspace. Shake jars as berries are added to get a full pack. Cover with boiling syrup, leaving ½-inch headspace. Remove air bubbles; wipe jar rims. Cover at once with metal lids, and screw on bands. Process in boiling-water bath 10 minutes for pints; process 15 minutes for quarts.

PEACHES AND PEARS

Peel fruit; cut in halves or quarters, and remove cores or pits. Cut in slices, if desired. To prevent fruit from darkening during preparation, use commercial ascorbic-citric powder according to manufacturer's directions, or immerse the peeled fruit in a sugar-syrup or lemon-juice solution (3/4 cup lemon juice to 1 gallon water).

Prepare a medium syrup. (See chart.)

Hot Pack: Simmer peaches or pears in hot syrup 3 to 5 minutes. Pack hot fruit into hot jars, leaving ½-inch headspace. Cover fruit with boiling syrup, leaving ½-inch headspace. Remove air bubbles; wipe jar rims. Cover at once with metal lids, and screw on bands. Process in boiling-water bath 20 minutes for pints; process 25 minutes for quarts.

Cold Pack: Pack raw peaches or pears into hot jars, leaving ½-inch headspace. Cover fruit with boiling syrup, leaving ½-inch headspace. Remove air bubbles; wipe jar rims. Cover at once with metal lids, and screw on bands. Process in boiling-water bath 25 minutes for pints; process 30 minutes for quarts.

PLUMS

Peel plums, if desired. Prick plums in several places with a sterilized needle if not peeled. (This helps keep plums from bursting.)

Prepare a medium syrup. (See chart.) Use hot-pack method only.

Hot Pack: Simmer plums in hot syrup 2 minutes. Cover, remove from heat, and let stand 20 minutes. Pack hot plums into hot jars, leaving ½-inch headspace. Cover fruit with boiling syrup, leaving ½-inch headspace. Remove air bubbles; wipe jar rims. Cover at once with metal lids, and screw on bands. Process in boiling-water bath 20 minutes for pints; process 25 minutes for quarts.

WHOLE CRANBERRY SAUCE

4 cups sugar
4 cups water
8 cups fresh cranberries (about 2 pounds)

Combine sugar and water in a large Dutch oven; bring to a boil, and boil 5 minutes. Add cranberries; boil, without stirring, 6 to 8 minutes or until cranberry skins pop. Quickly spoon into hot sterilized jars, leaving ¼-inch headspace. Remove air bubbles; wipe jar rims. Cover at once with metal lids, and screw on bands. Process in boiling-water bath 10 minutes. Yield: 4 pints.

APPLESAUCE

20 large apples, quartered (about 7
    pounds)
3 cups water
2 cups sugar

Combine apples and water in a large
kettle; cook over medium heat until
tender. Pour off liquid. Put apple mixture through a sieve or colander. Add
sugar to apple pulp, and bring to a boil.

Pack hot applesauce into hot jars,
leaving ½-inch headspace. Remove air
bubbles; wipe jar rims. Cover at once
with metal lids, and screw on bands.
Process in boiling-water bath 20 minutes. Yield: about 5 pints.

PEAR-APPLE
MINCEMEAT

15 large pears, peeled and ground
    (about 7 pounds)
12 apples, peeled and chopped (about
    4½ pounds)
2¾ cups raisins, ground
2¼ cups firmly packed brown sugar
1 cup sugar
1 unpeeled orange, seeded and
    ground
½ cup vinegar (5% acidity)
1 tablespoon salt
2 teaspoons ground cinnamon
1 teaspoon ground nutmeg
1 teaspoon ground cloves
½ teaspoon ground ginger

Combine all ingredients in a large
Dutch oven; bring to a boil, stirring
constantly. Spoon hot mixture into hot
jars, leaving ¼-inch headspace. Remove
air bubbles; wipe jar rims. Cover at once
with metal lids, and screw on bands.
Process in boiling-water bath 25 minutes. Yield: 8 pints.

Note: To make Pear-Apple Mincemeat
Pie, see page 359.

CINNAMON-APPLE
RINGS

Ascorbic-citric powder
14 medium cooking apples,
    unpeeled (about 6 pounds)
4 cups sugar
1 quart water
1½ teaspoons ground cinnamon
10 to 12 drops red food coloring

Prepare ascorbic-citric solution according to manufacturer's directions;
set aside.

Core apples, and slice into ¼-inch
rings. Drop apple rings into ascorbic-citric solution, and set aside. (Do not allow
apples to stand in solution more than 20
minutes.)

Combine sugar, water, ground cinnamon, and food coloring in a large Dutch
oven and bring to a boil; boil 5 minutes.
Remove syrup from heat. Drain apple
rings, and add to syrup; let stand 10
minutes. Return apple mixture to heat,
and bring to a rolling boil; reduce heat
and simmer, uncovered, 20 minutes,
stirring occasionally. Remove from heat,
and let cool slightly.

Drain apples, reserving syrup. Bring
syrup to a boil. Pack hot apple rings into
hot jars, leaving ½-inch headspace.
Cover with boiling syrup, leaving ½-
inch headspace. Remove air bubbles;
wipe jar rims. Cover at once with metal
lids, and screw on bands. Process in
boiling-water bath 15 minutes for pints;
process 20 minutes for quarts. Yield: 6
pints or 3 quarts.

BRANDY-SPICED
PEACHES

(pictured on page 250)

1 (1-inch) cube gingerroot, sliced
2 (4-inch) sticks cinnamon
1 tablespoon whole allspice
1 tablespoon whole cloves
5 cups sugar, divided
3 cups vinegar (5% acidity)
1¼ cups peach brandy
¾ cup water
24 small, firm, ripe peaches,
    peeled

Place gingerroot, cinnamon sticks, allspice, and cloves on a piece of cheesecloth; tie ends securely. Combine spice
bag, 2 cups sugar, vinegar, brandy, and
water in a large Dutch oven; bring to a
boil. Add peaches; simmer 2 minutes or
until thoroughly heated. Remove from
heat; let peaches stand 3 to 4 hours.

Carefully remove peaches from syrup;
set peaches aside. Add 2 cups sugar to
syrup, and bring to a boil. Remove mixture from heat, and add peaches; cover
and let stand 24 hours.

Heat peaches thoroughly in hot syrup.
Pack hot peaches into hot sterilized jars,
leaving ½-inch headspace. Add remaining 1 cup sugar to syrup; bring to a boil.
Cover peaches with boiling syrup, leaving ½-inch headspace. Remove air bubbles; wipe jar rims. Cover at once with
metal lids, and screw on bands. Process
15 minutes in boiling-water bath. Yield:
6 pints.

Note: Three tablespoons pure brandy
flavor may be substituted for peach
brandy, if desired. If brandy flavor is
used, increase water to 2 cups.

GREEN, SNAP, OR WAX BEANS

Wash beans, trim ends, and string if necessary; cut into 1- to 2-inch lengths.

Hot Pack: Cover beans with boiling water, and boil 5 minutes. Pack hot beans loosely in hot jars, leaving ½-inch headspace. Add ½ teaspoon salt to pints and 1 teaspoon to quarts, if desired. Cover with boiling liquid, leaving ½-inch headspace. Remove air bubbles; wipe jar rims. Cover at once with metal lids, and screw on bands. Process in pressure canner at 10 pounds pressure (240°). Process pints for 20 minutes and quarts for 25 minutes.

Cold Pack: Pack beans tightly into hot jars, leaving ½-inch headspace. Add ½ teaspoon salt to pints and 1 teaspoon to quarts, if desired. Cover with boiling water, leaving ½-inch headspace. Remove air bubbles; wipe jar rims. Cover at once with metal lids, and screw on bands. Process in pressure canner at 10 pounds pressure (240°). Process pints for 20 minutes and quarts 25 minutes.

LIMA BEANS

Shell and wash young tender beans.

Hot Pack: Cover beans with boiling water, and boil 3 minutes. Pack hot beans loosely in hot jars, leaving ½-inch headspace. Add ½ teaspoon salt to pints, 1 teaspoon to quarts, if desired. Cover with boiling liquid, leaving ½-inch headspace. Remove air bubbles; wipe jar rims. Cover at once with metal lids, and screw on bands. Process in pressure canner at 10 pounds pressure (240°). Process pints for 40 minutes and quarts for 50 minutes.

Cold Pack: Pack beans loosely in hot jars, leaving ½-inch headspace. (Do not shake or press beans down.) Add ½ teaspoon salt to pints, 1 teaspoon to quarts, if desired. Cover with boiling water, leaving ½-inch headspace. Remove air bubbles; wipe jar rims. Cover jars at once with metal lids, and screw on metal bands. Process in pressure canner at 10 pounds pressure (240°). Process pints for 40 minutes and quarts for 50 minutes.

CORN

Husk corn, and remove silks; wash. Cut corn from cob at about two-thirds the depth of kernel; do not scrape cob.

Hot Pack: Add 2 cups boiling water to 4 cups cut corn; boil 3 minutes. Pack hot corn into hot jars, leaving 1-inch headspace. Add ½ teaspoon salt to pints and 1 teaspoon to quarts, if desired. Remove air bubbles; wipe jar rims. Cover at once with metal lids, and screw on bands. Process in pressure canner at 10 pounds pressure (240°). Process pints for 55 minutes and quarts for 1 hour and 25 minutes.

Cold Pack: Pack corn in hot jars, leaving 1-inch headspace. Do not pack. Add ½ teaspoon salt to pints and 1 teaspoon to quarts, if desired. Remove air bubbles; wipe jar rims. Cover with boiling water, leaving ½-inch headspace. Cover at once with metal lids, and screw on bands. Process in pressure canner at 10 pounds pressure (240°). Process pints for 55 minutes and quarts for 1 hour and 25 minutes.

Cold-Packing Whole Kernel Corn Step-By-Step

1. To can whole kernel corn, remove husks and silks from corn; wash corn.

2. Cut corn from cob at about two-thirds the depth of kernel; do not scrape.

3. For the cold pack method, pack corn into hot jars, leaving 1-inch headspace; add salt, if desired.

4. Cover with boiling water, leaving ½-inch headspace; wipe jar rims. Cover with metal lids; screw on bands.

BEETS

Select small, uniform beets. Wash beets carefully; remove tops, leaving 1 inch of stem. Leave taproot. Use hot-pack method only.

Hot Pack: Place beets in a saucepan; cover with boiling water, and boil about 15 minutes or until skins slip easily. Remove skins, and trim. Leave baby beets whole; cut large beets into quarters or slices. Pack hot beets into hot jars, leaving ½-inch headspace. Add ½ teaspoon salt to pints and 1 teaspoon to quarts, if desired. Cover with boiling water, leaving ½-inch headspace. Remove air bubbles; wipe jar rims. Cover at once with metal lids, and screw on metal bands. Process jars in pressure canner at 10 pounds pressure (240°). Process pints for 30 minutes and quarts for 35 minutes.

OKRA

Select young, tender pods of okra. Wash okra; trim stem ends. Use hot-pack method only.

5. Stagger jars on rack in a pressure canner containing 2 to 3 inches warm water. Process as directed.

Hot Pack: Cook 1 minute in boiling water; drain. Leave pods whole or cut into 1-inch slices.

Pack hot okra into hot jars, leaving ½-inch headspace. Add ½ teaspoon salt to pints and 1 teaspoon to quarts, if desired. Cover okra with boiling water, leaving ½-inch headspace. Remove air bubbles, and wipe jar rims. Cover jars at once with metal lids, and screw on metal bands. Process jars in pressure canner at 10 pounds pressure (240°). Process pints for 25 minutes, and process quarts for 40 minutes.

SUMMER SQUASH

Wash and trim ends from squash; do not peel. Cut squash into ½-inch slices; then cut slices into uniform pieces.

Hot Pack: Add just enough water to cover squash; bring to a boil. Pack hot squash loosely into hot jars, leaving ½-inch headspace. Add ½ teaspoon salt to pints and 1 teaspoon to quarts, if desired. Cover with boiling liquid, leaving ½-inch headspace. Remove air bubbles; wipe jar rims. Cover at once with metal lids, and screw on bands. Process in pressure canner at 10 pounds pressure (240°). Process pints for 30 minutes and quarts for 40 minutes.

Cold Pack: Pack squash tightly into hot jars leaving 1-inch headspace. Add ½ teaspoon salt to pints and 1 teaspoon to quarts, if desired. Cover with boiling water, leaving ½-inch headspace. Remove air bubbles; wipe jar rims. Cover jar at once with metal lids, and screw on metal bands. Process in pressure canner at 10 pounds pressure (240°). Process pints for 30 minutes and quarts for 40 minutes.

TOMATOES

Select just-ripe tomatoes. Peel tomatoes; remove stem and blossom ends. Leave whole, or cut into quarters. Use hot-pack method only.

Hot Pack: Bring tomatoes to a boil, stirring to keep from sticking; boil 5 minutes. Pack hot tomatoes into hot jars, leaving 1-inch headspace. Add ½ teaspoon salt to pints and 1 teaspoon to quarts, if desired. Cover tomatoes with boiling juice, leaving ½-inch headspace. Remove air bubbles; wipe jar rims. Cover at once with metal lids, and screw on bands. Process in boiling-water bath 35 minutes for pints; process 45 minutes for quarts.

SUCCOTASH

10 ears fresh corn
1½ quarts shelled fresh lima beans
1 tablespoon plus ½ teaspoon salt, divided
Boiling water

Place corn in a large Dutch oven, and cover with water. Bring to a boil, and cook 5 minutes. Remove from heat, and cool.

Cook beans, uncovered, in boiling water to cover 5 minutes. Drain beans, reserving liquid.

Cut corn from cob as for whole kernel corn; combine corn and beans. Pack into hot jars, leaving 1½-inch headspace. Pour in boiling bean liquid, leaving 1-inch headspace. (Supplement with boiling water if you don't have enough bean liquid.) Add ½ teaspoon salt to each pint, 1 teaspoon salt to each quart, if desired. Remove air bubbles; wipe jar rims. Cover at once with metal lids, and screw on bands. Process in pressure canner at 10 pounds pressure (240°). Process pints for 1 hour and quarts for 1 hour and 25 minutes. Yield: 7 pints or 3½ quarts.

Note: When reheating Succotash, add additional seasonings as desired.

TOMATO SAUCE

24 medium tomatoes (about 12½
   pounds), peeled and chopped
3 cups chopped onion
2 cups chopped celery
1½ cups chopped green pepper
1 tablespoon salt

Combine all ingredients in a large kettle. Bring to a boil; reduce heat, and simmer, uncovered, 30 minutes, stirring frequently. Remove from heat; put tomato mixture through a food mill or sieve, reserving tomato juice.

Bring juice to a boil; reduce heat, and simmer, uncovered, 2 hours or until thick, stirring frequently.

Quickly pour hot mixture into hot jars, leaving ½-inch headspace. Remove air bubbles; wipe jar rims. Cover at once with metal lids, and screw on bands. Process in boiling-water bath 45 minutes. Yield: 9 half pints.

Fresh from the canner: Homemade Catsup in pint jars; Tomato Sauce in half pint jars.

ZIPPY BARBECUE SAUCE

24 medium tomatoes (about 12¼
   pounds), peeled and chopped
2 cups chopped onion
2 cups chopped celery
1½ cups chopped green pepper
2 hot red peppers
1 cup firmly packed brown sugar
2 cloves garlic, crushed
1 tablespoon salt
1 tablespoon dry mustard
1 tablespoon paprika
1 teaspoon peppercorns, tied in
   cheesecloth bag
1 teaspoon hot sauce
⅛ teaspoon red pepper
1 cup vinegar (5% acidity)

Combine first 4 ingredients in a large Dutch oven. Bring to a boil; reduce heat, and simmer, uncovered, 30 minutes, stirring frequently. Remove from heat; put tomato mixture through a food mill, reserving juice. Bring juice to a boil;

reduce heat, and simmer, uncovered, 1 hour and 15 minutes. Add remaining ingredients, and simmer an additional 1½ hours, stirring frequently.

Quickly pour hot mixture into hot jars, leaving ¼-inch headspace. Remove air bubbles; wipe jar rims. Cover at once with metal lids, and screw on bands. Process in boiling-water bath 20 minutes. Yield: 3 pints.

HOMEMADE CATSUP

46 medium tomatoes (about 24
   pounds), sliced
3 medium onions, coarsely
   chopped
3 (3-inch) sticks cinnamon
1 tablespoon whole cloves
3 cloves garlic, chopped
3 cups vinegar (5% acidity)
1½ cups sugar
1 tablespoon salt
1 tablespoon paprika
⅛ teaspoon red pepper

Combine tomatoes and onion in two large kettles. Bring vegetables to a boil; reduce heat, and simmer, uncovered, 45 minutes, stirring frequently. Remove from heat; put tomato mixture through a food mill or sieve, reserving tomato juice. Set aside.

Tie cinnamon sticks, cloves, and garlic in a cheesecloth bag; add to vinegar in a small saucepan. Bring to a boil; reduce heat, and simmer, uncovered, 30 minutes. Remove spice bag; set spiced vinegar aside.

Cook reserved tomato juice, uncovered, in a large kettle over medium-high heat 2 hours or until volume is reduced by half, stirring frequently. Add vinegar and remaining ingredients. Cook tomato mixture, uncovered, 30 to 40 minutes or until thickened.

Quickly pour hot mixture into hot jars, leaving ½-inch headspace. Remove air bubbles; wipe jar rims. Cover at once with metal lids, and screw on bands. Process in boiling-water bath 20 minutes. Yield: 6 pints.

TOMATO SOUP BASE

14 quarts tomatoes, peeled and chopped (about 20 pounds)
7 medium onions, chopped (about 3¼ pounds)
1 stalk celery, chopped
14 sprigs fresh parsley, chopped
3 bay leaves
¾ cup plus 2 tablespoons butter or margarine
¾ cup plus 2 tablespoons all-purpose flour
½ cup sugar
3 tablespoons salt
2 teaspoons white pepper

Combine tomatoes, onion, celery, parsley, and bay leaves in a large kettle; bring to a boil over medium heat. Reduce heat to low, and simmer 15 to 20 minutes or until celery is tender. Put vegetable mixture through a food mill, reserving juice.

Melt butter in a large Dutch oven over low heat; add flour, stirring until smooth. Cook 1 minute, stirring constantly. Gradually add reserved juice; cook over medium heat, stirring constantly, until thickened and bubbly. Stir in sugar, salt, and pepper. (If a smoother consistency of soup base is desired, put through a sieve.)

Pour hot tomato soup into hot jars, leaving 1-inch headspace. Remove air bubbles; wipe jar rims. Cover at once with metal lids, and screw on bands. Process in boiling-water bath 45 minutes. Yield: 12½ pints.

Note: When reheating Tomato Soup Base, additional seasonings may be added, as desired.

BEEF STEW BASE WITH VEGETABLES

4 to 4½ pounds lean beef for stewing, cut into 1-inch cubes
3 tablespoons vegetable oil
3 quarts peeled and cubed potatoes (½-inch cubes)
2 quarts thinly sliced carrots
3 cups chopped celery
3 cups chopped onion
1½ tablespoons salt
1 teaspoon dried whole thyme
½ teaspoon pepper

Brown beef cubes in hot oil in a large kettle; drain well. Add remaining ingredients, stirring well. Add boiling water just until mixture is covered. Spoon hot mixture into hot jars, leaving 1-inch headspace. Remove air bubbles; wipe jar rims. Cover jars at once with metal lids, and screw on bands. Process in pressure-canner at 10 pounds pressure (240°). Process pints for 1 hour and quarts for 1 hour 15 minutes. Yield: 18 pints or 9 quarts.

Note: When reheating beef stew, add additional seasonings as desired.

CHICKEN AND RICE SOUP STOCK

1 (3- to 4-pound) broiler-fryer
1 large onion, sliced
2 stalks celery, cut into 1-inch pieces
3 cups hot cooked rice (cooked without fat)

Place chicken, onion, and celery in a Dutch oven; cover with water, and bring to a boil. Cover, reduce heat, and simmer 1 hour or until tender. Remove chicken, reserving broth; let cool. Bone chicken, and chop meat; set aside.

Strain broth mixture; skim fat from surface. Add chopped chicken to broth; return to a boil. Spoon ¾ cup hot rice into each of 4 hot jars. Add hot broth mixture, leaving 1-inch headspace. Remove air bubbles; wipe jar rims. Cover at once with metal lids, and screw on bands. Process in pressure canner at 10 pounds pressure (240°). Process quarts for 45 minutes. Yield: 4 quarts.

Note: When reheating soup stock, add seasonings as desired.

VEGETABLE SOUP BASE

2 quarts peeled, chopped tomatoes
1½ quarts peeled, cubed potatoes (½-inch cubes)
1½ quarts thinly sliced carrots
1 quart fresh shelled lima beans
1 cup fresh cut corn
2 cups sliced celery
2 cups chopped onion
1½ quarts water
Salt

Combine vegetables and water in a large kettle; bring to a boil over medium heat, stirring often. Boil 5 minutes.

Spoon mixture into hot jars, leaving 1-inch headspace; add ¼ teaspoon salt to each pint jar, and ½ teaspoon salt to each quart jar. Remove air bubbles; wipe jar rims. Cover at once with metal lids, and screw on bands. Process in pressure canner at 10 pounds pressure (240°). Process pints for 55 minutes and quarts for 1 hour 25 minutes. Yield: 14 pints or 7 quarts.

Note: When reheating soup base, add additional seasonings as desired.

Pickling

Summer is prime time for pickling and showing off blue ribbon results to friends, neighbors, and county fair judges. The pantry becomes a canvas, painted with jar after jar of red-speckled relishes and green pickle slices.

EQUIPMENT

You'll need much the same utensils for processing pickles as you do for high-acid canned goods—a water-bath canner with rack, standard canning jars, new metal lids, metal bands, jar filler or funnel, timer, jar lifter, narrow rubber spatula, and a slotted spoon. Since pickles are usually processed in a water bath for under 15 minutes, the canning jars need to be sterilized by boiling in water 15 minutes.

For fresh-pack pickles (pickles that are covered with a hot vinegar mixture and allowed to stand several hours), you'll need containers of unchipped enamelware, stainless steel, aluminum, or glass for heating the vinegar solution. You should use only a crock, stone, or glass jar or plastic container intended for use with food for brining pickles. Other materials, such as copper, brass, galvanized steel, or iron may affect the pickle product or be unsafe.

PUT THESE INGREDIENTS IN A PICKLE

Always start with just-ripe **produce** that is free from deformities, bruises, and blemishes. It's best to begin pickling within 24 hours after fruits or vegetables are picked. If it's not possible for you to start pickling right away, store the produce, unwashed, in the refrigerator, or spread it in a cool, ventilated area. Remember that cucumbers will deteriorate quickly at room temperature.

Be sure to select a pickling variety of cucumber; your local Extension office can help you determine the one most available in your area. If you plan to pickle them whole, choose unwaxed cucumbers since pickling solutions won't penetrate the wax.

Wash cucumbers well, especially around the stem end, since it can harbor undesirable bacteria, which affect the pickles. Be sure to remove the blossom end before pickling since enzymes stored there cause pickles to soften.

Vinegar and **salt** are essential for making pickles, and amounts should never be reduced or diluted. Vinegar provides the acidity necessary for preservation of fresh-pack pickles. Always use vinegar of at least 5% acidity (it's listed on the label). You may use cider or white vinegar, but cider vinegar can darken light-colored vegetables and fruits.

Be sure to use granulated uniodized pickling or canning salt. Table salt contains anti-caking ingredients, which may leave a white sediment on the pickles or cloud the brine.

Most pickling recipes call for some **sugar**, since it helps to plump the pickles and keep them crisp. Unless the recipe specifies brown sugar, use the regular white granulated kind.

Spices give pickles their distinctive flavor — dill, garlic, cinnamon, mustard seeds, and cloves are just a few typically used. It's best to start with fresh, whole spices; powdered ones may darken and cloud the pickle product. Tie spices in a cheesecloth bag so they may be removed easily.

The type of **water** in your area may affect your pickles. If you have

PICKLE PROBLEM CHART
Problems and Possible Causes

Soft or slippery pickles:
Blossom ends not removed
Vinegar of too low acidity used
Not enough salt in brine
Cucumbers not completely submerged in brine
Improper processing

Hollow pickles:
Cucumbers too large
Too much time between picking and brining
Improper brining process

Shriveled pickles:
Brine or vinegar too strong
Syrup too heavy
Overcooking or overprocessing
Too much time between picking and brining
Dry weather during vegetable growth

Dark or discolored pickles:
Hard water used
Spices left in pickles,
Iodized salt used
Ground spices used

Spoilage:
Processing time too short
Canning jars and/or new lids not used
Ingredients not measured accurately
Vinegar that has lost strength used
Unsterilized jars used

hard water, soften it by boiling it for 15 minutes. Then cover the water, and let it set for 24 hours. Remove any scum that forms, and slowly pour water from the container without disturbing the sediment. Discard sediment. As an alternative, distilled water may be used for making pickles, but it's expensive.

Lime and **alum** are additives that have sometimes been used to ensure crisp pickles, but they are no longer recommended or needed. If you follow up-to-date methods for pickling and processing, and start with good quality ingredients, your pickles will be crisp.

PACKING THE PICKLES

When pickles are ready, place firmly in sterilized canning jars without packing too tightly. Cover with boiling syrup or brine, leaving recommended headspace.

After adding boiling liquid to pickles, run a rubber spatula around the inside edge of jars to remove air bubbles. Don't use a metal utensil, since it may scratch the glass and cause the jar to break.

Wipe jar rims clean before putting the metal lids in place. Then screw on metal bands. These procedures should be followed by water-bath processing for all pickles.

PROCESSING PICKLES

Water-bath processing destroys yeasts, molds, and bacteria that cause spoilage and also inactivates enzymes that can change color, flavor, and texture. To water bath pickles, put the jars on a rack in the canner filled with simmering water. The water should cover the jar tops by 1 to 2 inches. Start to count processing time when water reaches a boil. If no processing time is given, process 10 minutes for pints and quarts. Some relishes and pickles made from vegetables other than cucumbers and cabbage may require longer processing times.

Pickles

KOSHER DILLS

(pictured on page 250)

4 pounds (4 inch) pickling cucumbers
14 cloves garlic, peeled and cut in half
¼ cup pickling salt
3 cups water
2¾ cups vinegar (5% acidity)
14 sprigs fresh dillweed
28 peppercorns

Wash cucumbers, and cut in half lengthwise.

Combine garlic, salt, water, and vinegar; bring to a boil. Remove garlic and place 4 halves into each hot sterilized jar. Pack cucumbers into jars, adding 2 sprigs dillweed and 4 peppercorns to each jar. Pour boiling vinegar mixture over cucumbers, leaving ½-inch headspace. Remove air bubbles; wipe jar rims. Cover jars at once with metal lids, and screw on metal bands. Process jars in boiling-water bath 10 minutes. Yield: 6 to 7 pints.

BREAD-AND-BUTTER PICKLES

(pictured on page 250)

4 quarts medium cucumbers
6 medium onions, sliced
2 green peppers, chopped
3 cloves garlic
⅓ cup pickling salt
Crushed ice
5 cups sugar
3 cups cider vinegar (5% acidity)
2 tablespoons mustard seeds
1½ teaspoons ground turmeric
1½ teaspoons celery seeds

Wash cucumbers, and slice thinly. Combine cucumber, onion, green pepper, garlic, and salt in a large Dutch oven. Cover with crushed ice; mix thoroughly, and let stand 3 hours. Drain.

Combine remaining ingredients, and pour over cucumber mixture. Heat thoroughly, just until boiling. Pack while boiling into hot sterilized jars, leaving ½-inch headspace. Remove air bubbles; wipe jar rims. Cover at once with metal

lids, and screw on metal bands. Process jars in boiling-water bath for 10 minutes. Yield: 8 pints.

OKRA PICKLES

(pictured on page 250)

3½ pounds small okra pods
7 cloves garlic
7 small fresh hot peppers
1 quart water
2 cups vinegar (5% acidity)
⅓ cup pickling salt
2 teaspoons dillseeds

Pack okra tightly into hot sterilized jars, leaving ½-inch headspace; place a garlic clove and a hot pepper in each.

Combine water, vinegar, pickling salt, and dillseeds in a saucepan; bring to a boil. Pour boiling vinegar mixture over okra, leaving ½-inch headspace. Remove air bubbles; wipe jar rims. Cover at once with metal lids, and screw on bands. Process in boiling-water bath 10 minutes. Yield: 7 pints.

MIXED VEGETABLE PICKLES

(pictured on page 250)

1 cup pickling salt
4 quarts cold water
1 quart sliced small cucumbers
    (1-inch slices)
2 cups sliced carrots (1½-inch slices)
2 cups sliced celery (1½-inch slices)
2 cups small boiling onions
2 sweet red peppers, cut into ½-inch strips
1 small cauliflower, broken into flowerets
6½ cups vinegar (5% acidity)
2 cups sugar
1 fresh hot red pepper, sliced crosswise
¼ cup mustard seeds
2 tablespoons celery seeds

Dissolve salt in water; pour over vegetables (except hot red pepper) in a large crock or plastic container. Cover and allow to stand in a cool place 12 to 18 hours. Drain well.

Combine vinegar, sugar, hot red pepper, and spices in a 10-quart Dutch oven; bring to a boil, and boil 3 minutes. Add vegetables; reduce heat, and simmer until thoroughly heated.

Pack hot mixture into hot sterilized jars; fill with hot liquid, leaving ¼-inch headspace. Remove air bubbles; wipe jar rims. Cover at once with metal lids, and screw on bands. Process in boiling-water bath 15 minutes. Yield: 6 pints.

PICKLED BEETS

(pictured on page 250)

8 to 9 pounds small fresh beets
1 tablespoon mustard seeds
1 teaspoon celery seeds
3½ cups vinegar (5% acidity)
3 cups sugar
1½ teaspoons pickling salt

Leave root and 1 inch of stem on beets; scrub with a brush. Place beets in a saucepan; add water to cover. Bring to a boil; cover, reduce heat, and simmer 35 to 40 minutes or until tender. Drain, reserving 2½ cups liquid; pour cold water over beets, and drain. Trim off beet root and stems; then rub off skins. Set beets aside.

Combine mustard seeds and celery seeds in a cheesecloth bag. Combine vinegar, reserved beet liquid, sugar, pickling salt, and spice bag in a Dutch oven. Bring mixture to a boil; reduce heat, and simmer 15 minutes.

Pack beets into hot jars, leaving ½-inch headspace. Pour boiling syrup over beets, leaving ½-inch headspace. Remove air bubbles; wipe jar rims. Cover at once with metal lids, and screw on bands. Process in boiling-water bath 30 minutes. Yield: 7 pints.

WATERMELON RIND PICKLES

1 large watermelon, quartered
Pickling salt
2 tablespoons plus 2 teaspoons whole cloves
16 (1½-inch) sticks cinnamon
½ teaspoon mustard seeds
8 cups sugar
1 quart vinegar (5% acidity)

Remove flesh from melon (reserve for other uses); peel watermelon. Cut rind into 1-inch cubes.

Place rind in a large crock or plastic container. Add water by the quart until it covers the rind; add ¼ cup pickling salt for each quart water, stirring until salt dissolves. Cover and let stand in a cool place 8 hours. Drain well.

Place rind in a 10-quart Dutch oven; cover with cold water. Bring to a boil, and boil until rind is almost tender. Drain and set aside.

Tie cloves, cinnamon, and mustard seeds in a cheesecloth bag. Combine spice bag, sugar, and vinegar in a Dutch oven. Bring to a boil; remove from heat, and let stand 15 minutes. Add rind to syrup. Bring to a boil; reduce heat to low, and cook until rind is transparent. Remove spice bag.

Pack hot rind into hot sterilized jars; fill with hot liquid, leaving ½-inch headspace. Remove air bubbles; wipe jar rims. Cover jars at once with metal lids, and screw on metal bands. Process jars in boiling-water bath 10 minutes. Yield: about 5 pints.

PEACH PICKLES

3 quarts cold water
¾ teaspoon ascorbic-citric powder
8 pounds small to medium-size firm, ripe peaches, peeled
6¾ cups sugar
1 quart vinegar (5% acidity)
4 (3-inch) sticks cinnamon
2 tablespoons whole cloves
1 (1-inch) piece fresh gingerroot

Combine water and ascorbic-citric powder in a large container. Drop peaches into water mixture; set aside.

Combine sugar and vinegar in a large Dutch oven; bring to a boil, and cook 5 minutes. Tie remaining ingredients in a cheesecloth bag, and add to syrup.

Drain peaches and add to syrup mixture. Cook, uncovered, about 3 minutes or just until peaches can be pierced with a fork. Remove from heat. Cover and let stand at room temperature 24 hours.

Bring peaches to a boil; pack hot peaches into hot sterilized jars, leaving ½-inch headspace. Pour boiling syrup over peaches, leaving ½-inch headspace. Remove air bubbles; wipe jar rims. Cover at once with metal lids, and screw on bands. Process in boiling-water bath 15 minutes. Yield: 6 pints.

CUCUMBER CHIPS

24 small cucumbers (about 4 to 5 inches), sliced ¼-inch thick
½ cup pickling salt
3 cups vinegar (5% acidity)
1 quart water
1 tablespoon ground turmeric
1 quart vinegar (5% acidity)
1 cup water
2 cups sugar
2 (3-inch) sticks cinnamon
1 (1-inch) piece fresh gingerroot
1 tablespoon mustard seeds
1 teaspoon whole cloves
2 cups firmly packed brown sugar

Place cucumbers in a large bowl; sprinkle with salt. Cover and let stand 3 hours. Drain well.

Combine 3 cups vinegar, 1 quart water, and turmeric in a large Dutch oven; bring to a boil, and pour over cucumbers. Cover and let stand until cooled to room temperature; drain. Rinse cucumbers, and drain again.

Combine 1 quart vinegar, 1 cup water, and 2 cups sugar in a Dutch oven. Tie spices in a cheesecloth bag, and add to vinegar mixture. Bring vinegar mixture to a boil; reduce heat, and simmer, un-covered, 15 minutes. Pour mixture over cucumbers. Let stand at least 12 hours in a cool place.

Drain syrup from cucumbers into a Dutch oven. Add brown sugar, and bring to a boil.

Pack cucumbers into hot sterilized jars, leaving ¼-inch headspace. Pour boiling syrup over cucumbers, leaving ¼-inch headspace. Remove air bubbles; wipe jar rims. Cover at once with metal lids, and screw on bands. Process in boiling-water bath 10 minutes. Yield: 4 pints.

Relishes

Chopped, seasoned, and pickled fruits and vegetables are known as pickle relishes. The pickling process for relishes is similar to that of most pickles, but more time is required in preparation because the produce must be chopped. A food processor is a great timesaver.

PEPPER RELISH

(pictured on page 250)

6 green peppers, minced
6 sweet red peppers, minced
6 medium onions, minced
1 hot pepper
2 cups vinegar (5% acidity)
1½ cups sugar
2 tablespoons plus 1 teaspoon mustard seeds

Combine all ingredients in a large Dutch oven, and bring to a boil. Reduce heat to medium; cook, uncovered, 30 minutes, stirring occasionally. Discard hot pepper.

Quickly spoon hot relish into hot sterilized jars, leaving ¼-inch head-space. Remove air bubbles; wipe jar rims. Cover at once at once with metal lids, and screw on bands. Process in boiling-water bath 10 minutes. Yield: 10 half pints.

TOMATO RELISH

32 medium tomatoes (about 16 pounds)
12 medium onions, finely chopped
3 red peppers, finely chopped
3 green peppers, finely chopped
3 tablespoons salt
2 cups firmly packed brown sugar
2 cups vinegar (5% acidity)
1 tablespoon ground cinnamon
1½ teaspoons ground allspice
1½ teaspoons ground cloves

Peel, core, and chop tomatoes. Combine tomatoes and next 4 ingredients in a large kettle. Bring to a boil; reduce heat to medium, and cook, uncovered, 25 minutes. Add remaining ingredients; reduce heat and simmer, uncovered, 1½ to 2 hours or until thickened.

Quickly pack hot mixture into hot sterilized jars, leaving ½-inch head-space. Remove air bubbles; wipe jar rims. Cover at once with metal lids, and screw on bands. Process in boiling-water bath 10 minutes. Yield: 12 pints.

HORSERADISH RELISH

1¾ pounds fresh horseradish
½ teaspoon salt, divided
1½ cups boiling vinegar (5% acidity)

Scrub horseradish root; peel and cut into 2-inch pieces.

Position knife blade in food processor bowl; add horseradish. Top with cover, and process until finely chopped. Pack horseradish into hot sterilized jars. Add ¼ teaspoon salt to each jar. Pour boiling vinegar into jars, covering horseradish, leaving ¼-inch headspace. Remove air bubbles; wipe jar rims. Cover at once with metal lids, and screw on bands. Process in boiling-water bath 10 minutes. Yield: 2 pints.

Note: Mixture will separate upon storage; stir before using.

CORN RELISH

4 cups fresh cut corn
3 medium-size green peppers, chopped
1 cup chopped onion
1 cup chopped cucumber
¼ cup chopped celery
1 (28-ounce) can whole tomatoes, undrained and chopped
1 cup sugar
2 teaspoons salt
1 teaspoon whole mustard seeds
¾ teaspoon ground turmeric
¼ teaspoon dry mustard
1½ cups vinegar (5% acidity)

Combine all ingredients in a large Dutch oven; simmer over low heat 20 minutes. Bring mixture to a boil.

Pack hot mixture into hot sterilized jars, leaving ¼-inch headspace. Remove air bubbles; wipe jar rims. Cover at once with metal lids, and screw on bands. Process in boiling-water bath 15 minutes. Yield: 4 pints.

CHOW-CHOW

2 quarts finely chopped cabbage
1 quart peeled, chopped green tomatoes
6 medium onions, chopped
6 green peppers, coarsely chopped
6 red peppers, coarsely chopped
¼ cup pickling salt
6 cups vinegar (5% acidity), divided
2 tablespoons prepared mustard
2½ cups sugar
2 tablespoons mustard seeds
1 tablespoon mixed pickling spices
1½ teaspoons ground turmeric
1 teaspoon ground ginger

Combine vegetables and salt; stir well. Cover and let stand 8 hours. Drain well.

Stir 2 tablespoons vinegar into mustard. Combine mustard, remaining vinegar, and remaining 5 ingredients in a large kettle. Bring to a boil; reduce heat,

and simmer, uncovered, 20 minutes. Add vegetables; simmer 10 minutes.

Spoon hot mixture into hot sterilized jars, leaving ¼-inch headspace. Remove air bubbles; wipe jar rims. Cover at once with metal lids, and screw on bands. Process in boiling-water bath 10 minutes. Yield: about 8 pints.

SWEET PICKLE RELISH

4 cups chopped cucumbers
2 cups chopped onion
1 green pepper, chopped
1 sweet red pepper, chopped
¼ cup pickling salt
1¾ cups sugar
1 cup cider vinegar (5% acidity)
1½ teaspoons celery seeds
1½ teaspoons mustard seeds

Combine first 4 ingredients; sprinkle with salt, and cover with cold water. Let stand 2 hours. Drain.

Combine sugar, vinegar, and spices in a large Dutch oven; bring to a boil, and add vegetables. Return to a boil; reduce heat, and simmer 10 minutes.

Pack hot mixture into hot sterilized jars, leaving ¼-inch headspace. Remove air bubbles; wipe jar rims. Cover at once with metal lids, and screw on bands. Process in boiling-water bath 10 minutes. Yield: 4 half pints.

PICCALILLI

4 cups chopped cabbage
3 cups chopped cauliflower
2 cups chopped onion
2 cups chopped green tomatoes
1 cup chopped sweet red pepper
3 tablespoons pickling salt
2½ cups vinegar (5% acidity)
1½ cups sugar
2 teaspoons dry mustard
2 teaspoons celery seeds
1 teaspoon ground turmeric
1 teaspoon mustard seeds
½ teaspoon ground ginger

Combine vegetables; sprinkle with salt. Cover and let stand 8 hours. Drain well. Rinse with cold water, and drain again.

Combine vinegar, sugar, and seasonings in a large Dutch oven. Bring to a boil; reduce heat, and simmer, uncovered, 10 minutes. Add vegetables, and simmer an additional 10 minutes. Return to a boil.

Spoon boiling mixture into hot sterilized jars, leaving ¼-inch headspace. Remove air bubbles; wipe jar rims. Cover at once with metal lids, and screw on bands. Process in boiling-water bath 10 minutes. Yield: 3 pints.

PEAR RELISH

16 pears, peeled, cored, and ground
6 medium onions, ground
8 green peppers, ground
4 sweet red peppers, ground
2 hot peppers, ground
6 cups vinegar (5% acidity)
6 cups sugar
3 tablespoons mustard seeds
2 tablespoons pickling salt
1 tablespoon ground turmeric
1 teaspoon ground allspice
1 teaspoon ground cinnamon
1 teaspoon ground ginger

Let pears, onion, and peppers stand in separate containers for 1 hour. Pour boiling water over each; drain very well. Combine pears, onion, peppers, vinegar, sugar, and seasonings in a large kettle. Bring to a boil; reduce heat and simmer, uncovered, 30 minutes.

Pour hot mixture into hot sterilized jars, leaving ¼-inch headspace. Remove air bubbles; wipe jar rims. Cover at once with metal lids, and screw on bands. Process in boiling-water bath 20 minutes. Let stand in a cool place for 1 month before using. Chill before serving. Yield: 10 pints.

Vinegars

Combine vinegar and a handful of garden herbs, and you'll have a fresh tasting seasoning you can use all year long. Just pour hot vinegar over herbs in a jar, and let stand two weeks.

You can use any fresh herb or combination of herbs. We tried some blends of two or more in our kitchens to take the guesswork out of teaming flavors. If you choose to come up with your own combinations, keep in mind that strong herbs such as basil, sage, and rosemary need to be mixed with milder flavored ones.

If you're blessed with an abundance of fresh herbs, mix up several batches of flavored vinegar to give as gifts. Be sure to place a fresh sprig of an appropriate herb in the bottle and attach some ideas or recipes for using the vinegar.

GARLIC-BASIL VINEGAR

½ cup fresh basil leaves
1 clove garlic, crushed
2 cups vinegar (5% acidity)
Additional sprigs of fresh basil (optional)

Slightly bruise basil, and place in a wide-mouth glass jar with garlic.

Place vinegar in a medium saucepan; bring to a boil. Pour vinegar over basil and garlic; cover with lid. Let stand at room temperature 2 weeks.

Strain vinegar into decorative jars, discarding basil and garlic residue; add additional sprigs of basil, if desired. Seal jars with a cork or other airtight lid. Yield: 2 cups.

TARRAGON-DILL VINEGAR

⅓ cup fresh tarragon leaves
¼ cup fresh dill
2 cups white wine vinegar (5% acidity)
Additional sprigs of tarragon and dill (optional)

Slightly bruise tarragon and dill, and place in a wide-mouth glass jar.

Place vinegar in a medium saucepan, and bring to a boil. Pour vinegar over herbs; cover with lid. Let stand at room temperature 2 weeks.

Strain vinegar into decorative jars, discarding herb residue. Add additional sprigs of fresh dill and tarragon, if desired. Seal jars with a cork or other airtight lid. Yield: 2 cups.

LEMON-MINT VINEGAR

1 lemon
¼ cup chopped fresh mint leaves
2 cups white wine vinegar (5% acidity)
Additional sprigs of fresh mint (optional)
Lemon rind strips (optional)

Cut a continuous spiral of rind from lemon, and place in a wide-mouth glass jar. Reserve remainder of lemon for other uses. Add mint to jar.

Place vinegar in a medium saucepan, and bring to a boil. Pour vinegar over mint and lemon rind; cover with lid. Let stand at room temperature 2 weeks.

Strain vinegar into decorative jars, discarding lemon and herb residue; add additional sprigs of fresh mint and lemon rind, if desired. Seal jars with a cork or other airtight lid. Yield: 2 cups.

Splash on the Herb Vinegar

When it comes to using flavored vinegars, stir them into some less obvious recipes besides those for salad dressings and marinades. For example, you'll find Garlic-Basil Vinegar adds a fabulous taste to fresh, hot green beans. Try Tarragon-Dill Vinegar in place of lemon or lime juice in a seviche marinade or to season cold, smoked salmon. If you enjoy the tangy lemon flavor of chicken piccata, add some Spicy Oregano-Lemon Vinegar to the thin slices of sautéed meat or sprinkle it over hot, buttered broccoli. Just a hint of mint is what you will detect when you mix Lemon-Mint Vinegar with vegetable oil and toss it with a fresh fruit salad. Or, add Five-Herb Vinegar to a vegetable soup or stew.

FIVE-HERB VINEGAR

½ cup chopped fresh rosemary
½ cup chopped fresh thyme
¼ cup chopped chive blossoms
¼ cup chopped fresh oregano
4 shallots, thinly sliced
1 sprig fresh parsley, chopped
12 peppercorns
3¾ cups white wine vinegar (5% acidity)
Additional sprigs of fresh rosemary, thyme, and oregano (optional)

Place first 7 ingredients in a large wide-mouth glass jar. Place vinegar in a medium saucepan; bring to a boil. Pour vinegar over herbs; cover with lid. Let stand at room temperature 2 weeks.

Strain vinegar into decorative jars, discarding herb residue; add additional sprigs of fresh rosemary, thyme, and oregano, if desired. Seal jars with a cork or other airtight lid. Yield: 4 cups.

Jellies, Jams, and Preserves

Southerners have a real weakness for sweet spreads. During the summer you'll find Southern cooks busily putting up jellies, jams, and preserves destined to lather homemade bread, to be sandwiched with peanut butter, or to be enjoyed in a slice of jam cake.

EQUIPMENT

Before you begin, check to see that you have all the necessary equipment: an 8- to 10-quart deep, heavy, flat-bottom kettle; a jelly bag or cheesecloth; a jelly, candy, or deep-fat thermometer; a timer; a jar filler or funnel; a boiling-water bath canner with a rack and lid; and jelly jars with metal rings and new lids. Jars need to be sterilized thoroughly since they won't be processed in the water bath longer than 15 minutes. To sterilize, place them in boiling water 15 minutes.

INGREDIENTS FOR SWEET SPREADS

The ingredients are simple for these tasty summer-fresh treats. Only fruit, sugar, acid, and fruit pectin are needed. Three-fourths of the fruit should be just ripe and the remaining one-fourth slightly underripe for the best jelled product.

The proper amount of sugar is important for achieving a good jell, so never reduce the recommended amount. Sugar contributes to the taste of the product and acts as a preservative, too. You can substitute mild-flavored honey or light corn syrup for some of the sugar, but adjustments are sometimes neces-

sary in other ingredient amounts. If you choose to use another sweetener, be sure to check with your local Extension agent for advice.

Acid and pectin, contained in the fruit itself, are necessary for jell formation, as well. Fruit contains varying amounts of both, depending on the type of fruit and the degree of ripeness. Pectin is at its highest quality in just-ripe fruit, and acid content is higher in underripe fruit. If the fruit is naturally low in acid, lemon juice may be added.

Some of the guesswork as to acidity level and doneness of the cooked mixture can be eliminated with the use of commercial pectin. A disadvantage to using added pectin is that the natural fruit flavor may be masked to some extent since more sugar is needed with this product.

WHEN MAKING JELLY

Be sure to follow recipe directions exactly, and never double the recipe. Each batch should start with no more than 4 to 6 cups juice.

When your recipe calls for juice extracted from fresh fruit, prepare fruit as the recipe directs first. Then pour fruit into a damp jelly bag or four thicknesses of damp cheesecloth, and allow juice to drip into a bowl. Jelly is clearer when allowed to drip rather than being squeezed or pressed from the bag. If using a fruit press, strain juice again.

When making jelly without added pectin, it's tricky to tell when the hot fruit mixture has reached the proper consistency since it will thicken as it cools. Use one of these methods to

test for the proper jelling point.

● To test for doneness, dip a cool metal spoon into boiling jelly and lift spoon out of steam so syrup runs off side of spoon. When two drops of the syrup form together and "sheet" off the spoon, the jellying point has been reached.

● For another doneness check, spoon a small amount of boiling jelly on a saucer and place it in the freezer a few minutes. If it jells, the mixture should be done. Be certain to remove remaining jelly from heat during this doneness test.

When jelly is done, remove from heat, skim off foam, and pour into hot sterilized jars, leaving ¼-inch headspace; wipe jar rims. Cover at once with metal lids, and screw on bands. Process as directed. (Jams and other fruit spreads that contain crushed, whole, or chunks of fruit require cooking to a slightly higher temperature than jellies, and the sheeting and freezer tests don't work for them. Follow your recipe for specific cooking directions.)

PROCESSING FRUIT SPREADS

Processing in a boiling-water bath is now recommended for all jellies and fruit spreads except for freezer fruit spreads to remove air so mold can't grow. Place jars on the rack in a water-bath canner with the water hot to gently boiling, and add additional water to reach 1 to 2 inches above tops of the jars. Cover and begin to count processing time when water returns to a boil. If no time is suggested in the recipe, process 5 minutes.

TIPS FOR PRESERVING FRUIT

● Jelly or jam that is runny can be remade with the addition of lemon juice or commercial pectin. Call your local Extension agent for proportions and directions.

● Jellied products should keep well at least one year if stored in a cool, dark, dry place. However, they should be used as soon as possible since flavor and quality begin to decrease within a few months.

● Mold on jellied products is the result of imperfect sealing or underprocessing. Discard the jar if mold is extensive. If it only slightly covers the top, remove the mold and ½-inch of the product underneath.

Biscuits demand the best in jams and jellies: from front left, Strawberry Preserves (page 271), Apple Jelly (page 268), Peach Preserves (page 271), and Concord Grape Jelly (269).

Jellies are sparkling clear gelatin-like spreads that are the result of cooking sugar and fruit juice or other liquid together.

APPLE JELLY

(pictured on page 267)

4 cups apple juice
1 (1¾-ounce) package powdered pectin
5 cups sugar

Combine apple juice and pectin in a large Dutch oven; bring to a boil, stirring occasionally. Add sugar, and bring mixture to a full, rolling boil. Boil 1 minute, stirring constantly. Remove mixture from heat, and skim off foam with a metal spoon.

Quickly pour hot jelly into hot sterilized jars, leaving ½-inch headspace; wipe jar rims. Cover at once with metal lids, and screw on bands. Process in boiling-water bath 5 minutes. Yield: 7 half pints.

QUICK GRAPE JELLY

2 cups bottled unsweetened grape juice
3½ cups sugar
1 (3-ounce) package liquid pectin

Combine grape juice and sugar in a large Dutch oven; bring to a boil, stirring constantly. Stir in pectin; boil 1 minute, stirring constantly. Remove from heat, and skim off foam with a metal spoon.

Quickly pour hot jelly into hot sterilized jars, leaving ½-inch headspace; wipe jar rims. Cover at once with metal lids, and screw on bands. Process in boiling-water bath 5 minutes. Yield: 4 half pints.

WINE JELLY

3 cups sugar
2 cups Burgundy
1 (3-ounce) package liquid pectin

Combine sugar and wine in a large Dutch oven. Cook over medium heat; stir until sugar dissolves (do not boil). Remove from heat; stir in pectin. Skim off foam with a metal spoon.

Quickly pour hot jelly into hot sterilized jars; wipe jar rims. Cover at once with metal lids, and screw on bands. Process in boiling-water bath 5 minutes. Yield: 4 half pints.

PEPPER JELLY

1½ cups minced green pepper
½ cup minced hot green pepper
7½ cups sugar
1½ cups vinegar (5% acidity)
2 (3-ounce) packages liquid pectin

Combine first 4 ingredients in a Dutch oven; bring to a boil. Boil 6 minutes, stirring frequently. Stir in pectin; boil 3 minutes, stirring frequently. Remove from heat, and skim off foam with a metal spoon.

Quickly pour hot jelly into hot sterilized jars, leaving ¼-inch headspace; wipe jar rims. Cover at once with metal lids, and screw on bands. Process in boiling-water bath 5 minutes. Yield: 7 half pints.

BLACKBERRY JELLY

About 3 quarts ripe blackberries
7½ cups sugar
2 (3-ounce) packages liquid pectin

Sort and wash berries; remove stems and caps. Crush enough berries, and press through a jelly bag or cheesecloth to extract 4 cups juice. Combine juice and sugar in a large saucepan, and stir well. Place over high heat; cook, stirring constantly, until mixture comes to a rapid boil. Boil hard 1 minute, stirring constantly. Add pectin, and bring to a full rolling boil; boil 1 minute, stirring constantly. Remove from heat, and skim off foam with a metal spoon.

Quickly pour hot jelly into hot sterilized jars, leaving ¼-inch headspace; wipe jar rims. Cover at once with metal lids, and screw on bands. Process in boiling-water bath 5 minutes. Yield: 8 half pints.

HERB JELLY

1½ cups white grape juice
½ cup water
3½ cups sugar
Prepared herbs (variations follow)
Food coloring (variations follow)
1 (3-ounce) package liquid pectin

Combine all ingredients except pectin in a large Dutch oven. Bring to a rolling boil, stirring constantly; cook 1 minute. Add pectin, and bring to a full rolling boil. Boil 1 minute, stirring frequently. Remove from heat, and skim off foam with a metal spoon.

Quickly pour hot jelly through a sieve into hot jars, leaving ¼-inch headspace; wipe jar rims. Cover at once with metal lids, and screw on bands. Process in boiling-water bath 5 minutes. Yield: 4 half pints.

Rosemary Jelly: Add 3 tablespoons fresh rosemary leaves, crushed, 8 drops red food coloring, and 8 drops yellow food coloring.

Thyme Jelly: Add 3 tablespoons fresh thyme leaves, crushed, and 8 drops red food coloring.

Basil Jelly: Add 2 tablespoons chopped fresh basil leaves, and 6 drops yellow food coloring.

Mint Jelly: Add ¾ cup fresh mint leaves, crushed, and 2 drops green food coloring.

1. To make Concord Grape Jelly, wash grapes, remove stems, and place in a Dutch oven. Crush grapes, and cook as recipe directs.

2. Gently press cooked grape mixture through a jelly bag or cheesecloth, extracting 4 cups juice. Add sugar and pectin, and cook as directed.

3. Remove cooked jelly mixture from heat, and skim off foam with a metal spoon.

4. Quickly pour jelly into hot sterilized jars, leaving ¼-inch headspace; wipe jar rims. Cover with metal lids, and screw on bands. Process.

CONCORD GRAPE JELLY

3½ pounds Concord grapes
½ cup water
7 cups sugar
1 (3-ounce) package liquid pectin

Sort and wash grapes; remove stems, and place in a Dutch oven. Crush grapes, and add water. Bring mixture to a boil; cover, reduce heat, and simmer 10 minutes. Press mixture through a jelly bag, extracting 4 cups juice. Cover and let sit 8 hours in a cool place.

Strain juice through a double thickness of damp cheesecloth. Combine juice and sugar in a large Dutch oven, and stir well. Place over high heat; cook, stirring constantly, until mixture comes to a rapid boil. Add pectin, and bring to a full rolling boil; boil 1 minute, stirring constantly. Remove from heat, and skim off foam with a metal spoon.

Quickly pour hot mixture into hot sterilized jars, leaving ¼-inch headspace; wipe jar rims. Cover at once with metal lids, and screw on bands. Process in boiling-water bath 5 minutes. Yield: 8 half pints.

One taste, and you'll be glad you made Concord Grape Jelly.

Jams are less firm than jellies and are made with crushed or finely chopped fruit rather than juice.

BLUEBERRY JAM

1½ quarts stemmed blueberries, crushed
¼ cup lemon juice
1 (1-inch) stick cinnamon
7 cups sugar
2 (3-ounce) packages liquid pectin

Combine first 4 ingredients in a Dutch oven; bring to a boil, stirring occasionally, until sugar dissolves. Boil mixture 2 minutes, stirring frequently; remove from heat. Discard cinnamon stick. Add pectin to mixture, and stir 5 minutes. Skim off foam with a metal spoon.

Quickly pour hot jam into hot sterilized jars, leaving ¼-inch headspace; wipe jar rims. Cover jars at once with metal lids, and screw on bands. Process in boiling-water bath 10 minutes. Yield: 5 half pints.

FREEZER STRAWBERRY JAM

3 cups crushed strawberries
5 cups sugar
¾ cup water
1 (1¾-ounce) package powdered pectin

Combine strawberries and sugar; let stand 20 minutes, stirring occasionally.

Combine water and pectin in a small saucepan; bring to a boil. Boil 1 minute, stirring constantly. Add to fruit, and stir 3 minutes. Quickly spoon into freezer containers or hot sterilized jars, leaving ½-inch headspace. Cover at once with plastic or metal lids, and screw on bands. Let stand at room temperature 24 hours; freeze. Yield: 7 half pints.

Note: Jam may be stored in refrigerator 3 weeks.

FIG JAM

6 quarts boiling water
6 quarts fresh figs
Sugar
1 quart water
8 slices lemon

Pour boiling water over figs; let stand 15 minutes. Drain and thoroughly rinse in cold water. Pat dry; remove stems. Crush and measure figs; place in a large Dutch oven. Add ½ cup sugar for each cup of crushed figs. Add 1 quart water. Bring to a rapid boil; reduce heat and simmer, uncovered, 3 hours or until thickened, stirring occasionally.

Ladle hot jam into hot sterilized jars, leaving ¼-inch headspace; add a slice of lemon to each jar. Wipe jar rims. Cover at once with metal lids, and screw on bands. Process in boiling-water bath 10 minutes. Yield: 8½ pints.

PEACH-PLUM FREEZER JAM

¾ pound fresh plums
1 pound fresh peaches, peeled and chopped
2 tablespoons lemon juice
½ teaspoon ascorbic-citric powder
4 cups sugar
¾ cup water
1 (1¾-ounce) package powdered pectin

Remove pits from plums (do not peel), and grind pulp finely. Measure 1¼ cups peaches and 1 cup ground plums. Combine fruit, lemon juice, and ascorbic-citric powder in a large bowl.

Add sugar to fruit, mixing well; let stand 10 minutes. Combine water and pectin in a small saucepan. Bring to a boil, and boil 1 minute, stirring constantly. Pour over fruit mixture, and stir 3 minutes.

Quickly pour into freezer containers or hot sterilized jars, leaving ¼-inch headspace. Cover at once with plastic or metal lids, and screw on bands, if appropriate. Let stand at room temperature 24 hours; then store in freezer. To serve, thaw jam. Yield: about 6 half pints.

MUSCADINE JAM

4 pounds muscadines
1 cup water
1 (1¾-ounce) package powdered fruit pectin
7½ cups sugar

Remove stems and skins from muscadines; set skins and pulp aside. Discard stems.

Combine pulp and 1 cup water in a Dutch oven. Bring to a boil; cover, reduce heat, and simmer 5 minutes. Press mixture through a sieve or food mill to remove seeds.

Place reserved skins in a large saucepan, and cover with water. Bring to a boil; cover, reduce heat, and simmer 5 to 10 minutes or until tender. Drain and chop skins, reserving liquid.

Combine pulp mixture and chopped skins. Place 6 cups fruit mixture, adding reserved liquid if necessary to make 6 cups, in a large Dutch oven. Stir in powdered fruit pectin, mixing well. Bring mixture to a rolling boil, stirring constantly. Add sugar; return to a rolling boil. Boil 1 minute, stirring constantly. Remove mixture from heat; skim off foam. Stir 5 minutes.

Quickly spoon hot mixture into hot jars, leaving ¼-inch headspace; wipe jar rims. Cover jars at once with metal lids, and screw on metal bands. Process jars in boiling-water bath 15 minutes. Yield: 5 pints.

STRAWBERRY PRESERVES

(pictured on page 267)

1½ quarts small strawberries
5 cups sugar
⅓ cup lemon juice

Wash and hull strawberries. Combine strawberries and sugar in a large Dutch oven; stir well, and let mixture stand 3 to 4 hours.

Slowly bring strawberry mixture to a boil, stirring occasionally, until sugar dissolves. Stir in lemon juice. Boil about 12 minutes or until berries are clear, stirring occasionally. Remove from heat, and skim off foam with a metal spoon.

Carefully remove fruit from syrup with a slotted spoon, and place in a shallow pan. Bring syrup to a boil; cook about 10 minutes or until syrup has thickened to desired consistency. Pour syrup over fruit. Cover loosely with paper towels, and let stand 12 to 24 hours in a cool place. Shake pan occasionally (do not stir) so berries will absorb syrup and remain plump. Skim off foam with a metal spoon.

Heat mixture in Dutch oven, and ladle hot preserves into hot jars, leaving ¼-inch headspace; wipe jar rims. Cover at once with metal lids, and screw on bands. Process in boiling-water bath 20 minutes. Yield: 4 half pints.

PEAR PRESERVES

10 large pears (about 5 pounds), peeled, cored, and chopped
4½ cups sugar
3 cups water
2 lemons, thinly sliced

Place pears in a 3-quart Dutch oven, and add water to cover. Bring to a boil; cover, reduce heat, and simmer 15 minutes or until pears are tender. Drain.

Combine sugar and 3 cups water in a 6-quart Dutch oven; bring to a boil, and cook 10 minutes (mixture will be a thin, transparent syrup). Remove from heat, and let cool 15 minutes.

Stir in pears and lemon slices; bring mixture to a rapid boil. Boil rapidly until pears are transparent (about 45 minutes), stirring occasionally.

Pour pear mixture into a shallow 13- x 9- x 2-inch pan; skim off foam with a metal spoon. Cover loosely with paper towels, and let stand in a cool place 12 hours. Shake pan occasionally (do not stir) so pears will absorb the syrup. Skim off foam with a metal spoon.

Heat fruit and syrup mixture in Dutch oven. Using a slotted spoon, spoon the hot fruit into hot jars. Bring syrup to a boil; pour boiling syrup over fruit, leaving ¼-inch headspace; wipe jar rims. Cover with metal lids; screw on bands. Process in boiling-water bath 20 minutes. Yield: 6 half pints.

PEACH PRESERVES

(pictured on page 267)

3 pounds peaches, peeled and quartered
4 cups sugar
1 cup honey
½ medium-size orange, quartered and seeded
½ teaspoon salt (optional)
¼ teaspoon almond extract

Combine peaches, sugar, and honey in a large Dutch oven. Cover and let stand about 45 minutes.

Position knife blade in food processor bowl. Add orange, and top with cover. Process until finely chopped. Measure orange, and add an equal amount of water. Cover and cook over medium heat about 10 minutes or until orange peel is soft.

Bring peaches slowly to a boil, stirring frequently, until sugar dissolves. Bring to a rapid boil, and cook 15 minutes, stirring constantly. Add orange mixture, return to a boil, and cook about 25 minutes or until mixture registers 221° on a candy thermometer; stir mixture frequently. Remove from heat; stir in salt, if desired, and almond extract. Skim off foam with a metal spoon.

Spoon hot preserves into hot jars, leaving ¼-inch headspace; wipe jar rims. Cover with metal lids; screw on bands. Process in boiling-water bath 15 minutes. Yield: 5 half pints.

PEAR BUTTER

10 large ripe pears (5 pounds), quartered and cored
1 cup water
2 cups sugar
½ teaspoon grated orange rind
3 tablespoons orange juice
¼ teaspoon ground nutmeg

Combine pears and water in a large Dutch oven. Cover and cook over medium-low heat 40 minutes or until pears are soft, stirring occasionally. Drain. Press pears through a sieve or food mill; measure 1 quart of puree. Combine 1 quart puree with remaining ingredients in a Dutch oven. Cook over medium heat, stirring frequently, 15 minutes or until mixture thickens. Remove from heat; skim off foam.

Quickly pour hot pear mixture into hot sterilized jars, leaving ¼-inch headspace; wipe jar rims. Cover at once with metal lids, and screw on bands. Process in boiling-water bath 10 minutes. Yield: 2 pints.

CRANBERRY CONSERVE

4 cups fresh cranberries
¾ cup water
3 cups sugar
¾ cup water
1 medium orange, peeled and finely chopped
½ cup chopped pecans or walnuts
⅓ cup raisins

Combine cranberries and ¾ cup water in a Dutch oven; bring to a boil. Cover, reduce heat, and simmer 6 to 8 minutes or until skins pop. Drain fruit, and put through a food mill. Add remaining ingredients; bring to a boil, stirring frequently. Reduce heat and simmer, uncovered, 30 minutes.

Quickly spoon hot conserve into hot jars, leaving ¼-inch headspace; wipe jar rims. Cover jars at once with metal lids, and screw on metal bands. Process in boiling-water bath 15 minutes. Yield: 4 half pints.

DRIED FRUIT CONSERVE

1½ cups (about ½ pound) chopped dried apricots
1⅓ cups (about ½ pound) chopped dried peaches
1⅓ cups (about ½ pound) chopped dried pears
1 medium orange, unpeeled, seeded, and chopped
3 cups water
2 cups sugar
½ cup raisins
1 tablespoon lemon juice
½ teaspoon ground cinnamon
⅛ teaspoon ground cloves
½ cup chopped pecans or walnuts

Combine dried fruit, orange, and water in a large Dutch oven, stirring well. Cover and cook over medium heat 12 to 15 minutes or until fruit is tender.

Stir in remaining ingredients except pecans; bring mixture to a boil. Boil rapidly 10 minutes, stirring frequently. Stir in pecans.

Quickly pour hot conserve into hot jars, leaving ¼-inch headspace; wipe jar rims. Cover jars at once with metal lids, and screw on metal bands. Process in boiling-water bath 15 minutes. Yield: 8 half pints.

More than a Bread Spread

Because of their saucy consistency and sweet flavor, marmalades, preserves, conserves, and jams often serve as sauces to top pound cake slices, miniature cheesecakes, and similar desserts. Just select a fruit spread with a compatible flavor.

Marmalades offer a tangy twist to basic jams; they contain citrus peel and fruit.

MIXED CITRUS MARMALADE

4½ quarts water, divided
1½ cups thinly sliced grapefruit rind
½ cup thinly sliced orange rind
1½ cups chopped grapefruit sections
¾ cup chopped orange sections
½ cup thinly sliced lemon
About 2¼ cups sugar

Combine 1½ quarts water, grapefruit rind, and orange rind in a large Dutch oven; bring to a boil. Boil, uncovered, 5 minutes; drain. Repeat procedure.

Combine remaining 1½ quarts water, boiled rind, chopped fruit, and lemon slices; bring mixture to a boil, and boil 5 minutes. Cover and let stand 12 to 18 hours in a cool place.

Uncover; bring mixture to a boil, and boil 35 to 40 minutes or until rind is tender. Measure amount of fruit and liquid; add 1 cup sugar per 1 cup fruit and liquid. Stir well; bring mixture to a boil, and boil until mixture registers 221° on a candy thermometer, stirring frequently.

Pour boiling marmalade into hot sterilized jars, leaving ¼-inch headspace; wipe jar rims. Cover at once with metal lids, and screw on bands. Process in boiling-water bath 10 minutes. Yield: 3 half pints.

ORANGE-PINEAPPLE MARMALADE

3 medium oranges
1 medium lemon
1 (20-ounce) can crushed unsweetened pineapple, drained
6¾ cups sugar
½ cup hot water
1 (6-ounce) jar maraschino cherries, drained and chopped

Wash oranges and lemon; cut in quarters. Remove seeds and membrane from each piece. Grind unpeeled fruit in meat grinder or food processor.

Combine ground fruit, pineapple, sugar, and water in a Dutch oven; bring to a boil over high heat. Reduce heat; simmer 30 minutes, uncovered, stirring often. Remove from heat; stir in cherries. Pour hot mixture into hot sterilized jars, leaving ¼-inch headspace; wipe jar rims. Cover jars at once with metal lids, and screw on metal bands. Process in boiling-water bath 10 minutes. Yield: 8 half pints.

Fresh From the Freezer

Freezing is probably the easiest method of food preservation, so if your schedule is busy, this is a quick way to put up fresh produce without much special equipment.

Just keep in mind that the key to the best frozen produce is selecting top-quality vegetables and fruit, freezing as quickly as possible, and using the proper containers. The sooner the produce is prepared and frozen after harvesting, the better the flavor will be.

EQUIPMENT

Whether you're freezing vegetables or fruits, you'll need the following items on hand for preparing the produce: knife, cutting board, colander, large measuring container, kitchen scales, and freezer containers. To freeze vegetables, you'll also need equipment for blanching, such as a blancher or a large Dutch oven or saucepan with a wire-mesh basket, and a timer. It's also handy to have another large container to fill with ice water for cooling the vegetables after blanching.

Freezer containers come in many forms. Rigid containers made of plastic or glass are especially good for food packed in liquid. Select freezer containers with straight sides and flat tops for easy stacking. Wide-mouth containers are most convenient for easy removal of partially thawed food. Lids for rigid containers should be tight fitting and can be reinforced with freezer tape.

Plastic freezer bags are the best flexible packaging for dry-packed vegetables and fruits. They may also be used for liquid packs. Wax freezer cartons used with the bags provide extra protection against tearing during storage, but do not use the cartons without freezer bags. See the chart on page 274 to determine headspace recommendations for each type of container.

FREEZING VEGETABLES

Start with just-harvested vegetables at the peak of flavor, and prepare amounts to fill only a few containers at a time. Discard damaged produce. Wash and drain before peeling or shelling, and prepare according to our chart directions.

For the best quality frozen product, most vegetables require **blanching** (exposure to boiling water or steam for a few minutes) to inactivate natural enzymes that cause loss of flavor, color, and texture. Blanching also gives vegetables a brighter color, helps retain nutrients, and destroys surface microorganisms.

Freezing Green Beans Step-By-Step

1. To freeze green beans, wash them, and cut off tips; cut lengthwise into 1- to 2-inch lengths.

2. Blanch beans by submerging in boiling water 3 minutes. Then plunge in ice water to stop the cooking process. Drain well.

3. Place beans in freezer containers, leaving ½-inch headspace. Seal container, and freeze.

4. For tray pack, spread beans in a single layer on a shallow tray, and freeze about 1 hour or until firm. Then package frozen beans, leaving no headspace.

It's important to follow the recommended blanching time for each vegetable. Overblanching causes a loss of color, flavor, and nutrients, while underblanching stimulates rather than inactivates enzymes.

Vegetables need to be cooled immediately after blanching to stop the cooking process. Then drain the vegetables well before packing to eliminate extra moisture, which can cause a noticeable loss of quality during freezing.

Follow these directions for blanching: Heat 1 gallon of water to boiling for each pound of prepared vegetables. (Use 2 gallons per pound for leafy green vegetables.) Place vegetables in a blanching basket, and submerge in boiling water. Cover and begin timing when water returns to a boil.

To stop the cooking process, plunge the basket in ice water, using 1 pound of ice for each pound of vegetables, or hold the vegetables under cold running water. Cool vegetables the same number of minutes recommended for blanching. Drain.

Blanching can be done in the microwave oven or by steaming, but these methods aren't as good as boiling. Research shows that enzymes may not be inactivated in microwave blanching. However, if you plan to use the microwave method, work with small quantities, and use the directions that were designed for your microwave oven.

After blanching, freeze vegetables in a **dry pack** or a **tray pack**. For a dry pack, place cooled vegetables in freezer containers, leaving the recommended headspace, and freeze.

In a tray pack, vegetables are frozen individually so that they remain loose in the package. Simply spread the vegetables in a single layer on a shallow tray, and freeze until firm, checking vegetables every 10 minutes after 1 hour.

Package, leaving no headspace, and freeze. For preparation directions and blanching times for individual vegetables, see the Vegetable Freezing Chart on page 276.

FREEZING FRUIT

Wash and drain fruit before peeling, shelling, pitting, or capping; do not soak the fruit.

Since fruit is naturally acidic, avoid galvanized, copper, or iron utensils in preparation. These materials can react with the acid and make the fruit unsafe.

Enzymes in some fruit, such as apples, peaches, pears, plums, figs, and persimmons, cause browning and loss of vitamin C when the fruit is exposed to air. This can be controlled with ascorbic acid (vitamin C) or a commercial mixture called ascorbic-citric powder.

Ascorbic acid is most effective in controlling browning. It's available in powder, crystalline, or tablet forms and can be found in most drugstores. If ascorbic acid is purchased in tablet form, crush the tablets. Use it according to the instructions included for each type of fruit pack listed. For crushed and pureed fruit, stir dissolved ascorbic acid directly into fruit.

Ascorbic-citric powder, a commercial mixture of ascorbic acid, sugar, and citric acid, also prevents darkening of fruit. Use the powder according to the manufacturer's directions.

Citric acid and lemon juice are occasionally used to prevent discoloration. But they aren't as effective as ascorbic acid and may mask natural fruit flavors.

Fruit may be frozen in one of three ways: unsweetened, with sugar, or in syrup. Sugar and syrup packs give the fruit the best texture and flavor. Berries, blanched apples, rhubarb, and figs freeze quite well unsweetened. Directions for each type of pack are included in the following text. Preparation instructions and recommended packs for individual fruit are listed in the Fruit Freezing Chart on page 277.

Syrup pack: While a 40% sugar syrup is recommended for most fruit

HEADSPACE FOR FILLED FREEZER CONTAINERS			
Liquid pack for vegetables or fruit packed in juice, sugar, syrup or water			
Wide-Mouth Containers		**Narrow-Mouth Containers**	
Pint	Quart	Pint	Quart
½ inch	1 inch	¾ inch	1½ inches
Dry pack for vegetables or fruit packed without added sugar or liquid			
Wide-Mouth Containers		**Narrow-Mouth Containers**	
Pint	Quart	Pint	Quart
½ inch	½ inch	½ inch	½ inch

SUGAR SYRUPS FOR FREEZING FRUIT

Type of Syrup	Sugar (Cups)	Water (Cups)	Yield (Cups)
30%	2	4	5
35%	2½	4	5⅓
40%	3	4	5½
50%	4¾	4	6½

Directions: Combine the sugar and warm water, stirring until sugar dissolves. Chill.

(see the chart on Sugar Syrups for Freezing Fruit), a lighter syrup may be used for mild-flavored fruit to keep from masking the flavor. A heavier, sweeter syrup may be needed for tart fruit, such as sour cherries.

Use the Sugar Syrups chart for directions for making the different syrup concentrations.

Use just enough cold syrup to cover the fruit—usually ½ to ⅔ cup for each pint. Stir dissolved ascorbic acid into syrup just before using to prevent darkening, if necessary. When using rigid containers, place crumpled wax paper between the fruit and the lid to submerge fruit with syrup. Seal, label, and freeze.

Sugar Pack: Spread fruit in a shallow tray, and sprinkle with ascorbic acid dissolved in water to prevent darkening, if necessary. Sprinkle fruit with recommended amount of sugar, and let stand 10 to 15 minutes to draw out juices and allow the sugar to dissolve. Stir gently to coat fruit, and package with juices. Seal, label, and freeze.

Unsweetened packs: For a **liquid pack**, fruit may be frozen unsweetened in water containing ascorbic acid, if needed, or in unsweetened juice. Package as for syrup pack, using chilled liquid.

For unsweetened **dry pack**, place fruit in containers, leaving recommended headspace, and freeze. Ascorbic acid dissolved in water may be sprinkled over fruit before packing, if necessary. Fruit pieces can be frozen separately in a **tray pack**, making it easy to measure fruit without thawing. To prepare a tray pack, spread fruit in a single layer; sprinkle with dissolved ascorbic acid, if necessary. Place tray in freezer, and freeze just until fruit is firm; package, leaving no headspace. Seal, label, and return to freezer.

PACKAGING THE FRUIT

Food will be more convenient to use if packed in amounts to be used for a single meal or recipe. Freezer containers should be no larger than ½-gallon capacity; food packed in larger containers freezes too slowly for a quality product.

Have all the food cooled before packing to help speed freezing. Be sure syrup or juice for liquid packs is chilled before using. Pack food tightly in the containers to leave as little air as possible, but leave recommended headspace to allow for expansion during freezing.

With freezer bags, press all the air from the bag starting at the bottom, working your way to the opening. Twist tightly, and double back the top of the bag. Secure with a rubber band, string, or twist tie.

When sealing food in rigid freezer containers, keep the edge free from food or moisture to ensure a good seal. The lids should be tight fitting and may be reinforced with freezer tape, if necessary.

FREEZING TIPS

- Freeze food as soon as it is packaged and sealed. Be sure to label with the date frozen, package contents, and amount.
- Place in the freezer only the amount of food that will freeze within 24 hours (about 2 or 3 pounds of food per cubic foot of freezer space is about right). Food is best frozen quickly, and overloading slows the freezing rate.
- Place packages in contact with the surface in the coldest part of the freezer. Leave some space between packages for air circulation. After a period of freezing, the packages may be stacked or stored close together.
- Freeze food at 0° or lower. For rapid freezing, set the temperature at -10° a day in advance. Once food is frozen, return the temperature setting to 0°. If food is stored above 0°, quality decreases.
- Accidentally thawed vegetables may be refrozen only if ice crystals are still present, or if the freezer temperature is 40° or below.
- Accidentally thawed fruit may be refrozen if it shows no signs of spoilage. You may want to use the thawed fruit for cooking or making jellies, jams, and sauces.
- Vegetables and most fruits retain good quality in the freezer for eight to twelve months, citrus fruit for four to six months.

VEGETABLE FREEZING CHART

Vegetable	Preparation	Blanching Time
Beans (butter, lima, and pinto)	Choose tender beans with well-filled pods. Shell and wash; then sort according to size.	Small beans, 2 minutes; medium beans, 3 minutes; large beans, 4 minutes
Beans (green, snap, and waxed)	Select tender young pods. Wash beans, and cut off tips. Cut lengthwise or in 1- or 2-inch lengths.	3 minutes
Corn (on the cob)	Husk corn, and remove silks; trim and wash.	Small ears, 7 minutes; medium ears, 9 minutes; large ears, 11 minutes
Corn (whole kernel)	Blanch ears first. Then cut kernels from cob about ⅔ depth of kernels.	4 minutes
Corn (cream-style)	Blanch ears first. Cut off tips of kernels. Scrape cobs with back of a knife to remove juice and hearts of kernels.	4 minutes
Greens (beet, chard, collards, mustard, spinach, turnip)	Select tender, green leaves. Wash thoroughly, and remove woody stems.	Collards, 3 minutes; other greens, 2 minutes
Okra	Select tender green pods. Wash and sort according to size. Remove stems at end of seed cells. After blanching, leave pods whole or slice crosswise.	Small pods, 3 minutes; large pods, 4 minutes
Peas (black-eyed and field)	Select pods with tender, barely mature peas. Shell and wash peas; discard hard, immature, and overly mature ones.	2 minutes
Peas (green)	Select tender young peas. Shell and wash.	1½ minutes
Peppers (green and sweet red)	Select crisp, tender, green or red pods. Wash peppers; cut off tops; remove seeds and membrane. Dice peppers; cut in halves, or cut in ½-inch strips or rings. Pack raw, or blanch, if desired.	(Blanching is optional.) Pepper halves, 3 minutes; strips or rings, 2 minutes
Peppers (hot)	Wash peppers; remove stems. Place in containers leaving no headspace.	Not required
Squash (summer)	Select young squash with small seeds and tender rind. Wash and cut into ½-inch slices.	3 minutes
Tomatoes	Raw: Dip tomatoes in boiling water 30 seconds to loosen skins. Core and peel. Chop or quarter tomatoes, or leave whole. Pack, leaving 1-inch headspace.	Stewed: Remove stem end and core from tomatoes; peel and quarter tomatoes. Cover and cook until tender (10 to 20 minutes). Place pan containing cooked tomatoes in cold water to cool. Pack, leaving recommended headspace for liquid pack.

FRUIT FREEZING CHART

Fruit	Preparation	Type of Pack (syrup, sugar, unsweetened, puree)	Remarks
Apples	Wash, peel, and core. For sugar pack, apples may be steam blanched 1½ to 2 minutes to retain shape and color.	**Syrup:** 40% **Sugar:** use ½ cup sugar/1 quart apples	To prevent browning, use ½ teaspoon ascorbic acid per quart of syrup for syrup pack. Sprinkle ¼ teaspoon ascorbic acid mixed with ¼ cup water over each quart for sugar pack.
Blackberries, Dewberries, Raspberries	Select fully ripe berries. Wash quickly; remove caps and drain.	**Syrup:** 40% **Sugar:** use ¾ cup sugar/1 quart berries **Unsweetened:** dry pack **Puree:** 1 cup sugar/1 quart pureed berries	Freeze well in unsweetened tray pack.
Blueberries, Huckleberries	Select fully ripe berries. For unsweetened pack, do not wash.	**Unsweetened:** dry pack **Puree:** 1 cup sugar/1 quart pureed berries	Wash berries frozen in unsweetened pack before using.
Figs	Select soft-ripe figs. Make sure they are not sour in centers. Sort, wash, and cut off stems; do not peel. Halve or leave whole.	**Syrup:** 35% **Unsweetened:** dry or liquid pack	To prevent browning, use ¾ teaspoon ascorbic acid per quart of syrup for syrup pack or per 1 quart water for unsweetened liquid pack. May use ½ cup lemon juice per quart syrup instead of ascorbic acid.
Peaches, Nectarines	Select firm, ripe peaches. Peel; halve or slice.	**Syrup:** 40% **Sugar:** use ⅔ cup sugar/1 quart peaches **Unsweetened:** liquid pack **Puree:** use 1 cup sugar/1 quart pureed peaches	To prevent browning, use ½ teaspoon ascorbic acid per quart of syrup for syrup pack or 1 teaspoon ascorbic acid per quart of water for unsweetened pack. Sprinkle ¼ teaspoon ascorbic acid mixed with ¼ cup water over each quart for sugar pack. Use ⅛ teaspoon ascorbic acid per quart of puree.
Pears	Peel pears; cut in halves or quarters, and remove cores. Heat pears in boiling syrup 1 to 2 minutes. Drain and cool. Chill the syrup.	**Syrup:** 40%	To prevent browning, use ¾ teaspoon ascorbic acid per quart of cold syrup.
Persimmons	Select orange-colored, soft-ripe persimmons. Peel, cut into quarters, and remove seeds. Press pulp through a sieve to puree.	**Sugar:** use 1 cup sugar/1 quart puree **Unsweetened:** dry pack	To prevent browning, use ⅛ teaspoon ascorbic acid per quart of puree.
Plums	Select firm, ripe plums. Sort and wash. Leave whole or cut into halves or quarters; remove pits.	**Syrup:** 40% to 50%	To prevent browning, use 1 teaspoon ascorbic acid per quart of syrup.
Strawberries	Select fully ripe, firm, deep-red berries. Wash a few at a time; drain and remove caps.	**Syrup:** 50% **Sugar:** use ¾ cup sugar/1 quart whole berries	Strawberries may be crushed or sliced for sugar pack.

Food Dehydration

More and more people are discovering that food dehydration is also a good way to preserve the summer taste and nutrients of fruits and vegetables. Vegetable soup made from your own dehydrated vegetables will certainly taste good during the winter, and dried vegetables as salad garnishes are a delicious supplement to out-of-season grocery produce.

All fruits and some vegetables are suitable to eat dry, and drying intensifies the flavors of the foods. Dried fruit can also be easily rehydrated (water added) and baked in breads or desserts.

CHOOSING YOUR DEHYDRATOR

Commercial dehydrators are available in a variety of sizes, shapes, and prices. Consider these variables, as well as the following factors.

Most dehydrators are cabinet models that have pull-out drying trays. Others are modular units with stackable trays. Dehydration racks are also offered with many convection ovens. We found that convection drying works as well as drying in a regular dehydrator. Just be sure that your convection oven has 140° (the most typical drying temperature) on its temperature dial.

Regular dehydrators either offer a thermostat to use in selecting a dehydration temperature, or they are set to dry automatically at about 140°. A timer is an optional but helpful feature on a dehydrator.

Choose a dehydrator with mesh-type trays; the mesh openings should be fine enough to contain small pieces of food but large enough to allow a good air flow. Make sure the trays are easy to remove and clean. In general, plastic trays are easier to keep clean than metal trays.

HOW TO DRY FOOD

Drying food is simple in a commercial dehydrator. Start with fresh, high-quality produce. Wash well and prepare it according to the Fruit and Vegetable Dehydration Chart on the opposite page. Discard any bruised or overripe areas. Make all slices the same size so that slices will dry in the same length of time.

Foods that brown easily after slicing require special treatment. Dilute commercial ascorbic-citric powder as the package directs, dip in the cut food, and pat dry.

Some foods require steam blanching before drying. Our chart will indicate whether steam blanching is necessary. To steam blanch, place 1 to 2 inches of water in a large saucepan and bring to a rolling boil. Place food no more than 2½ inches deep

Foods dried in a dehydrator take on a whole new look, texture, size, and lasting ability.

FRUIT AND VEGETABLE DEHYDRATION CHART

Fruit or Vegetable/ Preparation	Drying Time at 140°	Treatment/ Storage Time
Apples Peel and core; slice into ⅛-inch rings. Dip in ascorbic acid solution or steam blanch 8 minutes; pat dry.	Dry 4 to 5 hours or until leathery but still pliable. No moistness should remain in center.	Condition. Store up to 6 months.
Bananas Peel and slice ⅛-inch thick. Dip in ascorbic acid solution; pat dry.	Dry 4 to 6 hours or until slightly pliable but crisp.	Condition. Store up to 4 months.
Carrots Wash and scrape; slice ⅛-inch thick. Steam blanch 5 minutes; pat dry.	Dry 2 to 4 hours or until very tough and brittle.	Store up to 6 months.
Corn Husk ears and remove silk; wash and steam blanch whole ears 5 minutes. Cut corn from cobs.	Dry 5 to 7 hours or until brittle, stirring occasionally.	Store up to 8 months.
Green Peas Shell and wash peas. Steam blanch 3 minutes; pat dry.	Dry 5 to 6 hours until shriveled and hard.	Store up to 6 months.
Grapes Wash seedless grapes and steam blanch 30 seconds or until skins crack; pat dry.	Dry 32 to 34 hours or until grapes look like raisins and there's no moisture in center.	Condition. Store up to 6 months.
Green Beans Wash and string beans. Diagonally slice into 1-inch lengths. Steam blanch 4 minutes; pat dry and freeze on drying tray 40 minutes.	Dry 6 to 10 hours or until shriveled and brittle.	Store up to 6 months.
Green Peppers Wash, stem, and core. Cut into ½-inch cubes. Steam blanch 3 minutes; pat dry.	Dry 9 to 11 hours or until brittle.	Store up to 12 months.
Nectarines Wash, peel, and pit; slice ⅛-inch thick. Dip in ascorbic acid solution or steam blanch 5 minutes; pat dry.	Dry 5 to 6 hours or until leathery but still pliable. No moistness should remain in center.	Store up to 6 months.
Okra Wash and steam blanch 4 minutes. Slice ¼-inch thick.	Dry 4 to 6 hours or until tough.	Store up to 6 months.
Peaches Wash, peel, and pit; slice ⅛-inch thick. Dip in ascorbic acid solution or steam blanch 8 minutes; pat dry.	Dry 9 to 11 hours or until leathery, but still pliable and there's no moisture in center.	Condition. Store up to 6 months.
Pineapple Wash, peel, and remove thorny eyes. Core and slice crosswise ⅛-inch thick.	Dry 7 to 12 hours or until leathery and not sticky.	Condition. Store up to 8 months.
Tomatoes Wash and dip in boiling water 30 seconds. Peel away skins. Slice ⅛-inch thick.	Dry 5 to 7 hours or until tough.	Store up to 4 months.

Drying times given here are for reference only. Examine each batch of food carefully to determine exact doneness.

in the pan on a rack that holds the food just above the water. Cover the pan and allow food to steam as directed. Food should be loosely packed so that steam can penetrate it. After steaming, gently pat the food dry.

DRYING TIMES VARY

Drying times for the foods listed in our chart vary depending on the amount, type, and size of food being dried, humidity, dehydrator efficiency, and excess moisture in the food. Therefore, drying times given here are for reference only. Examine each batch of food carefully to determine exact doneness.

When properly dried, most fruits are leathery and vegetables are brittle. Periodically remove a piece of food, let it cool, then feel and taste it, checking its texture against that described in our drying chart. No more than 5% moisture should remain for dried vegetables, and no more than 10% to 15% for dried fruit. Adding new food to food already being dried will increase the drying time of the partially dried food.

AFTER FOODS ARE DRIED

Some fruit requires additional treatment after drying to prevent spoilage and to make sure the food is equally and thoroughly dry. To "condition" dried fruit, loosely pack it into plastic or glass containers, filling them about two-thirds full. Cover tightly and let stand 7 to 10 days, shaking container daily, to let the drier pieces absorb excess moisture from other pieces. Shake the containers each day to separate the pieces, and, if condensation occurs in the containers, return the fruit to the dehydrator for additional drying.

STORING AND USING DRIED FOODS

Dried foods require less than one-third the storage space of foods preserved by other techniques. Storage life of dried food varies with storage conditions and the amount of moisture remaining in the food. Once cooled, immediately transfer the food to proper storage containers. Package it first in plastic bags; then seal plastic bags in a container with a tight fitting lid. If dried food is not packaged well, it may reabsorb moisture from the atmosphere, which can lead to spoilage.

Wrap each type of food separately, and package it in bags in amounts that can be used within several days of opening. Label each container with the date and contents, and store it in a dark, cool, dry place.

The shelf life of dried foods depends on proper drying and storage. Check the chart for length of storage for each specific food, but remember that the food will not keep as long if it is not thoroughly dry or if it reabsorbs moisture from the atmosphere. Generally, the lower the storage temperature, the longer the food will last. Freezing dried foods is a common practice that prolongs storage life; the dried foods take up little space in the freezer since drying greatly reduces the bulk.

REHYDRATING DRIED FOODS

Many dried foods will rehydrate to a state that looks almost like the raw product. But sometimes there is a loss of texture. For this reason, dried food is often more suitable for inclusion in recipes than being eaten by itself. To rehydrate, soak the dried food in water to cover; then simmer it to make it tender.

Dehydrating Carrots Step-By-Step

1. To dry carrots, wash, scrape, and slice. Steam blanch 5 minutes; pat dry. Arrange on drying trays, and dry 4 to 6 hours.

2. Carrots are thoroughly dried when they shrivel and look very dry and brittle.

Dehydration saves storage space. These whole carrots are equal in weight to the original weight of the dried carrots; contrast with rehydrated carrots (foreground).

Salad Sprinkles and Vegetable Soup Mix are two tasty ways to use dried vegetables. Toss dried fruit into granola (after baking) or eat it as a snack.

SALAD SPRINKLES

⅓ cup grated Parmesan cheese
2 tablespoons dried sliced carrots
2 tablespoons dried diced green pepper
8 dried tomato slices
¼ teaspoon garlic salt
¼ teaspoon pepper
2 tablespoons sunflower kernels

Combine first 6 ingredients in container of an electric blender; process until vegetables are flaked. (Make sure blender is dry, or vegetables will clump together.) Combine vegetable mixture and sunflower kernels. Store in airtight container in cool, dry place for up to 1 month. Serve over shredded lettuce with desired dressing. Yield: ½ cup.

BEEF JERKY

1 (1-pound) flank steak
½ cup soy sauce
Garlic powder
Lemon-pepper seasoning

Slice steak across the grain into ¼-inch strips. Combine meat and soy sauce; toss to coat evenly. Drain and discard soy sauce.

Sprinkle both sides of strips lightly with seasonings. Place strips in a single layer on an ungreased baking sheet. Bake at 140° to 150° for 10 hours. (Do not allow temperature to go above 150°.) Let cool, and store in an airtight container. Yield: ½ pound.

Note: To prepare in a dehydrator, arrange beef slices in single layers on trays; dry 5 to 7 hours.

VEGETABLE SOUP MIX

¼ cup dried sliced carrots
¼ cup dried cut corn
¼ cup dried cut green beans
¼ cup dried green peas
¼ cup dried sliced okra
¼ cup dried sliced tomato
2 tablespoons dried diced green
   pepper

Combine all ingredients in a freezer container or plastic bag. Freeze up to 8 months. Yield: enough for 7 cups soup.

Vegetable Soup

1 package Vegetable Soup Mix
6½ cups water
3 chicken-flavored bouillon cubes
½ teaspoon pepper
¼ teaspoon onion powder
1 bay leaf

Combine vegetable soup mix and water in a large Dutch oven; let soak 1½ hours. Add remaining ingredients, and bring to a boil; cover, reduce heat, and simmer 1 hour or until vegetables are tender. Remove bay leaf. Yield: 7 cups.

Strawberry Leather Step-By-Step

1. To make Strawberry Leather, puree fresh strawberries into a smooth liquid, stir in lemon juice and corn syrup, and dehydrate on a plastic wrap-lined tray.

2. Roll Strawberry Leather jellyroll fashion; then cut into small logs and cover tightly with plastic wrap.

3. To shape cake decorations, simply cut the leather into desired shapes, and press pieces together firmly to make them adhere. Wooden picks secure decorations to cake.

STRAWBERRY LEATHER

Strawberry Leather is made by pureeing fresh strawberries into a smooth liquid, then drying the puree in a thin sheet (in a convection oven or dehydrator) to a leather-like texture and appearance. The leather will hold its shape when pulled from the drying tray.

To store fruit leather, roll it jellyroll fashion and cut into 2-inch logs; seal each tightly in plastic wrap. Store in a cool dry place for up to a week or in the freezer for up to 6 months.

To shape cake-decorating flowers or bows from Strawberry Leather, simply cut the leather into desired shapes and gently press pieces together to make them stick. Insert one end of a wooden pick just through the bottom of the design, and insert the other end of the wooden pick into the cake.

About 3 cups fresh strawberries
1 tablespoon lemon juice
1 tablespoon light corn syrup

Place strawberries in container of an electric blender; process until smooth. Measure 2 cups of strawberry puree; stir in lemon juice and corn syrup.

Line a 15- x 10- x 1-inch jellyroll pan with heavy-duty plastic wrap, and tape plastic wrap to pan at corners. Pour pureed strawberry mixture into prepared pan and spread, leaving a 1-inch margin on all sides. (Adjust the size and shape of the pan, if necessary, to fit your dehydrator. Keep the layer of strawberry mixture at the same thickness.)

Dry in convection oven or dehydrator at 150° for 7½ to 8 hours or until surface is dry and no longer sticky.

Remove leather from pan while still warm; beginning with short end, roll up jellyroll fashion. Cut into logs, and wrap in plastic wrap. Yield: 5 (2-inch) logs.

MEATS

Whether it's a pot roast for Sunday dinner, a beautifully glazed ham for the holidays, or barbecued ribs still sizzling from the grill, Southerners enjoy eating all kinds of meat. And with so many different cuts to choose from, and so many ways to prepare them, the cook can hardly be at a loss for possibilities when someone asks, "What's for dinner?"

EQUIPMENT

You'll need two types of roasting pans. One should be deep and have a lid, much like a Dutch oven. The other should be a shallow roasting pan with a rack that you can use for dry heat roasting; it won't have a lid. You'll also want a good quality heavy skillet with a lid.

A meat mallet is frequently called for to pound various cuts of meat. And if you're particular about whether your roast is cooked to rare or medium-rare, invest in a meat thermometer. It's the only way to be certain your meat is cooked to the degree of doneness you desire.

WHAT AND HOW MUCH MEAT TO BUY

All fresh meat that is sold across state lines carries a stamp that says "U. S. Inspected and Passed" so you can be sure the meat is accurately labeled, is of good quality, and was processed under sanitary conditions. You may not actually see the stamp on meat packaged for retail sale, since the stamp is placed on larger wholesale cuts.

Marinate Spicy Beef Tenderloin (page 289) 8 hours; then cook it just to the degree of doneness you prefer. Serve the leftover marinade on the side.

The grading of meat is a voluntary program in which beef, veal, and lamb are judged on the basis of quality and taste. You'll find the grades in a shield-shaped stamp indicating, in descending order of grade, USDA PRIME, CHOICE, SELECT, STANDARD, COMMERCIAL, and UTILITY. PRIME is usually available only to restaurants. CHOICE is what you normally see in markets. Grades below SELECT are used by packers of processed meats and are not available at the meat counter. Pork is usually not graded at the consumer level because much of it is processed into sausage and ham and carries a packer's guarantee of quality.

These purple stamps that indicate inspection and grading need not be cut away from the meat; they're made from harmless vegetable dyes.

When buying meat, consider the cost per serving rather than the cost per pound. A lot of bone and fat in cheaper cuts of meat reduces the amount of edible meat, actually making some more expensive cuts your best buy.

Boneless meats, such as ground beef, stew meat, and boneless roasts and steaks, usually serve three to four people per pound. Roasts and steaks with only a moderate amount of bone will serve two to three people per pound. For boney meats, like spareribs, allow ¾ to 1 pound per serving.

STORING AND FREEZING MEAT

Place meat in the coldest part of your refrigerator as soon as possible after purchase. Prepackaged meat may be stored unopened in its wrapper; use ground meat within two days, and larger roasts and steaks within two to four days. Or, freeze it without rewrapping, and use it within two weeks. For longer freezer storage, overwrap the original package with special moistureproof, vaporproof freezer paper. Roasts and steaks will stay fresh in the freezer six to twelve months. Freeze ground meat or stew meat only three to four months. Leftover cooked meat will maintain good quality up to three months. Meat that has been frozen and thawed should be used immediately, and don't plan to refreeze it once thawed.

COOKING METHODS FOR MEAT

To determine the best way to cook a cut of meat, it's important to know whether the cut is classified as a "tender" or "less tender" one. Tenderness is determined by the location of the cut on the carcass. Tender cuts come mainly from the rib, loin, and short loin sections, the areas along the backbone. These sections include the more expensive cuts, such as rib roast, rib-eye steaks, and sirloin steaks. When preparing them, you'll want to roast, broil, pan-broil, or fry—cooking methods especially suited to tender cuts.

The less tender cuts, usually less expensive, include the chuck, foreshank, brisket, short plate, tip, and round. These are taken from the shoulder, legs, breast, and flanks, or areas with heavy muscle development. The additional muscle or connective tissue makes the cuts from these areas tougher. But by using the proper cooking method, you can make them fork-tender. Braising and cooking in liquid are two methods that make tough cuts, such as round steak, as tender as a fine steak.

Here are some specifics on the various cooking methods.

Roasting: To roast means to cook by dry heat in an oven without the addition of liquid. Roasting is best for large tender cuts of meat, such as rib roast and rolled rump roast.

Place the roast, fat side up, on a rack in a shallow roasting pan. The fat self-bastes the roast during cooking. Insert a meat thermometer so the bulb sits in muscle tissue, not in fat or against a bone. Don't cover the roast or add water. Cook at 275° to 325° until it reaches the degree of doneness you desire.

Broiling: To broil means to cook by direct heat in an oven. This method is ideal for cooking tender steaks, such as rib eye, porterhouse, or sirloin, and ground meat patties.

Set the oven on broil. Depending on the thickness of the cut, place the meat 2 to 5 inches from the broiler element (steaks and patties that are ¾ to 1 inch thick need to be 2 to 3 inches from the element—thicker cuts should cook 3 to 5 inches from the heat source). Broil until the top browns; the meat should be about half cooked at this point. Season with salt and pepper now. (Don't salt before cooking because salt draws out the moisture and inhibits browning.) Turn and brown the other side. Season again, if desired, before serving.

Pan-Broiling: To pan-broil is to cook by direct heat in a pan. This method is used for cooking the same cuts as for broiling, but the cooking is done in a skillet or on a griddle, not the oven.

When pan-broiling, don't add fat or water to the skillet unless the cut is extremely lean and a bit of fat is needed to prevent sticking. Spray the pan with vegetable cooking spray if you like. Cook the meat slowly over medium low heat, turning occasionally, making sure the meat browns evenly. Don't overcook; this method is faster than broiling. Also, don't let fat accumulate as you cook, or you'll be frying, not pan-broiling.

Pan-Frying: Fried meats are cooked in oil over medium heat. For pan-frying, use a small amount of oil; for deep fat frying, use enough oil to completely cover the meat. Pan-frying is best for tender meat, such as cubed beef steaks about ¼ to 1 inch thick or round steak, tenderized by pounding.

To fry, heat oil over medium heat. When hot, add the meat and brown it. Don't cover the skillet because you'll lose crispness. Continue to cook on medium heat until done, turning occasionally. Remove from pan and serve. Lower the heat if the fat begins smoking.

Braising: Braised meats are cooked slowly in a small amount of liquid. The slow cooking and moisture are vital for tenderizing tough cuts of meat. Top and bottom round steak, flank steak, arm pot roasts, and blade roasts are all good choices for braising.

To braise, first brown the meat in a small amount of fat; then pour off the pan drippings. The browning adds flavor and improves the appearance. Season the meat; add a small amount of liquid, such as bouillon, soup, tomato juice, or water. Cover tightly, and simmer until tender. Depending on the size of the meat cut, braising could take 1 to 4 hours. You may want to make gravy with the pan drippings.

Cooking in Liquid: To cook in liquid, cover the meat completely with water. Corned beef, beef brisket, and stew meat are best prepared using this method.

First, brown the meat, then cover with water and add seasonings. Cover with a lid, and simmer gently until tender. Boiling tends to dry out the meat and increases shrinkage. If vegetables are to be cooked with the meat, add them near the end of the cooking time. That way, they'll have just enough time to cook without overcooking.

IF YOUR MEAT NEEDS TENDERIZING

You can use several techniques to make less tender cuts of meat more tender. Using tenderizers means you can cook more cuts of meat by dry heat methods, and you can reduce the cooking time for some of those cooked by moist heat.

Consider *marinating* the meat in an acid marinade such as wine, vinegar, or citrus juice. This softens the connective tissue of the meat and makes it more tender. Let the meat marinate several hours in the refrigerator before cooking. Don't let it marinate any longer than this, or the texture of the meat can break down too much.

Pounding the meat with a meat mallet also tenderizes the connective tissue. Having the butcher run thin cuts of meat through the "cubing machine" serves the same function.

Commercial meat tenderizers are also available. They are derivatives of certain tropical fruits that contain a natural tenderizing agent (papain). Be sure to follow package directions. The meat can become mushy if you use more meat tenderizer than directed or leave the tenderizer on for longer than recommended.

DEPEND ON A MEAT THERMOMETER

Suggested cooking times for cuts of meat aren't always accurate, because the shape and thickness of the meat will vary, as will the temperature of the meat before it is cooked. You can't visually judge the doneness either. For the most accurate results, use a meat thermometer when cooking large roasts.

Insert the meat thermometer at an angle into the thickest part of the meat, making sure the bulb doesn't touch fat or bone. Have the top of the thermometer as far away as possible from the heating element.

Meat continues to cook slightly after it's removed from the heat source, especially large roasts. For this reason, remove the meat when it registers about 5° lower than the desired temperature. Watch and make sure the temperature indeed rises to the desired level as it stands.

Beef

From grilled hamburgers to a roasted tenderloin prepared to just the right degree of doneness, beef offers more variety in cuts and cooking methods than any other type of meat. Unfortunately, the names of cuts vary from state to state, and even from store to store, making it sometimes difficult to locate the exact cut of meat that a recipe calls for. The names of cuts specified in our recipes seem to be the most commonly found ones, but ask your butcher for advice if you're unable to locate a particular one.

WHAT TO LOOK FOR

Beef should have bright red meat and white fat; the bone should be red. Look for beef that is fine-textured, firm, and slightly moist. The most tender beef has a delicate network of fat running through it, called marbling. This fat dissolves during cooking and serves as a self-baster helping to keep the meat tender and moist.

Ground beef offers more variety in labeling than other cuts of beef. Federal regulations allow that meat labeled "ground beef" can contain up to 30% fat. "Lean ground beef" or "ground chuck" can contain up to 20% fat, while "extra-lean ground beef" or "ground round" can have no more that 15% fat. You can see the difference in these meats at a glance. The more fat the meat contains, the paler the meat will be. The price will also decrease. Just because ground beef is cheaper doesn't make it a better buy. Most of the fat cooks out of the meat anyway and will only be discarded. Expect more shrinkage in recipes made from ground beef.

Beef

• RETAIL CUTS •
WHERE THEY COME FROM
HOW TO COOK THEM

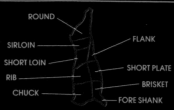

ROUND
SIRLOIN
SHORT LOIN
RIB
CHUCK
FLANK
SHORT PLATE
BRISKET
FORE SHANK

ROUND

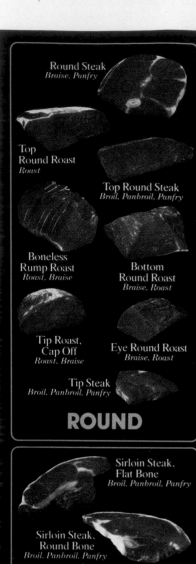

Round Steak
Braise, Panfry

Top Round Roast
Roast

Top Round Steak
Broil, Panbroil, Panfry

Boneless Rump Roast
Roast, Braise

Bottom Round Roast
Braise, Roast

Tip Roast, Cap Off
Roast, Braise

Eye Round Roast
Braise, Roast

Tip Steak
Broil, Panbroil, Panfry

SIRLOIN

Sirloin Steak, Flat Bone
Broil, Panbroil, Panfry

Sirloin Steak, Round Bone
Broil, Panbroil, Panfry

Top Sirloin Steak
Broil, Panbroil Panfry

FORE SHANK & BRISKET

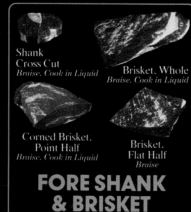

Shank Cross Cut
Braise, Cook in Liquid

Brisket, Whole
Braise, Cook in Liquid

Corned Brisket, Point Half
Braise, Cook in Liquid

Brisket, Flat Half
Braise

CHUCK

Chuck Eye Roast
Braise, Roast

Boneless Top Blade Steak
Braise, Panfry

Arm Pot Roast
Braise

Boneless Shoulder Pot Roast
Braise

Cross Rib Pot Roast
Braise

Mock Tender
Braise

Blade Roast
Braise

Under Blade Pot Roast
Braise, Roast

7-Bone Pot Roast
Braise

Short Ribs
Braise, Cook in Liquid

Flanken-Style Ribs
Braise, Cook in Liquid

THIS CHART APPROVED BY
NATIONAL LIVE STOCK & MEAT BOARD

SHORT LOIN

T-Bone Steak
Broil, Panbroil, Panfry

Boneless Top Loin Steak
Broil, Panbroil, Panfry

Porterhouse Steak
Broil, Panbroil, Panfry

Tenderloin Roast
Roast, Broil

Tenderloin Steak
Broil, Panbroil, Panfry

RIB

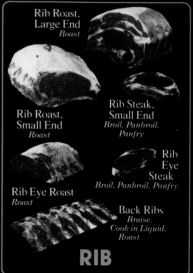

Rib Roast, Large End
Roast

Rib Roast, Small End
Roast

Rib Steak, Small End
Broil, Panbroil, Panfry

Rib Eye Roast
Roast

Rib Eye Steak
Broil, Panbroil, Panfry

Back Ribs
Braise, Cook in Liquid, Roast

FLANK & SHORT PLATE

Flank Steak
Broil, Braise, Panfry

Flank Steak Rolls
Braise, Broil, Panbroil, Panfry

Skirt Steak
Braise, Broil, Panbroil, Panfry

OTHER CUTS

Ground Beef
Broil, Panfry, Panbroil, Roast (Bake)

Cubed Steak
Panfry, Braise

Beef for Stew
Braise, Cook in Liquid

Cubes for Kabobs
Broil, Braise

BEEF FROM THE MICROWAVE

Many cooks have been disappointed with the results when they've cooked beef in their microwave oven. The key to success is selecting a cut that is suitable for microwaving, and following certain cooking techniques.

The microwave oven is not a good choice for roasts normally cooked by dry heat methods. Meat will not brown in a microwave oven, nor will it end up with the same outside texture it develops when roasted in a conventional oven.

Some pot roasts do well in the microwave, however. They're best microwaved in an oven roasting bag at MEDIUM LOW (30% power). Using MEDIUM LOW instead of HIGH power prolongs the cooking time, but ensures more uniform doneness and reduces shrinkage.

Some meat loaves work well in the microwave, too, and they cook significantly quicker than when cooked conventionally. Meat loaves that have a sauce or cheese topping are more pleasing than plain loaves since the meat will not brown. When adapting conventional recipes for the microwave, shape the meat into a round loaf to eliminate corners that might overcook.

It's easy to brown ground beef in the microwave to speed you up in recipes that call for the beef already cooked. Just crumble 1 pound of beef into a microwave-safe bowl, cover with heavy-duty plastic wrap, and microwave at HIGH for 5 to 7 minutes or until done, stirring twice. Drain well.

TIMETABLE FOR ROASTING BEEF

Cut	Approximate Weight in Pounds	Internal Temperature	Approximate Total Cooking Times at 325°F. in Hours
Standing ribs* (10-inch ribs)	4	140°F. (rare)	1¾
		160°F. (medium)	2
		170°F. (well done)	2½
	6	140°F. (rare)	2
		160°F. (medium)	2½
		170°F. (well done)	3½
	8	140°F. (rare)	2½
		160°F. (medium)	3
		170°F. (well done)	4½
Rolled ribs	4	140°F. (rare)	2
		160°F. (medium)	2½
		170°F. (well done)	3
	6	140°F. (rare)	3
		160°F. (medium)	3¼
		170°F. (well done)	4
Rolled rump	5	140°F. (rare)	2¼
		160°F. (medium)	3
		170°F. (well done)	3¼
Sirloin tip	3	140°F. (rare)	1½
		160°F. (medium)	2
		170°F. (well done)	2¼

Standing ribs (8-inch ribs) allow 30 minutes longer

BEEF AU JUS

1 (7-pound) rolled rib roast
Salt and pepper

Sprinkle roast with salt and pepper; place roast, fat side up, on rack in a roasting pan. Insert meat thermometer, making sure it does not touch fat or bone. Bake at 325° for 2½ hours or until meat thermometer registers 150° (medium-rare). Bake until thermometer registers 160° for medium or 170° for well done. Transfer roast to platter, reserving drippings and meat particles in roasting pan; cover roast with aluminum foil. Pour pan drippings into a measuring cup; skim off fat, and reserve drippings. (Chill pan drippings for easy removal of fat, if desired.)

Add 1 cup boiling water to meat particles in roasting pan; stir well to scrape crusty particles from bottom of pan. Stir in reserved drippings. Cook mixture over medium heat until reduced by about half. Strain drippings; discard. Season gravy as desired, and serve with roast. Yield: 12 servings.

Note: One-half teaspoon beef-flavored bouillon granules per cup of drippings may be stirred into drippings if richer flavor is desired.

Carving a Beef Rib Roast

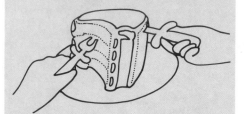

Place roast on platter with the large end down. Insert carving fork just below the first rib. Slice horizontally from the fat side of the meat through to the rib bone.

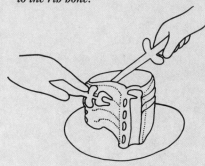

Slice along the rib bone to release each slice. Slide knife under each slice; lift and remove slice to plate.

STANDING RIB ROAST

1 (6½-pound) standing rib roast
Salt and pepper
Yorkshire Pudding (page 85)
Spiced crabapples (optional)
Fresh parsley sprigs (optional)

Sprinkle roast with salt and pepper. Place roast, fat side up, on rack in a shallow roasting pan. Insert meat thermometer, making sure it does not touch fat or bone.

Bake roast at 325° as follows, depending on the desired degree of doneness: rare, 20 minutes per pound or 140° on meat thermometer; medium, 25 minutes per pound or 160°; well done, 35 minutes per pound or 170°.

Remove rib roast to a serving platter, reserving ¼ cup clear pan drippings to make Yorkshire Pudding. Garnish the rib roast with spiced crabapples and fresh parsley sprigs, if desired. Serve the rib roast with Yorkshire Pudding. Yield: 12 servings.

SPICY RIB-EYE ROAST

1 (6-pound) boneless rib-eye roast
⅓ to ½ cup coarse or cracked pepper
½ teaspoon ground cardamom
1 cup soy sauce
¾ cup red wine vinegar
1 tablespoon tomato paste
1 teaspoon paprika
½ teaspoon garlic powder

Trim excess fat from roast. Combine pepper and cardamom; pat onto roast.

Place roast in a large, shallow dish.

Combine soy sauce and next 4 ingredients; pour over roast. Cover and marinate 8 hours in refrigerator, turning occasionally.

Remove roast from marinade; discard marinade. Wrap roast in foil, and place in a shallow pan. Insert meat thermometer, making an opening so thermometer does not touch foil. Bake at 325° for 2 hours or until thermometer registers 140° (rare) or 160° (medium). Yield: 12 to 14 servings.

Beef Wellington Step-By-Step

1. To make Beef Wellington, spread one side of partially baked tenderloin with liverwurst mixture.

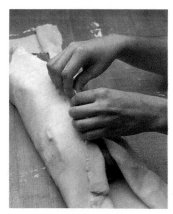

2. Invert tenderloin onto rolled pastry, liverwurst side down. Spread meat with remaining liverwurst, and cover with pastry.

3. Cut and arrange decorations on Wellington using leftover scraps of pastry. Moisten bottom of decorations so they'll adhere.

4. Brush egg yolk and milk mixture over the pastry to make it brown nicely. Bake as directed.

SPICY BEEF TENDERLOIN

(pictured on page 282)

1 cup port wine
1 cup soy sauce
½ cup olive oil
1 tcaspoon pcppcr
1 teaspoon dried whole thyme
½ teaspoon hot sauce
4 cloves garlic, crushed
1 bay leaf
1 (5- to 6-pound) beef tenderloin, trimmed
Watercress
Tomato roses

Combine first 8 ingredients; mix well. Place tenderloin in a large shallow dish; pour wine mixture over top, and cover tightly. Refrigerate 8 hours, turning occasionally.

Uncover tenderloin; drain off and reserve marinade. Place tenderloin on a rack in a pan; insert meat thermometer, making sure it does not touch fat. Bake at 425° for 45 to 60 minutes or until thermometer registers 140° (rare), basting occasionally with marinade. (Bake until thermometer registers 150° for medium-rare or 160° for medium.) Garnish with watercress and tomato roses. Serve leftover marinade on the side. Yield: 10 to 12 servings.

BEEF WELLINGTON

1 (7-pound) beef tenderloin, trimmed
1 (8-ounce) package liverwurst spread
1 cup chopped fresh mushrooms
2 tablespoons bourbon
1 (16-ounce) package frozen puff pastry, thawed
1 egg yolk
1 tablespoon milk
Fresh parsley sprigs

Place tenderloin on a rack in a shallow roasting pan, tucking small end of meat underneath. Bake, uncovered, at 425° for 25 to 30 minutes. Remove from oven, and let stand 30 minutes.

Combine liverwurst spread, mushrooms, and bourbon. Set aside.

Roll pastry to a 20- x 14-inch rectangle on a lightly floured surface. Spread one-third of liverwurst mixture over top of tenderloin. Place tenderloin lengthwise in middle of pastry, top side down. Spread remaining liverwurst mixture over sides of tenderloin. Bring sides of pastry up, and overlap slightly to form a seam, trimming off excess pastry. Reserve all pastry trimmings. Trim ends of pastry to make even; fold over ends of pastry to seal. Invert roast.

Combine egg yolk and milk; brush evenly over pastry. Roll out pastry trimmings; cut into decorative shapes and arrange on top of pastry, as desired. Brush shapes with remaining yolk mixture. Bake, uncovered, in a lightly greased 13- x 9- x 2-inch pan at 425° for 30 minutes. Let stand 10 minutes before slicing. Garnish with parsley. Yield: 12 to 15 servings.

Serve Beef Wellington proudly at your next dinner party. Starting with frozen puff pastry makes it an easier task than guests would imagine.

MARINATED BEEF TENDERLOIN

1 cup catsup
2 teaspoons prepared mustard
½ teaspoon Worcestershire sauce
1½ cups water
2 (0.7-ounce) envelopes Italian salad dressing mix
1 (4- to 6-pound) beef tenderloin, trimmed

Combine first 5 ingredients; stir well. Spear meat in several places, and place in a zip top heavy-duty plastic bag. Pour marinade in bag, and seal tightly. Place bag in a shallow pan, and refrigerate 8 hours, turning occasionally.

Drain off and reserve marinade. Place tenderloin on a rack in a pan; insert meat thermometer, making sure it does not touch fat. Bake at 425° for 30 to 45 minutes or until thermometer registers 140°(rare). (Bake until thermometer registers 150° for medium-rare or 160° for medium.) Baste occasionally with marinade while baking. Remove to serving platter; serve remaining marinade with meat. Yield: 10 to 12 servings.

BEEF BOURGUIGNON

1 (4- to 5-pound) boneless sirloin tip roast, cut into 1½-inch cubes
1 cup Burgundy or other dry red wine
1 cup water
2 (10¾-ounce) cans cream of mushroom soup, undiluted
1 (2.5-ounce) package dry onion soup mix
¾ pound fresh mushrooms, sliced
1 cup chopped green pepper
1 pound pearl onions, peeled
½ teaspoon garlic powder
10 cherry tomatoes (optional)
Fresh parsley sprigs
Hot cooked rice

Place beef in a 5-quart casserole. Combine wine, water, soup, and soup mix; stir well, and pour over beef. Stir in mushrooms, green pepper, onions, and garlic powder. Cover and bake at 325° for 3 hours, stirring occasionally. Stir in cherry tomatoes, if desired. Garnish with parsley sprigs. Serve over rice. Yield: 10 to 12 servings.

BEEF AND VEGETABLE KABOBS

½ cup vegetable oil
¼ cup soy sauce
¼ cup vinegar
½ teaspoon pepper
2 pounds sirloin tip roast, cut into 1½-inch cubes
6 small onions
½ pound fresh mushrooms
1 cup cherry tomatoes
1 large green pepper, cut into 1-inch pieces

Combine first 4 ingredients in a large shallow container. Add meat; cover and marinate in refrigerator 4 hours.

Parboil onions 3 to 5 minutes; drain.

Remove meat from marinade. Alternate meat and vegetables on skewers. Grill kabobs over medium coals 8 minutes on each side or to desired degree of doneness, basting often with marinade. Yield: 6 servings.

PINEAPPLE-BEEF KABOBS

2 (20-ounce) cans pineapple chunks
½ cup firmly packed brown sugar
⅔ cup cider vinegar
⅔ cup catsup
¼ cup soy sauce
2 teaspoons ground ginger
1½ teaspoons liquid smoke
3 pounds boneless sirloin tip roast, cut into 1½-inch cubes
½ pound fresh mushrooms
2 small onions, quartered
2 medium-size green peppers, cut into 1-inch pieces
Seasoned Rice (page 343)

Drain pineapple, reserving juice. Combine pineapple juice and next 6 ingredients, stirring well; pour into a large shallow dish. Add meat; cover and marinate 8 hours in refrigerator.

Drain meat, reserving marinade. Pour marinade into a saucepan; bring to a boil. Add mushrooms; reduce heat and simmer, uncovered, 10 minutes. Drain; reserve marinade. Set mushrooms aside.

Alternate meat, fruit, and vegetables on skewers. Grill kabobs over medium-hot coals 6 to 8 minutes on each side or to desired degree of doneness, brushing often with marinade. Serve kabobs with Seasoned Rice. Yield: 8 servings.

COMPANY POT ROAST

½ cup chopped onion
¼ cup butter or margarine, melted
1 (3½- to 4-pound) chuck roast
1 bay leaf, quartered
2 tablespoons grated orange rind
¼ teaspoon ground allspice
⅛ teaspoon pepper
1 (10½-ounce) can consommé, diluted

Sauté onion in butter in a large Dutch oven until tender; add meat, and brown on both sides. Combine seasonings and diluted consommé; pour over meat. Cover and simmer 2½ hours. Remove bay leaf. Yield: 6 to 8 servings.

○ *Microwave Directions:* Combine onion and melted butter; set aside. Place chuck roast in a roasting bag in a 12- x 8- x 2-inch baking dish; pour onion and butter over roast. Sprinkle seasonings over roast. Add diluted consommé. Tie bag loosely with string or a ½-inch-wide strip cut from open end of bag (do not use twist tie).

Microwave at MEDIUM LOW (30% power) for 33 to 37 minutes per pound or to desired degree of doneness, turning bag over and rotating dish every 30 minutes. Let stand 10 to 15 minutes in bag before serving. Remove bay leaf.

POT ROAST WITH SPAGHETTI

1 (2½- to 3-pound) boneless chuck
   roast
8 cloves garlic
Salt and pepper
1 tablespoon vegetable oil
3 (8-ounce) cans tomato sauce
2 tablespoons vinegar
1 teaspoon ground nutmeg
½ teaspoon ground allspice
6 to 8 whole cloves
Hot cooked spaghetti

Make 8 slits in roast, and insert 1 clove garlic in each slit; sprinkle roast with salt and pepper. Brown roast on all sides in hot oil in a Dutch oven.

Combine tomato sauce, vinegar, and spices; pour over roast. Cover and simmer 2 hours and 30 minutes or until tender. Remove and discard garlic cloves. Remove roast to serving platter; keep warm. Cook sauce over medium-high heat 3 to 5 minutes or until reduced to 3 cups. Cut roast into serving pieces, and serve with spaghetti and sauce. Yield: 4 to 6 servings.

QUICK SAUERBRATEN

1 (4-pound) chuck roast
1 tablespoon vegetable oil
¾ cup chopped onion
3 tablespoons brown sugar
1 teaspoon salt
1 teaspoon coarsely ground pepper
1 teaspoon ground ginger
⅛ teaspoon ground cloves
⅛ teaspoon ground allspice
1 bay leaf
1 cup water
⅔ cup red wine vinegar
½ cup water
½ cup all-purpose flour

Brown roast on both sides in hot oil in a large Dutch oven. Combine onion, brown sugar, salt, pepper, ginger, cloves, allspice, bay leaf, 1 cup water, and vinegar; mix well, and pour over roast. Cover and simmer 2½ to 3 hours or until roast is tender, turning once. Remove roast to serving platter. Remove bay leaf.

Stir ½ cup water into flour; stir into pan drippings. Cook, stirring constantly, until gravy is smooth and thickened. Pour gravy over roast, and serve. Yield: 6 servings.

ZESTY POT ROAST

1 (8-ounce) bottle Italian salad
   dressing
1 (3- to 4-pound) boneless chuck
   roast
1 (10½-ounce) can beef broth,
   undiluted
1 cup water
4 to 6 carrots, cut into 1½-inch
   pieces
1 (10-ounce) package frozen cut
   green beans
All-purpose flour

Pour dressing over roast in a shallow dish; cover and refrigerate 8 hours, turning occasionally.

Remove roast from marinade, reserving marinade. Place roast in a Dutch oven; add beef broth and water. Cover and simmer 2 hours. Add carrots, and cook 5 minutes. Add green beans and reserved marinade, and cook for 20 to 25 minutes.

Remove roast and vegetables to a platter; keep warm. Measure liquid, and return to Dutch oven. Combine 1 tablespoon flour for every 1 cup liquid, and 2 tablespoons water; stir well. Stir flour mixture into liquid in Dutch oven. Cook over medium heat, stirring constantly, until thick and bubbly. Serve gravy with roast. Yield: 6 to 8 servings.

POT ROAST WITH SOUR CREAM GRAVY

1 (2- to 2½-pound) boneless chuck
   roast
2 tablespoons vegetable oil
½ cup water
3 medium potatoes, peeled and
   quartered
3 medium carrots, cut into 2-inch
   pieces
3 medium onions, quartered
1 tablespoon all-purpose flour
1 (8-ounce) carton commercial sour
   cream
¼ teaspoon salt
⅛ teaspoon pepper

Brown roast on all sides in hot oil in a large Dutch oven; add water. Cover, reduce heat, and simmer 2½ hours. Add vegetables; cover and simmer 30 minutes or until vegetables are tender, adding additional water if needed.

Remove roast and vegetables to a serving dish. Drain off drippings, leaving 2 tablespoons drippings in pan; reserve remaining drippings. Stir flour into drippings in pan; cook over medium heat until browned, stirring constantly. Add enough water to reserved drippings to make 1 cup; stir into flour and cook, stirring constantly, until smooth and slightly thickened. Add sour cream, salt, and pepper; cook, stirring constantly, until thoroughly heated. Serve gravy with roast. Yield: 5 to 6 servings.

Put on a Pot Roast

The low cost and ease of preparing pot roasts make them a popular dinner choice, but don't make them predictable. These recipes team a cooking liquid, seasonings, and vegetables. Zesty Pot Roast with Italian salad dressing, carrots, and green beans is a unique example. Another version of pot roast is served over spaghetti.

BEEF MARENGO

1 (4-pound) boneless chuck
  roast
2 tablespoons vegetable oil
1 cup chopped onion
1 cup chopped celery
1 clove garlic, crushed
1 cup Chablis or other dry
  white wine, divided
2 (8-ounce) cans tomato sauce
2 bay leaves
1 teaspoon dried whole
  oregano
½ teaspoon dried whole
  rosemary
½ teaspoon salt
½ teaspoon pepper
1 pound fresh mushrooms,
  sliced
2 tablespoons butter or
  margarine, melted
1 tablespoon all-purpose flour
2 tablespoons water
Chopped fresh parsley (optional)
Hot cooked noodles

Trim excess fat from roast; cut meat
into 1-inch cubes.

Brown meat in hot oil in a large Dutch
oven; remove meat. Add onion, celery,
and garlic to pan drippings; sauté until
tender. Drain. Add meat, ½ cup wine,
and next 6 ingredients to vegetable mixture. Bring to a boil; cover, reduce heat,
and simmer 1 hour or until meat is
tender, stirring occasionally. Discard
bay leaves.

Sauté mushrooms in butter until
tender. Drain.

Combine flour and water; stir until
smooth. Stir flour mixture, sautéed
mushrooms, and remaining ½ cup wine
into meat mixture. Cover and cook over
medium heat 15 minutes.

Transfer mixture to a chafing dish, if
desired; sprinkle with chopped parsley,
if desired. Serve over noodles. Yield: 8 to
10 servings.

OVEN POT ROAST

1 (3- to 4-pound) chuck or rump
  roast
All-purpose flour
Pepper
¼ cup butter or margarine, melted
½ (1.25-ounce) envelope dry onion
  soup mix
1 (10¾-ounce) can cream of
  mushroom soup, undiluted
½ cup dry Vermouth or white
  wine
1 (4.5-ounce) jar whole
  mushrooms, undrained

Dredge roast in flour and pepper.
Brown roast in butter in a heavy skillet;
place roast in a 4-quart casserole dish
with lid. Combine soup mix, mushroom
soup, and Vermouth; pour over roast.
Cover and bake at 325° for 2½ hours.
Pour mushrooms over roast, and bake
an additional 30 minutes. Yield: 6 to 8
servings.

HOT TAMALES

1 (3-pound) shoulder or chuck
  roast
4 cloves garlic
1 teaspoon salt
2 dozen dried cornhusks
3 large, dried chiles
2 teaspoons shortening
1½ teaspoons all-purpose flour
¾ teaspoon ground cumin
¾ teaspoon salt
3 cups instant corn masa
1 teaspoon salt
½ cup plus 1 tablespoon
  shortening
Picante sauce (optional)

Combine first 3 ingredients in a Dutch
oven. Add water to cover; bring to a
boil. Cover, reduce heat, and simmer 2½
hours or until meat is tender. Drain
meat, reserving broth; set broth aside.
Shred meat with a fork; set aside.

Cover dried cornhusks with hot
water; let stand several hours or until
softened. Drain well. If husks are too
narrow overlap 2 husks to make a wide
one. If too wide, tear off one side.

Remove and discard seeds from
chiles; place in a saucepan, and cover
with water. Bring to a boil; reduce heat,
and simmer 20 to 25 minutes or until
chiles are tender. Drain chiles, reserving
¾ cup water; place softened chiles in
container of an electric blender. Add
reserved water, and blend 1 minute or
until smooth; set aside.

Melt 2 teaspoons shortening in a
small saucepan; add flour and cumin,
stirring until smooth. Cook 1 minute,
stirring constantly. Remove from heat,
and stir in ½ cup chile mixture and ¾
teaspoon salt; add to shredded meat,
stirring well. Set aside.

Bring reserved beef broth to a boil.
Combine corn masa, 1 teaspoon salt,
and ½ cup plus 1 tablespoon shortening
in a large bowl. Stir in 1 cup plus 2 to 3
tablespoons hot beef broth to make a
stiff dough. Add the remaining chile
mixture to the dough, mixing well.

Place 2½ to 3 tablespoons masa dough
(depending on size of husk) in the center of each husk, spreading to within ½
inch of edge. Place 2 tablespoons meat
mixture in center. Fold short ends of
husks to center, enclosing filling; roll up
from unfolded side. Tie with string or
strip of softened cornhusk.

Place a cup in center of a steaming
rack or metal colander inside a large pot.
Add enough water to fill pot below rack
level and keep tamales above water.
Stand tamales on folded ends around the
cup. Bring water to a boil. Cover and
steam 1 hour or until tamale dough pulls
away from husk; add more water as
necessary. Serve with picante sauce, if
desired. Yield: about 2 dozen.

Note: Steamed tamales may be frozen.
Allow to cool; place in a plastic bag, or
wrap them securely in aluminum foil,
and place in freezer. To reheat, follow
steaming procedure until tamales are
thoroughly heated.

JAVA ROAST

½ small onion
2 cloves garlic
1 (4- to 5-pound) shoulder or chuck
  roast
1 cup vinegar
2 tablespoons vegetable oil
2 cups strong coffee
2 cups water
1 teaspoon salt
½ teaspoon pepper

Cut onion and garlic into small strips; pierce roast at intervals, inserting onion and garlic in slits. Place roast in a large dish, and pour vinegar over top. Cover dish, and refrigerate 8 hours; drain off the vinegar.

Brown roast on all sides in hot oil in a large Dutch oven; add coffee, water, salt, and pepper. Cover, reduce heat, and simmer 3 to 3½ hours or until tender. Yield: 8 to 10 servings.

CRACKED PEPPER STEAK

2 (8- to 12-ounce) rib-eye steaks, 1½
  inches thick
¼ teaspoon garlic powder
Salt
¼ cup chopped green onions
¼ cup butter or margarine, melted
1 teaspoon cracked black pepper,
  divided

Sprinkle both sides of steaks with garlic powder and salt; set aside.

Sauté green onions in butter in a large skillet until crisp-tender. Remove onions, and set aside.

Sprinkle ½ teaspoon pepper in the skillet; add steaks, and cook over medium heat 8 minutes. Sprinkle remaining ½ teaspoon pepper over top of steaks; turn and continue cooking 8 minutes or until steaks reach desired degree of doneness.

Remove steaks to serving platter, and sprinkle with onions. Yield: 2 servings.

INDIVIDUAL BEEF WELLINGTONS

6 (4- to 5-ounce) tenderloin steaks
½ teaspoon salt
¼ teaspoon pepper
½ cup chopped onion
⅓ cup vegetable oil
1 cup red wine
2 tablespoons brandy
½ teaspoon fines herbes
1 tablespoon butter or margarine,
  melted
Mushroom Filling
Pastry (recipe follows)
2 egg yolks
2 teaspoons water
Reserved juice from Mushroom
  Filling
1 (14½-ounce) can beef broth,
  undiluted
1 tablespoon tomato paste
2 tablespoons cornstarch
¼ cup Madeira or other dry sweet
  wine

Sprinkle steaks with salt and pepper, and place in a shallow dish. Sauté onion in hot oil until tender. Add wine, brandy, and herbs. Pour mixture over steaks; cover and marinate in refrigerator 8 hours.

Drain steaks, reserving marinade. Sauté steaks in 1 tablespoon butter in a skillet just until lightly browned on both sides. Place steaks in dish; cover and refrigerate 2 hours.

Prepare Mushroom Filling; chill at least 2 hours.

Prepare pastry; chill 2 hours. Roll pastry into an 18-inch square on a lightly floured surface; cut into six 9- x 6-inch rectangles. Spread center of each pastry rectangle with ⅓ cup Mushroom Filling; top with a steak.

Combine egg yolks and water; brush edges of pastry with egg mixture. Fold pastry over, and pinch edges and ends together. Trim excess pastry, reserving scraps. Place Wellingtons, seam side down, on a lightly greased baking sheet. Brush with egg mixture; repeat after 1 minute. Roll pastry trimmings; cut into decorative shapes, and arrange on Wellingtons, if desired. Brush with remaining egg mixture. Bake at 400° for 25 minutes or until golden brown.

Combine reserved marinade, mushroom juice, beef broth, and tomato paste in a saucepan; cook over medium heat 25 minutes. Combine cornstarch and Madeira; stir into broth mixture and cook, stirring constantly, until thickened. Serve with Wellingtons. Yield: 6 servings.

Mushroom Filling

2 pounds fresh mushrooms, finely
  chopped
¼ cup minced green onions
2 tablespoons butter or margarine,
  melted
½ cup Madeira or other dry sweet
  wine
⅛ teaspoon salt
¼ teaspoon pepper

Sauté mushrooms and green onions in butter until tender. Drain; reserve liquid. Add Madeira; cook until evaporated. Add salt and pepper. Yield: 2⅓ cups.

Pastry

3 cups all-purpose flour
½ teaspoon salt
¾ cup plus 2 tablespoons chilled
  butter or margarine, cubed
¼ cup shortening, chilled
½ cup ice water

Combine flour and salt in a large bowl; cut in chilled butter and shortening with a pastry blender until mixture resembles coarse meal. Sprinkle ice water evenly over surface; stir with a fork until dry ingredients are moistened. Shape dough into a ball. Yield: enough for 6 individual Wellingtons.

Note: You may substitute 1½ pounds frozen puff pastry for homemade pastry.

STEAK DIANE FLAMBÉ

2 (8-ounce) rib-eye steaks
½ cup sliced fresh mushrooms
¼ cup chopped green onions
2 tablespoons butter or margarine, melted
2 tablespoons brandy
1 tablespoon Worcestershire sauce
½ teaspoon dry mustard
⅛ teaspoon salt
⅛ teaspoon pepper

Pound steaks with a meat mallet to flatten slightly, if desired. Sauté mushrooms and green onions in butter in a large skillet until tender. Push mushroom mixture to one side of skillet. Add steaks, and brown on both sides. Remove from heat.

Heat brandy in a long-handled saucepan just long enough to produce fumes (do not boil). Remove brandy from heat, ignite, and pour over steaks. When flames die down, remove steaks from skillet. Add last 4 ingredients to mushroom mixture in skillet; blend well. Cook 1 minute.

Place steaks on serving platter, and spoon mushroom mixture over top. Yield: 2 servings.

STEAK CONTINENTAL

1 clove garlic, minced
2 to 3 tablespoons soy sauce
1 tablespoon catsup
1 tablespoon vegetable oil
½ teaspoon pepper
½ teaspoon dried whole oregano
3 pounds boneless sirloin steak

Combine first 6 ingredients in a small bowl, stirring well.

Score steak ¼ inch deep on both sides; rub in garlic mixture. Place steak in a large shallow dish; cover and refrigerate 8 hours.

Grill over medium-hot coals 12 to 15 minutes on each side or to desired degree of doneness. Yield: 4 to 6 servings.

STEAK WITH MUSHROOM BROWN SAUCE

2 tablespoons lemon juice
2 tablespoons Worcestershire sauce
2 tablespoons molasses
1 teaspoon seasoned pepper
½ teaspoon seasoned salt or Creole seasoning
2 pounds boneless sirloin steak
2 recipes Mushroom Brown Sauce (page 436)

Combine first 5 ingredients, stirring well; pour into a large shallow dish. Add steak; cover and refrigerate at least 1 hour, turning once.

Drain steak, reserving marinade. Grill steak over hot coals 8 to 12 minutes on each side or to desired degree of doneness, basting often with marinade. Spoon Mushroom Brown Sauce over steak to serve. Yield: 4 servings.

BEEF TERIYAKI STIR-FRY

1½ pounds boneless sirloin steak
¼ cup teriyaki sauce
¼ cup water
2 tablespoons brown sugar
2 tablespoons Worcestershire sauce
½ teaspoon minced fresh garlic
1 tablespoon vegetable oil
1½ cups diagonally sliced carrots
1½ cups diagonally sliced celery
1 cup chopped onion
1 tablespoon vegetable oil
1 tablespoon cornstarch
1 cup hot cooked rice

Partially freeze steak; slice diagonally across grain into 3- x ¼-inch strips.

Combine next 5 ingredients in a large bowl. Add meat; cover and marinate in the refrigerator 4 to 6 hours, stirring occasionally.

Pour 1 tablespoon oil around top of preheated wok, coating sides; heat at medium high (325°) for 2 minutes. Add vegetables and stir-fry 4 minutes; remove from wok.

Pour 1 tablespoon oil around top of wok. Remove steak from marinade, reserving marinade; add steak to wok. Stir-fry until browned.

Combine cornstarch and reserved marinade, stirring well; stir mixture into beef. Cook, stirring constantly, until thickened.

Combine vegetables and rice; place on serving dish. Spoon meat mixture over rice. Yield: 6 servings.

To slice strips for stir-frying: First partially freeze the meat; then slice it cross the grain into thin strips.

STIR-FRY BEEF AND SNOW PEAS

1 pound boneless sirloin steak
1 tablespoon soy sauce
2 teaspoons cornstarch
2 carrots, scraped
¼ cup peanut or vegetable oil
1 (2-ounce) package cellophane noodles
1 (6-ounce) package frozen snow pea pods, thawed and drained
2 tablespoons peanut or vegetable oil
2 slices gingerroot
1 tablespoon peanut or vegetable oil
1 (15-ounce) can baby corn cobs, drained
1 (15-ounce) can straw mushrooms, drained
2 tablespoons soy sauce
2 tablespoons rice wine
1 teaspoon cornstarch

Partially freeze steak; slice steak diagonally across grain into 2- x ¼-inch strips. Combine soy sauce and 2 teaspoons cornstarch; pour over steak, and marinate 1 hour at room temperature or 8 hours in refrigerator.

Cut 4 or 5 lengthwise triangular grooves ⅛-inch deep at even intervals down length of carrots. Slice carrots ⅛-inch thick. Set aside.

Pour ¼ cup oil into preheated wok; heat oil to about 325°. Add cellophane noodles, a small amount at a time; fry 2 or 3 seconds or until noodles expand and turn white. Remove from wok, and drain on paper towels. Arrange around border of serving platter.

Drain oil from wok. Add snow pea pods to wok; stir-fry 1 to 2 minutes. Remove from wok, and arrange around inside border of cellophane noodles.

Pour 2 tablespoons oil around top of wok, coating sides. Add gingerroot and steak; stir-fry 4 to 5 minutes. Remove from wok.

Pour 1 tablespoon oil around top of wok, coating sides. Add carrots, corn, and mushrooms; stir-fry 2 to 3 minutes. Combine last 3 ingredients, stirring well; add to carrot mixture, and cook until thickened, stirring constantly. Stir in steak. Pour steak mixture into center of platter. Yield: 4 to 6 servings.

MEXICAN STEAK

1¼ pounds boneless round
   steak
2 tablespoons butter or
   margarine, melted
1 (4-ounce) can chopped green
   chiles, drained
1 (8-ounce) jar taco sauce
½ cup (2 ounces) shredded
   Monterey Jack cheese

Trim excess fat from steak. Cut steak into 4 pieces, and pound to ¼-inch thickness using a meat mallet.

Brown steak in butter, and place in a lightly greased shallow 2-quart casserole. Top with green chiles and taco sauce. Cover and bake at 350° for 40 minutes. Sprinkle with shredded cheese; bake, uncovered, an additional 5 minutes. Yield: 4 servings.

LEMON STEAK CUTLETS

1½ to 2 pounds boneless round
   steak
2 eggs, beaten
1 teaspoon grated lemon rind
3 tablespoons lemon juice
¾ teaspoon salt
¾ teaspoon pepper
1½ cups dry breadcrumbs
Vegetable oil

Trim excess fat from steak; pound steak to ¼-inch thickness using a meat mallet. Cut the steak into serving-size portions.

Combine eggs, lemon rind, lemon juice, salt, and pepper; beat well. Dip steak into egg mixture; dredge in breadcrumbs, coating evenly. Cook steak portions in hot oil until done, turning once. Yield: 6 to 8 servings.

To tenderize and flatten meat: Pound slices using a meat mallet.

PEPPER STEAK

1½ pounds round steak
2 tablespoons vegetable oil
2 medium tomatoes, peeled and
   coarsely chopped
2 medium-size green peppers,
   thinly sliced
1 small onion, sliced
1 cup water
¼ cup soy sauce
½ teaspoon pepper
½ teaspoon beef-flavored
   bouillon granules
¼ teaspoon garlic powder
¼ teaspoon ground ginger
2 tablespoons cornstarch
2 tablespoons water
Hot cooked rice

Pound steak to ¼-inch thickness using a meat mallet. Cut steak into serving-size pieces.

Brown steak in hot oil in a large skillet; drain. Return to skillet, and add tomatoes, green pepper, onion, water, soy sauce, pepper, bouillon granules, garlic powder, and ginger. Cover, reduce heat, and simmer 55 minutes, stirring occasionally.

Combine cornstarch and water, stirring well. Gradually stir mixture into steak mixture. Simmer 5 minutes, stirring constantly. Serve over rice. Yield: 4 servings.

BEEF STEAKS PARMESAN

1 (32-ounce) jar spaghetti sauce
1 teaspoon dried whole basil
⅛ teaspoon garlic powder
2 (1-pound) top round steaks,
   ½-inch thick
½ teaspoon pepper
1 cup (4 ounces) shredded
   mozzarella cheese
2 eggs
1 tablespoon milk
½ cup herb-seasoned stuffing mix
½ cup grated Parmesan cheese
⅓ cup all-purpose flour
2 tablespoons vegetable oil
¼ cup grated Parmesan cheese
Hot cooked noodles

Combine spaghetti sauce, basil, and garlic powder in a saucepan. Bring mixture to a boil; reduce heat and simmer 15 to 20 minutes. Set aside.

Trim excess fat from steaks. Sprinkle steaks with pepper, and pound to ⅛-inch thickness using a meat mallet. Cut each steak into 4 pieces. Place about ¼ cup mozzarella cheese in center of 4 steak pieces. Top with remaining steak pieces; secure with wooden picks.

Combine eggs and milk; beat well. Combine stuffing mix and ½ cup Parmesan cheese.

Dredge steaks in flour, and dip in egg mixture; dredge in stuffing mixture. Brown steaks in hot oil. Remove to lightly greased shallow 2-quart casserole; top with sauce, and sprinkle with ¼ cup Parmesan cheese. Cover and bake at 350° for 1 hour. To serve, cut each steak in half; serve over noodles. Yield: 8 servings.

STEAK FINGERS

1 pound boneless round steak
1 cup all-purpose flour
1 teaspoon salt
1 teaspoon pepper
1 egg
1 tablespoon milk
Vegetable oil

Trim excess fat from steak; pound steak to ⅛-inch thickness using a meat mallet, and cut into 4- x 1-inch strips.

Combine flour, salt, and pepper.

Combine egg and milk; beat well. Dredge steak strips in flour mixture; dip strips in egg mixture, and dredge again in flour mixture.

Heat about 2 inches of oil in a large skillet to 375°. Fry steak fingers in hot oil until browned. Drain on paper towels. Serve immediately. Yield: 4 servings.

SWISS STEAK WITH VEGETABLES

1 pound boneless round steak
¼ cup all-purpose flour
½ teaspoon salt
½ teaspoon pepper
2 tablespoons vegetable oil
3 large carrots, sliced
1 large onion, sliced
2 stalks celery, sliced
2 (8-ounce) cans tomato sauce
1 cup water
1 tablespoon butter or margarine
1½ teaspoons beef-flavored bouillon
   granules
2 teaspoons browning and seasoning
   sauce
Hot cooked noodles or rice

Trim excess fat from steak, and cut steak into serving-size pieces.

Combine flour, salt, and pepper; dredge steak in flour mixture, and lightly pound floured steak using a meat mallet. Brown steak in hot oil in a skillet; place in a shallow 2-quart casserole. Spoon vegetables over meat.

Combine tomato sauce, water, butter, bouillon granules, and browning and seasoning sauce in skillet; cook over medium heat until bouillon granules dissolve. Pour sauce over vegetables. Cover casserole, and bake at 350° for 1 hour and 10 minutes. Serve over noodles. Yield: 4 servings.

COUNTRY-FRIED STEAK

1½ to 2 pounds boneless round
   steak
⅓ cup all-purpose flour
¼ teaspoon salt
¼ teaspoon pepper
3 tablespoons vegetable oil
2 small onions, sliced
1 cup water
¼ cup all-purpose flour
¾ cup milk
¼ cup brewed coffee
2 teaspoons Worcestershire sauce
¼ teaspoon salt
¼ teaspoon pepper

Trim excess fat from steak; pound steak to ¼-inch thickness using a meat mallet. Cut into serving-size pieces.

Combine ⅓ cup flour, ¼ teaspoon salt, and ¼ teaspoon pepper. Dredge steak in flour mixture; lightly pound floured steak. Cook steak in hot oil in skillet until browned, turning steak once. Add sliced onion and water; cover, reduce heat, and simmer 30 minutes or until tender. Remove steak, reserving drippings in skillet.

Add ¼ cup flour to drippings in skillet, stirring until smooth. Cook until browned, stirring constantly. Gradually add milk and coffee; cook over medium heat, stirring constantly, until thickened. Stir in last 3 ingredients. Serve steak with gravy. Yield: 4 to 6 servings.

LONDON BROIL

1 (1½-pound) flank steak
⅓ cup vegetable oil
1 tablespoon red wine vinegar
2 cloves garlic, minced
Salt
Freshly ground pepper

Trim excess fat from steak; score steak on both sides in 1½-inch squares. Set steak in a deep bowl. Combine oil, vinegar, and garlic; pour over meat, and marinate 3 hours in refrigerator turning once. Remove meat from marinade, and place on a lightly greased rack in broiler pan. Broil 4 inches from heat 4 to 5 minutes. Sprinkle with salt and pepper, and turn. Broil an additional 4 to 5 minutes. Sprinkle with salt and pepper. To serve, slice across grain into thin slices. Yield: 4 to 6 servings.

ORIENTAL FLANK STEAK

1 (1½-pound) flank steak
5 green onions, chopped
¾ cup vegetable oil
½ cup soy sauce
1½ teaspoons ground ginger
¾ teaspoon garlic powder
3 tablespoons honey
2 tablespoons vinegar

Place steak in a large shallow dish. Combine remaining ingredients, stirring well. Pour over steak; cover and marinate in refrigerator 8 hours, turning steak occasionally.

Drain steak, reserving marinade. Grill over hot coals 10 minutes on each side or to desired degree of doneness, basting often with marinade. To serve, slice steak across grain into thin slices. Yield: 4 to 6 servings.

GRILLED FLANK STEAK

2 (1¼-pound) flank steaks
¼ cup vinegar
¼ cup vegetable oil
1 small onion, finely chopped
1 clove garlic, crushed
½ teaspoon dried whole basil
½ teaspoon dry mustard
⅛ teaspoon hot sauce

Place steak in a large shallow dish. Combine remaining ingredients, stirring well. Pour marinade mixture over steak; cover and marinate in refrigerator 8 hours, turning occasionally.

Drain steak. Grill over hot coals 8 minutes on each side or to desired degree of doneness. Slice across grain into thin slices. Yield: 8 servings.

FAJITAS

½ cup olive oil
⅓ cup lime juice
¼ cup red wine vinegar
⅓ cup finely chopped onion
1 teaspoon sugar
1 teaspoon dried whole oregano
½ teaspoon salt
½ teaspoon pepper
¼ teaspoon ground cumin
3 cloves garlic, minced
2 pounds flank or skirt steak
8 to 12 flour tortillas

Combine first 10 ingredients in a shallow dish, and stir well.

Pound steak to ¼-inch thickness using a meat mallet. Add steak to marinade, turning to coat both sides. Cover dish, and refrigerate 8 hours.

Remove steak from marinade; drain well. Grill steak over medium coals 6 to 7 minutes on each side or to desired doneness. Slice into thin slices.

Wrap tortillas in aluminum foil, and bake at 325° for 15 minutes. Wrap tortillas around meat and choice of toppings: picante sauce, guacamole, salsa verde, chopped tomatoes, and sour cream. Yield: 4 to 6 servings.

BARBECUED BEEF BRISKET

1 (4- to 5-pound) beef brisket
½ teaspoon celery salt
¼ teaspoon garlic powder
⅛ teaspoon onion powder
2 tablespoons liquid smoke
⅓ cup Worcestershire sauce
¾ cup commercial barbecue sauce

Sprinkle beef with celery salt, garlic powder, and onion powder. Place in a shallow dish. Pour liquid smoke and Worcestershire sauce over meat; cover with aluminum foil, and refrigerate 8 hours, turning once.

Cover and bake at 300° for 4 hours or until tender. Pour off liquid, reserving ½ cup. Combine barbecue sauce and ½ cup liquid, stirring well. Pour sauce over beef; bake, uncovered, an additional 30 minutes. To serve, slice across grain into thin slices. Yield: 8 to 10 servings.

BRAISED BRISKET CARBONNADE

1 (3½- to 4-pound) beef brisket
2 medium onions, sliced
2 (12-ounce) cans beer
¼ cup firmly packed brown sugar
1 tablespoon Dijon mustard
1 tablespoon beef-flavored bouillon granules
1 teaspoon coarsely ground pepper
¼ teaspoon dried whole thyme
1 bay leaf
2 cloves garlic, minced
Pot Roast Gravy (page 444)
4 slices bacon, cooked and crumbled

Trim excess fat from brisket. Place brisket in a large Dutch oven; cover with onion slices. Combine beer, brown sugar, mustard, bouillon granules, pepper, thyme, bay leaf, and garlic; pour over meat. Cover and bake at 350° for 2½ to 3 hours or until tender. Remove meat to a platter, and keep warm. Skim fat from pan juices; remove bay leaf.

Measure pan drippings, and prepare Pot Roast Gravy using pan drippings, multiplying recipe by amount of drippings. Stir bacon into gravy. Slice meat across grain into thin slices, and serve with gravy. Yield: 8 servings.

REUBEN CASSEROLE

1 (32-ounce) jar sauerkraut, drained
2 medium tomatoes, thinly sliced
2 tablespoons commercial Thousand Island salad dressing
2 tablespoons butter or margarine
4 (2.5-ounce) packages sliced corned beef, shredded
2 cups (8 ounces) shredded Swiss cheese
1 (10-ounce) can refrigerated buttermilk flaky biscuits
2 rye crackers, crushed
¼ teaspoon caraway seeds

Spread sauerkraut in a 13- x 9- x 2-inch baking dish. Arrange tomato slices on top; spread with dressing, and dot with butter. Cover with corned beef and cheese. Separate each biscuit into 3 thin layers; arrange over casserole. Sprinkle with cracker crumbs and caraway seeds. Bake at 425° for 10 minutes or until the biscuits are golden. Yield: 6 servings.

CORNED BEEF AND CABBAGE

1 medium cabbage
4 slices bacon
1½ to 2 teaspoons crushed red pepper
⅛ teaspoon salt
2½ cups water
1 (12-ounce) can corned beef, sliced

Wash cabbage, and cut into 4 wedges (do not separate leaves).

Cook bacon in a Dutch oven until crisp; remove and drain bacon, reserving 3 tablespoons drippings in Dutch oven. Crumble bacon.

Combine cabbage, bacon, red pepper, salt, and water in Dutch oven. Cover and cook over medium heat 30 minutes. Add corned beef, and cook an additional 10 minutes. Yield: 4 servings.

HEARTY BEEF SHORTRIBS

3 tablespoons all-purpose flour
2 tablespoons brown sugar
1 teaspoon salt
⅛ teaspoon coarsely ground pepper
3 pounds beef shortribs
2 tablespoons shortening
½ cup coarsely chopped onion
¼ teaspoon whole allspice
1 small bay leaf
¾ cup water
8 medium carrots
8 small whole onions
Prepared horseradish (optional)

Combine flour, sugar, salt, and pepper; dredge ribs in flour mixture. Reserve remaining flour mixture.

Melt shortening in a large Dutch oven; add ribs, and cook over medium heat until browned, turning meat frequently to brown evenly. Drain meat; discard drippings. Stir in remaining flour mixture, chopped onion, allspice, bay leaf, and water.

Cover, reduce heat, and simmer 1 hour and 45 minutes or until meat is fork tender. Add carrots and whole onions; cover and simmer 30 minutes or until vegetables are tender. Discard bay leaf. Serve with horseradish, if desired. Yield: 4 servings.

BEEF-VEGETABLE LOAF

2 pounds ground beef
2 cups soft breadcrumbs
2 eggs
½ cup chopped onion
¼ cup chopped celery
¼ cup grated carrot
¼ cup chopped green pepper
1 (16-ounce) can whole tomatoes, drained and chopped
1½ teaspoons salt
1 teaspoon dry mustard
½ teaspoon pepper
½ teaspoon dried whole oregano
¼ cup catsup
2 tablespoons water

Combine first 12 ingredients, mixing well. Shape mixture into a 9-inch loaf; place on rack of a lightly greased broiler pan. Bake at 350° for 1 hour. Combine catsup and water; pour over meat loaf, and bake an additional 15 minutes. Yield: 8 servings.

BASIC MEAT LOAF

1½ pounds ground beef
2 (8-ounce) cans tomato sauce, divided
1 cup soft breadcrumbs
2 eggs, slightly beaten
2 tablespoons dried minced onion flakes
¾ teaspoon salt
¼ teaspoon pepper
2 teaspoons dried parsley flakes
1 teaspoon Worcestershire sauce

Combine ground beef, ½ cup tomato sauce, and next 5 ingredients; mix well. Shape meat mixture into a loaf. Place on rack of a lightly greased broiler pan. Bake at 350° for 1 hour.

Combine remaining tomato sauce and last 2 ingredients; stir well. Pour over meat loaf, and bake an additional 5 minutes. Yield: 6 servings.

▢ *Microwave Directions:* Combine ground beef, ½ cup tomato sauce, and next 5 ingredients; mix well. Shape meat mixture into a 7-inch round loaf. Place on a microwave-safe rack in a 12- x 8- x 2-inch baking dish. Cover with wax paper. Microwave at HIGH for 14 to 16 minutes or until almost firm to the touch, turning dish after 8 minutes.

Combine remaining tomato sauce and last 2 ingredients; stir well. Pour over meat loaf, and microwave at HIGH for 1 to 2 minutes. Let stand 5 minutes before serving.

Hurry-up Meat Loaves: Shape meat mixture into 6 individual loaves; place on rack of a lightly greased broiler pan. Bake at 450° for 25 minutes or to desired degree of doneness. Add topping as directed for whole meat loaf.

SAUCY MEATBALLS

1 pound ground beef
½ cup soft breadcrumbs
¾ teaspoon salt
½ teaspoon pepper
¼ teaspoon ground allspice
¼ teaspoon ground nutmeg
1 egg, beaten
¼ cup milk
2 tablespoons vegetable oil
3 tablespoons all-purpose flour
¼ teaspoon pepper
1½ cups beef broth
1 (8-ounce) carton commercial sour cream
Hot cooked rice or noodles

Combine first 8 ingredients, mixing well; shape into 1½-inch meatballs. Brown in hot oil in a large skillet. Drain; reserve drippings in skillet. Add flour and ¼ teaspoon pepper to drippings; mix well. Gradually add broth, stirring until smooth. Cook over medium heat 1 minute, stirring constantly. Remove from heat; cool. Add sour cream and meatballs; cook over medium heat, stirring constantly, until heated. Serve over rice. Yield: 4 servings.

POPOVER PIZZA

1 pound ground beef
1 large onion, chopped
1 (1.5-ounce) package
  spaghetti sauce mix
1 (15-ounce) can tomato
  sauce
½ cup water
2 cups (8 ounces) shredded
  mozzarella cheese
2 eggs
1 cup milk
1 tablespoon vegetable oil
1 cup all-purpose flour
¼ teaspoon salt
½ cup grated Parmesan cheese

Cook ground beef and onion in a large skillet until meat is browned, stirring to crumble meat; drain. Add sauce mix, tomato sauce, and water, stirring well; simmer 10 minutes.

Spoon meat mixture into a lightly greased 13- x 9- x 2-inch pan; sprinkle with mozzarella cheese.

Beat eggs, milk, and oil until foamy. Add flour and salt; beat until smooth. Pour batter over meat mixture, spreading evenly. Sprinkle with Parmesan cheese. Bake at 400° for 30 minutes or until the top is puffed and golden brown. Cut into squares; serve hot. Yield: 6 servings.

ITALIAN BEEF AND POTATO CASSEROLE

1½ pounds ground chuck
1½ cups chopped onion
2 cloves garlic, minced
1 (32-ounce) jar spaghetti sauce
⅓ cup water
1 teaspoon dried whole basil
1 teaspoon dried whole oregano
¼ teaspoon pepper
4 medium potatoes, peeled and
  thinly sliced
2 cups (8 ounces) shredded
  mozzarella cheese

Cook ground chuck, onion, and garlic in a large skillet over medium heat until meat is browned, stirring to crumble meat; drain. Add spaghetti sauce, water, basil, oregano, and pepper, stirring well.

Spoon one-third of meat mixture into a lightly greased 13- x 9- x 2-inch baking dish. Top with half of potato slices; cover with one-third of meat mixture. Add remaining potato slices and remaining meat mixture. Cover with aluminum foil. Bake at 375° for 1 hour or until potatoes are tender. Remove foil; sprinkle cheese over casserole. Bake an additional 5 minutes or until cheese melts. Let casserole stand 10 minutes before serving. Yield: 6 to 8 servings.

BEEFY NOODLE CASSEROLE

1 (5-ounce) package fine egg noodles
½ cup sliced fresh mushrooms
½ cup diced celery
¼ cup chopped onion
¼ cup chopped green pepper
2 tablespoons butter or margarine,
  melted
1⅓ pounds lean ground beef
1 (17-ounce) can cream-style corn
1 (16-ounce) can whole tomatoes,
  undrained and chopped
1 (10¾-ounce) can tomato soup,
  undiluted
1 teaspoon dried whole oregano
½ teaspoon salt
½ teaspoon pepper
⅛ teaspoon garlic powder
2 teaspoons Worcestershire sauce
1 cup (4 ounces) shredded American
  cheese (optional)

Cook noodles according to package directions; drain and set aside.

Sauté mushrooms, celery, onion, and green pepper in butter in a large Dutch oven until tender. Add beef; cook until browned, stirring occasionally. Drain. Stir in corn and next 7 ingredients. Add noodles; spoon mixture into a greased,

deep 3-quart casserole. Cover and bake at 325° for 25 minutes or until hot and bubbly. Sprinkle with cheese, and bake, uncovered, 3 minutes or until cheese melts. Yield: 6 to 8 servings.

◻ *Microwave Directions:* Cook noodles according to package directions; drain and set aside.

Combine mushrooms, celery, onion, green pepper, and butter in a 3-quart microwave-safe bowl. Cover loosely with heavy-duty plastic wrap; microwave at HIGH for 3 to 4 minutes or until vegetables are tender, stirring after 2 minutes. Crumble beef into vegetables; cover and microwave at HIGH for 5 to 6 minutes or until meat is done, stirring twice. Drain.

Stir in corn and next 7 ingredients. Add noodles; spoon mixture into a deep 3-quart microwave-safe casserole. Cover and microwave at MEDIUM HIGH (70% power) for 9 to 11 minutes or until heated. Sprinkle with cheese; cover and microwave at MEDIUM for 2 to 3 minutes or until cheese melts.

EASY STROGANOFF

1 pound ground beef
1 medium onion, chopped
2 tablespoons all-purpose flour
½ teaspoon garlic salt
¼ teaspoon pepper
1 (4-ounce) can sliced mushrooms,
  drained
1 (10¾-ounce) can cream of
  mushroom soup, undiluted
1 (8-ounce) carton commercial sour
  cream
Hot cooked noodles

Cook ground beef and onion in a large skillet until meat is browned, stirring to crumble meat; drain. Stir in flour and next 3 ingredients; cook and stir 1 minute. Stir in soup. Simmer 10 minutes, stirring occasionally. Add sour cream, and heat thoroughly. Serve over noodles. Yield: 4 servings.

EGGPLANT MOUSSAKA

1½ pounds ground beef
3 tablespoons chopped onion
1 (8-ounce) can tomato sauce
2 tablespoons minced fresh
   parsley
¼ teaspoon salt
⅛ teaspoon pepper
⅛ teaspoon ground cinnamon
1 cup water
3 medium eggplants
Olive oil
2 cups (8 ounces) shredded
   mozzarella cheese, divided
⅓ cup butter or margarine
⅓ cup plus 2 tablespoons
   all-purpose flour
1 (12-ounce) can evaporated
   milk
1 cup water
2 eggs, beaten
1 teaspoon ground nutmeg

Cook ground beef and onion in a large skillet until meat is browned, stirring to crumble meat; drain. Stir in tomato sauce and next 5 ingredients. Cover and simmer 45 minutes.

Peel eggplants, and cut into ¼-inch slices. Cook in hot oil until slightly tender; drain and cool. Arrange slices in a lightly greased 13- x 9- x 2-inch baking dish; top with meat mixture, and sprinkle with 1 cup cheese.

Melt butter in a heavy saucepan over low heat; add flour, stirring until smooth. Cook 1 minute, stirring constantly. Gradually add milk and 1 cup water; cook over medium heat, stirring constantly, until thickened and bubbly. Stir in eggs, nutmeg, and remaining 1 cup cheese. Pour sauce over meat mixture. Bake at 350° for 45 minutes or until top is golden brown. Cool slightly before cutting into squares. Yield: 6 servings.

SPICY CABBAGE AND BEEF ROLLS

1 green cabbage
1 pound ground beef
3 tablespoons chopped onion
3 tablespoons chopped green pepper
3 tablespoons chopped celery
1 tablespoon Worcestershire sauce
¾ cup cooked rice
½ teaspoon salt
Dash of pepper
1 (6-ounce) can tomato paste
⅓ cup water
1 (10-ounce) can tomatoes with
   green chiles, undrained and
   chopped
¼ teaspoon seasoned salt

Remove 10 outer leaves of cabbage; cook leaves in boiling salted water 5 to 8 minutes or until just tender; drain and set aside. Reserve remaining cabbage for other uses.

Combine next 8 ingredients, mixing well. Place equal portions of meat mixture in center of each cabbage leaf. Fold 2 opposite ends over and place rolls, seam side down, in a lightly greased 13- x 9- x 2-inch baking dish.

Combine tomato paste and water, mixing well. Stir in tomatoes with green chiles and seasoned salt; pour over cabbage rolls. Cover and bake at 350° for 1 hour. Yield: 5 servings.

BEEF-STUFFED PEPPERS

4 large green peppers
1 pound ground beef
1 medium onion, chopped
1 (8-ounce) can tomato sauce
1 (8¾-ounce) can whole kernel
   corn, drained
2 teaspoons chili powder
½ teaspoon salt
½ cup (2 ounces) shredded Cheddar
   cheese

Cut off tops of green peppers; remove centers and discard. Cook peppers 5 minutes in boiling water; drain peppers, and set aside.

Cook ground beef and onion in a large skillet until meat is browned, stirring to crumble meat; drain well. Stir in tomato sauce and next 3 ingredients.

Stuff peppers with meat mixture, and place in a baking dish. Bake at 350° for 15 minutes. Sprinkle tops of peppers with cheese; bake an additional 5 minutes. Yield: 4 servings.

BEEF TACOS

1 pound ground beef
1 medium onion, chopped
Commercial taco sauce
1 tablespoon Worcestershire
   sauce
1½ teaspoons chili powder
1 teaspoon garlic salt
½ teaspoon dried whole
   oregano
¼ teaspoon dried whole
   rosemary, crushed
¼ teaspoon ground cumin
¼ teaspoon pepper
Commercial taco shells
2 to 3 cups shredded lettuce
2 large tomatoes, chopped
1 cup (4 ounces) shredded
   Cheddar cheese

Cook ground beef and onion in a skillet until meat is browned, stirring to crumble meat. Drain. Stir in 3 tablespoons taco sauce, Worcestershire sauce, and seasonings; simmer 5 minutes or until thoroughly heated.

Spoon about 2 tablespoons meat mixture into each taco shell; top meat with lettuce, tomatoes, cheese, and 1 to 2 tablespoons taco sauce. Repeat procedure with remaining ingredients. Yield: 6 servings.

BEST-EVER ENCHILADAS

1 pound ground beef
1 large onion, chopped
1½ tablespoons all-purpose flour
1 tablespoon chili powder
1 teaspoon garlic powder
¾ teaspoon salt
¼ teaspoon ground cumin
¼ teaspoon rubbed sage
1 (16-ounce) can stewed tomatoes, undrained
12 corn tortillas
¼ cup vegetable oil
1 medium onion, chopped
½ cup sliced ripe olives
Enchilada Sauce
2 cups (8 ounces) shredded Monterey Jack cheese

Cook ground beef and large onion in a large skillet until meat is browned, stirring to crumble meat; drain. Add flour and seasonings; cook 1 minute, stirring constantly. Gradually stir in tomatoes; cook until thoroughly heated.

Fry tortillas, one at a time, in hot oil for 3 to 5 seconds on each side or just until softened, adding more oil, if necessary. Drain tortillas on paper towels.

Combine medium onion and olives; sprinkle over tortillas. Spoon about 2 tablespoons meat filling on each tortilla; roll tightly, and place in a 13- x 9- x 2-inch baking dish. Pour Enchilada Sauce over tortillas; bake at 350° for 15 minutes. Sprinkle with cheese; bake an additional 5 minutes. Yield: 6 servings.

Enchilada Sauce

1 (10½-ounce) can beef consommé, undiluted
½ cup butter or margarine, melted
½ cup all-purpose flour
8 cloves garlic, pressed
2 (8-ounce) cans tomato sauce
2 tablespoons chili powder
2 teaspoons rubbed sage
1 teaspoon ground cumin

Pour consommé into measuring cup; add enough water to measure 2 cups.

Combine consommé and remaining ingredients in a medium saucepan, stirring until smooth. Cook over medium heat, stirring constantly, until smooth and thickened. Yield: about 4 cups.

BEEFY CHIMICHANGAS

1 pound lean ground beef
½ cup finely chopped onion
1 (16-ounce) can refried beans
2 teaspoons chili powder
½ teaspoon ground cumin
2 cloves garlic, minced
3 (8-ounce) cans tomato sauce
10 to 12 (10-inch) flour tortillas
1 (4-ounce) can chopped green chiles, drained
1 canned jalapeño pepper, seeded and chopped
Vegetable oil
1½ cups (6 ounces) shredded Cheddar or Monterey Jack cheese

Cook ground beef in a large skillet until browned, stirring to crumble. Drain well. Stir in onion, next 4 ingredients, and ½ cup tomato sauce.

Spoon about ⅓ cup of meat mixture off center of a tortilla. Fold the edge nearest filling up and over filling, just until mixture is covered. Fold in opposite sides of tortilla to center; roll up. Secure with wooden picks. Repeat with remaining meat filling and tortillas.

Combine remaining tomato sauce, green chiles, and jalapeño pepper in a saucepan; cook over medium heat just until heated.

Fry chimichangas in deep hot oil 2 to 3 minutes or until golden brown, turning once. Drain well on paper towels. Remove wooden picks. Arrange chimichangas on serving plates. Spoon hot tomato sauce over tops, and immediately sprinkle with shredded cheese. Yield: 10 to 12 servings.

Note: Filled uncooked chimichangas may be sealed in airtight plastic bags and frozen up to 2 months. Thaw in refrigerator, and fry as directed.

SAUCY HAMBURGER STEAKS

1 pound ground beef
⅓ cup milk
2 tablespoons Burgundy or other dry red wine
2 slices bread, crusts removed and bread crumbled
1 egg, beaten
½ teaspoon salt
½ teaspoon pepper
1 tablespoon vegetable oil
2 recipes Mushroom Brown Sauce (page 436)

Combine first 7 ingredients; mix well, and shape into 4 patties. Cook patties in hot oil in a large skillet until browned on each side.

Add Mushroom Brown Sauce, and simmer 5 minutes. Yield: 4 servings.

BASIC BURGERS

1 pound ground beef
1 egg, beaten
¼ cup soft breadcrumbs
¼ teaspoon salt
⅛ teaspoon pepper
2 teaspoons Worcestershire sauce
4 hamburger buns

Combine first 6 ingredients, mixing well. Shape into 4 patties. Grill over medium coals about 15 minutes or to desired degree of doneness, turning once. Serve on buns. Yield: 4 servings.

Broiling: Place patties on broiler pan; broil 3 inches from heat about 10 minutes or to desired doneness, turning once.

Pan-Frying: Heat a heavy skillet until hot. Add patties; cook over medium heat about 8 minutes or to desired degree of doneness, turning once.

Mushroom Burgers: Sauté ¼ pound fresh mushrooms, sliced, in 2 tablespoons butter or margarine until tender; sprinkle with ⅛ teaspoon salt and ¼ teaspoon dried whole oregano. Spoon over patties.

Aloha Burgers: Place 1 canned unsweetened pineapple slice on each cooked patty. Top each with 1 slice mozzarella cheese and 1 green pepper ring. Broil or grill until cheese melts.

Onion Burgers: Sauté 1 medium onion, sliced, in 2 tablespoons butter or margarine until tender. Sprinkle with ⅛ teaspoon salt and ¼ teaspoon dried whole basil. Spoon over patties.

Bacon-Cheese Burgers: Top each cooked patty with 1 slice Cheddar cheese and 1 slice cooked bacon, halved. Broil or grill until cheese melts.

Pizza Burgers: Spread 1½ to 2 tablespoons commercial pizza sauce on each cooked patty; top each with 1 slice mozzarella cheese and 3 pepperoni slices. Broil or grill until cheese melts.

SEASONED HAMBURGERS

⅓ cup catsup
2 tablespoons molasses
1½ tablespoons Worcestershire sauce
1 teaspoon salt
½ teaspoon pepper
¼ teaspoon ground nutmeg
¼ teaspoon ground cinnamon
1 small onion, cut into wedges
1 clove garlic
2 bay leaves
3 pounds ground beef

Combine all ingredients except meat in container of an electric blender or food processor, and process until smooth. Add to meat, mixing well. Shape into 8 to 10 patties.

Grill patties 3 to 5 inches from the hot coals 7 minutes on each side or to desired degree of doneness. Yield: 8 to 10 servings.

POOR BOY FILLETS

1 pound ground beef
1 (4-ounce) can mushroom stems and pieces, drained
¼ cup grated Parmesan cheese
3 tablespoons finely chopped pimiento-stuffed olives
2 tablespoons finely chopped green pepper
2 tablespoons finely chopped onion
⅛ teaspoon salt
½ teaspoon lemon-pepper seasoning
12 slices bacon

Shape ground beef into a 12- x 7½-inch rectangle on wax paper. Sprinkle next 7 ingredients evenly over beef. Begin at short end, and roll jellyroll fashion, lifting wax paper to help support beef as you roll. Carefully slide roll onto a baking sheet, seam side down. Smooth and shape beef roll with your hands. Cover roll, and refrigerate at least 2 hours.

Cook bacon until transparent (not crisp); drain. Cut beef roll into 6 even slices. Wrap 2 slices of bacon around edges of each fillet, and secure with wooden picks.

Grill the fillets 4 to 5 inches from hot coals 8 minutes on each side or to desired degree of doneness. Yield: 6 servings.

LIVER WITH HERBS

6 slices bacon
½ cup all-purpose flour
½ teaspoon salt
¼ teaspoon pepper
1½ pounds thinly sliced beef liver
1 small onion, chopped
2 tablespoons chopped fresh parsley
2 tablespoons butter or margarine, melted
1 tablespoon lemon juice
1 teaspoon dried whole tarragon

Cook bacon in a large skillet until crisp; remove bacon, reserving the drip-

pings in skillet. Drain and crumble bacon, and set aside.

Combine flour, salt, and pepper; dredge liver in flour mixture, and brown in reserved bacon drippings. Remove liver to a warm platter, and top with crumbled bacon.

Sauté onion and parsley in butter; stir in lemon juice and tarragon. Pour over liver. Yield: 4 to 6 servings.

LIVER STROGANOFF

1½ pounds calf or beef liver
All-purpose flour
2 tablespoons butter or margarine, melted
1 cup sliced fresh mushrooms
½ cup chopped green onions
2 tablespoons chopped fresh parsley
2 cloves garlic, minced
¼ cup butter or margarine, melted
3 tablespoons all-purpose flour
1 (10½-ounce) can consommé, undiluted
½ teaspoon freshly ground pepper
6 drops of hot sauce
1 (8-ounce) carton commercial sour cream
Hot cooked noodles or rice

Dredge liver in flour; cook in 2 tablespoons butter in a large skillet just until it loses its pink color and is lightly browned. Remove and set aside to cool. Cut into narrow strips.

Sauté mushrooms, green onions, parsley, and garlic in ¼ cup butter. Blend in 3 tablespoons flour; cook 1 minute, stirring constantly. Gradually stir in consommé; add pepper and hot sauce. Cook over medium heat, stirring constantly, until thickened and bubbly.

Add liver to sauce, and simmer 10 minutes. Remove from heat, and stir in sour cream. Heat thoroughly, but do not boil. Serve over hot cooked noodles. Yield: 4 to 6 servings.

STEAK AND KIDNEY PIE

1 beef kidney (about 1 pound)
1 pound boneless sirloin steak, cut into ¾-inch cubes
¼ cup all-purpose flour
3 tablespoons vegetable oil
2 cups water
1 small onion, coarsely chopped
2 medium carrots, scraped and sliced
1 tablespoon Worcestershire sauce
½ cup water
3 tablespoons all-purpose flour
1 teaspoon salt
¼ teaspoon pepper
Pastry for single crust 9-inch pie

Trim membrane and fat from kidney. Place kidney in a medium saucepan, and cover with water. Bring to a boil; cover, reduce heat, and simmer about 1½ hours or until meat is tender. Drain and cut into ½-inch cubes; set aside.

Dredge beef cubes in ¼ cup flour. Brown beef cubes in hot oil. Add 2 cups water, onion, carrots, and Worcestershire. Cover and simmer 30 minutes.

Combine ½ cup water, 3 tablespoons flour, salt, and pepper, stirring until flour dissolves; stir into beef and vegetables. Stir in kidney. Cook over medium heat, stirring constantly, until thickened and bubbly. Pour into a lightly greased 2-quart casserole.

Roll pastry on a lightly floured surface to ⅛-inch thickness; cut pastry to make it 1-inch larger than casserole top. Place pastry on meat mixture. Turn edges under, and flute. Cut slits in top of pastry for steam to escape. Bake at 400° for 12 to 15 minutes or until pastry is golden brown. Let stand 10 minutes before serving. Yield: 6 servings.

SPANISH-STYLE LIVER

1 small onion, thinly sliced
2 tablespoons chopped green pepper
3 tablespoons butter or margarine, melted
½ cup chopped fresh mushrooms
1 clove garlic
1 (16-ounce) can whole tomatoes, undrained and chopped
½ teaspoon salt
⅛ teaspoon pepper
½ cup all-purpose flour
½ teaspoon salt
¼ teaspoon pepper
1¾ pounds sliced beef liver
¼ cup olive or vegetable oil
Italian parsley (optional)

Sauté onion and green pepper in butter until tender. Add chopped mushrooms, garlic, tomatoes, ½ teaspoon salt, and ⅛ teaspoon pepper; simmer vegetables over low heat 50 to 60 minutes or until thickened. Remove and discard garlic clove. Set sauce aside, and keep warm.

Combine flour, ½ teaspoon salt, and ¼ teaspoon pepper in a shallow bowl. Dredge liver in flour mixture, and brown on both sides in hot oil.

Place cooked liver on a heated platter, and serve sauce over top. Garnish platter with Italian parsley, if desired. Yield: 6 to 8 servings.

Veal

The most delicately flavored of all meats, veal is simply very young beef. Having such a mild flavor makes it especially suitable for use in recipes with fancy sauces and pungent seasonings.

Because veal comes from young calves, it is usually very lean, has no marbling, and little external fat. Good veal is pale pink in color. The redder the meat, the older the veal. Bones should be porous and red. Any fat that is visible should be very pale in color.

Veal requires careful cooking because its lack of fat can cause it to become tough and dry. Never broil it; most veal responds best to slow cooking at low temperatures. Moist heat cooking works especially well. Exceptions are veal chops, cutlets, and scallops, which are best when quickly pan-fried.

TIMETABLE FOR ROASTING VEAL		
Cut	Approximate Weight in Pounds	Approximate Total Cooking Times at 325°F. in Minutes Per Pound (170°F. internal temp.)
Rib roast	3 to 5	35 to 40
Loin	4 to 6	30 to 35
Sirloin or round	6 to 8	25 to 35
Boneless shoulder or rump	3 to 6	35 to 40

VEAL ROAST WITH VEGETABLES

1 (3½- to 4-pound) boneless veal round roast
¼ cup vegetable oil
¼ cup lemon juice
1 teaspoon prepared mustard
¼ teaspoon ground nutmeg
1 clove garlic, minced
1 large green pepper, cut into strips
½ pound fresh mushrooms, sliced
1 large onion, sliced and separated into rings
1 (10½-ounce) can chicken broth, undiluted

Place roast on rack of a roasting pan; insert meat thermometer. Combine oil, lemon juice, mustard, nutmeg, and garlic; brush over roast, reserving remaining mixture. Bake at 325° for 2 hours.

Remove from oven, and remove veal from roasting pan; remove rack, drain fat, and place veal directly in pan. Place vegetables around veal. Pour remaining oil mixture and chicken broth over veal. Bake an additional 30 minutes or until meat thermometer registers 170°.

Arrange meat on a platter, and spoon vegetables around meat. Serve with pan drippings, if desired. Yield: 8 servings.

LEMON-VEAL PICCATA

⅔ cup all-purpose flour
1 teaspoon salt
½ teaspoon pepper
¼ teaspoon garlic powder
1 pound thin veal cutlets (about 8)
⅓ cup butter or margarine
⅓ cup lemon juice
1 tablespoon chopped fresh parsley

Combine first 4 ingredients. Dredge veal in flour mixture.

Melt butter in a large skillet over medium heat. Add veal, and cook about 1 minute on each side; drain on paper towels. Add lemon juice to skillet; cook until thoroughly heated. Return veal to skillet; sprinkle with parsley, and heat briefly. To serve, spoon lemon mixture over veal. Yield: 4 servings.

VEAL PARMIGIANA

2 (15-ounce) cans tomato sauce
1 tablespoon butter or margarine, melted
1 tablespoon Worcestershire sauce
1 teaspoon dried whole oregano
1 teaspoon dried whole basil
¼ teaspoon garlic powder
¼ teaspoon pepper
2 eggs
¼ teaspoon pepper
2 pounds veal cutlets, cut into serving-size pieces
About 4 cups soft breadcrumbs
½ cup olive oil
¼ cup grated Parmesan cheese
1 (8-ounce) package sliced mozzarella cheese

Combine first 7 ingredients in a saucepan; cook over medium heat, about 5 minutes, stirring occasionally. Set aside.

Combine eggs and pepper; beat well. Flatten cutlets with a meat mallet to ⅛-inch thickness, if necessary. Dip cutlets in egg, and dredge in breadcrumbs. Cook cutlets in hot oil 4 minutes on each side or until browned. Place in a lightly greased 13- x 9- x 2-inch baking dish. Pour sauce over veal, and sprinkle with Parmesan cheese. Cover and bake at 350° for 30 minutes. Uncover and top with mozzarella cheese; bake an additional 5 minutes or until cheese melts. Yield: 6 servings.

Veal

• RETAIL CUTS •
WHERE THEY COME FROM
HOW TO COOK THEM

LEG (ROUND)
SIRLOIN
LOIN
RIB
SHOULDER
FORESHANK & BREAST

Rib Roast
Roast

Boneless Rib Roast
Roast

Crown Roast
Roast

Boneless Rib Chop
Braise. Panfry. Broil

Rib Chop
Braise. Panfry. Broil

Short Ribs
Braise. Cook in Liquid

RIB

Blade Roast
Braise. Roast

Arm Roast
Braise. Roast

Blade Steak
Braise. Panfry

Arm Steak
Braise. Panfry

Boneless Shoulder Arm Roast
Braise. Roast

Boneless Shoulder Eye Roast
Braise. Roast

SHOULDER

Boneless Rump Roast
Braise. Roast

Round Steak
Braise. Panfry

Top Round Steak
Braise. Panfry

Leg Cutlet
Braise. Panfry. Broil

LEG (ROUND)

Breast
Braise. Roast

Boneless Breast Roast
Braise. Roast

Cross Cut Shank
Braise. Cook in Liquid

Riblet
Braise. Cook in Liquid

Shank
Braise. Cook in Liquid

FORESHANK & BREAST

THIS CHART APPROVED BY
NATIONAL LIVE STOCK & MEAT BOARD

Loin Roast
Roast

Boneless Loin Roast
Roast

Loin Chop
Braise. Panfry. Broil

Kidney Chop
Braise. Panfry

Top Loin Chop
Braise. Panfry. Broil

Butterfly Chop
Braise. Panfry. Broil

LOIN

Sirloin Roast
Roast

Boneless Sirloin Roast
Roast

Sirloin Steak
Braise. Panfry. Broil

Top Sirloin Steak
Braise. Panfry. Broil

SIRLOIN

Veal for Stew
Braise. Cook in Liquid

Ground Veal
Panfry. Broil

Cubes for Kabobs
Braise

Cubed Steak
Braise. Panfry

OTHER CUTS

Veal Schnitzel looks impressive but takes only a few minutes to prepare.

ROLLED VEAL CUTLETS

¼ cup chopped onion
¼ cup chopped celery
2 tablespoons chopped green pepper
¼ cup butter or margarine, melted
3 cups bread cubes
4 slices bacon, cooked and crumbled
2 tablespoons dry white wine
¼ teaspoon salt
⅛ teaspoon pepper
½ teaspoon poultry seasoning
6 veal cutlets (about 1½ pounds)
⅓ cup all-purpose flour
¼ cup vegetable oil
1½ cups water
1 teaspoon beef-flavored bouillon
   granules
2 tablespoons cornstarch
¼ cup water
¼ teaspoon salt
⅛ teaspoon pepper
Fresh parsley sprigs

Sauté first 3 ingredients in butter until tender; stir in bread cubes and next 5 ingredients. Place about one-sixth of vegetable mixture in center of each veal cutlet; fold edges over, and secure with a wooden pick.

Dredge veal in flour, and brown on all sides in hot oil in a heavy skillet. Add 1½ cups water and bouillon granules; cover and cook over low heat 30 minutes. Remove veal, keeping warm.

Combine cornstarch and ¼ cup water, stirring until blended. Stir into drippings in skillet; cook over medium heat until thickened and bubbly. Stir in ¼ teaspoon salt and ⅛ teaspoon pepper. Spoon over veal; garnish with parsley. Yield: 6 servings.

VEAL SCHNITZEL

1 pound (¼-inch-thick) veal cutlets
   (about 6)
3 eggs
1 teaspoon salt
¾ teaspoon coarsely ground pepper
¾ cup all-purpose flour
1½ cups soft breadcrumbs
¾ cup butter or margarine
5 ounces Gruyère cheese, thinly
   sliced
3 tablespoons dried parsley flakes
   (optional)
Twists of lemon (optional)
Fresh parsley sprigs (optional)

Place cutlets between sheets of wax paper; flatten to ⅛-inch thickness using a meat mallet or rolling pin.

Combine eggs, salt, and pepper; beat well. Dredge cutlets in flour; dip in egg mixture, and coat with breadcrumbs.

Melt butter in a large skillet over medium heat; add cutlets, and cook 4 to 5 minutes. Turn cutlets, and top with cheese. Cover and cook an additional 3 to 4 minutes. Sprinkle with parsley flakes, if desired. Garnish with lemon twists and fresh parsley, if desired. Yield: 6 servings.

VEAL OSCAR

1½ pounds veal cutlets, cut into
   serving-size pieces
⅓ cup all-purpose flour
⅛ teaspoon salt
⅛ teaspoon pepper
⅛ teaspoon garlic powder
⅓ cup butter or margarine, melted
1 cup fresh lump crabmeat
½ cup chopped green onions
2 teaspoons Worcestershire sauce
2 (10-ounce) packages frozen
   asparagus spears, cooked (optional)
Béarnaise Sauce (page 438)
Chopped fresh parsley

Flatten cutlets to ¼-inch thickness, if necessary. Combine flour and seasonings; dredge cutlets in flour mixture. Cook veal in melted butter in a large skillet until browned on both sides. Remove meat, and keep warm, reserving drippings in skillet.

Add crabmeat, green onions, and Worcestershire sauce to drippings in skillet; cook over medium heat, stirring occasionally, until mixture is thoroughly heated.

Arrange asparagus over each piece of veal, if desired. Spoon crabmeat mixture evenly over asparagus; top with Béarnaise Sauce. Sprinkle with parsley. Yield: 6 to 8 servings.

VEAL SCALLOPINI

1 pound thin veal cutlets (about 8)
¼ cup vegetable oil
¾ cup chopped onion
¼ pound fresh mushrooms, sliced
1 clove garlic, minced
2 tablespoons all-purpose flour
¾ teaspoon salt
¼ teaspoon pepper
1 cup Chablis or other dry white
   wine
½ cup water

Cook cutlets in hot oil 4 minutes or until browned. Drain on paper towels; reserve drippings in skillet.

Sauté onion, mushrooms, and garlic in reserved drippings. Add flour, salt, and pepper to sautéed vegetables, stirring well. Cook 1 minute, stirring constantly. Gradually add wine and water; cook over medium heat, stirring constantly, until mixture is thickened and bubbly. Add cutlets; cover and simmer 15 minutes. Transfer cutlets to a warm platter; spoon sauce over top. Yield: 4 servings.

VEAL MEATBALLS

1 pound ground veal
½ cup fine dry breadcrumbs
¼ cup milk
1 egg, beaten
2 tablespoons chopped fresh parsley
¾ teaspoon pepper
½ teaspoon salt
1 clove garlic, minced
2 tablespoons vegetable oil
2 tablespoons all-purpose flour
¾ cup milk
1 (16-ounce) carton commercial sour
   cream
1 (4-ounce) can sliced mushrooms,
   undrained
1 teaspoon browning and seasoning
   sauce
¼ teaspoon salt
⅛ teaspoon pepper
1 (5-ounce) package egg noodles,
   cooked

Combine first 8 ingredients; shape into 1½-inch balls. Brown in hot oil 5 minutes in a large skillet. Remove meatballs, reserving drippings in skillet. Add flour to drippings; cook 1 minute, stirring constantly. Gradually add milk; cook over medium heat, stirring constantly, until thickened. Stir in next 5 ingredients. Return meatballs to skillet, and cook over low heat 10 minutes.

Serve meatballs and sauce over hot cooked noodles. Yield: 4 to 6 servings.

Lamb

Lamb is meat from sheep slaughtered when less than a year old. The meat of older sheep, called mutton, is popular in England, but is rarely seen in the United States.

Look for lamb with a bright pink color, pink bones, and white fat. If the meat and bones are dark red, it usually means the meat is older.

A parchment-like skin usually surrounds chops, steaks, and roasts. Called fell, this skin is sometimes left on whole roasts to hold in natural juices while the lamb cooks. If left on individual steaks, however, the skin will shrink and cause the steaks to curl. If your butcher hasn't trimmed the fell from steaks, remove it yourself before cooking.

Most cuts of lamb are tender enough to be cooked by one of the dry heat methods. Cuts that are less tender work best when cooked by moist heat methods.

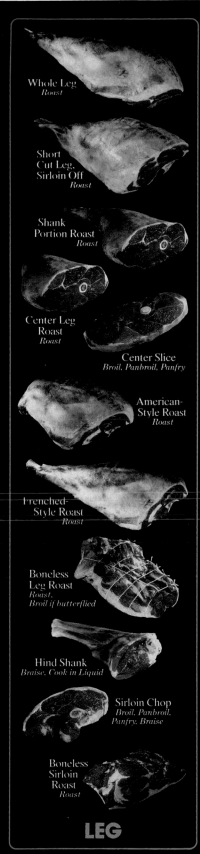
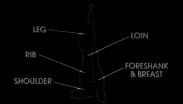

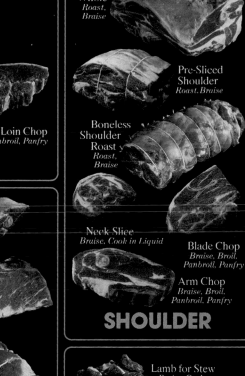

1185500 06-406

RACK OF LAMB WITH HERBED MUSTARD GLAZE

½ cup prepared mustard
2 tablespoons soy sauce
1 teaspoon dried whole rosemary
¼ teaspoon ground ginger
1 clove garlic
1 egg
2 tablespoons olive oil
2 (2-pound) racks of lamb

Combine first 6 ingredients in container of an electric blender; process 15 seconds or until smooth. Add oil to mustard mixture, one drop at a time; process on low speed until light and creamy.

Place lamb, fat side up, on rack in a shallow roasting pan; insert meat thermometer, making sure it does not touch fat or bone. Brush mustard mixture on lamb. Bake at 325° for 1 hour and 20 to 30 minutes or until meat thermometer registers 160°. Yield: 6 servings.

ROAST LEG OF LAMB

1 (6-pound) leg of lamb
2 teaspoons salt
1 teaspoon freshly ground pepper
1 teaspoon dried whole rosemary
¼ cup butter or margarine, melted
Mint Sauce (page 442) or commercial mint jelly
Fresh mint leaves

Place lamb, fat side up, in a shallow roasting pan. Combine seasonings and butter; brush butter mixture evenly over lamb. Insert meat thermometer, making sure it does not touch fat or bone. Bake at 325° for 2½ hours or until meat thermometer registers 160°. Let stand 10 minutes before carving. Serve with Mint Sauce, and garnish with fresh mint. Yield: 8 servings.

Serve Roast Leg of Lamb with a homemade Mint Sauce and a leafy fresh mint garnish.

TIMETABLE FOR ROASTING LAMB			
Cut	Approximate Weight in Pounds	Internal Temperature	Approximate Total Cooking Times at 325°F. in Hours
Leg			
Whole (bone in)	6 to 7	160°F. (medium)	2½ to 3¾
Half (bone in)	3 to 4	160°F. (medium)	2 to 2¾
Shoulder (boneless)	4 to 6	160°F. (medium)	2½ to 3¾
Rib roast*	1½ to 2½	160°F. (medium)	1 to 1⅔
Crown roast (unstuffed)*	2 to 3	160°F. (medium)	1 to 1½

*Oven set at 375°F. and not preheated.

STUFFED LEG OF LAMB

1 (5- to 7-pound) leg of lamb, boned
1 (6-ounce) package herb-seasoned
   stuffing mix
1½ tablespoons butter or margarine,
   melted
½ teaspoon celery seeds
¼ teaspoon pepper
1 (8-ounce) can crushed pineapple,
   drained
2 cloves garlic, sliced
1 tablespoon butter or margarine,
   softened
¼ teaspoon ground ginger
1 tablespoon lemon juice
¼ cup red currant jelly

Place lamb, fat side up, in a shallow roasting pan.

Combine stuffing mix, melted butter, celery seeds, pepper, and pineapple. Pack mixture into pocket of lamb. Fasten open edges of lamb with skewers.

Make several slits on outside of lamb, and insert garlic slices. Rub outside of lamb with softened butter, and sprinkle with ginger and lemon juice. Insert meat thermometer, making sure it does not touch fat.

Bake at 325° for 1 hour and 30 minutes. Glaze lamb with currant jelly, and bake an additional 15 minutes or until meat thermometer registers 160°. Let stand 10 minutes before carving. Yield: 10 servings.

Carving a Leg of Lamb

Place shank bone to carver's right. Cut 2 or 3 slices from thin side parallel to leg bone. Turn leg over so it rests on cut side. Steady leg with carving fork, and make vertical slices down to leg bone.

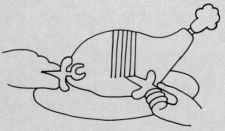

Cut horizontally along the leg bone to release slices.

LAMB STEAKS WITH BÉARNAISE SAUCE

2 tablespoons soy sauce
1 tablespoon catsup
1 tablespoon vegetable oil
½ teaspoon coarsely ground pepper
1 clove garlic, minced
4 (1-inch-thick) lamb sirloin chops
Béarnaise Sauce (page 438)

Combine first 5 ingredients, stirring well. Brush garlic mixture over both sides of each lamb chop. Place chops in a large shallow dish. Cover and refrigerate 8 hours.

Grill chops over medium coals 5 to 8 minutes on each side or to desired degree of doneness. Serve with Béarnaise Sauce. Yield: 4 servings.

DIJON LAMB CHOPS

4 to 6 lamb rib chops
1 lemon, cut in half
Garlic powder
Freshly ground pepper
1 cup chopped fresh parsley
⅓ cup Dijon mustard
1 tablespoon plus 1 teaspoon wheat
   bran
Vegetable cooking spray

Trim fat from lamb chops. Rub both sides with lemon; sprinkle lightly with garlic powder and pepper.

Combine parsley and next 2 ingredients; mix well, and press on all sides of chops. Place chops in a 12- x 8- x 2-inch baking dish coated with cooking spray; bake, uncovered, at 500° for 4 minutes. Reduce heat to 350°, and bake chops an additional 15 minutes or to desired degree of doneness. Yield: 4 to 6 servings.

BROILED LAMB CHOPS

⅓ cup firmly packed brown sugar
¼ cup soy sauce
2 tablespoons catsup
1 tablespoon lemon juice
½ teaspoon ground ginger
¼ teaspoon salt
¼ teaspoon pepper
⅛ teaspoon garlic powder
4 (1-inch-thick) lamb rib chops

Combine the first 8 ingredients; stir until smooth.

Broil chops 10 inches from heat about 25 minutes, basting often with sauce, and turning once. Yield: 4 servings.

BRAISED LAMB SHANKS

2 to 2½ pounds lamb shanks
1 tablespoon vegetable oil
½ cup chopped onion
½ cup chopped celery
½ cup water
½ cup catsup
2 teaspoons Worcestershire sauce
½ teaspoon salt
¼ teaspoon pepper
1 clove garlic, minced

Cook shanks in hot oil in a large skillet until browned. Drain well. Add remaining ingredients to skillet. Cover and cook over medium heat 1 to 1½ hours or until shanks are tender, stirring occasionally. Add additional water to skillet as necessary. Yield: 2 servings.

SHISH KABOBS TERIYAKI

¼ cup soy sauce
¼ cup vegetable oil
2 tablespoons vinegar
¼ teaspoon ground ginger
1 clove garlic, minced
1 pound boneless lamb, cut into
   1-inch cubes
4 cherry tomatoes
1 green pepper, cut into 1-inch pieces
1 (8-ounce) can pineapple chunks,
   drained
1 (8-ounce) can whole water
   chestnuts, drained
Hot cooked rice

Combine first 5 ingredients in a large shallow container. Add lamb; cover and marinate in refrigerator 4 hours. Remove lamb from marinade. Alternate lamb and next 4 ingredients on skewers.

Grill over medium coals 5 minutes on each side or to desired degree of doneness, basting frequently. Serve kabobs over rice. Yield: 4 servings.

CURRIED LAMB WITH RICE MOLD

1 pound boneless lamb
¾ cup sliced fresh mushrooms
¼ cup chopped onion
1 tablespoon butter or margarine,
   melted
1 tablespoon all-purpose flour
1 cup beef or lamb broth
1½ tablespoons bacon drippings
½ teaspoon curry powder
½ teaspoon salt
⅛ teaspoon pepper
Curried Rice Mold (page 345)
Assorted condiments

Partially freeze lamb; slice diagonally across grain into 2- x ¼-inch strips. Set lamb aside.

Sauté mushrooms and onion in butter in a large skillet; add flour, stirring until smooth. Cook 1 minute, stirring constantly. Gradually add broth; cook over medium heat, stirring constantly, until gravy is thickened and bubbly. Set gravy aside.

Stir-fry lamb in hot bacon drippings in a heavy skillet; drain. Add gravy mixture, curry powder, salt, and pepper; cover and simmer 10 minutes or until lamb is tender.

Invert Curried Rice Mold onto a serving platter. Spoon lamb and gravy into rice mold, and surround mold with several of the following condiments: chopped tomato, chopped green pepper, shredded carrot, toasted slivered almonds, bean sprouts, raisins, and flaked coconut. Yield: 4 servings.

Pork

Originally known as the fattiest type of meat on the market, today's pork has a new reputation. With so many people watching their cholesterol intake, producers now breed pork to be significantly lower in fat to keep the flavorful meat a popular consumer choice. Today's pork contains about the same amount of cholesterol as beef.

Almost all cuts of pork are tender and almost all cuts can be cooked by one of the dry heat methods. When selecting fresh pork, look for a bright pink color. Pork takes on a gray color when it's been in the meat case too long. The bones should be pink, and the fat white. Choose pork that has a high proportion of meat to fat or bone.

Although today's pork is virtually free of any trichinae (parasites), it is still recommended that pork be cooked until well done. An internal temperature of 140° will kill any parasites possibly present in pork, so our meat chart and recipe recommendations to cook fresh pork to 160° should prevent any problem of this nature. When fresh pork has been cooked to the proper internal temperature, there should no longer be any trace of pink. Just be sure not to overcook the meat, or it can be dry and tough.

Fresh pork is not frequently microwaved. Pockets of fat scattered throughout the meat can sometimes give false temperature readings.

To roast: Cook any type of roast with the fat side up, even if you have trimmed most of the fat away; the fat will partially melt as the meat roasts, and it will self-baste the meat.

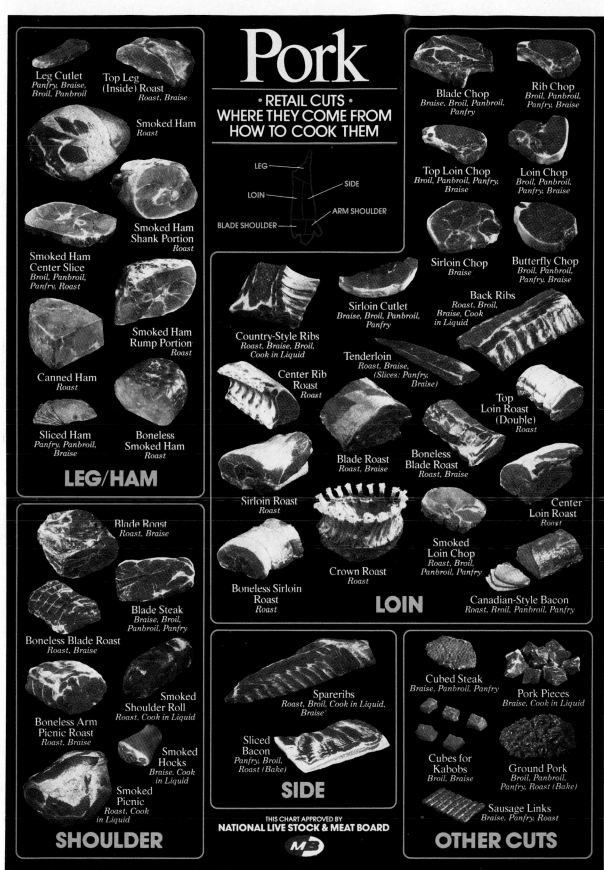

Pork

• RETAIL CUTS •
WHERE THEY COME FROM
HOW TO COOK THEM

LEG
LOIN
SIDE
ARM SHOULDER
BLADE SHOULDER

LEG/HAM

Leg Cutlet
Panfry, Braise, Broil, Panbroil

Top Leg (Inside) Roast
Roast, Braise

Smoked Ham
Roast

Smoked Ham Shank Portion
Roast

Smoked Ham Center Slice
Broil, Panbroil, Panfry, Roast

Smoked Ham Rump Portion
Roast

Canned Ham
Roast

Sliced Ham
Panfry, Panbroil, Braise

Boneless Smoked Ham
Roast

LOIN

Blade Chop
Braise, Broil, Panbroil, Panfry

Rib Chop
Broil, Panbroil, Panfry, Braise

Top Loin Chop
Broil, Panbroil, Panfry, Braise

Loin Chop
Broil, Panbroil, Panfry, Braise

Sirloin Chop
Braise

Butterfly Chop
Broil, Panbroil, Panfry, Braise

Sirloin Cutlet
Braise, Broil, Panbroil, Panfry

Back Ribs
Roast, Broil, Braise, Cook in Liquid

Country-Style Ribs
Roast, Braise, Broil, Cook in Liquid

Tenderloin
Roast, Braise, (Slices: Panfry, Braise)

Center Rib Roast
Roast

Top Loin Roast (Double)
Roast

Blade Roast
Roast, Braise

Boneless Blade Roast
Roast, Braise

Sirloin Roast
Roast

Center Loin Roast
Roast

Crown Roast
Roast

Smoked Loin Chop
Roast, Broil, Panbroil, Panfry

Boneless Sirloin Roast
Roast

Canadian-Style Bacon
Roast, Broil, Panbroil, Panfry

SHOULDER

Blade Roast
Roast, Braise

Blade Steak
Braise, Broil, Panbroil, Panfry

Boneless Blade Roast
Roast, Braise

Smoked Shoulder Roll
Roast, Cook in Liquid

Boneless Arm Picnic Roast
Roast, Braise

Smoked Hocks
Braise, Cook in Liquid

Smoked Picnic
Roast, Cook in Liquid

SIDE

Spareribs
Roast, Broil, Cook in Liquid, Braise

Sliced Bacon
Panfry, Broil, Roast (Bake)

OTHER CUTS

Cubed Steak
Braise, Panbroil, Panfry

Pork Pieces
Braise, Cook in Liquid

Cubes for Kabobs
Broil, Braise

Ground Pork
Broil, Panbroil, Panfry, Roast (Bake)

Sausage Links
Braise, Panfry, Roast

THIS CHART APPROVED BY
NATIONAL LIVE STOCK & MEAT BOARD
M3

Carving a Crown Roast

Remove any stuffing from the center of the roast. Steady the roast with the carving fork. Slice between the ribs, removing one chop at a time.

STUFFED CROWN PORK FLAMBÉ

1 (16-rib) crown roast of pork
Salt and pepper
3 green onions, sliced
¼ cup butter or margarine, melted
4 large fresh mushrooms, sliced
2 cooking apples, peeled and diced
3 cups herb-seasoned stuffing mix
1 cup applesauce
3 tablespoons brandy
1 (10-ounce) jar apricot preserves
¼ cup brandy
1 (9-ounce) jar sweet pickled kumquats, drained
¼ cup brandy

Season roast with salt and pepper; place roast, bone ends up, on rack in a shallow roasting pan. Insert meat thermometer without touching fat or bone.

Sauté green onions in butter until tender. Add mushrooms; cook, stirring constantly, until tender. Add apples; cook 1 minute, stirring constantly. Stir in next 3 ingredients; spoon into center of roast. Cover stuffing and exposed ends of ribs with aluminum foil.

Heat preserves and ¼ cup brandy; set ¼ cup aside. Bake roast at 325° for 2 hours or until thermometer registers 160°, basting with ¾ cup preserves every 10 minutes after 1 hour.

Remove from oven, and let stand 15 minutes; place on serving platter. Garnish bone tips with kumquats. Heat reserved ¼ cup preserves mixture; remove from heat. Pour ¼ cup brandy over heated mixture. Ignite and pour over roast. Yield: 8 servings.

PINEAPPLE PORK ROAST

1 small onion, sliced
¼ cup sliced celery
¼ cup sliced carrots
1 (3-pound) rolled boneless pork loin roast
Salt and pepper
1 small bay leaf, crumbled
½ cup pineapple juice
¼ cup soy sauce
¼ cup apricot preserves
1 teaspoon cornstarch

Arrange vegetables in a greased roasting pan. Season roast with salt and pepper; place roast over vegetables, fat side up, and sprinkle bay leaf on top.

Insert meat thermometer horizontally into one end of roast. Bake at 325° for 30 to 45 minutes or until browned; turn roast over, and bake 30 minutes to brown bottom side. Turn roast over again, and drain off drippings.

Combine pineapple juice and soy sauce; pour over roast, and bake 15 minutes or until thermometer registers 160°.

Remove roast from oven; strain and reserve drippings from vegetables, and sprinkle vegetables over roast.

Combine preserves and cornstarch; add to drippings. Cook over medium heat until thickened, stirring constantly with a whisk or wooden spoon. Spoon some of the glaze over roast; let stand 10 minutes. Serve with remaining glaze. Yield: 8 to 10 servings.

TIMETABLE FOR ROASTING FRESH PORK

Cut	Approximate Weight in Pounds	Internal Temperature	Approximate Cooking Times at 325°F. in Minutes Per Pound
Loin			
Center	3 to 5	160°F.	25 to 30
Half	5 to 7	160°F.	30 to 35
End	3 to 4	160°F.	35 to 40
Roll	3 to 5	160°F.	30 to 35
Boneless top	2 to 4	160°F.	25 to 30
Crown	4 to 6	160°F.	25 to 30
Picnic shoulder			
Bone in	5 to 8	160°F.	25 to 30
Rolled	3 to 5	160°F.	30 to 35
Boston shoulder	4 to 6	160°F.	35 to 40
Leg (fresh ham)			
Whole (bone in)	12 to 16	160°F.	18 to 20
Whole (boneless)	10 to 14	160°F.	20 to 25
Half (bone in)	5 to 8	160°F.	25 to 30
Tenderloin			
Roast at 375°F.	½ to 1	160°F.	20 to 30 minutes total
Back ribs		well done	1½ to 2½ hours
Country-style ribs		well done	1½ to 2½ hours
Spareribs		well done	1½ to 2½ hours
Pork loaf	1½ to 2	well done	1 to 1½ hours

Bacon strips baste and flavor Pork St. Tammany as it bakes; each slice reveals a tasty wild rice and apricot stuffing.

PORK ST. TAMMANY

1 (6-ounce) package long-grain and wild rice mix
½ cup boiling water
½ cup chopped dried apricots
2 green onions, finely chopped
½ cup chopped fresh mushrooms
¼ cup chopped green pepper
2 tablespoons butter or margarine, melted
3 tablespoons chopped pecans
1 tablespoon chopped fresh parsley
⅛ teaspoon garlic salt
⅛ teaspoon pepper
Dash of red pepper
1 (5- to 6-pound) rolled boneless pork loin roast
4 slices bacon
Canned apricot halves (optional)
Fresh parsley sprigs (optional)

Cook rice according to package directions. Set aside.

Pour boiling water over apricots; let stand 20 minutes to soften. Drain.

Sauté green onions, mushrooms, and green pepper in butter until tender. Stir in rice, apricots, pecans, parsley, and seasonings.

Remove strings and slice roast in half lengthwise, if not purchased sliced. Slice pork pieces lengthwise in half again, slicing to but not through one side. Lay pieces side by side, and spoon stuffing mixture evenly over pork. Beginning with 1 long side, roll pork jellyroll fashion, and tie securely with heavy string at 2-inch intervals. Place roast on a lightly greased rack in a shallow roasting pan. Place bacon lengthwise over roast. Insert meat thermometer into thickest part of roast, making sure it does not touch fat or stuffing.

Place an aluminum foil tent over roast. Bake at 325° for 3 hours or until meat thermometer registers 160° (30 to 35 minutes per pound). Remove foil for the last 30 to 40 minutes of baking. Remove roast from oven; let stand 5 minutes. Remove string; slice and garnish with apricot halves and parsley, if desired. Yield: 12 to 15 servings.

PORC À L'ORANGE

1 (4-pound) pork loin roast
1 clove garlic, sliced
1 teaspoon dried whole
　rosemary, crushed
½ teaspoon salt
¼ teaspoon pepper
2 tablespoons Dijon mustard
2 tablespoons orange
　marmalade
⅔ cup orange juice, divided
2 oranges, thinly sliced
　(optional)
Fresh parsley (optional)
1 to 2 tablespoons Grand
　Marnier or other orange-flavored
　liqueur
2 teaspoons cornstarch

When buying roast, ask the butcher to saw across the rib bones at the base of the backbone of roast, to separate the ribs from the backbone. Cut small slits in fat of loin, and insert slivers of garlic into slits. Rub the roast with rosemary, salt, and pepper.

Place meat, fat side up, on rack in a shallow roasting pan; insert meat thermometer, making sure it does not touch fat or bone. Bake at 325° for 2 hours or until meat thermometer registers 160° (30 minutes per pound).

Combine mustard, marmalade, and 2 tablespoons orange juice, stirring well. About 15 minutes before roast is done, brush with mustard mixture. Bake an additional 15 minutes. Remove roast to serving platter. Garnish with orange slices and parsley, if desired.

Skim fat from roasting pan, leaving 2 tablespoons drippings in pan; combine remaining orange juice, Grand Marnier, and cornstarch; add to pan drippings, mixing well. Cook over medium heat, stirring constantly, until thickened and bubbly. Serve with roast. Yield: 10 to 12 servings.

HERBED PORK ROAST

3 tablespoons vegetable oil
1 teaspoon dry mustard
1 teaspoon dried whole thyme
1 teaspoon dried marjoram leaves
½ teaspoon salt
½ teaspoon pepper
1 clove garlic, crushed
1 (4- to 5-pound) rolled boneless pork
　loin roast
¾ cup dry white wine

Combine first 7 ingredients. Score roast; rub on seasonings. Wrap roast in aluminum foil; refrigerate 8 hours.

Remove roast from foil. Place roast, fat side up, on rack in a shallow roasting pan. Insert meat thermometer, making sure it does not touch fat. Bake, uncovered, at 325° for 2 to 2½ hours or until thermometer registers 160° (30 to 35 minutes per pound), basting frequently with wine. Let stand 10 to 15 minutes before slicing. Yield: 12 servings.

PRUNE-STUFFED PORK LOIN ROAST

¾ cup dry sherry, divided
1 (12-ounce) package whole pitted
　prunes
2 cups apple cider
1 (8-ounce) can pineapple slices,
　drained
1 tablespoon grated fresh gingerroot
1 teaspoon seasoned salt
1 teaspoon lemon-pepper seasoning
1 (6- to 8-pound) boneless double
　pork loin roast, cut for rolling

Heat ¾ cup sherry in a saucepan just long enough to produce fumes (do not boil); remove from heat, and ignite. Let flames die down, and set aside.

Combine prunes and cider in a medium saucepan. Bring to a boil; reduce heat and simmer, uncovered, 20 minutes. Remove from heat; stir in ½ cup of heated sherry. Pour remaining ¼ cup sherry over pineapple; set aside.

Combine seasonings; rub on roast. Place one roast on a roasting rack, fat side down. Reserve 4 prunes in liquid; remove remaining prunes with a slotted spoon and place on roast. Place remaining roast, fat side up, atop prunes. Tie roast at 2- to 3-inch intervals with cord.

Insert meat thermometer into thickest part of roast, making sure it does not touch prunes or fat. Bake at 325° for 30 to 35 minutes per pound or until thermometer reaches 160°, basting often with reserved prune liquid.

Remove pineapple from sherry. Garnish roast with pineapple slices and reserved prunes. Serve roast with pan drippings. Yield: 14 to 16 servings.

Fresh ham is meat from the hind leg of pork that has not been cured or smoked. Fresh ham looks and tastes more like a pork roast than what people tend to think of when they hear the term "ham."

MAPLE-BAKED FRESH HAM WITH RAISIN SAUCE

1 (5- to 7-pound) pork leg half
　(fresh ham)
14 to 16 whole cloves
1 cup maple-flavored syrup
½ teaspoon ground ginger
¼ teaspoon ground nutmeg
¼ teaspoon ground allspice
Raisin Sauce (page 441)

Score fat on ham in a diamond design, and stud with cloves. Place ham, fat side up, on a rack in a roasting pan. Insert meat thermometer, making sure it does not touch fat or bone.

Combine syrup, ginger, nutmeg, and allspice; stir well, and pour over ham. Bake, uncovered, at 325° for 2 to 3 hours or until meat thermometer registers 160° (25 to 30 minutes per pound). Baste ham with drippings every 20 to 30 minutes. If ham browns too quickly, cover loosely with foil. Serve hot or cold with Raisin Sauce. Yield: 10 to 14 servings.

SUNSHINE GLAZED FRESH HAM

1 (10- to 12-pound) pork leg (fresh ham)
Whole cloves
1 (6-ounce) can frozen orange juice concentrate, thawed and undiluted
½ cup molasses
¼ cup prepared mustard
1 tablespoon grated orange rind
Peach halves (optional)
Fresh parsley sprigs (optional)

Place ham, fat side up, on a rack in a shallow roasting pan. Score fat on ham in a diamond design, and stud with cloves. Insert meat thermometer, making sure it does not touch fat or bone.

Combine orange juice and next 3 ingredients. Brush ham with juice mixture. Bake, uncovered, at 325° for 3 to 4 hours or until meat thermometer registers 160° (18 to 20 minutes per pound). Baste ham with juice mixture every 30 minutes. Garnish with peach halves and fresh sprigs of parsley, if desired. Yield: about 20 servings.

SMOKED PORK SHOULDER

1 cup catsup
1 cup vinegar
½ cup butter or margarine
2½ tablespoons Worcestershire sauce
1½ teaspoons dried onion flakes
1½ teaspoons hot sauce
¾ teaspoon salt
⅛ teaspoon pepper
Dash of red pepper
1 small clove garlic, minced
1 (6- to 8-pound) Boston butt roast
Hamburger buns (optional)

Combine first 10 ingredients in a saucepan, and bring to a boil; reduce heat, and simmer 10 minutes. Set aside.

Prepare charcoal fire in smoker, and let burn 10 to 15 minutes. Place water pan in smoker; fill with ½ cup sauce and about 4 quarts water.

Trim skin from roast. Place roast on food rack, and baste generously on all sides with sauce.

Cover with smoker lid; cook 9 to 11 hours or to desired degree of doneness. Thinly slice roast, and serve with remaining sauce. Serve on buns, if desired. Yield: 10 to 12 servings.

Note: Leftover sauce may be refrigerated and reheated for basting grilled chicken or other meats.

SPICY BARBECUED PORK

1 (5- to 6-pound) Boston butt roast
2 medium onions, sliced
4 or 5 whole cloves
1 (18-ounce) bottle hickory smoke-flavored barbecue sauce
⅛ teaspoon hot sauce
Hamburger buns (optional)

Cover pork roast with water in a large Dutch oven. Add onion and cloves; cover and cook over medium heat 3 hours or until pork is tender. Drain meat, and shred with a fork. Combine shredded pork, barbecue sauce, and hot sauce in Dutch oven. Cover and cook over low heat 15 to 20 minutes, stirring occasionally. Serve on buns, if desired. Yield: 10 to 12 servings.

Spicy Barbecued Beef: Substitute 1 (5- to 6- pound) rump roast for pork.

ROAST PORK TENDERLOIN

2 tablespoons butter or margarine, melted
1 teaspoon dried whole rosemary, crushed
1 teaspoon dried whole thyme
1 large clove garlic, minced
2 (1- to 1½-pound) pork tenderloins
⅓ cup orange marmalade
2 tablespoons brandy

Combine first 4 ingredients; brush tenderloins with butter mixture. Place tenderloins, fat side up, on rack in a shallow roasting pan. Insert meat thermometer into thickest part of meat, making sure it does not touch fat. Drizzle remaining butter mixture over meat.

Bake at 375° for 15 to 20 minutes. Combine marmalade and brandy; brush over roast. Bake an additional 15 to 20 minutes or until meat thermometer registers 160° (20 to 30 minutes per pound). Yield: 6 servings.

Carving a Whole Ham

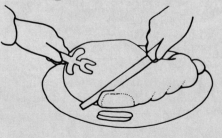

Place the shank bone to the carver's right. Cut 2 or 3 slices from the thin side of the ham parallel to the leg bone. Turn ham over so it rests on cut side.

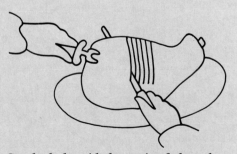

Steady the leg with the carving fork, and make vertical slices down to the leg bone. Cut horizontally along the bone to release slices.

PINEAPPLE PORK

1 (20-ounce) can pineapple chunks
1½ pounds boneless pork, trimmed
    of fat and cut into 1-inch cubes
1 tablespoon vegetable oil
1 medium onion, chopped
¼ cup firmly packed brown sugar
2 tablespoons cornstarch
½ teaspoon salt
½ cup water
⅓ cup vinegar
2 tablespoons catsup
1 tablespoon soy sauce
1 large green pepper, cut into 1-inch
    pieces
Hot cooked rice

Drain pineapple, reserving juice.

Cook pork in hot oil in a large skillet until browned. Drain. Add onion, and cook until tender. Combine sugar, cornstarch, and salt in a small bowl. Gradually add water, stirring until smooth. Stir in pineapple juice, vinegar, catsup, and soy sauce. Add to pork, stirring constantly; cook over medium heat until sauce thickens. Cover, reduce heat, and simmer 45 minutes or until meat is tender. Stir in the pineapple and green pepper; cover and cook 3 minutes. Serve with rice. Yield: 4 to 6 servings.

To reduce fat content: Trim away excess fat before cooking.

HURRY CURRY

8 pork tenderloin slices (about 1½
    pounds)
¼ cup butter or margarine, melted
    and divided
1 clove garlic, crushed
½ cup chopped onion
1 cup chopped tart apple
2 teaspoons curry powder
¼ teaspoon ground cardamom
1 tablespoon all-purpose flour
1 teaspoon crystallized ginger
¼ teaspoon salt
⅛ teaspoon pepper
1 (10½-ounce) can chicken broth,
    undiluted
1 teaspoon lemon juice
¼ cup chutney

Brown pork in 2 tablespoons butter in a large skillet. Remove and cut into bite-size pieces; set aside.

Add remaining butter, garlic, and onion to skillet; cook until onion is transparent. Add apple and curry powder; cook, stirring constantly, over low heat until apple is tender. Add cardamom, flour, ginger, salt, and pepper; stir until blended. Gradually add chicken broth, stirring constantly. Stir in lemon juice. Bring to a boil; reduce heat, and simmer about 10 minutes. Stir in pork and chutney; cover and simmer 10 minutes. Serve over rice with several condiments, such as toasted slivered almonds, raisins, or coconut. Yield: 6 servings.

PORK CHOPS AND CREAM GRAVY

4 to 6 (½-inch-thick) pork chops
Salt and pepper
¼ cup vegetable oil
2 tablespoons all-purpose flour
1½ cups milk
½ teaspoon browning and seasoning
    sauce
¼ teaspoon salt
⅛ teaspoon pepper

Trim excess fat from pork chops; sprinkle pork chops lightly with salt and pepper. Brown chops on both sides in hot oil, and drain on paper towels. Reserve 2 tablespoons drippings in skillet.

Add flour to skillet, stirring until smooth. Cook 1 minute, stirring constantly. Gradually add milk; cook over medium heat, stirring constantly, until thickened and bubbly. Stir in seasoning sauce, ¼ teaspoon salt, and ⅛ teaspoon pepper. Add pork chops to gravy; cover and simmer 45 minutes, turning chops occasionally. Yield: 4 to 6 servings.

TANGY BARBECUED PORK CHOPS

½ cup maple syrup
½ cup catsup
1 tablespoon Worcestershire
    sauce
1 tablespoon steak sauce
1 tablespoon prepared
    mustard
1 tablespoon vinegar
1 tablespoon vegetable oil
1 teaspoon lemon juice
¼ teaspoon salt
⅛ teaspoon pepper
Dash of ground cloves
6 to 8 (¾- to 1-inch-thick)
    pork chops

Combine first 11 ingredients in a small saucepan. Bring to a boil; reduce heat, and simmer 5 minutes.

Grill chops over medium coals 10 minutes on each side. Baste with sauce, and grill an additional 15 to 20 minutes or to desired degree of doneness, basting frequently with sauce, and turning meat occasionally. Yield: 6 to 8 servings.

PORK CHOPS AND SPANISH RICE

1 cup uncooked long-grain rice
2 tablespoons vegetable oil
4 (1-inch-thick) pork chops
3 cups coarsely chopped tomatoes
1 small green pepper, chopped
1 small onion, chopped
1 teaspoon salt
¼ teaspoon pepper
½ teaspoon prepared mustard
⅓ cup water

Sauté rice in hot oil in a large skillet 3 to 5 minutes or until browned, stirring constantly. Remove rice, and set aside.

Add pork chops to skillet, and brown on both sides. Combine rice, tomatoes, and next 5 ingredients; spoon over pork chops. Add water; cover and simmer 45 to 50 minutes or until pork chops are tender. Yield: 4 servings.

PRUNE-STUFFED PORK CHOPS

2 cups soft breadcrumbs
1 cup chopped prunes
2 tablespoons butter or margarine, melted
1 teaspoon lemon juice
½ teaspoon salt
6 (1¼-inch-thick) pork chops, cut with pockets
Salt
½ cup seasoned dry breadcrumbs
1 cup pineapple juice, divided

Combine first 5 ingredients, stirring well; stuff into pockets of chops, and secure openings with wooden picks. Sprinkle chops with salt, and dredge in seasoned dry breadcrumbs.

Place chops in a lightly greased 13- x 9- x 2-inch baking dish; pour ½ cup pineapple juice over chops. Cover and bake at 350° for 30 minutes. Add remaining ½ cup pineapple juice, and bake, uncovered, an additional 30 minutes. Yield: 6 servings.

BOURBON-BRAISED PORK CHOPS

¼ cup all-purpose flour
½ teaspoon salt
¼ teaspoon pepper
4 (1-inch-thick) pork chops
1 tablespoon vegetable oil
4 orange slices
2 tablespoons brown sugar
2 tablespoons cornstarch
⅛ teaspoon ground allspice
1 cup water
¼ cup orange juice
2 tablespoons bourbon
¼ cup currants or raisins

Combine flour, salt, and pepper; dredge chops in flour mixture. Brown on both sides in oil in a large skillet. Place an orange slice on each chop.

Combine brown sugar, cornstarch, and allspice in a small saucepan; gradually stir in water. Cook over medium heat, stirring constantly, until mixture thickens and comes to a boil. Cook 1 minute, stirring constantly. Remove from heat; stir in orange juice, bourbon, and currants. Spoon over pork chops. Cover, reduce heat, and simmer 1 hour or until pork chops are tender, stirring occasionally. Yield: 4 servings.

PORK AND RICE BAKE

2 pounds pork shoulder blade steaks (½-inch-thick)
1 tablespoon vegetable oil
¼ cup water
1 (10½-ounce) can chicken broth, undiluted
1 cup uncooked long-grain rice
½ cup chopped onion
1 cup water
1 (10-ounce) package frozen green peas

Brown steaks on both sides in hot oil in a large skillet. Add ¼ cup water. Cover and simmer 45 minutes. Remove steaks from skillet.

Stir broth, rice, onion, and 1 cup water into drippings; add steaks. Cover and simmer 20 to 25 minutes or until liquid is absorbed. Stir in peas; cook 5 to 8 minutes. Yield: 6 servings.

OVEN RIBS

½ cup molasses
¼ cup vinegar
¼ cup prepared mustard
2 tablespoons Worcestershire sauce
½ teaspoon salt
½ teaspoon hot sauce
4 pounds spareribs

Combine first 6 ingredients in a saucepan; bring mixture to a boil. Remove from heat, and set aside.

Cut ribs into serving-size pieces; place meaty side down in a large shallow pan. Bake, uncovered, at 450° for 30 minutes. Drain off excess fat. Reduce heat to 350°. Turn ribs over, and bake an additional 50 to 60 minutes. Brush ribs with sauce during last 30 minutes of cooking. Yield: 4 to 6 servings.

SAUCY SPARERIBS

3 pounds spareribs
½ cup chopped onion
1 clove garlic, minced
¼ cup butter or margarine, melted
2 (8-ounce) cans tomato sauce
⅓ cup water
¼ cup Worcestershire sauce
2 tablespoons lemon juice
2 tablespoons vinegar
2 teaspoons chili powder
4 dashes of hot sauce

Cut ribs into serving-size pieces. Place ribs in shallow pan. Bake, uncovered, at 325° for 1½ hours. Drain off pan drippings, and discard.

Sauté onion and garlic in butter in a saucepan. Add remaining ingredients; bring to a boil. Pour over ribs; continue baking 45 minutes or until tender, basting occasionally. Yield: 3 to 4 servings.

SMOKY RIBS

3 cups catsup
½ cup firmly packed brown sugar
½ cup molasses
¼ cup prepared mustard
2 tablespoons vinegar
2 tablespoons liquid smoke
2 tablespoons Worcestershire sauce
Red pepper to taste
6 pounds country-style pork ribs
½ teaspoon garlic salt
¼ teaspoon pepper

Combine first 8 ingredients; set aside.

Cut ribs into serving-size pieces; place in a large Dutch oven. Cover ribs with water; add garlic salt and pepper. Bring water to a boil; cover, reduce heat, and simmer 30 minutes. Drain well.

Grill ribs, 5 inches from heat, over slow coals 45 minutes or to desired degree of doneness, turning frequently. Brush ribs with sauce during last 15 minutes. Heat remaining sauce, and serve with ribs. Yield: 6 to 8 servings.

LITTLE MEAT PIES

2 teaspoons shortening
2 teaspoons all-purpose flour
1½ pounds ground pork
½ pound ground beef
2 large onions, finely chopped
6 green onions, chopped
1 tablespoon chopped fresh parsley
1 teaspoon salt
¼ teaspoon rubbed sage
⅛ teaspoon garlic powder
⅛ teaspoon pepper
Dash of red pepper
Meat Pie Pastry
Vegetable oil

Combine shortening and flour in a large Dutch oven; cook over medium heat, stirring constantly, until roux is caramel colored. Add pork, beef, onion, parsley, and seasonings. Cook over medium heat until meat is browned, stirring to crumble. Drain and cool.

Divide Meat Pie Pastry into 22 equal portions. Roll out each portion into a 5-inch circle. Place about 2 tablespoons meat mixture in center of each circle, and fold pastry in half. Moisten edges with water, and press with a fork to seal.

Fry pies in 1 inch hot oil (375°) until browned, turning once. Drain on paper towels. Yield: 22 pies.

Meat Pie Pastry

4 cups all-purpose flour
2 teaspoons baking powder
1 teaspoon salt
½ cup shortening, melted
2 eggs, slightly beaten
½ cup plus 2 tablespoons milk

Combine first 3 ingredients. Add shortening, stirring until blended. Combine eggs and milk, stirring well. Pour milk mixture into flour mixture; stir until blended, adding more milk if necessary. Yield: pastry for 22 pies.

SCRAMBLED EGGS AND BRAINS

Brains have a very soft consistency. A short blanching period makes them firmer, after which they can be fried, braised, or creamed. They should be cooked within a day of purchasing.

½ pound pork or veal brains
2 tablespoons lemon juice
6 eggs, beaten
3 tablespoons chopped green onions
¼ teaspoon salt
⅛ teaspoon pepper
3 tablespoons butter or margarine

Place brains in a bowl, and cover with cold water. Add lemon juice, and let soak 30 minutes. Drain and rinse under cold water. Trim any outer membranes with a sharp knife. Place brains in a saucepan; cover with water. Bring to a boil; reduce heat and simmer, uncovered, 20 minutes. Drain well, and chop coarsely.

Combine eggs, green onions, salt, and pepper, stirring well. Stir in brains.

Melt butter in a large nonstick skillet. Add egg mixture. Cook over low heat, stirring gently to allow uncooked portion to flow underneath. Cook until eggs are set but still moist. Do not stir constantly. Yield: 4 servings.

Smokers

Smokers, both charcoal and electric, are fast becoming one of the most popular cooking appliances. Long, slow cooking in a smoker with a self-basting water pan guarantees succulent meats and frees you to do other things.

What's more, most people are delighted by distinctive flavors that result from smoking. Not just hickory, but apple and maple wood from your yard and herbs from your garden can all be used for rich, sweet flavoring of smoked foods. Part of the fun of smoking foods is experimenting with different flavorings.

Leave space around each food item on the grill to allow even cooking and smoke penetration. Don't open the smoker after everything is set, particularly during the first few hours. You'll lose both smoke and moisture and prolong the cooking time required.

Occasionally you may need to add more water to the pan during cooking. You'll hear a sizzling sound if the pan is empty, so don't lift the lid to check; simply pour water through the grill.

Cooking times will vary with the outside temperature, cut of meat, quality of charcoal, and degree of doneness you desire.

Color is not an accurate test for doneness. Smoked pork and poultry are often pink even though they're thoroughly cooked. For large cuts of meat, it's best to use a meat thermometer to determine internal temperature and degree of doneness.

Ham and Sausage

The leg of pork becomes ham after it's cured with seasonings and/or smoked. The label on the ham should identify the type of processing, and whether or not the ham has been cooked.

Ham labeled "fully cooked" does not require further heating and may be eaten cold. Heating it to an internal temperature of 140° brings out more flavor in the ham than serving it cold, however.

Ham marked "cook-before-eating" must be cooked to an internal temperature of 160°. If the wrapping doesn't indicate whether or not the ham has been fully cooked, assume that it needs cooking.

WHAT KIND TO BUY

You'll find ham available either boneless or bone-in. Bone-in hams are marketed whole, in halves, in butt or shank portions, or as center-cut slices. The butt half generally has a higher proportion of meat to bone and is more expensive than the shank portion.

Boneless hams are easy to slice and have little or no waste. They are often the best buy, although the price is higher. Boneless hams are sold whole or cut into halves, quarters, or pieces.

Canned hams are always boneless and are fully cooked during the canning process. A small amount of unflavored gelatin is added to canned hams before sealing to absorb the natural juices as the ham cooks during processing and to cushion the ham during shipping. This causes the jelled substance common in canned hams.

Some hams are labeled "water-added," which means that a seasoned water solution was injected before smoking. Water-added hams are usually lower in price because part of their weight is water.

Bacon is sold in slices that vary in thickness. Its flavor also varies, depending on the smoking and curing process used. Bacon may be very lean or fat, depending on the origination of its cut.

Pork tenderloin that is cured and smoked is known as Canadian bacon. It's boneless and is usually very lean. Sausage is made from seasoned ground pork.

STORING HAM

Cured hams will keep in the refrigerator up to one week, whether cooked or uncooked. Refrigerate canned hams both before and after opening unless they are otherwise marked; unopened they will keep up to one year unless the label says something different.

Freezing is not generally recommended for ham because of flavor and texture changes, but these changes are minimal if the ham is frozen less than two months in an airtight container. Don't freeze canned hams, as the expansion during freezing may damage the seams of the can.

HAM TAKES TO THE MICROWAVE

Microwave ovens significantly reduce the cooking time for hams and yield the same juicy tenderness you enjoy from the conventional oven. For the microwave, we recommend only hams labeled "fully cooked" so you won't have to worry about the safety of the ham if your thermometer reading is off or if the ham cooks unevenly.

When selecting cuts of ham to

TIMETABLE FOR ROASTING SMOKED PORK

Cut	Approximate Weight in Pounds	Internal Temperature	Approximate Cooking Times at 325°F. in Minutes Per Pound
Ham (cook before eating)			
Whole	10 to 14	160°F.	18 to 20
Half	5 to 7	160°F.	22 to 25
Shank portion	3 to 4	160°F.	35 to 40
Butt portion	3 to 4	160°F.	35 to 40
Ham (fully cooked)			
Whole	10 to 12	140°F.	15 to 18
Half	5 to 7	140°F.	18 to 24
Loin	3 to 5	160°F.	25 to 30
Picnic shoulder (cook before eating)	5 to 8	160°F.	30 to 35
Picnic shoulder (fully cooked)	5 to 8	140°F.	25 to 30
Shoulder roll (butt)	2 to 4	160°F.	35 to 40
Canadian-style bacon	2 to 4	160°F.	35 to 40

1. For Sweet-and-Sour Glazed Ham, slice away skin from ham using a sharp knife.

2. Score fat on ham in a diamond design; use a ruler to help you cut straight lines, if necessary.

3. Insert a whole clove in center of each diamond.

4. Place ham, fat side up, on rack in roasting pan; insert meat thermometer. Be sure it does not rest in fat or bone.

cook in the microwave, choose cuts of ham no larger than halves so they'll cook more evenly. Most recipes that call for chopped cooked ham work especially well in the microwave.

When cooking ham halves, remember that the upper, cut edge of a ham cooks faster than the center, so shield this area with a narrow strip of aluminum foil; this will reduce energy received and slow the cooking process. Before shielding, however, check the manufacturer's directions with your oven; some older models can be damaged by the use of foil.

Make sure the shield is at least 3 inches from the top of the oven and 1 inch from the walls. Fold the foil smoothly over the cut edge of the ham; if it is not smooth or if it touches the walls, it may cause an arc (spark of electricity). If an arc occurs, flatten the foil and continue microwaving.

Cook ham halves and slices on MEDIUM (50% power) or MEDIUM HIGH (70% power). Sugar used in curing ham attracts microwaves and can cause overcooking or uneven cooking when microwaved at HIGH. Recipes that mix chopped ham with other ingredients can generally be cooked on HIGH.

CRANBERRY-ORANGE GLAZED HAM

1 (16- to 18-pound) smoked fully cooked ham
Whole cloves
2½ cups firmly packed brown sugar, divided
1⅓ cups cranberry juice cocktail
½ cup honey
¼ cup cider vinegar
1½ tablespoons all-purpose flour
3 tablespoons prepared mustard
3 tablespoons butter or margarine
2 to 3 oranges, sliced
About 6 maraschino cherries, halved

Slice skin from ham. Score fat on ham in a diamond design, and stud with cloves. Place ham, fat side up, on rack in a shallow roasting pan. Insert meat thermometer, making sure it does not touch fat or bone. Bake at 325° for 3 to 3½ hours.

Combine ½ cup sugar, cranberry juice, honey, cider vinegar, flour, mustard, and butter in a saucepan, mixing well. Bring to a boil, and cook 1 minute.

Coat exposed portion of ham with remaining sugar. Place orange slices on ham, securing in centers with wooden picks; leave tips of picks exposed. Place cherry half on each pick.

Pour hot cranberry mixture over ham; bake an additional 1 hour or until thermometer registers 140°, basting ham with pan juices twice. Yield: 25 to 30 servings.

Sweet-and-Sour Glazed Ham glistens from its spicy basting sauce.

SWEET-AND-SOUR GLAZED HAM

2 cups apple jelly
2 tablespoons prepared mustard
2 tablespoons lemon juice
½ teaspoon ground cloves
1 (5- to 7-pound) smoked fully
   cooked ham half
Whole cloves
Fresh parsley sprigs

Combine first 4 ingredients in a saucepan; bring to a boil over medium heat, stirring occasionally. Set aside.

Slice away skin from ham. Score fat on ham in a diamond design, and stud with whole cloves. Place ham, fat side up, on rack in a shallow roasting pan. Insert meat thermometer, making sure it does not touch fat or bone. Bake, uncovered, at 325° for 1½ to 2 hours or until thermometer registers 140° (18 to 24 minutes per pound); baste every 15 to 20 minutes with sauce. Heat remaining sauce, and serve with ham. Garnish with parsley. Yield: 10 to 14 servings.

☐*Microwave Directions:* Combine first 4 ingredients in a 4-cup glass measure. Microwave at HIGH for 1 to 2 minutes or until thoroughly heated, stirring after 1 minute. Set aside.

Slice away skin from ham. Score fat on ham in a diamond design, and stud with whole cloves. Place ham, fat side up, on rack in a 12- x 8- x 2-inch baking dish. Insert microwave-safe meat thermometer, making sure it does not touch fat or bone. Shield upper cut edge of ham with a 1½-inch wide strip of aluminum foil. Cover entire dish with heavy-duty plastic wrap. Microwave at MEDIUM (70% power) for 8 to 10 minutes per pound or until thermometer registers 140°, basting 4 times during cooking. Turn ham over after half the cooking time has elapsed. (Rearrange foil strip when ham is turned.) Let stand 10 minutes before serving. Garnish with parsley.

Country hams are produced by using a dry cure, and a long slow smoking and drying process. They are usually heavily salted and require soaking before cooking.

COUNTRY HAM IN APPLE CIDER

1 (12- to 14-pound) uncooked country ham
2 quarts apple cider
1 tablespoon whole cloves
½ cup firmly packed brown sugar
2 tablespoons prepared mustard
Fresh parsley sprigs (optional)

Place ham in a very large container; cover with water, and soak 8 hours. Pour off water. Scrub ham in warm water with a stiff brush, and rinse well. Place ham, skin side down, in a large roasting pan. Pour cider over ham, and sprinkle with cloves. Insert meat thermometer into ham, making sure it does not touch fat or bone. Cover and bake at 325° for 2½ to 3 hours.

Carefully remove ham from pan juices; remove skin. Place ham, fat side up, on a cutting board; score fat in a diamond design. Return ham to roaster, fat side up. Combine brown sugar and mustard, stirring well. Coat exposed portion of ham with sugar mixture. Continue baking, uncovered, 30 minutes or until meat thermometer registers 142° (about 15 minutes per pound).

Remove ham from roaster; discard pan drippings. To serve, thinly slice ham; garnish with parsley, if desired. Yield: 24 to 26 servings.

COUNTRY HAM WITH RED-EYE GRAVY

6 (¼-inch-thick) slices country ham
2 tablespoons butter or margarine, melted
2 tablespoons firmly packed brown sugar
½ cup strong black coffee

Cut gashes in fat to keep ham from curling. Sauté ham in butter in a heavy skillet over low heat until lightly browned, turning several times. Remove ham from skillet, and keep warm.

Stir sugar into pan drippings; cook over low heat until sugar dissolves, stirring constantly. Add coffee, stirring well; simmer 5 minutes. Serve gravy over ham. Yield: 6 servings.

HONEY-GLAZED HAM STEAK

½ cup firmly packed brown sugar
½ cup honey
½ teaspoon dried mustard
6 whole cloves
1 (1-inch thick) smoked fully cooked ham steak (about 2 pounds)
2 slices canned pineapple
4 maraschino cherries, halved

Combine brown sugar, honey, mustard, and cloves in a small saucepan; stir well. Bring to a boil; boil 2 minutes, stirring occasionally.

Place ham on rack of a shallow roasting pan; bake at 325° for 10 minutes. Arrange pineapple slices and cherries on top of ham; spoon on glaze. Bake an additional 15 minutes, basting twice with drippings. Yield: 6 servings.

GOLDEN GRILLED HAM

1 (1-inch-thick) smoked fully cooked ham steak (about 2 pounds)
1 cup ginger ale
1 cup orange juice
½ cup firmly packed brown sugar
3 tablespoons vegetable oil
1 tablespoon wine vinegar
2 teaspoons dry mustard
¾ teaspoon ground ginger
½ teaspoon ground cloves

Score fat edge of ham. Combine remaining ingredients; pour over ham in a shallow baking dish. Refrigerate 8 hours, or let stand at room temperature 1 hour, spooning marinade over ham several times.

Grill ham over slow coals about 15 minutes on each side, brushing frequently with marinade. Heat remaining marinade, and serve with ham. Yield: 4 to 6 servings.

HAM SPAGHETTI SKILLET

4 slices bacon
½ cup chopped onion
¼ cup chopped green pepper
2 cups chopped cooked ham
1 clove garlic, minced
1 (28-ounce) can whole tomatoes, undrained and chopped
1 (7-ounce) package spaghetti, cooked and drained
1 cup (4 ounces) shredded Cheddar cheese

Cook bacon in a large skillet until crisp; remove bacon, reserving 1 to 2 tablespoons drippings in skillet. Drain bacon on paper towels; crumble bacon, and set aside.

Sauté onion and green pepper in reserved drippings in skillet until vegetables are tender. Add ham, and cook until lightly browned. Add garlic and tomatoes; cover, reduce heat, and simmer 30 minutes, stirring occasionally.

Stir cooked spaghetti into ham mixture, and sprinkle with cheese. Simmer, uncovered, 10 minutes. Sprinkle spaghetti with bacon before serving. Yield: 4 to 6 servings.

CREAMY HAM TOWERS

½ teaspoon chicken-flavored
  bouillon granules
½ cup hot water
1½ cups milk
¼ cup butter or margarine
¼ cup all-purpose flour
½ cup (2 ounces) shredded
  American cheese
1 teaspoon prepared mustard
1 teaspoon Worcestershire sauce
2 cups cubed cooked ham
⅓ cup sliced ripe olives
2 tablespoons chopped pimiento
2 tablespoons minced fresh parsley
1 (10-ounce) package frozen patty
  shells, baked

Dissolve bouillon granules in hot water; stir in milk, and set aside.

Melt butter in a heavy saucepan over low heat; add flour, stirring until smooth. Cook 1 minute, stirring constantly. Gradually add bouillon mixture; cook over medium heat, stirring constantly, until thickened and bubbly. Add cheese, mustard, and Worcestershire sauce, stirring until cheese melts. Stir in ham, olives, pimiento, and parsley. Heat thoroughly. Spoon filling into patty shells. Yield: 6 servings.

◻ *Microwave Directions:* Dissolve bouillon granules in hot water; stir in milk, and set aside.

Place butter in a 1½-quart glass bowl. Microwave at HIGH for 55 seconds or until melted. Add flour, stirring until smooth. Gradually add bouillon mixture, stirring well. Microwave at HIGH for 5 to 6 minutes or until thickened and bubbly, stirring after 2 minutes, and then at 1-minute intervals. Add cheese, mustard, and Worcestershire sauce, stirring until cheese melts. Stir in ham, olives, pimiento, and parsley. Microwave at HIGH for 1 to 2 minutes or until thoroughly heated. Spoon filling into patty shells.

HAM AND CHEESE KABOBS

1 (20-ounce) can pineapple chunks
½ cup orange marmalade
2 teaspoons dried mustard
¼ teaspoon ground cloves
1 pound cooked ham, cut into 1-inch
  cubes
½ pound Swiss cheese, cut into
  1-inch cubes

Drain pineapple, reserving 2 tablespoons juice. Combine reserved juice, marmalade, mustard, and cloves; set mixture aside.

Thread ham, cheese, ham, then pineapple on 12-inch skewers. (Cheese must be between and touching ham to prevent rapid melting.) Repeat procedure until all ingredients are used.

Place kabobs 4 to 5 inches from hot coals. Brush with sauce. Grill 3 to 4 minutes or until cheese is partially melted and ham is heated, brushing frequently with sauce. Serve immediately. Yield: 4 to 6 servings.

HAM TETRAZZINI

1 (7-ounce) package spaghetti
½ pound fresh mushrooms, sliced
¼ cup chopped onion
¼ cup butter or margarine, melted
¼ cup all-purpose flour
2 cups milk
2 cups half-and-half
½ teaspoon salt
¼ teaspoon pepper
⅛ teaspoon garlic powder
¾ cup grated Parmesan cheese,
  divided
2 cups diced cooked ham
1 (2.2-ounce) can sliced ripe olives,
  drained

Cook spaghetti according to package directions, omitting salt. Drain well, and set aside.

Sauté mushrooms and onion in butter in a large skillet until tender. Add flour, stirring until smooth. Cook 1 minute, stirring constantly. Gradually add milk and half-and-half, stirring constantly, until mixture is thickened and bubbly. Stir in seasonings and ½ cup Parmesan cheese.

Spoon half of spaghetti into a lightly greased 12- x 8- x 2-inch baking dish. Pour one-third of sauce over spaghetti; sprinkle with half each of ham and olives. Repeat layers, ending with sauce over last layer of olives. Sprinkle the remaining ¼ cup Parmesan cheese over casserole. Bake at 350° for 25 minutes. Yield: 6 servings.

◻ *Microwave Directions:* Cook spaghetti according to package directions, omitting salt. Drain and set aside.

Combine mushrooms, onion, and butter in a 2-quart casserole. Cover with heavy-duty plastic wrap, and microwave at HIGH for 4 to 5 minutes or until tender. Add flour, stirring until smooth. Gradually add milk and half-and-half, stirring until blended. Microwave at HIGH for 10 to 14 minutes or until thickened and bubbly, stirring at 2-minute intervals. Stir in seasonings and ½ cup Parmesan cheese.

Spoon half of spaghetti into a lightly greased 12- x 8- x 2-inch baking dish. Pour one-third of sauce over spaghetti; sprinkle with half each of ham and olives. Repeat layers, ending with sauce over last layer of olives. Sprinkle the remaining ¼ cup Parmesan cheese over casserole.

Cover with heavy-duty plastic wrap. Microwave at HIGH for 6 to 8 minutes or until thoroughly heated, giving dish a half-turn after 3 minutes. Let stand 5 minutes before serving.

SUPREME HAM LOAF

1 pound ground cooked ham
1 pound ground fresh pork
2 eggs, slightly beaten
½ teaspoon onion powder
¼ teaspoon salt
¼ teaspoon seasoned pepper
1 cup cracker crumbs
¾ cup firmly packed brown sugar
1½ teaspoons dry mustard
¼ cup vinegar
1 cup whole-berry cranberry sauce

Combine first 7 ingredients; mix well. Shape mixture into a 9- x 5-inch loaf; place in a lightly greased 12- x 8- x 2-inch baking dish.

Combine sugar, mustard, and vinegar; mix well and spoon half over ham loaf. Bake at 350° for 1 hour and 20 minutes, basting twice with remaining sugar mixture. Top loaf with cranberry sauce, and bake an additional 10 minutes. Yield: 8 servings.

○*Microwave Directions:* Combine first 7 ingredients; mix well. Shape mixture into a 7-inch round loaf; place loaf in a lightly greased 12- x 8- x 2-inch baking dish.

Combine sugar, mustard, and vinegar; mix well and spoon half over ham loaf. Cover with wax paper; microwave at HIGH for 10 to 14 minutes or until almost firm to the touch, giving dish a half-turn after 6 minutes, and basting with remaining sugar mixture. Top with cranberry sauce; microwave at HIGH for 2 to 3 minutes or until cranberry sauce is thoroughly heated. Let stand 5 minutes before serving.

SAUCY HAM BALLS

1½ pounds ground pork
1 pound ground cooked ham
2 cups cracker crumbs
2 eggs, beaten
½ cup milk
Raisin Sauce (recipe follows)

Combine first 5 ingredients; chill. Shape into 10 balls; place in a lightly greased 12- x 8- x 2-inch baking dish. Bake at 350° for 15 minutes. Pour raisin sauce over ham balls; cover and bake 25 minutes. Uncover and bake an additional 20 minutes, basting ham balls occasionally with pan drippings. Yield: 8 to 10 servings.

Raisin Sauce

1 cup firmly packed brown
  sugar
½ cup vinegar
½ cup water
¼ cup raisins
1 teaspoon dry mustard

Combine all ingredients in a small saucepan. Cook over medium heat until sugar dissolves and mixture is thoroughly heated, stirring constantly. Yield: 1½ cups.

○*Microwave Directions:* Combine first 5 ingredients; chill. Shape into 10 balls; arrange in a ring as much as possible in a lightly greased 12- x 8- x 2-inch baking dish.

Cover dish with wax paper, and microwave at HIGH for 4 to 5 minutes. Pour raisin sauce over ham balls; cover with wax paper. Microwave at HIGH for 14 to 16 minutes, basting with pan drippings and rearranging ham balls every 5 minutes.

Raisin Sauce: Combine all ingredients in a 2-cup glass measure. Microwave sauce mixture at HIGH for 1 to 2 minutes or until sugar dissolves and mixture is thoroughly heated, stirring after 1 minute.

BACON

Fry: Cook bacon in a heavy skillet for 6 to 8 minutes or until crisp, turning once. Drain on paper towels.

Broil: Place bacon on rack of broiler pan. Broil 5 inches from heat for 3 to 4 minutes or until done, turning once. Drain on paper towels.

Bake: Place bacon on rack in a shallow baking pan. Bake at 400° for 12 to 15 minutes or until done. Drain on paper towels.

Microwave: Place bacon on rack in a 12- x 8- x 2-inch baking dish; cover with paper towels. Microwave as follows: 1 slice for 1 to 2 minutes, 2 slices for 2 to 3 minutes, 3 slices for 3 to 4 minutes, 4 slices for 3½ to 4½ minutes, 5 slices for 4 to 5 minutes, 6 slices for 5 to 6 minutes, 7 slices for 6 to 7 minutes, 8 slices for 6 to 8 minutes. Drain on paper towels.

GLAZED CANADIAN BACON

1 (¾-pound) package Canadian
  bacon, thinly sliced, or 2 (6-ounce)
  packages sliced Canadian bacon
¼ cup firmly packed brown sugar
1½ teaspoons all-purpose flour
¼ teaspoon dry mustard
1 tablespoon water
Dash of ground cloves
Chopped fresh parsley (optional)

Remove outer casing from bacon, if necessary. Place bacon in a lightly greased 12- x 8- x 2-inch baking dish.

Combine sugar, flour, mustard, water, and cloves, stirring well. Pour sugar mixture over bacon. Cover and bake at 350° for 20 minutes or until thoroughly heated. Garnish with parsley, if desired. Yield: 4 servings.

○*Microwave Directions:* Remove outer casing from bacon, if necessary.

Place bacon in a lightly greased 12- x 8- x 2-inch baking dish.

Combine sugar, flour, mustard, water, and cloves, stirring well. Pour sugar mixture over bacon; cover with wax paper. Microwave at HIGH for 2 to 3 minutes. Garnish with fresh parsley, if desired.

BEANS AND FRANKS

2 (16-ounce) cans pork and beans
1 (16-ounce) package frankfurters, cut into ½-inch pieces
1 medium onion, chopped
½ cup catsup
½ cup molasses
1 tablespoon prepared mustard
¼ teaspoon liquid smoke
⅛ teaspoon hot sauce

Combine all ingredients; stir well. Spoon mixture into a lightly greased 8-inch square baking dish. Bake, uncovered, at 350° for 1 hour, stirring after 30 minutes. Yield: 6 to 8 servings.

◻*Microwave Directions:* Combine all ingredients; stir well. Spoon mixture into a lightly greased 8-inch square baking dish; cover dish loosely with wax paper. Microwave at HIGH for 20 to 25 minutes or until mixture is desired thickness, stirring every 5 minutes.

GRILLED STUFFED FRANKS

1 (8-ounce) can tomato sauce
2 tablespoons spicy brown mustard
1 tablespoon sugar
½ teaspoon garlic powder
8 frankfurters
¼ pound Cheddar cheese, cut into 2½- x ¼-inch strips
8 slices bacon
8 hot dog buns (optional)

Combine tomato sauce, mustard, sugar, and garlic powder in a small saucepan, stirring well. Cook over medium heat 5 minutes or until thoroughly heated, stirring constantly. Set aside.

Slice frankfurters lengthwise to make a pocket. Stuff each pocket with cheese. Wrap each frankfurter with bacon, securing with a wooden pick.

Grill frankfurters over hot coals 10 minutes, turning and basting with sauce frequently. Serve with remaining sauce and hot dog buns, if desired. Yield: 8 servings.

CORN DOG BITES

1 cup all-purpose flour
1½ teaspoons baking powder
½ teaspoon salt
⅔ cup cornmeal
1 tablespoon sugar
2 tablespoons melted bacon drippings
1 egg, beaten
1 to 1¼ cups buttermilk
½ teaspoon baking soda
1 (16-ounce) package frankfurters
Vegetable oil
Prepared mustard, catsup, picante sauce (optional)

Combine flour, baking powder, salt, cornmeal, and sugar; stir in bacon drippings. Combine egg, buttermilk, and soda; mix well. Stir into flour mixture, mixing well. Cut each frankfurter into 10 pieces. Dip frankfurter sections into batter, coating completely. (Use wooden picks to aid in dipping.) Fry in 3 to 4 inches hot oil (375°) until golden, turning once; drain on paper towels.

Insert party picks, and serve immediately. Serve with desired condiments. Yield: about 10 servings.

Corn Dogs: Insert wooden sticks or skewers into whole frankfurters; dip frankfurters into batter, and fry in 3 to 4 inches hot oil until golden.

PEPPERONI AND CHEESE LOAF

1 (1-pound) loaf frozen bread dough
1 egg, beaten
½ cup grated Parmesan cheese
1 (3½-ounce) package sliced pepperoni
2 cups (8 ounces) shredded mozzarella cheese
½ teaspoon dried whole oregano
1 egg, beaten

Thaw dough, and allow to rise according to package directions. Roll dough out on a lightly floured surface to a 15- x 12-inch rectangle.

Combine 1 egg and Parmesan cheese, stirring well; spread dough with egg mixture, leaving a ½-inch margin at edges. Layer with pepperoni and mozzarella cheese; sprinkle with oregano. Fold each side of dough over cheese; press to seal sides and ends. Lay loaf on a lightly greased baking sheet, seam side down. Brush top of loaf with beaten egg. Bake at 375° for 30 minutes. Cut into slices to serve. Yield: 4 servings.

PORK SAUSAGE RING

2 pounds bulk pork sausage
2 eggs, slightly beaten
1½ cups cracker crumbs
1 cup peeled, chopped cooking apple
¼ cup minced onion
½ cup milk
Scrambled eggs (optional)
Fresh parsley sprigs (optional)

Combine first 6 ingredients, mixing well. Press into a greased 6½-cup ring mold; unmold onto a 15- x 10- x 1-inch jellyroll pan. Bake at 350° for 50 minutes or until done. Immediately remove to serving platter. Spoon scrambled eggs into center and around sides, if desired. Garnish with parsley sprigs, if desired. Yield: 8 to 10 servings.

CORN AND SAUSAGE CASSEROLE

1 pound bulk pork sausage, cooked and crumbled
4 eggs, beaten
1 (17-ounce) can cream-style corn
1 cup soft breadcrumbs
¼ teaspoon pepper
⅓ cup cracker crumbs
2 tablespoons chopped fresh parsley

Combine first 5 ingredients; stir well. Spoon into a lightly greased 8-inch square baking dish; sprinkle with cracker crumbs. Bake at 350° for 45 minutes. Sprinkle casserole with parsley. Yield: 6 servings.

SAUCY SAUSAGE CASSEROLE

1 (6-ounce) package long-grain and wild rice mix
1 pound bulk pork sausage
1 pound ground beef
1 large onion, chopped
1 (10¾-ounce) can cream of mushroom soup, undiluted
½ cup water
1 (4-ounce) can sliced mushrooms, drained
1 (8-ounce) can sliced water chestnuts, drained
3 tablespoons soy sauce
1 (2½-ounce) package sliced almonds, toasted

Cook rice mix according to package directions; set aside.
Cook sausage, ground beef, and onion in a large skillet until meat is browned, stirring to crumble meat. Drain.
Combine meat mixture, rice, and remaining ingredients except almonds. Spoon mixture into a lightly greased 12- x 8- x 2-inch baking dish; sprinkle with almonds. Bake at 350° for 15 to 20 minutes or until thoroughly heated. Yield: 8 servings.

SAUSAGE BURGERS

3 eggs, beaten
¼ cup Worcestershire sauce
2 teaspoons hot sauce
½ teaspoon seasoned salt
½ teaspoon seasoned pepper
⅛ teaspoon garlic powder
⅛ teaspoon onion powder
3 pounds ground chuck
1 pound bulk pork sausage

Combine first 7 ingredients, mixing well. Add beef and sausage; mix well. Cover and refrigerate 8 hours. Shape into 16 patties. Grill patties 3 to 5 inches from hot coals 8 minutes on each side or until done. Yield: 16 servings.
Note: Grilled patties may be frozen. Place patties in a single layer on aluminum foil; seal securely, and freeze. Thaw in refrigerator. Heat patties in aluminum foil at 350° for 30 minutes or until thoroughly heated. Patties may also be frozen uncooked; stack patties between sheets of wax paper, and seal stacks securely in plastic bags.

SAUSAGE SKILLET DINNER

1 pound bulk pork sausage
½ cup chopped green pepper
¼ cup chopped onion
1 cup uncooked elbow macaroni
1 (16-ounce) can whole tomatoes, undrained
1 (8-ounce) can tomato sauce
2 tablespoons sugar
1 teaspoon chili powder
½ teaspoon salt
½ cup commercial sour cream
Grated Parmesan cheese

Cook first 3 ingredients in a skillet until sausage is browned; stir to crumble. Drain; stir in next 6 ingredients. Cover, reduce heat, and simmer 20 to 25 minutes; stir occasionally. Stir in sour cream; cook until heated. Sprinkle with cheese. Yield: 6 servings.

SAUSAGE PIZZA SUPREME

1 small green pepper, chopped
1 large onion, chopped
2 small cloves garlic, minced
3 tablespoons chopped fresh parsley
1 tablespoon vegetable oil
1 (28-ounce) can whole tomatoes, undrained
1 (6-ounce) can tomato paste
1½ teaspoons dried whole oregano
¼ teaspoon pepper
2 (12-inch) thick or thin pizza crusts (recipes follow)
3 cups (12 ounces) shredded mozzarella cheese
2 cups (8 ounces) shredded Cheddar cheese
1 pound bulk pork sausage
1 (3½-ounce) package sliced pepperoni
1 (2.2-ounce) can sliced ripe olives, drained
1⅓ cups sliced fresh mushrooms
¾ cup sliced green onions
2 small green peppers, sliced into rings
½ to 1 cup grated Parmesan cheese

Sauté first 4 ingredients in hot oil in a Dutch oven until tender; set aside.
Place tomatoes in container of an electric blender or food processor, and process until smooth; add to onion mixture. Stir in tomato paste, oregano, and pepper. Bring to a boil; reduce heat, and simmer 1 hour or until sauce is reduced to about 3½ cups, stirring occasionally.
Spread sauce evenly over each pizza crust, leaving a ½-inch border around edges. Combine cheeses; sprinkle 1¼ cups cheese mixture over each pizza.
Cook sausage over medium heat until browned, stirring to crumble. Drain well. Sprinkle sausage over pizzas.
Layer pepperoni and next 4 ingredients on pizzas, and bake at 450° for 15 minutes. Sprinkle with remaining shredded cheese, and bake an additional 5 minutes. Top with Parmesan cheese. Yield: two 12-inch pizzas.

Thick Crust

1½ cups warm water (105° to 115°)
3 tablespoons vegetable oil
1 tablespoon sugar
1 teaspoon salt
2 packages dry yeast
4½ cups all-purpose flour

Combine first 4 ingredients in a mixing bowl; sprinkle yeast over mixture, stirring until dissolved. Gradually add flour, mixing well after each addition.

Turn dough out onto a lightly floured surface, and knead until smooth and elastic. Shape into a ball, and place in a greased bowl, turning to grease top. Cover and let rise in a warm place (85°), free from drafts, 1 hour or until doubled.

Punch dough down, and divide in half. Lightly grease hands, and pat dough evenly into 2 lightly greased 12-inch pizza pans. Cover and let rise in a warm place (85°), free from drafts, 1 hour or until doubled in bulk. Bake at 450° for 5 minutes. Yield: two 12-inch pizza crusts.

Thin Crust

1 cup warm water (105° to 115°)
2 tablespoons vegetable oil
2 teaspoons sugar
½ teaspoon salt
1 package dry yeast
3 cups all-purpose flour

Combine first 4 ingredients in a mixing bowl; sprinkle yeast over mixture, stirring until dissolved. Gradually add flour, mixing well after each addition.

Turn dough out onto a lightly floured surface, and knead until smooth and elastic. Shape into a ball, and place in a greased bowl, turning to grease top. Cover and let rise in a warm place (85°), free from drafts, 1 hour or until doubled.

Punch dough down, and divide in half. Lightly grease hands, and pat dough evenly into 2 lightly greased 12-inch pizza pans. Bake at 450° for 5 minutes. Yield: two 12-inch pizza crusts.

SAUSAGE-RICE CASSEROLE

2 pounds bulk pork sausage
1 medium onion, chopped
1 medium-size green pepper, chopped
1 cup chopped celery
1 cup uncooked long-grain rice
½ cup slivered almonds, toasted
2 (0.4-ounce) envelopes instant chicken noodle soup mix
1 (8-ounce) can water chestnuts, drained and chopped
2½ cups water

Cook sausage in a large skillet until browned, stirring to crumble meat; drain off drippings. Remove from heat. Stir in next 7 ingredients. Place in a greased 13- x 9- x 2-inch baking dish; pour water over top. Cover and bake at 350° for 1 hour. Yield: 8 servings.

SMOKED SAUSAGE JAMBALAYA

1 pound smoked sausage, cut into ½-inch slices
1 pound ground beef
1 medium-size green pepper, chopped
½ cup chopped green onions
5 cloves garlic, minced
1 (28-ounce) can tomatoes, undrained
½ teaspoon salt
¼ teaspoon pepper
1 cup uncooked long-grain rice
1½ cups water

Cook sausage in Dutch oven until browned; remove sausage, and discard the drippings.

Add ground beef, green pepper, green onions, and garlic to Dutch oven; cook until beef is browned. Drain. Add tomatoes, salt, pepper, and sausage. Cover; simmer 20 minutes.

Add rice and water to meat mixture; cover and cook 25 minutes or until rice is tender. Yield: 6 to 8 servings.

SAUSAGE AND KRAUT

4 slices bacon
½ cup chopped onion
1 pound Polish sausage, sliced
¼ cup dry white wine
1 teaspoon beef-flavored bouillon granules
1 bay leaf
1 cup water
1 (16-ounce) can sauerkraut, drained
2 teaspoons cornstarch
2 tablespoons water

Cook bacon in a large Dutch oven until crisp; drain bacon, reserving drippings in the skillet. Crumble bacon, and set aside.

Cook onion in reserved drippings until tender. Drain. Stir in sausage, wine, bouillon granules, bay leaf, and 1 cup water. Cover and cook over medium heat 30 minutes. Remove bay leaf. Stir in sauerkraut.

Combine cornstarch and 2 tablespoons water, mixing well. Stir into sausage mixture; cook over medium heat until thoroughly heated. Spoon into serving dish; sprinkle bacon on top. Yield: 4 servings.

☐ *Microwave Directions:* Place bacon on a rack in a 12- x 8- x 2-inch baking dish; cover with paper towels. Microwave at HIGH for 3½ to 4½ minutes or until bacon is crisp. Drain bacon, reserving drippings; crumble bacon, and set aside.

Stir onion, sausage, wine, bouillon granules, bay leaf, and 1 cup water into reserved drippings. Microwave at HIGH for 4 to 6 minutes or until sausage is done. Remove bay leaf. Stir in sauerkraut; microwave at HIGH for 1 minute.

Combine cornstarch and 2 tablespoons water, mixing well. Stir into sausage mixture. Microwave at HIGH for 2 to 2½ minutes. Spoon into serving dish; sprinkle bacon on top.

Wild Game

Game hunting is a typical pastime in the South during the season, and when the rewards are brought home, it's time for a hunter's feast.

Many cooks are afraid to prepare game because it has the reputation of being tough and dry. Since game lacks the marbling of most domestic animals, it can be tough and dry if not prepared properly. Marinating and cooking by moist heat methods will ensure a tender, juicy product.

VENISON ROAST WITH WINE GRAVY

1 (5- to 6-pound) venison roast
3 cups dry white wine
1 large onion, thinly sliced
12 black peppercorns
12 whole cloves
6 whole allspice
1 bay leaf
¼ teaspoon salt
3 tablespoons all-purpose flour
¼ cup water

Remove any white membrane surrounding roast. Place roast in a shallow dish. Combine wine, onion, and seasonings; pour over roast. Cover and marinate 8 hours in refrigerator, turning meat occasionally.

Remove roast from marinade, reserving marinade. Brown roast in a Dutch oven. Insert meat thermometer, making sure it does not touch fat or bone. Add marinade to roast; cover and bake at 350° for 2 hours or until meat thermometer registers 170°.

Remove and discard bay leaf. Remove roast, reserving marinade. Combine flour and water, stirring until smooth. Add flour mixture to marinade; cook over medium heat, stirring constantly, until thickened. Serve gravy with roast. Yield: 10 to 12 servings.

GRILLED VENISON STEAKS

1 (12- to 14-pound) venison hindquarter
1 (16-ounce) bottle commercial Italian salad dressing
1 (2.75-ounce) package dry onion soup mix
¾ cup butter or margarine, melted
2 teaspoons pepper

Separate each muscle of the hindquarter, and cut away from bone. Slice each muscle across the grain into 1-inch-thick slices (reserve remaining meat for other uses). Remove and discard the white membrane surrounding each steak.

Combine salad dressing and soup mix in a large shallow dish, stirring well; add steaks. Cover and marinate in refrigerator 1 hour, turning once.

Combine butter and pepper, stirring well; set aside. Remove steaks from marinade. Grill about 5 inches from hot coals 8 to 10 minutes on each side or until done, basting frequently with butter mixture. Yield: 10 to 12 servings.

COUNTRY-FRIED VENISON

2 pounds (¾-inch-thick) venison steaks
1 cup all-purpose flour
¼ teaspoon salt
¼ teaspoon seasoned salt
⅛ teaspoon pepper
¼ cup bacon drippings, divided
2 cloves garlic, minced
1 quart water
⅓ cup all-purpose flour
1½ teaspoons browning and seasoning sauce
½ teaspoon salt
⅛ teaspoon pepper
1 medium onion, thinly sliced
½ pound fresh mushrooms, sliced
Hot cooked rice

Prepare venison by trimming all fat and removing connective tissues. Cut meat into serving-size pieces, and pound each piece to ¼- to ½-inch thickness using a meat mallet. Combine 1 cup flour, ¼ teaspoon salt, seasoned salt, and ⅛ teaspoon pepper; dredge venison in flour mixture.

Heat 1 tablespoon bacon drippings in a large, heavy skillet; add garlic, and sauté until golden. Remove garlic, and set aside. Add remaining bacon drippings to skillet; cook venison until lightly browned on both sides. Remove from skillet, and set aside.

Gradually stir about ½ cup water into ⅓ cup flour, stirring until smooth; add remaining water. Stir flour mixture into pan drippings; cook over medium heat, stirring constantly, until thickened. Stir in browning and seasoning sauce, ½ teaspoon salt, and ⅛ teaspoon pepper.

Return venison and garlic to skillet; cover, reduce heat, and simmer 30 minutes. Add onion; cover and simmer 15 minutes. Add mushrooms; cover and simmer 15 minutes. Serve over rice. Yield: 6 servings.

VENISON AND TOMATOES

3 slices bacon, chopped
¾ pound ground venison
½ cup chopped onion
1 teaspoon chili powder
¾ teaspoon salt
½ teaspoon paprika
¼ teaspoon pepper
1 (16-ounce) can stewed tomatoes, undrained
Hot cooked rice

Fry chopped bacon in large skillet until crisp; add ground venison, chopped onion, chili powder, salt, paprika, and pepper to bacon and drippings in skillet. Cook mixture over medium heat until meat is browned, stirring to crumble.

Add tomatoes to skillet; cover, reduce heat, and simmer 40 minutes. Serve over rice. Yield: 3 to 4 servings.

FRIED RABBIT

2 (1½-pound) young rabbits, dressed and quartered
1 teaspoon salt
1 cup all-purpose flour
¼ teaspoon red pepper
1 cup vegetable oil
¼ cup all-purpose flour
2 cups milk
½ teaspoon salt
¼ teaspoon pepper

Sprinkle rabbits with 1 teaspoon salt. Combine 1 cup flour and red pepper; dredge rabbit in flour mixture, coating pieces well.

Brown rabbit on all sides in hot oil in a large skillet. Cover, reduce heat, and cook over low heat 40 to 45 minutes or until rabbit is tender and golden brown, turning once. Drain well.

Pour off pan drippings, reserving ¼ cup drippings in skillet. Add ¼ cup flour, stirring until smooth. Cook mixture 2 minutes, stirring constantly. Gradually add the milk to mixture; cook over medium heat, stirring constantly, until gravy is thickened and bubbly. Stir in ½ teaspoon salt and ¼ teaspoon pepper. Serve gravy with Fried Rabbit. Yield: 8 servings.

SQUIRREL FRICASSEE

¼ cup all-purpose flour
¼ teaspoon salt
⅛ teaspoon pepper
2 squirrels, dressed and cut in half
2 tablespoons vegetable oil
1 cup water
2 sprigs fresh parsley
¼ teaspoon dried whole marjoram
¼ teaspoon dried whole oregano
⅛ teaspoon ground allspice
⅛ teaspoon ground cloves
1 cup water
1 teaspoon lemon juice
1 tablespoon all-purpose flour
Hot cooked rice

Combine ¼ cup flour, salt, and pepper in a plastic bag; shake well. Place squirrel in bag; shake well.

Brown squirrel in hot oil in a heavy skillet. Add 1 cup water, parsley, and seasonings. Bring to a boil; cover, reduce heat, and simmer 45 minutes to 1 hour or until squirrel is tender, adding small amount of additional water if necessary. Remove squirrel to serving platter; discard parsley.

Combine 1 cup water, lemon juice, and 1 tablespoon flour; stir well. Gradually add to skillet, stirring constantly. Cook over low heat until thick and bubbly. Serve over rice. Yield: 2 servings.

PASTA, RICE, & CEREAL

The basic foods—pasta, rice, and cereal—play an important part in our daily diet. Even the simplest of kitchens has at least a few of these staples on hand, and as every cook has discovered, they are equally at home on the breakfast, lunch, or dinner menu.

So wholesome and packed with nutrients, these foods often replace meat on the dinner table. Teamed with certain dry beans and peas, they provide an economical and low-fat source of high quality protein.

These foods have little flavor when cooked and served without seasonings, and that leaves plenty of room for skillful cooks to create tasty combinations, such as garlic-cheese grits and rice sprinkled with a selection of savory herbs.

Pasta, rice, and cereal come in a myriad of forms that each require specific cooking and handling techniques. Therefore, we've devoted a separate section to each product.

They're all simple to cook, however, and require no equipment other than what you'll normally find in the well-stocked kitchen.

COOKING IN THE MICROWAVE

Microwaved pasta, rice, and cereal are often controversial subjects because they take about the same amount of time to microwave as they do to cook conventionally. When we found we didn't save time by cooking in the microwave, we gave con-

The flavor of Fettuccine Alfredo (page 335) depends on the quality of a few simple ingredients. Freshly grated Parmesan will add much flavor to this dish.

ventional directions only.

Because microwave ovens cook unevenly, a step or two is often added to microwave directions that you won't see in the conventional directions. Recipes often specify to give the dish a half-turn or to stir after half the cooking time is over. Conventional directions usually don't have you do anything to the dish as it cooks.

Always use the dish size specified in microwave directions. Pasta, rice, and cereal mixtures tend to boil higher in the microwave than they do on the cooktop, and using a smaller dish will increase the risk of the mixture boiling over.

A microwave oven is a good way to reheat many dishes of this type. Most can be reheated on HIGH power; those with delicate ingredients, such as eggs and cheese, should reheat at MEDIUM HIGH (70% power). The times will vary depending on the amount being reheated and other ingredients they contain.

Pasta

Pasta may have originated in Italy, but surely a Southerner would have invented it soon if an Italian hadn't. It bakes up into casseroles and serves as a base for all types of sauces—some meaty, some cheesy, and some subtly seasoned with a variety of herbs and spices and served on the side.

Pasta comes in about as many shapes as there are ways to prepare it. The most common are spaghetti and macaroni, but even these two types take on different looks. Spaghetti comes in a variety of thicknesses, all with a different name, and macaroni comes short, long, straight, and curved. Then there are sea shells, corkscrews, and bow ties, just to name a few. Types of pastas are fairly interchangeable in recipes, as long as you substitute a similar size and thickness. Check the package label for cooking times of the different varieties.

THE ART OF COOKING PASTA

The cooking time for pasta depends on its size and shape, but the test for doneness is the same—"al dente" as the Italians put it, which means "to the tooth." When properly cooked, pasta should be pliable but firm and no longer starchy.

You'll need a large pot with a tight-fitting lid for cooking pasta. The recommended amount of water is generally 3 quarts per ½ pound of pasta. Bring the water to a full rolling boil; add a small amount of salt if desired. You can also add a tablespoon of oil to the cooking water to prevent pasta from sticking together.

Add pasta to the rapidly boiling water, and cook it for the specified length of time. For spaghetti or other pasta that is too long for the pot, hold the handful of it by one end and gently push the other end into the boiling water until the pasta softens enough to submerge into the water. Make sure the water boils continuously; cook, uncovered, the length of time the package directs.

When close to being done, check the pasta once a minute until it is tender; then drain it in a colander. Transfer to a warm dish, and serve immediately. Do not rinse the pasta.

Slightly undercook pasta that will be further cooked in a casserole, so it will not be overcooked after it bakes.

STORING COOKED PASTA

Refrigerate leftover pasta up to 4 days, or freeze it up to a month. Reheat pasta chilled or frozen by plunging it in boiling water until thoroughly heated. Drain and serve.

The first half of this section is devoted to pasta dishes served as a side dish. Following that are classic pasta recipes with meaty and cheesy sauces suitable for the main dish.

LEMON VERMICELLI

⅓ cup milk
3 tablespoons butter or margarine
1 (7-ounce) package vermicelli
¼ cup lemon juice
⅓ cup grated Parmesan cheese

Combine milk and butter in a saucepan; cook over low heat until butter melts. Set aside, and keep warm.

Cook vermicelli according to package directions; drain. Place in a bowl, and toss with lemon juice; let stand 1 minute. Add cheese and warm milk mixture, tossing well. Yield: 4 servings.

SPAGHETTI ETCETERA

1 (7-ounce) package spaghetti
3 tablespoons olive oil
2 small onions, thinly sliced
2 cloves garlic, crushed
½ pound fresh mushrooms, sliced
3 slices bacon, cooked and crumbled
6 ripe olives, sliced
1 (2-ounce) can anchovy fillets, chopped
⅓ cup chopped fresh parsley
Grated Parmesan cheese

Cook spaghetti according to package directions, omitting salt; drain.

Heat oil in a large skillet; add onion and garlic, and sauté 3 to 5 minutes. Stir in mushrooms and next 3 ingredients; cover and cook over low heat 15 minutes. Stir in parsley. Spoon over spaghetti, and toss gently. Sprinkle with cheese. Yield: 6 servings.

SHELL MACARONI BAKE

1 (8-ounce) package seashell macaroni
¼ cup chopped onion
1 (2-ounce) jar diced pimiento, drained
1 tablespoon butter or margarine, melted
2 cups (8 ounces) shredded Cheddar cheese
1 (10¾-ounce) can cream of mushroom soup, undiluted
1 (2½-ounce) jar sliced mushrooms, drained
½ cup mayonnaise
⅓ cup sliced almonds, toasted

Cook macaroni according to package directions, omitting salt; drain.

Sauté onion and pimiento in butter until onion is crisp-tender. Combine all ingredients. Spoon into a greased shallow 2-quart casserole. Bake at 350° for 30 minutes. Yield: 6 to 8 servings.

NOODLES ROMANOFF

1 (8-ounce) package wide egg noodles
1 (16-ounce) carton commercial sour cream
¼ cup butter or margarine, melted
¼ teaspoon salt
¼ teaspoon freshly ground pepper
1 clove garlic, minced (optional)
¼ cup grated Parmesan cheese
Chopped fresh parsley

Cook noodles according to package directions; drain. Stir sour cream, butter, salt, pepper, and garlic, if desired, into noodles. Spoon mixture into a lightly greased 2-quart baking dish; sprinkle with Parmesan cheese. Cover and bake at 350° for 20 minutes. Sprinkle with parsley. Yield: 6 servings.

Mushroom-Noodles Romanoff: Sauté ½ pound fresh mushrooms, sliced, in 2 tablespoons butter until tender; drain. Stir cooked mushrooms into noodles with the sour cream.

SPAGHETTI ALLA CARBONARA

1 (1-pound) package spaghetti
3 eggs, beaten
1 cup grated Parmesan cheese, divided
½ cup whipping cream
8 slices bacon, cooked and crumbled
¼ cup chopped fresh parsley
¼ teaspoon dried whole basil
1 clove garlic, crushed
¼ cup butter or margarine

Cook spaghetti according to package directions, omitting salt; drain well, and keep warm.

Combine eggs and ½ cup cheese, stirring well. Heat whipping cream in a heavy saucepan. Stir in bacon, parsley, basil, and garlic.

Combine spaghetti, egg mixture, whipping cream mixture, and butter; toss gently until butter melts. Spoon spaghetti into a serving bowl, and sprinkle with remaining ½ cup cheese. Yield: 6 to 8 servings.

FETTUCCINE ALFREDO

(pictured on page 332)

You'll notice a big difference in Fettuccine Alfredo when you use freshly grated Parmesan cheese. A food processor makes grating the hard cheese an easy task, and the rich taste makes it well worth the effort.

8 ounces uncooked fettuccine
½ cup butter
½ cup whipping cream
¾ cup grated Parmesan cheese
¼ teaspoon white pepper
2 tablespoons chopped fresh parsley

Cook fettuccine according to package directions, omitting salt. Drain well; place in a large bowl.

Combine butter and whipping cream in a small saucepan; cook over low heat until butter melts. Stir in cheese, pepper, and parsley. Pour mixture over hot fettuccine; toss until fettuccine is coated. Yield: 4 servings.

MACARONI AND CHEESE

1 (8-ounce) package elbow macaroni
¼ cup butter or margarine
¼ cup all-purpose flour
2 cups milk
1 teaspoon salt
2 cups (8 ounces) shredded Cheddar cheese
1 egg, beaten
Paprika

Cook macaroni according to package directions, omitting salt. Drain well, and set aside.

Melt butter in a heavy saucepan over low heat; add flour, stirring until smooth. Cook 1 minute, stirring constantly. Gradually add milk; cook over medium heat, stirring constantly, until thickened and bubbly. Stir in salt and cheese, stirring until cheese melts. Gradually stir about one-fourth of hot mixture into egg; add to remaining hot mixture, stirring constantly.

Stir cheese sauce into macaroni; pour into a lightly greased 1¾-quart baking dish. Sprinkle with paprika. Bake at 350° for 35 minutes. Yield: 4 to 6 servings.

⬭ *Microwave Directions:* Cook macaroni according to package directions, omitting salt. Drain and set aside.

Place butter in a 1-quart glass measure; microwave at HIGH for 55 seconds or until melted. Add flour, stirring until smooth. Gradually add milk and salt, stirring well. Microwave at HIGH for 6 to 7½ minutes or until thickened, stirring after 2 minutes, then at 1-minute intervals. Add cheese, and stir until melted. Gradually stir about one-fourth of hot mixture into egg; add to remaining hot mixture, stirring constantly.

Stir cheese sauce into macaroni; pour into a lightly greased 1¾-quart baking dish. Cover and microwave at MEDIUM HIGH (70% power) for 8 to 10 minutes, stirring after 4 minutes. Sprinkle with paprika, and let dish stand 2 minutes before serving.

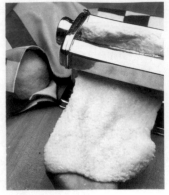

1. *To make Homemade Pasta, beat eggs in a large mixing bowl with a wire whisk.*

2. *Gradually add enough flour and water to form a soft dough.*

3. *Knead dough gently, and divide in half.*

4. *Working with one portion at a time, pass dough through smooth rollers of pasta machine on widest setting. Repeat process of dusting with flour, folding in half, and rolling until dough is smooth and pliable.*

HOMEMADE PASTA

If you enjoy pasta, you can double the enjoyment by making your own. The procedure takes some practice, but once you get the knack, it's simple and fun. And pasta purists maintain that there's a world of difference in terms of flavor and texture between the homemade and store-bought varieties.

The differences between brands of flour account for the range in flour and water amounts in our recipe. Start with the minimum amount of flour and water; if the dough seems too dry, add a few more drops of water. If too sticky, knead in a little extra flour. The dough should be firm at the beginning. It will soften as it is kneaded and worked through the pasta machine. Work with the dough and give it a chance to soften before you add extra water, or you might have to add more flour later. Experience is the best guide to knowing when the dough is the right consistency.

Homemade versions cook faster than commercial pasta (in just 1 to 2 minutes). To cook, add it to boiling water with salt and a small amount of oil.

3 eggs
3 to 4 cups all-purpose flour
1 teaspoon salt
2 to 4 tablespoons water
3 quarts boiling water
1 teaspoon salt
1 tablespoon olive oil

Beat eggs in a large mixing bowl, using a wire whisk. Add one-fourth of flour and 1 teaspoon salt; beat with a wire whisk until blended. Work in remaining flour and 2 to 4 tablespoons water (add a tablespoon at a time) to form dough. Knead dough gently, and divide in half. Working with one portion at a time, pass dough through smooth rollers of pasta machine on widest setting. Generously dust dough with flour, and fold in half. Repeat rolling, dusting, and folding procedure about 10 times or until dough becomes smooth and pliable.

Cut dough into 2 pieces. Pass each piece through rollers. Continue moving width gauge to narrower settings; pass dough through rollers once at each setting, dusting with flour, if needed.

Roll dough to thinness desired, about 1/16 inch. Pass each dough sheet through the cutting rollers of machine. Hang noodles on a wooden drying rack (dry no longer than 30 minutes). Repeat with remaining portion of dough.

Combine boiling water, 1 teaspoon salt, and olive oil in a large Dutch oven. Add noodles; cook 2 to 3 minutes or until tender. Use in recipes that call for cooked noodles. Yield: 10 cups.

5. Once smooth, pass dough through narrower settings until desired thinness is reached, dusting with flour, if needed.

6. Pass dough through desired cutting rollers of pasta machine.

7. Dry pasta on a wooden rack no longer than 30 minutes.

Served alone or with a sauce, Homemade Pasta will taste fresher than any you've ever eaten.

HOMEMADE RAVIOLI

Once you've made your own ravioli, you'll be spoiled forever. The flavor and texture of homemade versions are unmatched by canned types. And you'll enjoy the fun of rolling your own using a special ravioli rolling pin.

Homemade ravioli in no way resembles (nor should it) the canned versions. Ravioli is often served with a mushroom or tomato sauce, but our simple topping of melted butter and Parmesan cheese will win compliments every time.

1 cup ricotta cheese
1 (10-ounce) package frozen chopped spinach, thawed and squeezed almost dry
½ cup grated Parmesan cheese
2 egg yolks
2 tablespoons butter or margarine, softened
½ teaspoon ground nutmeg
½ teaspoon salt
¼ teaspoon pepper
1 recipe Homemade Pasta
4 quarts water
½ teaspoon salt
½ cup butter or margarine, melted
Grated Parmesan cheese
Chopped fresh parsley

Combine ricotta cheese, spinach, ½ cup Parmesan cheese, egg yolks, 2 table-spoons butter, and seasonings, stirring well; set aside.

Prepare dough for Homemade Pasta; divide dough into 4 equal portions. Set 2 portions aside. Pass each of 2 pieces of dough, one at a time, through rollers of pasta machine, starting at widest setting. Continue moving width gauge to narrower settings, passing dough through rollers once at each setting, dusting with flour, if needed. Roll dough to desired thinness, about 1/16-inch thick and 36- x 6-inches.

Place 2 strips of dough on a lightly floured work surface. Roll each rectangle of dough with a ravioli rolling pin, using heavy pressure to make indentations. Spoon 1 teaspoon spinach mixture in center of each square of pattern on one rectangle of dough. Brush water along lines of pattern and edge of dough. Carefully align remaining rectangle over filled rectangle so rolled ravioli indentations are aligned. Use a fluted pastry wheel to cut through both layers of dough along pattern lines. Allow ravioli to air dry about 1 hour.

Repeat above rolling and filling procedures with the remaining dough and filling ingredients.

Bring water and ½ teaspoon salt to a boil in a large Dutch oven. Cook half of ravioli in boiling water 10 to 12 minutes; drain. Cook remaining ravioli.

Dip ravioli in melted butter; place on baking sheets in a single layer, and sprinkle with Parmesan cheese. Broil 3 to 4 minutes or until lightly browned. Place in serving container, and sprinkle with parsley. Yield: 6 to 8 servings.

LINGUINE WITH CLAM SAUCE

8 ounces uncooked linguine
2 (6½-ounce) cans minced clams, undrained
½ medium onion, chopped
1 clove garlic, minced
¼ cup olive oil
1 tablespoon chopped fresh parsley
⅛ teaspoon freshly ground pepper
⅓ cup grated Parmesan cheese

Cook linguine in a Dutch oven according to package directions. Drain and return to Dutch oven; set aside. Drain clams, reserving liquid; set clams aside.

Sauté onion and garlic in hot oil in a medium saucepan until tender. Add clam liquid, and simmer 15 minutes. Stir in clams, parsley, pepper, and cheese. Heat thoroughly. Add clam mixture to linguine, tossing well. Cook over medium heat until thoroughly heated. Serve immediately. Yield: 4 servings.

SEAFOOD LINGUINE

1 medium onion, chopped
3 cloves garlic, minced
½ green pepper, chopped
⅓ cup chopped fresh parsley
¼ cup olive oil
1 (15-ounce) can tomato sauce
1 (28-ounce) can tomatoes, undrained and chopped
½ cup water
1 tablespoon lemon juice
1 teaspoon dried whole basil
1 teaspoon dried whole oregano
¼ teaspoon salt
¼ teaspoon pepper
1 dozen cherrystone clams in shells (optional)
1 pound unpeeled medium-size fresh shrimp
1 pound fresh lump crabmeat
1 (12-ounce) package linguine or spaghetti
Grated Parmesan cheese

Sauté onion, garlic, green pepper, and parsley in hot oil in a Dutch oven. Add next 8 ingredients; simmer 20 minutes or until thickened, stirring occasionally.

Scrub clams thoroughly, discarding any shells that are cracked or open. Add clams to sauce; cover and simmer about 5 to 10 minutes. Peel and devein shrimp; add shrimp and crabmeat. Simmer an additional 10 minutes or until clams open and shrimp turn pink.

Cook linguine according to package directions; drain. Place on warm platter, and top with sauce. Sprinkle with Parmesan cheese. Yield: 6 to 8 servings.

VEGETABLE FETTUCCINE

2 small zucchini, unpeeled and cut into thin strips
2 carrots, pared and cut into thin strips
1 cup sliced fresh mushrooms
2 green onions, cut into 1-inch pieces
1 clove garlic, minced
¼ cup butter or margarine, melted
1 (15-ounce) can garbanzo beans, drained
½ teaspoon dried whole basil
½ teaspoon salt
¼ teaspoon pepper
1 (8-ounce) package fettuccine
½ (8-ounce) package spinach fettuccine
¾ cup grated Parmesan cheese
2 egg yolks
1 cup whipping cream
¼ cup grated Parmesan cheese

Sauté first 5 ingredients in butter in a large skillet 5 minutes. Stir in beans, basil, salt, and pepper; set aside.

Cook fettuccine separately in two Dutch ovens according to package directions, omitting salt; drain. Combine fettuccine and vegetables in one Dutch oven; toss gently. Simmer mixture until heated, stirring occasionally. Stir in ¾ cup Parmesan cheese.

Beat egg yolks and whipping cream until foamy; add to fettuccine mixture, tossing gently. Cook over medium heat until thickened, stirring gently. Place on a serving platter; sprinkle with ¼ cup Parmesan cheese. Yield: 6 to 8 servings.

PASTA PRIMAVERA

3 cloves garlic, minced
⅓ cup pine nuts or sliced almonds
3 tablespoons olive oil
1½ cups sliced broccoli flowerets
1½ cups fresh or frozen snow pea pods
1 cup sliced zucchini
1 cup frozen green peas
10 large fresh mushrooms, sliced
6 fresh or frozen asparagus spears, cut into 1-inch pieces
¼ cup chopped fresh parsley
2 teaspoons dried whole basil
½ teaspoon salt
¼ teaspoon pepper
12 cherry tomatoes, halved
1 (12-ounce) package spaghetti
⅓ cup butter or margarine
1 cup whipping cream
½ cup grated Parmesan cheese

Sauté garlic and pine nuts in hot oil in a large Dutch oven 2 to 3 minutes or until pine nuts are lightly browned, stirring frequently. Add broccoli and next 9 ingredients; cook, stirring occasionally, 5 minutes or until vegetables are crisp-tender. Stir in tomatoes. Chill vegetable mixture at least 1 hour.

Cook spaghetti according to package directions; drain. Rinse with cold water, and drain.

Melt butter in a large saucepan; stir in whipping cream and cheese. Cook, stirring constantly, until cheese melts. Add spaghetti, and toss gently. Cover and chill mixture at least 1 hour. To serve, spoon vegetable mixture over spaghetti. Yield: 6 to 8 servings.

Note: Pasta Primavera may be served hot. If so, do not rinse pasta and do not chill vegetable mixture.

EASY SPAGHETTI

1 pound ground beef
1 small onion, chopped
1 (28-ounce) can tomatoes,
  undrained and chopped
2 (6-ounce) cans tomato paste
1 teaspoon dried whole oregano
1 teaspoon dried whole basil
½ teaspoon garlic powder
Hot cooked spaghetti
Grated Parmesan cheese

Cook ground beef and onion in a large skillet until meat is browned, stirring to crumble meat; drain well. Stir in tomatoes, tomato paste, and seasonings. Cook over medium heat, stirring occasionally, about 20 minutes. Serve sauce over spaghetti, and sprinkle with cheese. Yield: 4 to 6 servings.

Italian Spaghetti: Substitute 1 pound link Italian sausage for ground beef. Cut sausage into ½-inch pieces. Sauté sausage and onion in 2 tablespoons hot vegetable oil until sausage is almost done; drain well, and proceed with recipe.

▢ *Microwave Directions:* Crumble beef into a 2-quart casserole; add onion. Cover with lid or wax paper, and microwave at HIGH for 4 to 6 minutes or until done, stirring twice. Drain off excess drippings.

Stir in tomatoes, tomato paste, and seasonings. Cover and microwave at HIGH for 10 to 12 minutes, stirring after 6 minutes. Serve over spaghetti, and sprinkle with cheese.

SPICY SPAGHETTI

2 pounds ground beef
2 large onions, chopped
2 medium-size green peppers,
  chopped
1 cup chopped celery
2 to 3 cloves garlic, minced
1 (4-ounce) can sliced mushrooms,
  undrained
3 (6-ounce) cans tomato paste
1 (16-ounce) can whole tomatoes,
  undrained and coarsely chopped
3 (8-ounce) cans tomato sauce
2 tablespoons Worcestershire sauce
2 teaspoons chili powder
2 teaspoons dried whole oregano
1 teaspoon dried Italian seasoning
½ teaspoon salt
3 drops of hot sauce
2 bay leaves
¾ cup water
¼ cup Burgundy
Hot cooked spaghetti
Grated Parmesan cheese

Cook first 5 ingredients in a Dutch oven until meat is browned, stirring to crumble meat. Drain; stir in next 12 ingredients. Cover, reduce heat, and simmer 1 hour. Stir occasionally.

Remove bay leaves; stir in Burgundy. Spoon sauce over spaghetti. Sprinkle with cheese. Yield: 8 to 10 servings.

SPAGHETTI WITH MEATBALLS

½ cup chopped onion
2 tablespoons butter or margarine,
  melted
1 (28-ounce) can tomatoes,
  undrained and chopped
1 (6-ounce) can tomato paste
1 tablespoon chopped fresh parsley
¼ teaspoon pepper
Dash of ground oregano
1 pound ground beef
2 tablespoons grated onion
½ teaspoon salt
¼ teaspoon pepper
2 tablespoons vegetable oil
Hot cooked spaghetti

Sauté onion in butter in a large skillet. Add tomatoes, and next 4 ingredients. Cook over medium heat 20 minutes, stirring occasionally.

Combine ground beef and next 3 ingredients; mix well. Shape into 1½-inch meatballs. Cook in oil over medium heat until no longer pink; drain. Add meatballs to sauce; cook over low heat 15 minutes. Serve sauce over spaghetti. Yield: 4 servings.

▢ *Microwave Directions:* Combine onion and butter in a 2-quart casserole; cover with paper towels. Microwave at HIGH for 2 minutes. Add tomatoes, and next 4 ingredients. Cover with paper towels, and microwave at HIGH for 12 to 14 minutes, stirring mixture after 6 minutes.

Combine ground beef and next 3 ingredients; mix well. Shape into 1½-inch meatballs. Place meatballs in a 12- x 8- x 2-inch baking dish, omitting oil. Cover with heavy-duty plastic wrap. Microwave at HIGH for 3 to 4 minutes. Turn meatballs over, and rearrange in dish. Cover and microwave at MEDIUM LOW (30% power) for 3 to 4 minutes or until done; drain well. Add meatballs to sauce; cover and microwave at HIGH for 2 to 3 minutes. Serve sauce over spaghetti.

To cook long pasta: Hold pasta by the handful in boiling water, pushing gently, until it softens enough to submerge.

Dress each serving of Cream Cheese Lasagna with a green pepper ring; then slice between the rings.

CREAM CHEESE LASAGNA

1 pound ground beef
½ cup chopped onion
1 (8-ounce) can tomato sauce
1 (6-ounce) can tomato paste
¼ cup water
1 tablespoon dried parsley flakes
2 teaspoons dried Italian seasoning
1 teaspoon beef-flavored bouillon
  granules
¼ teaspoon garlic powder
1 (8-ounce) package cream cheese,
  softened
1 cup cottage cheese
¼ cup commercial sour cream
2 eggs, beaten
½ (16-ounce) package lasagna
  noodles, cooked and drained
1 (4-ounce) package sliced pepperoni
2 cups (8 ounces) shredded
  mozzarella cheese
½ cup grated Parmesan cheese
Green pepper rings

Cook beef and onion in a heavy skillet until meat is browned, stirring to crumble meat; drain. Stir in tomato sauce and next 6 ingredients; cook over low heat 10 minutes.

Combine the cream cheese, cottage cheese, sour cream, and eggs; stir well.

Spoon a small amount of meat sauce into a lightly greased 12- x 8- x 2-inch baking dish. Layer with half each of lasagna noodles, cheese mixture, pepperoni, meat sauce, and mozzarella cheese; repeat layers with remaining ingredients. Sprinkle with Parmesan cheese. Cover and bake at 350° for 30 minutes. Top lasagna with green pepper rings. Let stand 10 minutes before serving. Yield: 6 servings.

◻️ *Microwave Directions:* Crumble ground beef into a 2-quart casserole; add onion. Cover with wax paper, and microwave at HIGH for 4 to 6 minutes or until meat is done, stirring twice. Drain. Stir in tomato sauce and next 6 ingredients. Cover and microwave at HIGH for 2 to 3 minutes or until thoroughly heated, stirring once.

Combine the cream cheese, cottage cheese, sour cream, and eggs; stir mixture well.

Spoon a small amount of meat sauce into a lightly greased 12- x 8- x 2-inch baking dish. Layer with half each of lasagna noodles, cheese mixture, mozzarella, pepperoni, and meat sauce; repeat layers with the remaining ingredients. Sprinkle casserole with Parmesan cheese.

Cover and microwave at MEDIUM HIGH (70% power) for 6 to 8 minutes or until thoroughly heated, giving dish a half-turn after 5 minutes. Top with green pepper rings. Let stand 10 minutes before serving.

SPINACH LASAGNA

Although Spinach Lasagna contains no meat, the noodles and cheese make it hearty and nutritious enough to serve as a main dish.

1 (1½-ounce) package spaghetti sauce mix
1 (6-ounce) can tomato paste
1 (15½-ounce) can tomato sauce
2½ cups water
2 eggs, beaten
1 (16-ounce) carton ricotta or cottage cheese
1 (10-ounce) package frozen chopped spinach, thawed and drained
½ cup grated Parmesan cheese, divided
½ (16-ounce) package lasagna noodles
2 (6-ounce) packages mozzarella cheese slices

Combine spaghetti sauce mix, tomato paste, tomato sauce, and water in a medium saucepan; bring tomato mixture to a boil over medium heat. Remove from heat. Set aside.

Combine eggs, ricotta cheese, spinach, and ¼ cup Parmesan cheese, stirring well. Set aside.

Spread 1 cup tomato mixture in a lightly greased 13- x 9- x 2-inch baking dish. Layer half each of uncooked lasagna noodles, spinach mixture, mozzarella cheese, and tomato mixture; repeat layers. Sprinkle with remaining ¼ cup Parmesan cheese.

Cover dish securely with aluminum foil. Bake at 350° for 1 hour. Let lasagna stand 10 minutes before serving. Yield: 6 servings.

CLASSIC LASAGNA

1 pound ground beef
1 clove garlic, minced
1 teaspoon dried parsley flakes
1 teaspoon dried whole basil
1 (16-ounce) can tomatoes, undrained
2 (6-ounce) cans tomato paste
½ (16-ounce) package lasagna noodles
2 eggs, beaten
2 (12-ounce) cartons cream-style cottage cheese or ricotta cheese
½ teaspoon pepper
½ cup grated Parmesan cheese
1 pound sliced mozzarella cheese

Cook beef until browned, stirring to crumble; drain. Add garlic and next 4 ingredients; simmer 15 minutes or until thick, stirring occasionally.

Cook lasagna noodles according to package directions; drain.

Combine eggs, cottage cheese, pepper, and Parmesan cheese, stirring well.

Spread about ½ cup meat sauce in a greased 13- x 9- x 2-inch baking dish. Layer half each of noodles, cottage cheese mixture, mozzarella cheese, and meat sauce. Repeat layers. Cover and bake at 350° for 30 minutes; let stand 10 minutes. Yield: 6 to 8 servings.

VERMICELLI PIE

½ (12-ounce) package vermicelli
2 tablespoons butter or margarine
⅓ cup grated Parmesan cheese
2 eggs, well beaten
1 pound ground beef
½ cup chopped onion
¼ cup chopped green pepper
1 (8-ounce) can stewed tomatoes, undrained
1 (6-ounce) can tomato paste
¾ teaspoon dried whole oregano
½ teaspoon garlic salt
1 cup cream-style cottage cheese
½ cup (2 ounces) shredded mozzarella cheese
8 to 12 pepperoni slices

Cook vermicelli according to package directions; drain. Stir butter and Parmesan cheese into hot vermicelli. Add eggs, stirring well. Spoon into a greased 10-inch pieplate. Use a spoon to shape noodles into a pie shell. Bake at 350°, uncovered, for 9 minutes or until set.

Combine beef, onion, and green pepper in a large skillet. Cook over medium heat until meat is browned, stirring to crumble; drain well. Stir in tomatoes, tomato paste, and seasonings. Cover and cook 10 minutes, stirring occasionally.

Spread cottage cheese evenly over pie shell. Top with meat sauce. Cover with foil, and bake at 350° for 15 minutes; sprinkle with mozzarella, and top with pepperoni. Bake, uncovered, about 5 minutes. Let stand 10 minutes before serving. Yield: 6 to 8 servings.

◻*Microwave Directions:* Cook vermicelli according to package directions; drain. Stir butter and Parmesan cheese into hot vermicelli. Add eggs, stirring well. Spoon into a greased 10-inch pieplate. Use a spoon to shape noodles into a pie shell. Microwave at HIGH, uncovered, 3 minutes or until set.

Crumble beef into a shallow 2-quart casserole; add onion and green pepper. Cover with heavy-duty plastic wrap, and microwave at HIGH for 5 to 6 minutes, stirring at 2-minute intervals; drain. Stir in tomatoes, tomato paste, and seasonings. Cover and microwave at HIGH for 3½ to 4 minutes, stirring once.

Spread cottage cheese evenly over pie shell. Top with meat sauce. Cover with heavy-duty plastic wrap, and microwave at HIGH for 6 to 6½ minutes; sprinkle with mozzarella cheese, and top with pepperoni. Microwave, uncovered, at HIGH for 30 seconds. Let stand 10 minutes. Yield: 6 to 8 servings.

CANNELLONI

12 cannelloni shells
3 (8-ounce) cans tomato
   sauce
2 tablespoons grated
   Parmesan cheese
1 pound ground beef
¼ cup chopped onion
1 clove garlic, minced
1 (10-ounce) package frozen
   chopped spinach, thawed
   and drained
⅓ cup grated Parmesan cheese
2 tablespoons milk
2 eggs, slightly beaten
½ teaspoon dried whole
   oregano
¼ cup butter or margarine
¼ cup plus 2 tablespoons
   all-purpose flour
2 cups half-and-half
⅛ teaspoon white pepper

Cook cannelloni shells according to package directions; drain and set aside.

Combine tomato sauce and 2 tablespoons Parmesan cheese; spread 1 cup tomato mixture in a lightly greased 13- x 9- x 2-inch baking dish; set aside dish and remaining sauce.

Cook beef, onion, and garlic in a large skillet until beef is browned, stirring to crumble meat; drain well. Add spinach; sauté 3 minutes. Add ⅓ cup Parmesan cheese, milk, eggs, and oregano; stir well. Stuff cannelloni shells with beef mixture. Place filled cannelloni on tomato mixture in baking dish; set aside.

Melt butter in a heavy saucepan over low heat; add flour, stirring until smooth. Cook 1 minute, stirring constantly. Gradually add half-and-half; cook over medium heat, stirring constantly, until mixture is thickened and bubbly. Stir in pepper. Pour over cannelloni; spoon remaining tomato mixture over cream sauce. Bake, uncovered, at 375° for 20 minutes. Yield: 6 servings.

CREAMY CHICKEN MANICOTTI

8 manicotti shells
1 (10¾-ounce) can creamy
   chicken mushroom soup,
   undiluted
½ cup commercial sour cream
2 cups chopped cooked chicken
¼ cup chopped onion
2 tablespoons butter or margarine,
   melted
1 (4-ounce) can sliced mushrooms,
   undrained
1 cup (4 ounces) shredded Cheddar
   or Monterey Jack cheese

Cook manicotti shells according to package directions, omitting salt; drain shells, and set aside.

Combine soup and sour cream; stir well. Combine half of soup mixture and chicken; stir well. Set aside remaining soup mixture. Stuff manicotti shells with chicken mixture; place in a greased 12- x 8- x 2-inch baking dish.

Sauté onion in butter in a large skillet until tender; add mushrooms. Stir reserved soup mixture into mushroom mixture. Spoon over manicotti; bake, uncovered, at 350° for 15 minutes. Sprinkle with cheese, and bake an additional 5 minutes. Yield: 4 servings.

ITALIAN-STYLE MANICOTTI

1 pound link Italian sausage
¼ cup water
1 pound ground beef
1 medium onion, chopped
3 (10¾-ounce) cans tomato
   puree
1 (6-ounce) can tomato paste
1 teaspoon dried whole basil
½ teaspoon pepper
1 cup water
1 (8-ounce) package manicotti
   shells
2 (16-ounce) cartons ricotta or
   cottage cheese
1 (8-ounce) package mozzarella
   cheese, diced
2 eggs, lightly beaten
¾ teaspoon dried whole basil
½ teaspoon salt
2 tablespoons chopped fresh parsley
   (optional)
Grated Parmesan cheese

Place sausage and ¼ cup water in a large heavy skillet; cover and cook over medium heat 5 minutes. Uncover sausage, and brown well; drain on paper towels, and set aside.

Drain drippings from skillet, if necessary. Cook ground beef and onion in skillet until meat is browned, stirring to crumble; drain. Stir in tomato puree and next 4 ingredients. Cover, reduce heat, and simmer 45 minutes, stirring occasionally.

Cut sausage links into bite-size pieces, and add to sauce; cook 15 minutes, stirring occasionally.

Cook manicotti shells according to package directions. Combine ricotta and next 5 ingredients; stuff cheese mixture into manicotti shells.

Spoon half of sauce into a lightly greased 13- x 9- x 2-inch baking dish. Arrange stuffed shells over sauce. Spoon remaining sauce over shells; sprinkle with Parmesan cheese. Bake at 350° for 20 minutes or until thoroughly heated. Let stand 5 minutes before serving. Yield: 6 to 8 servings.

Note: Stuffed manicotti may be frozen before baking. Wrap securely, and freeze. To cook, cover with aluminum foil, and bake frozen manicotti at 375° for 1 hour; uncover and bake an additional 15 minutes.

Rice

The delicate flavor of rice teams readily with all types of foods. Season it subtly, and it's a complementary side dish for highly seasoned entrées. Pack it with flavor, and it may be just the spark to set off a mildly seasoned meat.

TYPES OF RICE

There are enough kinds of rice on supermarket shelves to confuse even the most educated shopper. Here are the most common.

● You're probably most familiar with *regular white rice*. It comes in short, medium, and long grain. The shorter the grain, the softer and more moist the end product. In our country, short-grain rice is usually used only for puddings, since it is too moist as a side dish. Medium-grain rice is often the choice for rice molds. The fluffiest type of rice is long grain, and it is the one most frequently chosen by Southerners for side dishes.

● *Parboiled* rice is put through a special process before milling to help it retain vitamins and minerals. It is available only in long grain, and it cooks up lighter and fluffier than most regular rice.

● *Precooked* rice is the choice of many who have little time to spend cooking. It's fully cooked and dehydrated, and requires only a short rehydrating process.

● Less bran is removed from *brown rice,* so more nutrients are retained. Brown rice takes longer to cook than regular rice and ends up with a firmer texture.

● *Wild rice* is actually not rice at all but a grain that is served as a side dish like rice. The dark grains of wild rice have a nutty taste and take longer to cook than regular rice. Wild rice needs rinsing in three changes of hot water prior to cooking. (Don't rinse other types of rice.) More expensive than rice, it is often sold blended with brown or regular rice to stretch it.

COOKING RICE

Each type of rice requires a different cooking time, a different amount of water, and yields a different amount of the cooked grain. Check the package for specifics about the type of rice you purchase.

Cook rice, tightly covered, in the designated amount of water until all liquid is absorbed. Resist the urge to peek or stir as it cooks; this can make rice gummy. Be careful not to overcook the rice, as this causes gumminess, too.

BASIC RICE

2½ cups water
½ teaspoon salt
1 cup uncooked long-grain rice

Bring water and salt to a boil in a medium saucepan; add rice. Cover, reduce heat, and simmer 20 minutes or until rice is tender and water is absorbed. Yield: 4 servings.

☐ *Microwave Directions:* Use very hot tap water instead of cool water when microwaving rice. Combine hot water, salt, and rice in a deep 2-quart casserole. Cover with heavy-duty plastic wrap, and microwave at HIGH for 5 minutes. Stir well. Cover and microwave at MEDIUM (50% power) for 12 to 14 minutes or until rice is tender and water is absorbed. Let stand 2 to 4 minutes. Fluff rice with a fork.

Herbed Rice: Cook rice in canned diluted chicken broth instead of water; omit salt. Stir 2 tablespoons chopped fresh parsley, basil, oregano, or thyme into cooked rice. (If substituting dried herbs, use 2 teaspoons of each, and add before cooking rice.)

Nutty Raisin Rice: Add ⅓ cup raisins with salt. Sauté ½ cup sliced almonds in 1 tablespoon melted butter or margarine until lightly browned; stir into cooked rice.

Onion Rice: Substitute onion salt for salt. Sauté ½ cup chopped white part of green onions in 2 tablespoons melted butter or margarine; stir into cooked rice. Stir 2 tablespoons raw green onion tops into cooked rice.

Orange Rice: Substitute ½ cup orange juice for ½ cup of the water. Stir in 1 tablespoon grated orange rind along with the salt.

Rice and Green Peas: Add 2 tablespoons butter and ½ teaspoon ground nutmeg with the salt. Stir 1 cup cooked frozen green peas into cooked rice. Serves 6.

SEASONED RICE

1½ cups uncooked long-grain rice
1½ cups water
1 (10½-ounce) can beef consommé, undiluted
2 tablespoons chopped green pepper
2 tablespoons butter or margarine
1 teaspoon Worcestershire sauce
1 teaspoon soy sauce
⅛ teaspoon onion powder

Combine all ingredients in a Dutch oven; bring mixture to a boil. Cover, reduce heat, and simmer 20 minutes or until rice is tender and liquid is absorbed. Yield: 8 servings.

Too often rice is just spooned into a dish and served on the side, but it can have a bigger impact if you mold it. The texture of rice makes it suitable for molding into a variety of shapes that will win new respect for the popular grain.

If you plan to serve rice as part of a buffet, consider making a single large mold. If you're having table service, individual rice molds will make a striking presentation on each dinner plate.

Almost any type of mold will work. Plastic salad molds work fine, as do regular mixing bowls. For individual-size molds, choose brioche pans, small salad molds, custard cups, or empty tuna cans.

MOLDING RICE

2 cups water
½ teaspoon salt
1 cup uncooked medium-grain rice
4 cherry tomato roses (optional)
Fresh watercress or parsley sprigs (optional)

Combine water and salt in a heavy saucepan; bring to a boil. Gradually add rice, stirring constantly. Cover, reduce heat, and simmer 15 minutes or until rice is tender and water is absorbed.

Press hot rice into 4 oiled 6-ounce custard cups, and immediately invert onto serving plates, or press into one oiled 3-cup mold and let stand 5 minutes before unmolding. Top with tomato roses and watercress or parsley, if desired. Yield: 4 servings.

To mold rice: Pack hot cooked rice into greased custard cups; invert immediately onto serving dish, and garnish.

EASY OVEN RICE

1 (10½-ounce) can French onion soup, undiluted
¼ cup butter or margarine, melted
1 (4½-ounce) jar sliced mushrooms
1 (8-ounce) can sliced water chestnuts
1 cup uncooked long-grain rice

Combine soup and butter; stir well. Drain mushrooms and water chestnuts, reserving liquid. Add enough water to reserved liquid to measure 1⅓ cups.

Add mushrooms, water chestnuts, reserved liquid, and rice to soup mixture; stir well. Pour into a lightly greased 10- x 6- x 2-inch baking dish. Cover and bake at 350° for 1 hour and 10 minutes or until rice is tender and liquid is absorbed. Yield: 6 servings.

Microwave Directions: Combine soup and butter; stir well. Drain mushrooms and water chestnuts, reserving liquid. Add enough water to reserved liquid to measure 1⅓ cups.

Add mushrooms, water chestnuts, reserved liquid, and rice to soup mixture; stir well. Pour into a lightly greased 10- x 6- x 2-inch baking dish. Cover with heavy-duty plastic wrap. Microwave at HIGH for 5 minutes. Give dish a quarter-turn; microwave at MEDIUM LOW (30% power) for 30 to 35 minutes or until rice is tender and liquid is absorbed, giving dish a quarter-turn at 10-minute intervals.

EGG FRIED RICE

⅓ cup chopped green onions
1 cup frozen green peas
2 tablespoons vegetable oil
3 cups cooked long-grain rice
1 egg, slightly beaten
3 tablespoons soy sauce

Sauté green onions and peas in hot oil 2 minutes. Add rice, and cook until thoroughly heated. Push rice mixture to sides of skillet, forming a well in center. Pour egg into well, and cook until set, stirring occasionally. Stir rice mixture into egg; add soy sauce, stirring well. Yield: 6 servings.

Sausage Fried Rice: Cook 1 pound Italian sausage, casings removed, in a large skillet, stirring to crumble; drain. Stir sausage into Egg Fried Rice, and cook until thoroughly heated.

RICE STRATA

3 cups cooked long-grain rice
2 cups (8 ounces) shredded Cheddar or American cheese
1 (2-ounce) jar diced pimiento
4 eggs, slightly beaten
2½ cups milk
½ teaspoon seasoned pepper
½ teaspoon dry mustard
¼ teaspoon hot sauce

Layer half each of rice, cheese, and pimiento in a lightly greased 13- x 9- x 2-inch baking dish. Repeat layers. Combine remaining ingredients, mixing well; pour milk mixture over the rice layers. Cover and bake at 325° for 45 minutes; uncover and bake an additional 30 minutes or until mixture is firm. Yield: 8 servings.

Note: Rice Strata may be chilled overnight before baking. After assembly, cover and refrigerate overnight. Let stand at room temperature 30 minutes. Cover and bake at 325° for 45 minutes; uncover and bake an additional 30 minutes or until firm.

Vegetable Rice will complement all types of entrées, from mildly seasoned to spicy.

VEGETABLE RICE

¾ cup thinly sliced green onions
2 tablespoons vegetable oil
1 cup uncooked long-grain rice
½ cup minced green pepper
¼ cup minced fresh parsley
2 cups water
2 teaspoons chicken-flavored
  bouillon granules
¼ teaspoon pepper
Green onion fan

Sauté green onions in hot oil in a large skillet until tender. Add rice and next 5 ingredients; cover and simmer 20 minutes or until rice is tender and liquid is absorbed. Garnish with a green onion fan. Yield: 4 to 6 servings.

CURRIED RICE MOLD

2 cups water
2 teaspoons chicken-flavored
  bouillon granules
1 cup uncooked medium-grain rice
2 tablespoons slivered almonds
2 tablespoons butter or margarine,
  melted
½ teaspoon curry powder
¼ teaspoon ground turmeric
¼ cup raisins

Combine water and bouillon granules in a large heavy saucepan; bring to a boil. Gradually add rice, stirring constantly. Cover, reduce heat, and simmer 15 to 20 minutes or until rice is tender and water is absorbed.

Sauté almonds in butter until golden. Stir almonds, curry powder, turmeric, and raisins into cooked rice. Pack hot rice mixture into a well-oiled 4-cup mold, pressing firmly with back of spoon; let stand 5 minutes. Invert onto serving platter. Yield: 4 servings.

Saffron Rice Mold: Substitute ⅛ teaspoon ground saffron for ½ teaspoon curry powder. Omit ground turmeric and raisins.

CHILE-CHEESE RICE

1 cup chopped onion
¼ cup butter or margarine, melted
4 cups cooked long-grain rice
2 (8-ounce) cartons commercial sour
  cream
1 cup cream-style cottage cheese
1 bay leaf, crumbled
½ teaspoon salt
¼ teaspoon pepper
3 (4-ounce) cans chopped green
  chiles, drained
2 cups (8 ounces) shredded sharp
  Cheddar cheese

Sauté onion in butter in a large saucepan until tender. Remove from heat; stir in next 7 ingredients.

Spoon half of rice mixture into a lightly greased 2-quart casserole. Top with half of cheese. Top with remaining rice mixture. Bake at 375°, uncovered, 20 minutes. Sprinkle with remaining cheese; bake an additional 5 minutes. Yield: 8 to 10 servings.

◻*Microwave Directions:* Combine onion and butter in a 2-quart glass bowl; microwave at HIGH 2 minutes or until tender. Stir in next 7 ingredients.

Spoon half of rice mixture into a lightly greased 2-quart casserole. Top with half of cheese. Top with remaining rice mixture. Microwave at HIGH for 10 to 13 minutes or until set. Sprinkle immediately with cheese; cover and let stand 3 minutes.

DIRTY RICE

½ pound chicken livers, chopped
½ pound bulk pork sausage
1 cup chopped onion
½ cup chopped celery
1 bunch green onions, chopped
2 tablespoons chopped fresh parsley
1 clove garlic, minced
⅓ cup butter or margarine, melted
½ teaspoon dried whole thyme
½ teaspoon dried whole basil
½ teaspoon pepper
¼ teaspoon hot sauce
3 cups cooked long-grain rice
1 (10¾-ounce) can chicken broth, undiluted

Sauté chicken livers and sausage in a skillet until browned; remove from skillet, drain, and set aside.

Sauté onion, celery, green onions, parsley, and garlic in butter in skillet until tender. Add chicken livers, sausage, and remaining ingredients; mix well. Cook over medium heat until thoroughly heated, stirring constantly. Yield: about 8 servings.

SPANISH RICE

¼ cup plus 2 tablespoons chopped green pepper
2 tablespoons chopped celery
1 clove garlic, crushed
1½ tablespoons vegetable oil
1 (14½-ounce) can whole tomatoes, undrained and chopped
¼ cup tomato sauce
¾ cup uncooked long-grain rice
1 bay leaf
Dash of red pepper
½ teaspoon beef-flavored bouillon granules
½ cup boiling water
1 teaspoon chili powder
½ teaspoon sugar

Sauté first 3 ingredients in hot oil in a large skillet until tender; drain.

Drain tomatoes, reserving liquid. Add enough water to tomato liquid to measure 1 cup. Add tomatoes, tomato liquid, tomato sauce, rice, bay leaf, and red pepper to green pepper mixture, stirring well. Bring mixture to a boil; cover, reduce heat, and simmer 10 minutes.

Dissolve bouillon granules in boiling water; add to rice mixture. Stir in remaining ingredients. Spoon into an 8-inch square baking dish. Cover and bake at 350° for 35 minutes. Remove bay leaf. Yield: 4 to 6 servings.

Beefy Spanish Rice: Brown 1 pound ground beef with green pepper, celery, and garlic; drain well.

Pilaf, a classic Turkish dish, is a long-time Southern favorite. Rice is sautéed in butter and simmered with either vegetables, meat, poultry, or fish.

A variation of pilaf, paella originated in Spain. Traditional paella is a flavorful blend of saffron-flavored rice and either vegetables, meat, or seafood.

NUTTY PILAF

⅓ cup chopped onion
¼ cup butter or margarine, melted
1 cup uncooked long-grain rice
¼ cup raisins, divided
2 cups water
2 chicken-flavored bouillon cubes
⅛ teaspoon salt
⅛ teaspoon pepper
Pinch of ground thyme
Pinch of ground oregano
¼ cup coarsely chopped salted peanuts
1 tablespoon vegetable oil
¼ cup plus 1 tablespoon coarsely chopped almonds, toasted and divided

Sauté onion in butter in a medium skillet until tender. Add rice; cook over low heat until lightly browned, stirring frequently. Pour into a lightly greased

1½-quart baking dish; sprinkle with 3 tablespoons raisins.

Combine water and bouillon cubes in a small saucepan; bring to a boil. Stir in salt, pepper, thyme, and oregano; pour over rice. Cover and bake at 350° for 25 minutes or until rice is tender.

Sauté chopped peanuts in hot oil; stir 2 tablespoons peanuts and ¼ cup almonds into rice. Garnish pilaf with the remaining raisins, peanuts, and almonds. Yield: 4 to 6 servings.

GARDEN PAELLA

1 cup chopped onion
1 green pepper, chopped
1 sweet red pepper, chopped
¼ cup butter or margarine, melted
1½ cups uncooked long-grain rice
2 (10¾-ounce) cans chicken broth, undiluted
¾ cup water
2 ripe tomatoes, chopped
1 tablespoon tomato paste
¼ to ½ teaspoon pepper
½ teaspoon dried whole saffron, crushed or ¼ teaspoon ground saffron
Dash of Worcestershire sauce
¾ pound broccoli, cut into 1-inch pieces
2 small zucchini, cut into ½-inch pieces
1 (10-ounce) package frozen green peas
12 fresh or frozen asparagus spears, cut into 1-inch pieces

Sauté onion, green pepper, and red pepper in butter in a heavy ovenproof Dutch oven until tender. Stir in rice and next 7 ingredients, and bring to a boil. Remove from heat; cover and bake at 350° for 30 minutes.

Stir remaining vegetables into rice mixture. Cover and bake an additional 45 minutes or until liquid is absorbed and vegetables are crisp-tender. Yield: 12 servings.

BROWN RICE WITH VEGETABLES

1½ cups uncooked brown rice
¼ pound fresh mushrooms, sliced
2 small green peppers, chopped
1 large onion, chopped
1 clove garlic, minced
2 tablespoons butter or margarine, melted
2 cups peeled, chopped tomato
2 tablespoons soy sauce
1 tablespoon minced fresh cilantro or parsley
⅛ teaspoon pepper

Cook brown rice according to package directions; set aside.

Sauté mushrooms, green peppers, onion, and garlic in butter in a large skillet 5 to 7 minutes or until vegetables are tender. Stir in cooked rice and remaining ingredients; cook until thoroughly heated. Yield: 8 servings.

HERBED BROWN RICE

2 tablespoons chopped onion
1 large clove garlic, minced
2 tablespoons butter or margarine, melted
1 cup uncooked brown rice
1⅓ cups water
1 (10¾-ounce) can chicken broth, undiluted
1 tablespoon chopped fresh parsley
¼ teaspoon ground thyme
⅛ teaspoon pepper
1 bay leaf

Sauté onion and garlic in butter until onion is tender; add remaining ingredients. Bring to a boil; cover, reduce heat, and simmer 35 to 40 minutes or until rice is tender and liquid is absorbed. Discard the bay leaf. Yield: 4 to 6 servings.

WILD RICE WITH VEGETABLES

2 scallions, chopped
1 tablespoon butter or margarine, melted
1 (6-ounce) package long-grain and wild rice mix
1 (10¾-ounce) can chicken broth, undiluted
⅔ cup water
1 (6-ounce) package frozen snow pea pods, thawed and drained
4 large mushrooms, sliced
1 (8-ounce) can sliced water chestnuts, drained
1 tablespoon vegetable oil

Sauté scallions in butter in a large skillet. Add rice mix, broth, and water; bring to a boil. Cover, reduce heat, and simmer 20 to 25 minutes or until rice is tender and liquid is absorbed.

Sauté snow pea pods, mushrooms, and water chestnuts in hot oil 1 to 2 minutes. Toss vegetables with rice mixture. Yield: 6 servings.

To prepare wild rice: Rinse wild rice in 3 changes of hot water before cooking. Don't rinse other types of rice.

PECAN WILD RICE

1 (4-ounce) package wild rice
1 small onion, chopped
1 cup chopped pecans
¼ cup butter or margarine, melted
1 teaspoon seasoned salt
2 to 3 tablespoons chopped fresh parsley

Wash wild rice in 3 changes of hot water; drain. Cook wild rice according to package directions, omitting salt.

Sauté onion and pecans in butter; add seasoned salt. Stir in wild rice, and cook until thoroughly heated. Sprinkle with parsley. Yield: 4 to 6 servings.

MUSHROOM WILD RICE

1 (4-ounce) package wild rice
2 cups water
1 tablespoon beef-flavored bouillon granules
½ pound fresh mushrooms, sliced
¼ cup butter or margarine, melted
1 tablespoon lemon juice
2 tablespoons minced onion
1 tablespoon minced fresh parsley
⅛ teaspoon garlic powder
½ cup coarsely chopped pecans, toasted

Wash wild rice in 3 changes of hot water; drain. Combine rice, 2 cups water, and bouillon granules in a medium saucepan; bring to a boil. Cover, reduce heat to low, and simmer 30 to 45 minutes or until rice is tender and water is absorbed.

Sauté mushrooms in butter and lemon juice until tender. Stir mushrooms, onion, parsley, garlic powder, and pecans into rice. Yield: 4 to 6 servings.

Grits and Other Cereals

Grits may be one of the South's best kept secrets. These small flakes of hulled, dried corn are eaten more here than in other regions of the country. Hominy, whole kernels of the same corn, is almost as popular as grits. It's served alone, as an entrée when meat is added, or as an interesting side dish when teamed with other ingredients.

You'll find oatmeal on breakfast tables throughout the winter months. Bulgur and barley are cereals not served as often in our region but they work well as a side dish served much like rice, and they add nutrients and fiber to the diet.

When cooking, add cereals to boiling water in a slow, steady stream. This prevents lumping, as the boiling water instantly surrounds and plumps the individual granules.

HEARTY CHEESE GRITS

6 cups water
½ teaspoon salt
1½ cups uncooked regular grits
½ cup butter or margarine
4 cups (1 pound) shredded medium-sharp Cheddar cheese, divided
3 eggs, beaten

Combine water and salt; bring to a boil. Stir in grits; cook until done, following package directions. Remove from heat. Add butter and 3¾ cups cheese; stir until cheese melts. Add a small amount of hot grits to eggs, stirring well; stir egg mixture into remaining hot grits. Pour grits into a lightly greased 2½-quart baking dish. Bake at 350° for 1 hour and 10 minutes. Sprinkle with remaining ¼ cup cheese; bake an additional 5 minutes. Yield: 8 servings.

☐ *Microwave Directions:* Combine first 3 ingredients in a 3-quart baking dish. Microwave at HIGH for 14 to 16 minutes or until grits are done, stirring every 5 minutes. Remove from microwave. Add butter and 3¾ cups cheese; stir until cheese melts. Add a small amount of hot grits to eggs, stirring well; stir egg mixture into remaining hot grits. Microwave at HIGH for 12 to 14 minutes, giving dish a half-turn every 5 minutes. Sprinkle with remaining ¼ cup cheese; cover and let stand 5 minutes.

Note: Cheese grits baked in a microwave oven will be slightly moister than when baked conventionally.

GARLIC CHEESE GRITS

4½ cups water
1 cup uncooked regular grits
½ cup butter or margarine
1 (6-ounce) roll process cheese food with garlic
2 eggs, beaten

Bring water to a boil in a large saucepan; add grits. Cover, reduce heat, and simmer 10 minutes. Add butter and cheese, stirring until cheese melts. Stir a small amount of hot grits into eggs; add to remaining hot grits, stirring constantly. Pour mixture into a lightly greased 1¾-quart casserole. Bake at 350° for 1 hour. Yield: 6 to 8 servings.

☐ *Microwave Directions:* Combine water and grits in a 3-quart glass bowl. Microwave at HIGH for 14 to 16 minutes, stirring after 7 minutes. Add butter and cheese, stirring until cheese melts. Stir a small amount of hot grits into eggs; add to remaining hot grits, stirring constantly. Pour mixture into a lightly greased 1¾-quart casserole. Microwave at HIGH for 10 to 12 minutes.

Note: Garlic Cheese Grits baked in a microwave oven will be slightly moister than when baked conventionally.

COUNTRY GRITS AND SAUSAGE

2 cups water
½ cup uncooked quick-cooking grits
4 cups (16 ounces) shredded sharp Cheddar cheese
4 eggs, beaten
1 cup milk
½ teaspoon dried whole thyme
⅛ teaspoon garlic powder
2 pounds mild bulk pork sausage, cooked, crumbled, and drained

Bring water to a boil; stir in grits. Return to a boil; reduce heat and cook 4 minutes, stirring occasionally.

Combine grits and cheese; stir until cheese melts. Combine eggs, milk, thyme, and garlic powder; mix well. Add a small amount of hot grits mixture to egg mixture, stirring well. Stir egg mixture into remaining hot grits mixture. Add sausage, stirring well. Pour into a lightly greased 12- x 8- x 2-inch baking dish. Bake at 350° for 30 minutes or until set. Yield: 8 servings.

Note: Casserole may be covered and refrigerated overnight, if desired. When ready to bake, remove from refrigerator, and let stand at room temperature for 15 minutes. Bake at 350° for 50 to 55 minutes or until set.

☐ *Microwave Directions:* Combine water and grits in a 2-quart glass bowl; microwave at HIGH for 7 to 9 minutes, stirring after 5 minutes.

Combine grits and cheese; stir until cheese melts. Combine eggs, milk, thyme, and garlic powder; mix well. Add a small amount of hot grits mixture to egg mixture, stirring well. Stir egg mixture into remaining hot grits mixture. Add sausage, stirring well. Pour into a lightly greased 12- x 8- x 2-inch baking dish. Microwave at HIGH for 14 to 16 minutes, giving dish a half-turn after 7 minutes.

SLICED CHEESE GRITS

1 cup quick-cooking grits
1 quart milk
½ teaspoon salt
¼ teaspoon white pepper
½ cup (2 ounces) shredded Swiss
   cheese
⅓ cup grated Parmesan cheese

Combine first 4 ingredients in top of a double boiler. Cook over boiling water 30 to 40 minutes or until grits are thick, stirring occasionally. Add additional water to double boiler, if necessary.

Spread grits mixture evenly in a lightly greased 13- x 9- x 2-inch pan. Let stand at room temperature until grits are firm. Cut grits into 12 rectangular slices. Arrange slices, long sides overlapping, in a lightly greased 8-inch square baking dish. Bake at 400° for 25 minutes. Sprinkle with cheeses; cover and let stand 5 minutes. Yield: 6 servings.

GRITS AND TOMATO MEDLEY

8 slices bacon
1 medium onion, chopped
2 small green peppers, finely chopped
1 (16-ounce) can tomatoes, undrained
   and chopped
6 cups water
1 teaspoon salt
1½ cups uncooked regular grits

Cook bacon in a large skillet until crisp; remove bacon, reserving 2 tablespoons drippings in skillet. Drain and crumble bacon; set aside.

Sauté onion and green pepper in drippings until tender; stir in tomatoes. Bring to a boil; reduce heat and simmer 30 minutes, stirring occasionally.

Bring water and salt to a boil; add grits. Cook 10 to 20 minutes or until grits are thickened, stirring frequently. Remove from heat; stir in tomato mixture. Spoon into serving dish; sprinkle bacon on top. Yield: 8 servings.

HOMINY-CHILI CASSEROLE

1 (15-ounce) can chili with beans
1 (2.2-ounce) can sliced ripe olives,
   drained and divided
1 small onion, finely chopped
1 (15½-ounce) can golden hominy,
   drained
1 cup (4 ounces) shredded sharp
   Cheddar cheese

Combine chili and half of olives; spoon into a lightly greased 1½-quart casserole. Top with onion and hominy, and bake at 350° for 25 minutes. Sprinkle with cheese and remaining olives; bake an additional 5 minutes. Yield: 4 servings.

CHILE-CHEESE HOMINY

¼ cup chopped onion
2 tablespoons butter or margarine,
   melted
2 (15½-ounce) cans golden hominy,
   drained
2 (4-ounce) cans chopped green
   chiles, drained
1 (8-ounce) carton commercial sour
   cream
1 teaspoon chili powder
⅛ teaspoon pepper
1½ cups (6 ounces) shredded
   Cheddar cheese, divided

Sauté onion in butter in a large skillet 5 minutes. Add hominy, next 4 ingredients, and ½ cup cheese; stir well. Pour into a lightly greased 10- x 6- x 2-inch baking dish; bake at 400° for 20 minutes. Sprinkle remaining 1 cup cheese over top; bake an additional 5 minutes or until cheese melts. Yield: 6 to 8 servings.

□ *Microwave Directions:* Combine onion and butter in a 1½-quart bowl; cover loosely with wax paper. Microwave at HIGH for 2 to 3 minutes or until onion is tender. Add hominy, next 4 ingredients, and ½ cup cheese; stir well.

Pour into a lightly greased 10- x 6- x 2-inch baking dish; microwave at HIGH for 8 to 10 minutes or until thoroughly heated. Sprinkle with remaining 1 cup cheese; cover and let stand 3 minutes.

SPICED OATMEAL AND RAISINS

4 cups water
2 cups quick-cooking oats, uncooked
1 cup raisins
1 teaspoon ground cinnamon
½ teaspoon salt
½ teaspoon ground nutmeg
Sugar
Milk

Bring water to a boil in a saucepan; stir in oats, raisins, and seasonings. Cook 1 minute, stirring occasionally. Cover, remove from heat, and let stand a few minutes. Serve with sugar and milk. Yield: 6 servings.

SEASONED BULGUR

1 cup uncooked bulgur wheat
⅓ cup chopped onion
⅓ cup chopped celery
2 tablespoons butter or margarine,
   melted
1 (10¾-ounce) can chicken broth,
   undiluted
¾ cup water
1 tablespoon minced fresh parsley

Sauté bulgur, onion, and celery in butter in a medium saucepan. Add chicken broth and water; bring to a boil. Cover, reduce heat, and simmer 15 to 20 minutes or until liquid is absorbed and bulgur is tender. Stir in parsley. Yield: 6 servings.

Seasoned Barley: Substitute 1 cup pearl barley for bulgur wheat.

PIES & PASTRIES

It's no wonder that you see so many pie safes in antique stores around our part of the country—the South is probably better known for its pies and pastries than any other dessert. It doesn't matter whether it's a pecan pie, coconut cream pie, or a fresh peach cobbler; one sight of a tender and flaky filled pastry starts taste buds tingling. And they're "easy as pie" to make!

EQUIPMENT

You can bake tender flaky pies with very little equipment—two knives to cut shortening into the flour, a rolling pin, and a pieplate—but a few extra items can simplify the process. A pastry blender will cut shortening into the flour easier than knives, and a pastry wheel will speed up cutting pastry strips. Pastry wheels come with either a plain edge, a fluted edge, or both.

If you have trouble with pastry sticking to your rolling pin or work surface, a stockinette cover for your rolling pin and a pastry cloth for your work surface may help. You'll also appreciate a wire rack on which to cool your pies; it will help keep crusts from becoming soggy.

Non-shiny pieplates or piepans, such as those of ovenproof glass or dull metal, work best. Shiny metal pans reflect heat and keep the pastry from browning properly. Always use the size pieplate or piepan specified in the recipe. Standard sizes are 8, 9, and 10 inches in diameter, and measure 1¼ inches deep.

The decorative slicing of the pears in Pear-Almond Tart (page 358) makes a beautiful presentation.

COMMERCIAL CRUSTS

You'll find a wide variety of convenience pastries on the market to help you bake pies and pastries in a hurry. Packaged dry piecrust mix and rolled flat rounds of pastry are two types that allow you to use your own pieplate and flute the crust yourself to give your pie a "homemade" look.

Frozen pastry shells and crumb crusts already in the pan offer good quality but hold less filling than most homemade pastries with which our pies were tested. Even though their packages may state they are 9-inch pastries, most are not an equivalent substitute. You can purchase individual tart size pastries in which to bake the extra filling, if desired. Piecrusts frozen in the pan labeled "deep dish" are closer to homemade size than the regular frozen crusts.

FREEZING PIES AND PASTRIES

You can freeze balls of uncooked pastry up to two months if they are wrapped properly. The balls of pastry can be thawed overnight in the refrigerator.

Or, if you prefer to go ahead and roll the pastry, roll it into circles about three inches larger all around than your pieplates, stack the pastry circles on a baking sheet with two sheets of plastic wrap between each, and freeze. After an initial freezing, the stack of frozen pastry circles should be wrapped, labeled and refrozen. Thaw the frozen circles at room temperature about 10 minutes before using.

You can also freeze baked or unbaked pastry directly in a pieplate. Unbaked frozen pastry can be baked in its frozen state; bake frozen pastry as the recipe directs, and then add two or three additional minutes of baking time. When thawed, pastry will be slightly more fragile than if it had not been frozen.

Some baked pies freeze well, especially fruit pies. However, the texture of the pastry may lose some crispness in the freezing and defrosting process and the texture of the fruit will soften slightly, too.

To freeze baked pies, freeze them unwrapped first, then wrap them securely, label, and return them to the freezer. Use frozen pies within two months. Thaw baked pies at room temperature 30 minutes, then bake at 350° until warm, if reheating is desired.

Do *not* freeze cream, custard, chiffon, or pies that contain a meringue crust or topping.

MICROWAVING PIES AND PASTRIES

You can bake pastry and pies in the microwave oven, but the end results are not the same as when baked conventionally. The pastry will not brown, and pastry and fillings have to be cooked separately. Adjustments in the amounts of liquid sometimes need to be made, also. For these reasons, we have not included microwave directions for pies. If you want to bake pies in your microwave oven, the cookbook distributed with your microwave oven is the best guide.

Pastry

The secret to making flaky pastry is to measure ingredients accurately and mix them properly. If proportions of fat to flour to liquid are off even slightly or if you overwork the dough, your pastry can be tough, soggy, or crumbly.

MAKING BASIC PASTRY

Cut the shortening into the flour using a pastry blender or two knives until the mixture resembles coarse meal. During baking, the fat particles melt, and the pockets of air left make the pastry flaky.

Sprinkle cold water, one tablespoon at a time, over the flour mixture; stir with a fork just enough to moisten the dry ingredients. Don't overwork the dough—the more you handle it, the more gluten will develop, toughening the pastry. Add the minimum amount of water that will moisten the flour mixture; too much can make pastry tough and soggy.

Shape the dough into a ball, cover with plastic wrap, and chill at least one hour. Chilling makes the dough easier to handle and helps prevent the crust from being soggy.

Lightly dust the rolling surface with flour, and place the chilled dough in the center; flatten the dough with the side of your hand. Carefully roll the dough from the center to the outer edges; do not roll back and forth across the dough, as this will stretch it and cause it to shrink during baking.

Lift the pastry periodically as you roll it to make sure it is not sticking. If it does stick, loosen it with a spatula, and sprinkle more flour on the work surface. Mend pastry cracks or breaks with little strips of pastry cut from the edges.

Roll the pastry to ⅛-inch thickness and about two inches larger in diameter than the pieplate. To transfer the pastry to the pieplate, carefully fold the dough in half, then into

quarters. Place the point of the fold in the center of the pieplate, and carefully unfold. Try not to pull at the dough, as it will stretch.

Trim the edges of the dough, leaving about ½-inch overhang. (Kitchen shears or scissors are easier to use than a knife.) Fold the overhanging dough under, pressing firmly against the pieplate edge to seal. Then flute as desired.

FLUTE A PRETTY FINISH

The simplest finish for the piecrust edge is a plain flute as shown in our step-by-step photographs for Basic Pastry. To make it, place one index finger on the outside edge of the pie, and place your other index finger and thumb on the inside of the pie, flanking your first finger; pinch the pastry with fingers in this position to flute the edge. Repeat the flute about every ¼ inch.

For other decorative piecrust finishes, see pages 354 and 356.

Basic Pastry Step-By-Step

1. To make Basic Pastry, cut the shortening into flour and salt with a pastry blender until the mixture resembles coarse meal.

2. Sprinkle cold water, one tablespoon at a time, over crumb mixture. Stir just until dry ingredients are moistened.

3. Then gather dough into a ball; cover and chill dough thoroughly.

4. Roll dough with a rolling pin to ⅛-inch thickness on a lightly floured surface.

5. Carefully fold dough into quarters and transfer to pieplate; unfold pastry, and fit into pieplate. Trim edge.

6. Pinch edge of pastry with your fingers to flute; repeat about every ¼ inch.

7. When baking the pastry shell without a filling, prick bottom and sides generously before baking. Do not prick shell if it is to be filled.

BASIC PASTRY

8-inch crust:

1 cup all-purpose flour
½ teaspoon salt
⅓ cup plus 1 tablespoon shortening
2 to 3 tablespoons cold water

9-inch crust:

1¼ cups all-purpose flour
½ teaspoon salt
⅓ cup plus 2 tablespoons shortening
3 to 4 tablespoons cold water

10-inch crust:

1⅓ cups all-purpose flour
½ teaspoon salt
½ cup shortening
3 to 4 tablespoons cold water

Combine flour and salt; cut in shortening with pastry blender until mixture resembles coarse meal. Sprinkle cold water (1 tablespoon at a time) evenly over surface; stir with a fork until dry ingredients are moistened. Shape into a ball; chill.

To fit into pieplate, roll dough to ⅛-inch thickness on a lightly floured surface. Place in pieplate; trim off excess pastry along edges. Fold edges under and flute.

For baked pastry shell, prick bottom and sides of pastry shell generously with a fork. Bake pastry at 450° for 10 to 12 minutes or until pastry is golden brown. Yield: pastry for one 8-inch, 9-inch, or 10-inch pie.

SINGLE OR DOUBLE CRUSTS

Pies not topped with a crust are known as single-crust pies. For this type, flute the edge before adding the filling. If the filling is unbaked, such as for a chiffon or lemon meringue pie, bake the crust before adding the filling.

Our pastry recipes give directions for baking the crust without fillings. Be sure to prick the bottom and sides of the crust well with a fork to keep the pastry from puffing during baking. Do not prick the pastry if the filling will be baked in the crust.

Double-crust pies have both a top and bottom crust, and the filling is baked inside the pastry. To make double-crust pies, use a pastry recipe specifically for this type pie, or make two batches of a recipe for a single-crust pie. Divide the pastry into two equal portions; keep one portion chilled as you work with the other.

To make a double-crust pie, line the pieplate with one portion of the

To make a decorative cutout for a top crust: Make cutout freehand or with cookie cutters; then moisten the back and gently press it onto the crust.

PASTRY PROBLEM CHART
Problems and Possible Causes

Tough pastry:
  Too little fat
  Too much water
  Overmixing
  Too much flour
  Kneading the dough

Crumbly crust:
  Too little water
  Too much fat
  Self-rising flour used
  Insufficient mixing

Soggy lower crust:
  Filling too moist
  Oven temperature too low
  Too much liquid in pastry

Crust shrinks:
  Too much handling
  Pastry stretched in pan
  Dough uneven in thickness
  Rolling dough back and forth with
    rolling pin

pastry following directions for a single-crust pie, omitting the fluting at that stage; then add the unbaked filling. Roll the remaining pastry about one inch larger in diameter than the pieplate.

Moisten the edge of the bottom pastry with water; fit the top crust over the filling. Trim the edge of the pastry so there's a ½-inch overhang. Fold the overhang under the edge of the bottom pastry, pressing firmly to seal. Then flute the edge. Either prick the pastry with a fork or cut slits using a sharp knife. These openings are necessary to allow steam to escape during baking.

Lattice toppings make especially pretty finishes for double-crust fruit pies. They require the same amount of pastry as regular double-crust pies. For a lattice-topped pie, roll and fit the bottom pastry as you would for a double-crust pie, leaving

a 1-inch overhang around the edge. Roll out the remaining pastry, and cut into 10 or 14 (½-inch) strips. Use a fluted pastry wheel for a decorative effect, if desired.

Moisten the edge of the pastry in the pieplate. Place five or seven of the strips evenly across the pie going in the same direction, leaving ½- to ¾-inch space between strips; fold every other strip back a little over half-way. Place one of the remaining strips across the center of the pie at right angles to the first strips. Carefully fold back the flat strips and unfold the folded ones. Place another strip parallel to the center strip, leaving ½- to ¾-inch space between strips. Repeat the folding and unfolding process and adding cross-strips until the lattice is woven. Trim edge, and press the ends of the strips to seal the pastry. Flute the edge.

To weave a lattice crust: Place strips across the pie going in one direction; then repeat the process of alternately folding back every other strip and laying a strip perpendicular to the original strips until pie is woven.

FOOD PROCESSOR PASTRY

Our recipe for Food Processor Pastry is your best bet if you want to make pastry in your food processor, although many other pastry recipes will work in your processor if you're skilled at using the processor for this task. Follow the pulsing directions given with the Food Processor Pastry carefully; it's easy to "over-process" your pastry, which makes it tough.

DOUBLE-CRUST PASTRY

2 cups all-purpose flour
1 teaspoon salt
⅔ cup plus 2 tablespoons
    shortening
4 to 5 tablespoons cold water

Combine flour and salt; cut in shortening with pastry blender until mixture resembles coarse meal. Sprinkle cold water (1 tablespoon at a time) evenly over surface; stir with a fork until dry ingredients are moistened. Shape into a ball; chill. Yield: pastry for one double-crust pie.

OIL PASTRY

1¼ cups all-purpose flour
½ teaspoon salt
¼ cup plus 2 tablespoons vegetable
    oil
3 to 4 tablespoons cold water

Combine flour and salt; add oil, stirring until mixture resembles coarse meal. Sprinkle with water (1 tablespoon at a time), stirring quickly. Gather dough into a ball.

To fit into pieplate, roll dough to ⅛-inch thickness on a lightly floured surface. Place in a 9-inch pieplate; trim off excess pastry along edges. Fold edges under and flute.

For baked pastry shell, prick bottom and sides of pastry generously with a fork. Bake at 450° for 12 to 14 minutes or until golden brown. Yield: pastry for one 9-inch pie.

Appliqué with Pastry

With cookie cutters, you can make pastry cutouts to appliqué on top of a double-crust pie. To make the cutout adhere, moisten the back, and gently press it onto the top crust. Make several slits in the top crust to let the steam escape, making them at the seam where the appliqué joins the top crust so as not to interfere with the pastry design.

HANDY PASTRY

4 cups all-purpose flour
1 teaspoon baking powder
1 teaspoon salt
1 tablespoon sugar
1¾ cups shortening
1 egg, beaten
½ cup cold water
1 tablespoon vinegar

Combine flour, baking powder, salt, and sugar in a large bowl; cut in shortening with pastry blender until mixture resembles coarse meal. Stir in egg, water, and vinegar. Divide dough into 5 equal parts; shape each into a ball and wrap tightly. Chill. May be stored up to 2 weeks in refrigerator.

To fit into pieplate, roll each ball of dough to ⅛-inch thickness on a lightly floured surface. Place in a 9-inch pieplate; trim off excess pastry along edges. Fold edges under and flute.

For baked pastry shell, prick bottom and sides of pastry generously with a fork. Bake at 450° for 10 to 12 minutes or until golden brown. Yield: pastry for five 9-inch pies.

FOOD PROCESSOR PASTRY

1 cup all-purpose flour
¼ teaspoon salt
¼ cup shortening
¼ cup cold water

Position knife blade in food processor bowl; add flour and salt. Top with cover, and process pulsing 3 or 4 times or until combined. Add shortening to flour mixture. Process pulsing 5 or 6 times or until mixture resembles coarse meal. With processor running, slowly add water (1 tablespoon at a time); process only until dough begins to form a ball and leaves sides of bowl. Cover and chill 30 minutes.

To fit into pieplate, roll dough to ⅛-inch thickness on a lightly floured surface. Place in a 9-inch pieplate; trim off excess pastry along edges. Fold edges under and flute.

For baked pastry shell, prick bottom and sides of pastry generously with a fork; bake at 425° for 10 to 12 minutes or until golden brown. Yield: pastry for one 9-inch pie.

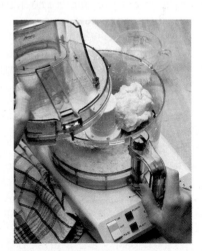

To process pastry in a food processor: Process pastry just until the dough begins to form a ball; if processed too long, the pastry will be tough.

Make a spiral fluted crust design by pinching the pastry at an angle between your thumb and index finger.

Cut a scalloped edge for piecrust by rolling the tip of a teaspoon around the edge of pastry.

Give pastry a forked design by gently pressing a fork around a scalloped or plain edge. Dip fork in flour, if necessary, to keep it from sticking to pastry.

Press a twirled rope around the edge of a pie. Cut strips of pastry about ½-inch wide; moisten edge of pastry shell, and twist rope with one hand, while pressing rope with other hand where it joins pastry.

WHOLE WHEAT PASTRY

¾ cup whole wheat flour
⅓ cup all-purpose flour
¼ teaspoon salt
⅓ cup plus 2 tablespoons shortening
3 to 4 tablespoons cold water

Combine flours and salt; cut in shortening with pastry blender until mixture resembles coarse meal. Sprinkle cold water (1 tablespoon at a time) evenly over surface; stir with a fork until dry ingredients are moistened. Shape into a ball; chill.

To fit into pieplate, roll dough to ⅛-inch thickness on a lightly floured surface. Place in a 9-inch pieplate; trim off excess pastry along edges. Fold edges under and flute.

For baked pastry shell, prick bottom and sides of pastry generously with a fork. Bake at 400° for 12 to 15 minutes or until golden brown. Yield: pastry for one 9-inch pie.

TART PASTRY

1½ cups all-purpose flour
½ teaspoon baking powder
½ teaspoon salt
¼ cup butter
¼ cup shortening
4 to 6 tablespoons milk

Combine flour, baking powder, and salt; cut in butter and shortening with pastry blender until mixture resembles coarse meal. Sprinkle milk evenly over surface of mixture; stir with a fork until dry ingredients are moistened. Shape into a ball; chill.

Roll dough to ⅛-inch thickness on a lightly floured surface. Fit pastry into an 11- x 7½- x 1-inch tart pan or into six 4-inch tart pans.

For baked tart shells, prick bottom of pastry generously with a fork. Bake at 450° for 12 to 15 minutes or until lightly browned. Yield: pastry for one 11- x 7½- x 1-inch tart or six 4-inch tarts.

OATMEAL PIE CRUST

1 cup all-purpose flour
2 tablespoons sugar
½ teaspoon salt
½ cup shortening
½ cup regular oats, uncooked
3 to 4 tablespoons water

Combine flour, sugar, and salt; cut in shortening with pastry blender until mixture resembles coarse meal. Stir in oats. Sprinkle cold water (1 tablespoon at a time) evenly over surface of mixture; stir with a fork until dry ingredients are thoroughly moistened. Shape mixture into a ball; chill.

Roll dough on a lightly floured surface to fit a 9-inch pieplate. Place in pieplate; trim off excess pastry along edges. Fold edges under and flute. Prick bottom and sides of pastry generously with a fork. Bake at 425° for 10 to 12 minutes. Yield: one 9-inch pastry shell.

For a braided crust, moisten edge of pastry shell, and interlace two ¼-inch wide pastry strips as you wrap them around the pie. Gently press pastry to the edge of the pie to make braid adhere.

To apply cutouts, moisten the edge of the piecrust, and gently press small cutouts around the edge, overlapping slightly.

Make a Design of Slits

Traditional double-crust pies call for a few slits to allow steam to escape from the filling during baking. Why not add enough slits to create a decorative pattern on top, such as a striking display of diagonal lines. You can reproduce almost any shape with simple designs. You can even monogram your initials. Just use a sharp knife so you can make the cuts cleanly and without tearing or stretching the pastry.

To make a crumb crust smooth and even: Place a slightly smaller pieplate atop the crumb-filled pieplate; press the smaller pieplate firmly all around sides and bottom.

Crumb Crusts

Crumb crusts are not true pastries, but they're easy to make and go well with pies that have a cold filling. When teamed with chilled fillings, crumb crusts are usually baked slightly to set the crumbs. When used for frozen fillings, crumb crusts need no baking.

To make a smooth crust, the crumbs should be fine and uniform in size. You can make your own crumbs in the food processor or place broken crackers in a plastic bag and roll with a rolling pin until finely crushed. You can also purchase commercially ground crumbs in an assortment of favorite flavors—graham cracker, chocolate wafer, and gingersnap.

When making a crumb crust, press a slightly smaller pieplate atop the crumb-filled pieplate to make the crust smooth and even.

GRAHAM CRACKER CRUST

1 (5⅓-ounce) packet graham crackers, crushed (about 1⅔ cups)
¼ cup sugar
¼ cup plus 2 tablespoons butter or margarine, melted

Combine all ingredients, mixing well. Firmly press crumb mixture evenly over bottom and sides of a 9-inch pieplate.

For frozen pies, crust may be used without baking. For other pies, bake at 350° for 7 to 9 minutes. Yield: one 9-inch crust.

GINGERSNAP CRUMB CRUST

1½ cups gingersnap crumbs
¼ cup sifted powdered sugar
⅓ cup butter or margarine, melted

Combine all ingredients, mixing well. Firmly press crumb mixture evenly over bottom and sides of a 9-inch pieplate.

For frozen pies, crust may be used without baking. For other pies, bake at 375° for 4 to 5 minutes. Yield: one 9-inch crust.

CHOCOLATE WAFER CRUST

1¼ cups chocolate wafer crumbs
⅓ cup butter or margarine, melted

Combine crumbs and butter, mixing well. Firmly press crumb mixture evenly over bottom and sides of a 9-inch pieplate.

For frozen pies, crust may be used without baking. For other pies, bake at 350° for 6 to 8 minutes. Yield: one 9-inch crust.

Fruit Pies

If anything is better than a plump, juicy peach, perhaps it's a plump, juicy peach pie. Crowned with flaky pastry and blended with butter, sugar, and spices, fruit pies rate high on the list of favorite desserts among Southerners of all ages.

You can store most fruit pies at room temperature for short periods of time, but refrigerate pies that contain eggs or dairy products as soon as they cool.

COUNTRY APPLE PIE

Pastry for double-crust 9-inch pie
6 cups peeled, sliced cooking apples
1 tablespoon lemon juice
½ cup sugar
½ cup firmly packed brown sugar
2 tablespoons all-purpose flour
½ teaspoon ground cinnamon
¼ teaspoon ground nutmeg
2 tablespoons butter or margarine

Roll half of pastry to ⅛-inch thickness on a lightly floured surface. Place in a 9-inch pieplate; set aside.

Combine apples and lemon juice in a large mixing bowl. Combine sugars, flour, cinnamon, and nutmeg, mixing well. Spoon over apple mixture, tossing gently. Spoon filling evenly into pastry shell, and dot with butter.

Roll remaining pastry to ⅛-inch thickness; transfer to top of pie. Trim off excess pastry along edges. Fold edges under and flute. Cut slits in top crust for steam to escape. Cover edges of pastry with strips of aluminum foil to prevent excessive browning. Bake at 450° for 15 minutes. Reduce heat to 350°, and bake an additional 35 minutes. Yield: one 9-inch pie.

To prevent edges of a pie from over-browning: Cut the center from a large piece of aluminum foil, and gently cover edges of the pastry.

APPLE CIDER PIE

Pastry for double-crust 9-inch pie
1 cup apple cider
⅔ cup sugar
6½ cups peeled, sliced cooking apples
2 tablespoons cornstarch
2 tablespoons water
½ teaspoon ground cinnamon
1 tablespoon butter or margarine

Roll half of pastry to ⅛-inch thickness on a lightly floured surface. Place in a 9-inch pieplate; set aside.

Combine cider and sugar in a large saucepan; bring to a boil. Add apples; cook, uncovered, 8 minutes or until apples are tender. Drain, reserving syrup. Add enough water to syrup to measure 1⅓ cups liquid; return syrup mixture and apples to saucepan. Combine cornstarch and 2 tablespoons water, stirring well; add to apple mixture. Stir in cinnamon; cook, stirring constantly, until thickened. Stir in butter. Spoon mixture into pastry shell.

Roll remaining pastry to ⅛-inch thickness; transfer to top of pie. Trim off excess pastry along edges. Fold edges under and flute. Cut slits in top of crust for steam to escape. Bake at 375° for 45 to 50 minutes. Cover edges of pastry with strips of aluminum foil to prevent excessive browning, if necessary. Serve warm or cool. Yield: one 9-inch pie.

PEAR-ALMOND TART

(pictured on page 350)

1 recipe Tart Pastry (page 356)
¾ cup slivered almonds
½ cup sugar
1 egg
1 tablespoon butter or margarine, melted
2 cups water
2 tablespoons lemon juice
3 large fresh pears
¼ cup sugar
3 tablespoons sliced almonds
2 tablespoons butter or margarine, melted
¼ cup plus 2 tablespoons apricot preserves
¼ cup water
2 tablespoons sugar
1 tablespoon Kirsch

Roll dough to ⅛-inch thickness on a lightly floured surface. Fit pastry into an 11- x 7½- x 1-inch tart pan. Set aside.

Position knife blade in processor bowl. Add ¾ cup almonds; process 40 to 50 seconds or until finely ground. Add ½ cup sugar, egg, and 1 tablespoon melted butter; process until blended. Spread evenly over pastry.

Combine 2 cups water and lemon juice; stir well. Peel and core pears. Dip pears in lemon juice mixture; drain well. Cut pears in half vertically, and then cut into ⅛-inch-thick lengthwise slices, keeping slices in order as they are cut. Arrange slices over almond mixture in the shape of 6 pear halves, letting slices fan out slightly. Top with ¼ cup sugar; sprinkle with 3 tablespoons almonds, and drizzle with 2 tablespoons melted butter. Bake at 400° for 40 to 50 minutes or until golden brown.

Combine preserves, ¼ cup water, and 2 tablespoons sugar; cook over low heat, stirring constantly, until sugar dissolves. Press mixture through a sieve, reserving syrup. Discard preserves. Stir Kirsch into syrup. Carefully brush syrup over tart. Remove tart from pan before serving. Yield: 6 servings.

PEAR-APPLE MINCEMEAT PIE

Pastry for double-crust 9-inch pie
4½ cups Pear-Apple Mincemeat (page 255)
¼ cup sugar
2 tablespoons butter or margarine

Roll half of pastry to ⅛-inch thickness on a lightly floured surface. Place in a 9-inch pieplate; set aside.

Combine mincemeat and sugar in a heavy saucepan; bring to a boil, stirring frequently. Spoon mincemeat mixture into prepared pastry shell; dot top of mincemeat with butter.

Roll remaining pastry to ⅛-inch thickness; transfer to top of pie. Trim off excess pastry along edges. Fold edges under and flute. Cut slits in top crust for steam to escape. Cover edges of pastry with strips of aluminum foil to prevent excessive browning. Bake at 375° for 30 to 40 minutes, removing foil last 15 minutes of baking. Yield: one 9-inch pie.

LITTLE FRIED PIES

4 cups dried apples or peaches
2 cups water
½ cup sugar
½ teaspoon ground cinnamon
Fried pie pastry (recipe follows)
Vegetable oil
Sugar

Combine apples and water in a large saucepan; bring to a boil. Cover, reduce heat, and simmer about 30 minutes or until tender. Cool; mash slightly, if necessary. Stir in ½ cup sugar and cinnamon, and set aside.

Divide pastry into thirds; roll each portion to ¼-inch thickness on wax paper. Cut into 5-inch circles.

Place about 2 tablespoons apple mixture on half of each pastry circle. To seal pies, dip fingers in water, and moisten edges of pastry circles; fold circles in half, making sure edges are even. Press edges of filled pastry firmly together using a fork dipped in flour.

Heat ½ inch of oil to 375° in a large skillet. Fry pies until golden brown on both sides, turning once. Drain well on paper towels. Sprinkle with sugar while warm. Yield: 1 dozen.

Fried Pie Pastry

3 cups all-purpose flour
1 teaspoon salt
¾ cup shortening
1 egg, beaten
¼ cup water
1 teaspoon vinegar

Combine flour and salt; cut in shortening with pastry blender until mixture resembles coarse meal. Combine egg and water; sprinkle over flour mixture. Add vinegar, and lightly stir with a fork until dry ingredients are moistened. Shape into a ball. Wrap pastry in wax paper; chill at least 1 hour. Yield: pastry for about 1 dozen 5-inch pies.

FRESH PEACH PIE

6 cups peeled, sliced fresh peaches
1⅓ cups sugar
¼ cup all-purpose flour
½ teaspoon ground nutmeg
¾ teaspoon vanilla extract
3 tablespoons butter or margarine
Pastry for double-crust 9-inch pie
Vanilla ice cream (optional)

Combine peaches, sugar, flour, and nutmeg in a saucepan; set aside until syrup forms. Bring mixture to a boil; reduce heat to low, and cook 10 minutes or until peaches are tender, stirring often. Remove from heat; add vanilla and butter, blending well.

Roll out half of pastry to ⅛-inch thickness on a lightly floured surface. Place pastry in a 9-inch pieplate; trim off excess pastry along edges. Spoon peach filling into pastry shell.

Roll remaining pastry to ⅛-inch thickness; cut into ½-inch strips. Arrange strips, lattice fashion, across top of pie. Trim strips even with edges; fold edges under and flute. Bake at 425° for 10 minutes. Reduce heat to 350° and bake an additional 30 minutes or until crust is browned. Serve with ice cream, if desired. Yield: one 9-inch pie.

PRIZE-WINNING CHERRY PIE

1 cup sugar
3 tablespoons cornstarch
¼ teaspoon salt
⅔ cup grenadine syrup
2 (16-ounce) packages frozen cherries, thawed
½ teaspoon almond extract
2 tablespoons butter or margarine
Pastry for double-crust 9-inch pie
2 teaspoons milk

Combine first 3 ingredients in a medium saucepan, stirring to remove lumps.

Stir grenadine syrup into sugar mixture. Cook over medium heat until smooth, stirring constantly. Add cherries; simmer until liquid is thickened and transparent (about 4 minutes), stirring gently once or twice. Add almond extract and butter, stirring until butter melts; cool.

Roll half of pastry to ⅛-inch thickness on a lightly floured surface. Place in a 9-inch deep-dish pieplate; trim off excess pastry along edges. Pour cooled cherry mixture into pastry shell.

Roll remaining pastry to ⅛-inch thickness; transfer to top of pie. Trim off excess pastry along edges. Fold edges under and flute. Cut slits in top crust for steam to escape. Brush top of pastry shell lightly with milk. Bake at 400° for 55 minutes or until golden brown. Cool pie before serving. Yield: one 9-inch pie.

Note: Two pounds fresh cherries, pitted, may be substituted for 2 (16-ounce) packages frozen cherries, if desired; use ¼ cup cornstarch instead of 3 tablespoons cornstarch.

PLUM GOOD PIE

8 fresh plums (about 1 pound)
2 tablespoons all-purpose flour
Pastry shell (recipe follows)
1 teaspoon ground cinnamon
⅔ cup sugar
2 eggs, beaten

Cut each plum into 8 wedges; discard pits. Sprinkle flour evenly in bottom of partially baked pastry shell. Arrange plum wedges side by side in pastry shell, overlapping slightly. Combine cinnamon and sugar; sprinkle over plums. Pour eggs over top, covering surface evenly.

Bake at 400° for 30 minutes or until lightly browned. Yield: one 10-inch pie.

Pastry Shell

1¼ cups all-purpose flour
2 tablespoons sugar
½ cup butter or margarine, melted
1 tablespoon vinegar

Combine flour and sugar; add butter and vinegar, mixing well. Roll pastry out to fit a 10-inch piepan; press evenly into bottom and halfway up sides of lightly greased 10-inch piepan. Prick bottom with a fork. Bake at 400° for 10 minutes. Yield: one 10-inch pastry shell.

Make Tarts in a Hurry

For a quick dessert for the family, purchase commercial individual-size tarts and take your choice of the following fillings:

● Fill tarts with a scoop of ice cream, and top with fresh fruit.

● Spoon butterscotch or fudge sauce in bottom of tart, and scoop ice cream on top.

● Fill tarts with your favorite pudding, and top with whipped cream.

● Slice fresh fruit into the tarts, and brush sieved melted jam over the fruit.

BLACKBERRY CRUMB PIE

1 cup sugar
1 (8-ounce) carton commercial sour cream
3 tablespoons all-purpose flour
⅛ teaspoon salt
4 cups fresh blackberries
1 unbaked 9-inch pastry shell
1 tablespoon sugar
¼ cup fine dry breadcrumbs
1 tablespoon sugar
1 tablespoon butter or margarine, melted

Combine first 4 ingredients; stir well.

Place blackberries in unbaked pastry shell; sprinkle 1 tablespoon sugar over berries. Spread sour cream mixture over berries. Combine breadcrumbs, 1 tablespoon sugar, and butter; sprinkle over top. Bake at 375° for 45 to 50 minutes or until center of pie is firm. Yield: one 9-inch pie.

Blueberry Crumb Pie: Substitute an equal amount of blueberries for blackberries.

Serve the Pie à la Mode

It's an old Southern custom to top many fruit pies with a scoop of ice cream. If you have a large crowd to serve, scoop the ice cream balls a day ahead of time, and freeze them on a baking sheet. Then you can serve fruit pie à la mode quickly and neatly!

You'll enjoy making Fancy Fruit Tarts; arrange the fruit differently for each individual serving.

FRESH RHUBARB PIE

Pastry for double-crust 9-inch pie
1½ cups sugar
2½ tablespoons cornstarch
¼ teaspoon ground nutmeg
½ teaspoon grated orange rind
¼ cup orange juice
2 tablespoons butter or margarine
4 cups sliced rhubarb

Roll half of pastry to ⅛-inch thickness on a lightly floured surface. Place in a 9-inch pieplate; trim off excess pastry along edges. Cover with plastic wrap, and chill until ready to fill.

Combine sugar, cornstarch, and nutmeg in a heavy saucepan, stirring to blend cornstarch well. Stir in orange rind, juice, and butter. Cook over medium heat, stirring constantly, until thickened and bubbly. Stir in rhubarb. Spoon rhubarb mixture into prepared pastry shell.

Roll remaining pastry to ⅛-inch thickness; cut into ½-inch strips. Arrange strips, lattice fashion, across top of pie. Trim strips even with edges; fold edges under and flute. Bake at 425° for 10 minutes. Reduce heat to 350° and bake an additional 30 minutes or until crust is browned. Yield: one 9-inch pie.

FANCY FRUIT TARTS

1 recipe Tart Pastry (page 356)
3 egg yolks
¼ cup sugar
2½ tablespoons all-purpose flour
¾ cup milk
3 tablespoons butter or margarine
¾ teaspoon vanilla extract
3 cups assorted fruit (blueberries, raspberries, grape halves, sliced peaches, or sliced strawberries)
½ cup pineapple preserves

Roll pastry to ⅛-inch thickness on a lightly floured surface. Cut and fit pastry into six 4-inch shallow tart or quiche pans. Bake at 450° for 12 to 15 minutes or until lightly browned.

Combine egg yolks, sugar, and flour in a medium saucepan, stirring until blended. Stir in milk. Cook over medium heat, stirring constantly, just until mixture comes to a boil. Reduce heat, and simmer 1 minute. Cool to lukewarm, and add butter and vanilla; stir until butter melts. Cover and chill thoroughly.

Spoon custard mixture evenly into tart shells. Top with fruit as desired. Cook preserves over low heat until melted. Press preserves through a sieve to remove lumps. Brush strained preserve liquid lightly over fruit. Yield: 6 servings.

Custard and Cream Pies

These pies don't call for a lot of fancy ingredients and they don't take a long time to make, but they're some of the creamiest and tastiest desserts you'll ever eat—especially when you dress the fillings with your favorite fruit or chocolate. Some of our pies are flavored with butterscotch and coffee as well.

When baking custard pies, avoid messy spills by placing the pastry-lined pieplate on the oven rack before pouring in the filling. Check for doneness with the knife test: when a knife inserted in the center comes out clean, the pie is done. The filling will still be somewhat shaky, but will firm up upon cooling.

Cream pies are easy to make, although their satiny-smooth texture can be intimidating.

If your cream pies are thickened with cornstarch or flour, never add it directly to a hot mixture, because it will cause the mixture to lump. Usually the thickening agent is blended with cold liquid before the cooking process begins.

Whether thickened with cornstarch or flour, cook the filling until it comes to a full boil; then boil and stir for 1 minute. The filling may look a little thin immediately after cooking, but will thicken as it cools.

If your recipe says to chill the filling before adding a topping, press wax paper or plastic wrap directly on the surface of the filling to prevent a skin from forming as the filling is cooling.

Cream or custard pies should be thoroughly cooled before serving. Otherwise the filling will not be firm enough. Always store leftover cream or custard pies in the refrigerator.

EGG CUSTARD PIE

1 unbaked 9-inch pastry shell
4 eggs, slightly beaten
⅔ cup sugar
1 teaspoon vanilla extract
¼ teaspoon salt
¼ teaspoon ground nutmeg
2¼ cups milk
Additional ground nutmeg

Bake pastry shell at 400° for 5 minutes. Let cool.

Combine eggs, sugar, vanilla, salt, and ¼ teaspoon nutmeg; beat until blended. Gradually stir in milk; mix well. Pour filling into pastry shell; sprinkle with additional nutmeg.

Bake at 400° for 15 minutes; reduce heat to 325°, and bake an additional 35 minutes or until a knife inserted in center comes out clean. Cool to room temperature before serving. Store in refrigerator. Yield: one 9-inch pie.

LUSCIOUS CARAMEL BANANA PIE

1 (14-ounce) can sweetened condensed milk
2 to 3 bananas
1 (9-inch) graham cracker crust
1 cup whipping cream
¼ cup sifted powdered sugar
1 or 2 (1⅛-ounce) English toffee-flavored candy bars, crumbled

Pour sweetened condensed milk into an 8-inch pieplate. Cover pieplate with aluminum foil.

Pour about ¼-inch hot water in a larger shallow pan. Place covered pieplate in pan. Bake at 425° for 1 hour and 20 minutes or until condensed milk is thick and caramel colored (add hot water to pan as needed). Remove foil when done, and set aside.

Cut bananas into ⅛-inch slices, and place on crust. Spread caramelized milk over bananas. Cool at least 30 minutes.

Beat whipping cream until foamy; gradually add powdered sugar, beating until soft peaks form. Spread over caramel layer. Sprinkle with crumbled candy. Chill at least 3 hours before serving. Yield: one 9-inch pie.

BUTTERMILK PIE

½ cup butter or margarine, softened
2 cups sugar
3 tablespoons all-purpose flour
3 eggs
1 cup buttermilk
1 teaspoon vanilla extract
1 unbaked 9-inch pastry shell

Cream butter at high speed of an electric mixer; gradually add sugar, beating well. Add flour, and beat until smooth. Add eggs; beat until blended. Add buttermilk and vanilla; beat well. Pour filling into pastry shell. Bake at 400° for 5 minutes; reduce heat to 350°, and bake an additional 45 minutes or until set. Cool to room temperature; then chill. Yield: one 9-inch pie.

LEMON CHESS PIE

2 cups sugar
1 tablespoon all-purpose flour
1 tablespoon cornmeal
¼ teaspoon salt
¼ cup butter or margarine, melted
2 teaspoons grated lemon rind
¼ cup lemon juice
¼ cup milk
4 eggs
1 unbaked 9-inch pastry shell

Combine sugar, flour, cornmeal, and salt. Add butter, lemon rind, lemon juice, and milk; mix well. Add eggs, one at a time, beating well with a wire whisk after each addition. Pour into pastry shell. Bake at 350° for 50 minutes. Yield: one 9-inch pie.

VANILLA CREAM PIE

¾ cup sugar
¼ cup plus 2 teaspoons cornstarch
⅛ teaspoon salt
3 egg yolks, beaten
3 cups milk
1½ tablespoons butter or margarine
1½ teaspoons vanilla extract
1 baked 9-inch pastry shell
¾ cup whipping cream
⅓ cup sifted powdered sugar

Combine sugar, cornstarch, and salt in a heavy saucepan; stir well. Combine egg yolks and milk; gradually stir into sugar mixture. Cook over medium heat, stirring constantly, until mixture thickens and boils. Boil 1 minute, stirring constantly. Remove from heat; stir in butter and vanilla. Immediately pour into pastry shell. Cover filling with wax paper. Let cool 30 minutes; then chill until firm.

Beat whipping cream until foamy; gradually add powdered sugar, beating until soft peaks form. Spread whipped cream over filling. Chill. Yield: one 9-inch pie.

Chocolate Cream Pie: Add ¼ cup cocoa when combining sugar and cornstarch.

Coconut Cream Pie: Add ½ cup flaked coconut with vanilla. Sprinkle ¼ cup toasted flaked coconut over whipped cream.

Banana Cream Pie: Slice 2 small bananas into pastry shell before adding filling.

Butterscotch Cream Pie: Substitute ¾ cup firmly packed dark brown sugar for ¾ cup sugar; reduce vanilla to ¾ teaspoon and add ¾ teaspoon butter flavoring.

A sprinkling of toasted coconut on top hints at the flavor inside Coconut Cream Pie.

FRENCH SILK PIE

2 (1-ounce) squares unsweetened chocolate
½ cup butter or margarine, softened
¾ cup sugar
2 eggs
1 (4-ounce) carton frozen whipped topping, thawed (about 1¾ cups)
1 baked 9-inch pastry shell
¾ cup whipping cream
2 tablespoons powdered sugar
Shaved chocolate (optional)

Place chocolate in top of a double boiler; bring water to a boil. Reduce heat to low; cook until chocolate melts. Let chocolate cool.

Cream butter; gradually add sugar, beating at medium speed of an electric mixer until light and fluffy. Stir in chocolate. Add eggs, one at a time, beating 5 minutes after each addition. Fold in whipped topping, and spoon mixture into pastry shell. Chill 2 hours.

Beat whipping cream until foamy; gradually add powdered sugar, beating until soft peaks form. Spread whipped cream on pie; garnish with shaved chocolate, if desired. Yield: one 9-inch pie.

BOSTON CREAM PIE

⅓ cup shortening
⅔ cup sugar
2 eggs
1 cup sifted cake flour
1 teaspoon baking powder
Pinch of salt
½ cup milk
½ teaspoon butter flavoring
½ teaspoon vanilla extract
Cream filling (recipe follows)
Chocolate glaze (recipe follows)

Cream shortening; gradually add sugar, beating well. Add eggs, one at a time, beating well after each addition.

Combine flour, baking powder, and salt; add to creamed mixture alternately with milk, beginning and ending with flour mixture. Stir in butter flavoring and vanilla. Pour batter into a greased and floured 9-inch round cakepan. Bake at 325° for 25 to 30 minutes or until a wooden pick inserted in center comes out clean. Cool in pan 10 minutes; remove from pan, and cool completely.

Split cake layer in half horizontally to make 2 layers. Spread cream filling between layers; spread chocolate glaze over top. Refrigerate until ready to serve. Yield: 8 to 10 servings.

Cream Filling

½ cup sugar
¼ cup cornstarch
¼ teaspoon salt
2 cups milk
4 egg yolks, slightly beaten
1 teaspoon vanilla extract

Combine first 3 ingredients in a heavy saucepan. Add milk and egg yolks; stir with a wire whisk until blended. Cook over medium heat, stirring constantly, until mixture comes to a boil. Boil 1 minute or until thickened, stirring constantly; remove from heat. Stir in vanilla. Cool. Yield: 2 cups.

Chocolate Glaze

2 tablespoons butter or margarine
1 (1-ounce) square unsweetened chocolate
1 cup sifted powdered sugar
¼ cup boiling water

Combine butter and chocolate in top of a double boiler; bring water to a boil. Reduce heat to low; cook until chocolate melts. Cool slightly. Add sugar and water; beat until smooth. Yield: ¾ cup.

CHOCOLATE MOCHA CRUNCH PIE

Mocha Pastry Shell
1 (1-ounce) square unsweetened chocolate
½ cup butter or margarine, softened
¾ cup firmly packed brown sugar
2 teaspoons instant coffee powder
2 eggs
2 cups whipping cream
½ cup sifted powdered sugar
1½ tablespoons instant coffee powder
½ (1-ounce) square semisweet chocolate, grated (optional)

Prepare Mocha Pastry Shell; set aside.

Place 1 square chocolate in top of a double boiler; bring water to a boil. Reduce heat to low; cook until chocolate melts. Let cool.

Cream butter at medium speed of an electric mixer. Gradually add brown sugar, and beat at medium speed 2 to 3 minutes, scraping sides of bowl occasionally. Stir in melted chocolate and 2 teaspoons coffee powder. Add eggs, one at a time, beating 5 minutes after each addition.

Pour filling into cooled pastry shell. Refrigerate at least 6 hours.

About 1 or 2 hours before serving, combine whipping cream, powdered sugar, and 1½ tablespoons coffee powder in a large, chilled mixing bowl. Whip cream until soft peaks form (do not overbeat). Spoon over chilled filling. Sprinkle with grated chocolate, if desired. Chill. Yield: one 9-inch pie.

Mocha Pastry Shell

1 piecrust stick, crumbled or ½ (11-ounce) package piecrust mix
1 (1-ounce) square unsweetened chocolate, grated
¾ cup finely chopped walnuts
¼ cup firmly packed brown sugar
1 tablespoon water
1 teaspoon vanilla extract

Use a fork to combine crumbled piecrust stick and chocolate in a medium bowl. Stir in walnuts and sugar. Combine water and vanilla; sprinkle over pastry mixture. Mix with fork until mixture forms a ball.

Line a 9-inch pieplate with aluminum foil; place a circle of wax paper over foil in the bottom of pieplate. Press pastry mixture evenly into pieplate.

Bake at 375° for 15 minutes; cool completely. Invert crust on an 8½-inch pieplate; remove foil and wax paper. Return to 9-inch pieplate. Yield: one 9-inch pastry shell.

Pipe the Cream Like a Professional

Many cream pies are sinfully topped with whipped cream. To give yours a professional look, pipe the fluffy topping from a decorating bag fitted with a large star tip. You can pipe the whipped cream freeform, or try a lattice or spiral design. And if you aren't pleased with the end result, you're not stuck with it! Just spread the whipped cream with a spatula, and sprinkle on some nuts or grated chocolate.

Meringue Pies

Some of the most classic pies are those topped with fluffy white meringue—mountains of it! Lemon and chocolate versions are probably the most common.

Cookbooks are full of directions for preventing meringue from weeping; sometimes the directions work, and sometimes they don't. We've accepted the fact that meringue occasionally weeps, even when made "exactly by the directions." Extra humidity in the air is sometimes the problem, while deviating from standard procedure can be the culprit.

When making meringue, separate the eggs while cold, but let them come to room temperature before beating the whites. Use only copper, metal, or glass bowls (never plastic ones), and make sure the bowls and beaters are grease-free.

Add the sugar to meringue gradually (one tablespoon at a time), and beat until the sugar dissolves. To be sure sugar is dissolved, rub a small amount of meringue between your fingers; it will not feel grainy if the sugar is dissolved.

When beaten enough, meringue should look glossy and have sharp peaks and almost invisible air pockets. At this point, spoon the meringue onto hot filling, and seal it to the edges of the pie. Bake it immediately as recipe directs, and cool it away from drafts.

Let meringue pies cool completely before serving; if sliced immediately the filling would probably run. They are best made several hours before serving. Refrigeration can cause meringue to become slightly sticky, but you do need to refrigerate any leftovers. Use a wet knife to make slicing easier.

CHOCOLATE MERINGUE PIE

1 cup sugar
3 tablespoons cornstarch
Dash of salt
2 cups milk
3 eggs, separated
1 (1-ounce) square unsweetened chocolate
1 tablespoon butter or margarine
1 teaspoon vanilla extract
1 baked 9-inch pastry shell
½ teaspoon cream of tartar
¼ cup plus 2 tablespoons sugar

Combine 1 cup sugar, cornstarch, and salt in a heavy saucepan; mix well.

Combine milk and egg yolks; beat with a wire whisk 1 to 2 minutes or until frothy. Gradually stir into sugar mixture, mixing well.

Cook over medium heat, stirring constantly, until thickened and bubbly. Remove from heat; add chocolate, butter, and vanilla, stirring until chocolate and butter melt. Spoon mixture into pastry shell; set aside.

Beat egg whites (at room temperature) and cream of tartar at high speed of an electric mixer 1 minute. Gradually add ¼ cup plus 2 tablespoons sugar, 1 tablespoon at a time, beating until stiff peaks form and sugar dissolves (2 to 4 minutes).

Spread meringue over hot filling, sealing to edge of pastry. Bake at 350° for 10 to 12 minutes or until golden brown. Yield: one 9-inch pie.

LIME MERINGUE PIE

4 eggs, separated
1 (14-ounce) can sweetened condensed milk
½ cup lime juice
1 (9-inch) graham cracker crust
½ teaspoon cream of tartar
¼ cup plus 2 tablespoons sugar

Beat egg yolks at medium speed of electric mixer until thick and lemon colored. Add sweetened condensed milk and lime juice, stirring well. Spoon filling into graham cracker crust.

Beat egg whites (at room temperature) and cream of tartar at high speed of an electric mixer 1 minute. Gradually add sugar, 1 tablespoon at a time, beating until stiff peaks form and sugar dissolves (2 to 4 minutes).

Spread meringue over filling, sealing to edge of pastry. Bake at 350° for 12 to 15 minutes or until golden brown. Yield: one 9-inch pie.

Key Lime Meringue Pie: We found Key limes to have a tarter taste than common Persian limes. When using Key limes for this pie, reduce lime juice to ⅓ cup, and add ⅓ cup sifted powdered sugar when the sweetened condensed milk is added.

1. To make Lemon Meringue Pie, combine sugar, cornstarch, and salt, stirring to blend cornstarch well. Add milk, and cook until mixture thickens.

2. Beat egg yolks at high speed of an electric mixer until thick and lemon colored. Stir about one-fourth of hot mixture into yolks; add to remaining hot mixture.

3. Stir lemon rind, juice, and butter into thickened mixture, and pour into pastry shell.

4. For meringue, beat egg whites and cream of tartar until foamy.

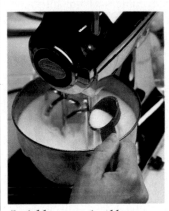

5. Add sugar, 1 tablespoon at a time, beating until stiff peaks form.

6. Spread meringue over lemon filling, sealing to edge of pastry.

Enjoy Lemon Meringue Pie piled high with fluffy meringue.

LEMON MERINGUE PIE

1 cup sugar
3 tablespoons cornstarch
¼ teaspoon salt
2 cups milk
4 eggs, separated
1 teaspoon grated lemon rind
⅓ cup lemon juice
3 tablespoons butter or
  margarine
1 baked 9-inch pastry shell
½ teaspoon cream of tartar
¼ cup plus 2 tablespoons sugar
½ teaspoon vanilla extract

Combine 1 cup sugar, cornstarch, and salt in a heavy saucepan. Gradually add milk, stirring until blended. Cook over medium heat, stirring constantly, until mixture thickens and comes to a boil. Boil 1 minute, stirring constantly. Remove from heat.

Beat egg yolks at high speed of an electric mixer until thick and lemon colored. Gradually stir about one-fourth of hot mixture into yolks; add to remaining hot mixture, stirring constantly. Cook over medium heat, stirring constantly, 2 to 3 minutes. Remove from heat; stir in lemon rind, lemon juice, and butter. Spoon into pastry shell.

Beat egg whites (at room temperature) and cream of tartar at high speed of an electric mixer 1 minute. Gradually add ¼ cup plus 2 tablespoons sugar, 1 tablespoon at a time, beating until stiff peaks form and sugar dissolves (2 to 4 minutes). Beat in vanilla. Spread meringue over hot filling, sealing to edge. Bake at 350° for 12 to 15 minutes or until browned. Yield: one 9-inch pie.

MOCHA MERINGUE PIE

In contrast to the typical meringue pie, Mocha Meringue Pie sports a crisp meringue as the crust. This type of meringue is baked for a long time in a very slow oven to achieve its characteristic crunch.

3 egg whites
½ teaspoon baking powder
Pinch of salt
¾ cup sugar
1 cup chocolate wafer crumbs
½ cup chopped pecans
1 teaspoon vanilla extract
1 quart coffee ice cream, softened
1 cup whipping cream
½ cup sifted powdered sugar
Chocolate curls or grated chocolate
About ½ cup Kahlúa or other
　coffee-flavored liqueur

Beat egg whites (at room temperature) at high speed of an electric mixer until frothy; add baking powder and salt, beating slightly. Gradually add sugar, 1 tablespoon at a time; continue beating until stiff and glossy. Fold in chocolate wafer crumbs, chopped pecans, and vanilla.

Spoon meringue into a greased 9-inch pieplate; use spoon to shape meringue into a pie shell, swirling sides high. Bake at 350° for 30 minutes; cool.

Spread ice cream evenly over meringue crust; cover pie, and freeze at least 8 hours.

Combine whipping cream and powdered sugar, beating until light and fluffy; spread on pie. Garnish with chocolate curls or grated chocolate; freeze pie until firm.

Let pie stand at room temperature 10 minutes before slicing. Pour 1 tablespoon Kahlúa over each serving. Yield: one 9-inch pie.

Note: This pie is thick and rich. It will easily yield 8 servings.

Chilled and Frozen Pies

Pies that call for chilling or freezing make excellent choices for entertaining because you can prepare them a day or two ahead of time, and then forget about them until it's time for dessert.

Chilled pies often contain unflavored gelatin which gives them a characteristic lightness. When making gelatin pies, it's important to dissolve the gelatin properly to insure that the mixture is smooth.

First, soften the gelatin in a small amount of cold liquid as your recipe directs. Then stir the gelatin mixture in hot liquid or over low heat until all gelatin granules dissolve and the mixture is smooth. Cool the mixture slightly before folding in the remaining ingredients; chill until set.

For ice cream pies, soften ice cream about 10 to 15 minutes before spooning it into a piecrust; then return the pie to the freezer for at least 8 hours.

Most ice cream pies need to sit at room temperature about 8 to 10 minutes before serving so they will be softer and slice more easily.

Chilled pies start with a baked pastry or crumb crust. Freezer pies also require a baked pastry crust, but baking crumb crusts is not necessary for this type of pie.

LEMON CHIFFON PIE

1 envelope unflavored gelatin
¼ cup cold water
4 eggs, separated
1 cup sugar
1½ teaspoons grated lemon rind
½ cup lemon juice
⅛ teaspoon salt
½ cup sugar
½ cup whipping cream, whipped
1 (9-inch) graham cracker crust
Lemon slices (optional)

Soften gelatin in cold water; set aside.

Beat egg yolks until thick and lemon colored. Combine yolks, 1 cup sugar, lemon rind, juice, and salt in a saucepan; stir until smooth. Cook over medium heat, stirring constantly, 5 minutes or until thickened. Remove from heat; add gelatin, and stir until gelatin granules dissolve. Cool.

Beat egg whites (at room temperature) until foamy; gradually add ½ cup sugar, 1 tablespoon at a time, beating until soft peaks form. Fold egg whites and whipped cream into lemon mixture; pour into crust. Chill until set. Garnish with lemon slices, if desired. Yield: one 9-inch pie.

Note: Recipe makes enough filling for 2 pies if using commercial graham cracker crusts.

PINEAPPLE-CHEESE PIE

¼ cup cold milk
1 envelope unflavored gelatin
½ cup milk
⅔ cup sugar
⅛ teaspoon salt
1 (8-ounce) package cream cheese, softened and cut into pieces
1 tablespoon lemon juice
1 teaspoon vanilla extract
1 (8-ounce) carton commercial sour cream
1 (8¼-ounce) can crushed pineapple, undrained
1 (9-inch) graham cracker crust

Combine ¼ cup cold milk and gelatin in container of an electric blender; process at low speed to soften gelatin. Heat ½ cup milk in a small saucepan; add to gelatin mixture, and process until gelatin granules dissolve. Scrape sides of blender with spatula. Add sugar and next 5 ingredients; blend until smooth. Drain pineapple, reserving 3 tablespoons syrup. Add pineapple and reserved syrup to blender mixture; process until smooth. Pour into crust. Chill 3 hours or until firm. Yield: one 9-inch pie.

RAISIN BOURBON PIE

¼ cup bourbon
¾ cup golden raisins
1 envelope unflavored gelatin
¼ cup cold water
¾ cup sugar
3 tablespoons cornstarch
1¼ cups milk
2 eggs, well beaten
1 tablespoon butter or margarine
½ teaspoon vanilla extract
1 cup whipping cream, whipped
1 baked 9-inch pastry shell
Ground nutmeg

Combine bourbon and raisins; cover and let stand 8 hours.
Soften gelatin in cold water; set aside.

Combine sugar and cornstarch in a heavy saucepan. Gradually stir milk and eggs into sugar mixture. Cook over medium heat, stirring constantly, until mixture thickens and boils. Boil 1 minute, stirring constantly. Add butter and gelatin, stirring until gelatin granules dissolve. Chill 30 minutes, but do not let mixture gel. Add raisin mixture and vanilla; blend. Fold in whipped cream; pour into pastry shell. Sprinkle with nutmeg. Chill at least 4 hours before serving. Yield: one 9-inch pie.

BLACK BOTTOM ICE CREAM PIE

1 cup chocolate ice cream, softened
1 (9-inch) gingersnap crumb crust
1 quart vanilla ice cream, softened
½ cup semisweet chocolate morsels
¼ cup whipping cream
¼ teaspoon vanilla extract

Spread chocolate ice cream in bottom of crust; cover and freeze until firm. Spread vanilla ice cream over chocolate layer; cover and freeze until firm.
Combine chocolate morsels and whipping cream in a small heavy saucepan; cook over low heat until chocolate melts, stirring constantly. Remove from heat, and stir in vanilla. Cool completely. Drizzle sauce over top of pie, and freeze until ready to serve. Yield: one 9-inch pie.

GRASSHOPPER ICE CREAM PIE

3¼ cups miniature marshmallows
2 tablespoons milk
¼ cup green crème de menthe
2 tablespoons white crème de cacao
1 cup whipping cream, whipped
1 pint vanilla ice cream, softened
1 (9-inch) chocolate wafer crust
Additional whipped cream for garnish

Combine marshmallows and milk in top of double boiler; bring water to a boil. Reduce heat to low; cook until marshmallows melt, stirring frequently. Remove from heat; cool, stirring occasionally. Add crème de menthe and crème de cacao; fold in whipped cream.
Spread ice cream evenly in crust, and pour marshmallow mixture over ice cream. Freeze at least 6 hours. Garnish with additional whipped cream. Yield: one 9-inch pie.

ICE CREAM PIE WITH BUTTERSCOTCH SAUCE

1 cup graham cracker crumbs
½ cup finely chopped walnuts
¼ cup butter or margarine, melted
1 pint coffee ice cream, softened
1 pint vanilla ice cream, softened
Butterscotch Sauce

Combine graham cracker crumbs, walnuts, and butter, mixing well; press firmly into a buttered 9-inch pieplate. Bake at 375° for 8 to 10 minutes; cool.
Spoon coffee ice cream into cooled crust, and spread evenly; freeze until almost firm. Spread vanilla ice cream over coffee layer and freeze until firm. To serve, slice and top with warm Butterscotch Sauce. Yield: one 9-inch pie.

Butterscotch Sauce

3 tablespoons butter or margarine
1 cup firmly packed brown sugar
½ cup half-and-half
1 cup chopped walnuts, toasted
1 teaspoon vanilla extract

Melt butter in a heavy saucepan over low heat; add brown sugar, and cook 5 to 8 minutes, stirring constantly. Remove from heat and gradually stir in half-and-half. Cook 1 minute, and remove from heat. Stir in walnuts and vanilla. Yield: about 1½ cups.

Vegetable and Nut Pies

When fall rolls around, thoughts turn to sweet potato and pumpkin pies. One or the other is often found at family Thanksgiving feasts.

Surely it was the pecan pie that made Southern pies famous. Other nuts work *almost* as well as our region's prized nut, however, and you'll find several variations in these nut pie recipes.

PECAN TASSIES

¾ cup firmly packed light brown sugar
¾ cup chopped pecans
1 egg
1 tablespoon butter or margarine, softened
1 teaspoon vanilla extract
Dash of salt
Tart shells (recipe follows)
Powdered sugar (optional)

Combine first 6 ingredients; mix until blended. Spoon mixture into tart shells, filling three-fourths full. Bake at 350° for 20 minutes or until browned. Dust with powdered sugar before serving, if desired. Yield: 2 dozen.

Tart Shells

1 cup all-purpose flour
1 (3-ounce) package cream cheese, softened
¼ cup plus 3 tablespoons butter, softened

Combine flour, cream cheese, and butter; stir until blended. Shape dough into 24 balls; chill. Place in greased 1¾-inch tart pans, shaping each ball into a shell. Yield: 2 dozen.

FAVORITE PECAN PIE

½ cup butter or margarine, melted
1 cup sugar
1 cup light corn syrup
4 eggs, beaten
1 teaspoon vanilla extract
¼ teaspoon salt
1 unbaked 9-inch pastry shell
1 to 1¼ cups pecan halves

Combine butter, sugar, and corn syrup; cook over low heat, stirring constantly, until sugar dissolves. Let cool slightly. Add eggs, vanilla, and salt to mixture; mix well.

Pour filling into unbaked pastry shell, and top with pecan halves. Bake at 325° for 50 to 55 minutes. Serve warm or cold. Yield: one 9-inch pie.

Rum Pecan Pie: Prepare recipe as directed above, adding 3 tablespoons rum with the eggs; mix well.

MACADAMIA PIE

3 eggs, slightly beaten
⅔ cup sugar
1 cup light corn syrup
1½ cups salted macadamia nuts, chopped
2 tablespoons butter or margarine, melted
1 teaspoon vanilla extract
1 unbaked 9-inch pastry shell

Combine eggs, sugar, and corn syrup, mixing well; stir in macadamia nuts, butter, and vanilla. Pour filling into pastry shell.

Bake at 325° for 55 minutes or until filling is set. Yield: one 9-inch pie.

Peanut Pie: Substitute an equal amount of peanuts for macadamia nuts.

SWEET POTATO PIE

2 cups cooked, mashed sweet potatoes
1 cup firmly packed brown sugar
½ cup butter or margarine, softened
2 eggs, separated
½ teaspoon ground ginger
½ teaspoon ground cinnamon
½ teaspoon ground nutmeg
¼ teaspoon salt
½ cup evaporated milk
¼ cup sugar
1 unbaked 10-inch pastry shell
Whipped topping (optional)

Combine sweet potatoes, brown sugar, butter, egg yolks, spices, and salt in a large mixing bowl; beat until light and fluffy. Add evaporated milk; beat just until blended.

Beat egg whites (at room temperature) until foamy; gradually add sugar, 1 tablespoon at a time, beating until stiff peaks form. Fold into potato mixture. Pour filling into pastry shell. Bake at 400° for 10 minutes; reduce heat to 350°, and bake an additional 45 to 50 minutes or until set. Cool. Top with dollops of whipped topping, if desired. Yield: one 10-inch pie.

Pumpkin Pie: Substitute an equal amount of cooked, mashed pumpkin for sweet potatoes.

Pie From Fresh Pumpkin

To bake fresh pumpkin for pumpkin pie, purchase a small cooking pumpkin that weighs about 2½ pounds. Wash the pumpkin, and cut in half crosswise. Place halves, cut-side down, on a 15- x 10- x 1-inch jellyroll pan. Bake at 325° for 45 minutes or until fork tender; cool 10 minutes. Peel pumpkin, and discard seeds. Puree pulp in a food processor or mash thoroughly. Yield will be about 2¼ cups mashed.

Cobblers and Other Family Favorites

Pastries, such as juicy fruit cobblers and apple dumplings, belong in a category to themselves. There's no good way to classify them other than as salt-of-the-earth family favorites. Most aren't considered complete without a scoop of ice cream.

CRUSTY PEACH COBBLER

About 8 cups sliced fresh peaches
2 cups sugar
2 to 4 tablespoons all-purpose flour
½ teaspoon ground nutmeg
1 teaspoon vanilla extract
⅓ cup butter or margarine
Pastry for double-crust pie
Vanilla ice cream

Combine first 4 ingredients in a Dutch oven; set aside until syrup forms. Bring peach mixture to a boil; reduce heat to low, and cook 10 minutes or until tender. Remove from heat; add vanilla and butter, stirring until butter melts.

Roll half of pastry to ⅛-inch thickness on a lightly floured surface; cut into an 8-inch square. Spoon half of peaches into a lightly buttered 8-inch square pan; top with pastry square. Bake at 475° for 12 minutes or until lightly browned. Spoon remaining peaches over baked pastry square.

Roll remaining pastry to ⅛-inch thickness, and cut into 1-inch strips; arrange in lattice design over peaches. Bake an additional 15 to 18 minutes or until browned. Spoon into serving bowls, and top each with a scoop of ice cream. Yield: 8 servings.

Layers of pastry and juicy fresh peaches make Crusty Peach Cobbler hard to resist.

SOUTHERN BLACKBERRY COBBLER

3 cups fresh blackberries or 2 (16-ounce) packages frozen blackberries, thawed
¾ cup sugar
3 tablespoons all-purpose flour
1½ cups water
1 tablespoon lemon juice
Crust (recipe follows)
2 tablespoons butter or margarine, melted
Ice cream (optional)

Place berries in a lightly greased shallow 2-quart baking dish. Combine sugar and flour; stir in water and lemon juice. Pour mixture over berries, and bake at 425° for 15 minutes.

Place crust over hot berries; brush with butter. Bake at 425° for 20 to 30 minutes or until crust is golden brown.

Serve warm with ice cream, if desired. Yield: 6 to 8 servings.

Crust

1¾ cups all-purpose flour
2 teaspoons baking powder
¾ teaspoon salt
2 to 3 tablespoons sugar
¼ cup shortening
¼ cup plus 2 tablespoons whipping cream
¼ cup plus 2 tablespoons buttermilk

Combine first 4 ingredients. Cut in shortening with pastry blender until mixture resembles coarse meal; stir in whipping cream and buttermilk. Knead dough 4 or 5 times; roll out on a lightly floured surface. Cut dough to fit baking dish. Yield: crust for 1 cobbler.

OLD-FASHIONED APPLE DUMPLINGS

3 cups all-purpose flour
2 teaspoons baking powder
1 teaspoon salt
1 cup shortening
¾ cup milk
6 small Winesap, York, or cooking apples
¼ cup firmly packed brown sugar, divided
1½ teaspoons ground cinnamon, divided
¼ cup butter or margarine, divided
1½ cups sugar
1½ cups water
1 tablespoon butter or margarine
¼ teaspoon ground cinnamon
¼ teaspoon ground nutmeg

Combine first 3 ingredients; cut in shortening with pastry blender until mixture resembles coarse meal. Gradually add milk, stirring to make a soft dough. Roll dough to ¼-inch thickness on a lightly floured surface, shaping into a 21- x 14-inch rectangle; cut dough with a pastry cutter into six 7-inch squares.

Peel and core apples. Place one apple on each pastry square. Fill core of each with 2 teaspoons brown sugar, and sprinkle each with ¼ teaspoon cinnamon. Dot each with 2 teaspoons butter. Moisten edges of each dumpling with water; bring corners to center, pinching edges to seal. Place dumplings in a lightly greased 12- x 8- x 2-inch baking dish. Bake at 375° for 35 minutes.

Combine 1½ cups sugar, 1½ cups water, 1 tablespoon butter, ¼ teaspoon cinnamon, and nutmeg in a medium saucepan; bring to a boil. Reduce heat, and simmer 4 minutes, stirring occasionally until butter melts and sugar dissolves. Pour syrup over dumplings; serve immediately. Yield: 6 servings.

QUICK FRUIT CRISP

4 to 5 cups sliced fresh apples, peaches, or pears
1 tablespoon lemon juice
⅔ cup firmly packed brown sugar
2 tablespoons all-purpose flour
½ cup regular oats, uncooked
½ teaspoon ground cinnamon
Dash of salt
⅓ cup butter or margarine
Vanilla ice cream (optional)

Place fruit in a lightly greased 8-inch square baking dish; sprinkle with lemon juice. Combine sugar, flour, oats, cinnamon, and salt; cut in butter with pastry blender until mixture resembles coarse crumbs. Sprinkle crumb mixture over fruit. Bake at 350° for 30 minutes or until fruit is tender and topping is browned. Serve with ice cream, if desired. Yield: 6 servings.

Note: One 21-ounce can fruit pie filling may be substituted for fresh fruit, if desired. Reduce brown sugar to ¼ cup if making substitution.

CRUSTLESS BROWNIE PIE

1 cup sugar
½ cup all-purpose flour
¼ cup cocoa
½ cup butter or margarine, softened
2 eggs
1 teaspoon vanilla extract
Pinch of salt
½ cup chopped pecans or walnuts
Whipped cream or ice cream

Combine first 7 ingredients; beat 4 minutes at medium speed of an electric mixer. Stir in pecans. Spread batter evenly in a buttered 9-inch pieplate. Bake at 325° for 35 to 40 minutes or until a wooden pick inserted in center comes out clean. (Pie will puff, then fall slightly.) Serve with whipped cream. Yield: one 9-inch pie.

Cream Puff Pastry

The dough credited for making cream puffs is called by the professionals *pâte à chou*, which in lay terms is cream puff pastry. When baked, the famous pastry magically rises and creates a center cavity just the right size to hold a filling.

Both cream puffs and eclairs start from this same pastry, but they are different in the shapes and fillings.

Both look prettiest when piped from a decorating bag; any large fluted tip will work well. You can also make the pastries by just spooning the dough onto the baking sheet, and they'll bake up smooth instead of fluted. Whether spooning or piping the dough, make all the puffs the same size so they'll bake evenly. Space the puffs two to three inches apart on the baking sheet, for they indeed "puff" during baking.

Bake the cream puffs as soon as the pastry is made; the longer you wait to bake them, the less they will rise. You can bake the puffs a day ahead, and store them in an airtight container, if desired. However, don't fill cream puffs more than four hours before serving.

Cream Puff Pastry Step-By-Step

1. For Cream Puff Pastry, combine water and butter in a saucepan; bring to a boil.

2. Add flour and salt to butter mixture.

3. Stir vigorously until mixture leaves sides of pan and forms a ball. Let cool 4 to 5 minutes.

4. Add eggs one at a time, beating with a wooden spoon after each addition.

5. Spoon dough into mounds on baking sheet, and bake as directed. Cut tops from baked puffs, and pull out soft dough inside.

CREAM PUFF PASTRY

⅔ cup water
⅓ cup butter or margarine
⅔ cup all-purpose flour
⅛ teaspoon salt
3 eggs

Combine water and butter in a medium saucepan; bring to a boil. Add flour and salt, all at once, stirring vigorously over medium-high heat until mixture leaves sides of pan and forms a smooth ball. Remove from heat, and cool 4 to 5 minutes.

Add eggs, one at a time, beating thoroughly with a wooden spoon after each addition; then beat until dough is smooth. Shape and bake pastry immediately according to recipe directions. Yield: enough for one 7-inch or eight 2-inch cream puffs.

STRAWBERRY CREAM PUFFS

1 recipe Cream Puff Pastry
¾ cup whipping cream
¼ to ⅓ cup sifted powdered sugar
3 cups fresh strawberries, sliced
Mint leaves

Drop Cream Puff Pastry into 8 equal mounds 3 inches apart on an ungreased baking sheet. Bake at 400° for 30 to 35 minutes or until golden brown and puffed. Cool away from drafts. Cut top off cream puffs; pull out and discard soft dough inside.

Beat whipping cream until foamy; gradually add powdered sugar, beating until soft peaks form. Fold three-fourths of sliced strawberries into whipped cream; fill cream puffs with strawberry mixture. Arrange remaining sliced strawberries on top. Replace tops of cream puffs. Garnish with mint leaves. Yield: 8 servings.

Fill cream puffs with whipped cream and strawberries, and serve as Strawberry Cream Puffs.

CHOCOLATE ECLAIRS

1 recipe Cream Puff Pastry
Pudding (recipe follows)
Chocolate frosting (recipe follows)

Drop Cream Puff Pastry by level one-fourth cupfuls 2 inches apart on ungreased baking sheets, shaping each portion into a 4½- x 1½-inch rectangle. Bake at 400° for 40 minutes or until golden brown and puffed. Cool away from drafts.

Cut off top of each eclair; pull out and discard soft dough inside. Fill bottom halves with pudding, and cover with top halves. Spread chocolate frosting over top of each. Yield: 7 servings.

Pudding

⅓ cup sugar
1½ tablespoons cornstarch
1½ cups milk
1 egg, beaten
1 tablespoon butter or margarine
1 teaspoon vanilla extract

Combine sugar and cornstarch in a heavy saucepan, stirring until blended. Gradually stir in milk, egg, and butter. Cook over medium heat, stirring frequently, until thickened and bubbly. Cook 1 minute longer. Remove from heat, and stir in vanilla. Cool completely. Yield: 2 cups.

Chocolate Frosting

2 tablespoons butter or margarine
¼ cup milk
½ cup semisweet chocolate morsels
1½ to 2 cups sifted powdered sugar

Combine butter and milk in a heavy saucepan; cook over medium heat, stirring constantly, until butter melts. Remove from heat. Add chocolate morsels, and beat until smooth; cool.

Gradually stir in enough powdered sugar to make mixture a good spreading consistency. Yield: 1 cup.

GIANT FRUIT PUFF

1 recipe Cream Puff Pastry
3 egg yolks
½ cup sugar
3½ tablespoons cornstarch
¼ teaspoon salt
1½ cups milk
1 tablespoon butter or margarine
1 teaspoon vanilla extract
½ cup whipping cream, whipped
6 fresh strawberries
1 kiwifruit, peeled and sliced

Spread ½ cup Cream Puff Pastry into a 7-inch circle on a lightly greased baking sheet. Spoon remaining pastry into decorating bag fitted with a No. 5 or 6B large fluted tip. Pipe pastry around outside edge of pastry circle, leaving a 3½-inch circle in center. Bake at 425° for 15 minutes; reduce heat to 375°, and bake an additional 25 minutes or until puffed and golden; cool on wire rack. Beat egg yolks at high speed of an electric mixer until thick and lemon colored. Set aside.

Combine sugar, cornstarch, and salt in a medium saucepan; stir in milk, and bring to a boil, stirring constantly. Boil 1 minute, and remove from heat. Gradually stir about one-fourth of hot mixture into egg yolks; add to remaining hot mixture, stirring constantly. Cook, stirring constantly, over medium-low heat 3 to 4 minutes. Remove from heat, and gently stir in butter and vanilla. Cover with wax paper, and allow mixture to cool completely. Fold in whipped cream.

Spoon mixture in center of puff, and arrange fruit on top; chill. Serve within 4 hours. Yield: 6 servings.

Experiment with Cream Puff Fillings

Don't limit cream puffs to the traditional shapes and fillings. You can make them any size you want, and adjust the baking time accordingly. For spur-of-the-moment dessert fillings, try sliced fruit and whipped cream, pudding, or your favorite flavor of ice cream. You can even serve cream puffs as appetizers or luncheon entrées with fillings like chicken or seafood salad.

Phyllo Pastry

The paper-thin pastry called phyllo originated in the Middle East, but its unique crispness has made it popular in America too. The most noted dessert made from this pastry is Baklava, crisp sheets of phyllo layered with ground nuts and spices and drenched with a honey syrup.

Because phyllo pastry is so thin and fragile, only the experts make it at home. Commercially prepared phyllo is too tasty and convenient to pass up; you'll find it in the freezer section of your supermarket.

Handle phyllo pastry carefully. Thaw phyllo in the package as the label directs. If used before completely thawed, the pastry will tear.

Work with only one sheet at a time; keep the remainder covered with a damp towel. Brush each sheet with butter to make the layers crisp.

If you refreeze thawed phyllo pastry, it will become drier and easier to break.

BAKLAVA

1 (17¼-ounce) package frozen phyllo pastry, thawed
1 cup butter, melted
1 cup ground walnuts
⅓ cup ground almonds
2 tablespoons sugar
½ teaspoon ground cinnamon
½ teaspoon ground nutmeg
Syrup (recipe follows)

Cut phyllo in half crosswise, and cut each half to fit a 13- x 9- x 2-inch pan. Cover with a slightly damp towel.

Lightly butter bottom of a 13- x 9- x 2-inch pan. Layer 10 sheets of phyllo in pan, brushing each sheet with melted butter. Set aside.

Combine walnuts, almonds, sugar, and spices, mixing well. Sprinkle one-third of nut mixture over phyllo in pan; drizzle with a little melted butter. Top nut mixture with 11 sheets of phyllo, brushing each sheet with butter; repeat twice with remaining nut mixture, phyllo, and butter, ending with buttered phyllo. Cut into diamond shapes. Bake at 350° for 50 minutes. Cool thoroughly. Drizzle warm syrup over pastries. Let stand at room temperature 24 hours. Yield: about 3 dozen.

Syrup

1 cup sugar
½ cup water
2 teaspoons lemon juice
2½ tablespoons honey

Combine sugar, water, and lemon juice. Bring to a boil; reduce heat and simmer, uncovered, 7 minutes. Stir in honey. Yield: 1 cup.

LITTLE PHYLLO CHEESECAKES

8 sheets commercial frozen phyllo pastry, thawed
½ cup butter or margarine, melted
3 (3-ounce) packages cream cheese, softened
½ cup sifted powdered sugar
1½ teaspoons grated orange rind
1 tablespoon orange juice
½ cup orange marmalade
2 teaspoons orange juice

Place one sheet of phyllo on a damp towel (keep remaining phyllo covered). Lightly brush phyllo with melted butter. Layer 3 more sheets phyllo on first sheet, brushing each sheet with butter. Repeat to make another stack of 4 sheets phyllo. Cut each stack of phyllo into 3-inch squares using kitchen shears.

Brush miniature muffin cups with melted butter. Place one square of layered phyllo into each muffin cup, pressing gently in center to form a pastry shell. Bake at 350° for 8 to 10 minutes or until golden. Gently remove from pan, and let cool on wire racks.

Combine cream cheese, powdered sugar, orange rind, and 1 tablespoon orange juice in a small mixing bowl; beat at high speed of an electric mixer until blended and smooth. Spoon 1½ teaspoons cream cheese mixture into each pastry shell.

Combine orange marmalade and 2 teaspoons orange juice; top each cheesecake with ½ teaspoon orange marmalade mixture. Yield: 40 pastries.

Note: Phyllo shells may be made up to 2 days in advance, and stored in an airtight container. Fill shells up to 4 hours before serving, and keep chilled until ready to serve.

PINEAPPLE PHYLLO BUNDLES

1 (8-ounce) can crushed pineapple, undrained
3 tablespoons sugar
1 tablespoon cornstarch
2 teaspoons butter or margarine
½ teaspoon grated lemon rind
1½ teaspoons lemon juice
16 sheets commercial frozen phyllo pastry, thawed
1 cup butter or margarine, melted

Drain pineapple, reserving 2 tablespoons juice.

Combine sugar and cornstarch in a small saucepan; stir well. Add reserved pineapple juice; cook over medium heat, stirring constantly, until mixture boils. Boil 1 minute, and remove from heat. Add crushed pineapple, butter, lemon rind, and lemon juice; stir until butter melts. Set aside.

Place 1 sheet of phyllo on a damp towel (keep remaining phyllo covered). Lightly brush phyllo with melted butter. Top with another sheet of phyllo, and brush with butter. Spoon about one-fourth of pineapple mixture in center of phyllo. Fold sides of phyllo over pineapple mixture, wrapping filling like a package. Wrap phyllo package in another sheet of buttered phyllo. Place package in center of another sheet of buttered phyllo. Draw edges of phyllo up and over package, twisting and squeezing together in center. Pull ends up and out to resemble a flower. Place on a lightly greased baking sheet; repeat with remaining phyllo and filling. Brush all bundles with melted butter. Bake at 375° for 15 minutes or until golden brown. Serve warm. Yield: 4 servings.

NUTTY PHYLLO NESTS

1¼ cups slivered almonds, lightly toasted
⅔ cup sugar
2 eggs
1 tablespoon butter or margarine, softened
12 sheets commercial frozen phyllo pastry, thawed
½ cup butter or margarine, melted
⅓ cup sugar
⅓ cup water
3 tablespoons honey
1 teaspoon lemon juice

Position knife blade in food processor bowl. Add almonds; top with cover, and process 50 seconds or until finely ground. Remove and set aside 3 tablespoons ground almonds. Add ⅔ cup sugar, eggs, and 1 tablespoon butter to almonds remaining in processor bowl; process until blended, and set aside.

Place 1 sheet of phyllo on a damp towel (keep remaining phyllo covered). Lightly brush phyllo with melted butter; fold in half lengthwise. Brush again with butter, and spread about 1½ tablespoons ground almond mixture down length of phyllo, leaving a 2-inch margin on 1 long side and a 1-inch margin on other 3 sides. Fold all margins of pastry over filling. Roll phyllo jellyroll fashion, starting with side with 2-inch margin. Wind strip loosely into a coil, and tuck end under coil. Place on a lightly greased baking sheet. Brush with melted butter. Repeat with remaining phyllo and almond mixture.

Bake at 375° for 16 minutes or until pastry is golden brown. Gently transfer to wire racks.

Combine ⅓ cup sugar, water, honey, and lemon juice; bring to a boil, and boil 4 minutes. Let cool slightly.

Drizzle half of honey mixture over warm pastries; sprinkle with reserved 3 tablespoons ground almonds, and drizzle remaining honey mixture over almonds. Serve pastries warm or cool. Yield: 1 dozen.

Puff Pastry

Puff pastry takes longer to make than other types of pastry, but the results are worth the time invested. Layer after layer of tender, flaky pastry carries these billowy desserts to new heights and hints at the buttery goodness inside.

Puff pastry may seem difficult to make, but it's not. The repetition of a simple rolling, folding, and chilling process alternates layers of dough with layers of butter and gives the dough its characteristic lightness. Two hours of chilling are essential between each rolling and folding stage—chilling keeps the butter firm and helps the layers rise evenly.

As you roll and fold the dough, sprinkle it lightly with flour to keep it from sticking, adding as little extra flour as possible. Excess flour toughens the pastry. After the rolling, folding, and chilling processes are completed, you can refrigerate the dough for a couple of days before shaping it. If storing it longer, wrap it in plastic wrap and freeze it in an airtight container up to two months. Thaw it in the refrigerator at least 8 hours before using it.

Keep the dough smooth and level when rolling it out for final shaping; this will insure an even rising during the baking process.

Baking sheets for puff pastry are generally not greased. When baking larger items, sprinkle the baking sheet with water to keep the dough from retracting.

Just before baking, brush the pastry with an egg yolk glaze to give it a pretty shine; then freeze the pastry, uncovered, for 10 minutes to firm up the butter in the dough. Bake it immediately after removal from the freezer.

BASIC PUFF PASTRY

¼ cup butter
1¾ cups all-purpose flour, chilled
½ cup cold water
¾ cup butter, softened
¼ cup all-purpose flour, chilled

Cut ¼ cup butter into 1¾ cups flour with pastry blender until mixture resembles coarse meal. Sprinkle cold water (1 tablespoon at a time) evenly over surface; stir with a fork until dry ingredients are moistened. Shape into a ball, and wrap in wax paper. Chill 15 minutes.

Combine ¾ cup butter and ¼ cup flour; stir until smooth. Shape mixture into a 6-inch square on wax paper. Chill 5 minutes.

Roll pastry into a 15-inch circle on a lightly floured surface; place chilled butter mixture in center of pastry. Fold left side of pastry over butter; fold right side of pastry over left. Fold upper and lower edges of pastry over butter, making a thick square.

Working quickly, place pastry, folded side down, on a lightly floured surface; roll pastry into a 20- x 8-inch rectangle. Fold rectangle into thirds, beginning with short side. Roll pastry into another 20- x 8-inch rectangle; again fold rectangle into thirds. Wrap pastry in wax paper, and chill about 2 hours.

Repeat rolling, folding, and chilling process 2 additional times. Chill 2 hours. Yield: one recipe Basic Puff Pastry.

PUFF PASTRY PATTY SHELLS

½ recipe Basic Puff Pastry
1 egg, beaten

Roll out Basic Puff Pastry to ⅜-inch thickness on a lightly floured surface. Cut pastry with a 3-inch cutter, cutting rounds as close together as possible to reduce scraps. Place rounds on an ungreased baking sheet. Using a 2-inch cutter, make an indentation about ¼-inch through center of pastry rounds, and lightly brush tops with beaten egg. Freeze 10 minutes.

Preheat oven to 450°; place pastry in oven. Reduce temperature to 400°, and bake 20 to 25 minutes or until puffed and golden brown. Remove to wire rack to cool. Remove centers of patty shells. Yield: 4 shells.

ALMOND COMBS

½ recipe Basic Puff Pastry
1 egg, beaten
½ cup ground almonds
2 tablespoons sugar
1 egg yolk
1 teaspoon water
¾ cup sifted powdered sugar
1 to 2 teaspoons milk

Roll pastry to a 12-inch square. Cut pastry into 4-inch squares.

Combine 1 egg, almonds, and 2 tablespoons sugar. Spoon about 1 tablespoon almond mixture in a strip down center of each square. Combine egg yolk and water; brush one side of each square with yolk mixture. Fold over opposite side, and press gently to seal. Make even 1-inch cuts along sealed edge, about ¼ inch apart; spread to form a comb. Place pastries on an ungreased baking sheet. Brush remaining egg yolk mixture over pastries. Freeze 10 minutes. Bake at 425° for 15 minutes or until puffed and golden brown. Transfer to a wire rack.

Combine powdered sugar and milk; drizzle mixture over hot pastries. Yield: 9 servings.

Note: One-half (17¼-ounce) package frozen puff pastry may be substituted for ½ recipe Basic Puff Pastry.

STRAWBERRY TART

½ recipe Basic Puff Pastry
1 egg yolk
1 teaspoon water
⅔ cup sugar
2½ tablespoons cornstarch
¾ cup lemon-lime carbonated beverage
Few drops of red food coloring
1 to 1½ pints whole strawberries
Fresh mint sprigs (optional)

Roll pastry into a 14½- x 7½-inch rectangle. Sprinkle a baking sheet with water, and shake off excess water. Place pastry on baking sheet.

Working quickly, cut a ¾-inch wide strip from each long side of pastry. Brush strips with water, and lay them, moist side down, on top of each long side of pastry rectangle, edges flush together. To complete pastry border, repeat procedure on short sides of rectangle, trimming away excess pastry at corners. Prick pastry generously with a fork, excluding the border.

Combine egg yolk and 1 teaspoon water; brush border of pastry with egg mixture. Freeze 10 minutes. Bake at 425° for 12 to 15 minutes or until puffed and golden brown. Gently remove pastry from baking sheet with spatulas, and let cool on a wire rack. Transfer to serving platter.

Combine sugar and cornstarch in a saucepan; gradually stir in carbonated beverage. Cook over low heat, stirring constantly, until smooth and thickened. Stir in red food coloring.

Wash strawberries, and remove stems. Arrange strawberries in pastry shell, stem end down. Spoon glaze over berries. Chill. To serve, garnish platter with mint leaves, if desired. Yield: 8 servings.

Note: One-half (17¼-ounce) package frozen puff pastry may be substituted for ½ recipe Basic Puff Pastry.

NAPOLEONS

1 recipe Basic Puff Pastry
Napoleon Cream
1 cup sifted powdered sugar
1 teaspoon vanilla extract
1 tablespoon hot water
½ cup semisweet chocolate morsels
1 teaspoon shortening

Divide puff pastry in half lengthwise. Roll each half into a 15- x 6-inch rectangle. Sprinkle two baking sheets with water; shake off excess water. Carefully transfer pastry to baking sheets.

Prick pastry well with a fork. Trim sides with a sharp knife, if necessary, to make edges even. Freeze 10 minutes. Bake at 425° for 15 minutes or until pastry is puffed and golden brown. Gently remove pastry from baking sheets with spatulas, and cool on wire racks.

Trim sides of pastry again, if necessary, to make edges even. Carefully split each layer in half horizontally, using a long serrated knife. Set aside the prettiest bottom layer for top of Napoleon.

Place one pastry strip on serving platter, browned side down; spread evenly with one-third Napoleon Cream. Repeat layering twice. Top with reserved bottom layer, browned side up.

Combine powdered sugar, vanilla, and water; spoon glaze over top pastry layer, spreading evenly.

Combine chocolate and shortening in top of a double boiler; bring water to a boil. Reduce heat to low; cook until chocolate melts. Let cool slightly; then spoon into a decorating bag fitted with metal tip No. 2. Pipe 5 lengthwise strips of chocolate evenly across top of glaze. Pull a wooden pick crosswise through chocolate at ¾-inch intervals, reversing the pulling direction each time. Refrigerate 30 minutes before serving. To serve, cut into 1½-inch crosswise slices using a serrated knife. Yield: 10 servings.

Napoleon Cream

¾ cup sugar
¼ cup cornstarch
⅛ teaspoon salt
1½ cups milk
4 egg yolks
1½ teaspoons vanilla extract
½ cup whipping cream, whipped

Combine first 3 ingredients in a heavy saucepan, stirring until cornstarch is blended. Stir in milk. Cook over low heat, stirring constantly, until mixture is thickened.

Beat egg yolks until thick and lemon colored. Gradually stir about one-fourth of hot mixture into yolks; add to remaining hot mixture, stirring constantly. Cook, stirring constantly, until mixture thickens. Remove from heat, and stir in vanilla. Cover filling with a sheet of wax paper, and chill thoroughly. Gently fold whipped cream into chilled filling. Yield: 2½ cups.

Note: One (17¼-ounce) package frozen puff pastry may be substituted for Basic Puff Pastry.

CREAM HORNS

½ recipe Basic Puff Pastry
1 egg yolk
1 teaspoon water
¾ cup whipping cream
3 tablespoons powdered sugar
1 teaspoon grated chocolate

Roll pastry into a 15- x 9-inch rectangle. Cut into 9 (15- x 1-inch) strips. Starting at tip of mold, wrap one strip around an ungreased 4-inch metal cream horn mold, winding strip spiral-fashion and overlapping edges about ¼ inch. Place on a lightly greased baking sheet, end of strip down. Repeat with remaining strips. Combine egg yolk and water; brush over entire pastry. Freeze 10 minutes.

Bake at 425° for 10 to 12 minutes or until puffed and golden brown. Remove from oven, and gently slide molds from pastry. Turn oven off. Return pastry to oven for 10 minutes. Remove from oven, and cool completely on a wire rack.

Combine whipping cream and powdered sugar; beat at high speed of an electric mixer until soft peaks form. Spoon whipped cream into a decorating bag fitted with metal tip No. 4B. Pipe whipped cream into pastry horns. Sprinkle grated chocolate over tops of cream horns. Chill until ready to serve. Yield: 9 servings.

Note: One-half (17¼-ounce) package frozen puff pastry may be substituted for ½ recipe Basic Puff Pastry.

APPLE FOLDOVERS

1 recipe Basic Puff Pastry
1 egg yolk
1 teaspoon water
6 cups peeled, sliced apples
¾ cup firmly packed brown sugar
¾ cup chopped pecans
3 tablespoons butter or margarine, melted
1½ tablespoons lemon juice
2 teaspoons cornstarch
Powdered sugar

Roll pastry into a 17- x 13-inch rectangle. Cut pastry into 4-inch squares; place squares on ungreased baking sheets.

Combine egg yolk and water; brush edges of pastry with yolk mixture.

Fold each square of pastry into a triangle; press edges of foldovers together with a fork. Bake at 425° for 13 to 15 minutes or until foldovers are puffed and golden brown. Let foldovers cool on a wire rack.

Combine apples, brown sugar, pecans, butter, lemon juice, and cornstarch in a medium saucepan, stirring until cornstarch dissolves; bring to a boil. Reduce heat to low; cook, uncovered, about 10 minutes or until apples are tender.

Slice foldovers in half horizontally, not cutting completely through long side of pastry.

Spoon hot filling into foldovers; sprinkle tops with powdered sugar. Yield: 1 dozen.

Note: One (17¼-ounce) package frozen puff pastry may be substituted for Basic Puff Pastry.

Cream Horns Step-By-Step

1. *Start with Basic Puff Pastry, cutting butter into flour with pastry blender. Sprinkle water, 1 tablespoon at a time, over flour mixture, and stir until dry ingredients are moistened. Shape dough into a ball; chill.*

2. *Roll pastry into a circle on lightly floured surface; place prepared square of butter in center of pastry, and fold pastry over butter.*

3. *Roll pastry into a 20- x 8-inch rectangle, and fold into thirds; roll into another rectangle, and again fold. Cover and chill 2 hours. Repeat rolling, folding, and chilling process 2 times.*

4. *Roll pastry into a 15- x 9-inch rectangle, and cut into 9 lengthwise strips.*

*Cream Horns are filled with
sweetened whipped cream;
sprinklings of grated chocolate
adorn the tops.*

5. *Wind strip of pastry
around cream horn mold,
starting at tip of mold, and
overlapping edges slightly.
Bake as directed.*

POULTRY

The dream of a good life guarantees a chicken in every pot, and that goal has often been realized in the South. Poultry of all kinds has long been a Southern favorite, whether it's fried chicken on the Sunday dinner table, Cornish hens for company, or baked quail at the end of the hunt. Today, poultry is an increasingly popular "best seller" at the meat counter because of its high protein and low fat content and its marvelous versatility as a menu item.

Health enthusiasts today frequently promote poultry as the ideal meat, nutritionally speaking. They have even introduced some lighter ways of cooking the favorite fowl, such as Chicken Piccata and Skillet Chicken With Vegetables.

Readily available in many convenient forms, poultry, especially chicken, has become a staple item in the kitchen. Whole, cut up, or in its chopped cooked form, poultry can easily be stocked in the freezer until needed, and then defrosted quickly in the microwave. Many of our recipes are quick to cook, too.

EQUIPMENT

If you plan to bone your own poultry breasts, you'll want to purchase a long thin boning knife; it will do the job much quicker and neater than other knives.

The only other specialty equipment you'll need is for roasting and stuffing poultry. For stuffing poultry, purchase skewers and cord for trussing the cavities. You'll need a large

Serve Chicken-in-a-Garden (page 395) as a meal in itself; it's packed with chicken, vegetables, and flavor.

roasting pan, and a bulb baster or basting brush to make basting the bird easier.

In addition, a meat thermometer is almost essential for roasting poultry. You'll want to be sure the meat

is done; overdone poultry will be tough and dry.

WHICH CHICKEN IS WHICH?

The type of poultry to buy depends on how you want to cook it. If your recipe calls for a cut-up chicken, you can cut up a broiler-fryer yourself, buy it precut from the supermarket, or you can take advantage of packaged chicken "parts," buying all legs or thighs if dark meat is your preference, or all breasts if white meat is your choice.

Aside from chicken pieces, you can buy whole domestic birds that range in weight from 1-pound Cornish hens to 30-pound turkeys. Choose the bird your recipe specifies or whatever best meets the needs of your family. Domestic birds usually available in your supermarket include the following.

● *Cornish hens* are the smallest members of the poultry family. They range in weight from 1 to 2 pounds and are found in the frozen meat section. One serving per bird is usually the standard, but larger Cornish hens can be split to make two servings.

- The most commonly purchased type of whole bird is probably the *broiler-fryer*, ranging in weight from 1½ to 4 pounds. These are good all-purpose birds that can be broiled, fried, roasted, braised, stewed, or barbecued.

- *Roasters* are a little larger than broiler-fryers, weighing in from 4 to 6 pounds. They are good for oven roasting or cooking on the rotisserie.

- *Hens* or stewing chickens range from 3 to 8 pounds. They are more mature than the birds previously mentioned and are usually tougher. They're recommended only for long, slow simmering to tenderize them.

- Ranging from 3 to 6 pounds, *ducklings* have a lower proportion of meat to bone than most poultry. Plan on at least 1 pound of duckling per serving. Ducklings are only available in the frozen meat section.

- *Geese* range from 6 to 15 pounds, and they, too, have a lower proportion of meat to bone. They are also only available frozen.

- *Turkeys* are the largest domestic birds, ranging from 4 to 30 pounds. Count on one serving per pound for a turkey up to 12 pounds, and about ¾ pound per serving for larger turkeys. They are available year-round in the frozen meat section, and fresh around the holidays.

STORING POULTRY

Fresh poultry is one of the most perishable of foods. As soon as you get it from the grocery store, wrap it in plastic wrap, and store it in the coldest part of your refrigerator up to two days. If you're unable to use it within that time, place poultry in a freezerproof bag; freeze up to three months. Freeze giblets and livers separately from the whole bird.

The safest way to thaw poultry is to let it sit in the refrigerator. Overnight is usually long enough for most birds. Large turkeys may take up to three days.

Many cooked poultry dishes can be frozen; casseroles especially freeze well. Avoid freezing poultry dishes that contain either mayonnaise or hard-cooked egg in them. Let smaller dishes cool completely before wrapping and freezing them; let larger items cool in the refrigerator, and then wrap airtightly and freeze. Remember to never freeze stuffed poultry.

A CHICKEN IN EVERY MICROWAVE

The natural tenderness of chicken makes it an excellent choice for microwave cooking. Many dishes can be ready to serve in a fraction of the time required with conventional preparation, and the chicken remains moist and tender.

We've included microwave directions for our recipes that are indeed quicker in the microwave, and for those that compare favorably to the end product cooked in a conventional oven. Follow these tips when cooking poultry in the microwave.

- To take advantage of the speed of a microwave oven, select a broiler-fryer rather than a stewing hen. Because stewing hens are larger and have a tougher skin, they must be microwaved at MEDIUM (50% power). This means that the cooking time will be almost as long as conventional preparation; in addition, the skin will not tenderize well during microwaving.

- Since microwave energy first

TIMETABLE FOR ROASTING POULTRY

Kind of Poultry	Ready-to-Cook Weight in Pounds	Oven Temperature	Internal Temperature	Approximate Total Roasting Time in Hours
Chicken (unstuffed)*	1½ to 2	400°F.	185°F.	1
	2 to 2½	375°F.	185°F.	1 to 1¼
	2½ to 3	375°F.	185°F.	1¼ to 1½
	3 to 4	375°F.	185°F.	1½ to 2
	4 to 5	375°F.	185°F.	2 to 2½
Capon (unstuffed)	4 to 7	325°F.	185°F.	2½ to 3
Cornish Hen (stuffed)	1 to 1½	375°F.	185°F.	1 to 1¼
Duckling (unstuffed)	3½ to 5½	325°F.	190°F.	2 to 3
Goose (unstuffed)	7 to 9	350°F.	190°F.	2½ to 3
	9 to 11	350°F.	190°F.	3 to 3½
	11 to 13	350°F.	190°F.	3½ to 4
Turkey (stuffed)†	4 to 8	325°F.	185°F.	3 to 3¾
	8 to 12	325°F.	185°F.	3¾ to 4½
	12 to 16	325°F.	185°F.	4½ to 5½
	16 to 20	325°F.	185°F.	5½ to 6½
	20 to 24	325°F.	185°F.	6½ to 7½

Stuffed chickens require about 5 additional minutes per pound.
†Unstuffed turkeys require about 5 minutes less per pound.

enters food at the edge of the dish, arrange chicken pieces so the meatier portions are around the outside of the dish.

● Rearranging the chicken pieces about halfway through microwaving will promote even cooking; turning them also promotes even cooking. However, crumb-coated chicken should not be turned because the coating will not be crisp.

● Plain chicken will neither brown nor become crisp when microwaved as it does when cooked conventionally. However, a browned appearance can be achieved by brushing the chicken with a mixture of melted butter and a brown sauce, such as soy sauce, teriyaki sauce, or browning and seasoning sauce.

● Check for doneness by cutting into chicken pieces next to the bone. Test several pieces in different areas of the baking dish. If some require additional cooking, remove those that are done and briefly microwave the remainder.

Broiler-Fryers

You'll find broiler-fryers more plentiful in supply than any other type of poultry in the meat case. You'll also see it in more forms than any other—whole, cut up, boneless, and in a host of individually packaged parts. Just pick the form your recipe calls for, or substitute an equivalent amount of the pieces your family prefers.

When you'd like a roasted turkey but don't want the leftovers, try a broiler-fryer. The taste and texture are about the same, but chicken cooks faster and provides a family-size yield.

WILD RICE-STUFFED CHICKEN

1 (6-ounce) package long grain and wild rice mix
3 tablespoons butter or margarine, melted
½ teaspoon dried whole thyme, crushed
⅛ teaspoon onion powder
1½ cups seedless green grapes, halved
1 (3- to 3½-pound) broiler-fryer
Salt
2 tablespoons soy sauce
2 tablespoons white wine
Green grapes (optional)

Cook rice mix according to package directions. Add butter, thyme, onion powder, and 1½ cups grapes; stir well.

Season cavity of chicken with salt; place chicken, breast side up, on a rack in a shallow roasting pan. Stuff lightly with half of rice mixture. Truss chicken, and bake at 375° for 1½ hours. Combine soy sauce and wine; use to baste chicken during last 30 minutes of baking.

Spoon remaining rice mixture into a lightly greased 1-quart casserole; bake at 375° for 15 to 20 minutes. Remove chicken to serving platter, and spoon rice around it. Garnish with grapes, if desired. Yield: 4 to 6 servings.

◻ *Microwave Directions:* Cook rice mix according to package directions. Add butter, thyme, onion powder, and 1½ cups grapes; stir well.

Season cavity of chicken with salt, and stuff lightly with half of rice mixture. Truss chicken, and place, breast side down, on a microwave roasting rack in a 12- x 8- x 2-inch baking dish. Microwave at HIGH for 3 minutes. Microwave at MEDIUM (50% power) for 20 minutes. Turn chicken, breast side up. Combine soy sauce and wine; baste chicken with soy mixture. Microwave at MEDIUM for 25 to 30 minutes or until drumsticks are easy to move.

Spoon remaining rice mixture into a lightly greased 1-quart casserole. Micro-wave at HIGH for 6 to 8 minutes or until thoroughly heated. Remove chicken to serving platter, and spoon rice around it. Garnish with grapes, if desired.

What About Oven Cooking Bags?

We receive many questions about cooking poultry as well as other foods in oven cooking bags. The bags offer a convenient way to cook poultry in your oven, and the mess is confined to the bag—not your oven walls. No basting is required when cooking with this method. When cooking a turkey or other poultry that is usually roasted, the skin will not be crisp, because you're actually braising the bird rather than roasting it. The meat should be moist and tender, however.

Directions for microwave or conventional cooking are on the package of oven cooking bags.

HERB-ROASTED CHICKEN

1 (3- to 3½-pound) broiler-fryer
3 cloves garlic, halved
2 bay leaves
⅓ cup mixed fresh basil, oregano, and thyme leaves
¼ cup butter or margarine, melted
2 teaspoons chopped fresh basil
2 teaspoons chopped fresh oregano
2 teaspoons chopped fresh thyme
½ teaspoon salt
¼ teaspoon pepper
¼ teaspoon paprika
Additional fresh herbs for garnish

Rub skin of chicken with cut side of 2 pieces of garlic. Place all garlic halves, bay leaves, and mixed herbs in cavity of chicken. Truss chicken.

Combine butter, chopped herbs, salt, pepper, and paprika. Place chicken, breast side up, in a shallow roasting pan; brush chicken generously with butter mixture. Bake, uncovered, at 375° for 1½ hours or until done, basting occasionally with remaining butter mixture during last half of baking. Remove chicken to serving platter; garnish with fresh herbs. Yield: 4 servings.

☐ *Microwave Directions:* Rub skin of chicken with cut side of 2 pieces of garlic. Place all garlic halves, bay leaves, and mixed herbs in cavity of chicken. Truss chicken using wooden picks.

Combine butter, chopped herbs, salt, pepper, and paprika. Place chicken, breast side down, on a microwave roasting rack; brush chicken generously with butter mixture. Microwave at HIGH for 3 minutes. Microwave at MEDIUM (50% power) for 20 minutes. Turn chicken, breast side up, and brush with butter mixture. Microwave at MEDIUM for 25 to 35 minutes or until drumsticks are easy to move, basting twice with butter mixture. Remove chicken to serving platter; garnish with fresh herbs.

Recipes calling for split or quartered broiler-fryers are sized for hearty appetites. Cut the pieces after cooking if you'd like to serve more.

BAKED CHICKEN

1 (2½- to 3-pound) broiler-fryer, split
1 lemon, halved
2 teaspoons salt
½ teaspoon paprika
¼ teaspoon pepper
½ cup butter or margarine, melted and divided

Place chicken, skin side up, in a shallow roasting pan. Rub chicken with lemon, squeezing out juice occasionally. Combine salt, paprika, and pepper; sprinkle over chicken; brush with ¼ cup butter. Bake, uncovered, at 450° for 10 minutes. Baste with remaining butter. Reduce heat to 350°; cover and bake an additional 35 minutes or until tender. Yield: 2 to 4 servings.

Cutting Up A Whole Chicken Step-By-Step

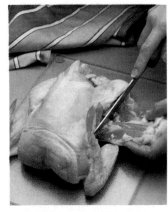

1. To cut up a whole chicken, grasp leg, and pull away from body. Cut through skin to expose joint. Bend thigh back until bones break at hip joint. Cut through hip joint.

2. Separate legs and thighs by cutting through skin at knee joint; break joint, and cut two pieces apart.

3. Remove wings by cutting through skin and joint on inside of wings.

4. Separate breast from back by cutting along each side of backbone between rib joints.

ZIPPY BARBECUED CHICKEN

2 cups apple cider vinegar
½ cup commercial barbecue
  sauce
¼ cup vegetable oil
1 tablespoon crushed red
  pepper
1½ teaspoons pepper
½ teaspoon salt
½ teaspoon ground red pepper
2 (2½- to 3-pound) broiler-fryers,
  quartered

Combine first 7 ingredients in a medium saucepan. Bring mixture to a boil; reduce heat, and simmer 2 to 3 minutes, stirring occasionally. Set sauce aside.

Place chicken, skin side up, on grill. Grill over medium coals 15 minutes.

Dip each chicken quarter in barbecue sauce, and return chicken to grill, skin side down. Grill an additional 35 to 40 minutes or until chicken is tender, basting with sauce every 10 minutes. Yield: 8 servings.

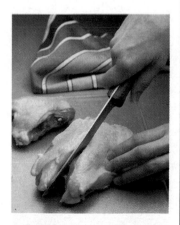

5. *Split breast into two lengthwise pieces by cutting along breastbone.*

CHICKEN MARENGO

1 cup sliced fresh mushrooms
2 tablespoons butter or margarine,
  melted
1 (2½- to 3-pound) broiler-fryer,
  cut up
2 to 3 tablespoons olive or
  vegetable oil
2 green onions, sliced
1 clove garlic, minced
½ cup dry white wine
2 tomatoes, peeled, cut in wedges,
  and seeded
¾ teaspoon salt
¼ teaspoon dried whole thyme
⅛ teaspoon pepper
1 tablespoon minced fresh
  parsley

Sauté mushrooms in butter 2 minutes; set aside.

Cook chicken in hot oil in a large skillet until browned. Remove chicken from skillet, and set aside, reserving pan drippings.

Sauté green onions and garlic in reserved drippings until onion is tender. Stir in wine, tomatoes, salt, thyme, and pepper, scraping bottom of skillet. Add chicken; cover, reduce heat, and simmer 30 minutes or until chicken is tender. Add mushrooms, and sprinkle with parsley. Yield: 4 servings.

HONEY CHICKEN

¼ cup butter or margarine,
  melted
½ cup honey
¼ cup prepared mustard
3 tablespoons lemon juice
1½ teaspoons paprika
1 (2½- to 3-pound) broiler-fryer,
  cut up and skinned
⅛ teaspoon salt
⅛ teaspoon pepper

Combine butter, honey, mustard, lemon juice, and paprika, stirring well. Lightly sprinkle chicken with salt and pepper, and place chicken, meaty side down, in a lightly greased 12- x 8- x 2-inch baking dish. Pour honey mixture over chicken; cover dish and refrigerate 3 to 4 hours.

Remove chicken pieces from refrigerator; bake, covered, at 325° for 30 minutes. Remove cover, and turn chicken pieces; bake an additional 30 minutes or until done, basting occasionally with pan drippings. Yield: 4 servings.

☐*Microwave Directions:* Combine butter, honey, mustard, lemon juice, and paprika; stir well. Lightly sprinkle chicken with salt and pepper; place chicken, meaty side down, in a lightly greased 12- x 8- x 2-inch baking dish. Pour honey mixture over chicken; cover and refrigerate 3 to 4 hours.

Remove chicken from refrigerator. Cover with heavy-duty plastic wrap; microwave at HIGH for 18 to 22 minutes or until chicken pieces are done, rotating dish a quarter-turn and basting with sauce every 5 minutes.

BUTTERMILK FRIED CHICKEN

¾ cup buttermilk
1 teaspoon salt
¼ teaspoon pepper
1 (2½- to 3-pound) broiler-fryer,
  cut up
1 cup all-purpose flour
1½ cups vegetable oil

Combine buttermilk, salt, and pepper; stir well. Skin chicken, if desired. Place chicken in a shallow container, and pour mixture over top. Cover and let stand 20 minutes, turning once. Remove chicken.

Dredge chicken in flour, coating well. Cook in hot oil (350°) until browned, turning to brown both sides. Reduce heat to 275°; cover and cook 25 minutes. Uncover and cook an additional 5 minutes. Drain on paper towels. Yield: 4 servings.

DIXIE FRIED CHICKEN

1 (2½- to 3-pound) broiler-fryer,
  cut up
½ teaspoon salt
⅛ teaspoon pepper
2 cups all-purpose flour
1 teaspoon red pepper
1 egg, slightly beaten
½ cup milk
Vegetable oil
Cream Gravy (page 444)
Watercress (optional)

Season chicken with salt and pepper.
Combine flour and red pepper; set aside.
Combine egg and milk; dip chicken in
egg mixture, and dredge in flour mixture, coating well.

Heat 1 inch of vegetable oil in a skillet
(350°); place chicken in skillet. Cover
and cook chicken over medium heat 20
to 25 minutes or until golden brown;
turn occasionally. Drain chicken on
paper towels. Serve with Cream Gravy,
and garnish with watercress, if desired.
Yield: 4 servings.

OVEN-FRIED CHICKEN

1 cup dry breadcrumbs
¼ cup grated Parmesan cheese
¾ teaspoon salt
¼ teaspoon garlic powder
¼ teaspoon pepper
1 (2½- to 3-pound) broiler-fryer,
  cut up and skinned
½ cup butter or margarine, melted

Combine first 5 ingredients. Dip
chicken in butter, and dredge in breadcrumb mixture. Place in a greased 12- x
8- x 2-inch baking dish. Bake at 350° for
1 hour or until tender. Yield: 4 servings.

☐ *Microwave Directions:* Combine
first 5 ingredients. Dip chicken in butter, and dredge in breadcrumb mixture.
Place in a greased 12- x 8- x 2-inch
baking dish with meatier portions to
outside of dish. Cover with paper
towels, and microwave at HIGH for 8 to
10 minutes. Rearrange chicken (do not
turn) so uncooked portions are to outside of dish. Cover and microwave at
HIGH for 9 to 12 minutes or until done.

SEASONED COUNTRY-FRIED CHICKEN

1 cup all-purpose flour
2 teaspoons pepper
1 teaspoon salt
1 teaspoon paprika
½ teaspoon poultry seasoning
¼ teaspoon garlic powder
1 egg, beaten
½ cup milk
1 (2½- to 3-pound) broiler-fryer,
  cut up
Vegetable oil

Combine first 6 ingredients in a plastic bag; shake to mix, and set aside.
Combine egg and milk; mix well.

Skin chicken, if desired. Place 2 or 3
pieces in bag; shake well. Dip in egg
mixture; return to bag and shake again.
Repeat with remaining chicken.

Heat 1 inch of oil in a large skillet to
350°; add chicken and fry 15 minutes or
until golden brown, turning to brown
both sides. Drain on paper towels. Yield:
4 servings.

Dixie Fried Chicken Step-By-Step

1. To make Dixie Fried
Chicken, season cut-up
chicken with salt and pepper;
dip in egg and milk mixture.

2. Dredge chicken in a
mixture of flour and red
pepper, coating well.

3. Fry chicken in hot oil,
covered, until golden brown,
turning occasionally. Drain
well.

4. Prepare Cream Gravy
using drippings of chicken. To
avoid lumping, stir gravy
vigorously as milk is added.

OVEN-BARBECUED CHICKEN

Southerners can barbecue chicken outdoors almost all year long, but if the weather keeps you indoors, consider this version barbecued in the oven.

½ cup all-purpose flour
1 teaspoon paprika
½ teaspoon salt
⅛ teaspoon pepper
1 (2½- to 3-pound) broiler-fryer, cut up
¼ cup butter or margarine, melted
½ cup catsup
½ medium onion, chopped
2 tablespoons water
1 tablespoon vinegar
1 tablespoon Worcestershire sauce
½ teaspoon salt
½ teaspoon chili powder
¼ teaspoon pepper

Combine first 4 ingredients; stir well. Dredge chicken in flour mixture. Pour butter into a 13- x 9- x 2-inch pan. Arrange chicken in pan, skin side down. Bake at 350° for 30 minutes.

Combine remaining ingredients, stirring well.

Remove chicken from oven, and turn; spoon sauce over chicken. Bake an additional 30 minutes. Yield: 4 servings.

Sunday dinner in the South often centers around Dixie Fried Chicken with Cream Gravy.

COUNTRY CAPTAIN

½ cup all-purpose flour
1 teaspoon salt
½ teaspoon pepper
1 (2½- to 3-pound) broiler-fryer, cut up
Vegetable oil
2 medium onions, chopped
2 medium-size green peppers, chopped
1 clove garlic, minced
2 (16-ounce) cans tomatoes, undrained and chopped
¼ cup currants
2 teaspoons curry powder
¾ teaspoon salt
½ teaspoon white pepper
½ teaspoon ground thyme
2 cups hot cooked rice
½ cup slivered almonds, toasted

Combine flour, 1 teaspoon salt, and ½ teaspoon pepper. Skin chicken, if desired. Dredge chicken in flour mixture. Fry chicken in ½ inch hot oil until browned; drain well and arrange chicken in a 13- x 9- x 2-inch baking dish. Reserve 2 tablespoons drippings in skillet.

Sauté onion, green pepper, and garlic in reserved pan drippings until tender. Add tomatoes, currants, curry powder, ¾ teaspoon salt, ½ teaspoon white pepper, and thyme; stir well, and spoon over chicken. Cover and bake at 350° for 55 minutes to 1 hour or until done.

Remove chicken to large serving platter, and spoon rice around chicken. Spoon sauce over rice, and sprinkle with almonds. Yield: 4 servings.

Marinate the Chicken

Enhance the flavor of plain baked or grilled chicken by refrigerating it several hours in a flavorful marinade. Our chapter on sauces offers a variety of well-seasoned choices. Drain the chicken, and bake or grill it as usual; baste it with marinade as it cooks.

DIJON CHICKEN BREASTS

Chicken breasts offer an easy way to serve chicken in equal-sized portions, and there are so many ways to prepare these tender pieces of meat. Dijon Chicken Breasts are a simple version cooked on the grill.

1 tablespoon Dijon mustard
4 chicken breast halves, skinned
¼ teaspoon freshly ground black pepper
⅓ cup butter or margarine
2 teaspoons lemon juice
½ teaspoon garlic salt
1 teaspoon dried whole tarragon

Spread mustard on both sides of chicken, and sprinkle with pepper. Cover and refrigerate 2 to 4 hours.

Melt butter; stir in lemon juice, garlic salt, and tarragon.

Place chicken on grill over medium coals; baste with butter sauce. Cover and grill 20 minutes. Remove cover, and grill 30 to 35 minutes or until done, turning and basting every 10 minutes. Yield: 4 servings.

☐*Microwave Directions:* Spread mustard on both sides of chicken, and sprinkle with pepper. Cover and refrigerate 2 to 4 hours.

Place butter in a 1-cup glass measure. Microwave at HIGH for 1 minute or until melted; stir in lemon juice, garlic salt and tarragon.

Arrange chicken on a microwave roasting rack. Brush with butter sauce, and microwave at HIGH for 10 minutes. Rearrange chicken (do not turn) so that uncooked portions are to outside of dish; brush with butter sauce. Microwave at HIGH for 10 to 15 minutes or until chicken is done, brushing with butter sauce every 5 minutes.

Chicken Breasts, Minus the Bone

When the bones are removed from chicken breasts, you have tender meat for an endless variety of dishes. You can buy boneless chicken breasts prepackaged in the meat section of most supermarkets to save a little time, or you can bone the breasts at home to save a little money.

To bone a chicken breast, pull the skin from the chicken, and discard skin. Split the breast in half lengthwise if it's not already split. Place chicken breast half on work surface, bone side down. Starting at the breastbone side of the chicken, slice meat away from the bone using a boning knife (or other thin sharp knife), cutting as close as possible to the bone.

CHICKEN PICCATA

6 chicken breast halves, skinned and boned
⅓ cup all-purpose flour
1 teaspoon salt
¼ teaspoon pepper
¼ cup butter or margarine
¼ cup lemon juice
1 lemon, thinly sliced
2 tablespoons chopped fresh parsley

Place each piece of chicken between 2 sheets of wax paper; flatten to ¼-inch thickness using a meat mallet or rolling pin. Combine flour, salt, and pepper; dredge chicken in flour mixture.

Melt butter in a large skillet over medium heat. Add chicken, and cook 3 to 4 minutes on each side or until golden brown. Remove chicken, and drain on paper towels; keep warm. Add lemon juice and lemon slices to pan drippings in skillet; cook until thoroughly heated. Pour lemon mixture over chicken; sprinkle with parsley. Yield: 6 servings.

*To flatten chicken breasts:
Place chicken between wax
paper, and pound with a meat
mallet to desired thickness. This
yields a thinner breast that rolls
or stuffs easily and cooks
quickly.*

ORANGE-AVOCADO CHICKEN

6 chicken breast halves, skinned
¼ cup butter or margarine, melted
1 teaspoon grated orange rind
1 cup orange juice, divided
½ cup chopped onion
¾ teaspoon salt
1 teaspoon paprika
½ teaspoon ground ginger
½ teaspoon dried whole tarragon, crushed
1 teaspoon cornstarch
2 oranges, peeled and sliced crosswise
1 avocado, peeled and sliced

Brown chicken in butter; add orange rind, ½ cup orange juice, onion, and seasonings. Reduce heat to low; cover and cook 50 minutes or until tender. Remove to serving dish; keep warm.

Combine remaining ½ cup juice and cornstarch, stirring until smooth; add to pan drippings. Cook over low heat, stirring constantly, until thickened.

Arrange orange and avocado slices around chicken; pour orange sauce over top before serving. Yield: 6 servings.

IMPERIAL CHICKEN BAKE

½ cup dry breadcrumbs
¼ cup plus 2 tablespoons grated Parmesan cheese
1½ tablespoons minced fresh parsley
½ teaspoon salt
⅛ teaspoon pepper
6 chicken breast halves, skinned and boned
¼ cup milk
¼ cup butter or margarine, melted
1 small clove garlic, crushed
Juice of 1 lemon
Paprika

Combine first 5 ingredients. Dip each breast in milk, and dredge in breadcrumb mixture. Arrange in a lightly greased 12- x 8- x 2-inch baking dish.

Combine butter, garlic, and lemon juice; drizzle over chicken. Sprinkle with paprika. Bake at 350° for 40 minutes or until tender. Yield: 6 servings.

CHICKEN IN WINE SAUCE

4 chicken breast halves, skinned and boned
Salt
Ground nutmeg
¼ cup butter or margarine, melted
1 sweet red pepper, cut into strips
¼ cup chopped green onions
½ pound fresh mushrooms, sliced
1⅓ cups dry white wine
1 tablespoon plus 1 teaspoon cornstarch
2 tablespoons dry white wine
Hot cooked rice

Sprinkle chicken with salt and nutmeg; brown each side in butter in a heavy skillet. Add red pepper, green onions, mushrooms, and 1⅓ cups wine. Bring to a boil; cover, reduce heat, and simmer 15 minutes. Remove chicken.

Combine cornstarch and 2 tablespoons wine; mix well, and stir into skillet. Cook, stirring constantly, until thickened.

Serve chicken and sauce over rice. Yield: 4 servings.

EASY BAKED CHICKEN BREASTS

8 chicken breast halves, skinned and boned
8 (4- x 4-inch) slices Swiss cheese
1 (10¾-ounce) can cream of chicken soup or cream of mushroom soup, undiluted
¼ cup dry white wine
1 cup herb-seasoned stuffing mix, crushed
2 to 3 tablespoons butter or margarine, melted
Parsley (optional)

Arrange chicken in a lightly greased 12- x 8- x 2-inch baking dish. Top with cheese slices.

Combine soup and wine; stir well. Spoon sauce over chicken; sprinkle with stuffing mix. Drizzle butter over crumbs; bake at 350° for 45 minutes. Garnish with parsley. Yield: 8 servings.

◯*Microwave Directions:* Arrange chicken in a lightly greased 12- x 8- x 2-inch baking dish. Top with cheese.

Combine soup and wine, stirring well. Spoon sauce evenly over chicken, and sprinkle with stuffing mix. Drizzle butter over crumbs. Cover with wax paper, and microwave at HIGH for 18 to 20 minutes; let stand 5 minutes. Continue microwaving briefly if not done after standing. Garnish with parsley.

CHINESE CHICKEN

2 cloves garlic, minced
2 tablespoons vegetable oil
6 chicken breast halves, skinned and boned
2 (4.5-ounce) jars sliced mushrooms, undrained
1 cup canned diluted beef broth
¼ cup soy sauce
2 tablespoons instant minced onion
⅛ teaspoon curry powder
Pinch of ground ginger
2 stalks celery, cut into ½-inch pieces
1 (8-ounce) can bamboo shoots, drained
1 medium-size green pepper, diced
½ cup fresh bean sprouts
Hot cooked rice

Sauté garlic in hot oil in a large skillet 1 minute. Add chicken, and cook until browned. Combine mushrooms and next 5 ingredients; pour over chicken. Cover, reduce heat, and simmer 35 minutes. Add remaining ingredients except rice; cook, uncovered, 5 to 7 minutes or until vegetables are crisp-tender. Serve over rice. Yield: 6 servings.

GRILLED CHICKEN WITH TARRAGON MAYONNAISE

4 chicken breast halves, skinned and boned
½ cup commercial Italian salad dressing
2 tablespoons tarragon vinegar
½ teaspoon dried whole tarragon
1 clove garlic, minced
½ cup mayonnaise
3 tablespoons chopped fresh parsley
1 tablespoon minced onion
1 tablespoon lime juice
½ teaspoon dried whole tarragon
Lime slices

Place chicken between 2 sheets of wax paper; flatten to ½-inch thickness using a meat mallet or rolling pin.

Combine salad dressing, vinegar, ½ teaspoon tarragon, and garlic in a jar; cover tightly, and shake vigorously. Pour over chicken in a shallow dish; cover and refrigerate 6 hours.

Remove chicken from marinade, reserving marinade. Place chicken on lightly greased rack of a broiler pan. Broil 6 inches from heat source 4 minutes on each side or until done, basting occasionally with marinade. Let chicken cool slightly; cover and chill thoroughly.

Combine mayonnaise, parsley, onion, lime juice, and ½ teaspoon tarragon, stirring well. Chill thoroughly.

Arrange chilled chicken on platter; garnish with lime slices, and serve with mayonnaise mixture. Yield: 4 servings.

BAKED CHICKEN AND ARTICHOKE HEARTS

6 chicken breast halves, skinned and boned
½ teaspoon salt
½ teaspoon paprika
¼ teaspoon pepper
¼ cup butter or margarine, melted
1 (14-ounce) can artichoke hearts, drained and halved
¼ pound fresh mushrooms, sliced
2 tablespoons all-purpose flour
⅔ cup canned diluted chicken broth
3 tablespoons dry sherry

Sprinkle chicken with salt, paprika, and pepper. Brown chicken in butter over low heat; transfer to a lightly greased shallow 2-quart casserole, reserving drippings in skillet. Arrange artichoke hearts between chicken breasts.

Sauté mushrooms in reserved drippings 4 to 5 minutes. Stir in flour, and cook 1 minute. Gradually add chicken broth and sherry; cook over medium heat, stirring constantly, until mixture is thickened and bubbly. Pour over chicken and artichokes. Cover and bake at 375° for 40 minutes. Yield: 6 servings.

CHICKEN CACCIATORE

8 chicken breast halves, skinned and boned
½ teaspoon salt
¼ teaspoon pepper
All-purpose flour
⅓ cup olive oil
1 large onion, chopped
3 to 4 cloves garlic, minced
½ pound fresh mushrooms, sliced in half
2 (16-ounce) cans whole tomatoes, undrained and quartered
1 (4-ounce) jar whole pimientos, sliced and undrained
½ cup vermouth
3 bay leaves
1 teaspoon dried whole thyme
1 teaspoon dried whole oregano
¼ teaspoon freshly ground pepper
2 medium-size green peppers, cut into strips
Hot cooked spaghetti

Sprinkle chicken with salt and pepper; dredge in flour, shaking off excess. Heat oil in a Dutch oven over medium-high heat; add chicken, and sauté 4 to 5 minutes on each side or until golden brown. Remove chicken from Dutch oven; drain on paper towels.

Add onion and garlic to Dutch oven; sauté over medium heat 5 minutes. Stir in mushrooms and next 7 ingredients; add chicken, and bring to a boil. Reduce heat and simmer, uncovered, 30 minutes, stirring occasionally. Stir in green pepper; cook an additional 30 minutes, stirring occasionally. Remove bay leaves; serve over spaghetti. Yield: 8 servings.

Add flavor to Skillet Chicken With Vegetables by drizzling tarragon-wine sauce over the chicken and vegetables.

SKILLET CHICKEN WITH VEGETABLES

2 large carrots, cut into julienne strips
2 stalks celery, cut into julienne strips
1 tablespoon butter or margarine
¼ teaspoon salt
⅛ teaspoon pepper
4 chicken breast halves, skinned and boned
¼ cup all-purpose flour
1 teaspoon salt
¼ teaspoon pepper
¼ cup butter or margarine
1½ teaspoons chopped fresh tarragon or ½ to ¾ teaspoon dried whole tarragon
½ cup dry white wine

Cook carrots and celery in a small amount of boiling water until crisp-tender; drain and return to saucepan. Stir in 1 tablespoon butter, ¼ teaspoon salt, and ⅛ teaspoon pepper; set aside.

Place each piece of chicken between 2 sheets of wax paper, and flatten to ¼-inch thickness using a meat mallet or rolling pin. Combine flour, 1 teaspoon salt, and ¼ teaspoon pepper; dredge chicken in flour mixture.

Melt ¼ cup butter in a large skillet over medium heat. Add chicken, and cook 3 to 4 minutes on each side or until golden brown.

Remove chicken, reserving drippings in skillet. Drain chicken on paper towels; keep warm.

Add tarragon and wine to pan drippings, stirring well. Arrange vegetables on individual serving plates; place chicken on top of vegetables. Spoon wine sauce over vegetables and chicken. Yield: 4 servings.

CHICKEN BREASTS LOMBARDY

8 chicken breast halves, skinned and boned
½ cup all-purpose flour
½ cup butter or margarine, melted and divided
1 cup sliced mushrooms
½ cup Marsala wine
⅓ cup chicken broth
½ cup shredded Fontina or mozzarella cheese
½ cup grated Parmesan cheese

Place chicken between 2 sheets of wax paper; flatten to ⅛-inch thickness using a meat mallet or rolling pin.

Dredge chicken lightly with flour. Place 4 pieces at a time in 2 tablespoons melted butter in a large skillet; cook over low heat 3 to 4 minutes on each side or until chicken is golden brown.

Place chicken in a lightly greased 13- x 9- x 2-inch baking dish, overlapping edges. Repeat procedure with remaining chicken, adding 2 tablespoons butter. Reserve drippings.

Sauté mushrooms in remaining ¼ cup butter. Sprinkle evenly over chicken.

Stir wine and chicken broth into pan drippings in skillet. Simmer 10 minutes, stirring occasionally. Spoon sauce evenly over chicken. Bake at 400° for 10 minutes.

Combine cheeses, and sprinkle over chicken. Bake an additional 5 minutes. Yield: 8 servings.

Note: Instead of Marsala wine, ½ cup white wine plus 2 tablespoons brandy may be used.

CHICKEN ROCKEFELLER

1 (10-ounce) package frozen chopped spinach, thawed and well drained
1 egg, beaten
⅓ cup commercial sour cream
½ teaspoon salt
½ teaspoon ground nutmeg
⅛ teaspoon red pepper
½ cup Italian-style breadcrumbs
2 tablespoons grated Parmesan cheese
6 chicken breast halves, skinned and boned
Pepper
3 tablespoons butter or margarine, melted

Combine first 6 ingredients, stirring well; set aside. Combine breadcrumbs and Parmesan cheese; set aside.

Place each chicken breast between 2 sheets of wax paper; flatten to ¼-inch thickness using a meat mallet or rolling pin. Sprinkle with pepper. Place spinach mixture evenly in center of each chicken breast. Fold long sides of chicken over spinach mixture; fold ends over and secure with a wooden pick. Roll chicken in breadcrumb mixture, and place in a lightly greased 12- x 8- x 2-inch baking dish. Sprinkle with remaining breadcrumb mixture, and drizzle with butter. Bake at 350° for 35 to 40 minutes. Yield: 6 servings.

◻*Microwave Directions:* Combine first 6 ingredients, stirring well; set aside. Combine breadcrumbs and Parmesan cheese; set aside.

Place each chicken breast between 2 sheets of wax paper; flatten to ¼-inch thickness using a meat mallet or rolling pin. Sprinkle with pepper. Place spinach mixture evenly in center of each chicken breast. Fold long sides of chicken over spinach mixture; fold ends over and secure with a wooden pick. Roll chicken in breadcrumb mixture, and place in a lightly greased 12- x 8- x 2-inch baking dish. Sprinkle with remaining breadcrumb mixture, and drizzle with butter. Cover with wax paper, and microwave at HIGH for 10 to 12 minutes or until done, rotating dish after 5 minutes, and rearranging chicken so uncooked portions are to outside of dish.

CHICKEN-EGGPLANT PARMIGIANA

4 chicken breast halves, skinned and boned
¾ cup fine dry breadcrumbs
¼ teaspoon salt
⅛ teaspoon pepper
1 egg, beaten
⅓ cup vegetable oil
1 small eggplant, peeled and cut into 4 (½-inch-thick) slices
1 (15½-ounce) jar commercial meatless spaghetti sauce
2 tablespoons grated Parmesan cheese
1 cup (4 ounces) shredded mozzarella cheese

Place each piece of chicken between 2 sheets of wax paper. Flatten each chicken piece to ¼-inch thickness using a meat mallet or rolling pin.

Combine breadcrumbs, salt, and pepper. Dip chicken in egg, and coat with breadcrumbs. Place chicken on a baking sheet; cover and chill 10 minutes.

Sauté chicken in vegetable oil over medium-low heat 5 minutes on each side or until golden brown. Remove chicken from skillet, and place in a 12- x 8- x 2-inch baking dish.

Sauté eggplant in oil remaining in skillet over medium heat until golden brown on both sides; drain eggplant on paper towels.

Place 1 slice eggplant on each chicken breast half. Spoon spaghetti sauce over eggplant; sprinkle with grated Parmesan cheese. Bake at 375° for 15 minutes. Top each eggplant slice with mozzarella cheese, and bake an additional 5 minutes or until cheese melts and sauce is bubbly. Yield: 4 servings.

CHICKEN KIEV

½ cup butter, softened
1 tablespoon chopped fresh parsley
½ teaspoon dried whole rosemary
¼ teaspoon salt
⅛ teaspoon pepper
6 chicken breast halves, skinned and boned
⅓ cup all-purpose flour
1 egg, well beaten
1½ to 2 cups soft breadcrumbs
Vegetable oil

Combine butter and seasonings; blend thoroughly. Shape butter mixture into a stick; cover and freeze about 45 minutes or until firm.

Place each piece of chicken between 2 sheets of wax paper. Flatten each chicken piece to ¼-inch thickness using a meat mallet or rolling pin.

Cut stick of butter mixture into 6 pats; place a pat in center of each chicken breast. Fold long sides of chicken over butter; fold ends over and secure with a wooden pick. Dredge each piece of chicken in flour, dip in egg, and coat with breadcrumbs.

Fry chicken in 1 inch hot oil (350°), cooking 5 minutes on each side or until browned. Yield: 6 servings.

CHICKEN ROMANOFF

1 (5-ounce) package egg noodles
1 (12-ounce) carton small-curd cottage cheese
1 (8-ounce) carton commercial sour cream
¾ cup chopped green onions
2 tablespoons butter or margarine, melted
⅛ teaspoon pepper
1 clove garlic, crushed
6 chicken breast halves, skinned and boned
3 (1-ounce) slices Monterey Jack cheese, halved
2 eggs, beaten
1 cup fine, dry breadcrumbs
⅓ cup butter or margarine
1 chicken-flavored bouillon cube
1 cup boiling water
½ cup chopped onion
½ cup chopped green pepper
2 tablespoons butter or margarine, melted
2 tablespoons all-purpose flour
¼ teaspoon salt
¼ teaspoon pepper
1 (4-ounce) can sliced mushrooms, drained
1 (2-ounce) jar diced pimiento, drained

Cook egg noodles according to package directions; drain. Rinse with cold water, and drain again. Combine next 6 ingredients; stir well. Add noodles, and toss lightly; set aside.

Place each piece of chicken between 2 sheets of wax paper; flatten to ¼ inch thickness using a meat mallet or rolling pin. Place a slice of cheese over each piece of chicken, and top with 1 to 2 tablespoons of noodle mixture. Fold long sides of chicken over noodles and cheese; fold ends over and secure with wooden picks. Spoon remaining noodle mixture into a lightly greased 12- x 8- x 2-inch baking dish; set aside.

Dip chicken in egg; coat with breadcrumbs. Melt ⅓ cup butter in a heavy skillet; brown chicken on all sides. Place chicken over noodles in baking dish.

Dissolve bouillon cube in boiling water. Sauté onion and green pepper in 2 tablespoons butter until tender. Add flour; stir until smooth. Cook 1 minute; stir constantly. Gradually add bouillon mixture; cook over medium heat, stirring constantly, until thickened. Stir in last 4 ingredients; pour over chicken. Bake, uncovered, at 400° for 20 to 30 minutes. Yield: 6 servings.

COMPANY CHICKEN CORDON BLEU

8 chicken breast halves, skinned and boned
¼ teaspoon salt
¼ teaspoon white pepper
2 eggs, beaten
1 cup milk
4 (1-ounce) slices cooked ham, cut in half
4 (1-ounce) slices Swiss cheese, cut in half
⅓ cup all-purpose flour
1⅓ cups fine dry breadcrumbs
Vegetable oil
Mushroom Sauce (optional)

Place each piece of chicken between 2 sheets of wax paper; flatten to ¼-inch thickness using a meat mallet or rolling pin. Sprinkle with salt and pepper.

Combine eggs and milk; brush chicken pieces with milk mixture. Place a ham slice and cheese slice in center of each chicken piece. Brush top of cheese slices with milk mixture. Fold short ends of chicken over ham and cheese; roll up, beginning with one unfolded side. Secure with wooden picks. Dredge chicken in flour; dip in remaining milk mixture, and coat well with breadcrumbs. Cover and chill 1 hour.

Heat ½ inch oil in a heavy skillet (350°); add chicken, and pan-fry over medium heat 20 minutes or until golden brown, turning frequently. Drain well. Serve with Mushroom Sauce, if desired. Yield: 8 servings.

Mushroom Sauce

1 (10¾-ounce) can mushroom soup, undiluted
1 (8-ounce) carton commercial sour cream
1 (4-ounce) can sliced mushrooms, drained
⅓ cup dry sherry

Combine all ingredients; cook over medium heat, stirring occasionally, until thoroughly heated. Yield: 2½ cups.

Whether you cook a whole chicken and remove the meat from the bone or use leftover chopped cooked chicken, there's no substitute for the tender chunks of meat in favorites like Old-Fashioned Chicken and Dumplings and Chicken Pot Pie.

When you have leftover chopped cooked chicken, remember that you can place the leftovers in freezer bags, and freeze them up to 1 month.

OLD-FASHIONED CHICKEN AND DUMPLINGS

1 (2½- to 3-pound) broiler-fryer
2 quarts water
1 teaspoon salt
½ teaspoon pepper
2 cups all-purpose flour
½ teaspoon baking soda
½ teaspoon salt
3 tablespoons shortening
¾ cup buttermilk

Place chicken in a Dutch oven; add water and 1 teaspoon salt. Bring to a boil; cover, reduce heat, and simmer 1 hour or until tender. Remove chicken, and let it cool slightly. Bone chicken, cutting meat into bite-size pieces; set aside. Bring broth to a boil; add pepper.

Combine flour, soda, and ½ teaspoon salt; cut in shortening until mixture resembles coarse meal. Add buttermilk, stirring with a fork until dry ingredients are moistened. Turn dough out onto a well-floured surface, and knead lightly 4 or 5 times.

For drop dumplings, pat dough to ¼-inch thickness. Pinch off dough in 1½-inch pieces, and drop into boiling broth. Reduce heat to medium-low, and cook 8 to 10 minutes or to desired consistency, stirring occasionally. Stir in chicken. Yield: 4 to 6 servings.

Note: For rolled dumplings, roll dough to ¼-inch thickness. Cut dough into 4- x ½-inch pieces. Drop dough, one piece at a time, into boiling broth, gently stirring after each addition.

CHICKEN POT PIE

1 (3- to 3½-pound) broiler-fryer, cut up
1 (20-ounce) package frozen mixed vegetables
3¾ cups all-purpose flour
1¼ teaspoons salt
1¼ cups shortening
8 to 10 tablespoons cold water
¼ cup butter or margarine
½ cup all-purpose flour
1½ teaspoons salt
¼ to ½ teaspoon pepper
⅛ teaspoon ground nutmeg
1 tablespoon butter or margarine, melted

Cook chicken in boiling water to cover for 45 minutes or until tender; drain, reserving broth. Bone chicken; cut meat into bite-size pieces. Set aside.

Bring broth to a boil; add frozen vegetables, and simmer 10 minutes. Drain vegetables, reserving 1 quart broth. Set both aside.

Combine 3¾ cups flour and 1¼ teaspoons salt; cut in shortening with pastry blender until mixture resembles coarse meal. With a fork, stir in enough cold water, 1 tablespoon at a time, to moisten dry ingredients. Shape dough into a ball; remove two-thirds of dough. Cover and chill remaining one-third of dough.

Roll two-thirds dough into a 16- x 12-inch rectangle. Fit into the bottom and on sides of a 13- x 9- x 2-inch baking dish. Trim edges even with baking dish; set aside.

Melt butter in a large heavy saucepan over low heat; add ½ cup flour, stirring until smooth. Cook 1 minute, stirring constantly. Gradually add chicken broth; cook over medium heat, stirring constantly, until thickened and bubbly. Stir in 1½ teaspoons salt, pepper, nutmeg, chicken, and vegetables; pour into pastry-lined dish.

Roll remaining pastry into a 14- x 10-inch rectangle on a lightly floured surface. Place on top of pie; fold edges under, and flute. Cut several slits in top to allow steam to escape. Cut designs from extra pastry and arrange on top crust, if desired. Brush with 1 tablespoon melted butter. Bake at 400° for 30 to 35 minutes. Yield: 6 servings.

CHEESY CHICKEN SPAGHETTI

1 (6-pound) hen
1 (10-ounce) package spaghetti
1½ cups chopped onion
1 cup chopped green pepper
1 cup chopped celery
1 (4-ounce) jar diced pimiento, drained
1 (6-ounce) jar sliced mushrooms, drained
1 (16-ounce) package American cheese, cubed
½ teaspoon salt
½ teaspoon pepper

Place hen in a Dutch oven; add water to cover. Bring to a boil; cover, reduce heat, and simmer 1½ hours or until tender. Remove hen, reserving 6 cups broth; let hen cool slightly. Bone hen, and cut meat into bite-size pieces; set meat aside.

Bring 1 quart reserved stock to a boil; gradually add spaghetti. Cook, uncovered, over medium heat 10 to 13 minutes. Do not drain.

Combine onion, green pepper, celery, and remaining 2 cups reserved broth in a medium saucepan. Bring to a boil; reduce heat and simmer 10 minutes or until tender. Drain.

Combine chicken, spaghetti, cooked vegetables, pimiento, and mushrooms, stirring well. Add cheese cubes, salt, and pepper, stirring until cheese melts. Yield: 8 servings.

CHICKEN KABOBS

½ cup vegetable oil
¼ cup soy sauce
¼ cup Chablis or other dry white wine
¼ cup light corn syrup
1 tablespoon sesame seeds
2 tablespoons lemon juice
¼ teaspoon garlic powder
¼ teaspoon ground ginger
4 chicken breast halves, skinned, boned, and cut into 1½-inch pieces
1 small green pepper, cut into 1-inch pieces
1 medium onion, quartered
8 large fresh mushroom caps
8 cherry tomatoes

Combine first 8 ingredients; stir well. Add chicken; cover and marinate at least 2 hours in refrigerator.

Remove chicken from marinade, reserving marinade. Alternate chicken and vegetables on skewers, placing tomatoes on ends of skewers. Grill about 6 inches from medium-hot coals for 15 to 20 minutes or until done, turning and basting often with marinade. Yield: 4 servings.

QUICK AND EASY CHICKEN DIVAN

2 (10-ounce) packages frozen broccoli spears, thawed and cut into 2-inch pieces
2 cups diced cooked chicken or turkey
8 slices process American cheese
1 (12-ounce) can evaporated milk or 1½ cups half-and-half
1 (10¾-ounce) can cream of mushroom soup, undiluted
⅓ cup grated Parmesan cheese
Paprika

Arrange broccoli in a lightly greased 12- x 8- x 2-inch baking dish; top with chicken. Place cheese over chicken.

Combine milk and soup, stirring well.

Pour mixture over cheese. Bake at 350° for 25 minutes. Sprinkle with Parmesan cheese and paprika. Bake an additional 5 minutes. Yield: 4 to 6 servings.

☐*Microwave Directions:* Arrange broccoli in a lightly greased 12- x 8- x 2-inch baking dish; top with chicken. Place cheese slices over chicken.

Combine milk and soup, stirring well. Pour mixture over cheese. Microwave at HIGH for 9 to 10 minutes, giving dish a half-turn after 5 minutes. Sprinkle with Parmesan cheese and paprika.

ORANGE CHICKEN STIR-FRY

3 tablespoons vegetable oil
6 chicken breast halves, skinned, boned, and cut into 1-inch pieces
2 tablespoons grated orange rind
1 teaspoon freshly grated gingerroot
¼ teaspoon hot sauce
4 green onions, cut into ¼-inch slices
1 cup orange juice
⅓ cup soy sauce
¼ cup sugar
1½ tablespoons cornstarch
2 oranges, peeled, seeded, and sectioned
Hot cooked rice

Pour oil around top of preheated wok, coating sides; allow to heat at medium-high (325°) for 2 minutes. Add chicken and stir-fry 2 minutes or until lightly browned. Remove from wok, and drain well on paper towels. Add orange rind, gingerroot, and hot sauce to wok; stir-fry 1½ minutes.

Return chicken to wok; stir-fry 3 minutes. Combine green onions, orange juice, soy sauce, sugar, and cornstarch; mix well. Add orange juice mixture and orange sections to chicken; stir-fry 3 minutes or until thickened. Serve over rice. Yield: 6 servings.

CHICKEN-IN-A-GARDEN

(pictured on page 380)

6 chicken breast halves, skinned, boned, and cut into 1-inch pieces
3 tablespoons peanut or vegetable oil, divided
2 tablespoons soy sauce, divided
3 tablespoons cornstarch, divided
½ teaspoon garlic powder
¼ teaspoon pepper
3 green peppers, cut into 1-inch pieces
1 cup diagonally sliced celery (1-inch pieces)
8 scallions, cut into ½-inch slices
1 (6-ounce) package frozen snow pea pods, thawed and drained
¾ cup water
¾ teaspoon chicken-flavored bouillon granules
⅛ teaspoon ground ginger
3 medium tomatoes, peeled and cut into eighths
Hot cooked rice

Combine chicken, 1 tablespoon oil, 1 tablespoon soy sauce, 1½ teaspoons cornstarch, garlic powder, and pepper; stir well, and let stand 20 minutes.

Pour remaining 2 tablespoons oil around top of preheated wok, coating sides; heat at medium high (325°) for 2 minutes. Add green pepper, and stir-fry 4 minutes. Add celery, scallions, and pea pods; stir-fry 2 minutes. Remove vegetables from wok, and set aside.

Combine remaining 1 tablespoon soy sauce and remaining 2½ tablespoons cornstarch; stir in water, bouillon granules, and ginger. Set mixture aside.

Add chicken to wok, and stir-fry 3 minutes; add stir-fried vegetables, tomatoes, and bouillon mixture. Stir-fry over low heat (225°) for 3 minutes or until thickened and bubbly. Serve over rice. Yield: 6 servings.

CURRIED CHICKEN

4 chicken breast halves, skinned,
　　boned, and cut into bite-size pieces
¼ cup all-purpose flour
¼ cup butter or margarine, melted
½ cup chopped onion
¼ cup chopped celery
¼ cup raisins
¾ cup chicken broth
1½ cups half-and-half
1 tablespoon curry powder
¼ teaspoon salt
⅛ teaspoon pepper
Hot cooked rice
Assorted condiments

Dredge chicken in flour; brown chicken in butter in a large skillet. Remove chicken, reserving drippings in skillet. Set chicken aside.

Sauté onion, celery, and raisins in reserved drippings until tender; add chicken broth. Cook, uncovered, over low heat 5 minutes. Stir in half-and-half, curry powder, salt, and pepper. Simmer, uncovered, 10 minutes. Add chicken, and simmer 10 minutes. Serve over rice with several of the following condiments: flaked coconut, toasted almonds, peanuts, chutney, chopped green pepper, chopped hard-cooked egg, crumbled bacon. Yield: 4 servings.

CHICKEN CROQUETTES

¼ cup butter or margarine
¼ cup all-purpose flour
1 cup milk
½ teaspoon salt
⅛ teaspoon pepper
2 cups minced cooked chicken
1 egg, beaten
1 tablespoon milk
⅓ cup all-purpose flour
1 cup soft breadcrumbs
Vegetable oil

Melt butter in a heavy saucepan over low heat; add ¼ cup flour, stirring until smooth. Cook 1 minute, stirring constantly. Gradually add 1 cup milk; cook over medium heat, stirring constantly, until thickened and bubbly. Stir in salt and pepper. Remove from heat; stir in chicken. Cover and chill about 1 hour.

Shape chicken mixture into 6 balls or logs. Combine egg and 1 tablespoon milk; mix well, and set aside. Dredge croquettes in ⅓ cup flour; then dip into egg and milk mixture, and coat each croquette with breadcrumbs.

Fry croquettes in deep hot oil (370°) for 3 to 5 minutes or until golden brown. Drain croquettes on paper towels. Yield: 6 servings.

CREAMED CHICKEN

½ pound fresh mushrooms,
　　sliced
⅓ cup chopped green pepper
1 medium onion, chopped
¼ cup butter or margarine,
　　melted
⅓ cup all-purpose flour
2 cups canned diluted chicken
　　broth
1 cup half-and-half
2 cups chopped cooked chicken
　　or turkey
½ teaspoon ground nutmeg
Dash of pepper
3 tablespoons dry sherry
1 (2-ounce) jar diced pimiento,
　　drained
½ cup sliced almonds, toasted
8 patty shells or hot cooked rice

Sauté mushrooms, green pepper, and onion in butter until tender. Add flour, stirring until smooth. Cook 1 minute, stirring constantly. Gradually add chicken broth and half-and-half; cook over medium heat, stirring constantly, until thickened and bubbly. Stir in chicken, seasonings, sherry, pimiento, and almonds; cook until thoroughly heated. Spoon mixture into patty shells or over rice. Yield: 8 servings.

SWEET-AND-SOUR CHICKEN

3 tablespoons soy sauce
1 egg
1 tablespoon dry sherry
¼ teaspoon pepper
¼ teaspoon garlic powder
¼ cup cornstarch
6 chicken breast halves, skinned,
　　boned, and cut into ½-inch cubes
Vegetable oil
1 (15¼-ounce) can pineapple
　　chunks, undrained
½ cup chopped onion
2 tablespoons vegetable oil
2 cups thinly sliced carrot sticks
1¼ cups water
3 chicken-flavored bouillon cubes
¼ cup firmly packed brown sugar
2 tablespoons cornstarch
¼ teaspoon ground ginger
¼ cup catsup
2 tablespoons vinegar
1 tablespoon soy sauce
1 large green pepper, cut into thin
　　strips
Scrambled rice (recipe follows)

Combine first 6 ingredients, stirring well. Add chicken, stirring to coat. Heat 1-inch vegetable oil in a heavy skillet; cook chicken until lightly browned. Drain.

Drain pineapple, reserving juice for rice. Set pineapple aside.

Sauté onion in 2 tablespoons oil until tender. Add carrots, water, and bouillon cubes. Bring to a boil; cover, reduce heat, and simmer 5 minutes.

Combine sugar, 2 tablespoons cornstarch, and ginger; stir in catsup, vinegar, and 1 tablespoon soy sauce, stirring well. Gradually stir cornstarch mixture into vegetable mixture. Cook over medium heat, stirring constantly, until thickened and bubbly. Stir in chicken, green pepper, and pineapple; cover and simmer 5 minutes. Serve over scrambled rice. Yield: 6 servings.

Scrambled Rice

Reserved pineapple juice
1 tablespoon butter or margarine
¾ teaspoon salt
1 cup uncooked long-grain rice
4 eggs, beaten
4 green onions, chopped

Add enough water to reserved juice to make 2¼ cups. Combine juice mixture, butter, and salt in a 10-inch skillet; bring to a boil. Stir in rice; cover and cook over medium heat 15 minutes or until rice is done. Push rice to one side of skillet; pour eggs into other side, and top with green onions. Cook eggs until partially set; stir eggs and rice together, and cook until done. Yield: 3 cups.

CHEESY CHICKEN TETRAZZINI

1 cup water
¼ teaspoon salt
⅛ teaspoon pepper
4 boneless chicken breast halves
6 cups water
½ teaspoon salt
1 tablespoon olive oil
1 (7-ounce) package spaghetti
1 medium-size green pepper, chopped
¼ cup butter or margarine, melted
2½ tablespoons all-purpose flour
1 cup milk
¼ cup dry white wine
1 (10¾-ounce) can cream of mushroom soup, undiluted
1 (4-ounce) can sliced mushrooms, drained
1 (2-ounce) jar diced pimiento
⅛ teaspoon garlic powder
½ cup grated Parmesan cheese
3 cups (12 ounces) shredded Cheddar cheese, divided
½ cup sliced almonds, toasted

Combine first 3 ingredients in a saucepan; bring to a boil. Cut chicken into ½-inch cubes using kitchen shears. Add chicken; cover, reduce heat, and simmer 10 minutes or until done. Drain chicken.

Combine 6 cups water and next 2 ingredients in a Dutch oven; bring to a boil. Add spaghetti, and cook 10 minutes or until almost tender. Drain well, and set aside.

Sauté green pepper in butter in a Dutch oven until tender. Add flour, and stir well. Stir in milk, next 6 ingredients, and 2 cups cheese. Cook over medium heat, stirring constantly, 10 minutes or until thoroughly heated. Stir in chicken.

Spread half of spaghetti in a greased 12- x 8- x 2-inch baking dish; spread half of chicken mixture evenly over spaghetti. Repeat layers. Bake at 350° for 15 minutes. Sprinkle with remaining 1 cup cheese and almonds; bake an additional 5 minutes. Yield: 6 to 8 servings.

◻*Microwave Directions:* Combine first 3 ingredients in a 1½-quart casserole. Cut chicken into ½-inch cubes using kitchen shears. Add chicken to casserole. Cover with heavy-duty plastic wrap; microwave at MEDIUM HIGH (70% power) for 6 to 9 minutes or until done. Drain chicken.

Combine 6 cups water and next 2 ingredients in a 12- x 8- x 2-inch baking dish. Cover with heavy-duty plastic wrap, and microwave at HIGH for 10 minutes. Add spaghetti; cover and microwave at HIGH for 6 minutes, stirring after 4 minutes. Let stand 3 minutes; drain well, and set aside.

Combine green pepper and butter in a 2-quart baking dish. Cover with heavy-duty plastic wrap, and microwave at HIGH for 4 minutes or until crisp-tender. Add flour, and stir well. Stir in milk, next 6 ingredients, and 2 cups cheese. Cover with heavy-duty plastic wrap and microwave at MEDIUM HIGH for 6 to 8 minutes or until thoroughly heated, stirring twice. Stir in chicken.

Spread half of spaghetti in a greased 12- x 8- x 2-inch baking dish; spread half of chicken mixture evenly over spaghetti. Repeat layers. Sprinkle remaining cheese over casserole; top with almonds. Cover with heavy-duty plastic wrap, and microwave at MEDIUM HIGH for 5 minutes or until thoroughly heated, giving dish a half-turn after 3 minutes.

CHICKEN CRÊPES

3 cups finely chopped cooked chicken
1½ cups freshly grated Parmesan cheese, divided
¼ pound finely chopped fresh mushrooms
1 tablespoon butter or margarine, melted
½ teaspoon salt
¼ teaspoon pepper
¼ teaspoon ground nutmeg
⅓ cup butter or margarine
⅓ cup all-purpose flour
3 cups milk
1 cup whipping cream
1 recipe Basic Crêpes (page 86)

Combine chicken and 1 cup cheese; set aside.

Sauté mushrooms in 1 tablespoon butter until tender. Stir in salt, pepper, and nutmeg.

Melt ⅓ cup butter in a heavy saucepan over low heat; add flour and cook 1 minute, stirring constantly. Gradually add milk; cook over medium heat, stirring constantly, until thickened and bubbly. Stir in whipping cream.

Combine chicken mixture, mushroom mixture, and ⅔ cup sauce, stirring well. Spoon ⅓ cup mixture into center of each crêpe, and roll up tightly; place crêpes, seam side down, in a lightly greased 13- x 9- x 2-inch baking dish. Pour remaining sauce over crêpes, and bake at 350° for 25 minutes. Sprinkle with remaining ½ cup Parmesan cheese, and bake an additional 5 minutes. Yield: 8 servings.

CHICKEN ENCHILADAS

¼ cup butter or margarine
¼ cup all-purpose flour
1 (10¾-ounce) can chicken broth, undiluted
¾ cup water
1 (8-ounce) carton commercial sour cream
2 canned jalapeño peppers, seeded and chopped
12 corn tortillas
Vegetable oil
¾ cup chopped cooked chicken
2 cups (8 ounces) shredded Monterey Jack cheese, divided
¾ cup chopped onion
Chopped fresh parsley
Enchilada Relish

Melt butter in a heavy saucepan over low heat; add flour, stirring until smooth. Cook 1 minute, stirring constantly. Gradually add chicken broth and water; cook over medium heat, stirring constantly, until thickened and bubbly. Stir in sour cream and chopped peppers. Pour half of sour cream sauce into a lightly greased 12- x 8- x 2-inch baking dish; set aside dish and remaining sour cream sauce.

Fry tortillas, one at a time, in 2 tablespoons oil in a medium skillet 5 seconds on each side or just until tortillas are softened; add additional oil, if necessary. Drain on paper towels.

Place 1 tablespoon each of chicken, cheese, and onion on each tortilla; roll up tortillas, and place, seam side down, in reserved baking dish. Pour remaining sour cream sauce over top. Bake, uncovered, at 425° for 20 minutes. Sprinkle remaining 1¼ cups cheese on top; bake an additional 5 minutes or until cheese melts. Garnish tortillas with parsley, and serve with Enchilada Relish. Yield: 6 servings.

Enchilada Relish

1 large tomato, finely chopped
½ cup finely chopped onion
1 to 2 canned jalapeño peppers, seeded and chopped
¼ cup tomato juice
½ teaspoon salt

Combine all ingredients; stir well. Chill. Yield: 1 cup.

CHICKEN LIVERS EN BROCHETTE

1½ pounds chicken livers
⅓ cup vegetable oil
3 tablespoons wine vinegar
1 teaspoon salt
¾ to 1 teaspoon dried whole tarragon
⅛ teaspoon pepper
6 pearl onions
1 green pepper, cut into 1-inch cubes
12 cherry tomatoes

Place livers in a shallow container. Combine next 5 ingredients in a jar; cover and shake. Pour marinade over livers; cover and chill 2 hours.

Cook onions in small amount of boiling water 8 to 10 minutes or until just tender; drain.

Drain livers, reserving marinade. Arrange livers and vegetables on skewers; brush with marinade. Broil 6 to 8 inches from heat 10 to 12 minutes, turning and brushing occasionally with marinade. Yield: 6 servings.

FRIED CHICKEN LIVERS

½ cup all-purpose flour
½ teaspoon salt
¼ teaspoon pepper
1 pound chicken livers, cut in half
Vegetable oil
Sweet-and-Sour Plum Sauce

Combine first 3 ingredients; stir well.

Dredge livers in flour mixture.

Fry livers in deep hot oil (350°) for 3 minutes or until golden brown. Drain livers well on paper towels. Serve immediately with Sweet-and-Sour Plum Sauce. Yield: 4 servings.

Sweet-and-Sour Plum Sauce

¾ cup red plum jam
2 teaspoons vinegar
⅛ teaspoon hot sauce

Combine all ingredients in a saucepan; cook until thoroughly heated. Serve hot or cold. Store in refrigerator. Yield: about ¾ cup.

CHICKEN LIVERS AND RICE

1 pound chicken livers
1 pound fresh mushrooms, sliced
3 tablespoons butter or margarine, melted
1 cup uncooked long-grain rice
3 tablespoons butter or margarine, melted
1 (10½-ounce) can beef broth, undiluted
1 (10¾-ounce) can cream of mushroom soup, undiluted
¼ cup dry sherry

Sauté chicken livers and mushrooms in 3 tablespoons butter in a large skillet 5 to 8 minutes or until livers are browned. Remove livers and mushrooms from skillet; set aside. Reserve pan drippings in a small bowl.

Sauté rice in 3 tablespoons butter until golden. Add beef broth, mushroom soup, sherry, and reserved drippings to rice; stir well. Cover and simmer 20 minutes or until liquid is absorbed. Stir livers and mushrooms into rice; cook until thoroughly heated. Yield: 4 to 6 servings.

Turkey and Other Domestic Birds

Although some people serve pork and beef for their holiday meals, many demand the traditional roast turkey on their table. A highly seasoned dressing, usually consisting of cornbread in the South, is served alongside or sometimes spooned into the turkey and baked as stuffing. Served on the side, Giblet Gravy (page 445) tops off both the turkey and dressing.

Young turkeys weigh as little as 4 pounds, while tom turkeys can tip the scales at 20 to 30 pounds—perfect for holiday feasts. Generally, the larger the bird, the more economical it is, since larger birds have a higher ratio of meat per pound.

The goose and duckling also make choice offerings for holiday meals. Since both contain more fat than other domestic birds, prick their skin all over with a fork before roasting to let extra fat escape during cooking. Do not brush with additional fat before or during roasting as you do other birds.

THAW THE BIRD CAREFULLY

You'll probably buy your turkey frozen, and it's very important that the turkey be properly thawed before cooking. The best way is to let it thaw in the refrigerator. Leave the turkey in its original wrapper, place on a tray (to catch drippings), and refrigerate until the bird thaws. Depending on its size, allow two to four days for thawing. A 4- to 12-pound turkey will take one to two days, a 12- to 20-pound will take two to three days, and a 20- to 24-pound will take as long as three to four days. Thawing in the refrigerator instead of at room temperature is the safest method to use because it re-

duces the risk of bacterial growth.

If the bird must be thawed at room temperature due to lack of time, try this method: Leave the bird in its wrapper, and place in a heavy grocery sack, closing the opening. Put the bird on a tray, and let it thaw in a cool room away from heat. Check the turkey frequently. Once thawed, the turkey should be cooked immediately. Remember to allow enough thawing time, since it will take quite a while for the bird to thaw.

STUFFING THE TURKEY

Be sure to remove the giblets from the turkey before stuffing it. Use them for making gravy. Rinse the turkey thoroughly before stuffing, and pat dry. Do not salt the cavity if the bird is to be stuffed. Stuff the turkey immediately before roasting. Never stuff it the night before.

COOKING THE TURKEY

To roast a turkey, first place it breast side up on a rack in a shallow roasting pan. Brush with vegetable oil. Cook it in a 325° oven, uncovered, without adding any water to the pan. Baste the bird occasionally during cooking with pan drippings or melted butter, if desired.

The most accurate way to determine doneness of the turkey is to use a meat thermometer. The thermometer should be inserted in the thickest part of the thigh muscle, making sure the bulb doesn't touch bone. When the thermometer registers 185°, the turkey is done. Check for doneness by moving the drumstick up and down—the joint should give easily. Also, press the drumstick with your fingers. The meat will be soft if the turkey is done.

CARVING THE TURKEY

Let the turkey stand at room temperature at least 15 minutes before carving. Make sure you have the proper carving utensils; you'll need a knife with a very sharp edge, and a large two-tined carving fork. Carving may be done on a cutting board in the kitchen, or on the serving platter at the table.

Carve the bird with the breast side up. Insert the carving fork to steady the turkey as you work. Cut the skin between the thigh and breast; bend the leg away from the bird to expose the leg joint. Slice through the joint, and remove the leg.

Cut through the joint that separates the thigh and drumstick. Slice the dark meat from the bones of the leg and thigh rather than placing them whole on the serving platter.

The wing tips were twisted underneath the turkey before roasting, so you should be able to carve the turkey without removing them. You can slice them away at the shoulder joint, if necessary, to make carving easier.

To carve the breast, hold the bird securely with carving fork. Beginning at the meaty area above the shoulder joint, cut thin slices diagonally through the meat (across the grain) the entire length of the breast. Carve from one side of the turkey at a time, carving only as much meat as is needed to serve at a time.

STORING THE LEFTOVERS

Always chill leftover meat, dressing, and gravy separately, even if the dressing was baked in the turkey. Cooked turkey may be chilled up to two days. For longer storage, freeze meal-size portions.

OLD-FASHIONED CORNBREAD DRESSING

2 cups cornmeal
2 teaspoons baking powder
1 teaspoon baking soda
½ teaspoon salt
2 eggs, beaten
2 cups buttermilk
2 tablespoons bacon drippings, melted
3 stalks celery, chopped
1 medium onion, chopped
⅓ cup butter or margarine, melted
12 slices day old bread, crumbled
2 to 2½ cups turkey or chicken broth
1 cup milk
2 eggs, beaten
¼ teaspoon salt
1 teaspoon poultry seasoning
½ teaspoon rubbed sage
¼ teaspoon pepper

Combine cornmeal, baking powder, baking soda, and salt in a large bowl; add 2 eggs, buttermilk, and melted bacon drippings, stirring well.

Place a well-greased 10-inch cast-iron skillet in a 450° oven for 4 minutes or until hot. Remove skillet from oven; spoon batter into skillet. Bake at 450° for 35 minutes or until cornbread is lightly browned. Cool; crumble cornbread into a large bowl.

Sauté celery and onion in butter until tender. Add sautéed vegetables and remaining ingredients to crumbled cornbread, stirring well. Spoon dressing into a lightly greased 13- x 9- x 2-inch pan. Bake at 350° for 25 to 30 minutes. Yield: 8 servings.

Note: One (10¾-ounce) can chicken broth and 1 cup water may be substituted for homemade chicken broth.

Dressing may be spooned into turkey cavities. Spoon any remaining dressing into a lightly greased 2-quart casserole; bake at 350° for 25 to 30 minutes.

PEANUT DRESSING

1½ cups finely chopped celery
¾ cup finely chopped onion
½ cup chopped fresh parsley
¾ cup butter or margarine, melted
12 cups soft breadcrumbs
2 cups salted peanuts, chopped
1 egg, beaten
1 tablespoon rubbed sage
1 teaspoon salt
1 teaspoon pepper
4½ cups water

Sauté first 3 ingredients in butter in a large Dutch oven until tender. Add remaining ingredients; stir well. Spoon dressing into a lightly greased 13- x 9- x 2-inch pan; bake at 350° for 45 minutes to 1 hour or until lightly browned around edges. Yield: 10 to 12 servings.

Note: Dressing may be spooned into turkey cavities. Spoon any remaining dressing into a lightly greased 2-quart casserole; bake at 350° for 45 minutes.

Stuffing a Turkey Step-By-Step

1. Before stuffing a turkey, rinse thoroughly inside and out; pat dry. Spoon dressing into both cavities.

2. If excess skin around tail has been cut away, tuck legs under flap of skin to hold them in place. You can't truss turkeys with excess skin cut away.

3. If excess skin is intact, close cavity with skewers, and truss with heavy cord. Tie ends of legs to tail with cord.

4. Lift wing tips up and over back, and tuck under bird.

SAUSAGE-CORNBREAD DRESSING

10 (2-inch) cornbread muffins, crumbled (about 5⅓ cups)
6 slices sandwich bread, crumbled
2 (10¾-ounce) cans chicken or turkey broth, undiluted
2 cups water
2 medium onions, chopped
4 stalks celery, chopped
3 tablespoons butter or margarine, melted
½ pound mild bulk pork sausage
2 eggs, beaten
¼ teaspoon pepper

Soak cornbread and sandwich bread in chicken broth and water in a large bowl about 10 minutes; stir until liquid is absorbed.

Sauté onion and celery in butter until tender. Add sausage, and cook over low heat until sausage is browned; drain. Add sausage mixture, eggs, and pepper to bread mixture; stir well.

Spoon dressing into a lightly greased 13- x 9- x 2-inch baking dish. Bake at 350° for 1 hour or until lightly browned. Yield: 8 servings.

Note: Five cups homemade unsalted chicken broth may be substituted for canned broth and water; additional salt may need to be added.

5. *Place turkey on a roasting rack, breast side up, and brush with vegetable oil. Insert meat thermometer in meaty part of thigh, making sure it does not touch bone. Roast as directed.*

CAJUN DRESSING

1 pound hot bulk pork sausage
1 small onion, chopped
1 small green pepper, chopped
1½ stalks celery, chopped
1 (1.15-ounce) envelope instant chicken noodle soup mix
1 cup uncooked long-grain rice
3 cups water

Brown sausage in a Dutch oven, stirring to crumble; drain. Add remaining ingredients, and stir well. Place mixture in a lightly greased 12- x 8- x 2-inch baking dish. Cover and bake at 350° for 1 hour or until moisture is absorbed. Yield: 8 servings.

BREAD DRESSING

1 (1-pound) loaf day old bread, cubed
1½ teaspoons poultry seasoning
½ teaspoon pepper
1 cup canned diluted chicken broth
2 eggs, slightly beaten
¾ cup chopped onion
¾ cup chopped celery
½ cup butter or margarine, melted

Combine first 5 ingredients in a large bowl; set aside.

Sauté onion and celery in butter until tender. Add to bread mixture, stirring well. Spoon into a lightly greased 2-quart casserole. Cover and bake at 325° for 20 minutes. Yield: 6 servings.

Note: Dressing is too moist to bake in a turkey.

MOIST CORNBREAD DRESSING

6 cups cornbread crumbs
5 cups toasted soft breadcrumbs
6 chicken-flavored bouillon cubes
4 cups boiling water
1 cup finely chopped celery
1 cup finely chopped onion
1 cup finely chopped green pepper
¼ cup butter or margarine, melted
½ pound bulk pork sausage
1 teaspoon poultry seasoning
½ teaspoon salt
¼ teaspoon pepper
4 eggs, beaten
1 cup finely chopped pecans

Combine cornbread crumbs and breadcrumbs in a large bowl. Dissolve bouillon cubes in boiling water; pour over crumb mixture, and stir well.

Sauté celery, onion, and green pepper in butter until tender; add to crumb mixture, stirring well.

Brown sausage in a heavy skillet; drain. Stir sausage and remaining ingredients into cornbread mixture. Spoon into a lightly greased 13- x 9- x 2-inch baking dish; bake at 350° for 45 minutes. Yield: 8 servings.

Note: Dressing is too moist to bake in a turkey.

Dressing Like Mom Made

Southerners are hard to please when it comes to turkey dressing. It seems that everyone wants it like their mother used to make, but no one's mother made it the same. The main variation lies in the moistness of the dressing. If you prefer yours more moist than most, add a little more broth or other liquid—add a little less if you prefer it on the dry side. The holiday meal just isn't right if the dressing's not right!

The traditional Roast Turkey is a regular holiday guest in many Southern homes. Giblet Gravy is in the background.

ROAST TURKEY

1 (12- to 14-pound) turkey
Salt (optional)
Vegetable oil or melted butter or
    margarine
Curly endive (optional)
Cherry tomatoes (optional)
Mushrooms (optional)

Remove giblets and neck from turkey; reserve for other uses, if desired. Rinse turkey thoroughly with cold water; pat dry. Sprinkle cavity with salt if you are not going to stuff turkey. If stuffing is desired, lightly stuff dressing into body cavities of turkey. If excess skin around tail has been cut away, tuck legs under flap of skin around tail. If excess skin is intact, close cavity with skewers, and truss. Tie ends of legs to tail with cord. Lift wingtips up and over back, and tuck under bird.

Place turkey on a roasting rack, breast side up; brush entire bird with vegetable oil. Insert meat themometer in meaty part of thigh, making sure it does not touch bone. Bake at 325° until meat themometer reaches 185° (refer to Poultry Roasting Chart on page 382). If turkey starts to brown too much, cover loosely with aluminum foil.

When turkey is two-thirds done, cut the cord or band of skin holding the drumstick ends to the tail; this will ensure that the thighs are cooked internally. Turkey is done when drumsticks are easy to move up and down. Let stand 15 minutes before carving. Garnish with endive, tomatoes, and mushrooms, if desired. Yield: 20 to 24 servings.

SMOKED TURKEY

1 (10- to 15-pound) turkey
1 tablespoon salt
1 tablespoon sugar
1 tablespoon ground cinnamon
1 apple, cored, peeled, and
   quartered
2 medium onions, quartered
4 stalks celery with leaves, cut into
   thirds

Remove giblets and neck from turkey; reserve for other uses. Rinse turkey; pat dry. Sprinkle cavity with salt.

Combine sugar and cinnamon; dredge apple in cinnamon mixture. Stuff apple quarters, onion quarters, and celery stalks into cavity of turkey; close cavity with skewers. Tie ends of legs to tail with cord; lift wing tips up and over back so they are tucked under bird.

Prepare charcoal fire in smoker, and let burn 10 to 15 minutes. Soak hickory chips in water at least 15 minutes. Place water pan in smoker, and fill with water. Place hickory chips on coals.

Place turkey on food rack. Cover with smoker lid; cook 8 to 12 hours or until meat thermometer reaches 185° when inserted in meaty part of thigh, making sure it does not touch bone. Smoking may take 9 to 12 hours. Refill water pan, and add charcoal as needed.

Remove turkey from food rack; cover and chill. Thinly slice turkey to serve. Yield: 14 to 18 servings.

Smoking Poultry

Hickory wood with its strong dense-flavored smoke is the old standby used for smoking. And you can increase the hickory flavor by adding a handful of cracked hickory nuts on the coals. In addition to hickory, other woods used for smoking are mesquite, oak, maple, and wood from fruit or nut trees. Apple wood is a particular favorite for smoking chicken or turkey.

CIDER BAKED TURKEY BREAST

1 (5- to 5½-pound) turkey breast
1½ cups apple cider
¼ cup soy sauce
2 tablespoons cornstarch
½ cup apple cider

Place turkey breast, skin side up, in a large roasting pan; bake at 450° for 30 minutes or until skin is crisp.

Combine 1½ cups cider and soy sauce; pour over turkey. Insert meat thermometer in meaty portion of breast, making sure it does not touch bone. Cover and bake at 325° until meat thermometer registers 170° (about 1½ hours); baste turkey frequently with cider mixture.

Combine cornstarch and ½ cup cider, stirring well; stir into pan drippings. Return to oven and bake, uncovered, until sauce is thickened. Transfer turkey to serving platter; serve with sauce. Yield: 12 to 16 servings.

☐*Microwave Directions:* Place turkey, skin side down, in a 12- x 8- x 2-inch baking dish. Cover with wax paper, and microwave at HIGH for 18 to 20 minutes.

Combine 1½ cups cider and soy sauce; pour over turkey. Cover with tent of wax paper. Microwave at MEDIUM (50% power) for 35 to 40 minutes, giving dish a quarter-turn and basting once. Turn breast, skin side up, and microwave at MEDIUM for 35 to 40 minutes or until juices run clear when turkey is pierced with a fork, giving dish a quarter-turn and basting once. When done, a microwave meat thermometer should register 175° when placed in thickest part of turkey breast. (Microwave temperature is higher than conventional temperature.)

Combine cornstarch and ½ cup cider, stirring well; stir into pan drippings. Microwave at HIGH for 5 to 6 minutes or until sauce thickens, stirring after 2 minutes, then at 1-minute intervals.

STUFFED TURKEY ROLL

12 ounces ground pork
1 (10-ounce) package frozen
   chopped spinach, thawed and well
   drained
1 egg, beaten
½ cup soft breadcrumbs
⅓ cup minced onion
2 cloves garlic, minced
¾ teaspoon dried whole thyme
¾ teaspoon dried whole rosemary,
   crushed
½ teaspoon salt
½ teaspoon freshly ground pepper
1 (3-pound) boneless turkey breast
¼ cup butter or margarine, melted

Combine first 10 ingredients; set aside.

Lay turkey breast flat on wax paper, skin side down. Remove tendons, and trim fat, keeping skin intact. From center, slice horizontally (parallel with skin) through thickest part of each side of breast almost to outer edge; flip cut piece and breast fillets over to enlarge breast. Pound breast to flatten and form a more even thickness.

Spoon stuffing mixture in center of width of turkey breast, leaving a 2-inch border at sides. Fold in sides of turkey breast over filling; roll up turkey breast over filling, starting from bottom. (Roll should be about 12 to 14 inches long.)

Tie turkey breast roll securely in several places with string; place, seam side down, on a rack in a roasting pan. Insert meat thermometer, making sure bulb rests in meat of turkey. Pour butter evenly over roll. Bake at 425° for 30 minutes, basting often with pan drippings. Reduce heat to 350° and bake an additional 20 to 30 minutes or until meat thermometer registers 170°, basting often. Let stand 10 minutes before slicing. Yield: 10 servings.

STUFFED GOOSE

1 (9- to 10- pound) dressed goose
3 cups cooked rice
1½ cups peeled and chopped
  cooking apples
½ cup raisins
½ cup chopped onion
1 teaspoon dried whole rosemary
½ teaspoon salt
⅛ teaspoon pepper
1 egg, beaten
Fresh parsley (optional)
Orange slices (optional)

Remove giblets and neck from goose; reserve for other uses. Rinse goose thoroughly with water; pat dry. Prick skin with a fork at 2-inch intervals.

Combine rice and next 7 ingredients, stirring well. Spoon mixture into cavity; close with skewers. Truss goose, and place, breast side up, on rack in a roasting pan. Insert meat thermometer in thigh, making sure it does not touch bone. Bake, uncovered, at 350° for 2 to 2½ hours or until meat thermometer registers 185°. Place goose on a serving platter; garnish with parsley and orange slices, if desired. Yield: 5 to 7 servings.

Make Plans for the Leftovers

Even small portions of leftover cooked chicken or turkey can stretch a long way when you're creative with your menu planning. Just flip through our chapters on soups, salads, and appetizers and sandwiches, and you'll find that leftover chicken is a valuable resource. Also, look to the section in this chapter for ways to use chopped cooked chicken.

If you won't have time to use the leftovers within two days, package them in small portions, and freeze until needed.

ORANGE-RUM ROAST DUCKLING

1 (4- to 4½-pound) dressed
  duckling
1½ teaspoons ground tarragon
½ teaspoon salt
⅛ teaspoon pepper
1 stalk celery, cut into 2-inch
  pieces
1 carrot, scraped and cut into
  2-inch pieces
1 apple, cored and coarsely
  chopped
2 tablespoons chopped green
  onions
½ thin-skinned orange, seeded and
  coarsely ground
1 tablespoon butter or margarine,
  melted
⅓ cup orange marmalade
¼ cup firmly packed brown
  sugar
3 tablespoons rum

Remove giblets and neck from duckling; reserve for other uses, if desired. Rub cavity of duckling with tarragon, salt, and pepper; stuff with celery, carrot, and apple. Close cavity of duckling with skewers; truss. Prick skin with a fork at 2-inch intervals. Place duckling, breast side up, on rack in a shallow roasting pan. Cover and bake at 375° for 1 hour. Insert meat thermometer in thigh, making sure it does not touch bone. Cover duckling loosely with aluminum foil; bake an additional 1 to 1½ hours or until meat thermometer registers 185°. Let cool to touch.

Strain drippings, reserving 2 tablespoons; set aside.

Remove and discard stuffing; halve duckling by cutting down both sides of backbone as close as possible to bone. Cut duckling in half down breast sides, removing breast bones. Place duckling halves in a baking dish; set aside, and keep warm.

Sauté green onions and orange in butter until tender; stir in reserved drippings, marmalade, and brown sugar. Bring to a boil. Cook 5 minutes; stir constantly. Stir in rum. Spoon over duckling. Yield: 2 to 4 servings.

☐ *Microwave Directions:* Remove giblets and neck from duckling; reserve for other uses, if desired. Rub cavity of duckling with tarragon, salt, and pepper; stuff with celery, carrot, and apple. Close cavity of duckling with wooden picks; truss. Prick skin with a fork at 2-inch intervals. Place duckling, breast side down, on a microwave roasting rack in a 12- x 8- x 2-inch baking dish. Cover with a tent of wax paper. Microwave at HIGH for 11 minutes.

Turn duckling, breast side up, and give duckling a half-turn. Cover with wax paper. Microwave at HIGH for 18 to 21 minutes or until juices run clear when pierced with a fork between leg and thigh. Microwave meat thermometer should register 185° when inserted between leg and thigh. Let cool to touch.

Strain drippings, reserving 2 tablespoons; set aside.

Remove and discard stuffing; halve duckling by cutting down both sides of backbone as close as possible to bone. Cut duckling in half down breast sides, removing breast bones. Place duckling halves in a baking dish; set aside, and keep warm.

Combine green onions, orange, and butter in a 1-quart glass bowl; cover with heavy-duty plastic wrap, and microwave at HIGH for 2 to 3 minutes or until tender. Stir in reserved drippings, marmalade, and brown sugar. Cover and microwave 3 minutes or until thickened, stirring at 1-minute intervals.

SWEET-AND-SOUR ROAST DUCKLING

1 (3½- to 4-pound) dressed duckling
Salt and pepper
1 tablespoon vinegar
¼ cup red currant jelly
¼ cup orange juice
1 teaspoon cornstarch
Orange slices
Fresh parsley sprigs

Remove giblets and neck from duckling; reserve for other uses. Sprinkle cavity with salt and pepper. Prick skin with fork at 2-inch intervals. Place duckling, breast side up, on rack in roasting pan. Insert thermometer in thigh, making sure it doesn't touch bone. Bake, uncovered, at 325° for 2 to 2½ hours or until meat thermometer registers 185°.

Combine 1 tablespoon pan drippings, vinegar, jelly, orange juice, and cornstarch in a small saucepan; stir well. Cook over medium heat, stirring constantly, until thickened and bubbly.

Cut duckling in half or quarters; garnish with orange slices and parsley. Serve with sauce. Yield: 2 to 4 servings.

☐ *Microwave Directions:* Remove giblets and neck from duckling; reserve for other uses. Sprinkle cavity with salt and pepper. Prick skin with a fork at 2-inch intervals. Place duckling, breast side down, on a microwave roasting rack placed in a 12- x 8- x 2-inch baking dish. Cover with a tent of wax paper. Microwave at HIGH for 12 minutes.

Turn duckling breast side up, and give duckling a half-turn. Cover with wax paper. Microwave at MEDIUM (50% power) for 35 to 40 minutes or until juices run clear when pierced with a fork between leg and thigh. Microwave thermometer should register 185° when inserted between leg and thigh.

Combine 1 tablespoon pan drippings, vinegar, jelly, orange juice, and cornstarch in a 2-cup glass measure; stir well. Microwave at HIGH for 2½ to 3½ minutes or until thickened and bubbly,

stirring after 1 minute, and then at 2-minute intervals.

Cut duckling in half or quarters; garnish with orange slices and parsley. Serve with sauce.

CORNISH HENS WITH ORANGE GLAZE

4 (1½- to 2-pound) Cornish hens
½ teaspoon salt
½ teaspoon dried whole basil
½ teaspoon dried whole tarragon
½ teaspoon dried whole thyme
½ teaspoon ground savory
⅛ teaspoon pepper
¼ cup butter or margarine, melted
¼ cup orange marmalade
Watercress
Peeled orange slices

Remove giblets from hens. Rinse hens with cold water, and pat dry. Combine seasonings, stirring well. Sprinkle cavities with half of seasonings, and close cavities. Secure with wooden picks; truss. Brush skins with butter, and sprinkle with remaining seasonings.

Place hens, breast side up, on a rack in a shallow roasting pan. Pour water into pan to cover bottom (about ⅛-inch deep). Place in upper half of oven, and bake at 325° for 45 minutes.

Brush hens with butter, and spoon 1 tablespoon marmalade on each breast. Bake an additional 35 to 45 minutes or until juices run clear when thigh is pierced with a fork. Garnish chicken with watercress and orange slices. Yield: 4 servings.

☐ *Microwave Directions:* Remove giblets from hens. Rinse hens with cold water, and pat dry. Combine seasonings, stirring well. Sprinkle cavities of hens with half of seasonings, and close cavities. Secure with wooden picks; truss. Brush skins with butter, and sprinkle with remaining seasonings.

Place hens, breast side down, on a

microwave roasting rack placed in a 12- x 8- x 2-inch baking dish. Pour water in dish to cover bottom (about ⅛-inch deep). Cover with a tent of wax paper. Microwave at HIGH for 15 minutes.

Turn hens, breast side up, and give each a half-turn on rack. Brush with butter, and spoon 1 tablespoon marmalade on breast of each hen. Cover with wax paper, and microwave at HIGH for 18 to 20 minutes, turning dish after 10 minutes, or until juices run clear when thigh is pierced with a fork. Let stand 4 to 6 minutes before serving. Garnish with watercress and orange slices.

CORNISH HENS WITH WILD RICE STUFFING

1 (6-ounce) package long grain and wild rice mix
1 medium onion, minced
3 tablespoons butter or margarine, melted and divided
1 large apple, peeled, cored, and coarsely shredded
1 egg, beaten
1 tablespoon minced fresh parsley
⅛ teaspoon ground thyme
6 to 8 (1- to 1½-pound) Cornish hens
Salt and pepper

Prepare rice according to package directions.

Sauté onion in 2 tablespoons butter.

Combine rice, onion, apple, egg, parsley, and thyme; stir well, and set aside.

Remove giblets from hens; reserve for other uses. Rinse hens with cold water, and pat dry; sprinkle cavities with salt and pepper.

Stuff hens with rice mixture, and close cavities. Secure with wooden picks; truss. Place hens, breast side up, in a shallow pan, and brush with remaining 1 tablespoon butter. Bake at 350° for 1 to 1½ hours or until juices run clear when thigh is pierced with a fork. Yield: 6 to 8 servings.

BRANDY-BUTTERED CORNISH HENS

4 (1½-pound) Cornish hens
Salt and pepper
Pecan Stuffing
⅓ cup butter or margarine, melted
3 tablespoons apricot-, peach-, or
 plum-flavored brandy
Fresh parsley sprigs
Apple slices
Green grapes

Remove giblets from hens; reserve for other uses, if desired. Rinse hens with cold water, and pat dry; sprinkle cavities with salt and pepper.

Stuff hens with Pecan Stuffing, and close cavities. Secure with wooden picks; truss. Brush hens with butter, and sprinkle generously with pepper. Combine remaining butter and brandy.

Place hens, breast side up, in a shallow pan. Bake at 350° for 1 to 1½ hours or until juices run clear when thigh is pierced with a fork, basting frequently with brandy mixture. Garnish with parsley, apple slices, and grapes. Yield: 4 servings.

Pecan Stuffing

1 cup apple juice
¼ cup apricot-, peach-, or
 plum-flavored brandy
¼ cup butter or margarine
1 (8-ounce) package cornbread
 stuffing mix
¾ cup chopped pecans

Combine first 3 ingredients in a saucepan; cook over medium heat, stirring occasionally, until butter melts. Add stuffing mix and pecans; stir lightly. Yield: enough stuffing for 4 Cornish hens.

⬭ *Microwave Directions:* Remove giblets from hens; reserve for other uses,

Brandy-Buttered Cornish Hens glisten with the flavorful basting mixture; pecan stuffing hides inside the birds.

if desired. Rinse hens with cold water, and pat dry; sprinkle cavities with salt and pepper.

Stuff hens with Pecan Stuffing, and close cavities. Secure with wooden picks; truss. Brush hens with butter, and sprinkle generously with pepper. Combine remaining butter and brandy, and set aside.

Place hens, breast side down, on a microwave roasting rack placed in a 12- x 8- x 2-inch baking dish. Cover hens with a tent of wax paper. Microwave at HIGH for 15 minutes.

Turn hens, breast side up, and give each a half-turn on rack. Brush with brandy mixture. Cover with wax paper, and microwave at HIGH for 16 to 20 minutes or until juices run clear when thigh is pierced with a fork. Baste with brandy mixture, and turn uncooked portions to outside every 5 minutes. Let stand 4 to 6 minutes before serving. Garnish with parsley, apple slices, and grapes.

Pecan Stuffing: Combine first 3 ingredients in a 1-quart glass measure. Microwave at HIGH for 3 minutes. Combine juice mixture, stuffing mix, and pecans, stirring lightly.

Assuming the hunters are successful, the head cook has to then take over with an assortment of ways to serve the bounty. Most wild birds are prepared much like similar domestic birds, so there are only a few basics to remember.

Wild birds tend to be leaner than domestic ones, which can make them tough. Moist heat cooking methods are often preferable to dry heat methods, especially for older, tougher birds. Wild birds that are roasted need basting frequently and are often topped with bacon to keep them tender and juicy as they cook.

SHERRIED BAKED DUCK

1 cup dry sherry
½ cup water
2 tablespoons vegetable oil
1 tablespoon butter or margarine
½ teaspoon white pepper
1½ teaspoons dried parsley flakes
¼ teaspoon red pepper
1 (2-ounce) bottle onion juice
4 wild ducks, cleaned
Salt
4 bay leaves
1 large onion, quartered
Orange slices (optional)

Place sherry in a heavy medium saucepan; heat just until warm (do not boil). Remove from heat; ignite sherry, and let stand until flames disappear. Add next 7 ingredients; heat well.

Sprinkle ducks with salt. Place 1 bay leaf and an onion quarter in cavity of each duck; place ducks, breast side down, in a large roaster.

Pour half of hot sherry mixture over ducks; cover and bake at 350° for 3 hours or until tender, basting occasionally with pan drippings.

Reheat remaining sherry mixture, and pour mixture over ducks; cool. Cover ducks, and let stand in refrigerator 1 to 2 hours or until ready to reheat and serve, if desired.

Cut ducks in half, and return to roaster. Cover and bake at 350° for 30 minutes or until hot. Place ducks on serving platter; garnish with orange slices and fresh parsley sprigs, if desired. Yield: 4 servings.

Note: This dish is best when prepared a day in advance. Store in refrigerator, and reheat before serving.

PHEASANTS WITH PORT WINE SAUCE

2 (2-pound) pheasants, cleaned
2 tablespoons butter or margarine, melted
¼ teaspoon salt
¼ teaspoon pepper
¼ teaspoon onion powder
¼ teaspoon dried whole thyme
¼ teaspoon ground nutmeg
¼ teaspoon dried parsley flakes
2 slices bacon
¼ cup canned diluted chicken broth
¼ cup port wine
Grapes (optional)
Port Wine Sauce

Brush pheasants with butter; place, breast side up, on a rack in a large roasting pan, and broil 5 minutes. Remove from oven; rub each pheasant with ⅛ teaspoon each of salt, pepper, onion powder, thyme, nutmeg, and parsley. Place a strip of bacon lengthwise over each pheasant. Insert meat thermometer in breast or thigh of one bird, making sure it does not touch bone. Cover and bake at 375° for 1 hour.

Combine broth and port wine, stirring well. Remove bacon from pheasants. Continue to bake, uncovered, until meat thermometer registers 185° (35 to 45 minutes), basting frequently with broth mixture. Garnish with grapes, if desired. Serve with Port Wine Sauce. Yield: 6 servings.

Port Wine Sauce

½ cup red currant jelly
½ cup port wine
¼ cup catsup
1½ teaspoons cornstarch
½ teaspoon Worcestershire sauce

Combine all ingredients in a saucepan, stirring until cornstarch dissolves. Bring to a boil, stirring constantly, and cook 1 minute. Yield: 1¼ cups.

◻*Microwave Directions:* Brush pheasants with butter. Rub each pheasant with ⅛ teaspoon each of salt, pepper, onion powder, thyme, nutmeg, and parsley. Place pheasants, breast side down, on a microwave roasting rack in a 12- x 8- x 2-inch baking dish. Cover with a tent of wax paper. Microwave at HIGH for 10 minutes.

Combine broth and wine, stirring well. Set aside.

Turn pheasants, breast side up, and give pheasants a half-turn. Place a strip of bacon lengthwise over each pheasant, and cover with wax paper. Microwave at HIGH for 27 to 30 minutes or until juices run clear when pierced with a fork between leg and thigh, basting pheasants at 4-minute intervals with broth mixture. Meat thermometer should register 185° when inserted in center between leg and thigh. Remove bacon. Garnish with grapes, if desired. Serve with Port Wine Sauce.

Port Wine Sauce: Combine all ingredients in a 2-cup glass measure, stirring until cornstarch dissolves. Microwave at HIGH for 3 to 5 minutes, stirring after 1 minute and then at 2-minute intervals.

SAUCY DOVES

1 cup all-purpose flour
1 teaspoon salt
½ teaspoon poultry seasoning
¼ teaspoon pepper
12 doves, cleaned
½ cup butter or margarine, melted
1 (8-ounce) can tomato sauce
1 (4-ounce) can mushroom stems and
  pieces, drained
1 medium onion, diced
½ cup milk
12 French bread slices, toasted

Combine flour, salt, poultry season-ing, and pepper; dredge doves in flour mixture. Brown doves in butter in a large skillet; add tomato sauce, mush-rooms, and onion. Cover and cook over low heat 20 minutes or until tender. Remove doves, and keep warm.

Add milk to pan drippings, scraping sides and bottom of skillet. Cook, stir-ring constantly, until thoroughly heated.

Place doves on toasted bread; spoon sauce over doves. Yield: 6 servings.

DOVES WITH APPLE DRESSING

12 doves, cleaned
½ teaspoon salt
¼ teaspoon pepper
½ cup water
⅓ cup butter or margarine
2 tablespoons lemon juice
1 tablespoon all-purpose flour
½ cup water
½ teaspoon beef-flavored bouillon
  granules
Apple Dressing

Place doves in a large skillet. Sprinkle salt and pepper over doves. Pour ½ cup water into skillet. Cover and cook over medium heat 20 minutes. Remove cover, and continue cooking until most of water is gone.

Add butter and lemon juice to doves. Cook doves, turning occasionally, until

browned. Remove doves, and set aside.

Add flour to drippings in skillet; cook over low heat until lightly browned, stir-ring occasionally. Add ½ cup water and bouillon granules; cook over medium heat, stirring constantly, until thick-ened. Arrange 2 doves over each square of Apple Dressing, and spoon gravy over top. Yield: 6 servings.

Apple Dressing

3 cups crumbled cornbread
2 cups peeled and chopped cooking
  apples
½ cup chopped celery
1 small onion, chopped
¼ cup butter or margarine, melted
½ teaspoon salt
½ teaspoon poultry seasoning
½ cup milk
1 egg, slightly beaten

Combine all ingredients. Spoon into a lightly greased 8-inch square pan. Bake at 375° for 30 minutes. Cut into 6 squares. Yield: 6 servings.

BAKED QUAIL WITH MUSHROOMS

⅓ cup all-purpose flour
½ teaspoon salt
½ teaspoon pepper
8 quail
½ pound fresh mushrooms, sliced
½ cup butter or margarine, divided
¼ cup plus 1 tablespoon all-purpose
  flour
2 cups canned diluted chicken broth
½ cup dry sherry
Hot cooked rice

Combine ⅓ cup flour, salt, and pep-per. Dredge quail in flour mixture, and set aside.

Sauté mushrooms in 2 tablespoons butter in a large skillet 4 minutes. Re-move mushrooms from skillet; drain and set aside.

Melt remaining 6 tablespoons butter

in skillet; brown quail on both sides. Remove quail to a 1½-quart casserole. Add ¼ cup plus 1 tablespoon flour to drippings in skillet; cook 1 minute, stir-ring constantly. Gradually add chicken broth and sherry; cook over medium heat, stirring constantly, until gravy is thickened. Stir in mushrooms.

Pour mushroom gravy over quail. Cover and bake at 350° for 1 hour. Serve over rice. Yield: 4 servings.

FRIED QUAIL

1 cup all-purpose flour
1 teaspoon salt
½ teaspoon pepper
1 egg
½ cup milk
8 quail, cleaned
Vegetable oil
½ cup water
¼ cup all-purpose flour
2 cups milk
¼ teaspoon salt
⅛ teaspoon pepper

Combine first 3 ingredients; stir well, and set aside.

Combine egg and ½ cup milk, and beat until blended. Dredge quail in flour mixture, dip in egg mixture, and dredge again in flour mixture.

Heat ¼ inch of oil in a large skillet; add quail, and cook over medium heat 10 minutes or until golden brown, turn-ing occasionally. Drain on paper towels.

Pour off all but ½ cup oil from skillet. Add water and quail; cover and cook over medium heat 15 minutes. Remove quail to serving platter. Drain off drip-pings, reserving ¼ cup in skillet.

Add ¼ cup flour to drippings in skil-let; cook over low heat, stirring until smooth. Cook 1 minute, stirring con-stantly. Gradually add 2 cups milk; cook over medium heat, stirring constantly, until thickened and bubbly. Stir in ¼ teaspoon salt and ⅛ teaspoon pepper. Serve gravy over quail. Yield: 4 servings.

QUAIL WITH RED PLUM SAUCE

8 quail, cleaned and split down back
¾ cup all-purpose flour
1 teaspoon salt
½ teaspoon pepper
½ cup butter or margarine, divided
½ cup chopped onion
⅓ cup chopped mushrooms
½ cup dry white wine
¼ cup dry sherry
Dash of salt and pepper
8 (¾-inch-thick) slices French bread, toasted
Red Plum Sauce

Spread quail open, and pat dry with paper towels. Combine flour, 1 teaspoon salt, and ½ teaspoon pepper; dredge quail in flour mixture, and set aside.

Melt 2 tablespoons butter in a skillet; add onion and mushrooms, and sauté 4 minutes. Remove onion and mushrooms from skillet, and set aside.

Melt ¼ cup butter in skillet, and brown quail on both sides. Remove to a 13- x 9- x 2-inch pan. Add wine to drippings in skillet; bring to a boil, scraping sides and bottom of skillet with back of spoon. Pour over quail. Bake at 350° for 30 minutes.

Combine onion mixture, remaining 2 tablespoons butter, sherry, dash of salt and pepper; stir well. Spread mixture on toasted bread, and broil 6 inches from heat until bubbly.

Place quail on each toast slice, and serve with Red Plum Sauce. Yield: 4 servings.

Red Plum Sauce

1 cup red plum jam
Grated rind of 1 lemon
Grated rind of 1 orange
3 tablespoons lemon juice
½ cup orange juice
1 tablespoon cornstarch
½ teaspoon dry mustard

Combine all ingredients, stirring well. Cook over medium heat, stirring constantly. Bring to a boil, and boil 1 minute. Serve hot. Yield: 1½ cups.

SALADS & DRESSINGS

Some of the simplest yet most delightful foods come from the salad bowl. And as Southerners are becoming more conscious of fiber and vitamins in their diets, salads have taken on an increased importance in menu planning. Simply dressed fresh green salads can serve as appetizers. Heartier salads and fruit serve as accompaniments to the main meal. Meat salads or salads full of high protein ingredients, such as cheese, eggs, and beans, can be entrées for light lunches or dinners. There are even fruit salads rich enough for dessert, especially those with nuts and sweet dressings.

EQUIPMENT

It's not necessary to have a lot of special equipment to be a connoisseur of fine salads. Many people do enjoy having a large wooden salad bowl in which to toss fresh greens like the pros, although any large container will do.

A good sharp knife for chopping and dicing fresh vegetables is essential, and if you're lucky enough to own a food processor, you'll save a lot of time shredding, slicing, and chopping fresh salad ingredients.

STAY AWAY FROM THE FREEZER

Because they're usually made up of fresh fruits and vegetables, most salads aren't good candidates for freezing. The texture of fresh fruits and vegetables will never be the same after freezing. Also, mayonnaise, a common binding ingredient

Laden with salad greens and other vegetables, Ham and Cheese Toss (page 413) makes a hearty main-dish salad. Serve the creamy dressing on the side.

for salads, tends to break down upon freezing.

Never freeze a gelatin salad that contains fruits or vegetables. The low freezer temperatures can extract liquid from the fruits and vegetables and leave you with a soupy salad.

If you need to make a salad ahead of time, consider making one of our congealed versions or the many vegetable combinations that specify chilling overnight.

Also, you can precook and prechop some ingredients for salads and chill them in plastic bags for a day or two; wait to add the dressing until just before serving.

Homemade salad dressings can usually be made ahead and chilled for several days, assuming they don't contain extremely delicate or perishable ingredients. Allow oil-and-vinegar dressings to return to room temperature before serving. Shake them vigorously before serving to blend ingredients.

Salads From Greens

Because there are so many types of salad greens from which to choose, salads should never be boring. Not only do the looks of salad greens vary, so do the textures, flavors, and even colors. Refer to our lettuce photograph and these brief descriptions before your next trip to the produce market. Then select a few varieties new to you to mix and match in your salad bowl. Combine tangy greens with those milder in flavor, crisp greens with tender varieties, and pale greens with those flashier in color.

Iceberg lettuce turns up in more salads than any other green, probably because it is readily available, easy to store, and makes an especially crisp salad. It is probably the mildest in flavor of all greens, so it works well with greens of more pronounced flavor. Because it is so crisp, iceberg holds up well for

Leafy greens come in all sizes, shapes, and textures. See chart for identification.

Lettuce Identification Chart

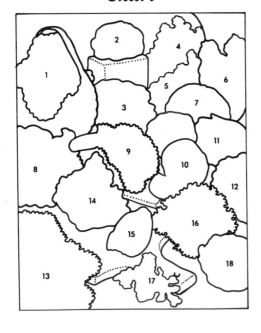

1. Spinach
2. Iceberg Lettuce
3. Romaine Lettuce
4. Green Leaf Lettuce
5. Red Leaf Lettuce
6. Nappa or Chinese Cabbage
7. Savoy Cabbage
8. Flowering Cabbage
9. Kale
10. Red Cabbage
11. Green Cabbage
12. Boston Lettuce
13. Curly Endive
14. Bibb Lettuce
15. Belgian Endive
16. Oakleaf Lettuce
17. Watercress
18. Radicchio

salads and sandwiches, makes nice lettuce cups, and works well as a bed of shredded lettuce.

Green and red leaf lettuce have delicate leaves that grow loosely rather than in heads like iceberg; the leaves are clustered only at the core. The color of most leaf lettuce is medium green; red-leafed varieties sport curly red-tipped edges. Leaf lettuce is crisp-textured when cold, but it wilts easily and should be used soon after purchase.

Romaine is a long, loaf-shaped head with coarse, crisp leaves and heavy ribs. Usually the leaves are torn into bite-size pieces, and the tough ribs discarded.

Bibb or **butterhead** is a small, cup-shaped head of lettuce with deep green veins. The veins and ribs of Bibb are less prominent than in other lettuces, giving this lettuce a soft texture. Its slightly sweet and nutty taste adds a unique flavor to salads.

Boston is similar in looks, taste, and texture to Bibb but is larger and has a more rounded head. It is generally available year-round.

Oakleaf, a very delicate variety, is usually only found in local markets in spring and summer. It is mild in flavor and adds a deep green color to salads.

For **spinach** salads, choose very young tender leaves, and trim away the tough stems. Wash spinach well, as dirt adheres tightly to the curly leaves.

Belgian endive sports long slender leaves light green in color. Its taste is slightly tangy and the texture very crisp. Belgian endive offers nice variety to a mixed green salad. Its crisp leaves hold up well and even make a nice base for appetizer dips or stuffings.

Curly endive or chicory has spiky, curly-edged leaves. Its texture is also slightly tangy, making it a nice green to combine with others.

The small and flat dark green leaves of **watercress** have a peppery taste that blends well with other greens. Its stem is tough and leggy, so you'll want to trim away most of it. The unique look of watercress makes it a nice garnish for all types of food—a pleasing change from overused parsley.

Purplish-red in color, **radicchio** has cup-shaped leaves that are tightly bunched together. It's slightly tangy in taste, and it makes an interesting addition to other salad greens. Radicchio also works well alone with a tangy dressing.

Today you'll find **cabbage** in several varieties. **Savoy** with its crinkly leaves is milder in flavor than common **green** and **red cabbage.** Also mild in flavor, **nappa** or **Chinese cabbage** grows in slender tight heads. **Flowering cabbage** comes in purple and green or white and green varieties; graceful curly leaves account for its name. **Kale,** also a member of the cabbage family, has curly green leaves. It is sometimes eaten cooked and sometimes tossed raw into salads.

"PICKING" YOUR GREENS

When buying leafy greens, avoid any that are oversized, spotted, limp, or beginning to yellow; they're past their prime. Choose a head that gives slightly when squeezed and has a good color—usually bright green. Lettuce that looks fresh and crisp has usually been stored properly in the store and should be a good choice. A brown core is a sign of oxidation and doesn't necessarily indicate poor quality. After lettuce is

cut during harvesting, the core naturally browns as the cut surface seals to keep the head fresh and to hold in nutrients.

The crisper drawer in your refrigerator is the best storage spot for greens. Gently rinse the leaves, and shake off excess moisture; store in plastic bags, and use within a day or two. Firm, crisp varieties like iceberg hold up longer than do more fragile varieties like watercress.

Arrange Salads for a Buffet

Salads should be simple, but sometimes you might want an especially eye-catching arrangement. Try radiating Belgian endive leaves around the outside of the salad bowl, or centering the salad with a nest of Aztec mushrooms or tomato roses. Serve dressing on the side for the more elaborate "arranged" salads.

HAM AND CHEESE TOSS

(pictured on page 410)

8 cups mixed salad greens
2 cups cooked ham strips
1½ cups sliced zucchini
1½ cups cauliflower flowerets
1 cup Swiss cheese strips
1 (8-ounce) carton commercial
   sour cream
¼ cup chili sauce
1 tablespoon milk
1 tablespoon minced fresh chives
Dash of red pepper

Combine first 5 ingredients in a large bowl; toss well.

Combine remaining ingredients; stir well. Serve dressing with salad. Yield: 6 servings.

QUICK SPINACH SALAD

½ pound fresh spinach
⅓ cup mayonnaise
3 tablespoons frozen orange
   juice concentrate, thawed
1 red apple, unpeeled
4 slices bacon, cooked and
   crumbled
Freshly ground pepper to taste

Remove stems from spinach; wash leaves thoroughly, and pat dry. Tear into bite-size pieces. Combine mayonnaise and orange juice concentrate; stir well, and set aside.

Just before serving, chop apple. Combine spinach, apple, and bacon in a large bowl. Serve with dressing, and add freshly ground pepper to taste. Yield: 4 servings.

SPINACH-MUSHROOM SALAD

1 pound fresh spinach
¼ pound fresh mushrooms, sliced
3 hard-cooked eggs, chopped
1 bunch green onions, chopped
½ cup vegetable oil
3 tablespoons vinegar
⅓ cup sugar
¼ teaspoon salt
¼ teaspoon dry mustard
⅛ teaspoon freshly ground pepper
8 slices bacon, cooked and
   crumbled

Remove stems from spinach; wash leaves thoroughly, and pat dry. Tear into bite-size pieces. Combine spinach, mushrooms, eggs, and green onions in a large bowl.

Combine oil, vinegar, sugar, and seasonings in a jar. Cover tightly, and shake vigorously. Top spinach mixture with dressing just before serving. Sprinkle bacon over top. Yield: 6 servings.

To cut citrus slices: Starting at one end, slice away rind in one continuous strip. Then cut neat slices from pulp of fruit.

To section citrus: Once rind is removed, slice between membranes of fruit to remove easy-to-eat sections for garnishing or salad making.

WATERCRESS SALAD

3 cups torn fresh watercress
½ cup sliced fresh mushrooms
½ cup sliced canned hearts of palm
¼ cup slivered almonds, toasted
⅛ teaspoon salt
⅛ teaspoon pepper
¼ cup commercial creamy garlic
   salad dressing

Combine first 6 ingredients in a salad bowl. Add enough water to salad dressing to make ⅓ cup, mixing well. Pour over salad, and toss. Yield: 4 servings.

ORANGE-WALNUT SALAD

2 small heads Bibb lettuce, torn into
   bite-size pieces
1 pound fresh spinach, torn into
   bite-size pieces
2 oranges, peeled, seeded, and
   sectioned
½ medium onion, sliced and
   separated into rings
½ cup coarsely chopped walnuts
2 teaspoons butter or margarine,
   melted
Sweet-and-Sour Dressing (page 432)

Place first 4 ingredients in a large bowl. Sauté walnuts in butter until lightly browned; add to lettuce mixture. Toss with Sweet-and-Sour Dressing. Yield: 6 to 8 servings.

CHEF'S GARDEN SALAD

1 large head lettuce, torn into
   bite-size pieces
1 tomato, cut into wedges
1 small cucumber, sliced
½ cup sliced celery
½ cup chopped green pepper
½ cup Thousand Island dressing
1 cup julienne strips cooked ham
1 cup julienne strips cooked chicken
1 cup julienne strips Cheddar cheese
2 hard-cooked eggs, sliced
Additional Thousand Island dressing
   (optional)

Combine vegetables in a large bowl. Add ½ cup dressing, tossing well. Arrange ham, chicken, cheese, and eggs on salad. Serve with additional dressing, if desired. Yield: 6 servings.

TACO SALAD

1 pound ground beef
1 (1¼-ounce) envelope taco
  seasoning mix
1 (16-ounce) can cream-style corn
1 (16 ounce) can red kidney beans,
  drained
1 (7½-ounce) package tortilla chips,
  coarsely crushed
1 medium head lettuce, torn into
  pieces
2 cups (8 ounces) shredded
  Longhorn cheese
2 medium tomatoes, diced
Commercial taco sauce

Cook beef in a large skillet until browned, stirring to crumble. Drain. Stir in taco mix, corn, and beans. Cool slightly.

Layer half each of tortilla chips, meat mixture, lettuce, cheese, and tomatoes in a large serving bowl. Repeat layers. Serve immediately with taco sauce. Yield: 6 to 8 servings.

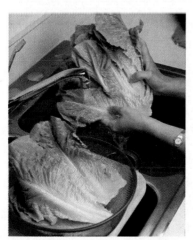

For crisp romaine: Break off each stalk, and rinse under cool running water. Shake off the excess moisture, and chill lettuce in a plastic bag for several hours or overnight.

Add Crunch to the Salad

Croutons commonly top salads to add that extra crunch to the greens. If you're out of croutons or want to try something different, you have many options. Toasted almonds, pecans, and walnuts add interesting flavor, as do sunflower kernels and cooked, crumbed bacon. Even small types of cereal seasoned and toasted like croutons add a tasty flavor and a change-of-pace appearance.

MEDITERRANEAN SPRING SALAD

½ pound new potatoes (5 small)
½ cup olive oil
2 tablespoons lemon juice
2 teaspoons dried whole oregano
¼ teaspoon salt
1 clove garlic, crushed
6 cups torn mixed salad greens
1 large tomato, cut into wedges
1 medium-size green pepper, thinly
  sliced into rings
1 small purple onion, thinly sliced
  and separated into rings
1 small cucumber, thinly sliced
½ cup crumbled feta cheese
1 (2-ounce) can anchovy fillets
  (optional)

Cook potatoes in boiling water to cover about 25 minutes or until tender; drain and cool slightly. Peel and thinly slice potatoes; place in a shallow bowl. Combine oil, lemon juice, oregano, salt, and garlic; mix well. Pour over potatoes; marinate 1 hour. Drain potatoes, reserving marinade.

Place salad greens in a large bowl. Arrange potatoes, tomato, green pepper, onion, cucumber, cheese, and anchovies (if desired) over salad greens. Toss with reserved marinade just before serving. Yield: 6 to 8 servings.

GREENS AND TUNA SALAD

½ head romaine, torn
½ head Bibb lettuce, torn
4 Belgian endive leaves, torn
½ head iceberg lettuce, torn
1 head Boston lettuce, torn
1 cup chopped cucumber
1 small onion, thinly sliced
2 (7-ounce) cans tuna, drained and
  flaked
4 hard-cooked eggs
½ cup olive oil
¼ cup lemon juice
1 teaspoon mayonnaise
½ teaspoon dry mustard
½ teaspoon salt
Dash of pepper

Combine first 8 ingredients in a large salad bowl. Cut 3 hard-cooked eggs into wedges; add to salad greens and tuna.

Press remaining egg through a sieve; add olive oil, lemon juice, mayonnaise, and seasonings just before serving, stirring well. Pour dressing over salad; toss gently. Yield: 6 to 8 servings.

To core a head of iceberg lettuce: Hold lettuce, core end down, and tap core on the counter. Then twist and remove core. If core is cut with a knife, the surrounding area will discolor quickly.

1. For Caesar Salad, first make homemade croutons from slices of French bread. Butter the bread, sprinkle with garlic powder, cut into cubes, and bake until crisp.

2. Combine dressing ingredients in a jar; cover tightly, and shake vigorously.

3. Coddle an egg by dipping it into boiling water 1 minute. Set aside to cool.

4. Toss torn salad greens with dressing. Break coddled egg over greens, and add lemon juice, pepper, and cheese; toss again gently.

CAESAR SALAD

This famous salad was created by accident. The story goes that a Mexican restauranteur named Caesar was overwhelmed by guests one day, and had to prepare a salad from the few simple ingredients on hand—romaine, eggs, Parmesan cheese, lemons, and dry bread. The guests were delighted.

1 large head romaine lettuce
¾ cup olive oil
3 tablespoons red wine vinegar
1 teaspoon Worcestershire sauce
½ teaspoon salt
¼ teaspoon dry mustard
1 large clove garlic, crushed
1 egg
1 lemon, halved
Freshly ground pepper
¼ cup grated Parmesan cheese
Garlic Croutons
1 (2-ounce) can anchovy fillets, drained (optional)

Wash romaine under cold running water. Trim core, and separate stalk into leaves; discard wilted or discolored portions. Shake leaves well to remove moisture. Place romaine in a large plastic bag; chill at least 2 hours.

Combine olive oil, vinegar, Worcestershire sauce, salt, mustard, and garlic in a jar. Cover tightly, and shake vigorously. Set aside.

Pour water to a depth of 2 inches in a medium saucepan; bring water to a rapid boil, and turn off heat. Carefully lower egg into water using a slotted spoon; let stand 1 minute. Remove egg from water, and set aside to cool.

Cut coarse ribs from large leaves of romaine; tear leaves into bite-size pieces, and place in a large salad bowl. Pour dressing over romaine; toss gently until well coated.

Break coddled egg over romaine; then squeeze juice from lemon halves over salad. Grind a generous amount of pepper over salad, and sprinkle with cheese. Toss. Top with Garlic Croutons; garnish with anchovies, if desired. Serve immediately. Yield: 4 to 6 servings.

Garlic Croutons

3 tablespoons butter or margarine, softened
3 (¾-inch-thick) slices French bread
¼ teaspoon garlic powder

Spread butter over both sides of bread slices; sprinkle with garlic powder. Cut slices into ¾-inch cubes. Place on a baking sheet, and bake at 350° for 15 minutes or until croutons are crisp and dry. Let croutons cool; then store in an airtight container. Yield: about 1½ cups.

Topped with croutons and anchovies, your homemade Caesar Salad will rival those tossed in many exclusive restaurants.

Vegetable Salads

Crisp vegetable salads add color and a unique freshness to the menu, and most of them are quick to make. Many are as simple as opening a can of vegetables and adding a seasoned marinade; most marinated salads keep well in the refrigerator for several days.

Salads made from fresh vegetables take a few extra minutes to make since you'll have to clean and prepare the vegetables, but their characteristic crispness and unmatched freshness make up for the extra time they take to put together. If you own a food processor, put it to work slicing and chopping for you.

CHILLED CORN SALAD

1 (12-ounce) can whole kernel corn, drained
1 small onion, chopped
½ cup chopped green pepper
2 tablespoons minced fresh parsley
2 tablespoons cider vinegar
1 tablespoon vegetable oil
¼ teaspoon salt
¼ teaspoon pepper
Lettuce leaves (optional)

Combine all ingredients except lettuce leaves. Cover and chill at least 4 hours. Serve on lettuce leaves, if desired. Yield: 4 to 6 servings.

CHICK-PEA SALAD

1 (19-ounce) can chick-peas, drained and rinsed
2 tablespoons finely chopped green pepper
2 tablespoons finely chopped onion
¼ cup vegetable oil
¼ cup sugar
2 tablespoons vinegar
1 tablespoon diced pimiento
⅛ teaspoon pepper

Combine first 3 ingredients. Combine remaining ingredients in a jar; cover tightly, and shake vigorously. Toss pea mixture with dressing. Cover and chill 8 hours. Yield: 4 servings.

MARINATED BEET SALAD

2 (16-ounce) cans sliced beets
½ cup sugar
2 teaspoons dry mustard
¾ cup cider vinegar
1 teaspoon celery seeds
½ cup finely chopped onion

Drain beets, reserving ½ cup juice; set aside. Combine sugar and dry mustard in a small saucepan; stir well. Add beet juice and vinegar; bring to a boil over medium heat. Remove from heat; stir in celery seeds.

Combine beets and chopped onion. Add vinegar mixture, tossing gently. Cover and chill salad at least 8 hours. Yield: 8 servings.

MARINATED VEGETABLE SALAD

1 cup sugar
¾ cup vinegar
½ cup vegetable oil
1 teaspoon pepper
½ teaspoon salt
1 (16-ounce) can French-style green beans, drained
1 (17-ounce) can green peas, drained
1 (12-ounce) can shoepeg whole kernel corn, drained
1 (2-ounce) jar diced pimiento, drained
1 cup chopped celery
1 green pepper, finely chopped
1 bunch green onions, chopped

Combine first 5 ingredients in a medium saucepan; bring to a boil, stirring to dissolve sugar. Cool.

Combine vegetables, and stir in vinegar mixture. Cover and chill at least 8 hours, stirring occasionally. Yield: 8 to 10 servings.

SAUERKRAUT SALAD

⅓ cup vinegar
3 tablespoons vegetable oil
½ cup sugar
1 (16-ounce) can sauerkraut, drained
½ cup chopped celery
½ cup chopped green pepper
½ cup chopped green onions
¼ cup grated carrot
1 (2-ounce) jar diced pimiento, undrained

Combine vinegar, oil, and sugar in a large bowl; stir well. Add remaining ingredients, stirring to coat all vegetables. Cover and chill at least 8 hours. Serve salad with a slotted spoon. Yield: 4 to 6 servings.

FIVE-BEAN SALAD

8 slices bacon
⅔ cup sugar
2 tablespoons cornstarch
¼ teaspoon salt
⅛ teaspoon pepper
¾ cup vinegar
½ cup water
1 (15½-ounce) can red kidney beans, drained
1 (16-ounce) can cut green beans, drained
1 (16-ounce) can lima beans, drained
1 (16-ounce) can wax beans, drained
1 (15-ounce) can garbanzo beans, drained
1 small onion, sliced and separated into rings

Cook bacon in a large Dutch oven until crisp; drain well, reserving ¼ cup drippings in Dutch oven. Crumble bacon, and set aside.

Add sugar, cornstarch, salt, and pepper to drippings; stir until smooth. Gradually add vinegar and water; cook over medium heat, stirring constantly, until thickened and bubbly.

Add beans to Dutch oven; cover and simmer 15 minutes. Add onion, tossing gently. Spoon salad into a 2½-quart serving dish, and sprinkle with crumbed bacon. Serve immediately. Yield: 10 to 12 servings.

CONFETTI POTATO SALAD

6 medium potatoes
4 green onions, thinly sliced
½ cup finely chopped green pepper
1 stalk celery, thinly sliced
1 small carrot, shredded
2 to 3 pimiento-stuffed olives, thinly sliced
3 hard-cooked eggs, chopped
½ cup commercial coleslaw dressing
3 tablespoons commercial sour cream
1 tablespoon lemon juice
Lettuce leaves (optional)
Paprika

Cook potatoes in boiling salted water to cover 30 minutes or until tender. Drain and cool slightly. Peel and dice potatoes. Combine potatoes, green onions, green pepper, celery, carrot, olives, and eggs in a large bowl.

Combine dressing, sour cream, and lemon juice; stir well. Add dressing to vegetable mixture, tossing gently. Serve on lettuce leaves, if desired, and sprinkle with paprika. Yield: 5 to 6 servings.

HOT GERMAN POTATO SALAD

4 medium potatoes
8 slices bacon
¼ cup sugar
2 tablespoons all-purpose flour
⅓ cup water
⅓ cup vinegar
1 small green pepper, chopped
1 small onion, chopped
¼ cup chopped celery
1 tablespoon chopped pimiento

Cook potatoes in boiling water to cover 30 minutes or until tender. Drain and cool slightly. Peel potatoes; cut into ½-inch cubes.

Cook bacon in a large skillet until crisp; remove bacon, reserving ¼ cup drippings in skillet. Crumble bacon, and set aside. Add sugar, flour, water, and vinegar to pan drippings, stirring well. Cook mixture over medium heat until slightly thickened.

Combine potatoes, bacon, green pepper, onion, celery, and pimiento in a large bowl; top with vinegar mixture, and toss gently. Yield: 6 servings.

CRISPY COLESLAW

1 small head cabbage, shredded
  (about 1½ pounds)
½ green pepper, chopped
½ red pepper, chopped
1 medium onion, chopped
1 cup sugar
½ cup plus 2 tablespoons vinegar
½ cup vegetable oil
1 teaspoon salt
1 teaspoon celery seeds

Combine cabbage, peppers, onion, and sugar in a large bowl; stir well. Cover and chill 2 hours.

Combine remaining ingredients in a saucepan; bring to a boil, stirring until salt dissolves. Pour over cabbage mixture; toss gently. Cover and chill at least 2 hours before serving. Will keep several days in the refrigerator. Yield: 6 to 8 servings.

CREAMY COLESLAW

1 small head cabbage, finely shredded
  (about 1½ pounds)
1 small carrot, shredded
½ cup diced green pepper
½ cup diced celery
¼ cup diced onion
½ cup mayonnaise
½ cup commercial sour cream
2 tablespoons sugar
2 tablespoons vinegar
1 tablespoon prepared mustard
½ teaspoon salt
½ teaspoon paprika
¼ teaspoon pepper

Combine vegetables; toss well, and set aside. Combine remaining ingredients; stir well. Pour dressing over vegetables; toss gently. Yield: 6 to 8 servings.

CUCUMBERS IN SOUR CREAM

3 large cucumbers
1 (8-ounce) carton commercial sour
  cream
3 tablespoons minced fresh chives
2 tablespoons lemon juice
½ teaspoon salt
¼ teaspoon pepper

Peel cucumbers, if desired, and thinly slice. Set aside.

Combine sour cream and remaining ingredients, stirring well. Stir cucumbers into sour cream mixture; cover and chill. Yield: 6 servings.

LAYERED GREEN PEA SALAD

1 (10-ounce) package frozen
  green peas, thawed
¼ cup chopped onion
¼ cup sliced celery
¼ teaspoon salt
⅛ teaspoon pepper
⅛ teaspoon dried whole basil
⅓ cup commercial sour cream
1 teaspoon sugar
¾ cup (3 ounces) shredded
  Cheddar cheese
6 slices bacon, cooked and
  crumbled

Layer first 9 ingredients in order given in a 1-quart serving bowl; cover and chill at least 4 hours. Top with bacon, and toss salad just before serving. Yield: 4 servings.

BASIL-TOMATO SALAD

5 medium tomatoes, sliced
⅓ cup sliced pitted ripe olives
½ cup (4 ounces) crumbled feta
  cheese
½ cup olive oil
⅓ cup wine vinegar
2 tablespoons finely chopped
  fresh basil or 2 teaspoons dried
  whole basil
1 clove garlic, minced
⅛ teaspoon coarsely ground
  pepper

Arrange tomatoes, olives, and cheese in a 13- x 9- x 2-inch dish. Combine remaining ingredients in a jar. Cover tightly, and shake vigorously. Pour dressing over tomato mixture, stirring gently. Cover and chill at least 4 hours. Yield: 8 servings.

LAYERED CAULIFLOWER SALAD

1 medium head cauliflower
1 medium head iceberg lettuce, torn into bite-size pieces
1 medium purple onion, chopped
½ pound bacon, cooked and crumbled
1 cup mayonnaise or salad dressing
3 tablespoons sugar
⅓ cup grated Parmesan cheese

Wash cauliflower; cut flowerets into bite-size pieces. Layer lettuce, onion, cauliflower, and bacon in a 3-quart bowl.

Combine mayonnaise and sugar; mix well. Spread mayonnaise mixture evenly over top of salad, sealing to edge of bowl. Sprinkle with Parmesan cheese.

Cover salad tightly, and chill at least 8 hours. Toss gently before serving. Yield: 8 to 10 servings.

GREEN-AND-WHITE VEGETABLE SALAD

1 pound fresh broccoli
1 medium head cauliflower, broken into flowerets
1½ cups finely chopped celery
6 green onions, finely chopped
¾ cup mayonnaise or salad dressing
¼ cup whipping cream
2 tablespoons sugar
½ teaspoon salt
¼ teaspoon pepper

Remove large leaves of broccoli, and cut off tough ends of lower stalks; discard. Wash broccoli thoroughly, and cut into 1-inch pieces. Combine broccoli, cauliflower, celery, and green onions in a large bowl.

Combine remaining ingredients, stirring until blended. Pour mayonnaise mixture over vegetables; toss lightly to coat. Cover and chill thoroughly. Yield: 8 to 10 servings.

FRESH ASPARAGUS SALAD

1 pound fresh asparagus
½ cup plain yogurt
1 small clove garlic, crushed
1 tablespoon chopped fresh parsley
¼ teaspoon salt
1 small head Boston or Bibb lettuce
1 hard-cooked egg yolk, sieved

Snap off tough ends of asparagus. Remove scales with knife or vegetable peeler. Cook asparagus in boiling water 6 to 8 minutes or until crisp-tender; drain. Chill.

Combine yogurt, garlic, parsley, and salt; stir well, and chill.

Place asparagus on bed of lettuce; top with yogurt dressing, and sprinkle with egg yolk. Yield: 4 servings.

CARROT-AMBROSIA SALAD

1 pound carrots, shredded
1 (20-ounce) can crushed pineapple, drained
1 (8-ounce) carton commercial sour cream
¾ cup flaked coconut
¾ cup golden raisins
2 tablespoons honey

Combine all ingredients, tossing well. Cover and chill. Yield: 6 to 8 servings.

ZUCCHINI SALAD

6 small zucchini, thinly sliced
1 sweet red or green pepper, sliced into thin strips
¼ cup chopped green onions
½ cup vegetable oil
3 tablespoons vinegar
½ teaspoon salt
½ teaspoon pepper
⅛ teaspoon garlic powder

Combine zucchini, red pepper, and green onions; toss lightly. Combine remaining ingredients; mix well, and pour over vegetables. Cover and chill at least 8 hours, stirring occasionally. Yield: 6 to 8 servings.

VEGETABLE-PASTA SALAD

1 cup uncooked corkscrew macaroni
2 small carrots, cut into 2-inch julienne strips
2 green onions, chopped
1 (2-ounce) jar diced pimiento, drained
¾ cup sliced celery
¼ cup frozen green peas, thawed
2 tablespoons chopped fresh parsley
10 cherry tomatoes, halved
¼ cup commercial Italian salad dressing
2 tablespoons mayonnaise
⅛ teaspoon pepper
Lettuce leaves

Cook macaroni according to package directions, omitting salt; drain. Rinse with cold water; drain.

Combine pasta and remaining ingredients except lettuce, tossing well; chill at least 1 hour. Spoon into a lettuce-lined bowl. Yield: 6 servings.

For pasta salads: Rinse cooked pasta to be used for salads under cool running water to keep it from becoming gummy. (Don't rinse hot pasta that is to be served with sauces.)

Spoon Vegetable-Rice Salad into a mold, if desired; then invert onto lettuce leaves.

COLORFUL RICE SALAD

1 (10-ounce) package frozen green peas, thawed
3 cups cooked rice
1 (4-ounce) jar diced pimiento, drained
6 green onions, chopped
4 hard-cooked eggs, chopped
2 cups (8 ounces) shredded Cheddar cheese
½ cup sliced pimiento-stuffed olives
½ cup chopped celery
⅓ cup sweet pickle relish
½ cup mayonnaise or salad dressing
Lettuce leaves (optional)
Cherry tomatoes (optional)

Combine first 9 ingredients; stir well. Add mayonnaise, tossing until well mixed. Cover and chill thoroughly. Serve on lettuce leaves, and garnish with cherry tomatoes, if desired. Yield: 8 servings.

VEGETABLE-RICE SALAD

1¼ cups uncooked long-grain rice
1 cucumber, peeled and chopped
Salt
1 large carrot, scraped and diced
⅓ pound fresh green beans,
  cut into ½-inch pieces
  (about 1 cup)
1 cup frozen green peas
1 sweet red pepper, chopped
2 tablespoons tarragon vinegar
½ teaspoon salt
½ teaspoon white pepper
¼ cup plus 1 tablespoon
  olive oil
Lettuce leaves

Cook rice according to package directions; chill.

Sprinkle cucumber generously with salt; cover and let stand 30 minutes. Rinse well.

Combine carrot, green beans, and green peas in a medium saucepan; cover with water, and cook 8 to 10 minutes or until crisp-tender. Drain vegetables, and rinse in cold water.

Combine cucumber, carrot, beans, peas, red pepper, and rice. Combine vinegar, ½ teaspoon salt, and pepper; gradually add oil, beating with a wire whisk until blended. Pour dressing over salad, and toss gently. Serve on lettuce leaves. Yield: 6 servings.

Note: The ingredients in Vegetable-Rice Salad make it cohesive enough to mold, if desired. Just spoon the mixture into a mold coated with vegetable cooking spray, packing rice gently with the back of a spoon. Chill 10 minutes; then invert onto lettuce leaves. Place a sweet red pepper flower in center of mold for garnish, if desired.

MINESTRONE SALAD

1 (8-ounce) package elbow macaroni
1 (16-ounce) can navy beans, drained
3 medium carrots, scraped and shredded
1½ cups chopped celery
¼ cup chopped fresh parsley
¾ cup mayonnaise
½ cup vegetable oil
2 tablespoons cider vinegar
½ teaspoon seasoned salt
¼ teaspoon seasoned pepper
Romaine
Tomato slices

Cook macaroni according to package directions, omitting salt; drain. Rinse with cold water, and drain.

Combine macaroni, navy beans, carrot, celery, and parsley; stir well. Combine mayonnaise and next 4 ingredients; stir well. Pour mayonnaise mixture over macaroni mixture, stirring well. Cover and chill at least 1 hour.

Line a salad bowl with romaine. Spoon macaroni salad into bowl; arrange tomato slices around edge. Yield: 8 servings.

A composed salad is one in which the ingredients are creatively arranged on a salad plate. Similar vegetables are usually grouped together, and the arrangement is based on color, size, and shape of the vegetables. Many salads work well for composing on individual salad plates, such as Salad Composée, Basil-Tomato Salad, and Crab Louis.

SALAD COMPOSÉE

2 medium carrots, cut into julienne strips
⅓ head cauliflower, cut into flowerets
½ bunch broccoli, cut into bite-size pieces
6 ounces fresh whole green beans
1 head romaine or leaf lettuce
24 to 30 cherry tomatoes
1 (16-ounce) can diced beets, drained
Vinaigrette Dressing

Cook first 4 vegetables separately in boiling, lightly salted water. Cook carrots, cauliflower, and broccoli 2 minutes; cook green beans 5 minutes or until crisp-tender. Immerse vegetables in ice water to cool; drain and chill.

Arrange lettuce on individual serving plates; arrange vegetables separately on lettuce, and serve with Vinaigrette Dressing. Yield: 6 to 8 servings.

Vinaigrette Dressing

1 cup olive oil
¼ cup wine vinegar
2 teaspoons dry mustard
½ teaspoon salt
2 shallots or scallions, minced

Combine all ingredients in a jar. Cover tightly, and shake vigorously. Yield: 1½ cups.

Fruit Salads

It's hard to find a salad more refreshing than one made of juicy fresh fruit—many salads of this type are sweet and satisfying enough to substitute as a dessert, such as Old-Fashioned Ambrosia and Summertime Melon Salad.

If served as a dessert, consider adding a simple but tasty cookie on the side. Don't prepare fruit salads too far ahead of time unless the recipe suggests it; if you prepare them too early, the fruit can become limp.

OLD-FASHIONED AMBROSIA

9 oranges, peeled, seeded, and sectioned
2 (20-ounce) cans crushed pineapple, drained
1 cup honey
1 to 2 teaspoons almond extract
1 cup flaked coconut

Combine all ingredients; cover mixture, and chill at least 8 hours. Yield: 6 to 8 servings.

BEST WALDORF SALAD

2 large tart red apples, unpeeled and diced
1 large green apple, unpeeled and diced
½ pound seedless green grapes, halved
½ cup coarsely chopped pecans
½ cup finely diced celery
⅓ cup raisins
¼ cup plus 2 tablespoons mayonnaise

Combine all ingredients, and stir well. Yield: 6 to 8 servings.

SUMMER FRUIT SALAD

1 fresh pineapple, peeled, cored, and cubed
1 quart fresh, hulled strawberries
½ cup fresh or frozen blueberries, thawed
½ cup fresh or frozen raspberries, thawed
1 (11-ounce) can mandarin oranges, drained
2 cups orange juice
½ cup sugar
¼ cup cream sherry
½ teaspoon almond extract
½ teaspoon vanilla extract

Combine first 5 ingredients in a large bowl. Combine remaining ingredients, stirring until sugar dissolves. Pour sherry mixture over fruit mixture, tossing lightly. Cover and chill 2 to 3 hours. Serve salad mixture with a slotted spoon. Yield: 10 servings.

CRUNCHY PEAR SALAD

3 pears, peeled, halved, and cored
2 teaspoons lemon juice
1 (3-ounce) package cream cheese, softened
3 tablespoons milk
¼ teaspoon dried whole tarragon
½ cup sliced celery
½ cup chopped dates
Lettuce leaves
¼ cup chopped walnuts or pecans

Sprinkle pear halves with lemon juice. Combine cream cheese, milk, and tarragon; beat until smooth. Stir in celery and dates. Spoon one-sixth of cheese mixture into each pear half. Arrange pear halves on a lettuce-lined platter; sprinkle with walnuts. Cover and chill 1 to 2 hours. Yield: 6 servings.

SAUCY FRUIT SALAD

1 egg yolk
1 tablespoon sugar
1 tablespoon orange juice
1 tablespoon vinegar
1 (8-ounce) carton commercial sour cream
2 cups mixed melon balls
1 cup seedless green grapes
1 cup sliced bananas
1 cup diced pineapple
1 cup sliced strawberries
1 cup orange sections
Flaked coconut

Combine first 4 ingredients in a saucepan; stir well. Cook over medium heat until thickened, stirring constantly. Remove from heat; chill. Fold in sour cream. Combine melon balls and next 5 ingredients; fold in dressing. Sprinkle coconut over top. Cover and chill. Yield: 6 to 8 servings.

To make melon balls: Plunge a melon baller into the seedless part of a melon, and turn the utensil with a circular motion to make smooth rounds. Reserve remaining melon pulp for other uses.

To make fruit cups: Cut tomatoes and other fruits into decorative containers for individual salads with a V-shaped knife. Cut crosswise all around the tomato, cutting just to the center. Twist the two sections apart, and scoop out the seedy center.

To cut a fresh pineapple: Slice it lengthwise into quarters. With a thin knife, slice away the core, and cut the pulp from the skin. Then cut the pulp crosswise into strips. Leave it in the shell for decorative serving, or cut strips into chunks for use in recipes.

To prevent darkening of fruits: When cutting avocados and other fruits that discolor quickly, immediately rub the cut surfaces with a lemon or dip in lemon juice.

SUMMERTIME MELON SALAD

½ (6-ounce) can frozen lemonade
   concentrate, thawed and undiluted
¼ cup orange marmalade
2 tablespoons Triple Sec or other
   orange-flavored liqueur
2 cups assorted melon balls
   (cantaloupe, honeydew, and
   watermelon)
½ cup halved fresh strawberries
1 small pineapple, peeled, cored, and
   cubed
3 small cantaloupes, halved and
   seeded
Mint leaves (optional)

Combine lemonade concentrate, marmalade, and Triple Sec; stir well. Combine melon balls, strawberries, and pineapple in a large bowl; pour lemonade mixture over fruit, stirring gently. Cover and chill at least 2 hours.

Spoon fruit mixture into cantaloupe halves; garnish with mint, if desired. Yield: 6 servings.

Summertime Melon Salad looks prettiest spooned into carved cantaloupe halves. A U-shaped knife was used to make the decorative cut on the melons.

FROSTY CRANBERRY SALAD

1 (16-ounce) can whole-berry
   cranberry sauce
1 (8-ounce) can crushed pineapple,
   drained
1 teaspoon lemon juice
1 (8-ounce) carton commercial sour
   cream
Lettuce leaves (optional)

Combine first 4 ingredients; stir until blended. Pour mixture into an 8½- x 4½- x 3-inch loafpan; cover and freeze until firm. Cut into 1-inch slices. Serve on lettuce leaves, if desired. Yield: 8 servings.

CANTALOUPE COOLER SALAD

1 large or 2 small cantaloupes
Lettuce leaves
1 large onion, thinly sliced and
   separated into rings
½ pound (about 12 slices) bacon,
   cooked and crumbled
Blender Poppy Seed Dressing
   (page 431)

Peel cantaloupe, and cut into bite-size pieces; arrange on lettuce leaves on individual salad plates. Top cantaloupe with onion rings and crumbled bacon. Drizzle Blender Poppy Seed Dressing over salad. Yield: 8 servings.

Salads That Hold Their Shape

Sparkling congealed salads laden with cut fruit and vegetables make pretty additions to a menu, especially when the salad is shaped in an upright mold and unmolded on a bed of lettuce. Gelatin makes these salads hold their shape, and it's important that the cook know how to use this product. There are two types of gelatin on the market, and they are not interchangeable.

TYPES OF GELATIN

Flavored gelatin comes in a wide assortment of fruit flavors and colors and has sugar added, so all recipes that specify flavored gelatin make sweet salads. For flavored gelatin,

To dissolve gelatin: Dissolve flavored gelatin in boiling water; then add cold water. Reverse the process for unflavored gelatin.

boiling water is stirred into gelatin until granules dissolve, and then the cold liquid and other ingredients are added. Follow the package label for exact proportions of solids this type of gelatin will support.

Unflavored gelatin is packaged in envelopes that contain enough to gel 2 cups liquid. It adds no color, flavor, or sugar to the recipe. When working with this type of gelatin, first soften the gelatin in cold water 1 to 5 minutes to make the particles swell. Then dissolve it by adding hot liquid, and cooking and stirring over low heat until it's clear and no granules remain.

With both types of gelatin, the granules must be properly dissolved before adding other ingredients, otherwise the end product will not be firm enough to hold its shape.

WATCH WHAT YOU ADD TO THE SALAD

You can add fruit, vegetables, and meat to the salad as specified on the gelatin package. Don't add more or the salad may not mold. In general, finely chop all added ingredients; large pieces may cause the salad to crumble upon slicing.

Lemon juice, vinegar, wine, and other acids will make the mold softer and more fragile. One to two tablespoons of an acid per cup of liquid are probably the most you'll want to add to a shaped dish. Never use fresh pineapple pulp or juice, kiwifruit, or papaya in a gelatin salad. This fresh fruit contains an enzyme that prevents gelatin from setting up; canned pineapple and juice is fine to use, as the canning process destroys the enzyme.

If serving your congealed salad outdoors in warm weather, place the plate on a bed of crushed ice rather than add extra gelatin. Too much gelatin will make the salad tough and rubbery.

SELECTING A MOLD

Use the size mold indicated in the recipe. If the mold is too small, you'll have too much gelatin mixture. If the mold is too large, the ingredients won't completely fill the mold, and you'll lose the effect of the shape. For ease in unmolding, lightly oil the mold with vegetable oil before adding the gelatin mixture.

CHILL TO THE CONSISTENCY OF UNBEATEN EGG WHITE

Chilling the gelatin mixture to the consistency of an unbeaten egg white means to refrigerate the mixture until it's only slightly thick or looks like an egg white from a just broken egg. Chilling takes 20 to 40 minutes, depending on the amount of mixture. Don't let the mixture congeal too much because then the solids are difficult to add. If the gelatin is too firm, set the container of gelatin in a bowl of warm water and stir until the mixture softens enough to add the solids.

UMOLDING THE SALAD

After your shaped dish has completely congealed, carefully unmold. To break the suction, run a knife around the edge of the mold. If the mold has fluted sides, press the edge of the salad lightly with your finger and gently pull away from the sides. Unmold the salad using the hot towel method. Wet a dish towel with hot water, and wring it out. Wrap the towel around the bottom and sides of the container, and let it stand for 1 or 2 minutes. Then place a serving platter on top of the mold and invert. If it doesn't unmold, repeat the process.

AMBROSIA CREAM CHEESE MOLD

1 envelope unflavored gelatin
½ cup cold water
1 (15½-ounce) can pineapple chunks, undrained
⅓ cup sugar
Juice of 1 lemon
2 (3-ounce) packages cream cheese, softened
1 orange, peeled, sectioned, and diced
½ cup chopped pecans
½ cup flaked coconut
Lettuce leaves (optional)
Lemon slices (optional)

Sprinkle gelatin over cold water; let stand 1 minute.

Drain pineapple, and reserve juice; add enough water to juice to make 1 cup. Place juice in a 2-quart saucepan; heat to boiling; add gelatin mixture, and stir until gelatin dissolves. Remove from heat; stir in sugar, lemon juice, and cream cheese, using a wire whisk to blend. Chill until consistency of unbeaten egg white; fold in pineapple chunks, orange, pecans, and coconut.

Spoon mixture into a lightly oiled 1-quart mold; cover and chill until firm. Unmold on lettuce; garnish with lemon slices, if desired. Yield: 6 servings.

HIDDEN TREASURE STRAWBERRY SALAD

3 (3-ounce) packages strawberry-flavored gelatin
1 cup boiling water
1 (10-ounce) package frozen sliced strawberries, partially thawed
1 (15¼-ounce) can crushed pineapple, drained
3 medium bananas, mashed
½ cup coarsely chopped pecans
1 (8-ounce) carton commercial sour cream

Dissolve gelatin in boiling water; stir in fruit and pecans. Pour half of gelatin mixture into oiled 12- x 8- x 2-inch dish; chill until firm. Store remaining mixture at room temperature.

Spread sour cream over congealed fruit mixture. Spoon remaining gelatin mixture over sour cream; cover and chill until firm. Yield: 12 servings.

PERFECTION SALAD

2 envelopes unflavored gelatin
1½ cups cold water
½ cup sugar
¼ teaspoon salt
1½ cups water
½ cup vinegar
2 tablespoons lemon juice
1½ cups finely shredded cabbage
¾ cup sliced celery
½ cup shredded carrot
½ cup chopped green pepper
½ cup sliced pimiento-stuffed olives

Sprinkle gelatin over 1½ cups cold water in a saucepan; let stand 1 minute. Add sugar and salt; cook over low heat, stirring until gelatin dissolves.

Stir 1½ cups water, vinegar, and lemon juice into gelatin mixture; chill until consistency of unbeaten egg white. Fold in remaining ingredients; pour into a lightly oiled 5-cup mold. Cover and chill until firm. Yield: 8 servings.

FALL FRUIT MOLD WITH GINGER DRESSING

1 (3-ounce) package apricot-flavored gelatin
2 cups boiling water
⅓ cup coarsely chopped dates
2 medium unpeeled pears, cored and diced (about 1 cup)
2 medium unpeeled apples, cored and diced (about 1 cup)
⅓ cup chopped walnuts
Lettuce leaves (optional)
Ginger Dressing

Dissolve gelatin in boiling water; stir in dates. Chill until consistency of unbeaten egg white.

Fold in pears, apples, and walnuts. Pour into a lightly oiled 4-cup mold; cover and chill until firm. Unmold on lettuce leaves, if desired; serve with Ginger Dressing. Yield: 6 servings.

Ginger Dressing

⅓ cup mayonnaise
⅓ cup commercial sour cream
2 tablespoons minced crystallized ginger

Combine all ingredients, stirring well. Chill. Yield: ⅔ cup.

CRANBERRY FRUIT SALAD MOLD

1 (8¼-ounce) can pineapple tidbits
2 (3-ounce) packages raspberry-flavored gelatin
2 cups boiling water
1 cup cold water
2 tablespoons lemon juice
½ unpeeled orange, seeded and quartered
2 cups fresh cranberries
¼ cup sugar
1 (11-ounce) can mandarin orange sections, drained

Drain pineapple, reserving ⅓ cup juice. Dissolve gelatin in boiling water; add cold water, reserved pineapple juice, and lemon juice. Chill until the consistency of unbeaten egg white.

Position knife blade in food processor bowl; add orange. Top with cover; process 1 minute or until chopped. Add cranberries, and process 1 minute. Combine cranberry mixture, sugar, pineapple, and mandarin oranges in a large bowl, stirring well. Stir cranberry mixture into gelatin. Pour into a lightly oiled 6-cup mold; cover and chill until firm. Yield: 10 to 12 servings.

1. *Start with unflavored gelatin. Sprinkle gelatin over 1½ cups tomato juice; let stand 1 minute for gelatin particles to swell.*

2. *Cook gelatin mixture over low heat until gelatin dissolves; stir in onion, salt, and remaining tomato juice.*

3. *Chill mixture until the consistency of unbeaten egg white. Fold in chopped vegetables, and spoon into an oiled mold. Chill.*

4. *Unmold salad on a lettuce-lined plate.*

Arrange lettuce in center of mold. Spoon Blue Cheese Dressing onto lettuce.

TOMATO ASPIC WITH BLUE CHEESE DRESSING

3 envelopes unflavored gelatin
1 (46-ounce) can tomato juice, divided
2 tablespoons grated onion
½ teaspoon salt
1 cup chopped green pepper
1 cup chopped celery
Lettuce leaves
1 (3-ounce) package cream cheese, softened
¼ cup milk
1 (4-ounce) package blue cheese, crumbled
Twist of lemon

Sprinkle gelatin over 1½ cups tomato juice; let stand 1 minute. Cook mixture over medium heat until gelatin dissolves. Stir in onion, salt, and remaining tomato juice. Chill until the consistency of unbeaten egg white. Fold in green pepper and celery; spoon into a lightly oiled 6-cup ring mold. Cover and chill until firm. Unmold onto a lettuce-lined plate; arrange a lettuce cup in center.

Combine cream cheese and milk; beat at medium speed of an electric mixer until blended. Add blue cheese, and beat until blended. Spoon dressing into center of mold, and garnish with a twist of lemon. Yield: 10 to 12 servings.

TUNA CONGEALED SALAD

2 envelopes unflavored gelatin
1 cup cold water
1 (10¾-ounce) can tomato soup, undiluted
¼ teaspoon pepper
2 (3-ounce) packages cream cheese, softened
1 cup mayonnaise
1 (9¼-ounce) can tuna, drained and flaked
1 cup diced celery
¼ cup chopped green pepper
¼ cup finely chopped onion
Lettuce leaves (optional)
Cherry tomatoes (optional)

Sprinkle gelatin over cold water; let stand 1 minute. Heat soup in a medium saucepan. Add softened gelatin mixture and pepper, stirring until gelatin dissolves; remove from heat.

Combine cream cheese and mayonnaise; add to soup mixture, stirring well. Stir in tuna and next 3 ingredients. Spoon into a lightly oiled 5-cup mold; cover and chill until firm. Unmold on lettuce-lined plate, and garnish with tomatoes, if desired. Yield: 6 to 8 servings.

CUCUMBER SALAD MOUSSE

4 medium cucumbers
3 envelopes unflavored gelatin
⅓ cup cold water
⅔ cup commercial sour cream
⅔ cup mayonnaise or salad dressing
1½ tablespoons grated onion
1 tablespoon lemon juice
¾ teaspoon salt
¼ teaspoon dried whole dillweed
⅓ cup whipping cream
Lettuce leaves
Cucumber slices (optional)

Peel cucumbers, and cut in half lengthwise; scoop out and discard seeds. Coarsely chop cucumbers, and place in container of an electric blender or food processor; process until smooth. Set aside 2⅔ cups puree.

Sprinkle gelatin over cold water in a small saucepan; let stand 1 minute. Cook over medium heat, stirring until gelatin is dissolved.

Combine sour cream, mayonnaise, onion, lemon juice, salt, and dillweed in a large bowl, mixing well; stir in 2⅔ cups cucumber puree and gelatin, and set aside.

Beat whipping cream until thickened but not stiff; fold into cucumber mixture. Pour mixture into 8 lightly oiled individual ½-cup molds; cover and chill until firm.

Unmold individual salads onto lettuce-lined salad plates, and garnish each with cucumber slices, if desired. Yield: 8 servings.

Meat and Seafood Salads

You'll enjoy serving these meat and seafood salads because they're hearty enough to be the main meal. Accompany them with French bread, breadsticks, or crackers, and perhaps fresh cut vegetables or a vegetable or fruit salad. Look for more meat salads in the section on green salads.

Since all of these salads include some type of cooked meat or seafood, remember to start preparation early if you plan to serve it for dinner. You'll want to leave plenty of time for the salad to chill.

TUNA-EGG SALAD

4 hard-cooked eggs
1 (9¼-ounce) can tuna, drained and flaked
1 cup sliced celery
¼ cup chopped green onions
¼ cup sweet pickle relish
¼ cup mayonnaise
¼ teaspoon lemon-pepper seasoning
⅛ teaspoon salt
3 drops of hot sauce

Coarsely chop 3 eggs. Combine chopped eggs and remaining ingredients except whole egg; stir well. Cover and chill. Slice remaining egg. Garnish salad with egg slices. Yield: 4 to 6 servings.

SEAFOOD SALAD

2 cups cooked shrimp, crabmeat, lobster, or tuna
3 hard-cooked eggs, chopped
¾ cup chopped celery
¼ to ⅓ cup mayonnaise
2 teaspoons lemon juice
⅛ teaspoon pepper
Salt to taste
Lettuce leaves (optional)
Lemon wedges (optional)

Combine first 7 ingredients; cover and chill. To serve, spoon mixture onto lettuce leaves, and garnish with lemon wedges, if desired. Yield: 4 servings.

CHICKEN SALAD

4 cups chopped cooked chicken
2 cups thinly sliced celery
¾ cup mayonnaise
¼ cup whipping cream
¼ cup sweet pickle relish
2 tablespoons minced onion
1 tablespoon lemon juice
½ teaspoon salt
White pepper to taste

Combine chicken and celery. Combine remaining ingredients, stirring well; add to chicken mixture, and toss well. Cover and chill. Yield: 6 servings.

MANDARIN CHICKEN SALAD

3 cups diced cooked chicken
1 cup diced celery
2 tablespoons lemon juice
1 tablespoon minced onion
½ teaspoon salt
⅓ cup mayonnaise
1 cup seedless green grapes
1 (11-ounce) can mandarin oranges, drained
1 (2-ounce) package slivered almonds, toasted
Leaf lettuce
Additional mandarin orange slices (optional)
Clusters of green grapes (optional)

Combine first 5 ingredients; stir well. Cover and chill.

Add mayonnaise, grapes, oranges, and almonds to chicken mixture; toss well. Serve on lettuce. Garnish with additional orange slices and grape clusters, if desired. Yield: 6 servings.

Mandarin Chicken Salad is a blend of the traditional chicken salad ingredients with fruits and nuts. It's fancy enough for company.

SALMON SALAD

1 (15½-ounce) can salmon
2 cups shredded cabbage
¼ cup diced celery
¼ cup sliced pitted ripe olives
½ cup mayonnaise
Lettuce leaves
Tomato wedges

Drain salmon, and flake with a fork. Add cabbage, celery, and olives; stir gently, and fold in mayonnaise. Cover and chill 2 hours.

To serve, spoon onto lettuce leaves, and garnish with tomato wedges. Yield: 4 to 6 servings.

CRAB LOUIS

5 cups mixed salad greens
3 large tomatoes, cut into wedges
6 hard-cooked eggs, quartered
18 pitted ripe olives
¾ cup chili sauce
¾ cup mayonnaise
¼ cup chopped green pepper
¼ cup chopped green onions
1 teaspoon lemon juice
1 pound cooked fresh crabmeat, drained and flaked

Arrange salad greens on individual salad plates. Arrange tomatoes, eggs, and olives over greens.

Combine chili sauce, mayonnaise, green pepper, green onions, and lemon juice; drizzle over salad. Top salad with crabmeat. Yield: 6 servings.

LOBSTER AND ORANGE SALAD

¼ cup whipping cream, whipped
2 tablespoons orange juice
1 tablespoon mayonnaise
¼ teaspoon prepared horseradish
¼ teaspoon grated orange rind
3 large oranges, peeled and sectioned
Lettuce leaves
1 (5-ounce) can lobster, drained and flaked, or 1 cup coarsely chopped cooked lobster, chilled
Ground nutmeg

Combine first 5 ingredients; stir well. Cover and chill 1 hour.

Arrange orange sections on lettuce leaves; top with lobster. Spoon dressing over lobster, and sprinkle with nutmeg. Yield: 2 to 4 servings.

SCALLOP-AVOCADO SALAD

1 pound fresh scallops
1 tomato, chopped
¼ cup chopped green onions
½ cup olive oil
3 tablespoons white wine vinegar
¼ cup chopped fresh basil leaves or 1 tablespoon plus 1 teaspoon dried whole basil
¼ teaspoon salt
⅛ teaspoon white pepper
2 avocados
¼ cup chopped walnuts, lightly toasted
Lettuce leaves

Place scallops in boiling water to cover; reduce heat and simmer 4 minutes. Drain. Combine scallops, tomato, and green onions in a bowl.

Combine oil, vinegar, basil, salt, and pepper in a jar. Cover tightly, and shake vigorously. Pour over scallop mixture. Cover and chill at least 8 hours.

Peel and dice avocado just before serving. Toss avocado and walnuts with scallop mixture, and spoon over lettuce leaves. Yield: 4 servings.

Neat Containers for Salads

Dress up plain chicken or seafood salad by serving it in a fruit or vegetable cup for company. A shell made from tomato, green pepper, avocado, melon, or pineapple makes an attractive presentation.

Dressings

The dressing is perhaps the most crucial component of a salad. If it's too salty, too bland, too oily, or too strongly seasoned, it can ruin the entire salad. The amount of dressing is critical, too. Too much dressing softens the greens and will settle in the bottom of the bowl.

When serving a dressed salad for company, either toss the entire salad with the dressing in a large bowl, using just enough to lightly coat the vegetables, and transfer the vegetables to the individual salad plates, or serve the dressing on the side for each guest to add.

MINT DRESSING

1 cup sugar
⅓ cup water
1 tablespoon lemon juice
½ cup loosely packed fresh mint leaves

Combine sugar, water, and lemon juice in a small saucepan; bring to a boil, stirring occasionally. Remove from heat.

Combine sugar mixture and mint leaves in container of an electric blender or food processor; process until leaves are finely chopped. Cover and chill dressing 2 to 3 hours. Serve dressing over fresh fruit. Yield: 1 cup.

PINEAPPLE-CREAM DRESSING

1 cup pineapple juice
2 egg yolks, beaten
Juice of 1 lemon
½ cup sugar
1 tablespoon prepared mustard
Dash of salt
1 cup whipping cream, whipped

Combine first 6 ingredients in a small saucepan. Cook over low heat, stirring occasionally, until smooth and thickened (about 30 minutes). Cool; fold in whipped cream just before serving. Serve over fruit. Yield: 2¾ cups.

BLENDER POPPY SEED DRESSING

¾ cup vegetable oil
⅓ cup honey
¼ cup red wine vinegar
2 tablespoons poppy seeds
1 tablespoon minced onion
1 tablespoon Dijon mustard
½ teaspoon salt

Combine all ingredients in container of an electric blender; process on low speed 30 seconds. Cover and chill; stir well before serving. Yield: 1⅓ cups.

HOMEMADE MAYONNAISE

Homemade Mayonnaise is a novelty to make and lacks the preservatives of some brands of commercial mayonnaise. Use it to bind simple salads or as a base to make other dressings, such as Chive Dressing, Green Goddess Dressing, or Thousand Island Dressing.

2 egg yolks
2 cups vegetable oil
2 tablespoons lemon juice
¾ teaspoon dry mustard
½ teaspoon salt
Dash of paprika
3 drops of hot sauce

Beat egg yolks in a deep, narrow bowl at high speed of an electric mixer until thick and lemon colored. Add oil, 1 tablespoon at a time; beat until mixture begins to thicken. Gradually add lemon juice, beating until thickened. Add remaining ingredients, stirring well. Spoon mayonnaise into a glass or plastic container; cover and chill. Do not store mayonnaise in a metal container. Yield: 2½ cups.

CHIVE DRESSING

¾ cup Homemade Mayonnaise
3 tablespoons chopped chives
1½ tablespoons lemon juice
⅛ teaspoon pepper

Combine all ingredients, stirring well; cover and chill. Yield: ¾ cup.
Note: Commercial mayonnaise may be substituted for Homemade Mayonnaise.

GREEN GODDESS DRESSING

⅓ cup coarsely chopped fresh parsley
1 cup Homemade Mayonnaise
⅓ cup chopped chives
3 tablespoons tarragon vinegar
1 tablespoon anchovy paste
⅛ teaspoon salt
1 clove garlic, crushed

Place parsley in container of an electric blender; process 1 minute. Add remaining ingredients; process until smooth. Cover and chill. Yield: 1¼ cups.
Note: Commercial mayonnaise may be substituted for Homemade Mayonnaise.

THOUSAND ISLAND DRESSING

1 cup Homemade Mayonnaise
½ cup chili sauce
3 tablespoons coarsely chopped pimiento-stuffed olives
1 tablespoon chopped fresh parsley
1 tablespoon diced pimiento
1 tablespoon honey
½ teaspoon lemon juice
¼ teaspoon onion powder
12 capers

Combine first 2 ingredients. Stir in remaining ingredients. Cover and chill at least 1 hour. Yield: about 2 cups.
Note: Commercial mayonnaise may be substituted for Homemade Mayonnaise.

YOGURT-DILL DRESSING

Try substituting yogurt for mayonnaise or sour cream when you want a dressing that's lower in fat. Its flavor is more tart than mayonnaise or sour cream-based dressings, but the consistency is very similar. (Don't substitute yogurt for sour cream when the dressing is cooked or when it's processed in a blender or food processor. These conditions can cause yogurt to break down.) Try this Yogurt-Dill Dressing over salad greens.

1 (8-ounce) carton plain low-fat yogurt
1½ tablespoons lemon juice
1 teaspoon chopped onion
½ teaspoon salt
¼ to ½ teaspoon dried whole dillweed
⅛ teaspoon freshly ground pepper
1 clove garlic, minced

Combine all ingredients, stirring well. Cover and chill dressing at least 1 hour. Yield: 1 cup.

SPICY FRENCH DRESSING

(pictured on page 432)

1 cup vegetable oil
½ cup catsup
½ cup honey
⅓ cup cider vinegar
½ teaspoon paprika
¼ teaspoon garlic powder
¼ teaspoon celery salt
⅛ teaspoon onion powder

Combine all ingredients in container of an electric blender; process on low speed 1 minute or until smooth. Cover and chill thoroughly. Stir well before serving. Yield: 2 cups.

Homemade dressings add that extra freshness to salad greens. From left: Spicy French Dressing (page 431), Herb Vinaigrette (page 433), and Blue Cheese Dressing (page 433).

BUTTERMILK DRESSING

1 cup mayonnaise
½ cup buttermilk
1 tablespoon parsley flakes
½ teaspoon onion powder
¼ teaspoon garlic powder
¼ teaspoon white pepper
⅛ teaspoon salt

Combine all ingredients, stirring well. Cover and chill dressing at least 4 hours. Serve with coleslaw or tossed salad. Yield: 1½ cups.

SWEET-AND-SOUR DRESSING

1 cup vegetable oil
½ cup vinegar
½ cup sugar
1 teaspoon salt
1 teaspoon celery seeds
1 teaspoon dry mustard
1 teaspoon paprika
1 teaspoon grated onion

Combine all ingredients in a jar. Cover tightly, and shake vigorously. Chill several hours. Shake again before serving over salad. Yield: 1¾ cups.

BLUE CHEESE DRESSING

(pictured on opposite page)

1 cup mayonnaise
¾ cup buttermilk
1½ (4-ounce) packages blue cheese, crumbled
7 drops of hot sauce
1 tablespoon dried Italian seasoning
1 tablespoon dried parsley flakes
1 teaspoon steak sauce
1 clove garlic, pressed

Combine all ingredients; stir well. Cover and chill. Yield: about 2¼ cups.

CREAMY CAESAR SALAD DRESSING

3 eggs
1 stalk celery, coarsely chopped
½ cup coarsely chopped onion
1 (2-ounce) can anchovies, drained
2 cloves garlic
2 tablespoons prepared mustard
1 tablespoon lemon juice
1 teaspoon pepper
2 cups vegetable oil

Combine first 8 ingredients in container of an electric blender; process until smooth. Add oil, ¼ cup at a time, processing after each addition. Cover and chill dressing thoroughly. Yield: about 3½ cups.

HOT BACON DRESSING

4 slices bacon
2 tablespoons cider vinegar
2 tablespoons water
1 tablespoon sugar
1 egg, beaten

Cook bacon in a large skillet until crisp; remove bacon, reserving drippings in skillet. Crumble bacon, and set aside.

Add vinegar, water, and sugar to drippings in skillet; bring to a boil. Remove from heat. Gradually stir one-fourth of hot mixture into beaten egg; add egg mixture to skillet, stirring constantly until blended. Cook over low heat, stirring constantly, until thickened. Stir in bacon. Immediately toss warm dressing over salad greens. Yield: about ½ cup.

HERB VINAIGRETTE

(pictured on opposite page)

1¼ cups vegetable oil
½ cup white wine vinegar
¼ cup chopped fresh basil, oregano, chives, or tarragon, or a combination of these herbs
½ teaspoon salt
⅛ teaspoon pepper

Combine all ingredients in a jar; cover tightly, and shake vigorously. Chill thoroughly. Yield: 2 cups.

CREAMY ITALIAN-STYLE SALAD DRESSING

1 cup mayonnaise
2 tablespoons vinegar
2 tablespoons olive oil
1 tablespoon milk
½ teaspoon garlic powder
½ teaspoon ground oregano

Combine all ingredients, stirring well. Cover and chill. Yield: 1 cup.

ZIPPY ITALIAN DRESSING

1⅓ cups vegetable oil
½ cup tarragon vinegar
¼ cup grated Parmesan cheese
10 pimiento-stuffed olives
2 green onions, coarsely chopped
3 or 4 cloves garlic
2 tablespoons chopped fresh parsley
1 tablespoon lemon juice
2 teaspoons freshly ground pepper
1½ teaspoons anchovy paste
1 teaspoon sugar
1 teaspoon dried whole basil
1 teaspoon dried whole oregano
¼ teaspoon salt

Combine all ingredients in container of an electric blender; blend well. Cover and chill at least 1 hour. Yield: 2 cups.

SAUCES

Most sauces are made from just a few simple ingredients, but the results are extraordinary. Sauces turn simple foods like steamed broccoli into company fare. And you can only imagine what a hot fudge sundae would be without a thick and chocolaty sauce.

EQUIPMENT

Sauces require little special equipment; your most frequently used tools will include a wooden spoon, a wire whisk, and a heavy saucepan. Some sauces based on eggs and cream require a double boiler to keep them from curdling, while others call for an electric blender to mix and chop ingredients.

STIRRING UP THE SAUCE

The base of many sauces is a butter and flour mixture called a roux; it's like the roux used in many gumbos, but it's not cooked as long, usually only 1 minute. This short cooking time is just long enough to release the starch from the flour, prevent the sauce from lumping, and eliminate a pasty flavor. This type sauce takes approximately 2 tablespoons flour to thicken 1 cup liquid.

Sauces made with a roux must be stirred constantly as they cook to prevent lumping. If you must leave a sauce for a moment while it is cooking, take it off the heat.

Cornstarch is another thickening agent commonly used for sauces. It has twice the thickening power of flour; about 1 tablespoon cornstarch

Spoon Mushroom Brown Sauce, a variation of Basic Brown Sauce (page 436), over any of your favorite cuts of beef.

will thicken 1 cup liquid. Sauces thickened with cornstarch have a more transparent look, so this thickening agent is commonly used for dessert sauces.

Never add cornstarch or flour directly to a hot mixture because it will lump. Instead, combine the cornstarch or flour with about twice as much cold liquid, and stir until smooth. Then gently stir the cold

mixture into the hot mixture. Cook, stirring gently, until it comes to a full boil. Boil for at least 1 minute. It takes only a short time for the starch granules to swell, absorb some of the liquid, and thicken the mixture.

Don't think that the longer you cook a cornstarch mixture, the thicker it will become. Overcooking can cause the sauce to become thin and runny. Remember, the mixture may look too thin while cooking but will thicken as it cools.

If you're making a sauce with an acid ingredient, such as lemon juice, cook the cornstarch mixture until thickened. Then remove from heat, and gently stir in the acid. If you cook an acid, it tends to reduce the thickening ability of the cornstarch and the result will be a runny sauce.

Eggs are another common thickening agent. Sauces such as hollandaise and béarnaise get their luscious consistency from eggs. Just remember that thickening with eggs can be tricky. They must be handled carefully to prevent curdling. Don't overcook the eggs or use heat that is too high. Rather, heat them slowly, and stir constantly.

When your recipe requires adding

eggs to a hot mixture, a special technique called tempering helps prevent lumping. First, beat the eggs slightly; warm them by gradually stirring in about one-fourth of the hot mixture. Then stir the tempered egg mixture into the remaining hot mixture. Cook, stirring constantly, until thickened. Try this method for a smooth and creamy mixture.

FREEZING SAUCES

You probably won't want to freeze sauces often since they usually have small yields and are so quick to make, but many sauces can be frozen. Flour-based and tomato-based sauces freeze best. Pack them in rigid plastic containers, leaving at least ½-inch headspace. Thaw sauces at room temperature or in the refrigerator, or cook them over very low heat in a heavy saucepan or double boiler, stirring gently. Use a wire whisk to smooth out sauces that have separated.

Gravy and other sauces with a high fat content don't freeze well.

For gravy, it's best to freeze the broth base, and thicken it as you reheat it.

MICROWAVING SAUCES

Making sauces is one of the best uses of a microwave oven. They're quick to make, and they usually don't entail the problems of lumping, scorching, and constant stirring.

A glass measure or casserole dish is ideal for microwaving sauces. Just be sure it's large enough to prevent the sauce from boiling over. A sauce yielding 1 to 2 cups should be cooked in a 1-quart container.

Microwave sauces need to be stirred occasionally to mix the cooked portion near the outside with the uncooked portion in the center. Stirring at 1- to 2-minute intervals is usually sufficient; check your recipe for specifics. The microwave oven is excellent for reheating leftover sauces and heating commercially prepared sauces. Sauces purchased or stored in glass containers can be heated in that container. (Remove

the lids first.) Sauces that aren't especially delicate (that is, they don't have a lot of eggs or heavy cream) can usually be heated at HIGH, stirring at 1-minute intervals. The times will vary depending on the amount of sauce reheated.

WHAT WENT WRONG

Lumps can sometimes be removed by pouring the sauce through a fine sieve or by whirling it in the blender. An overly thick sauce can be thinned by gradually adding milk, a tablespoon at a time, as the sauce cooks. If too thin, blend additional flour and milk or water together and add to the sauce, cooking and beating until thickened.

To rescue a curdled hollandaise or béarnaise sauce, combine a teaspoon of lemon juice and a tablespoon of curdled sauce. Beat with a wire whisk until mixture is thick and creamy. Gradually beat in remaining sauce, a tablespoon at a time, making sure each addition has thickened before adding the next.

Vegetable and Meat Sauces

From the basic brown and white sauces to the more sophisticated remoulade and mornay sauces, these recipes will suit your sauce needs over and over. None are exclusively for meats; none are exclusiviely for vegetables. Just glance through the recipes on the next few pages, and pick out a flavor you think will complement your menu.

BASIC BROWN SAUCE

4 thin slices onion
1½ tablespoons butter or margarine, melted
1½ tablespoons all-purpose flour
1 teaspoon beef-flavored bouillon granules
1 cup water
⅛ teaspoon pepper

Sauté onion in butter in a heavy skillet until onion is tender; discard onion. Cook butter over low heat until it begins to brown. Add flour, stirring until smooth. Cook 1 minute, stirring constantly. Add bouillon granules, and

gradually stir in water. Cook over medium heat, stirring constantly, until thickened and bubbly. Stir in pepper. Serve with beef or pork. Yield: 1 cup.

Bordelaise Sauce: Substitute ⅓ cup dry red wine for ⅓ cup of the water, and stir in ¾ teaspoon dried parsley flakes and ¼ teaspoon dried whole thyme; increase pepper to ¼ teaspoon. Serve with beef or pork.

Mushroom Brown Sauce: Sauté ½ cup sliced mushrooms in 2 tablespoons butter; drain and stir into Basic Brown Sauce. Serve with beef.

1. To make White Sauce, melt butter in a heavy saucepan; add flour, and stir until smooth.

2. Cook flour and butter mixture 1 minute, stirring constantly.

3. Gradually add milk, and cook over medium heat, stirring constantly, until thickened and bubbly.

4. Stir in desired seasonings; adding chopped fresh parsley turns it into Parsley Sauce.

WHITE SAUCE

Probably the most basic of all sauces, White Sauce can be transformed into a new and different sauce with the addition of selected seasonings, such as cheese, curry, or horseradish.

Thin White Sauce:

1 tablespoon butter or margarine
1 tablespoon all-purpose flour
1 cup milk
¼ teaspoon salt
Dash of white pepper

Medium White Sauce:

2 tablespoons butter or margarine
2 tablespoons all-purpose flour
1 cup milk
¼ teaspoon salt
Dash of white pepper

Thick White Sauce:

3 tablespoons butter or margarine
3 tablespoons all-purpose flour
1 cup milk
¼ teaspoon salt
Dash of white pepper

Melt butter in a heavy saucepan over low heat; add flour, stirring until smooth. Cook 1 minute, stirring constantly. Gradually add milk; cook over medium heat, stirring constantly, until thickened and bubbly. Stir in salt and pepper.

Serve over poached eggs, poultry, seafood, or vegetables. Yield: 1 cup.

☐ *Microwave Directions:* Place butter in a 1-quart glass measure. Microwave at HIGH for 45 seconds or until melted. Add flour, stirring until smooth. Gradually add milk, stirring well. Microwave at HIGH for 3 to 4 minutes or until thickened and bubbly, stirring after 2 minutes, then at 1-minute intervals.

Cheddar Cheese Sauce: Stir in 1 cup (4 ounces) shredded Cheddar cheese and ¼ teaspoon dry mustard with salt and pepper.

Curry Sauce: Stir in 1½ teaspoons curry powder and ⅛ teaspoon ground ginger with salt and pepper.

Dill Sauce: Stir in 1 teaspoon lemon juice and 1 tablespoon chopped fresh dillweed or 1 teaspoon dried dillweed with salt and pepper.

Horseradish Sauce: Stir in 1½ to 2 tablespoons prepared horseradish with salt and pepper.

Parsley Sauce: Stir in ¼ cup chopped fresh parsley with salt.

Velouté Sauce: Substitute 1 cup chicken, beef, or fish broth for milk. Omit salt if broth is salted.

Serve Parsley Sauce on the side, or spoon it over cooked vegetables.

HOLLANDAISE SAUCE

Hollandaise Sauce and its variations can be made by the cooktop or blender method, depending on your preference and equipment at hand. The blender version will be lighter in color and slightly thinner than the cooktop sauce.

3 egg yolks
⅛ teaspoon salt
Dash of red pepper
2 tablespoons lemon juice
½ cup butter or margarine

Cooktop Method

Beat egg yolks, salt, and red pepper in top of a double boiler; gradually add lemon juice, stirring constantly. Add about one-third of butter to egg mixture; cook over hot, not boiling water, stirring constantly, until butter melts.

Add another third of butter, stirring constantly; as sauce thickens, stir in remaining butter. Cook until thickened. Yield: about ¾ cup.

Blender Method

Place egg yolks, salt, red pepper, and lemon juice in container of an electric blender. Cover and blend at high speed about 5 seconds. Melt butter; with blender on high, gradually add melted butter in a slow steady stream. Blend about 30 seconds or until thickened. Yield: about ¾ cup.

Béarnaise Sauce: Combine 3 tablespoons white wine vinegar, 1 teaspoon minced green onion, and ¼ teaspoon coarsely ground pepper in a small saucepan; bring to a boil over medium heat. Reduce heat to low, and simmer until half the liquid evaporates. Pour mixture through a strainer, reserving liquid; discard solids. Let vinegar mixture cool slightly; stir in ½ teaspoon dried whole tarragon. Add to Hollandaise Sauce after butter is added. Immediately remove from heat. Serve sauce with vegetables, fish, or beef.

Mousseline Sauce: Cool Hollandaise Sauce to room temperature, if desired. Beat ¼ cup whipping cream until stiff peaks form. Fold whipped cream into sauce. Serve hot or cold over cooked vegetables or fish. Makes about 1 cup.

To make blender sauces: When adding liquids with blender running, remove the small center portion of the blender cap to prevent splatters; add liquid through center opening.

CHINESE HOT MUSTARD

Chinese Hot Mustard is similar to the mustard sauce often served in Chinese restaurants; a little of this pungent condiment goes a long way. Serve it with egg rolls and other Oriental dishes.

¼ cup dry mustard
1 teaspoon sugar
¼ cup boiling water
2 teaspoons vegetable oil

Combine mustard and sugar; stir in water and oil. Let stand 8 hours before serving. Store in refrigerator. Yield: about ⅓ cup.

MUSTARD SPREAD

½ cup sugar
¼ cup plus 1 tablespoon dry mustard
2 tablespoons all-purpose flour
½ teaspoon salt
1 cup milk
½ cup vinegar
1 egg yolk

Combine sugar, mustard, flour, and salt in a small saucepan; stir well. Combine remaining ingredients; beat well. Gradually stir milk mixture into mustard mixture; cook over low heat, stirring constantly, until thickened and bubbly. Cool thoroughly, and store in refrigerator. Serve as a meat or sandwich spread. Yield: 2 cups.

☐*Microwave Directions:* Combine sugar, mustard, flour, and salt in a 1-quart glass measure; stir well. Combine remaining ingredients; beat well. Gradually stir milk mixture into mustard mixture. Microwave at HIGH for 4 to 5 minutes or until thickened and bubbly, stirring after 2 minutes, then at 1-minute intervals. Cool thoroughly, and store in refrigerator.

CUCUMBER SAUCE

½ cup unpeeled, chopped cucumber
½ cup mayonnaise
½ cup commercial sour cream
1 to 2 tablespoons chopped chives
½ teaspoon dried parsley flakes
¼ teaspoon salt
¼ teaspoon dried whole dillweed

Combine all ingredients, stirring well. Cover and chill. Serve sauce with seafood, salmon loaf, or fresh vegetables. Yield: 1¼ cups.

HERBED YOGURT SAUCE

1 (8-ounce) carton plain low-fat yogurt
⅓ cup mayonnaise
¾ teaspoon dried whole thyme
¾ teaspoon dry mustard
½ teaspoon dried whole oregano
¼ teaspoon dried whole marjoram
1½ tablespoons tarragon vinegar
1 teaspoon soy sauce
1 clove garlic, minced

Combine all ingredients, stirring well. Cover and chill at least 1 hour. Serve over cooked, chilled vegetables or seafood. Yield: 1¼ cups.

FRESH PESTO

2 cups packed fresh basil, parsley, or coarsely chopped spinach
¾ cup grated Parmesan cheese
½ cup walnut pieces
2 large cloves garlic, cut in half
¼ teaspoon salt
¼ teaspoon freshly ground pepper
⅔ cup olive oil

Remove stems from basil. Wash leaves thoroughly in lukewarm water, and drain well.

Position knife blade in food processor bowl; add basil and next 5 ingredients, and top with cover. Process until smooth. With processor running, pour oil through food chute in a slow, steady stream until combined. Use immediately or place in an airtight container; refrigerate up to 1 week, or freeze up to 6 months. Yield: 1¾ cups.

Pesto Pointers

Pesto has many more uses than the one it's most known for—tossing with pasta. Our recipe makes 1¾ cups, just the right amount to toss over 1 pound of pasta. If you have leftovers, the mixture keeps well in an airtight container for up to a week in the refrigerator or freezes as long as six months. You might consider freezing the mixture in 1-tablespoon amounts in ice cube trays. Once frozen, pop the cubes from the tray, and store in a freezer bag. The following serving suggestions are so simple that you won't even need a recipe.

● Stir 2 tablespoons pesto into one 8-ounce carton of commercial sour cream for an instant dip for raw vegetables.

● Serve warmed pesto as a topper for baked potatoes. Allow about 1 tablespoon per potato.

● Spread a small amount of pesto over slices of French bread, and then toast before serving.

● Stir about 3 tablespoons pesto into a can of commercial tomato soup (diluted as the can directs). Soup with pesto will taste amazingly homemade!

● Try pesto as an omelet filling. Spoon about 2 tablespoons of the sauce over half of a three-egg omelet; then fold it over, and serve.

● Stir 2 tablespoons pesto into ½ cup softened unsalted butter. Serve the pesto butter as a bread spread or toss it with hot vegetables. Melt the butter for dipping shrimp or lobster.

Fresh Pesto and Herbed Yogurt Sauce complement all types of steamed fresh vegetables.

Liven up the bread and butter plates at your next dinner party by presenting guests with pretty herb butters. You can make them days in advance, and chill them until the impressive presentation.

These flavorful herb blends liven up grilled meats, steamed vegetables, and baked potatoes. Or use them as table butter for spreading on toast, rolls, or sandwiches. Reserve scraps from shaping the butter and that left after dinner for stirring into sauces or spreading on French bread slices before toasting.

GARLIC BUTTER

½ cup butter or margarine, softened
2 to 3 cloves garlic, minced

Cream butter until light and fluffy; blend in garlic. Spoon mixture into a butter crock, or shape as desired; chill until ready to serve. Yield: ½ cup.

Chive Butter: Stir in 2 tablespoons minced fresh or frozen chives. Omit garlic, if desired.

Herb Butter: Stir in 2 tablespoons minced fresh or 2 teaspoons dried whole basil, oregano, tarragon, or chervil, or a combination of the herbs. Omit garlic, if desired.

Parsley Butter: Stir in ¼ cup minced fresh parsley. Garlic may be omitted, if desired.

Colorful Sauce Containers

Make your own fresh vegetable containers to hold sauces. Cabbage, green pepper, and acorn squash work especially well. Cut a small slice from the bottom of the vegetable so it will sit flat, being careful not to cut into the cavity. Then cut a top slice from the vegetable, and carve out the pulp to leave a cavity for the sauce.

CLARIFIED BUTTER

1 cup butter

Melt butter over low heat. The fat will rise to the top, and the milk solids will sink to the bottom. Skim off the white froth that appears on top. Then strain off the clear, yellow butter, keeping back the sediment of milk solids. Chill clarified butter until ready to serve; then reheat. Yield: about ¾ cup.

Lemon Butter: Add ½ cup lemon juice to clarified butter, stirring well. Makes about 1¼ cups.

PICANTE SAUCE

Serve Picante Sauce as a dip for chips or as a sauce for meats and Tex-Mex entrées.

½ cup coarsely chopped onion
¼ cup chopped green pepper
1 clove garlic, minced
1 tablespoon olive or
vegetable oil
½ cup chopped tomato
1 to 2 tablespoons finely
chopped canned jalapeño pepper
¼ teaspoon dried whole
oregano
¼ teaspoon ground cumin
⅛ teaspoon salt
1½ tablespoons vinegar
1 (8-ounce) can tomato sauce

Sauté onion, green pepper, and garlic in hot oil. Combine vegetables and remaining ingredients except tomato sauce in container of an electric blender; process 2 to 3 seconds.

Combine vegetable mixture and tomato sauce, stirring well. Serve hot or cold. Yield: 1¾ cups.

CREOLE SAUCE

1 tomato, peeled and chopped
⅔ cup chopped onion
⅔ cup chopped green pepper
⅔ cup chopped celery
2 cloves garlic, minced
3 tablespoons butter or margarine,
melted
⅔ cup water
1 (8-ounce) can tomato sauce
1 chicken-flavored bouillon cube
½ teaspoon coarsely ground pepper
½ teaspoon dried whole oregano
½ teaspoon dried whole basil
¼ teaspoon red pepper
¼ teaspoon hot sauce
2 bay leaves

Sauté vegetables and garlic in butter in a large skillet. Stir in remaining ingredients. Bring to a boil; cover, reduce heat, and simmer 20 minutes, stirring occasionally. Remove bay leaves. Serve with chicken, seafood, or egg dishes. Yield: 2¾ cups.

◻*Microwave Directions:* Combine vegetables, garlic, and butter in a 2-quart casserole; cover with lid, and microwave at HIGH for 4 to 6 minutes or until vegetables are crisp-tender, stirring once. Stir in remaining ingredients; cover and microwave at HIGH for 8 to 10 minutes or until vegetables are done, stirring at 4-minute intervals. Remove bay leaves. Serve with chicken, seafood, or egg dishes.

MORNAY SAUCE

¼ cup butter or margarine
¼ cup all-purpose flour
2 cups milk
½ teaspoon salt
⅛ teaspoon white pepper
2 egg yolks
1 tablespoon whipping cream
¼ cup (1 ounce) shredded Swiss
cheese

Melt butter in a heavy 2-quart saucepan over low heat; add flour, stirring until smooth. Cook 1 minute, stirring constantly. Gradually add milk; cook over medium heat, stirring constantly, until thickened and bubbly. Stir in salt and pepper.

Beat egg yolks until thick and lemon colored; stir in whipping cream. Gradually stir about one-fourth of hot mixture into yolks; add to remaining hot mixture and cook, stirring constantly, until thickened (about 2 to 3 minutes). Add cheese; stir until melted. Remove from heat. Yield: 2¼ cups.

Be Creative With Sauces

Many times you can vary the liquid ingredients called for in a sauce recipe; for example, substitute chicken broth instead of milk in a white sauce. Just be sure to keep the amounts the same so the thickening agents will function properly. The only exception would be when substituting liquids with a higher acid content than the original liquid. (Some fruit juices and wine are high in acid.) Acids can alter the thickening ability of some thickening agents.

RAISIN SAUCE

1 cup firmly packed brown sugar
1½ tablespoons cornstarch
¾ cup raisins
½ cup water
2 tablespoons orange juice
2 tablespoons vinegar
1 tablespoon butter or margarine
⅛ teaspoon salt

Combine brown sugar and cornstarch in a small saucepan, stirring well; add remaining ingredients. Cook, uncovered, over low heat 15 minutes, stirring often. Serve with ham. Yield: 1 cup.

□*Microwave Directions:* Combine brown sugar and cornstarch in a 1-quart glass measure, stirring well; add remaining ingredients. Microwave at HIGH for 5 to 6 minutes or until thickened, stirring after 2 minutes, then at 1-minute intervals. Serve warm with ham.

TART CRANBERRY SAUCE

2 cups fresh cranberries
2 tablespoons water
2 tablespoons grated orange rind
½ teaspoon ground cinnamon
¼ teaspoon ground cloves
¼ teaspoon ground ginger
½ cup honey

Cook cranberries in water until cranberry skins pop (about 8 minutes). Stir in remaining ingredients. Serve warm or cold with turkey or ham. Yield: about 1½ cups.

□*Microwave Directions:* Combine cranberries and water in a 2-quart casserole. Cover with lid, and microwave at HIGH for 5 minutes or until cranberry skins pop. Stir in remaining ingredients. Serve warm or cold with turkey or ham.

JEZEBEL SAUCE

1 (18-ounce) jar pineapple preserves
1 (18-ounce) jar apple jelly
1 (1.12-ounce) can dry mustard
1 (5-ounce) jar prepared horseradish
1 tablespoon cracked peppercorns

Combine all ingredients; stir well. Pour sauce into airtight containers; store in refrigerator. Serve sauce over cream cheese with crackers as an appetizer spread or with pork or beef. Yield: 3⅔ cups.

TARTAR SAUCE

⅔ cup mayonnaise
2 tablespoons sweet pickle relish
1 tablespoon minced fresh parsley or 1 teaspoon dried parsley flakes
1 tablespoon capers
1 tablespoon grated onion
1 tablespoon lemon juice
Dash of hot sauce

Combine all ingredients, stirring well. Cover and chill several hours before serving. Yield: 1 cup.

ZIPPY COCKTAIL SAUCE

⅔ cup chili sauce
¼ cup lemon juice
2 to 3 tablespoons prepared horseradish
2 teaspoons Worcestershire sauce
¼ teaspoon hot sauce

Combine all ingredients, stirring until smooth. Cover and chill at least 2 hours. Yield: 1 cup.

REMOULADE SAUCE

1 cup mayonnaise
1 to 2 tablespoons lemon juice
1½ tablespoons Dijon mustard
1 tablespoon sweet pickle relish
1 teaspoon dried tarragon leaves
1 teaspoon dried chervil leaves
½ teaspoon anchovy paste

Combine all ingredients, stirring well. Cover and chill thoroughly. Serve with hot or cold meat, fish, or shellfish. Yield: 1 cup.

MINT SAUCE

¼ cup chopped fresh mint leaves
¼ cup light corn syrup
1½ tablespoons vinegar
1½ teaspoons cornstarch
¼ cup water

Combine mint leaves, corn syrup, and vinegar in a small saucepan. Combine cornstarch and water, stirring until blended. Add to mint mixture. Cook over medium heat until mixture thickens and bubbles, stirring constantly. Strain sauce, if desired. Yield: about ½ cup.

SWEET-AND-SOUR SAUCE

½ cup sugar
¼ cup white wine vinegar
2 tablespoons prepared mustard
1 teaspoon ground ginger
½ cup crushed pineapple, undrained
1 tablespoon cornstarch
½ cup pineapple juice

Combine sugar and vinegar in a small saucepan; cook over medium heat, stirring constantly, until sugar dissolves. Remove from heat; stir in mustard, ginger, and pineapple.

Combine cornstarch and juice, stirring until blended. Gradually stir about one-fourth of hot mixture into cornstarch mixture; add to remaining hot mixture, stirring constantly. Cook over medium heat, stirring constantly, until smooth and thickened. Yield: 1½ cups.

To keep sauces for later use: If a sauce is not to be served immediately, cover the surface entirely with plastic wrap or wax paper; this will prevent a thin skin from forming.

Marinades and Barbecue Sauces

Southerners grill outdoors almost all year-round, and any good outdoor chef needs a large variety of sauces and marinades from which to choose. We think you'll find this assortment varied enough in function and flavor to sauce up any meat or seafood you want to grill.

In general, the more you baste meat with a sauce, the more tender and juicy it will be; every 5 to 10 minutes is a good choice for most meats. For barbecue sauces and other sauces with a high sugar content, don't start basting before the last 30 or 45 minutes of cooking, or the sugar may start to burn on the meat.

OIL AND VINEGAR MARINADE

¼ cup vegetable oil
¼ cup red wine vinegar
¼ cup lemon juice
½ teaspoon sugar
½ teaspoon salt
½ teaspoon dried whole thyme
½ teaspoon pepper

Combine all ingredients; stir well. Use to marinate beef, pork, or poultry before cooking; use to baste during cooking. Yield: ¾ cup.

SWEET-AND-SOUR MARINADE

½ cup soy sauce
¼ cup pineapple juice
¼ cup vinegar
¼ cup firmly packed brown sugar
⅛ teaspoon garlic powder

Combine soy sauce, pineapple juice, vinegar, brown sugar, and garlic powder; stir well. Use to marinate beef or pork before cooking; use to baste during cooking. Yield: 1 cup.

ORIENTAL MARINADE

¾ cup soy sauce
⅔ cup vegetable oil
½ cup lemon juice
¼ cup Worcestershire sauce
¼ cup prepared mustard
2 cloves garlic, minced

Combine all ingredients; stir well. Use to marinate beef, pork, or chicken before cooking; use to baste during cooking. Yield: 2⅓ cups.

BURGUNDY MARINADE

½ cup Burgundy
¼ cup olive oil
1 clove garlic, minced
½ teaspoon coarsely ground pepper
½ teaspoon dried whole thyme
¼ teaspoon salt
¼ teaspoon dried whole rosemary, crushed
2 tablespoons chopped fresh parsley (optional)

Combine all ingredients; stir well. Use to marinate beef before cooking; use to baste during cooking. Yield: ¾ cup.

BUTTERY BASTING SAUCE

½ cup butter or margarine, melted
¼ cup lemon juice
3 tablespoons finely chopped onion
1 tablespoon Worcestershire sauce
1 teaspoon Dijon mustard
½ teaspoon salt
⅛ teaspoon pepper

Combine all ingredients in a saucepan. Bring to a boil; cover, reduce heat, and simmer 5 minutes. Use to baste chicken, pork chops, ribs, or kabobs. Yield: ¾ cup.

EASY BARBECUE SAUCE

1 (10-ounce) jar orange marmalade
1 (12-ounce) bottle chili sauce
¼ cup vinegar
1 tablespoon Worcestershire sauce
1½ teaspoons celery seeds

Combine all ingredients; stir well. Use to baste spareribs and other meats during cooking. Yield: 2 cups.

SOUTHERN BARBECUE SAUCE

2 cloves garlic, crushed
2 tablespoons butter or margarine, melted
1 cup catsup
1 cup water
¾ cup chili sauce
¼ cup firmly packed brown sugar
2 tablespoons prepared mustard
2 tablespoons Worcestershire sauce
1½ teaspoons celery seeds
½ teaspoon salt
1 or 2 dashes of hot sauce

Sauté garlic in butter 4 to 5 minutes in a medium saucepan. Add remaining ingredients; bring to a boil. Use to baste pork or chicken during cooking. Yield: 3½ cups.

◯*Microwave Directions:* Combine garlic and butter in a deep 1½-quart casserole; cover with lid. Microwave at HIGH for 1 minute. Add remaining ingredients; cover and microwave at HIGH for 8 to 10 minutes or until thoroughly heated. Use to baste pork or chicken during cooking.

FIERY BARBECUE SAUCE

½ cup water
½ cup catsup
⅓ cup firmly packed brown sugar
¼ cup Worcestershire sauce
¼ cup vinegar
¼ cup butter or margarine
2 tablespoons lemon juice
2 teaspoons dry mustard
2 teaspoons chili powder
2 teaspoons paprika
1 teaspoon red pepper
½ teaspoon salt

Combine all ingredients in a saucepan; cook over medium heat until sugar dissolves, stirring occasionally. Use as a basting sauce for pork chops or chicken during cooking. Yield: 2 cups.

◯*Microwave Directions:* Combine all ingredients in a 1-quart glass bowl. Cover with heavy-duty plastic wrap, and microwave at HIGH for 4 to 5 minutes or until mixture is thoroughly heated, stirring once. Use as a basting sauce for pork chops or chicken during cooking.

TANGY BARBECUE SAUCE

¾ cup chopped onion
¼ cup butter or margarine, melted
¾ cup catsup
⅓ cup lemon juice
2 tablespoons brown sugar
2 tablespoons water
2 tablespoons Worcestershire sauce
1½ tablespoons prepared mustard
1 teaspoon salt
½ teaspoon coarsely ground pepper

Sauté onion in butter in a medium saucepan until tender. Stir in remaining ingredients. Bring mixture to a boil; reduce heat and simmer, uncovered, 10 to 15 minutes. Use as a basting sauce for grilled beef, pork, or chicken. Yield: 1¼ cups.

WHITE BARBECUE SAUCE

1 cup mayonnaise
3 tablespoons vinegar
1 teaspoon coarsely ground pepper

Combine all ingredients, stirring well. Use as a basting sauce for grilled chicken. Yield: 1 cup.

Gravies

Gravies rely on the drippings from meat for their rich flavor and color. The drippings called for in recipes may be extended with bouillon or milk if the volume is too low; keep the proportions of liquid to thickening agents the same as in the recipe.

PAN GRAVY

Make Pan Gravy from the natural drippings left in the skillet or roasting pan by roasts, steaks, chops, or other meats.

Pan drippings (fat and juice)
2 tablespoons all-purpose flour
1 cup meat juices, broth, or water
¼ teaspoon salt
⅛ teaspoon pepper

Pour off all but 2 tablespoons pan drippings from pan. Add flour, stirring until smooth. Cook 1 minute, stirring constantly. Gradually add meat juice; cook over medium heat, stirring constantly, until thickened and bubbly. Stir in salt and pepper. Yield: 1 cup.

POT ROAST GRAVY

Make Pot Roast Gravy from the liquid in which pot roast has simmered. If the simmering liquid was highly seasoned, you might need to omit the salt and pepper.

¼ cup cold water
2 tablespoons all-purpose flour
1 cup broth from pot roast
¼ teaspoon salt
⅛ teaspoon pepper

Combine water and flour in a jar; cover tightly, and shake until thoroughly blended. Stir flour mixture slowly into broth in a saucepan. Cook over medium heat until thickened, stirring constantly. Add salt and pepper. Yield: 1¼ cups.

□*Microwave Directions:* Combine water and flour in a jar; cover tightly, and shake until thoroughly blended. Stir flour mixture slowly into broth in a 2-cup glass measure. Microwave at HIGH for 2½ to 3 minutes or until thickened, stirring at 1-minute intervals. Add salt and pepper.

Note: If pot roast broth is salty, salt in gravy recipe may be reduced or omitted.

CREAM GRAVY

Cream Gravy is the typical accompaniment to Southern fried chicken. In many homes, one is never served without the other. This gravy can also be made from drippings of meat other than fried chicken.

¼ cup pan drippings
¼ cup all-purpose flour
2½ to 3 cups hot milk
½ teaspoon salt
⅛ to ¼ teaspoon pepper

Pour off all except ¼ cup drippings from skillet in which chicken was fried; place skillet over medium heat. Add flour, and stir until browned. Gradually add hot milk; cook, stirring constantly, until thickened and bubbly. Stir in salt and pepper. Serve hot. Yield: 2¾ cups.

Doctoring a Light-Colored Sauce

If your sauce is not dark enough in color, add a few splashes of commercial browning and seasoning sauce. Be sure to add it before you add your other seasonings, as it does add flavor as well as color. You may want to reduce the other seasonings.

To make Cream Gravy or Pan Gravy: Stir flour into premeasured hot drippings that remain in skillet; cook and stir 1 minute until the mixture is smooth. Then add liquid and seasonings.

To make Pot Roast Gravy: Measure the amount of broth you want to thicken; combine ¼ cup water and 2 tablespoons flour for each cup of broth. Shake flour mixture in a jar, and stir into broth. Cook until thickened.

GIBLET GRAVY

Giblets and neck from 1 turkey or
   chicken
1 small onion, chopped
2 stalks celery, chopped
½ teaspoon salt
Pan drippings from 1 roasted turkey
   or chicken
3 tablespoons all-purpose flour
¼ cup water
1 hard-cooked egg, chopped
¼ teaspoon pepper

Combine giblets (except liver), neck, onion, celery, and salt in a saucepan. (Set liver aside.) Cover with water. Bring to a boil; cover, reduce heat, and simmer 45 minutes or until giblets are fork tender. Add liver, and simmer an additional 10 minutes. Drain, reserving broth. Remove meat from neck; coarsely chop neck meat and giblets. Set aside.

Skim fat from pan drippings of roasted poultry; discard fat. Add re-served broth to pan drippings; stir until sediment is loosened from bottom of roaster. Measure broth mixture; add water to equal 1½ cups, if necessary.

Combine flour and ¼ cup water in a medium saucepan; stir until smooth. Add broth mixture; cook over medium heat, stirring constantly, until thickened and bubbly. Stir in reserved neck meat, giblets, egg, and pepper. Serve hot with roasted poultry. Yield: 2 cups.

Dessert Sauces

Keep ingredients on hand to make an assortment of dessert sauces. They're a great way to personalize commercial ice cream or pound cake when unexpected company drops in or when someone in your family has an urge for something sweet.

HOT FUDGE SAUCE

¼ cup plus 2 tablespoons sugar
1 (5-ounce) can evaporated milk
¾ cup semisweet chocolate morsels
1½ teaspoons butter or margarine
½ teaspoon vanilla extract

Combine sugar, evaporated milk, and chocolate morsels in a small saucepan. Cook over medium heat, stirring until chocolate melts and mixture boils. Remove from heat, and stir in butter and vanilla. Serve hot over ice cream. Yield: 1 cup.

◯*Microwave Directions:* Combine sugar, evaporated milk, and chocolate morsels in a 1-quart glass bowl. Microwave at MEDIUM HIGH (70% power) for 4 to 5 minutes or until chocolate melts and mixture is very hot, stirring after 1 minute, then at 30-second intervals. Stir in butter and vanilla. Serve hot over ice cream.

Pour thick and creamy Hot Fudge Sauce over ice cream, and top with your favorite fruit and nuts.

CHOCOLATE SAUCE SUPREME

1 (6-ounce) package semisweet
  chocolate morsels
¼ cup butter or margarine
1 cup sifted powdered sugar
½ cup light corn syrup
¼ cup crème de cacao liqueur
  (optional)
¼ cup water
1 teaspoon vanilla extract
Dash of salt

Combine semisweet chocolate morsels and butter in top of a double boiler; bring water to a boil. Reduce heat to low; cook until chocolate melts.

Stir powdered sugar and remaining ingredients into chocolate mixture. Cook mixture over medium heat, stirring frequently, until sugar dissolves and sauce is smooth. Serve hot or cold over ice cream. Yield: 1¾ cups.

◻ *Microwave Directions:* Place semisweet chocolate morsels and butter in a 2-quart glass bowl; microwave at HIGH for 2 to 2½ minutes or until chocolate melts, stirring at 1-minute intervals. Stir in powdered sugar and remaining ingredients. Microwave at HIGH for 1 to 2 minutes or until sugar dissolves and sauce is smooth, stirring at 1-minute intervals. Serve hot or cold.

BUTTERSCOTCH SAUCE

2 cups firmly packed brown sugar
¾ cup plus 2 tablespoons light corn
  syrup
¼ cup butter or margarine
⅛ teaspoon salt
1 (5-ounce) can evaporated milk

Combine brown sugar, corn syrup, and butter in a saucepan; bring mixture to a boil over medium-low heat, stirring constantly. Remove from heat. Stir in salt and evaporated milk. Serve sauce warm over ice cream. Yield: 2½ cups.

◻ *Microwave Directions:* Combine sugar, syrup, and butter in a 1-quart glass measure; stir well. Microwave at HIGH for 3 to 4 minutes, stirring once. Stir in salt and milk. Serve warm over ice cream.

CREAMY CARAMEL SAUCE

1 cup sugar
½ cup butter
½ cup half-and-half

Sprinkle sugar into a large cast-iron skillet. Cook over medium heat, stirring

constantly with a wooden spoon, until sugar melts and turns light brown. Remove from heat; add butter, and stir until blended.

Return mixture to low heat; gradually add half-and-half to hot mixture, 1 table-

spoon at a time, stirring constantly. Continue to cook mixture over low heat, stirring constantly, 10 minutes or until mixture is thickened and creamy. Serve sauce warm over ice cream or pound cake. Yield: 1 cup.

PRALINE SAUCE

1½ cups chopped pecans
¼ cup butter or margarine
1¼ cups firmly packed light brown
  sugar
¾ cup light corn syrup
3 tablespoons all-purpose flour
1 (5-ounce) can evaporated milk

Spread pecans on a baking sheet; bake at 300° for 15 minutes. Set aside.

Melt butter in a medium saucepan;

add brown sugar, corn syrup, and flour, stirring well. Bring mixture to a boil; reduce heat and simmer 5 minutes, stirring constantly. Remove mixture from heat, and let cool to lukewarm. Gradually stir in evaporated milk and toasted pecans. Serve sauce warm over ice cream. Yield: 3 cups.

◻ *Microwave Directions:* Spread pecans on a large glass pizza plate. Mi-

crowave at HIGH for 5 to 6 minutes or until lightly toasted, stirring at 2-minute intervals.

Place butter in a 1-quart glass bowl; microwave at HIGH for 55 seconds or until melted. Add sugar, corn syrup, and flour, stirring well. Microwave at HIGH for 3 to 4 minutes or until mixture is very hot, stirring at 2-minute intervals. Gradually stir in milk and pecans. Serve warm over ice cream.

BRANDIED STRAWBERRY SAUCE

2 (10-ounce) packages frozen sliced
   strawberries, thawed
2 teaspoons cornstarch
⅓ cup red currant jelly
3 tablespoons brandy

Drain strawberries, reserving ½ cup juice. Reserve remaining juice for other uses. Set strawberries aside.

Combine ½ cup reserved juice and cornstarch in a small mixing bowl, stirring until smooth. Set aside.

Melt jelly over low heat in a heavy saucepan; add cornstarch mixture. Cook over medium heat, stirring constantly, until thickened and clear. Add reserved strawberries and brandy, stirring well. Serve warm or chilled over ice cream or pound cake. Yield: about 1¾ cups.

◻ *Microwave Directions:* Drain strawberries, reserving ½ cup juice. Reserve remaining juice for other uses. Set strawberries aside.

Combine ½ cup reserved juice and cornstarch in a small mixing bowl, stirring until mixture is smooth. Set aside.

Place jelly in a 4-cup glass measure. Microwave at HIGH for 1 minute or until melted; add cornstarch mixture. Microwave at HIGH for 2 minutes or until thickened and clear, stirring after 1 minute. Add reserved strawberries and brandy, stirring well. Microwave at HIGH for 1 minute.

Brandied Raspberry Sauce: Substitute 2 (10-ounce) packages frozen raspberries for strawberries.

PEACH-BLUEBERRY SAUCE

1 cup sliced fresh peaches, divided
1 cup fresh blueberries, divided
¾ cup sugar
⅓ cup water
⅛ teaspoon ground nutmeg

Combine ½ cup sliced fresh peaches, ½ cup fresh blueberries, and remaining ingredients in a small saucepan. Bring mixture to a boil, reduce heat, and simmer 10 minutes. Stir in remaining peaches and blueberries. Serve fruit sauce warm over ice cream, pancakes, waffles, or pound cake. Yield: 1½ cups.

◻ *Microwave Directions:* Combine ½ cup peaches, ½ cup blueberries, and remaining ingredients in a 2-quart glass bowl. Cover with heavy-duty plastic wrap, and microwave at HIGH for 4 to 5 minutes, stirring once. Stir in reserved peaches and blueberries. Serve fruit sauce warm over ice cream, pancakes, waffles, or pound cake.

FRESH LEMON SAUCE

1 cup water
½ cup sugar
2 tablespoons cornstarch
Pinch of salt
1 tablespoon butter or margarine
2 teaspoons grated lemon rind
⅓ cup lemon juice

Combine first 4 ingredients in a saucepan, stirring until smooth. Cook over medium heat, stirring until smooth and thickened. Add remaining ingredients; cook until heated. Serve over cake or date nut bread. Yield: about 1⅔ cups.

◻ *Microwave Directions:* Combine first 4 ingredients in a 2-cup glass measure, stirring until smooth. Microwave at HIGH for 3 minutes, stirring after 2 minutes, then at 1-minute intervals. Add remaining ingredients; microwave at HIGH for 1 minute, and stir well.

Fresh Orange Sauce: Substitute orange rind and juice for that of lemon. Increase juice to ⅔ cup, and decrease water to ⅔ cup.

SOUPS & STEWS

Soups offer more variety to menu planning than almost any other type food. You can team a light soup with a salad or sandwich; a hearty soup can be a complete meal with the addition of French bread. Soups can be casual enough for Sunday supper or formal enough to be first course of an elegant dinner. Hearty gumbos and chilies warm up a cold day, while chilled fruit or vegetable soups make just the right pick-me-up for a sultry summer day. First take note of the season and your mood, and then choose the soup.

EQUIPMENT

Soup making does not require much special equipment. A large Dutch oven or stock pot is all you'll need for most soups. Cream soups and purees do require that you have an electric blender or food processor to obtain the right consistency. Soups that simmer with a large number of whole herbs and spices often call for cheesecloth in which to confine the spices. Called a bouquet garni, the filled spice bag allows for easy removal of the spices after the soup is cooked.

MENU PLANNING WITH SOUPS

Our soup yields are given in cup measures rather than numbers of servings so you can be the judge, depending on how you plan to serve the soup. Allow ¾ to 1 cup soup when offering it as an appetizer. For an entrée, 1¼ to 1¾ cups is usually standard. Soups served as the main course tend to be heavier, meatier soups. Choose a lighter, more deli-

Spoon up a bowl of Gazpacho (page 455) for an appetizer or a light lunch. Offer breadsticks as a crunchy accompaniment.

cate soup for an appetizer; it should be just enough in taste and body to whet the appetite, especially if the main course will be filling.

CANNED SOUPS MAKE CONVENIENT ADDITIONS

Several of our soup recipes call for commercially canned soup as the base, with the addition of fresh or frozen vegetables, meats, or seasonings to expand and enhance the flavor. Since some brands of soups are condensed, while other similar soups are regular strength, be sure to use the exact name and ounce-size of the soups our recipes specify. If a recipe indicates a condensed soup, the recipe will note whether or not the soup needs diluting.

When our recipes call for chicken or beef broth, you can use our broth recipes or you can substitute commercially canned broth. Just remember that canned varieties are saltier than our homemade versions, so hold extra seasonings until the end. Bouillon cubes, granules, and powdered mixes diluted according to package directions may be used, but they too are saltier than our homemade broths.

STORING AND FREEZING SOUP

Most soups are actually better if refrigerated one or two days to give the flavors a chance to blend and intensify. Because of this, soups are an excellent make-ahead suggestion for entertaining or for accommodating a busy schedule.

Most soups also freeze well, especially thick gumbos, chilies, and stews, which tend to have a large yield anyway. Package soups and stews in pint or quart jars or plastic freezer containers, and label them with the soup name, the amount in the container, and the date it was frozen. Plan to use them within four to six months.

MICROWAVE WITH DISCRETION

We have included microwave directions for those soups that have few steps and yield small amounts. More complicated soups and those with large yields can actually take longer to cook in the microwave than on the cooktop. Of course your microwave will be useful in reheating leftovers in small quantities, whether or not the soup was initially cooked in the microwave. Cooking times will vary according to the ingredients in the soup and the amount of soup to be reheated.

Broth

Broth has the reputation of being difficult to prepare, but it's actually one of the simplest soups to make. A thin liquid in which meat, poultry, vegetables, or any combination of these has been cooked, broth forms the base for a variety of sauces and gravies.

Although broths may simmer for a long time, they don't require much work. It's not even necessary to peel or trim the vegetables since they'll be strained out after cooking. Just wash and cut them.

After the broth has cooked, strain it through several thicknesses of cheesecloth to remove meat, vegetables, and small particles. Allow the broth to cool thoroughly so the fat can rise to the surface and become firm. Chilling the broth is the quickest way of congealing the fat. Then just lift off the solidified fat for a lighter, healthier broth. If you need to defat the broth in a hurry, wrap an ice cube in cheesecloth, and skim it over the surface. The fat will congeal on contact with the ice and can easily be lifted off.

Fresh broth can be refrigerated only three to four days, but that's no reason not to make large quantities of it. Freeze the broth in containers of various sizes—anything from a cup to a quart. It's also handy to freeze broth in ice cube trays; transfer the cubes to a plastic bag once frozen. Each cube yields about 2 tablespoons of broth.

or granules may be substituted for freshly made chicken broth. The homemade version is not as salty as canned, bouillon cube, or granule versions. Also, turkey pieces may be substituted for chicken to make turkey broth.

CHICKEN BROTH

4 pounds chicken pieces
2 quarts water
1 onion, quartered
2 stalks celery
1 bay leaf
¾ teaspoon salt
½ teaspoon pepper
½ teaspoon dried parsley flakes
¼ teaspoon dried whole thyme
⅛ teaspoon dried whole marjoram

Combine all ingredients in a large Dutch oven. Bring to a boil; cover, reduce heat, and simmer 1 hour. Strain broth, reserving chicken and vegetables for other uses. Chill broth; remove fat from surface. Yield: about 8 cups.

Note: Canned chicken broth or chicken broth made with bouillon cubes

EGG DROP SOUP

Often served as the first course in an Oriental menu, the broth base of Egg Drop Soup shows off the soup's lacy strands of cooked egg.

2 (10¾-ounce) cans chicken broth, diluted
1 (2½-ounce) jar sliced mushrooms, undrained
2 green onions, chopped
2 cloves garlic
⅛ teaspoon white pepper
1 egg, slightly beaten
1 teaspoon sesame or vegetable oil

Combine first 5 ingredients in a Dutch oven. Bring to a boil; cover, reduce heat, and simmer 10 minutes. Remove garlic.

Combine egg and oil, stirring well. Slowly pour egg mixture into soup, stirring constantly. (The egg forms lacy strands as it cooks.) Serve immediately. Yield: 5 cups.

BEEF BROTH

2½ pounds cut-up beef shanks
2 quarts water
1 carrot, cut into eighths
1 onion, quartered
2 stalks celery
2 cloves garlic
1 bay leaf
¾ teaspoon salt
½ teaspoon pepper
¼ teaspoon dried whole thyme

Place beef in a 13- x 9- x 2-inch pan; bake at 400° for 20 minutes. Transfer beef and drippings to a large Dutch oven; add remaining ingredients. Bring to a boil; cover, reduce heat, and simmer 1½ to 2 hours. Strain broth, reserving meat and vegetables for other uses. Chill broth; remove fat from surface of broth. Yield: about 8 cups.

Note: Canned beef broth or beef broth made with bouillon cubes or granules may be substituted for freshly made beef broth. The homemade version is not as salty as canned, bouillon cube, or granule versions.

To defat soups: Chill meaty soups after cooking; the fat will rise to the surface and congeal. Skim off and discard the fat.

Finishing Touches for Soup

Keep the garnishes for soup simple. A sprinkling of chopped fresh herbs or green onions adds nice color to any soup, while croutons offer a little crunch. A slice of lemon, a little grated Parmesan cheese, or ground cooked egg white or yolk can add complementary color to many soups.

Creams and Purees

When your menu calls for an elegant appetizer soup or one for a light lunch or supper, choose one of these creams or purees. Most rely on an electric blender or food processor for their smooth texture, while others have that texture naturally by virtue of their ingredients.

Some of these soups are served hot, and some cold; others may be served at either temperature, depending on your preference and the season of the year.

The smooth texture of these soups suggests that they can be "sipping soups," rather than always served from a soup bowl. Consider serving them in mugs or wine glasses, depending on the formality of the occasion. However you serve them, plain cream soups are complemented by a garnish on top.

DRESSED-UP TOMATO SOUP

2 to 3 tablespoons packed fresh basil or parsley
2 tablespoons grated Parmesan cheese
1 small clove garlic, cut in half
⅛ teaspoon freshly ground pepper
1 (10¾-ounce) can tomato soup, diluted

Remove stems from basil. Wash leaves thoroughly in lukewarm water, and drain well.

Position knife blade in food processor bowl; add basil, cheese, garlic, and pepper, and top with cover. Process until mixture is smooth.

Combine basil mixture and tomato soup in a saucepan; cook over medium heat until thoroughly heated, stirring constantly. Yield: 3 cups.

CREAM OF PEANUT BUTTER SOUP

½ cup chopped celery
¼ cup chopped onion
1 tablespoon butter or margarine, melted
1 tablespoon all-purpose flour
2 (14½-ounce) cans chicken broth, undiluted
½ cup creamy peanut butter
½ cup milk or half-and-half
Chopped chives (optional)

Sauté celery and onion in butter in a Dutch oven until tender; add flour, stirring until smooth. Cook 1 minute, stirring constantly. Gradually add chicken broth; bring mixture to a boil. Add peanut butter and milk; reduce heat and simmer 5 minutes, stirring constantly (do not boil). Garnish soup with chives, if desired. Serve immediately. Yield: about 4 cups.

CRÈME VICHYSSOISE

2 cups coarsely chopped leeks with
  tops, or onions
3 cups peeled, sliced potatoes
3 cups water
4 chicken-flavored bouillon cubes
¼ teaspoon white pepper
3 tablespoons butter or margarine
2 cups half-and-half or milk
2 tablespoons chopped chives

Combine first 6 ingredients in a Dutch
oven; cook over medium heat until vegetables are tender. Puree in an electric
blender. Stir in half-and-half, and chill.
Garnish with chives. Yield: 6½ cups.

CREAM OF SQUASH
SOUP

*Cream of Squash Soup is a good
make-ahead choice, as the flavor actually
improves after a day of chilling. It can be
served hot or cold to complement the season
you serve it.*

1 small onion, minced
1 clove garlic, minced
3 tablespoons butter or margarine,
  melted
1½ pounds yellow squash, thinly
  sliced
1 (10¾-ounce) can chicken broth,
  undiluted
⅔ cup water
½ cup half-and-half
¼ teaspoon white pepper
Chopped fresh parsley

Sauté onion and garlic in butter in a
Dutch oven. Stir in squash, chicken
broth, and water; cover and simmer 15
minutes or until squash is tender. Spoon
mixture into container of an electric
blender, and process until smooth.

Return squash mixture to Dutch
oven; stir in half-and-half and pepper.
Cook over low heat, stirring constantly,
until well heated. Serve hot or chilled.
Garnish with parsley. Yield: 5 cups.

COLD CUCUMBER SOUP

1½ cups commercial sour cream
½ teaspoon dried whole dillweed
1 tablespoon Worcestershire sauce
1 tablespoon lemon juice
½ teaspoon celery salt
¼ teaspoon pepper
2 green onions, coarsely chopped
3 medium cucumbers, peeled, seeded,
  and coarsely chopped

Combine all ingredients in an electric
blender; process until smooth. Chill
thoroughly. Yield: 3½ cups.

CREAMY SPINACH SOUP

1 large onion, diced
3 tablespoons butter or margarine,
  melted
1 medium potato, cut into
  quarters
¼ cup diced cooked ham
2 beef-flavored bouillon cubes
¼ teaspoon salt
¼ teaspoon pepper
⅛ teaspoon ground nutmeg
1 clove garlic, minced
1 cup water
1 (10-ounce) package frozen
  chopped spinach, thawed and
  drained, or 1 pound fresh
  spinach, cooked and drained
3½ cups half-and-half or milk
Croutons (optional)
Grated Parmesan cheese (optional)

Sauté onion in butter in a large Dutch
oven. Add next 8 ingredients. Bring to a
boil; cover, reduce heat, and simmer 15
to 20 minutes or until potato is tender,
stirring occasionally.

Combine potato mixture and spinach
in container of an electric blender; process until smooth.

Return mixture to Dutch oven; stir in
half-and-half. Cook over low heat, stirring constantly, until heated. Garnish
each serving with croutons, and sprinkle
with cheese, if desired. Yield: 6 cups.

BORSCHT

1 (16-ounce) can whole beets,
  undrained
1 (10¾-ounce) can chicken broth,
  undiluted
1 (8-ounce) carton commercial sour
  cream
⅛ teaspoon white pepper
1½ teaspoons lemon juice
2 tablespoons chopped chives

Combine beets and broth in container
of an electric blender or food processor.
Process until smooth.

Combine beet puree, sour cream, pepper, and lemon juice; stir well. Chill.
Sprinkle each serving of soup with
chives. Yield: 4 cups.

CRAB BISQUE

¼ cup chopped mushrooms
2 tablespoons chopped onion
2 tablespoons chopped celery
2 tablespoons chopped carrot
3 tablespoons butter or margarine,
  melted
1 (14½-ounce) can chicken broth,
  undiluted
⅛ teaspoon salt
⅛ teaspoon red pepper
1½ cups half-and-half
½ cup dry white wine
½ pound fresh lump crabmeat

Sauté mushrooms, onion, celery, and
carrot in butter in a large saucepan over
low heat 2 minutes or until tender. Add
chicken broth, salt, and red pepper;
bring mixture to a boil, reduce heat, and
simmer 10 minutes.

Pour vegetable mixture into container
of an electric blender; process until
smooth. Combine vegetable puree, half-
and-half, wine, and crabmeat in a saucepan. Cook until thoroughly heated.
Yield: 6 cups.

BEER-CHEESE SOUP

3 cups milk
1 (12-ounce) can beer
1 (16-ounce) package process cheese
   spread, cubed
1½ teaspoons chicken-flavored
   bouillon granules
3 dashes of hot sauce
¼ cup plus 2 tablespoons all-purpose
   flour
¼ cup water

Combine milk and beer in a Dutch oven. Cook over low heat until thoroughly heated, stirring frequently. Add cheese spread, bouillon granules, and hot sauce. Cook over low heat until thoroughly heated, stirring constantly.

Combine flour and water, stirring until smooth. Gradually stir flour mixture into cheese mixture; cook over medium-low heat until thickened, stirring constantly (do not boil). Yield: 6 cups.

☐ *Microwave Directions:* Combine milk and beer in a 3-quart casserole. Microwave at HIGH for 4 to 5 minutes. Add cheese spread, bouillon granules, and hot sauce. Stir well with a wire whisk. Microwave at HIGH for 5 to 6 minutes or until cheese melts, stirring every 2 minutes.

Combine flour and water, stirring until smooth. Gradually stir flour mixture into cheese mixture; microwave at HIGH for 4 to 5 minutes or until thickened, stirring every minute.

Fruit Soups

Consider serving fruit soup as a delicate appetizer or a light ending to a meal. These soups are a little too sweet for a main course, but their refreshingly fresh flavors offer a novel way to satisfy that Southern sweet tooth.

CHILLED CANTALOUPE SOUP

3 medium cantaloupes, halved
¼ cup plus 2 tablespoons dry sherry
¼ cup sugar
¾ cup orange juice
Mint leaves

Discard seeds from cantaloupes. Scoop pulp from each cantaloupe, leaving shells ½ inch thick. Cut a thin slice from bottom of each shell, being careful not to cut a hole in shell.

Combine cantaloupe pulp, sherry, sugar, and orange juice in container of an electric blender; process until smooth. Chill mixture thoroughly. Serve in cantaloupe shells, and garnish with mint. Yield: 5 cups.

Swirl whipping cream into Rosy Berry Soup for an interesting garnish.

ROSY BERRY SOUP

2 (10-ounce) packages frozen
   raspberries or strawberries, thawed
2 cups Burgundy
2½ cups water
1 (3-inch) stick cinnamon
¼ cup sugar
2 tablespoons cornstarch
Whipping cream

Combine first 5 ingredients in a deep, ceramic, heatproof casserole or stainless steel saucepan (mixture will discolor aluminum). Bring mixture to a boil; reduce heat, and simmer 15 minutes.

Press raspberry mixture through a sieve, and return to casserole or saucepan; discard seeds. Combine cornstarch and ¼ cup raspberry liquid; stir well. Bring remaining liquid to a boil. Reduce heat to low, and stir in cornstarch mixture. Cook, stirring constantly, until slightly thickened. Chill 6 to 8 hours. Drizzle whipping cream in soup, and swirl in with a knife. Yield: 5 cups.

Vegetable Soups

Hot or cold, thick or thin, vegetable soups have always played an important role in Southern menu planning. They can often be made from leftovers, and most can be cooked well ahead of time and reheated.

When adding vegetables to homemade soup, remember that not all vegetables cook in the same length of time. Vegetables that take the longest to cook should be added first. Remember to cut like vegetables into pieces of the same size so they'll cook evenly. Frozen vegetables should be added after fresh, and canned vegetables need only to be reheated.

QUICK BROCCOLI SOUP

1 (10-ounce) package frozen chopped broccoli
1 (10¾-ounce) can cream of mushroom soup, undiluted
1½ cups milk
2 tablespoons butter or margarine
⅛ teaspoon pepper
1 cup (4 ounces) shredded Cheddar cheese

Cook broccoli in a large saucepan according to package directions, omitting salt; drain well. Stir in remaining ingredients. Cook over medium heat, stirring constantly, until thoroughly heated. Yield: about 4 cups.

☐*Microwave Directions:* Place broccoli in a 2-quart casserole. Cover with heavy-duty plastic wrap; microwave at HIGH for 7 to 8 minutes or until tender. Stir in remaining ingredients. Microwave at HIGH for 4 to 6 minutes or until thoroughly heated.

QUICK VEGETABLE SOUP

Quick Vegetable Soup may soon become one of your favorites. It's tasty and it's quick to make. Many cooks commonly have all the ingredients on hand and could make it at a moment's notice.

1 (14½-ounce) can stewed tomatoes, undrained
1 (8-ounce) can tomato sauce
1 (10-ounce) package frozen mixed vegetables
2 cups water
1½ teaspoons beef-flavored bouillon granules
⅛ teaspoon freshly ground pepper

Combine all ingredients in a Dutch oven. Bring to a boil; cover, reduce heat, and simmer 20 minutes, stirring occasionally. Yield: 7 cups.

FRESH VEGETABLE SOUP

1 (1 pound) meaty beef shank bone
2½ quarts water
1 (16-ounce) can stewed tomatoes, undrained and coarsely chopped
1½ cups lima beans
1 cup cut corn
½ cup chopped onion
1 large potato, peeled and cubed
1 carrot, scraped and sliced
1 tablespoon brown sugar (optional)
1 teaspoon salt
1 teaspoon dried Italian seasoning
½ teaspoon pepper
½ teaspoon hot sauce
1 bay leaf
1½ tablespoons all-purpose flour
1½ tablespoons water

Combine shank bone and 2½ quarts water in a large Dutch oven; bring to a boil. Cover, reduce heat, and simmer 1 hour. Remove from heat; cover and refrigerate 8 hours.

Discard excess fat on broth. Strain broth through several layers of cheesecloth. Return broth to Dutch oven.

Bring broth to a boil; add remaining ingredients, except flour and 1½ tablespoons water. Reduce heat and simmer, uncovered, 1 hour, stirring occasionally. Combine flour and water, stirring to make a paste. Add mixture to soup, stirring until blended. Cook, stirring constantly, until soup thickens. Remove bay leaf. Yield: 10 cups.

ELEGANT MUSHROOM SOUP

¾ cup chopped green onions
2 cups sliced fresh mushrooms
3 tablespoons butter or margarine, melted
2 tablespoons all-purpose flour
2 cups milk
1 cup water
2 teaspoons chicken-flavored bouillon granules

Sauté green onions and mushrooms in butter in a Dutch oven until onions are tender. Stir in flour; gradually add milk and water to mushroom mixture, stirring well. Add bouillon granules, and cook over low heat 10 minutes or just until thoroughly heated, stirring frequently. Yield: 4 cups.

☐*Microwave Directions:* Combine green onions, mushrooms, and butter in a 2-quart casserole. Cover with heavy-duty plastic wrap, and microwave at HIGH for 4 to 6 minutes or until onions are tender. Stir in flour; gradually add milk and water to mushroom mixture, stirring well. Add bouillon granules. Microwave at HIGH for 5 to 6 minutes or until thoroughly heated, stirring well after 3 minutes.

GAZPACHO

(pictured on page 448)

1 (10¾-ounce) can tomato soup, undiluted
1½ cups tomato juice
1¼ cups water
½ to 1 cup chopped cucumber
½ to 1 cup chopped tomato
½ cup chopped green pepper
½ cup chopped onion
2 tablespoons wine vinegar
1 tablespoon commercial Italian dressing
1 tablespoon lemon or lime juice
1 clove garlic, minced
¼ teaspoon pepper
¼ teaspoon hot sauce

Combine all ingredients; chill at least 6 hours. Yield: 6 cups.

MINESTRONE

¼ pound lean salt pork, finely diced
2½ quarts water
1 (16-ounce) can whole tomatoes, undrained and chopped
1 (15-ounce) can red kidney beans, undrained
1 (15-ounce) can white kidney beans, undrained
6 beef-flavored bouillon cubes
1 cup diced carrot
1 cup diced celery
1 cup shredded cabbage
1 cup chopped green onions
1 (10-ounce) package frozen chopped spinach
1 teaspoon dried whole basil
½ teaspoon freshly ground pepper
¾ cup uncooked macaroni
Grated Parmesan cheese

Sauté pork in a large Dutch oven until crisp; drain. Add remaining ingredients except macaroni and cheese. Bring to a boil; cover, reduce heat, and simmer 1 hour, stirring occasionally. Add macaroni; simmer 10 minutes. Sprinkle each serving with cheese. Yield: 18 cups.

LEEK SOUP

4 slices bacon, coarsely chopped
6 leeks, thinly sliced
¼ cup all-purpose flour
4 cups water
3 chicken-flavored bouillon cubes
2 potatoes, peeled and cubed
1 teaspoon dried whole basil
1 cup half-and-half or milk

Cook bacon in a Dutch oven over medium heat 5 minutes. Add leeks; sauté 5 minutes. Reduce heat to low; add flour, stirring until smooth. Cook 1 minute, stirring constantly. Gradually add water; cook over medium heat, stirring constantly, until thickened. Add bouillon cubes, potatoes, and basil; cover and simmer 45 minutes. Stir in half-and-half, and cook until thoroughly heated. Yield: 7 cups.

CHUNKY POTATO SOUP

3 tablespoons butter or margarine
¼ cup all-purpose flour
4 cups milk
2 cups diced potatoes
½ cup minced onion
½ to ¾ teaspoon salt
¼ to ½ teaspoon freshly ground pepper

Melt butter in a heavy saucepan over low heat; add flour, stirring until smooth. Cook 1 minute, stirring constantly. Gradually add milk; stir in potatoes, onion, salt, and pepper. Cook over medium heat, stirring frequently, until mixture is thickened and potatoes are done. Yield: 5 cups.

❑*Microwave Directions:* Place butter in a 2-quart casserole. Microwave at HIGH for 50 seconds or until melted. Add flour, stirring until smooth. Gradually add milk, stirring well. Add potatoes, onion, salt and pepper. Microwave at HIGH for 16 to 18 minutes or until mixture is thickened and potatoes are done, stirring twice.

LENTIL SOUP

1½ cups dried lentils
6 cups water
1 tablespoon beef-flavored bouillon granules
1 (16-ounce) can whole tomatoes, undrained and coarsely chopped
2 tablespoons parsley flakes
1 large onion, diced
1 medium carrot, thinly sliced
4 medium potatoes, peeled and cubed
1 bay leaf
½ teaspoon salt
¼ teaspoon pepper
1 clove garlic, crushed
1 cup chopped ham

Combine all ingredients in a large Dutch oven. Bring to a boil; cover, reduce heat, and simmer 1½ hours, stirring occasionally. Remove bay leaf. Yield: 12 cups.

SPLIT PEA SOUP

1 (16-ounce) package dried green split peas
2 quarts water
1 medium onion, chopped
1 medium carrot, diced
1 medium potato, diced
1 meaty ham bone
¼ to ½ teaspoon salt
¼ teaspoon pepper
¼ teaspoon dried whole tarragon

Sort and wash peas; place in a Dutch oven. Cover with water 2 inches above peas; let soak 8 hours.

Drain peas; add 2 quarts water, vegetables, ham bone, and seasonings. Bring to a boil; cover, reduce heat, and simmer 2½ to 3 hours, stirring occasionally. Remove bone; cut off meat, and dice. Discard bone. Return meat to soup, and simmer an additional 10 minutes. Yield: 12 cups.

1. *Begin by sautéing onion slices in butter until tender. Then blend in flour, stirring until smooth.*

2. *Stir in broth, water, and wine, and simmer 15 minutes.*

3. *Ladle soup over bread in individual serving bowls.*

4. *Top each bowl of soup with a slice of mozzarella, and sprinkle with Parmesan cheese. Broil until cheese melts.*

DOUBLE CHEESE FRENCH ONION SOUP

4 large onions, thinly sliced and
    separated into rings
½ cup butter or margarine, melted
1 tablespoon all-purpose flour
1 (10¾-ounce) can chicken broth,
    undiluted
1 (10½-ounce) can beef broth,
    undiluted
2 cups water
¼ cup dry white wine
⅛ to ¼ teaspoon pepper
8 (¾-inch-thick) slices French bread,
    toasted
8 slices mozzarella cheese
½ cup grated Parmesan cheese

Sauté onion in butter in a Dutch oven until tender. Blend in flour, stirring until smooth. Gradually add chicken broth, beef broth, water, and wine. Bring to a boil; reduce heat and simmer 15 minutes. Add pepper.

Place 8 ovenproof serving bowls on a baking sheet. Place 1 bread slice in each bowl; ladle soup over bread. Top with 1 cheese slice; sprinkle with Parmesan cheese. Broil 6 inches from heat until cheese melts. Yield: 8 cups.

Serve Double Cheese French Onion Soup as an appetizer or with a salad or sandwich.

Meat and Seafood Soups and Gumbos

Chock-full of meat and seafood, and sometimes vegetables, too, these hearty soups and gumbos are warm and satisfying for lunch or dinner. Along with a loaf of crusty French bread, they'll satisfy most appetites for a full meal. Heartier eaters can add a salad or sandwich to the menu.

Our sampling of gumbos had their origins deep in the Louisiana bayou country. All have as their base that flavorful brown roux that gives gumbos their characteristic color and texture. If you're one who enjoys the added flavor and thickening of gumbo filé, pass the powder at the table after serving the gumbo. Never add it to the pot while cooking, or your gumbo will become thick and stringy.

To prepare vegetables: Cut into uniform pieces so they cook in the same length of time.

CHICKEN NOODLE SOUP

1 (3½- to 4-pound) broiler-fryer
8 to 10 cups water
1 bay leaf
1 tablespoon chopped fresh parsley
1¼ teaspoons salt
¼ teaspoon pepper
¼ teaspoon dried whole basil
⅛ teaspoon celery seeds
⅛ teaspoon garlic powder
4 medium carrots, chopped
1 small onion, chopped
1 cup uncooked fine egg noodles

Combine first 9 ingredients in a large Dutch oven. Bring to a boil; cover, reduce heat, and simmer 1½ hours or until tender. Remove chicken from broth; discard bay leaf. Remove skin, bone chicken, and dice meat; set aside.

Add carrot and onion to broth; cover and simmer 30 minutes. Add chicken and noodles; cook an additional 15 minutes. Yield: 10 cups.

BEEFY VEGETABLE SOUP

2 pounds ground beef
½ cup butter or margarine
½ cup all-purpose flour
1½ quarts water
1 cup chopped onion
1 cup chopped carrot
1 cup chopped celery
1 (10-ounce) package frozen mixed vegetables
1 (28-ounce) can tomatoes, undrained and chopped
1 (15-ounce) can tomato sauce with tomato bits
1½ tablespoons beef-flavored bouillon granules
1½ teaspoons salt
2 teaspoons pepper

Brown ground beef in a large Dutch oven, stirring to crumble. Drain well, and set aside.

Melt butter in same Dutch oven; add flour and cook over low heat 3 to 5 minutes or until a smooth paste forms. Gradually add water, stirring constantly; cook over medium heat until bubbly, stirring occasionally. Add ground beef and remaining ingredients. Bring to a boil; reduce heat and simmer, uncovered, for 1 hour. Yield: 13 cups.

CREAMY CRAB SOUP

½ pound lump crabmeat
2 tablespoons butter or margarine
2 tablespoons all-purpose flour
3 cups half-and-half or milk
1 teaspoon chicken-flavored bouillon granules
⅛ teaspoon white pepper
¼ cup dry sherry
Chopped fresh parsley (optional)

Remove and discard cartilage from crabmeat; set aside.

Melt butter in a heavy saucepan over low heat; add flour, stirring until smooth. Cook 1 minute, stirring constantly. Gradually add half-and-half; cook over low heat, stirring constantly, until thickened and bubbly. Stir in crabmeat, bouillon granules, and pepper; cook over low heat 10 minutes (do not boil), stirring frequently. Stir in sherry, and cook 1 minute. Garnish with parsley, if desired. Yield: 4 cups.

◻*Microwave Directions:* Remove and discard cartilage from crabmeat; set aside.

Place butter in a 2-quart casserole. Microwave at HIGH for 45 seconds or until melted. Add flour, stirring until smooth. Gradually add half-and-half, stirring well. Microwave at HIGH for 2 minutes; stir well. Add crabmeat, bouillon granules, and pepper; microwave at HIGH for 4 to 5 minutes, stirring after 2 minutes. Stir in sherry, and microwave at HIGH for 1 minute. Garnish with parsley, if desired.

1. *Southern Seafood Gumbo starts with a base of oil and flour that's called a roux.*

2. *Cook oil and flour over medium heat, stirring constantly, until roux is the color of caramel.*

3. *Stir in celery, onion, green pepper, and garlic; cook 45 minutes, stirring occasionally. Add okra.*

4. *Add chicken broth, water, and seasonings; simmer 2½ hours, stirring occasionally.*

SOUTHERN SEAFOOD GUMBO

½ cup vegetable oil
½ cup all-purpose flour
4 stalks celery, chopped
2 medium onions, chopped
1 small green pepper, chopped
1 clove garlic, minced
½ pound okra, sliced
1 tablespoon vegetable oil
1 quart chicken broth
1 quart water
¼ cup Worcestershire sauce
1 teaspoon hot sauce
¼ cup catsup
1 small tomato, chopped
1 teaspoon salt
2 slices bacon or 1 small ham slice, chopped
1 bay leaf
¼ teaspoon dried whole thyme
¼ teaspoon dried whole rosemary
¼ teaspoon red pepper flakes
2 pounds unpeeled medium-size fresh shrimp
2 cups chopped cooked chicken
1 pound fresh crabmeat
1 (12-ounce) container fresh oysters, undrained (optional)
Hot cooked rice
Gumbo filé (optional)

5. *Add seafood and cooked chicken during the last 10 minutes of cooking.*

Serve Southern Seafood Gumbo over rice. Add gumbo filé to each serving, if desired.

Combine ½ cup oil and flour in a large Dutch oven; cook over medium heat, stirring constantly, until roux is caramel-colored (15 to 20 minutes). Stir in celery, onion, green pepper, and garlic; cook an additional 45 minutes, stirring occasionally.

Fry okra in 1 tablespoon hot oil until browned. Add to gumbo, and stir well over low heat for a few minutes. At this stage, the mixture may be cooled, packaged, and frozen or refrigerated for later.

Add broth and next 11 ingredients; simmer 2½ hours; stir occasionally.

Peel and devein shrimp; add shrimp, chicken, crabmeat, and oysters, if desired, during last 10 minutes of simmering period. Remove bay leaf. Serve over rice. Add gumbo filé, if desired. Yield: 14 cups.

HAM, SAUSAGE, AND CHICKEN GUMBO

1½ pounds ham, cut into ½-inch
    cubes
1½ pounds smoked sausage, cut into
    ½-inch slices
6 chicken thighs
¼ cup plus 2 tablespoons vegetable
    oil
¼ cup all-purpose flour
1 large onion, chopped
4 cloves garlic, minced
½ green pepper, chopped
2 quarts water
½ teaspoon crushed red pepper
½ teaspoon dried whole thyme
¼ teaspoon pepper
½ cup chopped green onion tops
Hot cooked rice
Gumbo filé (optional)

Brown each meat, one at a time, in oil in a large Dutch oven, removing to drain on paper towels.

Add flour to oil remaining in Dutch oven; cook over medium heat, stirring constantly, until roux is caramel-colored (10 to 15 minutes).

Add onion, garlic, and green pepper to roux; cook until vegetables are tender, stirring frequently. Gradually add water. Add ham, sausage, chicken, red pepper, thyme, and pepper. Bring to a boil; reduce heat and simmer, uncovered, 1½ to 2 hours, stirring occasionally. Cool and skim fat from top. Remove bones from chicken; coarsely chop chicken, and return to pot.

Bring gumbo to a boil; add green onion tops. Cook an additional 10 minutes. Serve over hot cooked rice. Add filé, if desired. Yield: 12 cups.

CHICKEN AND OYSTER GUMBO

1 (5-pound) hen
2½ quarts water
2 teaspoons salt
¾ cup vegetable oil
1 cup all-purpose flour
2 large onions, chopped
¼ cup chopped fresh parsley
1 teaspoon whole allspice
1 teaspoon crushed red pepper
5 bay leaves
½ teaspoon pepper
2 (12-ounce) containers fresh oysters,
    undrained
Salt to taste
2 teaspoons gumbo filé
Hot cooked rice

Combine hen, water, and 2 teaspoons salt in a Dutch oven. Bring to a boil; cover, reduce heat, and simmer 1½ hours or until tender. Remove hen from broth, reserving 8½ cups broth. Remove skin, bone hen, and cut meat into pieces. Set aside.

Combine oil and flour in a Dutch oven; cook over medium heat, stirring constantly, until roux is chocolate-colored (20 to 25 minutes).

Add onion and parsley to roux; cook 10 minutes, stirring frequently. Gradually add reserved broth to roux, stirring constantly. Combine allspice, red pepper, and bay leaves in a cheesecloth bag; add to broth mixture. Add pepper; simmer 2½ hours, stirring occasionally. Add chicken and oysters; simmer 10 minutes. Remove from heat, and discard spice bag. Add additional salt, if desired. Stir in filé. Serve over rice. Yield: about 14 cups.

Be Creative With Soup

Unlike recipes for cakes and candies, most soup recipes don't have to be followed precisely. You can usually add a little more or a little less of what's called for, or you can make substitutions or additions of similar ingredients. Soups also make good use of leftovers and might help you clean out the refrigerator.

Chowders, Stews, and Chilies

Although chowders, stews, and chilies are good year-round, they're typically thought of as more appropriate for winter menus. Often suitable as a main dish, each is thick with meat and vegetables, and skillfully seasoned with herbs and spices. Their flavor improves if they are made ahead, refrigerated, and then reheated. Most of these soups are suitable for freezing, too.

HAM AND CORN CHOWDER

½ cup coarsely chopped onion
½ cup butter or margarine, melted
1 (17-ounce) can cream-style corn
½ cup half-and-half
1 cup chopped cooked ham
⅛ teaspoon salt
⅛ teaspoon pepper

Sauté onion in butter in a Dutch oven until tender. Add remaining ingredients; cook over low heat until heated (do not boil). Yield: 4 cups.

◻ *Microwave Directions:* Combine onion and butter in a 2-quart casserole; cover with heavy-duty plastic wrap, and microwave at HIGH for 2 minutes or until onion is tender. Add remaining ingredients. Microwave at HIGH for 4 to 5 minutes or until thoroughly heated.

Little pimiento cutouts and a sprig of parsley top each serving of Vegetable Cheddar Chowder.

VEGETABLE CHEDDAR CHOWDER

3 cups water
3 chicken-flavored bouillon cubes
4 medium potatoes, peeled and diced
1 medium onion, sliced
1 cup thinly sliced carrots
½ cup diced green pepper
⅓ cup butter or margarine
⅓ cup all-purpose flour
3½ cups milk
4 cups (1 pound) shredded sharp
   Cheddar cheese
1 (2-ounce) jar diced pimiento,
   drained
¼ teaspoon hot sauce (optional)
Pimiento cutouts
Fresh parsley sprigs

Combine water and bouillon cubes in a Dutch oven; bring to a boil. Add vegetables; cover and simmer 12 minutes or until vegetables are tender.

Melt butter in a heavy saucepan over low heat; add flour, stirring until smooth. Cook 1 minute, stirring constantly. Gradually add milk; cook over medium heat, stirring constantly, until thickened and bubbly. Add cheese, stirring until melted.

Stir cheese sauce, pimiento, and hot sauce into vegetable mixture. Cook over low heat until thoroughly heated (do not boil). Garnish each serving with pimiento cutouts and a parsley sprig. Yield: 10 cups.

FISH CHOWDER

1 cup water
1 cup diced potatoes
3 slices bacon, chopped
1 medium onion, chopped
¾ pound fish fillets, cubed
⅛ teaspoon dried whole thyme
1 cup half-and-half
½ teaspoon salt
¼ teaspoon pepper
2 tablespoons chopped fresh parsley

Bring water to a boil in a Dutch oven; add potatoes. Cover and cook 10 minutes. Fry bacon until transparent; add onion, and cook until onion is soft and bacon is lightly browned. Add bacon, onion, bacon drippings, fish fillets, and thyme to potatoes. Simmer 10 minutes or until potatoes are tender. Stir in half-and-half, salt, and pepper; simmer 5 minutes. Sprinkle with parsley. Yield: 3½ cups.

NEW ENGLAND CLAM CHOWDER

2 (6½-ounce) cans minced clams,
   undrained
1 small onion, chopped
4 slices bacon, coarsely chopped
4 medium potatoes, finely diced
1 teaspoon salt
¼ teaspoon pepper
2 tablespoons cornstarch
4 cups milk, divided
2 tablespoons butter or margarine

Drain clams; reserve liquid. Set aside. Cook onion and bacon in a Dutch oven until bacon is browned. Stir in clam liquid, potatoes, salt, and pepper; cover and simmer until potatoes are tender.

Combine cornstarch and ¼ cup milk; add to potato mixture. Add butter, clams, and remaining 3¾ cups milk. Cook over medium heat, stirring constantly, until thickened (do not boil). Yield: about 8 cups.

MANHATTAN CLAM CHOWDER

4 slices bacon, coarsely chopped
1 onion, chopped
2 stalks celery, chopped
1 clove garlic, minced
2 cups water
2 cups diced potatoes
1 (28-ounce) can whole tomatoes, undrained and chopped
½ teaspoon salt
¼ teaspoon dried whole thyme
2 (6½-ounce) cans minced clams, undrained
2 tablespoons cornstarch

Cook bacon in a Dutch oven until lightly browned. Add onion, celery, and garlic; sauté until vegetables are tender. Add water and next 4 ingredients. Cover and cook over medium heat 20 minutes or until potatoes are tender.

Drain clams; reserve liquid. Add cornstarch to liquid; stir until smooth. Stir clams and liquid into vegetable mixture. Bring to a boil over medium heat, stirring constantly; cook 1 minute or until slightly thickened. Yield: 10 cups.

OYSTER STEW

2 green onions, chopped
2 tablespoons butter or margarine, melted
1 (12-ounce) container fresh Standard oysters, undrained
1 quart half-and-half or milk
¼ teaspoon salt
¼ teaspoon white pepper
⅛ teaspoon red pepper

Sauté green onions in butter in a Dutch oven until onions are tender. Add remaining ingredients to onion mixture. Cook over low heat until edges of oysters begin to curl and mixture is hot, but not boiling. Serve stew with crackers. Yield: 6 cups.

MEATBALL STEW

1½ pounds ground beef
1 egg, slightly beaten
¾ cup soft breadcrumbs
¾ cup finely chopped onion, divided
½ teaspoon salt
1 tablespoon vegetable oil
1 (10½-ounce) can beef broth, undiluted
2 (8-ounce) cans tomato sauce
½ teaspoon dried whole thyme
¼ teaspoon freshly ground pepper
2 (10-ounce) packages frozen mixed vegetables

Combine ground beef, egg, breadcrumbs, ¼ cup onion, and salt; mix well. Shape into 1-inch balls. Sauté meatballs and remaining ½ cup onion in hot oil until meatballs are browned; drain off excess drippings.

Combine beef broth, tomato sauce, seasonings, and vegetables in a Dutch oven. Cover and simmer over medium heat 10 minutes. Add meatballs; cover and simmer 5 minutes or until vegetables are tender and meatballs are done. Yield: 8 cups.

BEEF STEW WITH DUMPLINGS

2 pounds boneless beef chuck, cut into 1-inch cubes
¼ cup plus 1 tablespoon all-purpose flour
3 tablespoons vegetable oil
1 medium onion, sliced
1 small clove garlic, minced
1 teaspoon salt
¼ teaspoon pepper
¼ teaspoon dried whole thyme
1 small bay leaf
4 cups water
3 large potatoes, quartered
4 large carrots, cut in half crosswise
6 small onions
3 stalks celery, cut into 1-inch pieces
1 cup all-purpose flour
1 tablespoon chopped fresh parsley
1½ teaspoons baking powder
¼ teaspoon salt
½ cup milk

Dredge meat in ¼ cup plus 1 tablespoon flour, and brown in hot oil in a large Dutch oven. Stir in next 7 ingredients; cover, reduce heat, and simmer 2 hours. Add potatoes, carrots, onions, and celery; cover and cook over low heat 15 minutes.

Combine 1 cup flour, parsley, baking powder, and salt in a small bowl; make a well in center of mixture. Add milk, stirring just until moistened. Drop mixture by tablespoonfuls onto stew; cover and cook 15 minutes without removing cover. Yield: 10½ cups.

BRUNSWICK STEW

There are almost as many variations of Brunswick Stew as there are of barbecue sauce. This pork and chicken version seems to be most typical. While a bowl of steaming Brunswick Stew is good alone, it's often served as an accompaniment to Southern barbecue.

1 (4½-pound) pork roast
1 (4½-pound) hen
3 (16-ounce) cans whole tomatoes, undrained and chopped
1 (8-ounce) can tomato sauce
3 large onions, diced
2 small green peppers, diced
¾ cup vinegar
¼ cup sugar
¼ cup all-purpose flour
1 cup water
1 teaspoon salt
½ teaspoon pepper
½ teaspoon ground turmeric
2 tablespoons hot sauce
1 (16-ounce) package frozen shoepeg corn

Place roast, fat side up, on rack of a roasting pan. Insert meat thermometer, being careful not to touch bone or fat. Bake at 325° about 30 to 35 minutes per pound or until thermometer registers 160°. Cool. Trim and discard fat; cut pork into 2-inch pieces.

Place hen in a Dutch oven, and cover with water. Bring to a boil; cover, reduce heat, and simmer 2 hours or until tender. Remove hen from broth and cool. (Reserve broth for other uses.) Bone hen, and cut meat into 2-inch pieces.

Coarsely grind pork and chicken in food processor or with meat grinder. Combine ground meat, tomatoes, tomato sauce, onion, green pepper, vinegar, and sugar in a large Dutch oven. Combine flour and water, stirring until smooth; stir into meat mixture. Stir in salt, pepper, turmeric, and hot sauce. Cook over medium heat 30 minutes, stirring occasionally. Add water, if needed, to reach desired consistency. Stir in corn, and cook an additional 10 minutes. Yield: 22 cups.

Note: Brunswick Stew freezes well. To serve, thaw and cook until thoroughly heated.

KENTUCKY BURGOO

A stew of Southern origin, burgoo typically includes at least two types of meat and a garden's worth of vegetables.

1 (4- to 5-pound) hen
2 pounds beef or veal stew meat
1½ to 2 pounds beef or veal bones
1 stalk celery with leaves, cut into 1-inch pieces
1 carrot, cut into 1-inch pieces
1 small onion, quartered
1 (6-ounce) can tomato paste
3 quarts water
1 red pepper pod
1 to 1½ tablespoons salt
1½ to 2 teaspoons black pepper
½ teaspoon red pepper
2 tablespoons lemon juice
1 tablespoon Worcestershire sauce
6 onions, finely chopped
8 to 10 tomatoes, peeled and chopped
1 turnip, peeled and finely chopped
2 green peppers, finely chopped
2 cups fresh butterbeans
2 cups thinly sliced celery
2 cups finely chopped cabbage
2 cups sliced fresh okra
2 cups fresh cut corn

Combine first 14 ingredients in a large Dutch oven. Bring to a boil; cover, reduce heat, and simmer 1 hour. Cool. Strain meat mixture, reserving meat and liquid; discard vegetables. Remove bone, skin, and gristle from meat; finely chop meat. Return meat to liquid, and refrigerate 8 hours.

Remove fat layer on mixture, and add remaining ingredients. Bring mixture to a boil; reduce heat and simmer, uncovered, 3 hours or to desired consistency, stirring mixture frequently to prevent sticking. Yield: 30 cups.

Note: Kentucky Burgoo freezes well. To serve, thaw and cook until thoroughly heated.

SOUTHERN BOUILLABAISSE

The original bouillabaisse hailed from France and included fish typical of the region. The Southern version resembles the original stew, but boasts seafood plentiful in our area. Bouillabaisse is typically seasoned with saffron and served over slices of French bread.

1 large onion, coarsely chopped
2 cloves garlic, minced
¼ cup butter or margarine, melted
2 tablespoons all-purpose flour
2 cups water
1 cup coarsely chopped fresh tomato
1 (8-ounce) can tomato sauce
½ cup dry sherry
1 bay leaf
1 teaspoon salt
¼ teaspoon red pepper
¼ teaspoon dried whole thyme
⅛ teaspoon ground allspice
Pinch of ground saffron
1 pound unpeeled medium-size fresh shrimp
2 pounds red snapper, skinned and cut into large pieces
1 (12-ounce) container fresh oysters, undrained
Toasted French bread

Sauté onion and garlic in butter in a large Dutch oven until tender. Add flour, stirring until smooth. Cook 1 minute, stirring constantly. Gradually stir in water. Add tomato, tomato sauce, sherry, and seasonings. Bring to a boil; reduce heat and simmer, uncovered, 30 minutes. Peel and devein shrimp. Add shrimp, fish, and oysters; simmer 5 minutes or until shrimp are tender and fish flakes easily when tested with a fork. Remove bay leaf. Serve each portion over a slice of toasted French bread. Yield: 10 cups.

TEXAS CHUNKY CHILI

2 large onions, chopped
1 stalk celery, chopped
3 cloves garlic, minced
1 jalapeño pepper, finely chopped
1 tablespoon vegetable oil
3 pounds boneless chuck roast, diced
2 teaspoons dried whole oregano
½ teaspoon cumin seeds
1 (28-ounce) can whole tomatoes, undrained and chopped
1 (6-ounce) can tomato paste
¼ cup chili powder
½ teaspoon salt
3½ cups water

Sauté onion, celery, garlic, and jalapeño pepper in hot oil until tender; set vegetables aside.

Combine meat, oregano, and cumin in a Dutch oven. Cook until meat is browned; drain well. Add onion mixture, tomatoes, tomato paste, chili powder, salt, and water to meat mixture. Bring to a boil; reduce heat and simmer, uncovered, 1½ to 2 hours, stirring occasionally. Yield: 5 cups.

SPEEDY CHILI

1 pound ground beef
1 large onion, chopped
1 clove garlic, crushed
2 (8-ounce) cans tomato sauce
¼ teaspoon salt
⅛ teaspoon pepper
3 to 4 tablespoons chili powder
1 cup water

Combine first 3 ingredients in a Dutch oven; cook until beef is browned, stirring to crumble. Drain off drippings. Add remaining ingredients; cover, reduce heat, and simmer 30 minutes, stirring occasionally. Yield: about 4 cups.

❑ *Microwave Directions:* Combine first 3 ingredients in a 2-quart casserole. Cover with heavy-duty plastic wrap, and microwave at HIGH for 5 to 6 minutes or until meat is browned, stirring once. Drain off drippings. Add remaining ingredients; cover and microwave at HIGH for 10 to 12 minutes or to desired consistency, stirring after 6 minutes.

SAVORY CHILI

4 stalks celery with leaves, chopped
3 green onions, chopped
2 cloves garlic, minced
1 large onion, chopped
1 green pepper, chopped
1 tablespoon vegetable oil
2 pounds ground beef
1 (15-ounce) can tomato sauce
1 (6-ounce) can tomato paste
2 cups water
1 (1½-ounce) can chili powder
1 teaspoon salt
Dash of pepper
1 (16-ounce) can kidney beans, undrained
Condiments (optional)

Sauté first 5 ingredients in oil in a large Dutch oven until tender. Add ground beef, and brown, stirring to crumble meat. Drain well.

Add tomato sauce and next 5 ingredients to beef mixture; stir well. Bring to a boil; reduce heat and simmer, uncovered, 30 minutes or to desired consistency. Add beans the last 15 minutes.

Serve with the following condiments, if desired: shredded lettuce, shredded Cheddar cheese, diced onion, and tortilla chips. Yield: 10 cups.

Serve Savory Chili with a choice of colorful condiments.

VEGETABLES & SIDE DISHES

Vegetable and fruit side dishes are as much a part of the Southern life-style as are beaches and barbecue. In early summer, when farmers' markets and backyard gardens offer fresh produce, Southerners celebrate with sumptuous spreads of vegetable and fruit dishes.

While there are times when we'd all like to sit down to a dinner of vegetables prepared like grand-mother's—cooked for hours and sea-soned with fatback—for the most part we've changed the way we cook vegetables. The flavor is still full and fresh, but quicker cooking methods and alternate seasonings leave vege-tables with less fat and more fiber, nutrients, texture, and color than ever before. Here are the things you need to know about cooking vegeta-bles for today's life-style.

EQUIPMENT

If you frequently boil or steam vegetables, the most important equipment you can have is a variety of saucepans with tight-fitting lids. The tight-fitting lids enable you to use less water when cooking, be-cause less water will evaporate. Using less water means your vegeta-bles will retain more nutrients.

Equally beneficial is a steaming rack, which keeps vegetables out of direct contact with the water, lets

A simple sauce dramatically transforms plain cauliflower into Cauliflower With Herb Butter (page 476).

you use minimum water, and also promotes nutrient retention.

To encourage your use of vegeta-bles in their fresh form, the form that supplies the most nutrients, keep a sharp French knife on hand

for slicing, chopping, and dicing. Using the proper knife and cutting techniques will increase your speed and pleasure in preparing fresh veg-etables for eating raw and cooking.

BEST BUYS ON VEGETABLES

Fresh vegetables reward you with the fullest flavors, the most nutri-ents, and usually the best prices. Concentrate on buying vegetables that are in season. Not only will they be at their peak of quality and flavor, they'll also be available at the most reasonable price.

When buying fresh vegetables, look for freshness and crispness. Avoid vegetables that have soft or bruised spots. If vegetables are weary when you buy them, they won't improve once you get them home, and often a bruised or bad spot on one item will cause spoilage among the others.

When buying frozen vegetables, avoid packages that are limp or damp. These are definite signs that the vegetables have defrosted at least once. When vegetables thaw and are refrozen, nutrients, flavor, and texture are lost.

STORING YOUR PICK OF THE CROP

There is an art to storing fresh vegetables. Green leafy vegetables wilt quickly and change flavor as the water evaporates from them. To prevent this, rinse them under cool water, and drain thoroughly. Wrap them in paper towels, place in plastic bags, and refrigerate. Parsley and other fresh herbs should be rinsed and put into a container with their stems in the water. Secure a plastic bag over the top, and refrigerate.

Vegetables such as corn, beans, and peas lose sweetness within a short time as the sugar in their tissues turns to starch. Store them dry and unwashed in plastic bags in the refrigerator.

Just about all fresh vegetables, in fact, should be stored in plastic bags in the refrigerator. The exceptions are potatoes and onions. Store these in a cool, dry, well-ventilated place out of direct sunlight. However, don't store potatoes and onions together as they tend to hasten spoilage of each other.

FREEZING VEGETABLES

Most fresh vegetables require blanching prior to freezing to maintain good quality. Freezing fresh vegetables is discussed in detail in the chapter on food preservation.

Leftover cooked vegetables and casseroles usually freeze well, although the texture of reheated vegetables will not be quite as crisp as freshly cooked. Casseroles with a white sauce base freeze best; avoid freezing any casseroles that include mayonnaise or hard-cooked egg.

THE BASICS OF COOKING VEGETABLES

When we test any vegetable recipe, regardless of the cooking method used, we keep these basic cooking principles in mind:

● To retain as many of the nutrients as possible, avoid cutting vegetables into tiny pieces. When possible, leave the vegetables whole or cut them into large chunks; the larger the pieces the more nutrients retained.

● Use as little water as possible in cooking. (Reserve the vegetable water, and use when making soups or stews to increase the flavor and nutritional value.)

● Avoid overcooking vegetables, because this drives out nutrients and makes the vegetables limp. When the vegetables are bright in color and crisp-tender, they are ready to eat. Crisp-tender means they should be soft enough for a fork to penetrate, but not so soft that it penetrates without moderate resistance. At this stage, the vegetables will hold their shape best, provide the most flavor, and their texture will be neither mushy or flabby.

Boiling: This method is a popular way to cook vegetables, but it's easy to overdo. Use a shallow saucepan when cooking vegetables by this method, and use just enough water to barely cover them.

Bring the water to a boil over high heat; then add the vegetable. When the water returns to a boil, cover the pan, and reduce the heat so vegetables will boil gently. After a short cooking time, as little as 3 to 5 minutes for some vegetables, test them with a fork for doneness. Refer to our Vegetable Cooking Chart on pages 496-498 for directions for boiling many types of vegetables.

Steaming: Among the many ways to cook vegetables, steaming is one of our favorites. This method not only preserves nutrients, it also retains much of the color and texture of fresh vegetables.

To steam vegetables, use a pot with a tight-fitting lid and a steamer rack. Add water to depth of 1 inch in the pot, making sure the water does not touch the bottom of the rack. It's the steam from the water that cooks the vegetables, not the water.

Add the vegetables to the rack, and place it over the water. Cover and let the water boil over medium-high heat. The vegetables are done when crisp-tender. Depending on the vegetable used, you may need to add more water to complete the cooking process.

Stir-frying: Cooking at a high temperature for only a short period of time is the key to stir-frying. This ensures minimum nutrient loss while preserving the natural color and flavor of the vegetables.

Cut tender vegetables such as zucchini into large slices, or leave them whole as with fresh mushrooms. Cut less tender vegetables such as carrots and celery diagonally into smaller slices to expose the largest possible area to the heat.

Heat a small amount of oil in a large skillet or wok; rotate the skillet just long enough to coat the sides with the hot oil. Add the vegetables, and stir constantly until the vegetables are crisp-tender. Use a combination of vegetables, such as squash, zucchini, onion, and tomato, or stir-fry a single vegetable; then add your favorite seasonings.

Sautéing: This method is a close relative of stir-frying but doesn't require the high temperature needed to stir-fry. To sauté, cook vegetables in a small amount of oil over medium heat in a shallow skillet, just until crisp-tender.

MICROWAVING VEGETABLES

The microwave oven is rapidly becoming standard kitchen equipment, and some of the best foods to come out of these ovens are vegetables. They retain nutrients and natural flavor because they can be cooked with little or no water. Vegetables with a high water content, such as fresh corn on the cob, cook in their own juices. Here are tips for microwaving vegetables:

- Cover vegetables tightly unless otherwise stated in the recipe.
- Stir vegetable halfway into the cooking time to distribute the heat.
- Arrange smaller or more tender portions of vegetables toward the center of the dish. For example, place broccoli flowerets toward the center of the dish, extending the tougher stem ends toward the outer edge of the dish.
- Rotate dish during cooking to promote even cooking.
- Before cooking, pierce vegetables to be cooked in their skins, such as potatoes and acorn squash, to release excess steam.

When cooking commercially frozen vegetables in the microwave, you can cook them right in the box. Remove the outside wrapping (wax contained in wrappings of some brands can melt onto your hands; other brands contain foil), and place the box in a flat baking dish. (Use a paper platter if you want to eliminate dishwashing.) Prick the box several times with a fork to let steam escape, and microwave according to the time specified. Watch out for steam as you open the box.

To cook solid-pack frozen vegetables in a microwave-safe dish, remove them from the box and place them, icy side up, in the dish. Add 1 tablespoon water for each box you're cooking; cover with the glass lid made for the dish or with heavy-duty plastic wrap. Cooking times in a dish are often the same as in the box, but can be one or two minutes longer.

Always cook loose-pack vegetables in a dish, and add 2 tablespoons water per 16-ounce package since these vegetables contain fewer ice crystals.

Whether you're microwaving vegetables in the box or in a dish, you will need to stir the vegetables halfway through the cooking time. Simply untuck the box lid, or remove the glass lid or plastic wrap.

COOKING VEGETABLES

When your recipe calls for a certain amount of cooked vegetable or you want to cook vegetables by the simplest method, use the Vegetable Cooking Chart on pages 496-498 as a guide. Remember that cooking times may vary slightly, depending on the size and freshness of the produce.

Vegetables

MARINATED ARTICHOKE HEARTS

⅓ cup olive or vegetable oil
¼ cup vinegar
1 clove garlic, minced
1 tablespoon grated onion
⅛ teaspoon salt
⅛ teaspoon pepper
⅛ teaspoon dry mustard
⅛ teaspoon dried whole basil
1 (14-ounce) can artichoke hearts, drained and sliced in half

Combine first 8 ingredients in a medium bowl, mixing well. Add artichokes, and toss lightly. Cover and refrigerate at least 8 hours. Yield: 4 servings.

Intimidated by an Artichoke?

Many people shy away from trying this tasty vegetable because they just don't know how to eat it. Don't let that be the case with you.

Pluck the cooked leaves, one at a time, dipping the base of the leaf into clarified butter or whatever sauce it's served with. Turn the leaf meaty side down, and draw the leaf between the teeth, scraping off the meaty portion. Discard the remaining part of the leaf on the plate. If the leafy portion of the artichoke is stuffed, eat the stuffing along with the meaty portion of each leaf. Discard the remaining part of the leaf on the plate. If the center of the artichoke is stuffed, just use a fork for it.

When the leaves have been removed, there will remain a core of little leaves and a fuzzy "choke" (unless the choke was removed during preparation). Cut off the center core of leaves, and slice off the fuzzy choke with a knife and fork. The remaining "heart" is considered the prize portion of the vegetable; cut it into bite-size pieces, and dip it into the sauce to eat.

VEGETABLE-STUFFED ARTICHOKES

6 small artichokes
Lemon wedge
¾ teaspoon salt
2 green onions, chopped
3 tablespoons butter or margarine, melted
¼ cup all-purpose flour
1 cup half-and-half or milk
½ teaspoon salt
⅛ teaspoon pepper
Dash of hot sauce
½ cup diced carrots
½ cup frozen or canned green peas
½ cup chopped mushrooms
2 tablespoons dry white wine
½ cup soft breadcrumbs
Clarified Butter (page 440)
Lemon wedges
Lemon rind

Wash artichokes by plunging up and down in cold water. Cut off stem end, and trim about ½ inch from top of each artichoke. Remove any loose bottom leaves. With scissors, trim away about a fourth of each outer leaf. Rub top and edges of leaves with a lemon wedge to prevent discoloration.

Place artichokes in a large Dutch oven; add water to depth of 1 inch. Add ¾ teaspoon salt to water. Bring to a boil; cover, reduce heat, and simmer 25 minutes or until almost tender. Spread leaves apart; scrape out the fuzzy thistle center (choke) with a spoon. Set artichokes aside.

Sauté green onions in butter in a large skillet until tender. Add flour, stirring until smooth. Cook 1 minute, stirring constantly. Gradually add half-and-half; cook over medium heat, stirring constantly, until thickened and bubbly. Stir in salt, pepper, hot sauce, vegetables, and wine.

Spoon vegetable mixture into artichoke cavities. Arrange artichokes in a shallow baking dish; sprinkle breadcrumbs on top. Bake at 350° for 20 minutes or until tops are browned. Serve with Clarified Butter; garnish with lemon wedges and a twist of lemon rind. Yield: 6 servings.

MARINATED ASPARAGUS

1½ pounds fresh asparagus spears or 2 (14½-ounce) cans asparagus spears, drained
1 green pepper, chopped
1 small bunch green onions with tops, chopped
1 stalk celery, finely chopped
¾ cup vegetable oil
½ cup red wine vinegar
½ cup sugar
1 small clove garlic, minced
¼ teaspoon paprika
Pimiento strips

Snap off tough ends of asparagus. Remove scales from stalks with a knife or vegetable peeler, if desired. Cook asparagus, covered, in boiling water 6 to 8 minutes or until crisp-tender. Drain. (Do not cook canned asparagus.)

Place asparagus in a 13- x 9- x 2-inch baking dish. Combine green pepper and next 7 ingredients; stir well, and pour over asparagus; cover and chill at least 4 hours. Drain before serving; garnish with pimiento. Yield: 6 servings.

Vegetable-Stuffed Artichokes Step-By-Step

1. Prepare Vegetable-Stuffed Artichokes by first cutting off the stem end and slicing about ½-inch from the top of each artichoke.

2. Trim away about one-fourth of each outer leaf, using kitchen shears.

3. Rub top of artichoke and edges of leaves with lemon juice to prevent discoloration.

4. Place artichokes in a large Dutch oven; add water to depth of 1 inch. Add salt, and cook as directed.

Serve Vegetable-Stuffed Artichokes with lemon wedges and Clarified Butter for dipping.

5. After cooking, spread leaves apart, and scrape out the fuzzy thistle center (choke) with a spoon.

To prepare asparagus for cooking: Hold base of asparagus stalk, and snap off ends where they seem to break naturally. The end removed will be the tough part; what remains should be tender after cooking.

Make Your Own Breadcrumbs

Many vegetable recipes call for breadcrumbs, either as a filler ingredient or as a topping. You can always have fresh breadcrumbs on hand if you stockpile scraps and end pieces of bread in the freezer, make them into breadcrumbs, and freeze them again until needed. Even when frozen, they stay free-flowing enough to measure without thawing.

To make breadcrumbs, place torn pieces of bread in your food processor or electric blender, and process until ground. When making dry breadcrumbs, dry the bread first in a 250° oven; watch it carefully, as cooking time varies depending on the thickness and type of bread, and how stale it is.

Don't ignore leftover scraps of whole wheat, rye, or other types of bread; they make good breadcrumbs, too, either alone or in combination with white bread.

ASPARAGUS WITH ORANGE SAUCE

1½ pounds fresh asparagus spears
1½ teaspoons cornstarch
¼ cup orange juice
2 tablespoons grated orange rind
⅓ cup butter or margarine
¼ teaspoon white pepper
3 orange slices

Snap off tough ends of asparagus. Remove scales from stalks with a knife or vegetable peeler, if desired. Cook asparagus, covered, in small amount boiling water 6 to 8 minutes or until crisp-tender. Drain. Arrange on serving platter; keep warm.

Combine cornstarch and orange juice in a small saucepan; add orange rind, butter, and pepper. Bring mixture to a boil; reduce heat and simmer, uncovered, 7 minutes or until mixture thickens slightly, stirring constantly.

Pour sauce on asparagus; garnish with orange slices. Yield: 4 to 6 servings.

⬭*Microwave Directions:* Snap off tough ends of asparagus. Remove scales from stalks with a knife or vegetable peeler, if desired. Combine asparagus and ¼ cup water in a shallow 2-quart baking dish. Cover with lid, and microwave at HIGH for 6 to 8 minutes or until crisp-tender. Drain. Arrange on serving platter; keep warm.

Combine cornstarch and orange juice in a 2-cup glass measure; add orange rind, butter, and pepper. Microwave at HIGH for 2 minutes or until mixture thickens slightly, stirring after 1 minute.

Pour sauce on asparagus; garnish with orange slices.

ASPARAGUS GOLDENROD

1½ pounds fresh asparagus spears
2 tablespoons butter or margarine
2 tablespoons all-purpose flour
1 cup milk
¼ teaspoon salt
Dash of pepper
½ cup cottage cheese
Toast points (optional)
3 hard-cooked eggs, diced
Hard-cooked egg slices
Mint leaves

Snap off tough ends of asparagus. Remove scales from stalks with a knife or vegetable peeler, if desired. Cook asparagus, covered, in small amount boiling water 6 to 8 minutes or until crisp-tender. Drain.

Melt butter in a heavy saucepan over low heat; add flour, stirring until smooth. Cook 1 minute, stirring constantly. Gradually add milk; cook over medium heat, stirring constantly, until thickened and bubbly. Stir in salt and pepper. Fold in cottage cheese; cook over low heat 1 minute.

Place asparagus on toast, if desired, or arrange on serving platter; top with sauce, and sprinkle with diced egg. Garnish with egg slices and mint leaves. Yield: 6 servings.

⬭*Microwave Directions:* Snap off tough ends of asparagus. Remove scales from stalks with a knife or vegetable peeler, if desired. Combine asparagus and ¼ cup water in a shallow 2-quart casserole. Cover with lid, and microwave at HIGH for 6 to 8 minutes or until crisp-tender. Drain.

Place butter in a 1-quart glass measure. Microwave at HIGH for 45 seconds or until melted. Add flour, stirring until smooth. Gradually add milk, stirring well. Microwave at HIGH for 6 to 8 minutes or until thickened and bubbly, stirring after 2 minutes, then at 1-minute intervals. Stir in salt and pepper. Fold in cottage cheese. Microwave at HIGH for 30 seconds.

Place asparagus on toast, if desired, or arrange on serving platter; top with sauce, and sprinkle with diced egg. Garnish with egg slices and mint leaves.

CHUCKWAGON BEANS

2 medium onions, finely chopped
1 medium-size green pepper, finely
   chopped
1 (28-ounce) can pork and beans
¾ cup catsup
½ cup firmly packed brown sugar
½ cup molasses
1 teaspoon liquid smoke
Dash of hot sauce

Combine all ingredients, stirring well. Spoon bean mixture into a lightly greased 12- x 8- x 2-inch baking dish.

Bake bean mixture, uncovered, at 425° for 30 to 45 minutes or until mixture is bubbly. Yield: 6 servings.

◯*Microwave Directions:* Combine all ingredients, stirring well. Spoon bean mixture into a lightly greased 12- x 8- x 2-inch baking dish; cover dish loosely with wax paper. Microwave bean mixture at HIGH for 20 to 24 minutes or until mixture is thoroughly heated and desired thickness, stirring after 6 minutes, then at 4-minute intervals.

CREOLE BEANS AND RICE

1 pound dried red beans
¼ pound salt pork
3 cups chopped onion
1 bunch green onions, chopped
1 cup chopped fresh parsley
1 cup chopped green pepper
2 cloves garlic, pressed
1 teaspoon red pepper
1 teaspoon pepper
3 dashes of hot sauce
1 tablespoon Worcestershire sauce
1 (8-ounce) can tomato sauce
¼ teaspoon dried whole oregano
¼ teaspoon dried whole thyme
2 pounds Mettwurst or other
   smoked German sausage, cut into
   bite-size pieces
Hot cooked rice

Sort and wash beans; place in a large Dutch oven. Cover with water 2 inches above beans; let soak 8 hours. Drain. Cover beans with water, and add salt pork; bring to a boil. Cover, reduce heat, and simmer over low heat 45 minutes. Add remaining ingredients except sausage and rice; cover and cook over low heat 1 hour, stirring occasionally. Add sausage; cook, uncovered, over low heat 45 minutes, stirring occasionally. Serve over rice. Yield: 8 servings.

The creamy topping on Asparagus Goldenrod is filled with cottage cheese and sprinkled with diced egg. Hard-cooked egg slices and a mint sprig complete the garnish.

SOUTHERN BAKED BEANS

2 cups dried Great Northern beans
½ teaspoon salt
½ cup cubed salt pork
½ cup chopped onion
½ cup molasses
2 tablespoons catsup
½ teaspoon prepared mustard
¼ teaspoon pepper
2 cups hot water

Sort and wash beans; place in a large Dutch oven. Cover with water 2 inches above beans; let soak 8 hours. Drain.

Cover beans with water, and add salt; bring to a boil. Cover, reduce heat, and simmer 2 hours; drain if necessary.

Place beans in a greased 2½-quart baking dish; add salt pork and onion. Combine molasses, catsup, mustard, pepper, and 2 cups hot water; pour over beans. Cover and bake at 350° for 2 hours, stirring once. Yield: 8 servings.

GREEN BEANS AMANDINE

2 pounds fresh green beans
1 small ham hock
1 cup water
⅔ cup slivered almonds
⅓ cup minced onion
3 tablespoons butter or margarine, melted
1 teaspoon salt

Wash beans and remove strings. Cut beans into 1½-inch pieces. Place in a 5-quart Dutch oven; add ham hock and water. Bring to a boil; cover, reduce heat, and simmer 30 minutes. Drain off excess liquid.

Sauté almonds and onion in butter until onion is tender. Add to beans, along with salt; toss lightly. Yield: 8 servings.

GREEN BEAN CASSEROLE

1 (10¾-ounce) can cream of mushroom soup, undiluted
1 (3-ounce) package cream cheese, softened
3 (9-ounce) packages frozen French-style green beans, thawed
1 (8-ounce) can sliced water chestnuts, drained
1 clove garlic, minced
2 tablespoons finely chopped onion
¼ teaspoon pepper
1½ cups (6 ounces) shredded Cheddar cheese
1 (2-ounce) package slivered almonds, lightly toasted

Combine soup and cream cheese in a large saucepan. Cook over medium heat, stirring constantly, until cream cheese melts. Remove from heat; stir in green beans, water chestnuts, garlic, onion, pepper, and cheese.

Spoon mixture into a lightly greased 1¾-quart casserole; top with almonds. Bake, uncovered, at 375° for 30 minutes. Yield: 8 servings.

○*Microwave Directions:* Combine soup and cream cheese in a medium bowl. Microwave at MEDIUM HIGH (70% power) for 3 minutes or until cream cheese melts, stirring every minute. Stir in green beans, water chestnuts, garlic, onion, pepper, and cheese.

Spoon mixture into a lightly greased 1¾-quart casserole; top with almonds. Microwave at HIGH for 8 to 9 minutes or until thoroughly heated, giving dish a quarter-turn every 3 minutes.

Note: Two (16-ounce) cans French-style green beans may be substituted for frozen green beans, if desired. Drain before using.

LIMAS IN PIMIENTO-CHEESE SAUCE

1 pound shelled fresh lima beans (3 cups)
1 cup boiling water
¼ cup chopped onion
2 tablespoons butter or margarine, melted
1½ tablespoons all-purpose flour
1 cup milk
1 teaspoon salt
⅛ teaspoon pepper
1 (2-ounce) jar diced pimiento, drained
1 cup (4 ounces) shredded Cheddar cheese
4 slices bacon, cooked and crumbled

Cook beans in 1 cup boiling water 20 minutes or until tender; drain.

Sauté onion in butter until tender. Add flour, stirring until smooth. Cook 1 minute, stirring constantly. Gradually add milk; cook over medium heat, stirring constantly, until thickened and bubbly. Add salt, pepper, pimiento, and cheese; stir until cheese melts. Stir beans into sauce mixture. Spoon mixture into serving bowl, and sprinkle bacon over top. Yield: 4 to 6 servings.

Help for the Phrase "I Don't Like It"

If you have a hard time getting your family to eat vegetables, try a few fix-ups that might change the personality of the dish a little. Stir the cooked vegetables into a cream or cheese sauce, sprinkle with chopped toasted nuts such as pecans, almonds, and peanuts, or sprinkle crumbled cooked bacon over the top. Even a few strands of shredded cheese might be enough to spark interest in finicky eaters.

ORANGE-GINGER BEETS

1 pound fresh beets
½ teaspoon grated orange rind
¾ cup orange juice
2 teaspoons cornstarch
2 teaspoons sugar
½ teaspoon ground ginger
⅛ teaspoon salt
1 tablespoon butter or margarine

Leave root and 1 inch of stem on beets; scrub with a vegetable brush. Place beets in a saucepan; add water to cover. Bring to a boil; cover, reduce heat, and simmer 35 to 40 minutes or until tender. Drain; pour cold water over beets, and drain. Trim off roots and stems, and rub off skins; cut beets into julienne strips, and set aside.

Combine orange rind, orange juice, cornstarch, sugar, ginger, and salt in a small bowl, stirring well. Melt butter in a medium skillet; add beets and orange juice mixture. Place over medium heat; bring to a boil, and cook 1 minute, stirring constantly. Yield: 4 to 6 servings.

To prepare broccoli: Remove outer leaves and tough lower stalks. Slice off flowerets, including about 3 inches of the stem; cut flowerets into individual spears. Slice remaining stalks into thin strips.

SWEET-AND-SOUR BEETS

12 small beets
½ cup sugar
1 tablespoon cornstarch
½ teaspoon salt
2 whole cloves
½ cup vinegar
3 tablespoons orange marmalade
2 tablespoons butter or margarine

Leave root and 1 inch of stem on beets; scrub with a vegetable brush. Place beets in a saucepan; add water to cover. Bring to a boil; cover, reduce heat, and simmer 35 to 40 minutes or until tender. Drain; pour cold water over beets, and drain. Trim off stems and roots, and rub off skins.

Combine sugar, cornstarch, salt, and cloves in a heavy saucepan; stir in vinegar. Cook over medium heat, stirring constantly, until thickened and bubbly.

Add beets to sauce, and cook 15 minutes; stir in marmalade and butter. Yield: 4 to 6 servings.

ZESTY BROCCOLI SPEARS

1 pound fresh broccoli
3 tablespoons olive oil
3 tablespoons lemon juice
¼ teaspoon salt
⅛ teaspoon pepper
1 medium clove garlic, crushed

Trim off large leaves of broccoli, and remove tough ends of lower stalks. Wash broccoli thoroughly, and cut into spears. Cook in a small amount of boiling water 10 to 12 minutes or just until tender; drain. Chill thoroughly.

Combine remaining ingredients, stirring well; pour over chilled broccoli. Yield: 4 servings.

◻ Microwave Directions: Trim off large leaves of broccoli, and remove tough ends of lower stalks. Wash broccoli thoroughly, and cut into spears. Arrange broccoli in a shallow 2-quart baking dish, stem ends out; add ¼ cup water. Cover with lid, and microwave at HIGH for 6 to 8 minutes or just until tender; drain. Chill thoroughly.

Combine remaining ingredients, stirring well; pour over chilled broccoli.

Save Those Leftover Vegetables

Think before you throw leftover vegetables out. Stockpiled bits of plain cooked vegetables will make soup later in the week. Highly seasoned vegetables might add just the spark your homemade soup needs. Sautéed mushrooms and onions make wonderful pizza toppings. Other vegetables work well to fill an omelet.

BROCCOLI WITH SESAME

1 pound fresh broccoli
2 tablespoons sesame seeds
3 tablespoons peanut or vegetable oil
2 teaspoons minced garlic
½ cup sliced water chestnuts
3 tablespoons white wine
3 tablespoons soy sauce
½ teaspoon salt

Trim off large leaves of broccoli, and remove tough ends of lower stalks. Wash broccoli thoroughly. Cut away tops, and set aside. Cut stalks into ¼-inch slices; set aside.

Toast sesame seeds in an electric wok or skillet; remove and set aside. Pour oil into wok; heat at 325° for 3 minutes. Add garlic; stir-fry briefly. Add broccoli stalks; stir-fry 5 minutes. Add water chestnuts, wine, soy sauce, salt, and broccoli tops; stir well. Cover and cook 5 minutes; sprinkle sesame seeds over top. Yield: 4 to 5 servings.

BROCCOLI-SWISS CHEESE CASSEROLE

5 cups chopped fresh broccoli
1 (24-ounce) carton cottage cheese
3 eggs
¼ cup butter or margarine, melted
⅓ cup all-purpose flour
1 (8¾-ounce) can whole kernel corn, drained
2 cups (8 ounces) shredded Swiss cheese
¼ cup finely chopped onion
½ teaspoon salt
¼ teaspoon pepper
4 drops of hot sauce
8 slices bacon, cooked and crumbled

Cook broccoli, covered, in a small amount boiling water 10 minutes or until tender. Drain.

Combine cottage cheese, eggs, butter, and flour in container of an electric blender; process until smooth. Set aside. Combine broccoli, corn, and next 5 ingredients in a large bowl; stir in cottage cheese mixture. Spoon into a lightly greased 12- x 8- x 2-inch baking dish. Sprinkle bacon over casserole. Bake casserole at 350° for 45 minutes. Yield: 8 to 10 servings.

BROCCOLI WITH CHEESE SAUCE

1½ pounds fresh broccoli
½ teaspoon dried whole oregano
½ teaspoon salt (optional)
½ cup mayonnaise
¼ cup (1 ounce) shredded Cheddar cheese
¼ cup milk
2 tablespoons grated Parmesan cheese

Trim off large leaves of broccoli, and remove tough ends; wash thoroughly. Cut into spears. Place broccoli in a Dutch oven; add oregano and water to depth of 1 inch. Bring to a boil; cover, reduce heat, and simmer 10 to 15 minutes or until tender. Drain; place in a serving dish. Sprinkle broccoli with salt, if desired.

Combine the mayonnaise, Cheddar cheese, and milk in a saucepan; cook over low heat until cheese melts, stirring constantly. Spoon mixture over broccoli, and sprinkle Parmesan cheese over sauce. Yield: 4 to 6 servings.

Note: Two (10-ounce) packages frozen broccoli spears may be substituted for 1½ pounds fresh broccoli, if desired. Simmer just until tender.

☐*Microwave Directions:* Trim off large leaves of broccoli, and remove tough ends; wash thoroughly, and cut into spears. Arrange broccoli in a shallow 2-quart baking dish, with stem ends toward outside of dish; add oregano and ½ cup water. Cover with lid or heavy-duty plastic wrap, and microwave at HIGH for 8 minutes or until broccoli is tender. Drain and place in a serving dish. Sprinkle with salt, if desired.

Combine the mayonnaise, Cheddar cheese, and milk in a 1-cup glass measure. Microwave at MEDIUM HIGH (70% power) for 1 to 2 minutes or until cheese melts, stirring after 1 minute. Spoon mixture over broccoli, and sprinkle Parmesan cheese over sauce.

BROCCOLI SOUFFLÉ

1 (10-ounce) package frozen chopped broccoli, thawed
¼ cup butter or margarine
¼ cup plus 2 tablespoons all-purpose flour
1½ cups milk
½ teaspoon salt
¼ teaspoon pepper
⅛ teaspoon ground nutmeg
Dash of red pepper
1 cup (4 ounces) shredded Swiss cheese
4 eggs, separated

Cook broccoli according to package directions, omitting salt; drain well. Po-

To ensure even cooking of brussels sprouts: Cut a shallow "X" in stem end of sprouts; this allows the heat to penetrate through the stem.

sition knife blade in food processor bowl; add broccoli, and process until smooth. Set aside.

Cut an aluminum foil strip long enough to fit around a 1-quart soufflé dish, allowing a 1-inch overlap; fold foil lengthwise into thirds. Lightly oil one side of foil and bottom of dish. Wrap foil around dish, oiled side against dish, allowing it to extend 3 inches above rim to form a collar; secure with string.

Melt butter in a large heavy saucepan over low heat; add flour, stirring until smooth. Cook 1 minute, stirring constantly. Gradually add milk; cook over medium heat, stirring constantly, until thickened and bubbly. Stir in salt, pepper, nutmeg, red pepper, and cheese.

Beat egg yolks until thick and lemon colored. Gradually stir about one-fourth of hot sauce into yolks; add to remaining hot mixture, stirring constantly. Add broccoli, and stir well.

Beat egg whites (at room temperature) until stiff but not dry. Gently fold into broccoli mixture. Spoon into prepared dish. Bake at 350° for 50 to 55 minutes or until golden brown. Serve immediately. Yield: 6 servings.

Note: To omit collar, bake mixture in a 1½-quart soufflé dish.

BRUSSELS SPROUTS AMANDINE

1 pound fresh brussels sprouts
1 cup water
2 teaspoons chicken-flavored bouillon granules
1 (10¾-ounce) can cream of chicken soup, undiluted
1 (2-ounce) jar diced pimiento, undrained
⅛ teaspoon dried whole thyme
⅛ teaspoon pepper
½ cup sliced almonds, lightly toasted

Wash the brussels sprouts thoroughly, and remove discolored leaves. Cut off stem ends, and slash bottom of each sprout with a shallow X.

Place brussels sprouts, water, and bouillon granules in a medium saucepan. Cook over medium-high heat until mixture comes to a boil; cover, reduce heat, and simmer 8 minutes or until tender. Drain.

Combine soup, pimiento, thyme, and pepper in a greased 1½-quart casserole; stir in brussels sprouts, and sprinkle with almonds. Bake at 350° for 20 minutes or until hot and bubbly. Yield: 4 to 6 servings.

Note: Two (10-ounce) packages frozen brussels sprouts may be substituted for 1 pound fresh brussels sprouts.

◯*Microwave Directions:* Wash the brussels sprouts thoroughly, and remove discolored leaves. Cut off stem ends, and slash bottom of each sprout with a shallow X.

Combine brussels sprouts, water, and bouillon granules in a 1½-quart baking dish; cover with lid, and microwave at HIGH for 8 to 10 minutes or until tender, stirring once. Let stand 2 minutes; drain.

Combine soup, pimiento, thyme, and pepper in a greased 1½-quart casserole; stir in brussels sprouts, and sprinkle with almonds. Microwave at HIGH for 6 minutes or until hot and bubbly, giving dish a half-turn after 4 minutes.

BRUSSELS SPROUTS MEDLEY

1½ pounds fresh brussels sprouts
3 cups water
2 chicken-flavored bouillon cubes
1½ cups thinly sliced carrots
1½ cups sliced celery
⅓ cup butter or margarine
¾ cup dry roasted cashew halves
¼ teaspoon salt
¼ teaspoon dried whole thyme, crushed
⅛ teaspoon pepper

Wash brussels sprouts thoroughly, and remove discolored leaves. Cut off stem ends, and slash bottom of each sprout with a shallow X.

Place water and bouillon cubes in a medium saucepan; bring to a boil. Add brussels sprouts, carrots, and celery; return to a boil. Cover, reduce heat, and simmer 12 to 15 minutes or until vegetables are tender. Drain; place vegetables in a serving bowl.

Melt butter in a small skillet; add cashews and seasonings. Cook over low heat 3 to 4 minutes or until cashews are lightly toasted; pour over vegetables. Yield: 8 to 10 servings.

Note: Three (10-ounce) packages frozen brussels sprouts may be substituted for 1½ pounds fresh brussels sprouts.

CABBAGE CASSEROLE

1 medium-size green cabbage, cut into thin wedges
½ cup water
¼ cup butter or margarine
¼ cup all-purpose flour
2 cups milk
½ teaspoon salt
¼ teaspoon pepper
¾ cup (3 ounces) shredded Cheddar cheese
½ cup mayonnaise
3 tablespoons chili sauce
½ cup finely chopped onion
½ cup finely chopped green pepper

Combine cabbage wedges and water in a large saucepan; cover and cook over medium heat 15 minutes. Drain well, and place cabbage wedges in a 12- x 8- x 2-inch baking dish.

Melt butter in a heavy saucepan over low heat; add flour, stirring until smooth. Cook over low heat 1 minute, stirring constantly. Gradually add milk; cook over medium heat, stirring constantly, until mixture is thickened and bubbly. Stir in the salt and pepper. Pour mixture over cabbage, and bake at 375° for 20 minutes.

Combine cheese, mayonnaise, chili sauce, onion, and green pepper; stir well, and spread over cabbage. Bake at 400° for 20 minutes. Yield: 8 servings.

◯*Microwave Directions:* Combine cabbage and water in a 12- x 8- x 2-inch baking dish. Cover with heavy-duty plastic wrap, and microwave at HIGH for 12 to 15 minutes or until tender, turning wedges over and rearranging halfway through cooking time. Drain well, and return to baking dish.

Place butter in a 1-quart glass measure; microwave at HIGH for 55 seconds or until melted. Add flour, stirring until smooth. Gradually add milk, stirring well. Microwave at HIGH for 6 to 7 minutes or until thickened and bubbly, stirring twice. Stir in salt and pepper. Pour mixture over cabbage; microwave at HIGH for 4 minutes.

Combine cheese, mayonnaise, chili sauce, onion, and green pepper; stir well, and spread over cabbage. Microwave at HIGH for 5 to 6 minutes, giving dish a half-turn after 2 minutes.

CRISPY MARINATED CARROTS

1 pound carrots, scraped and thinly sliced
⅓ cup chopped onion
⅓ cup chopped green pepper
⅓ cup vinegar
⅓ cup sugar
3 tablespoons vegetable oil
1 teaspoon Worcestershire sauce
¼ teaspoon prepared mustard

Cook carrots in a small amount of boiling water about 5 minutes or until crisp-tender; drain. Combine carrots, onion, and green pepper.

Combine remaining ingredients in a jar. Cover tightly, and shake vigorously. Pour over vegetables; toss lightly with a fork. Cover and chill at least 8 hours. Yield: 4 to 6 servings.

◻ *Microwave Directions:* Place 1 cup water in a 1½-quart casserole. Microwave at HIGH for 1 minute. Add carrots; cover and microwave at HIGH for 5 to 6 minutes or until carrots are crisp-tender, stirring once. Drain. Combine carrots, onion, and green pepper.

Combine remaining ingredients in a jar. Cover tightly, and shake vigorously. Pour over vegetables; toss lightly with a fork. Cover and chill 8 hours.

CARROTS MADEIRA

¼ cup butter or margarine, melted
1½ pounds carrots, scraped and cut into julienne sticks
¼ cup Madeira wine
1 teaspoon salt
6 sprigs fresh parsley, minced
⅛ teaspoon dried tarragon leaves

Combine butter, carrots, wine, and salt in a heavy saucepan. Bring to a boil; cover, reduce heat, and simmer 15 minutes or until carrots are tender. Drain well; sprinkle with parsley and tarragon. Yield: 6 servings.

◻ *Microwave Directions:* Combine butter, carrots, wine, and salt in a 2-quart casserole. Cover with heavy-duty plastic wrap; microwave at HIGH for 12 minutes or until carrots are desired degree of doneness, stirring every 4 minutes. Drain well; sprinkle with parsley and tarragon.

ORANGE-RAISIN CARROTS

1 pound carrots, scraped and sliced
¾ cup water
½ teaspoon salt
1 tablespoon cornstarch
1 cup orange juice
½ cup raisins
1 tablespoon sugar

Combine carrots, water, and salt in a medium saucepan; bring to a boil. Cover, reduce heat, and simmer 5 to 8 minutes or until carrots are crisp-tender. Drain.

Combine cornstarch and orange juice; stir into carrots. Stir in raisins and sugar. Cook over medium heat, stirring constantly, until smooth and thickened. Yield: 4 to 6 servings.

◻ *Microwave Directions:* Combine carrots, water, and salt in a 1-quart baking dish. Cover with lid, and microwave at HIGH for 7 to 8 minutes or until carrots are crisp-tender. Drain.

Combine cornstarch and orange juice; stir into carrots. Stir in raisins and sugar. Cover with lid, and microwave at HIGH for 4 to 5 minutes or until smooth and thickened, stirring every 2 minutes.

A Trick with Cauliflower

You can arrange prepared flowerets to resemble a whole uncut head of cauliflower by grouping them with the stem ends down and to the center of the arrangement.

FRENCH-FRIED CAULIFLOWER AU GRATIN

1 small head cauliflower
2 eggs
2 tablespoons water
2½ cups fine cracker crumbs
Vegetable oil
Cheddar Cheese Sauce (page 437)

Remove large outer leaves of cauliflower. Break cauliflower into flowerets. Cook, covered, in a small amount of boiling salted water 8 minutes or until crisp-tender; drain.

Combine eggs and water; beat well. Dredge flowerets in cracker crumbs; then dip in egg. Dredge again in cracker crumbs. Deep fry in hot oil (375°) until golden brown. Drain on paper towels. Serve with Cheddar Cheese Sauce. Yield: 4 to 6 servings.

CAULIFLOWER WITH HERB BUTTER

(pictured on page 464)

1 large head cauliflower
Juice of 1 lemon
¼ cup plus 1 tablespoon butter or margarine, melted
1 tablespoon chopped fresh parsley
¼ teaspoon salt
1 tablespoon chopped fresh basil or ¼ teaspoon dried whole basil
1 small clove garlic, crushed
Lemon twists
Parsley sprigs

Remove large outer leaves of cauliflower. Break cauliflower into flowerets. Cook, covered, in a small amount of boiling water 8 to 10 minutes or until tender; drain. Arrange flowerets in serving dish, and sprinkle with lemon juice.

Combine butter and next 4 ingredients; pour herb butter evenly over flowerets. Garnish with lemon twists and parsley sprigs. Yield: 6 servings.

⊡*Microwave Directions:* Remove large outer leaves of cauliflower. Break cauliflower into flowerets. Place flowerets in a shallow 2-quart casserole; add ¼ cup water. Cover with lid, and microwave at HIGH for 8 to 10 minutes or until tender, stirring once. Drain cauliflower; arrange flowerets in serving dish, and sprinkle with lemon juice.

Combine butter and next 4 ingredients; pour herb butter evenly over flowerets. Garnish with lemon twists and parsley sprigs.

CHEESE-TOPPED CAULIFLOWER

1 medium head cauliflower
2 cups water
½ teaspoon salt
¾ cup (3 ounces) shredded sharp Cheddar cheese
½ cup mayonnaise
1 tablespoon diced pimiento
2 teaspoons Dijon mustard
2 tablespoons sliced almonds, toasted

Remove outer leaves and stalk of cauliflower; wash. Leave head whole.

Bring water and salt to a boil in a large saucepan; add cauliflower. Cover and cook 10 to 12 minutes or until tender. Drain cauliflower, and place in a serving dish; keep warm.

Combine cheese and next 3 ingredients in a heavy saucepan. Cook over low heat, stirring constantly, until cheese melts. Spoon over cauliflower; sprinkle with almonds. Yield: 4 to 6 servings.

⊡*Microwave Directions:* Remove outer leaves and stalk of cauliflower; wash. Leave head whole.

Combine cauliflower, water, and salt in a deep 2-quart baking dish. Cover with lid, and microwave at HIGH for 8 minutes or until tender, giving dish a half-turn after 4 minutes. Let stand, covered, 2 minutes; drain. Place in a serving dish; keep warm.

Combine cheese and next 3 ingredients in a 1-quart glass measure. Cover with heavy-duty plastic wrap, and microwave at HIGH for 1 to 2 minutes or until cheese melts, stirring once. Spoon mixture over cauliflower; sprinkle almonds over top.

CAULIFLOWER SOUFFLÉ

1 small head cauliflower
½ cup butter or margarine
¼ cup plus 2 tablespoons all-purpose flour
1½ cups milk
4 eggs, separated
1 (3-ounce) package cream cheese, cubed and softened
½ teaspoon salt
¼ teaspoon white pepper
⅛ teaspoon ground thyme

Remove large outer leaves of cauliflower. Break cauliflower into flowerets. Cook, covered, in a small amount of boiling salted water 8 to 10 minutes or until tender. Drain well; place cauliflower in container of an electric blender or food processor; process until smooth, and set aside.

Melt butter in a heavy saucepan over low heat; add flour, stirring until smooth. Cook 1 minute, stirring constantly. Gradually add milk; cook over medium heat, stirring constantly, until thickened and bubbly.

Beat egg yolks until thick and lemon colored. Gradually stir about one-fourth of hot white sauce into yolks; add to remaining white sauce, stirring constantly. Add cream cheese, stirring until melted. Add cauliflower, salt, pepper, and thyme; stir well.

Beat egg whites (at room temperature) until stiff but not dry. Gently fold into cauliflower mixture. Spoon into a 1½-quart soufflé dish. Bake at 350° for 55 minutes or until golden brown. Serve immediately. Yield: 6 servings.

CELERY STIR-FRY

1 small bunch celery, diagonally sliced ¼-inch thick
3 tablespoons butter or margarine, melted
2 green onions with tops, sliced
1 (2-ounce) jar diced pimiento, drained
¼ cup roasted cashew nuts
¼ teaspoon salt
⅛ teaspoon pepper

Sauté celery in butter in a large skillet until almost crisp-tender. Stir in remaining ingredients, and sauté until celery is crisp-tender. Yield: 4 to 6 servings.

⊡*Microwave Directions:* Combine celery and butter in a 1-quart baking dish. Cover with heavy-duty plastic wrap, and microwave at HIGH for 4 to 5 minutes or until almost crisp-tender. Stir in remaining ingredients; cover and microwave at HIGH for 3 minutes or until celery is crisp-tender.

SAUCY CELERY

4½ cups thinly sliced celery
¼ cup butter or margarine, melted
2 tablespoons all-purpose flour
1 cup milk
1 cup (4 ounces) shredded Cheddar cheese, divided
¼ teaspoon salt
1 (3-ounce) can mushroom stems and pieces, drained
3 tablespoons chopped green pepper

Sauté celery in butter in a large skillet until tender. Stir in flour; cook 1 minute, stirring constantly. Gradually add milk; cook, stirring constantly, until thickened. Add ¾ cup cheese and salt; stir until cheese melts. Stir in mushrooms and green pepper. Pour into a greased 1-quart shallow casserole. Bake at 350° for 15 minutes. Sprinkle with remaining ¼ cup cheese; bake an additional 5 minutes. Yield: 4 to 6 servings.

To prepare corn for creaming:
Cut off tips of corn; then scrape
milk and remaining pulp from
cob, using a small paring knife.

SOUTHERN-STYLE CREAMED CORN

6 medium ears fresh corn
¼ cup butter or margarine
¼ cup water
½ cup half-and-half or milk
2 teaspoons cornstarch
½ teaspoon salt
¼ teaspoon white pepper

Cut corn from cobs, scraping cobs well to remove all milk.

Combine corn, butter, and water in a heavy saucepan. Cover and cook over medium heat 10 minutes or until corn is done, stirring occasionally.

Combine remaining ingredients, beating with a wire whisk until cornstarch is blended; add to corn, stirring well. Cover and cook 3 minutes or until thickened and bubbly, stirring often. Yield: 4 to 6 servings.

⬭ *Microwave Directions:* Cut corn from cobs, scraping cobs well to remove all milk.

Combine corn, butter, and water in a 2-quart casserole, and cover with heavy-duty plastic wrap. Microwave at HIGH for 4 minutes; stir well. Cover and microwave at HIGH for 4 to 6 minutes or until corn is done.

Combine remaining ingredients, beating with a wire whisk until cornstarch is blended; add to corn, stirring well. Cover and microwave at HIGH for 3 to 5 minutes or until thickened and bubbly, stirring at 1-minute intervals.

SEASONED CORN ON THE COB

4 ears fresh corn
¼ cup butter or margarine, softened
1 teaspoon chopped chives
½ teaspoon salt
½ teaspoon prepared mustard
¼ teaspoon pepper

Remove husks and silks from corn just before cooking. Combine remaining ingredients, stirring well. Spread herb butter on corn, and place each ear on a piece of aluminum foil; wrap tightly.

Bake at 400° for 45 minutes, turning occasionally, or grill over medium coals 20 to 30 minutes, turning several times. Yield: 4 servings.

⬭ *Microwave Directions:* Remove husks and silks from corn just before cooking. Combine remaining ingredients, stirring well. Spread herb butter on corn, and place each ear on a piece of wax paper; wrap tightly. Arrange corn in a 12- x 8- x 2-inch baking dish; microwave at HIGH for 8 to 9 minutes or until corn is done, rearranging ears every 4 minutes.

CREAMY CORN PUDDING

3 tablespoons butter or margarine
3 tablespoons all-purpose flour
1 tablespoon sugar
¾ teaspoon salt
¾ cup milk
1 (17-ounce) can cream-style corn
3 eggs

Melt butter in a heavy saucepan over low heat; add flour, sugar, and salt, stirring until smooth. Cook 1 minute, stirring constantly. Gradually add milk; cook over medium heat, stirring constantly, until thickened and bubbly. Remove from heat, and stir in corn.

Beat eggs well. Gradually stir about one-fourth of hot mixture into beaten eggs; add to remaining hot mixture, stirring constantly.

Pour into a greased 1½-quart casserole. Bake at 350° for 1 hour. Yield: 6 servings.

CRISPY EGGPLANT FINGERS

1 medium eggplant
⅔ cup fine, dry breadcrumbs
⅓ cup grated Parmesan cheese
½ teaspoon salt
½ teaspoon celery salt
¼ teaspoon pepper
2 eggs
2 tablespoons milk
Vegetable oil

Peel eggplant; cut into finger-size strips.

Combine next 5 ingredients; stir well. Combine eggs and milk; stir well. Roll eggplant strips in breadcrumb mixture; dip in egg mixture, and roll again in breadcrumb mixture. Fry in hot oil (375°) until golden brown. Drain on paper towels. Yield: about 6 servings.

EGGPLANT PARMESAN

1 large eggplant
Salt
2 eggs, beaten
1½ cups cracker crumbs
Hot vegetable oil
Quick Italian Sauce
2 cups (8 ounces) shredded
  mozzarella cheese
¼ cup plus 2 tablespoons grated
  Parmesan cheese

Peel eggplant, and cut into ¼-inch slices. Sprinkle each slice with salt, and place in a bowl. Let stand 30 minutes; rinse and pat dry. Dip each slice in egg, and coat with cracker crumbs. Fry in hot oil until golden brown. Drain on paper towels.

Place half of eggplant in a lightly greased 12- x 8- x 2-inch baking dish; spread half of Quick Italian Sauce over eggplant. Top with half each of mozzarella and Parmesan cheeses; repeat layers. Bake at 350° for 20 to 25 minutes or until mixture is thoroughly heated. Yield: 6 servings.

Quick Italian Sauce

½ cup chopped onion
1 clove garlic, minced
1 tablespoon vegetable oil
1 (12-ounce) can tomato paste
1 (7¾-ounce) can tomato soup,
  undiluted
1¼ cups water
1½ teaspoons dried whole oregano
½ teaspoon ground basil

Sauté onion and garlic in hot oil until tender; stir in remaining ingredients. Bring to a boil; reduce heat and simmer 15 minutes, stirring occasionally. Yield: about 4 cups.

To remove bitterness from eggplant: Salt the cut eggplant, and let it stand 30 minutes. Then rinse, pat dry, and proceed with recipe.

STUFFED EGGPLANT CASSEROLE

2 small eggplants
4 slices bacon, cut into small pieces
½ cup sliced fresh mushrooms
¼ cup chopped onion
¼ cup chopped green pepper
2 cups peeled chopped tomato
¼ teaspoon salt
⅛ teaspoon pepper
1 cup (4 ounces) shredded
  mozzarella cheese

Wash eggplant; cut in half lengthwise. Remove pulp, leaving a ¼-inch shell; chop pulp. Set shells and pulp aside.

Combine bacon and next 3 ingredients in a large skillet; sauté until bacon is cooked. Add eggplant pulp, tomato, salt, and pepper; bring to a boil. Reduce heat; simmer 10 minutes, stirring occasionally.

Place eggplant shells in a 12- x 8- x 2-inch baking dish. Spoon hot mixture into shells; add water to dish to depth of ½ inch. Bake at 350° for 25 minutes.

Sprinkle with cheese; bake an additional 5 minutes. Yield: 4 servings.

☐ *Microwave Directions:* Wash eggplant, and cut in half lengthwise. Remove pulp, leaving a ¼-inch shell; set shells aside. Chop pulp, and set aside.

Place bacon in a 12- x 8- x 2-inch dish; cover with paper towels. Microwave at HIGH for 3½ minutes or until crisp. Drain bacon; reserve drippings in dish. Crumble bacon; set aside.

Add eggplant pulp, and remaining ingredients except cheese to drippings, stirring well. Cover with heavy-duty plastic wrap; microwave at HIGH for 7 to 9 minutes or until tender. Drain.

Place eggplant shells in a 12- x 8- x 2-inch baking dish. Spoon hot mixture into shells. Cover with wax paper, and microwave at HIGH for 7 to 9 minutes or until eggplant is just tender. Sprinkle with cheese; microwave at HIGH for 1 minute.

EGGPLANT-ZUCCHINI RATATOUILLE

1 large onion, thinly sliced
1 large green pepper, chopped
2 cloves garlic, minced
2 tablespoons vegetable oil
1 medium eggplant, peeled and
  cubed
3 medium zucchini, sliced
3 tomatoes, peeled and chopped
½ teaspoon salt
⅛ teaspoon pepper
Dash of dried whole oregano
2 to 4 tablespoons grated Parmesan
  cheese
2 tablespoons chopped fresh parsley

Sauté onion, green pepper, and garlic in hot oil in a large skillet until vegetables are crisp-tender. Stir in eggplant and zucchini; cook 5 minutes. Add tomatoes, salt, pepper, and oregano; stir well, and cook just until thoroughly heated. Sprinkle with cheese and parsley. Yield: 6 to 8 servings.

SWEET-AND-SOUR GREENS

2½ pounds fresh collard, kale, or
  mustard greens
6 slices bacon, chopped
½ cup water
¼ cup vinegar
½ cup sugar
½ teaspoon salt
⅛ teaspoon pepper

Remove stems from greens. Wash leaves thoroughly, and tear into bite-size pieces. Set aside.

Cook bacon in a large Dutch oven until crisp; remove bacon, reserving drippings in skillet. Set bacon aside.

Add water, vinegar, sugar, salt, and pepper to drippings in Dutch oven; bring to a boil. Add greens; cover and cook over medium heat 30 to 45 minutes or until greens are tender, adding additional liquid if necessary. Spoon into serving dish, and sprinkle bacon over top. Yield: 6 servings.

SPINACH WITH MUSHROOMS

3 tablespoons peanut or
  vegetable oil
1 cup sliced fresh mushrooms
1 onion, chopped
1 clove garlic, chopped
1 pound fresh spinach, washed and
  drained
1 tablespoon lemon juice
1 teaspoon salt
Dash of ground nutmeg
Lemon slices

Pour oil around top of preheated wok, coating sides; allow to heat at high (350°) for 2 minutes. Add mushrooms, onion, and garlic; stir-fry 3 minutes. Add spinach, and stir-fry 3 minutes or until spinach wilts. Sprinkle spinach mixture with lemon juice, salt, and nutmeg, tossing lightly. Garnish with lemon slices. Yield: 4 servings.

CREAMED SPINACH

1 pound fresh spinach
1 medium onion, chopped
1 clove garlic, crushed
¼ cup butter or margarine, melted
½ cup commercial sour cream
Dash of salt
¼ teaspoon pepper
Pinch of ground nutmeg
Paprika

Remove stems from spinach; wash leaves thoroughly, and tear into large pieces. Cook spinach in a small amount of boiling water 5 to 8 minutes or until tender. Drain; place on paper towels, and squeeze until barely moist.

Sauté onion and garlic in butter in a large skillet until tender. Stir in sour cream, salt, pepper, and nutmeg. Add spinach, and cook over low heat until thoroughly heated; sprinkle with paprika. Yield: 4 servings.

CHEESY SPINACH SOUFFLÉ

1 (10-ounce) package frozen
  chopped spinach
2 tablespoons minced onion
¼ cup butter or margarine, melted
¼ cup plus 1 tablespoon all-purpose
  flour
1½ cups milk
1 cup (4 ounces) shredded Cheddar
  cheese
½ teaspoon salt
⅛ teaspoon pepper
4 eggs, separated
⅛ teaspoon cream of tartar
2 tablespoons grated Parmesan
  cheese

Cook spinach according to package directions. Drain; place on paper towels, and squeeze until barely moist.

Cut a piece of aluminum foil long enough to fit around a 5-cup soufflé dish, allowing a 1-inch overlap; fold foil lengthwise into thirds. Lightly butter one side of foil and bottom of dish. Wrap foil around dish, buttered side against dish, allowing it to extend 3 inches above rim to form a collar. Secure foil with string. Set aside.

Sauté onion in butter in a large saucepan until tender. Add flour, and cook 1 minute, stirring constantly. Gradually add milk; cook over medium heat, stirring constantly, until thickened and bubbly. Add Cheddar cheese, salt, and pepper; stir until cheese melts. Stir in spinach.

Beat egg whites (at room temperature) and cream of tartar until stiff peaks form.

Beat egg yolks until thick and lemon colored; stir into spinach mixture. Fold in egg whites. Spoon into prepared soufflé dish; sprinkle with Parmesan cheese. Bake at 350° for 55 to 60 minutes. Remove collar, and serve immediately. Yield: 4 to 6 servings.

Note: One pound fresh spinach, chopped and cooked, may be substituted for frozen chopped spinach.

CREAMED SWISS CHARD

3 pounds fresh Swiss chard leaves
2 tablespoons butter or margarine
1½ tablespoons all-purpose flour
1 cup half-and-half or milk
½ teaspoon salt
¼ teaspoon pepper
¼ teaspoon ground nutmeg

Wash chard thoroughly. Remove and discard ribs from larger leaves. Coarsely chop chard.

Place chard in a large Dutch oven (do not add water). Cover and cook over medium heat 10 minutes or until tender. Drain chard well, and squeeze between paper towels until barely moist. Return chard to Dutch oven.

Melt butter in a heavy saucepan over low heat; add flour, stirring until smooth. Cook 1 minute, stirring constantly. Gradually add half-and-half;

cook over medium heat, stirring constantly, until thickened and bubbly. Stir in salt, pepper, and nutmeg. Stir creamed mixture into chard. Yield: 4 to 6 servings.

TURNIP GREENS WITH TURNIPS

2 pounds fresh turnip greens
6 slices bacon, chopped
4 cups water
3 medium turnips, peeled and diced
1 tablespoon sugar
½ teaspoon salt

Wash greens thoroughly; drain. Tear into bite-size pieces. Cook bacon in a Dutch oven until browned. Drain bacon, and set aside; reserve drippings in Dutch oven. Add greens and water. Cover and simmer 20 minutes. Stir in turnips, sugar, and salt. Cover and cook an additional 20 minutes or until desired degree of doneness. Spoon into serving dish; sprinkle bacon over top. Yield: 6 servings.

KOHLRABI STIR-FRY

1½ pounds kohlrabi
½ teaspoon salt
1 small onion, sliced and separated into rings
1 clove garlic, minced
¼ cup butter or margarine, melted
½ teaspoon dried whole basil
⅛ teaspoon freshly ground pepper

Trim off kohlrabi roots and tops; peel kohlrabi, and cut into julienne strips. Combine kohlrabi and salt in a Dutch oven; cover with water, and bring to a boil. Cover, reduce heat, and simmer 10 minutes or until almost tender. Drain.
Stir-fry kohlrabi, onion, and garlic in butter in a large skillet until vegetables are tender. Toss with basil and pepper. Yield: 4 to 6 servings.

BRAISED LEEKS

6 medium leeks
3 tablespoons butter or margarine
¾ cup water
¼ cup grated Parmesan cheese
1 tablespoon chopped fresh parsley
¼ teaspoon salt
¼ teaspoon freshly ground pepper

Remove root, tough outer leaves, and tops from leeks, leaving 2 inches of dark leaves. Wash leeks; split in half lengthwise to within 1 inch of bulb end.
Melt butter in a large skillet. Add leeks, tossing well to coat with butter. Cover and cook over medium heat 10 minutes. Add water, and bring to a boil. Cover, reduce heat, and simmer over low heat 15 minutes or until tender. Drain well.
Combine Parmesan cheese, parsley, salt, and pepper, and sprinkle over leeks. Yield: 4 to 6 servings.

MARINATED MUSHROOMS

2 pounds fresh mushrooms
¼ cup lemon juice
½ cup cider vinegar
¼ cup water
2 tablespoons finely chopped onion
1 to 2 tablespoons minced garlic
1 tablespoon chopped fresh parsley
½ teaspoon salt
⅛ teaspoon pepper
⅛ teaspoon dried whole oregano

Cover mushrooms with water in a large Dutch oven; add lemon juice, stirring well. Bring to a boil; reduce heat, and simmer 1 minute; drain.
Combine vinegar and remaining ingredients, stirring well; pour marinade over mushrooms, and toss lightly. Place mushroom mixture in a shallow container; cover and refrigerate 24 hours. Yield: 8 servings.

EASY SAUTÉED MUSHROOMS

¾ pound fresh mushrooms, sliced
½ cup diced green pepper
3 green onions with tops, finely chopped
1 clove garlic, minced
2 tablespoons butter or margarine, melted
½ teaspoon dried whole oregano
Dash of salt
Dash of pepper

Sauté vegetables and garlic in butter 8 to 10 minutes or until vegetables are tender. Stir in oregano, salt, and pepper. Yield: 2 to 4 servings.

◻ *Microwave Directions:* Combine vegetables, garlic, and butter in a 1½-quart baking dish; cover with heavy-duty plastic wrap. Microwave at HIGH for 4 to 5 minutes or until vegetables are tender, stirring once. Stir in oregano, salt, and pepper.
Note: Easy Sautéed Mushrooms may also be served as a topping for steak, chicken, or hamburgers.

SPINACH-STUFFED MUSHROOMS

24 large fresh mushrooms
¼ cup butter or margarine
⅓ cup finely chopped green pepper
3 tablespoons finely chopped celery
4 green onions, finely chopped
1 clove garlic, minced
1 (12-ounce) package frozen spinach soufflé, thawed

Clean mushrooms with damp paper towels. Remove mushroom stems, and reserve for other uses.

Melt butter in a skillet. Roll mushroom caps in butter; place in a 12- x 8- x 2-inch baking dish, cap side down. Sauté green pepper, celery, green onions, and garlic in butter remaining in skillet; stir in soufflé, and cook until thoroughly heated.

Spoon spinach mixture into mushroom caps; cover and bake at 350° for 15 minutes. Yield: 8 servings.

◻*Microwave Directions:* Clean mushrooms with damp paper towels. Remove mushroom stems, and reserve for other uses.

Place butter in a shallow 2-quart baking dish. Microwave at HIGH for 55 seconds or until melted. Roll mushroom caps in butter; place in a 12- x 8- x 2-inch baking dish, cap side down.

Place green pepper, celery, green onions, and garlic in butter remaining in dish; cover with heavy-duty plastic wrap, and microwave at HIGH for 2 to 3 minutes or until tender. Stir in soufflé, and microwave at HIGH for 2 minutes or until thoroughly heated.

Spoon spinach mixture into mushroom caps. Arrange 12 mushrooms at a time on a microwave-safe platter. Microwave each platter at HIGH for 3 to 5 minutes or until spinach mixture is set, turning once.

STEWED OKRA AND VEGETABLES

3 cups sliced okra
2 cups fresh cut corn
4 or 5 large ripe tomatoes, peeled and chopped
3 tablespoons butter or margarine, melted
½ teaspoon salt
¼ teaspoon pepper
4 slices bacon, cooked and crumbled (optional)

Thoroughly rinse okra; drain well. Combine okra, corn, tomatoes, butter, salt, and pepper in a large skillet; cover and simmer 15 minutes, stirring occasionally. Sprinkle with bacon, if desired. Yield: 8 servings.

Stewed Okra and Vegetables is a quick and easy way to serve summer vegetables at their finest.

FRIED OKRA

1 to 1¼ pounds fresh okra
½ to 1 cup cornmeal
Vegetable oil
Salt

Wash okra well; drain. Cut off tips and stem ends; cut okra crosswise into ½-inch slices.

Roll okra in cornmeal (okra should be very damp for cornmeal to adhere), and fry in hot oil (375°) until golden brown. Drain well on paper towels. Sprinkle lightly with salt. Yield: 4 servings.

1. Begin Favorite Fried Onion Rings with large Spanish or Bermuda onions. Peel and cut them into ½-inch slices.

2. Separate slices into rings, and place in a bowl of water; chill 30 minutes.

3. Dip the rings in batter, letting excess drip off.

4. Fry onion rings in deep hot oil until golden on both sides.

FAVORITE FRIED ONION RINGS

1 extra-large Spanish onion or 3
   large Bermuda onions
About 1 quart water
1 cup all-purpose flour
1 teaspoon salt
2 eggs
⅔ cup milk
1 tablespoon vegetable oil
Vegetable oil

Peel onion; cut into ½-inch slices, and separate into rings. Place rings in a large bowl of water; refrigerate 30 minutes. Drain on paper towels.

Combine flour and salt; stir well. Add eggs, milk, and 1 tablespoon oil; beat until smooth.

Dip rings into batter; fry in deep hot oil (375°) until golden on both sides (3 to 5 minutes). Drain well on paper towels. Yield: 4 to 6 servings.

No matter how high it's piled, a platter of Favorite Fried Onion Rings won't last very long.

SHERRIED CHEESE ONIONS

1½ pounds pearl onions, peeled
½ cup water
1 teaspoon salt
2 tablespoons butter or margarine
2 tablespoons all-purpose flour
1½ cups milk
½ cup (2 ounces) shredded mild
   Cheddar cheese
1½ tablespoons dry sherry
Paprika

Combine onions, water, and salt in a large saucepan; bring to a boil. Reduce heat, and cook 10 to 15 minutes or until tender. Drain well, and place onions in a greased 1-quart baking dish.

Melt butter in a heavy saucepan over low heat; add flour, stirring until smooth. Cook 1 minute, stirring constantly. Gradually add milk; cook over medium heat, stirring constantly, until thickened and bubbly. Add cheese; stir until cheese melts and sauce is smooth. Stir in sherry. Pour over onions; sprinkle with paprika. Bake at 350° for 20 minutes. Yield: 6 servings.

▢*Microwave Directions:* Combine onions, water, and salt in a 1½-quart baking dish; cover with heavy-duty plastic wrap. Microwave at HIGH for 8 to 10 minutes or until onions are tender. Drain well, and place onions in a greased 1-quart baking dish.

Place butter in a 1-quart glass measure. Microwave at HIGH for 45 seconds or until melted. Add flour, stirring until smooth. Gradually add milk, stirring well. Microwave at HIGH for 4 to 5 minutes or until thickened and bubbly, stirring after 2 minutes, then at 1-minute intervals. Add cheese, stirring until cheese melts and sauce is smooth. Stir in sherry, and pour sauce over onions. Sprinkle with paprika. Microwave at HIGH for 5 minutes.

Note: One and one-half pounds regular onions, peeled and sliced, may be substituted for 1½ pounds pearl onions.

BAKED STUFFED ONIONS

6 large Spanish onions
½ pound hot bulk pork sausage
¼ cup chopped green pepper
1 egg, beaten
1 cup cooked rice
½ cup soft breadcrumbs
½ teaspoon dried whole oregano
2 tablespoons chopped fresh
   parsley
2 tablespoons butter or margarine,
   melted
½ teaspoon paprika

Peel onions, and cut a slice from top. Cook onions in boiling salted water 12 to 15 minutes or until tender but not mushy. Cool. Remove center of onions, leaving shells intact; chop onion centers, and reserve ½ cup.

Cook sausage in a large skillet until browned, stirring to crumble; drain, reserving pan drippings. Sauté green pepper and reserved ½ cup onion in drippings until tender. Combine sausage, sautéed vegetables, egg, rice, breadcrumbs, oregano, and parsley. Fill onion shells with sausage mixture; place in a lightly greased shallow pan.

Combine butter and paprika; brush on onions. Cover and bake at 400° for 15 minutes. Uncover and bake an additional 5 minutes. Yield: 6 servings.

PARSNIP PATTIES

1 pound parsnips, scraped and
   shredded
2 green onions, chopped
1 egg
1 tablespoon all-purpose flour
½ teaspoon salt
⅛ teaspoon pepper
Vegetable oil

Cook parsnips, covered, in a very small amount of boiling water until almost done. Drain well; squeeze parsnips between paper towels to remove excess moisture. Combine parsnips, green onions, egg, flour, salt, and pepper, stirring well. Drop ¼ cup parsnip mixture at a time into ⅛-inch hot oil; press into 3-inch rounds with the back of a fork. Fry until golden brown, turning once. Yield: 6 patties.

GLAZED PARSNIPS

1 pound parsnips, scraped and
   thinly sliced
3 tablespoons butter or margarine,
   melted
¼ cup firmly packed brown sugar
1 tablespoon lemon juice
¼ teaspoon salt
⅛ teaspoon freshly ground pepper
1 tablespoon chopped fresh parsley
   (optional)

Cook parsnips in butter in a large skillet for 5 minutes, stirring occasionally. Cover skillet, and cook over low heat until parsnips are crisp-tender (about 5 minutes).

Remove cover from skillet; add brown sugar, lemon juice, salt, pepper, and parsley, if desired, and stir-fry over medium heat until parsnips are glazed. Yield: 4 servings.

HOPPING JOHN

2 cups dried black-eyed peas
½ pound salt pork, quartered
2 cups chopped onion
1 cup chopped green pepper
2½ cups water
1 cup uncooked long-grain rice
1 teaspoon salt
¼ teaspoon pepper
⅛ teaspoon red pepper

Sort and wash peas; place in a Dutch oven. Cover with water 2 inches above peas; let soak 8 hours. Drain. Return peas to saucepan; add salt pork, onion, and green pepper. Cover with water, and simmer, covered, 2 hours or until peas are tender and water has cooked very low.

Add 2½ cups water, rice, and seasonings to peas. Cover and cook over low heat 20 minutes or until rice is done. (Add additional water if necessary.) Yield: 8 to 10 servings.

SPICY HOT BLACK-EYED PEAS

1 pound fresh shelled
  black-eyed peas
½ cup water
3 slices bacon
1 (16-ounce) can whole tomatoes,
  undrained and chopped
1 cup chopped onion
1 large green pepper, chopped
1 clove garlic, minced
1 teaspoon salt
1 teaspoon ground cumin
1 teaspoon dry mustard
½ teaspoon curry powder
½ teaspoon chili powder
½ teaspoon pepper
Chopped fresh parsley

Combine peas and water. Bring to a boil; cover, reduce heat, and simmer 10 minutes or until peas are almost tender. Drain and set aside.

Cook bacon in a large skillet until crisp. Remove bacon, reserving drippings in skillet; crumble bacon, and set aside.

Stir peas and remaining ingredients except parsley, into bacon drippings in skillet. Bring to a boil; reduce heat and simmer 20 minutes, stirring occasionally. Pour mixture into a serving dish; sprinkle with bacon and parsley. Yield: 6 servings.

Note: One (17-ounce) can or 1 (16-ounce) package frozen black-eyed peas, drained, may be substituted for fresh. Do not cook canned or frozen peas before adding them to the recipe.

GREEN PEAS AND PEARL ONIONS

3 pounds fresh green peas
½ pound pearl onions, peeled
2 tablespoons butter or margarine
2 tablespoons all-purpose flour
1 cup milk
½ teaspoon salt
⅛ teaspoon pepper
Pinch of ground nutmeg

Shell and wash peas; cover peas and onions with water in a saucepan, and bring to a boil. Cover, reduce heat, and simmer 12 to 15 minutes or until peas are tender. Drain.

Melt butter in a heavy saucepan over low heat; add flour, stirring until smooth. Cook 1 minute, stirring constantly. Gradually add milk; cook over medium heat, stirring constantly, until mixture is thickened and bubbly. Stir in salt, pepper, and nutmeg. Spoon sauce over vegetables, and toss gently. Yield: 6 servings.

○*Microwave Directions:* Shell and wash peas. Combine peas, onions, and ⅓ cup water in a 2-quart casserole. Cover with heavy-duty plastic wrap, and microwave at HIGH for 10 to 12 minutes or until peas are tender. Drain.

Place butter in a 1-quart glass measure. Microwave at HIGH for 45 seconds or until melted. Add flour, stirring until smooth. Gradually add milk, stirring well. Microwave at HIGH for 2 to 3 minutes or until thickened and bubbly, stirring after 2 minutes. Stir in salt, pepper, and nutmeg. Spoon sauce over vegetables, and toss gently.

PEAS WITH SHERRY

2 pounds fresh green peas
¼ cup minced onion
1 (4-ounce) can sliced mushrooms,
  drained
2 tablespoons butter or margarine,
  melted
¼ cup dry sherry
¼ teaspoon salt
⅛ teaspoon dried marjoram leaves
Dash of pepper

Shell and wash peas; add enough boiling water to cover peas. Cover, reduce heat, and simmer 12 to 15 minutes or until tender. Drain.

Sauté onion and mushrooms in butter in a large skillet 5 minutes; stir in peas and remaining ingredients. Cook 1 minute. Yield: 4 servings.

Note: Two cups frozen peas may be substituted for fresh peas.

SKILLET SNOW PEAS

1 pound fresh snow pea pods or 2
  (6-ounce) packages frozen snow
  pea pods, thawed
2 green onions, chopped
1 clove garlic, minced
2 tablespoons soy sauce
⅛ teaspoon freshly ground pepper
2 tablespoons olive or vegetable oil

Wash snow pea pods; trim ends, and remove any tough strings. Sauté snow peas and next 4 ingredients in hot oil just until crisp-tender. Yield: 4 servings.

SAUTÉED RED AND GREEN PEPPERS

2 sweet red peppers, cut into ¼-inch strips
2 green peppers, cut into ¼-inch strips
1 small onion, sliced and separated into rings
1 clove garlic, minced
3 tablespoons olive or vegetable oil
½ teaspoon salt
½ teaspoon dried whole basil
¼ teaspoon freshly ground pepper

Sauté peppers, onion, and garlic in hot oil just until tender. Stir in salt, basil, and pepper. Yield: 4 to 6 servings.

RICE-STUFFED PEPPERS

4 medium-size green peppers
1 cup cooked rice
1 (14½-ounce) can stewed tomatoes, drained
¼ cup butter or margarine, melted
2½ tablespoons dry onion soup mix
½ cup (2 ounces) shredded Cheddar cheese

Cut off tops of green peppers; remove seeds. Cook peppers 5 minutes in boiling water to cover; drain and set aside.

Combine rice and next 3 ingredients; stir well. Fill peppers with rice mixture; place in a 1-quart baking dish. Pour hot water to depth of ½ inch into dish. Bake at 350° for 25 minutes. Sprinkle cheese over peppers; bake an additional 5 minutes. Yield: 4 servings.

OVEN-FRIED POTATOES

3 medium potatoes
¼ cup vegetable oil
1 tablespoon grated Parmesan cheese
½ teaspoon salt
¼ teaspoon garlic powder
¼ teaspoon paprika
¼ teaspoon pepper

Wash potatoes well, and cut each into ⅛-inch wedges. Place wedges, slightly overlapping, in a single layer in a 13- x 9- x 2-inch pan.

Combine the remaining ingredients. Brush potatoes with half of oil mixture. Bake, uncovered, at 375° for 45 minutes, basting occasionally with remaining oil mixture. Yield: 4 to 6 servings.

BACON-TOPPED CHEESE POTATOES

4 medium baking potatoes
Vegetable oil
½ cup commercial sour cream
¼ cup milk
¼ cup butter or margarine
¼ cup (1 ounce) shredded Cheddar or crumbled blue cheese
¾ teaspoon salt
Dash of pepper
4 slices bacon, cooked and crumbled

Wash potatoes, and rub skins with vegetable oil. Bake at 400° for 1 hour or until done. Allow potatoes to cool to touch. Cut a 1-inch lengthwise strip from top of each potato; carefully scoop out pulp, leaving shells intact.

Combine potato pulp and remaining ingredients except bacon in a medium mixing bowl. Beat at medium speed of an electric mixer until light and fluffy; stuff shells with potato mixture. Bake at 400° for 15 minutes; top with crumbled bacon. Serve hot. Yield: 4 servings.

☐ *Microwave Directions:* Wash potatoes; prick several times with a fork. Arrange potatoes on paper towels in microwave oven, leaving 1 inch between each. Microwave at HIGH for 12 to 14 minutes, turning and rearranging potatoes once. Let potatoes stand 5 minutes. Microwave again briefly if not done. Allow potatoes to cool to touch; Cut a 1-inch lengthwise strip from top of each potato; carefully scoop out pulp, leaving shells intact.

Combine potato pulp and remaining ingredients except bacon in a medium mixing bowl. Beat at medium speed of an electric mixer until light and fluffy; stuff shells with potato mixture. Arrange on a microwave-safe platter. Microwave at HIGH for 4 to 5 minutes or until hot; top with crumbled bacon. Serve hot.

HASH BROWN POTATOES

¼ cup bacon drippings
2 tablespoons butter or margarine
4 cups diced cooked potatoes
⅔ cup minced onion
2 tablespoons minced fresh parsley
½ teaspoon dried whole oregano
2 cloves garlic, minced
Salt and pepper to taste

Melt bacon drippings and butter in a 9-inch skillet. Add remaining ingredients, stirring gently until coated. Cook mixture, uncovered, turning occasionally until browned on all sides (about 20 minutes). Yield: 4 servings.

FRIED POTATO PATTIES

4 medium potatoes, peeled and shredded
1 small onion, finely chopped
1 egg, beaten
1 tablespoon all-purpose flour
1 teaspoon salt
¼ teaspoon pepper
⅛ teaspoon red pepper
Vegetable oil

Squeeze potatoes between paper towels to remove excess moisture. Combine all ingredients except vegetable oil, stirring well. Drop ¼ cup of potato mixture at a time into ⅛ inch hot oil; press into 3-inch rounds with the back of a fork. Fry until golden brown, turning once. Drain well. Yield: 6 servings.

DRESSED-UP POTATOES

10 medium potatoes, peeled and
   quartered
1 (8-ounce) carton commercial sour
   cream
1/4 cup plus 2 tablespoons milk
2 tablespoons chopped chives
2 teaspoons salt
1/4 teaspoon white pepper
1/8 teaspoon onion powder
1/8 teaspoon garlic powder
2 tablespoons butter or margarine,
   melted
2 tablespoons sliced almonds

Cook potatoes in boiling water to
cover 15 minutes or until tender. Drain
and mash. Add sour cream, milk, chives,
and seasonings to potato mixture, beating at medium speed of an electric mixer
until smooth. Spoon half of potato mixture into a greased 2-quart casserole.
Spoon remaining potato mixture into a
decorating bag fitted with large fluted tip
No. 8B. Pipe remaining potato mixture
into casserole. Drizzle butter lightly over
top; sprinkle with almonds. Bake at 400°
for 15 minutes. Place under broiler just
long enough to brown. Yield: 8 to 10
servings.

SCALLOPED POTATOES

1/4 cup butter or margarine
1/4 cup all-purpose flour
2 cups milk
1 teaspoon salt
1/2 teaspoon white pepper
1 (2-ounce) jar diced pimiento,
   drained
4 medium potatoes, peeled and sliced
   1/8-inch thick
2 small onions, thinly sliced and
   separated into rings
2 cups (8 ounces) shredded Cheddar
   cheese

Melt butter in a heavy saucepan over
low heat; add flour, stirring until
smooth. Cook 1 minute, stirring constantly. Gradually add milk; cook over
medium heat, stirring constantly, until
thickened and bubbly. Stir in salt, pepper, and pimiento.

Spoon 1/4 cup white sauce into a
greased 12- x 8- x 2-inch baking dish.
Top with half each of potatoes, onions,
remaining sauce, and cheese. Repeat
layers, using remaining potatoes,
onions, and sauce. Cover and bake at
350° for 55 to 60 minutes or until
tender. Sprinkle with remaining cheese,
and bake an additional 5 minutes. Yield:
8 servings.

Scalloped Ham And Potatoes:
Sprinkle 1 cup chopped cooked ham
over each layer of potatoes (total 2 cups
ham). Yield: 6 main dish servings.

CHILLED DILLED NEW POTATOES

2 pounds new potatoes, unpeeled
   and sliced
1/4 cup plus 1 tablespoon olive oil
1/4 cup white wine vinegar
3 tablespoons finely chopped green
   onions
1 teaspoon dried whole dillweed
1/2 teaspoon salt
1/2 teaspoon pepper
1 large clove garlic, minced

Cook potatoes, covered, in boiling
water to cover 15 minutes or until
tender; drain carefully, leaving skins intact. Combine oil and remaining ingredients, stirring well. Pour oil mixture
over potatoes, tossing gently to coat potatoes thoroughly. Chill potato mixture
at least 8 hours. Yield: 8 servings.

◻*Microwave Directions:* Place potatoes in a 3-quart casserole dish; add
about 3 tablespoons water. Cover with
lid, and microwave at HIGH for 8 to 10
minutes or until potatoes are barely
done, stirring at 4-minute intervals. Let
stand 3 minutes. Drain carefully, leaving
skins intact. Combine oil and remaining
ingredients, stirring well. Pour oil mixture over potatoes, tossing gently to coat
potatoes thoroughly. Chill at least 8
hours.

BROWNED NEW POTATOES

1 pound small new potatoes, peeled
2 tablespoons bacon drippings
1/4 teaspoon salt
1/4 teaspoon pepper
1 tablespoon molasses
1 tablespoon chopped fresh parsley
   (optional)

Cook potatoes in boiling water to
cover until almost tender (about 10 minutes); drain.

Heat bacon drippings in a heavy ovenproof skillet over medium heat; add potatoes and cook 10 minutes or until
lightly browned, turning frequently.
Sprinkle with salt and pepper. Bake at
400° for 30 minutes or until browned,
turning once. Stir in molasses and sprinkle with parsley, if desired. Serve immediately. Yield: 3 to 4 servings.

Plan a Spud Party

A baked potato, topped with chili,
guacamole, ham, salad, or just about
anything, can transform itself into a
meal, and a fun and casual party menu.
You could make the party a potluck by
asking each guest to bring a different
topping for the baked potatoes you
provide.

For the party, slice the baked potatoes in half and offer two or three
halves per person so that guests can
mix and match toppings as they desire.
Base the potatoes on a bed of lettuce
for color and crunch, and let guests
pile on the toppings. Follow the potatoes with a rich dessert, and you have a
meal.

Micro-Baked Potatoes

Rinse potatoes and pat dry; prick several times with a fork. Arrange potatoes in microwave oven, leaving 1 inch between each. (If microwaving more than 2 potatoes, arrange them in a circle.)

Microwave at HIGH according to the times below, turning and rearranging potatoes once. Let potatoes stand 5 minutes before serving. (If potatoes are not done after standing, microwave briefly and let stand 2 minutes.)

NUMBER OF POTATOES	MINUTES AT HIGH POWER
1	4 to 6
2	7 to 8
3	9 to 11
4	12 to 14
6	16 to 18

Note: *These times are for cooking medium-size potatoes (6 to 7 ounces). If potatoes are larger, allow more time.*

STUFFED SWEET POTATOES

6 medium-size sweet potatoes
½ cup orange juice
3 tablespoons butter or margarine
1 teaspoon salt
1 (8-ounce) can crushed pineapple, drained
½ cup chopped pecans

Wash sweet potatoes; bake at 375° for 1 hour or until done. Allow potatoes to cool to touch. Cut a 1-inch lengthwise strip from top of each potato; carefully scoop out pulp, leaving shells intact.

Combine potato pulp, orange juice, butter, and salt; beat at medium speed of an electric mixer until fluffy. Stir in pineapple. Stuff shells with potato mixture, and sprinkle with pecans. Bake at 375° for 12 minutes. Yield: 6 servings.

☐*Microwave Directions:* Wash sweet potatoes; prick several times with a fork. Arrange on paper towels in microwave oven, leaving 1 inch between each. Microwave at HIGH for 22 to 24 minutes, rearranging potatoes once. Let stand 5 minutes. Microwave again briefly if not done. Allow potatoes to cool to touch. Cut a 1-inch lengthwise strip from top of each potato; carefully scoop out pulp, leaving shells intact.

Combine potato pulp, orange juice, butter, and salt; beat at medium speed of an electric mixer until fluffy. Stir in pineapple. Stuff shells with potato mixture, and sprinkle with pecans. Arrange potatoes on a microwave-safe platter. Microwave at HIGH for 5 minutes or until hot.

FRENCH-FRIED SWEET POTATOES

3 medium-size sweet potatoes
Vegetable oil
Salt or powdered sugar (optional)

Cook sweet potatoes in boiling water 10 minutes; let cool to touch.

Peel sweet potatoes, and cut into finger-size strips or ¼-inch slices. Fry potatoes in hot oil (375°) until golden brown; drain on paper towels. Sprinkle with salt or powdered sugar, if desired. Yield: 4 servings.

SWEET POTATO CASSEROLE

6 medium-size sweet potatoes
½ cup sugar
2 eggs
1 teaspoon vanilla extract
⅓ cup milk
½ cup butter or margarine
⅓ cup firmly packed brown sugar
⅓ cup finely chopped pecans
2 tablespoons all-purpose flour
2 tablespoons butter or margarine

Cook sweet potatoes in boiling water 45 minutes to 1 hour or until tender. Let cool to touch; peel and mash.

Combine sweet potatoes, sugar, eggs, vanilla, milk, and ½ cup butter; beat at medium speed of an electric mixer until smooth. Spoon into a lightly greased 12- x 8- x 2-inch baking dish.

Combine brown sugar, pecans, flour, and 2 tablespoons butter; sprinkle mixture over casserole. Bake at 350° for 30 minutes. Yield: 8 servings.

CREAMY RUTABAGA

1 small rutabaga, peeled and diced
1½ cups water
½ teaspoon salt
¼ cup evaporated milk
2 tablespoons brown sugar
2 tablespoons butter or margarine
Ground nutmeg

Combine rutabaga, water, and salt in a saucepan. Bring to a boil; cover, reduce heat, and simmer 20 minutes or until very tender. Drain well.

Position knife blade in food processor bowl; add rutabaga, milk, brown sugar, and butter. Top with cover, and process 1 minute or until smooth. Spoon into a serving dish, and sprinkle with nutmeg. Yield: 4 servings.

NUTTY RUTABAGA

1 large rutabaga, peeled and
  diced
1¾ cups water
½ teaspoon salt
½ cup chopped pecans
3 tablespoons butter or margarine,
  melted
1½ tablespoons maple syrup

Combine rutabaga, water, and salt in a saucepan. Bring to a boil; cover, reduce heat, and simmer 15 to 20 minutes. Drain well.

Sauté pecans in butter in a large skillet 3 minutes. Add rutabaga and syrup, and toss gently over low heat. Yield: 6 servings.

COUNTRY CLUB SQUASH

2 pounds yellow squash, sliced
½ cup chopped onion
½ cup water
1 (8-ounce) carton commercial
  sour cream
½ teaspoon salt
¼ teaspoon pepper
¼ teaspoon dried whole basil
1 cup soft breadcrumbs
½ cup (2 ounces) shredded
  medium Cheddar cheese
⅓ cup butter or margarine,
  melted
½ teaspoon paprika
8 slices bacon, cooked and
  crumbled

Cook squash and onion in ½ cup boiling water until tender; drain and mash. Combine squash, sour cream, salt, pepper, and basil; pour into a greased 2-quart casserole. Combine breadcrumbs, cheese, butter, and paprika; sprinkle over squash mixture. Top with bacon. Bake at 300° for 20 minutes. Yield: 6 servings.

◻ *Microwave Directions:* Combine squash, onion, and water in a 12- x 8- x 2-inch baking dish; cover with heavy-duty plastic wrap. Microwave at HIGH for 11 to 13 minutes, stirring once, or until tender; drain and mash. Combine squash, sour cream, salt, pepper, and basil; pour into a greased 2-quart casserole. Combine breadcrumbs, cheese, butter, and paprika; sprinkle over squash mixture. Microwave at MEDIUM HIGH (70% power) for 10 minutes. Top with bacon.

STIR-FRIED SQUASH MEDLEY

3 tablespoons peanut or vegetable oil
¾ pound zucchini, sliced
¾ pound yellow squash, sliced
½ cup chopped onion
1 clove garlic, crushed
1 cup diced tomatoes
1 tablespoon Worcestershire sauce
2 tablespoons tomato paste
1 teaspoon salt

Pour oil around top of preheated wok, coating sides; allow to heat at medium high (325°) for 2 minutes. Add squash, onion, and garlic; stir-fry 2 minutes. Add remaining ingredients; simmer 8 to 10 minutes or until vegetables are crisp-tender, stirring occasionally. Yield: about 6 servings.

PATTYPAN-ZUCCHINI SKILLET

1 medium onion, sliced and
  separated into rings
½ cup chopped green pepper
2 tablespoons butter or margarine,
  melted
1 tablespoon sugar
1 teaspoon all-purpose flour
½ teaspoon salt
¼ teaspoon pepper
⅛ teaspoon garlic powder
1 medium pattypan squash, cubed
1 medium zucchini, sliced
3 medium tomatoes, quartered

Sauté onion and green pepper in butter in a large skillet until tender. Stir in sugar, flour, salt, pepper, and garlic powder. Add squash; cook over medium heat 4 minutes; add tomatoes, and cook until squash is crisp-tender. Yield: 6 servings.

PLANTATION SQUASH

6 medium-size yellow squash
1 (10-ounce) package frozen
  chopped spinach
1 (3-ounce) package cream cheese,
  softened
1 egg, well beaten
2 tablespoons butter or margarine,
  melted
½ to 1 teaspoon pepper
¾ teaspoon sugar
¼ teaspoon seasoned salt
¼ teaspoon onion salt
½ cup round buttery cracker
  crumbs
Paprika
4 slices bacon, cooked and
  crumbled

Wash squash thoroughly. Drop in boiling water; cover, reduce heat, and simmer 8 to 10 minutes or until tender but still firm. Drain and cool slightly; trim off stems. Cut squash in half lengthwise. Scoop out pulp, leaving firm shells; drain and mash pulp.

Cook spinach according to package directions, omitting salt; drain well, and add to squash pulp. Add cream cheese, mixing until blended. Stir in next 6 ingredients; spoon into squash shells.

Sprinkle squash with cracker crumbs, paprika, and bacon. Place on a lightly greased baking sheet; cover with foil, and bake at 325° for 30 minutes. Yield: 6 servings.

Note: To prepare ahead, spoon filling into shells, cover, and chill. When ready to bake, sprinkle with cracker crumbs, paprika, and bacon. Cover with foil, and bake at 325° about 30 minutes or until thoroughly heated.

Taming Fresh Garlic

Garlic tastes sharpest when uncooked and finely minced or crushed. Cooking the garlic and leaving the cloves whole or in large pieces tames the potent herb, and imparts a sweet, nutlike flavor.

Use garlic to season vegetables subtly by sautéing a clove lightly and discarding it before adding the vegetable to the cooking fat. For a touch of garlic flavor in a salad, rub a cut clove over a wooden salad bowl before tossing the salad.

ZUCCHINI SOUFFLÉ

¼ cup butter or margarine
¼ cup all-purpose flour
1⅓ cups milk
½ teaspoon salt
Dash of pepper
1 tablespoon minced onion
1¼ cups grated zucchini
5 eggs, separated
1 teaspoon cream of tartar
½ cup (2 ounces) shredded sharp
   Cheddar cheese

Cut a piece of aluminum foil long enough to fit around a 1½-quart soufflé dish, allowing a 1-inch overlap; fold foil lengthwise into thirds. Lightly butter one side of foil and bottom of dish. Wrap foil around dish, buttered side against dish, allowing it to extend 3 inches above rim to form a collar. Secure foil with string. Set aside.

Melt butter in a heavy saucepan over low heat; add flour, stirring until smooth. Cook 1 minute, stirring constantly. Gradually add milk; cook over medium heat, stirring constantly, until mixture is thickened and bubbly. Stir in salt, pepper, and onion; remove from heat, and let cool. Squeeze grated zucchini to remove as much liquid as possible; stir into sauce.

Beat egg yolks until thick and lemon colored; add to squash mixture, and stir well. Beat egg whites (at room temperature) and cream of tartar until stiff, but not dry; fold into squash mixture. Pour into prepared dish. Bake at 350° for 1 hour and 10 minutes; sprinkle with cheese, and bake an additional 5 minutes or until a knife inserted in center comes out clean. Yield: 6 to 8 servings.

Note: Soufflé may also be baked in a greased 2-quart casserole instead of soufflé dish.

To prepare spaghetti squash: After cooking squash, slice it in half, and remove seeds. Separate strands with a fork.

SPAGHETTI SQUASH TOSS

1 large spaghetti squash
2 cloves garlic, minced
1 medium onion, sliced and separated into rings
1 large green pepper, sliced into strips
2 tablespoons vegetable oil
1 (15-ounce) can tomato sauce
1 teaspoon dried whole oregano
1 teaspoon dried whole basil

Wash squash; cut in half lengthwise, and discard seeds. Place squash, cut side down, in a Dutch oven; add water to depth of 2 inches. Bring to a boil; cover, reduce heat, and simmer 20 to 25 minutes or until tender.

Drain squash, and cool. Using a fork, remove spaghetti-like strands; measure 5 cups of strands, and set aside.

Sauté garlic, onion rings, and green pepper in hot oil in a large skillet just until onion is tender. Stir in tomato sauce, oregano, and basil; cook an additional 5 minutes or until thoroughly heated. Toss sautéed vegetables with squash strands. Yield: 8 servings.

WHIPPED WINTER SQUASH

5 pounds hubbard or butternut squash
2 tablespoons butter or margarine
2 tablespoons brown sugar
⅓ cup golden raisins
½ teaspoon salt
¼ teaspoon ground nutmeg
⅛ teaspoon pepper
2 tablespoons finely chopped pecans
1 tablespoon brown sugar
1 tablespoon light corn syrup
1 tablespoon butter or margarine

Cut squash in half lengthwise, and remove seeds. Place cut side down in shallow pans; add water to depth of ½ inch. Cover and bake at 400° for 1 to 1½ hours or until tender. Drain. Scoop out pulp, and discard shell.

Combine squash pulp, 2 tablespoons butter, and 2 tablespoons brown sugar in a large mixing bowl; beat at medium speed of an electric mixer until smooth.

Spoon squash mixture into a large saucepan; cook over medium heat 5 minutes, stirring often. Stir in raisins, salt, nutmeg, and pepper; cook 10 minutes, stirring often. Spoon squash into a serving dish, and keep warm.

Combine remaining ingredients in a small saucepan; cook over medium heat until sugar dissolves, stirring constantly. Pour over squash. Yield: 6 to 8 servings.

GLAZED ACORN SQUASH RINGS

1 large acorn squash
⅓ cup orange juice
½ cup firmly packed brown sugar
¼ cup light corn syrup
¼ cup butter or margarine
2 teaspoons grated lemon rind
⅛ teaspoon salt
Fresh parsley sprigs (optional)

Cut squash into ¾-inch-thick slices; remove seeds and membrane. Arrange squash in a lightly greased 12- x 8- x 2-inch baking dish. Pour orange juice over squash. Cover; bake at 350° for 30 minutes.

Combine brown sugar and next 4 ingredients in a saucepan. Bring to a boil; reduce heat, and simmer 5 minutes. Pour sugar mixture over squash. Bake, uncovered, an additional 20 minutes or until squash is tender, basting occasionally. Garnish with parsley, if desired. Yield: 2 to 3 servings.

◻*Microwave Directions:* Cut squash into ¾-inch-thick slices; remove seeds and membrane. Stack slices to resemble uncut squash. Place stack in a lightly greased 12- x 8- x 2-inch baking dish. Pour orange juice into baking dish. Cover with heavy-duty plastic wrap, and microwave at HIGH for 10 to 12 minutes or until soft to the touch.

Combine brown sugar and next 4 ingredients in a 2-cup glass measure. Cover with heavy-duty plastic wrap, and microwave at HIGH for 2 to 3 minutes or until boiling, stirring once.

Overlap squash rings in orange juice in baking dish. Pour sugar mixture over squash. Cover with wax paper, and microwave at HIGH for 2 to 3 minutes. Rearrange rings in baking dish; cover with wax paper, and microwave at HIGH for 2 to 3 minutes or until done.

ROMANO-TOPPED TOMATOES

3 tomatoes, halved crosswise
Salt and pepper
2 tablespoons butter or margarine
2 tablespoons chopped fresh parsley
2 tablespoons grated Romano cheese
Fresh parsley sprigs

Sprinkle cut side of tomato halves with salt and pepper. Broil 3 to 5 minutes, about 4 inches from heat. Place 1 teaspoon butter, 1 teaspoon parsley, and 1 teaspoon cheese on each; broil 2 minutes. Garnish platter with parsley sprigs. Yield: 6 servings.

◻*Microwave Directions:* Sprinkle cut side of tomato halves with salt and pepper. Microwave at HIGH, uncovered, for 3 to 4 minutes or until thoroughly heated. Place 1 teaspoon butter, 1 teaspoon parsley, and 1 teaspoon cheese on each; microwave at HIGH for 1 to 2 minutes.

Romano-Topped Tomatoes makes a shapely and colorful side dish.

OREGANO TOMATOES

4 medium tomatoes, sliced
¼ cup vegetable oil
1½ tablespoons lemon juice
½ teaspoon salt
½ teaspoon dried whole oregano
⅛ teaspoon pepper
1 small clove garlic, minced

Place tomatoes in a shallow dish. Combine remaining ingredients; stir well, and pour over tomatoes. Cover and chill several hours, stirring once or twice. Yield: 6 servings.

FRIED GREEN TOMATOES

6 large, firm green tomatoes
Salt and pepper to taste
1 cup cornmeal
Bacon drippings or shortening

Cut tomatoes into ¼-inch slices. Season with salt and pepper; dredge in cornmeal. Heat bacon drippings in a heavy skillet; add tomatoes, and fry slowly until browned, turning once. Yield: 6 to 8 servings.

To peel a tomato: Dip the tomato into boiling water for 15 to 30 seconds; the skin will slip off easily. The tomato will not "cook" at all during this short blanching.

TOMATOES PROVENÇAL

4 slices bacon, diced
1 clove garlic, minced
1 medium onion, thinly sliced
¼ pound fresh mushrooms, sliced
1 tablespoon all-purpose flour
½ teaspoon seasoned salt
5 medium tomatoes
¼ cup plus 2 tablespoons grated Parmesan cheese, divided
1 tablespoon butter or margarine

Fry bacon in a medium skillet until crisp; remove bacon, reserving drippings in skillet. Drain bacon, and set aside. Sauté garlic, onion, and mushrooms in skillet until tender. Stir in bacon, flour, and seasoned salt.
Cut tomatoes into ½-inch slices. Place half of slices in a lightly greased 8-inch square baking dish. Spoon half of bacon mixture over tomatoes; sprinkle with 3 tablespoons Parmesan cheese. Repeat layers. Dot with butter. Bake at 350° for 25 minutes. Yield: 6 to 8 servings.

STEWED TOMATO BAKE

2 (14½-ounce) cans stewed tomatoes, undrained
1½ tablespoons cornstarch
1¼ teaspoons dried whole basil
½ teaspoon dried whole marjoram
½ teaspoon freshly ground pepper
10 round buttery crackers, crushed
3 tablespoons grated Parmesan cheese

Drain tomatoes, reserving juice. Add cornstarch to reserved juice, stirring until blended. Pour juice into a 1-quart baking dish. Add tomatoes, and sprinkle with basil, marjoram, and pepper. Bake at 450° for 15 minutes. Remove from oven, and stir gently.
Combine cracker crumbs and cheese; sprinkle evenly over tomatoes. Bake an

additional 5 minutes or until crumbs are browned. Yield: 4 to 6 servings.

▢ *Microwave Directions:* Drain tomatoes, reserving juice. Add cornstarch to reserved juice, stirring until blended. Pour juice into a 1-quart baking dish. Add tomatoes, and sprinkle with basil, marjoram, and pepper. Cover loosely with a paper towel, and microwave at HIGH for 5 to 7 minutes or until bubbly. Remove from oven; stir gently.
Combine cracker crumbs and cheese; sprinkle evenly over tomatoes. Microwave at HIGH for 2 minutes.

TANGY TURNIPS

3 medium turnips, peeled and sliced
1 teaspoon salt
4 slices bacon, diced
1 egg, beaten
¼ cup sugar
¼ cup vinegar

Place turnips in a saucepan; cover with water. Add salt, and bring to a boil; cover, reduce heat, and simmer 15 to 20 minutes or until turnips are tender. Drain and set aside.
Fry bacon in a large skillet until crisp. Combine egg, sugar, and vinegar, stirring well; stir into bacon and drippings. Pour mixture over turnips, and toss gently. Yield: about 4 servings.

▢ *Microwave Directions:* Place turnips in a shallow 1½-quart casserole. Add ¼ cup water and salt; cover with lid, and microwave at HIGH for 6 to 8 minutes or until turnips are tender, stirring twice. Let stand, covered, 2 minutes. Drain and set aside.
Place bacon in a shallow 1-quart casserole; cover with paper towels. Microwave at HIGH for 3½ to 4½ minutes or until bacon is crisp. Combine egg, sugar, and vinegar, stirring well; stir into bacon and drippings. Pour mixture over turnips, and toss gently.

MIXED VEGETABLE STIR-FRY

2½ tablespoons peanut or vegetable oil
10 to 12 large mushrooms, sliced
1 medium onion, sliced into rings
1 medium zucchini, thinly sliced
1 tablespoon soy sauce
½ teaspoon salt
¼ teaspoon pepper

Heat oil in a large skillet. Add remaining ingredients; stir-fry over high heat about 5 minutes or until zucchini is crisp-tender. Yield: 2 servings.

ORIENTAL VEGETABLE STIR-FRY

¼ cup peanut or vegetable oil
2 cups coarsely shredded Chinese cabbage
1 cup sliced green pepper
1 (16-ounce) can bean sprouts, drained
1 (8-ounce) can bamboo shoots, drained
1 (8-ounce) can water chestnuts, drained and sliced
3 cups coarsely chopped spinach
2 tablespoons soy sauce
½ teaspoon salt

Heat electric wok or skillet at 350° for 2 to 3 minutes; add oil, and heat 1 minute.

Add shredded cabbage, sliced green pepper, bean sprouts, bamboo shoots, and water chestnuts to oil in wok; stir-fry vegetables 5 minutes. Cover wok, and cook vegetables over low heat 3 to 5 minutes.

Stir in chopped spinach, soy sauce, and salt, and stir-fry vegetable mixture about 2 minutes or until spinach wilts. Yield: 6 servings.

Serve Fruit on the Side

Side dishes don't always have to be vegetables, as these tasty fruit concoctions prove. They're as satisfying as a vegetable dish and can be used for any brunch, lunch, or dinner menu.

HONEY APPLE RINGS

½ cup honey
2 tablespoons vinegar
¼ teaspoon salt
¼ teaspoon ground cinnamon
4 medium cooking apples, unpeeled, cored, and cut into ½-inch rings
Mint leaves
Cinnamon sticks

Combine honey, vinegar, salt, and cinnamon in a large skillet; bring to a boil. Add apple rings; reduce heat and simmer 8 to 10 minutes, turning apples once. Arrange on platter, and garnish with mint leaves and cinnamon sticks. Yield: 8 servings.

Mint leaves and cinnamon sticks jazz up the look of Honey Apple Rings.

SCALLOPED PINEAPPLE

3 eggs, well beaten
1½ cups sugar
3 cups 1-inch cubes fresh bread
1 (20-ounce) can crushed pineapple, undrained
⅓ cup butter or margarine, cut into 1-inch squares

Combine all ingredients, and stir well. Pour into a lightly greased 10- x 8- x 2-inch baking dish. Bake at 350° for 1 hour. Yield: 6 to 8 servings.

SPICED CRANBERRIES

4 cups fresh cranberries
3 cups sugar
2 cups water
1 teaspoon ground cinnamon
½ teaspoon ground cloves
Pinch of ground ginger

Wash cranberries and drain; set aside.

Combine remaining ingredients in a large saucepan; bring to a boil. Add cranberries; cook 7 minutes or until cranberry skins pop. Reduce heat, and simmer mixture 1 hour, stirring occasionally. Remove mixture from heat, and allow to cool. Chill until ready to serve. Yield: 3 cups.

RUM-BROILED GRAPEFRUIT

2 large grapefruits, halved crosswise
¼ cup light rum
¼ cup honey
2 maraschino cherries, halved

Remove seeds, and loosen sections of grapefruit halves. Sprinkle 1 tablespoon light rum over top of each grapefruit half; spread 1 tablespoon honey over top of each.

Broil grapefruit 4 inches from heat for 3 minutes or until bubbly and lightly browned. Top each with a cherry half. Yield: 4 servings.

◻*Microwave Directions:* Remove seeds, and loosen sections of grapefruit halves. Sprinkle 1 tablespoon rum over top of each grapefruit half; spread 1 tablespoon honey over top of each.

Arrange grapefruit halves on a microwave-safe platter. Microwave at HIGH for 5 to 6 minutes or until thoroughly heated, giving dish a half-turn after 3 minutes. Top each with a cherry half.

HONEY-BAKED BANANAS

4 firm ripe bananas, peeled and cut in half crosswise
2 teaspoons butter or margarine, melted
¼ cup honey
1 tablespoon orange juice
¼ cup chopped pecans

Brush bananas with butter, and place in a shallow baking dish. Combine honey and orange juice; stir well, and pour juice mixture over bananas. Sprin-kle with chopped pecans. Bake at 375° for 15 minutes. Do not overbake. Yield: 4 servings.

◻*Microwave Directions:* Brush bananas with butter, and place in a shallow baking dish. Combine honey and orange juice; stir well, and pour juice mixture over bananas. Sprinkle with chopped pecans. Microwave at HIGH for 1½ to 2 minutes or until bananas are heated, but still firm.

HOT BRANDIED FRUIT

2 (17-ounce) cans apricot halves
1 (29-ounce) can pear halves
1 (29-ounce) can peach halves
1 (20-ounce) can pineapple slices
1 (10-ounce) jar maraschino cherries
½ cup butter or margarine, melted
¾ cup firmly packed brown sugar
½ cup brandy
10 whole cloves
4 (3-inch) sticks cinnamon

Drain fruit, reserving all juice. Combine juices; stir well, and set aside ½ cup of fruit juice mixture. (Save remaining juice for other uses.)

Combine butter and sugar, stirring until smooth. Add reserved juice, brandy, and spices; stir until blended.

Combine fruit in a 12- x 8- x 2-inch baking dish; stir in brandy mixture. Bake at 350° for 30 minutes or until bubbly. Yield: 8 to 10 servings.

◻*Microwave Directions:* Drain fruit, reserving all juice. Combine juices; stir well, and set aside ½ cup of the fruit juice mixture. (Save remaining juice for other uses.)

Combine butter and sugar, stirring until smooth. Add reserved juice, brandy, and spices; stir until blended.

Combine fruit in a 12- x 8- x 2-inch baking dish, and pour in brandy mixture. Microwave at HIGH for 10 to 12 minutes or until thoroughly heated, stirring twice.

MARMALADE PEARS

⅓ cup orange marmalade
¼ cup orange juice
2 (16-ounce) cans pear halves,
  drained

Combine all ingredients in a large skillet. Cover and cook over medium heat until thoroughly heated, stirring gently. Spoon pears and juice into individual serving bowls. Yield: 6 servings.

☐ *Microwave Directions:* Combine marmalade and orange juice in an 8-inch square baking dish. Arrange pears, cut side down, in dish. Cover with heavy-duty plastic wrap, and microwave at HIGH for 4 to 5 minutes or until thoroughly heated. Let stand 2 minutes, basting pears occasionally with juice mixture. Spoon pears and juice into individual serving bowls.
Note: Cooked pear mixture may be refrigerated at least 8 hours and served cold.

COLD SWEET-AND-SOUR FRUIT

1 (16-ounce) can sliced peaches
1 (15¼-ounce) can pineapple chunks
¾ cup vinegar
1 cup sugar
8 whole cloves
1 (3-inch) stick cinnamon
12 fresh strawberries

Drain peaches and pineapple, reserving 1 cup juice. Combine fruit juice, vinegar, sugar, cloves, and cinnamon in a medium saucepan; cook over low heat until sugar dissolves. Remove from heat and let cool slightly. Add peaches, pineapple, and strawberries. Cover and chill several hours. Remove cinnamon stick and cloves. Serve with a slotted spoon. Yield: 8 servings.

OVEN-BAKED PEACHES WITH GINGER

¾ cup firmly packed brown sugar,
  divided
2 tablespoons butter or margarine
6 medium peaches, peeled and halved
  crosswise or 2 (16-ounce) cans
  peach halves, drained
2 tablespoons minced crystallized
  ginger
½ cup light rum
12 maraschino cherries
1 tablespoon butter or margarine

Sprinkle half of sugar in a 12- x 8- x 2-inch baking dish; dot with 2 tablespoons butter. Place peaches on top of sugar and butter; sprinkle with ginger. Pour rum over peaches; place cherry in center of each peach half, and sprinkle with remaining sugar. Dot with 1 tablespoon butter. Bake at 350° for 20 minutes. Spoon two peach halves and syrup into individual serving dishes. Yield: 6 servings.

Oven-Baked Apricots With Ginger: Substitute 8 medium-size fresh apricots or 1 (17-ounce) can apricot halves, drained, for peaches.

HOT CURRIED FRUIT

1 (29-ounce) can pear halves
1 (29-ounce) can peach halves
1 (20-ounce) can pineapple chunks
1 (16½-ounce) can pitted Royal Anne
  cherries
1 (17-ounce) can apricot halves
1 (11-ounce) can mandarin oranges
¼ cup sugar
3 tablespoons all-purpose flour
3 tablespoons butter or margarine
½ cup golden raisins
½ cup white wine
1 teaspoon curry powder

Drain fruit, reserving all juice. Combine juices, stir well, and set aside ¾ cup. (Reserve remaining juice for other uses.)
Combine sugar and flour in a medium saucepan, stirring well. Gradually stir in reserved ¾ cup fruit juice. Add butter and raisins, and cook over medium heat, stirring constantly, until mixture comes to a boil. Boil 1 minute, stirring constantly; remove from heat.
Gradually stir in wine and curry powder. Stir sauce into fruit, and spoon mixture into a 12- x 8- x 2-inch baking dish. Bake at 350° for 30 minutes. Yield: 8 to 10 servings.

☐ *Microwave Directions:* Drain fruit, reserving all juice. Combine juices, stir well, and set aside ¾ cup. (Reserve remaining juice for other uses.)
Combine sugar and flour in a 1-quart glass measure, stirring well. Gradually stir in reserved ¾ cup fruit juice. Add butter and raisins. Cover with heavy-duty plastic wrap, and microwave at HIGH for 3 to 4 minutes or until mixture is thoroughly heated, stirring once.
Gradually stir in wine and curry powder. Stir sauce into fruit, and spoon mixture into a 12- x 8- x 2-inch baking dish. Microwave at HIGH for 8 to 10 minutes or until thoroughly heated, stirring twice.

Vegetable	Servings	Preparation	Cooking Instructions (*Add salt, if desired*)	Compatible Seasonings and Sauces
Artichoke, globe	2 per pound (2 medium artichokes)	Wash; cut off stem and ½ inch from top. Remove loose bottom leaves. Cut off thorny tips with scissors. Rub cut surfaces with lemon.	Cook, covered, in small amount of boiling water 25 to 35 minutes.	Garlic butter, hollandaise sauce, vinaigrette
Artichoke, Jerusalem	3 per pound	Wash; peel. Leave whole or slice.	Cook, covered, in small amount of boiling water 15 minutes (slices) to 30 minutes (whole).	Butter, lemon juice, cream sauce
Asparagus	3 to 4 per pound	Snap off tough ends. Remove scales, if desired.	To boil: cook, covered, in small amount of boiling water 6 to 8 minutes or until crisp-tender. To steam: cook, covered, on a rack above boiling water 8 to 12 minutes.	Cheese sauce, hollandaise sauce, orange sauce, vinaigrette, lemon juice, mustard seeds, tarragon, dill
Beans, dried	6 to 8 per pound	Sort and wash. Cover with water 2 inches above beans; soak overnight. Drain.	Cover soaked beans with water. Bring to a boil; cover, reduce heat, and simmer 1½ to 2 hours or until tender.	Garlic, cumin, chili powder, bacon
Beans, green	4 per pound	Wash; trim ends, and remove strings. Cut into 1½-inch pieces.	Cook, covered, in small amount of boiling water 12 to 15 minutes.	Almonds, butter, bacon, basil, dill, savory, thyme
Beans, lima	2 per pound unshelled, 4 per pound shelled	Shell and wash.	Cook, covered, in small amount of boiling water 20 minutes.	Butter, cream sauce, oregano, sage, savory, tarragon, thyme
Beets	3 to 4 per pound	Leave root and 1 inch of stem; scrub with vegetable brush.	Cook, covered, in boiling water 35 to 40 minutes. Remove peel.	Butter, lemon juice, orange juice, wine vinegar, allspice, ginger
Broccoli	3 to 4 per pound	Remove outer leaves and tough ends of lower stalks. Wash; cut into spears.	To boil: cook, covered, in small amount of boiling water 10 to 15 minutes. To steam: cook, covered, on a rack above boiling water 15 to 20 minutes.	Cheese or hollandaise sauce, lemon-butter sauce, vinaigrette, dill, mustard seeds, tarragon
Brussels Sprouts	4 per pound	Wash; remove discolored leaves. Cut off stem ends; slash bottom with an X.	Cook, covered, in small amount of boiling water 8 to 10 minutes.	Cheese sauce, butter, caraway seeds, basil, dill, mustard seeds, sage, thyme
Cabbage	4 per pound	Remove outer leaves; wash. Shred or cut into wedges.	Cook, covered, in small amount of boiling water 5 to 7 minutes (shredded) or 10 to 15 minutes (wedges).	Cream or cheese sauce, butter, caraway seeds, dill, savory, tarragon
Carrots	4 per pound	Scrape; remove ends, and rinse. Leave tiny carrots whole; slice large carrots, or cut into strips.	Cook, covered, in small amount of boiling water 8 to 10 minutes (slices) or 12 to 15 minutes (strips).	Butter, brown sugar glaze, vinaigrette, dill, chives, ginger, mace, mint, nutmeg
Cauliflower	4 per medium head	Remove outer leaves and stalk. Wash. Leave whole, or break into flowerets.	Cook, covered, in small amount of boiling water 10 to 12 minutes (whole) or 8 to 10 minutes (flowerets).	Cream or cheese sauce, herb butter, basil, caraway seeds, mace, tarragon
Celery	4 per medium bunch	Separate stalks; trim off leaves and base. Rinse. Slice diagonally.	Cook, covered, in small amount of boiling water 10 to 15 minutes.	Butter, cream or cheese sauce, grated Parmesan cheese, mustard, thyme, tarragon

Vegetable	Servings	Preparation	Cooking Instructions (*Add salt, if desired*)	Compatible Seasonings and Sauces
Corn	4 per 4 large ears	Remove husks and silks. Leave corn on cob, or cut off tips of kernels, and scrape cob with dull edge of knife.	Cook, covered, in boiling water 10 minutes (on cob) or in small amount boiling water 8 to 10 minutes (cut).	Cream sauce, herb butter, garlic, chili powder, red pepper, basil
Cucumbers	2 per large cucumber	Peel, if desired; slice or cut into strips.	Generally served raw.	Sour cream, dill, basil, mint, tarragon
Eggplant	2 to 3 per pound	Wash and peel. Cut into cubes, or cut crosswise into slices.	To boil: cook, covered, in small amount of boiling water 8 to 10 minutes. To sauté: cook in small amount of butter or vegetable oil 5 to 8 minutes.	Grated Parmesan cheese, basil, curry, oregano, marjoram
Greens	3 to 4 per pound	Remove stems; wash thoroughly. Tear into bite-size pieces.	Cook, covered, in 1 to 1½ inches boiling water 5 to 8 minutes (spinach), 10 to 20 minutes (Swiss chard), 30 to 45 minutes (collards, turnip greens, mustard, kale).	Cream sauce, butter, onion, mushrooms, wine vinegar, lemon juice, horseradish, bacon, dill, marjoram, rosemary, nutmeg
Kohlrabi	3 to 4 per pound	Remove leaves; wash. Peel; dice, slice, or cut into strips.	Cook, covered, in small amount of boiling water 15 to 20 minutes.	Butter, cheese sauce, lemon juice, sour cream, chives, garlic, basil
Leeks	3 per pound	Remove root, tough outer leaves, and tops, leaving 2 inches of dark leaves. Wash thoroughly. Slice leeks, if desired.	Cook, covered, in small amount boiling water 12 to 15 minutes (whole) or 10 to 12 minutes (sliced).	Flavored butters, crumbled bacon, cream sauce, grated Parmesan cheese, mushroom sauce, dill, basil, thyme, rosemary
Mushrooms	4 per pound	Wipe with dry paper towels, or wash gently and pat dry. Cut off tips of stems. Slice, if desired.	Sauté in butter 5 minutes.	Cream sauce, vinaigrette, marjoram, oregano, rosemary, savory, tarragon
Okra	4 per pound	Wash and pat dry. Trim ends.	Cook, covered, in small amount of boiling water 5 to 10 minutes.	Butter, cream sauce, garlic, lemon juice, tomatoes, chives, basil, nutmeg
Onions	4 per pound	Peel; cut large onions into quarters or slices, or leave small onions whole.	Cook, covered, in small amount of boiling water 15 minutes or until tender. Or sauté slices in butter 3 to 5 minutes.	Cream or cheese sauce, brown sugar glaze, butter, basil, ginger, oregano, parsley, thyme
Parsnips	4 per pound	Scrape; cut off ends. Slice or cut into strips.	Cook, covered, in small amount of boiling water 15 to 20 minutes.	Cream sauce, brown sugar glaze, butter, Worcestershire, honey, parsley, nutmeg
Peas, black-eyed	2 per pound unshelled, 4 per pound shelled	Shell and wash.	Cook, covered, in small amount of boiling water 15 to 20 minutes or until tender.	Bacon, butter, garlic, red pepper, cumin, chili powder, basil
Peas, dried	6 to 8 per pound	Sort and wash. Cover with water 2 inches above peas; soak overnight. Drain.	Cover soaked peas with water. Bring to a boil; cover, reduce heat, and simmer 1½ to 2 hours or until tender.	Butter, garlic, red pepper, bacon, cumin, chili powder
Peas, green	2 per pound unshelled, 4 per pound shelled	Shell and wash.	Cook, covered in a small amount of boiling water 12 to 15 minutes.	Cream or cheese sauce, butter, garlic, marjoram, nutmeg, chervil, mint, rosemary, tarragon
Peas, snow	4 per pound	Wash; trim ends, and remove tough strings.	Cook, covered, in small amount of boiling water 3 to 5 minutes, or sauté in vegetable oil or butter 3 to 5 minutes.	Onion, garlic, soy sauce, basil

VEGETABLE COOKING CHART (continued)

Vegetable	Servings	Preparation	Cooking Instructions (*Add salt, if desired*)	Compatible Seasonings and Sauces
Peppers, green	1 per medium pepper	Cut off top, and remove seeds. Leave whole to stuff and bake; cut into thin slices or strips to sauté.	To bake: cook, covered, in boiling water 5 minutes; stuff and bake at 350° for 15 to 25 minutes. To sauté: cook in butter or vegetable oil 3 to 5 minutes.	Meat, vegetable, or rice stuffing; garlic, basil, oregano, fennel
Potatoes, all-purpose	3 to 4 per pound	Scrub potatoes; peel, if desired. Leave whole, or slice or cut into chunks.	Cook, covered, in small amount of boiling water 30 to 40 minutes (whole) or 15 to 20 minutes (slices or chunks).	Cream or cheese sauce, butter, bacon, sour cream, basil, chives, garlic, dill, oregano
Potatoes, baking	2 per pound	Scrub potatoes; rub skins with vegetable oil.	Bake at 400° for 1 hour or until done.	Butter, sour cream, cheese, chives, garlic, oregano, thyme
Potatoes, new	3 to 4 per pound	Scrub potatoes; peel, if desired.	Cook, covered, in boiling water to cover 15 minutes or until tender.	Cream or cheese sauce, butter, onion, lemon juice, vinaigrette, parsley
Potatoes, sweet	2 to 3 per pound	Scrub potatoes; leave whole to bake, or slice or cut into chunks to boil.	Bake at 375° for 1 hour or until done. To boil: cook in boiling water to cover for 20 to 30 minutes.	Butter, brown sugar glaze, marmalade, honey, maple syrup, allspice, cinnamon, nutmeg
Pumpkin	4½ to 5 cups cooked, mashed pumpkin per one 5-pound pumpkin	Slice in half crosswise. Remove seeds.	Place cut side on baking pan. Bake at 325° for 45 minutes or until tender. Cool; peel and mash.	Butter, brown sugar or maple syrup glaze, cinnamon, nutmeg, mace, ginger
Rutabagas	2 to 3 per pound	Wash; peel and slice or cube.	Cook, covered, in boiling water 15 to 20 minutes. Mash, if desired.	Butter, maple syrup, brown sugar, lemon, cinnamon, nutmeg
Squash, summer	3 to 4 pound	Wash; trim ends. Slice or dice.	To boil: cook, covered, in small amount of boiling water 8 to 10 minutes (slices) or 15 minutes (whole). To steam: cook, covered, on a rack over boiling water 10 to 12 minutes (sliced or diced).	Butter, cheese, onion, garlic, cinnamon, marjoram, dillweed, ginger, allspice, rosemary
Squash, spaghetti	2 per pound	Rinse; cut in half lengthwise, and discard seeds.	Place squash, cut side down, in Dutch oven; add 2 inches water. Bring to a boil; cover, reduce heat, and cook 20 minutes or until tender. Drain and separate strands with a fork.	Butter, onions, tomato sauce, basil, garlic, oregano
Squash, winter (acorn, butternut, hubbard)	2 per pound	Rinse; cut in half, remove seeds.	To boil: cook, covered, in boiling water 20 to 25 minutes. To bake: place cut side down in shallow baking dish; add ½ inch water. Bake, uncovered, at 375° for 30 minutes. Turn and season or fill; bake 20 to 30 minutes or until tender.	Brown sugar glaze, orange juice, apple filling, butter, crumbled bacon, candied ginger, cinnamon, nutmeg
Tomatoes	4 per pound (2 large tomatoes)	Wash; peel, if desired. Slice or cut into quarters.	Generally served raw or used as ingredient in cooked dishes.	Vinaigrette, grated Parmesan cheese, onion, chives, marjoram, oregano, sage, tarragon, basil
Turnips	3 per pound	Wash; peel and slice or cube.	Cook, covered, in boiling water to cover 15 to 20 minutes or until tender.	Sweet-and-sour sauce, butter, soy sauce, onion, bacon, chives, dill, thyme

APPENDICES

EQUIVALENT MEASUREMENTS

3 teaspoons...... 1 tablespoon	2 tablespoons (liquid).. 1 ounce	4 quarts... 1 gallon
4 tablespoons... ¼ cup	1 cup............................ 8 fluid ounces	⅛ cup....... 2 tablespoons
5⅓ tablespoons... ⅓ cup	2 cups............................ 1 pint (16	⅓ cup....... 5 tablespoons plus 1 teaspoon
8 tablespoons... ½ cup	fluid ounces)	⅔ cup....... 10 tablespoons plus 2 teaspoons
16 tablespoons... 1 cup	4 cups............................ 1 quart	¾ cup....... 12 tablespoons

METRIC MEASURE/CONVERSION CHART

Approximate Conversion to Metric Measures

When You Know . . .	Multiply by . . . Mass (weight)	To Find . . .	Symbol
ounces	28	grams	g
pounds	0.45	kilograms	kg
(volume)			
teaspoons	5	milliliters	ml
tablespoons	15	milliliters	ml
fluid ounces	30	milliliters	ml
cups	0.24	liters	l
pints	0.47	liters	l
quarts	0.95	liters	l
gallons	3.8	liters	l

COOKING MEASURE EQUIVALENTS

Metric Cup	Volume (Liquid)	Liquid Solids (Butter)	Fine Powder (Flour)	Granular (Sugar)	Grain (Rice)
1	250 ml	200 g	140 g	190 g	150 g
¾	188 ml	150 g	105 g	143 g	113 g
⅔	167 ml	133 g	93 g	127 g	100 g
½	125 ml	100 g	70 g	95 g	75 g
⅓	83 ml	67 g	47 g	63 g	50 g
¼	63 ml	50 g	35 g	48 g	38 g
⅛	31 ml	25 g	18 g	24 g	19 g

EQUIVALENT WEIGHTS AND MEASURES

Food	Weight or Count	Measure or Yield
Apples	1 pound (3 medium)	3 cups sliced
Bacon	8 slices cooked	½ cup crumbled
Bananas	1 pound (3 medium)	2½ cups sliced, or about 2 cups mashed
Bread	1 pound	12 to 16 slices
	About 1½ slices	1 cup soft crumbs
Butter or margarine	1 pound	2 cups
	¼-pound stick	½ cup
Cabbage	1 pound head	4½ cups shredded
Candied fruit or peels	½ pound	1¼ cups chopped
Carrots	1 pound	3 cups shredded
Cheese, American or Cheddar	1 pound	About 4 cups shredded
cottage	1 pound	2 cups
cream	3-ounce package	6 tablespoons
Chocolate morsels	6-ounce package	1 cup
Cocoa	1 pound	4 cups
Coconut, flaked or shredded	1 pound	5 cups
Coffee	1 pound	80 tablespoons (40 cups perked)
Corn	2 medium ears	1 cup kernels
Cornmeal	1 pound	3 cups
Crab, in shell	1 pound	¾ to 1 cup flaked

Food	Weight or Count	Measure or Yield
Crackers, chocolate wafers	19 wafers	1 cup crumbs
graham crackers	14 squares	1 cup fine crumbs
saltine crackers	28 crackers	1 cup finely crushed
vanilla wafers	22 wafers	1 cup finely crushed
Cream, whipping	1 cup (½ pint)	2 cups whipped
Dates, pitted	1 pound	3 cups chopped
Eggs	5 large	1 cup
whites	8 to 11	1 cup
yolks	12 to 14	1 cup
Flour, all-purpose or whole wheat	1 pound	3½ cups unsifted
cake	1 pound	4¾ to 5 cups sifted
Green pepper	1 large	1 cup diced
Lemon	1 medium	2 to 3 tablespoons juice; 2 teaspoons grated rind
Lettuce	1 pound head	6¼ cups torn
Lime	1 medium	1½ to 2 tablespoons juice; 1½ teaspoons grated rind
Macaroni	4 ounces (1 cup)	2¼ cups cooked
Marshmallows	11 large	1 cup
	10 miniature	1 large marshmallow
Marshmallows, miniature	½ pound	4½ cups
Milk, evaporated	5-ounce can	½ cup
evaporated	12-ounce can	1½ cups
sweetened condensed	14-ounce can	1¼ cups
Mushrooms	3 cups raw (8 ounces)	1 cup sliced cooked
Nuts, almonds	1 pound	1 to 1¾ cups nutmeats
	1 pound shelled	3½ cups nutmeats
peanuts	1 pound	2¼ cups nutmeats
	1 pound shelled	3 cups
pecans	1 pound	2¼ cups nutmeats
	1 pound shelled	4 cups
walnuts	1 pound	1⅔ cups nutmeats
	1 pound shelled	4 cups
Oats, quick-cooking	1 cup	1¾ cups cooked
Onion	1 medium	½ cup chopped
Orange	1 medium	⅓ cup juice; 2 tablespoons grated rind
Peaches or Pears	2 medium	1 cup sliced
Potatoes, white	3 medium	2 cups cubed cooked or 1¾ cups mashed
sweet	3 medium	3 cups sliced
Raisins, seedless	1 pound	3 cups
Rice, long-grain	1 cup	3 to 4 cups cooked
pre-cooked	1 cup	2 cups cooked
Shrimp, raw in shell	1½ pounds	2 cups (¾ pound) cleaned, cooked
Spaghetti	7 ounces	About 4 cups cooked
Strawberries	1 quart	4 cups sliced
Sugar, brown	1 pound	2⅓ cups firmly packed
powdered	1 pound	3½ cups unsifted
granulated	1 pound	2 cups

HANDY SUBSTITUTIONS

Ingredient Called For	Substitution
1 cup self-rising flour	1 cup all-purpose flour plus 1 teaspoon baking powder and ½ teaspoon salt
1 cup cake flour	1 cup sifted all-purpose flour minus 2 tablespoons
1 cup all-purpose flour	1 cup cake flour plus 2 tablespoons
1 teaspoon baking powder	½ teaspoon cream of tartar plus ¼ teaspoon baking soda
1 tablespoon cornstarch or arrowroot	2 tablespoons all-purpose flour
1 tablespoon tapioca	1½ tablespoons all-purpose flour

Ingredient Called For	Substitution
2 large eggs	3 small eggs
1 egg	2 egg yolks (for custard)
1 egg	2 egg yolks plus 1 tablespoon water (for cookies)
1 (8-ounce) carton commercial sour cream	1 tablespoon lemon juice plus evaporated milk to equal 1 cup
1 cup yogurt	1 cup buttermilk or sour milk
1 cup sour milk or buttermilk	1 tablespoon vinegar or lemon juice plus sweet milk to equal 1 cup
1 cup fresh milk	½ cup evaporated milk plus ½ cup water
1 cup fresh milk	3 to 5 tablespoons nonfat dry milk solids in 1 cup water
1 cup honey	1¼ cups sugar plus ¼ cup water
1 (1-ounce) square unsweetened chocolate	3 tablespoons cocoa plus 1 tablespoon butter or margarine
1 tablespoon chopped fresh herbs	1 teaspoon dried herbs or ¼ teaspoon powdered herbs
1 teaspoon dry mustard	1 tablespoon prepared mustard

CANNED FOOD GUIDE

Can Size	Number of Cups	Number of Servings	Foods
8-ounce	1 cup	2 servings	Fruits, Vegetables
10½- to 12-ounce (picnic)	1¼ cups	3 servings	Condensed Soups, Fruits and Vegetables, Meats and Fish, Specialties
12-ounce (vacuum)	1½ cups	3 to 4 servings	Vacuum-Packed Corn
14- to 16-ounce (No. 300)	1¾ cups	3 to 4 servings	Pork and Beans, Meat Products, Cranberry Sauce
16- to 17-ounce (No. 303)	2 cups	4 servings	Principle Size for Fruits and Vegetables, Some Meat Products
1 pound, 4 ounce (No. 2)	2½ cups	5 servings	Juices, Pineapple, Apple Slices
27- to 29-ounce (No. 2½)	3½ cups	7 servings	Fruits, Some Vegetables (Pumpkin, Sauerkraut, Greens, Tomatoes)
46-ounce (No. 3 cyl.)	5¾ cups	10 to 12 servings	Fruit and Vegetable Juices
6½-pound (No. 10)	12 to 13 cups	25 servings	Institutional Size for Fruits and Vegetables

CHEESE SELECTION GUIDE

Cheese	Flavor, Texture, and Color	Used For	Goes With
American	Very mild; creamy yellow	Sandwiches, snacks	Crackers, bread
Bel Paese (Italy)	Mild; spongy; creamy yellow interior	Dessert, snacks	Fresh fruit, crusty French bread
Brie (France)	Sharper than Camembert; soft, creamy, with edible crust	Dessert, snacks	Fresh fruit
Blue (France)	Piquant, spicy; marbled, blue veined, semisoft; creamy white	Dessert, dips, salads, appetizers, cheese trays	Fresh fruit, bland crackers
Brick (United States)	Mild; semisoft; cream-colored to orange	Sandwiches, appetizers, cheese trays	Crackers, bread
Camembert (France)	Mild to pungent; edible crust; creamy yellow	Dessert, snacks	Especially good with tart apple slices
Cheddar (England) (United States)	Mild to sharp; cream-colored to orange	Dessert, sandwiches, salads, appetizers, cheese trays; use as an ingredient in cooking	Especially good with apples or pears
Chèvre (French)	Goat cheese; very pungent; creamy	Relishes, appetizers, sauces	Crackers, fruit

Cheese	Flavor, Texture, and Color	Used For	Goes With
Cottage Cheese (United States)	Mild; soft, moist, large or small curd; white	Appetizers, fruit salads, snacks; use as an ingredient in cooking	Canned or fresh fruit
Cream Cheese (United States)	Mild; buttery, soft, smooth; white	Dessert, sandwiches, salads; use as an ingredient in cooking	Jelly and crackers
Edam (Holland)	Mild; firm with red wax coating	Dessert, appetizers, cheese tray	Fresh fruit
Feta (Greece)	Salty; crumbly, but sliceable; snow white	Appetizers; use as an ingredient in cooking	Greek salad
Fontina (Italy)	Nutty; semisoft to hard	Dessert, appetizers, sandwiches	Fresh fruit, crackers, bread
Gjetost (Norway)	Sweetish; firm, smooth; caramel-colored	Appetizers	Crackers
Gouda (Holland)	Mild, nutty; softer than Edam, with or without red wax coating	Dessert, appetizers	Fresh fruit, crackers
Gruyère (Switzerland)	Nutty; similar to swiss; firm with tiny holes	Dessert, appetizers	Fresh fruit
Jarlsberg (Norway)	Mild, nutty; firm	Sandwiches, snacks	Fresh fruit, bread
Havarti (Denmark)	Mild; rich and creamy	Snacks, sandwiches	Crackers, bread, fresh fruit
Liederkranz (United States)	Robust; texture of heavy honey, edible light-orange crust	Dessert, snacks	Fresh fruit, matzo, pumpernickel, sour rye, thinly sliced onion
Limburger (Belgium)	Robust, aromatic; soft, smooth; creamy white	Dessert	Fresh fruit, dark bread, bland crackers
Monterey Jack (United States)	Mild; semisoft; creamy white	Snacks, sandwiches, sauces, casseroles	Bread, crackers
Mozzarella (Italy)	Delicate, mild; semisoft; creamy white	Pizza; use as an ingredient in cooking	Italian foods
Muenster (Germany)	Mild to mellow; semisoft	Sandwiches, cheese trays	Crackers, bread
Parmesan (Italy)	Sharp, piquant; hard, brittle body; light yellow	Use grated as an ingredient in cooking; table use: young cheese, not aged	Italian foods; combine with Swiss for sauces
Pineapple Cheese (United States)	Sharp; firm, pineapple-shaped	Dessert, appetizers, salads, snacks	Fresh fruit
Port Salut (France)	Mellow to robust, fresh buttery flavor; semisoft	Dessert, appetizers, cheese trays	Fresh fruit, crackers
Provolone (Italy)	Mild to sharp, usually smoked, salty; hard; yellowish-white	Dessert, appetizers; use as an ingredient in cooking	Italian foods
Ricotta (Italy)	Bland but semisweet; soft; creamy white	An ingredient in main dishes, filling, or pastries	Fresh fruit
Romano (Italy)	Sharp; hard, brittle body; light yellow	Use grated as an ingredient in cooking; table use: young cheese, not aged	Italian foods, salads, sauces
Roquefort (France)	Sharp; semisoft, sometimes crumbly; blue veined	Desserts, dips, salads, appetizers	Bland crackers, fresh fruit, demitasse
Stilton (England)	Semisoft; slightly more crumbly than blue; blue veined	Dessert, cheese trays, dips, salads	Fresh fruit, bland crackers
Swiss (Switzerland)	Sweetish; nutty with large holes; pale yellow	Dessert, cheese trays, salads, sandwiches, appetizers, use as an ingredient in cooking	Fresh fruit, squares of crusty French bread

RECIPE INDEX

M preceding the page number indicates a recipe which includes microwave directions as well as conventional directions.

SUBJECT INDEX